Kant and the Unity of Reason

Purdue University Press Series in the History of Philosophy

Kant and the Unity of Reason

Angelica Nuzzo

Purdue University Press
West Lafayette, Indiana

Printed in the United States of America.

The cover image is from the grounds of Schloss Benrath, which was built in the mid-1700s outside of Düsseldorf, Germany, and represents the transition from late baroque to classical architecture. Photo by Thomas Bacher

Library of Congress Cataloging-in-Publication Data

Nuzzo, Angelica, date.
Kant and the unity of reason / Angelica Nuzzo.
p. cm. -- (Purdue University Press series in the history of philosophy)
Includes bibliographical references and index.
ISBN 1-55753-187-0 (case) -- ISBN 1-55753-188-9 (pbk.)
1. Kant, Immanuel, 1724–1804. Kritik der Urteilskraft. Einführung. 2. Reason. 3. Judgment. 4. Judgment (Aesthetics) I. Kant, Immanuel, 1724–1804. Kritik der Urteilskraft. Einführung. English & German. II. Title. III. Series.

B2784.N89 2004
121--dc22

2004021846

Contents

Preface

In this book I shall present an analysis, commentary, and comprehensive interpretation of Kant's *Critique of Judgment.* In accordance with the other volumes of this Purdue series, the central part of the book offers a detailed commentary on the published Introduction to the third *Critique.* The German text is reprinted along with a new English translation.

The book is divided into three parts. The first part, "Kant's Way to the *Critique of Judgment,*" introduces the reader to the main concepts and issues of Kant's critical philosophy. Herein I take up more specifically the crucial problem of the "system of the cognitive faculties" of the human mind as Kant conceives of it before the *Critique of Judgment.* My analysis is both historically and systematically oriented. Since this crucial issue lies at the very center of the Introduction to the third *Critique*, I consider its discussion in the *Critique of Pure Reason* and the *Critique of Practical Reason* respectively to be the best way to engage the reader in the pivotal topic of Kant's 1790 book.

My presentation and interpretation of the *Critique of Judgment* revolves around a central thesis. I propose to read Kant's critical project, which culminates precisely in the third *Critique*, as one of the most sophisticated attempts in the whole history of philosophy to articulate a complex notion of human "sensibility" as an alternative to both eighteenth-century empiricism and rationalism. At stake in Kant's work is the idea of human experience. The fundamental contribution of understanding and reason in experience cannot be fully appreciated if its sensible and sensuous component is not adequately taken into account. Kant's philosophical itinerary—*toward* the third *Critique* and *within* the third *Critique*—can be viewed as a progressive discovery of the complexity of human sensibility in its interplay with understanding and reason. For Kant, sensibility includes functions as different as sensation, intuition, perception, emotion, passion, drive, moral feeling, and feeling of pleasure and displeasure. Kant's discovery of an independent "faculty of judgment" is the discovery of the third *Critique.* Such a faculty is responsible for articulating the interplay between sensibility and rationality, the world of nature and the human mind in order to constitute human experience and the world of human relationships.

The central part of the volume, "The 'Introduction' to the Critique of Judgment," offers a detailed analytical commentary on the published Introduction to the 1790 *Critique.* Kant sets out to write this Introduction when his work on the *Critique of Judgment* is finally completed. I have chosen it because it constitutes a concluded text that, as opposed to the so-called "First Introduction," is not disproportionately long and may be viewed as an independent treatise. Moreover, both thematically and methodologically, this text provides an excellent and unique key to enter the vast and multiform world of the *Critique of Judgment.*

The Introduction consists of nine sections. I have divided my presentation of these sections into three groups, thereby following the important methodological suggestion that Kant makes at the very end of the text. For each section, I give a brief synopsis followed by the commentary.

The last part of the book, "The World of Experience: Beauty and Life," is a comprehensive exposition of the *Critique of Judgment* as a whole. Herein I follow the development of Kant's argument offering both a systematic overview of its structure and a more detailed analysis of the text. I have chosen to give priority to the internal reconstruction of Kant's argument in its integrity and to limit my discussion of Kant's historical sources, of the influence of the third *Critique* on later philosophies, and of the secondary literature.

The bibliography at the end of the volume has no pretension of completeness.

I have many debts of gratitude. The work for this book has been sustained by many institutions and people although the process of its creation has often seemed solitary and lonely. I wish to thank them all here.

My deepest gratitude to Adriaan Peperzak, who has been encouraging my work in philosophy from the very beginning and has suggested that I write this book for the Purdue series. DePaul University has supported my research with research grants in the summers of 1998 and 2000 and with an entire year of leave in 2000–01, which has made possible the completion of the book. A special thanks to David Farrell Krell, who was my challenging partner in a long Kant seminar throughout 1999–2000. My gratitude to George Di Giovanni, Tom Rockmore, and Gianna Gigliotti for their generosity, friendship, and insightful comments.

This project has been completed while I was the beneficiary of a fellowship provided by the Bunting Institute of Radcliffe College, Harvard, during my sabbatical leave in 2000–2001. I would like to thank this institution, which has allowed me to complete this book in the most stimulating community I could ever have dreamed of. I want to express my deepest gratitude to the director of the Bunting Institute, Rita Nakashima Brock, and to the staff for their enthusiastic help and support during this unique year. I now realize how the intellectual community at the Bunting has been the ideal interdisciplinary environment for working on the *Critique of Judgment*. I am fortunate to have been part of a working group at the Bunting in which I have discussed parts of this book and its main ideas. I have been challenged by philosophers, writers, visual artists, and historians of religion, art, and architecture who have helped me to see my topic from different and unexpected angles and have opened my mind to new interests and fruitful connections.

My thanks for editing the manuscript go to Myrna Patterson. Margaret Hunt has been a patient, generous, and scrupulous editor of the book.

My deepest debt is to Aurora. This book is better for her kindness, unlimited support, and inspiration. She has supported my efforts daily and with patience has endured my silence when I could not extricate myself from the world of ideas.

She has witnessed all my struggles with Kant as well as some small occasional victories over the text. She has inspired me with Bach and with her unique way of doing and undoing the world around her. I owe her more than she could suspect. To her this book is dedicated.

Note on the Text and Translation, Abbreviations

The German text of the Introduction to the *Critique of Judgment* is the text published in the Akademie edition, volume V. The English translation is my own. My translation aims at reproducing Kant's text literally. It should be read as an effort at comprehension that complements and integrates the work of the commentary. I do not intend to propose any emendation either to the excellent translation of the *Critique of Judgment* by W. Pluhar or to P. Guyer's very recent one or to the older work of J. C. Meredith. Besides Pluhar's, Guyer's, and Meredith's work, in my translation I have taken into account J. H. Bernard's English translation, the French version by A. Philonenko, and the most recent Italian translation by E. Garroni and H. Hohenegger.[1]

I have considered the ongoing discussion regarding the translation in different languages (English, Italian, French) of some crucial terms of Kant's third *Critique,* such as *Urteilskraft* and *Zweckmäßigkeit. Urteilskraft,* as opposed to *Urteil,* indicates the "power" or "faculty" or "capacity" to judge. Even though the English word *judgment* (also capitalized as *Judgment*) does retain the sense of a faculty, power or capacity, I have chosen to render *Urteilskraft* with "faculty of judgment." In spite of the inconsistency, however, I have preserved *Critique of Judgment* in the title of the work in order both to maintain the reference to a title that embodied an established tradition and to simplify phrases that would otherwise become exceedingly wordy. As for the terms *Zweckmäßigkeit* and *Zweck* and the translations "purposiveness" and "purpose," I endorse the persuasive considerations of Pluhar in his essay, "How to Render Zweckmäßigkeit in Kant's Third Critique."[2] Since neither the English *spirit* nor *mind* renders the precise meaning of the German term *Gemüt*, I have chosen to preserve the German throughout the text.

Both the original text of the Introduction and its translation show two reference numbers. In the margin I provide the page of the fifth volume of the Akademie edition (= AA) (in the German text, the end of the page is indicated with ||). The page number in the body of the text refers to the pagination of the original 1790 edition (in the German text the end of the page is indicated with |). In the commentary as well as in all references to the third *Critique*, I provide in order both the pagination of the original edition and that of the *Akademie* edition, the latter followed by the line number.

---

1. See the bibliography at the end of this volume.

2. In *Interpreting Kant,* ed. by Moltke S. Gram, Iowa City, University of Iowa Press, 1982, 85–98. See P. Guyer's different position in *Kant and the Claims of Taste,* Cambridge Mass., Cambridge University Press, 1997, 378 n.

The translation of other German texts in quotations are either my own or my own modifications of the English translations listed in the bibliography (emphasis in the text quoted is always my own unless differently indicated); in the case of the *Critique of Judgment,* I generally follow Pluhar's translation.

Abbreviations

Kants Gesammelte Schriften Herausgegeben von der Preußischen Akademie der Wissenschaften zu Berlin, Berlin, de Gruyter, 1902–83	**AA** followed by volume and page number
Critique of Pure Reason	**KrV** followed by the pagination of the B edition (1787) and the A edition (1781)
Critique of Practical Reason	**KpV** followed by the pagination of the original edition (A)
Critique of Judgment	**KU** followed by section number, the pagination of the original edition, and the pagination of AA V
"First Introduction" to the *Critique of Judgment*	**EE**
Introduction to the *Critique of Judgment*	**E**
Reflexionen from the *Handschriftliche Nachlaß*	**R** followed by the progressive number (in: AA, XIV–XXIII)

Part I

Kant's Way to the *Critique of Judgment*

Chapter 1

Kant's Philosophical Biography

This chapter presents a brief account of Kant's life and a general overview of the development of his thought throughout the wide range of his writings and interests. The presentation follows Kant's activity in a chronological and thematic order and discusses only the core ideas for each work. The purpose of this chapter is to show the complexity of Kant's itinerary toward the *Critique of Judgment.*

1. The Origins of Kant's Philosophy, 1746–1765

Immanuel Kant was born in the East Prussian town of Königsberg on April 22, 1724. His father, the son of Scottish emigrants, was a saddler of humble condition whose strict morality remained his son's most relevant memory. His mother, a devout Christian, was for her children a model of religious and moral integrity. Both of Kant's parents belonged to the pietistic confession of the Lutheran church. Kant spent his whole life in Königsberg, where he attended the Collegium Fridericianum (1732–40), and then the Albertus-Universität (1740–46). From 1747 to 1754, Kant was employed as a tutor in aristocratic families. In 1755 he started his academic career at the University of Königsberg. In 1770 he was appointed professor of Logic and Metaphysics; in the two summer semesters of 1786 and 1788, he was appointed rector. He remained active in his functions until 1801. He died on February 12, 1804. Kant's first biographers and friends, Ludwig Ernst Borowski, Bernhard Jachmann, and Ehregott Andreas Christoph Wasianski, gave accurate descriptions of Kant's character, habits, private and academic life, and humanity. They portray, albeit in quite different ways, a gentle and kind man of strict morality, fascinating in conversation and curious in his social life.[1]

At the beginning of the century, the University of Königsberg was under the guidance of Franz Albert Schultz, who established its pietistic orientation and in 1734 appointed Martin Knutzen as extraordinary professor for Logic and Metaphysics. Knutzen, who followed Wolff's philosophy in an unorthodox way, was an important teacher for Kant. His interests in natural science led him to abandon

1. See *Immanuel Kant. Sein Leben in Darstellungen von Zeitgenossen. Die Biographien von L. E. Borowski, R. B. Jachmann und A. Chr. Wasianski,* ed. by F. Gross, Berlin, 1912; see the material collected in: *Immanuel Kant im Rede und Gespräch,* ed. by R. Malter, Hamburg, Meiner, 1990; K. Vorländer, *Immanuel Kant. Der Mann und das Werk,* 2 vols., Leipzig, Meiner, 1924; one of the first English biographies is J. H. W. Stuckenberg, *The Life of Immanuel Kant,* London, Macmillan, 1882. One of the latest English biographies is M. Kuehn, *Kant: A Biography,* Cambridge, Cambridge University Press, 2001.

some of Leibniz's essential doctrines such as the preestablished harmony.[2] After 1740, however, with Friedrich II king, the cultural situation in Prussia changed radically. Friedrich II, who strongly opposed Pietism, appointed the French philosopher Maupertuis as president of the Berlin Academy. Thenceforth, this move gave a decisive antischolastic orientation to German philosophy. In 1740, Christian August Crusius started the publication of his works. Crusius represented, against Wolff and the Leibnizian tradition, the new empiricist development of German metaphysics. Kant's early philosophical interests were determined by this cultural climate.[3]

Kant's early writings were influenced by the scientific interests of his teacher, Knutzen, and show how his attempts to think of metaphysics *in relation* to natural science (1747–58) would eventually lead him to reflect upon the problem of metaphysics *as* science (1760–66). Kant reads and combines in interesting ways Leibniz and Newton, Knutzen and Crusius; against this background, he then turns to Rousseau and Hume. The scientific and cosmological orientation of Kant's thought is accompanied by a sensibility to moral questions that broaden into the fields of history, anthropology, and aesthetics (from the 1755 *Universal History of Nature and Theory of the Heavens* up to the important 1764 *Observations on the Feeling of the Beautiful and Sublime*).

Kant's first publication in 1747, "Thoughts on the True Estimation of Living Forces,"[4] discloses his early interests in the scientific culture of the time. In the framework of Leibniz's dynamism, Kant combines Knutzen's theory of the *infuxus physicus* with Newton's law of attraction; he pleads for a new determination of the notion of force and presents his first reflections on the problem of space. In 1754, Kant published two articles on scientific topics: "Examination of the Question, Whether the Earth, Since its First Origins, Has Changed Its Circular Motion Around Its Axis,"[5] where he claims that the length of a day increases as an effect of the tides; and "The Question, Whether the Earth Grows Older, Physically Examined,"[6] where he argues that the earth grows older and will eventually die because

2. B. Erdmann, *Martin Knutzen und seine Zeit. Ein Beitrag zur Geschichte der wolffischen Schule und insbesondere zur Entwicklungsgeschichte Kants,* Leipzig, L. Voss, 1876.

3. In my presentation I follow the chronological publication of Kant's works in the AA edition. For Kant's development in the years 1746–1781, see Frederick C. Beiser, "Kant's Intellectual Development, 1746–1781," in *The Cambridge Companion to Kant,* ed. by P. Guyer, Cambridge, Cambridge University Press, 1992, 26–61; M. Campo, *La genesi del criticismo kantiano,* Varese, Magenta, 1953; A. Guerra, *Introduzione a Kant,* Bari, Laterza, 1980.

4. "Gedanken über die wahre Schätzung der lebendigen Kräfte," AA, I, 1–181.

5. "Untersuchung der Frage, ob die Erde in ihren Umdrehung um die Achse . . . einige Veränderungen seit den ersten Zeiten ihres Ursprungs erlitten habe," AA, I, 183–191.

6. "Die Frage, ob die Erde veralte, physikalisch erwogen," AA, I, 193–213.

natural mechanisms, once manifested, cannot be restored. Kant's major work during these years is the *Universal History of Nature and Theory of the Heavens*[7] of 1755. Taking up Newton's theories, Kant presents a mechanistic reconstruction of the origins of the universe. In the preface, he addresses the problem of the conciliation between mechanism and teleology, science and faith. Having claimed that the planets, according to their distance from the sun, present a different material constitution and density, Kant draws a moral conclusion that places the human being—inhabitant of the earth—in an intermediary position as a being that participates both in the lightness of reason and in the heaviness of the body. According to the cosmological model outlined by Kant, intellectual and moral capacities are necessarily tied to the different weight and density of the subject's own body.

Kant's 1755 Latin work, *Principiorum primorum cognitionis metaphysicae nova dilucidatio*,[8] directly addresses for the first time the problem of metaphysics with an examination of the principles of knowledge. Kant analyzes traditional logical principles both in their formal and ontological significance. Accepting the results of Crusius's work, he pleads for a limitation of the validity of the principle of contradiction. Among the logical principles, he carefully examines the principle of sufficient reason—or, along with Crusius, the principle of "determining" reason. Since this principle ultimately governs the activity of the will, the analysis leads to the problem of the freedom of the will. Kant endorses a radical determinism closer to Wolff than to Crusius. Moreover, the analysis of the principles of succession and coexistence calls into consideration the concepts of space and time. The order of coexistence shows for Kant priority over succession and is seen as ultimately depending upon a *schema intellectus divini*.

Between 1756 and 1758, Kant published a series of writings dedicated to natural science. In 1756, he responded to the earthquake in Lisbon with three articles: "On the Causes of the Earthquakes in Occasion of the Misshapen in West Europe at the End of Last Year," "History and Natural Description of the Most Extraordinary Events of the Earthquake," and "Other Considerations on the Seismic Shocks Registered Recently,"[9] in which he argues against a form of extrinsic teleological explanation that sees a form of divine punishment in natural catastrophes; he looks instead for a different kind of teleology, able to reconcile science

7. *Allgemeine Naturgeschichte und Theorie des Himmels oder Versuch von der Verfassung und dem mechanischen Ursprunge des ganzen Weltgebäudes, nach Newtonischen Grundsätze abgehandelt,* AA, I, 215–368.

8. In AA, I, 385–416.

9. Respectively: "Von der Ursachen der Erdschütterungen bei Gelegenheit des Unglücks, welches die westliche Länder von Europa gegen das Ende des Jahres betroffen hat," AA, I, 417–427; "Geschichte und Naturbeschreibung der merkwürdigsten Vorfälle des Erdbebens," AA, I, 429–461; and "Fortgesetzte Betrachtungen der seit einigen Zeit wahrgenommenen Erderschütterungen," AA, I, 463–472.

and faith. In the "*Monadologia physica*"[10] (1756) and the "New Doctrine of Motion and Rest"[11] (1758), Kant assumed a new perspective on Leibniz's monadology and argued for the relative nature of space. In 1756, he taught physical geography[12] for the first time; in 1756–57, he initiated his courses on ethics. In 1759, he published "Some Considerations on Optimism"[13] against Crusius, a work that he would later repudiate.

In the 1760s, Kant's interests turned decisively to the problem of metaphysics. In "The False Subtlety of the Four Syllogistic Figures"[14] (1762), he started his polemic against traditional formal logic—a polemic that also emerges in "The Only Possible Basis for a Demonstration of the Existence of God"[15] (1763). Here Kant examines and criticizes the traditional proofs of god's existence and proposes two different proofs, namely a new ontological argument and a revised physico-theological argument. The ontological argument—albeit in the new form proposed—exhibits for Kant a logical completeness that grounds its priority over all other forms of proof (Kant would maintain this position until the first *Critique*). Kant's criticism of the traditional ontological proof is based upon his claim that "existence is not a predicate or a determination of a thing"[16] but the "absolute position of a thing,"[17] that is, the reference of the totality of its predicates to a subject. Kant argues that since the internal possibility of something presupposes an existence so that the possible is always grounded in something existing, and since it is impossible that nothing at all exists, then something must exist as a necessary being; this being is god.[18] Following Crusius, Kant distinguishes between logical and material possibility—between the mere logical condition that allows something to be thought (i.e., the principle of contradiction) and the material element of thought. This distinction remains crucial in the "Inquiry into the

---

10. In AA, I, 473–487.

11. "Neuer Lehrbegriff der Bewegung und Ruhe und der damit verknüpften Folgerungen in den ersten Gründen der Naturwissenschaft," AA, II, 13–25.

12. Cf. the *Vorlesungsverzeichnisse der Universität Königsberg (1720–1804),* ed. by M. Oberhausen, R. Pozzo, Stuttgart, Frommann, 1999. Kant taught physical geography fifty times in his career; cf. J. A. May, *Kant's Concept of Geography and Its Relation to Recent Geographical Thought,* Toronto-Buffalo, University of Toronto Press, 1970.

13. "Versuch einiger Betrachtungen über den Optimismus," AA, II, 27–35.

14. "Die falsche Spitzfindigkeit der vier syllogistischen Figuren erwiesen," AA, II, 45–61.

15. "Der einzig mögliche Beweisgrund zu einer Demonstration des Daseins Gottes," AA, II, 63–163.

16. "Beweisgrund," I, 1, §1, AA, II, 72.

17. "Beweisgrund," I, 1, §2, AA, II, 73.

18. The best study on Kant's "Beweisgrund" is K. Reich, *Kants Einzig mögliche Beweisgrund zu einer Demonstration des Daseins Gottes,* Hamburg, Meiner, 1937; see also D. Henrich, *Der ontologische Gottesbeweis. Sein Problem und seine Geschichte in der Neuzeit,* Tübingen, Mohr, 1960, 178 ff.

Clarity of the Principles of Natural Theology and Morals, In Response to the Question Posed by the Royal Academy of Sciences in Berlin"[19] (written in 1762 and published in 1764), in which Kant brings the problem of the nature and tasks of metaphysics to the foreground. He compares the method of mathematics with that of philosophy in relation to the question of the production of their object. While mathematics proceeds synthetically, philosophy proceeds analytically. The question is further developed in the "Attempt to Introduce the Concept of Negative Magnitudes into Philosophy" (1763).[20] If philosophy should not try to imitate mathematics, it can nonetheless benefit from the use of its procedures. The notion of "negative quantity" provides an example thereof. A negative quantity is not sheer logical negation but rather has a positive reality of its own.

In the *Observations on the Feeling of the Beautiful and Sublime* (1764),[21] Kant presents a theory of human conduct characterized by aesthetic, anthropological, and sociological elements. Kant analyzes the difference between the beautiful and the sublime as it manifests itself in the feeling of the human being in general, in the two sexes, and in different nations. Kant establishes a close relation between morals and aesthetics and pleads for a foundation of morality and virtue on universal principles. These principles are not "speculative rules, but rather the conscience of a feeling," namely the universal "feeling of beauty and dignity of human nature."[22] In the following years, Kant filled the pages of his own copy of the *Observations* with important remarks. These *Bemerkungen*[23] (remarks) witness the importance of Rousseau to the development of Kant's ethical theory. They show how the ideal of scientific knowledge as the highest value that Kant professed in his early years yields to a different idea of knowledge that must relate to human society and welfare. Kant further reflects on the relation between feeling and morality and maintains that feeling, which following Rousseau he judges as presently corrupted, cannot ground practical principles. Feeling is an expression of morality.

---

19. "Untersuchung über die Deutlichkeit der Grundsätze der natürlichen Theologie und der Moral. Zur Beantwortung der Frage, welche die Königl. Akademie der Wissenschaften zu Berlin auf das Jahr 1763 aufgegeben hat," AA, II, 273–301.

20. "Versuch den Begriff der negativen Grössen in die Weltweisheit einzuführen," AA, II, 165–204.

21. *Beobachtungen über das Gefühl des Schönen und Erhabenen,* AA, II, 105–256.

22. *Beobachtungen,* AA, II, 217.

23. *Bemerkungen zu den Beobachtungen über das Gefühl des Schönen und Erhabenen*, AA, XX, 1–192. G. Lehmann dates these remarks back to 1764–65. A detailed analysis is provided by J. Schmucker, *Die Ursprünge der Ethik Kants in seinen vorkritischen Schriften und Reflektionen,* Meisenheim a.G., Hain, 1961.

2. Toward the Critique of Reason, 1766–1781

The witty and polemic *Dreams of a Spirit-Seer Explained with the Dreams of Metaphysics*[24] of 1766 is a prelude to problems and themes of Kant's "critical" philosophy. With a skeptical attitude toward metaphysics, Kant compares the "visions" that metaphysics produces out of mere concepts through the magic power of words to the visions of the Swedish spirit-seer Swedenborg[25] who claimed to be able to communicate with the spirits of the dead. While he justifies the illusions of the spirit-seers as due to a physical illness that affects their sensibility, he attacks the fantasies of metaphysics as illusions created by "the blind trust in the apparent grounds of reason."[26] The result is a radical rejection of rational psychology (pneumatology) that constituted an essential part of traditional Leibnizian-Wolffian metaphysics. Against it, Kant argues for the necessity of establishing the limits of human reason. Metaphysics can raise claims of truth only insofar as it is understood as the "science of the *limits of human reason*" and as such is established "on the ground of experience and common understanding."[27] Since nothing can be positively known by us except what falls under our sensations,[28] the task of metaphysics is reduced to a destruction of the false opinions from which illusions arise. In his argument, Kant follows suggestions of Hume's first *Enquiry* (e.g., the idea of metaphysics as a "mental geography"); he renews Rousseau's polemic against the "vain subtlety" of philosophers and logicians and finds in Newton an inspiration for a "moral faith"[29] that opens up to the idea of a future life and a community of spirits.

In the *Dreams of a Spirit-Seer,* Kant's refutation of both Wolff's psychology and the illusions of the spirit-seer is based on a conception of space as the order of coexistence resulting from the interaction of substances, which was precisely Wolff's own way of conceiving space. Thereby, Kant constructed his refutation of Wolff playing Wolff against himself.[30] The significance of space for metaphysics is discussed again in the 1768 essay "On the Ultimate Ground of the Differentiation of Regions in Space,"[31] where Kant directly rejects Wolff's notion of

---

24. *Träume eines Geistersehers, erläutert durch die Träume der Metaphysik,* AA, II, 315–37.

25. See J. Ebbinghaus, "Kant und Swedenborg," in *Jahrbuch des Auslandsamtes der deutschen Dozentenschaft,* 1943.

26. *Träume,* AA, II, 356.

27. *Träume,* AA, II, 358.

28. *Träume,* AA, II, 351 f.

29. *Träume,* AA, II, 372 f.

30. See K. Reich, "Kants Behandlung des Raumbegriffs in den 'Träume eines Geistersehers' und im 'Unterschied der Gegenden im Raum,'" in his edition of Kant's *Träume,* Hamburg, Meiner, 1975, v–xviii.

31. "Von dem ersten Grunde der Unterscheidung der Gegenden im Raume," AA, II, 375–383.

space. His purpose is to demonstrate through "intuitive judgments of extension,"[32] the absolute reality of space. Against Leibniz and Wolff, Kant follows Newton's idea of absolute space. Space cannot be the order of coexistence, because in this case the relations that each part of a thing has with another would suffice to explain all the spatial properties of that thing: the right hand would be thoroughly identical with the left hand. Yet orientation is precisely the spatial property that can never be explained through mere logical relations. Kant's argument of the "incongruent counterparts"[33]—the nonidentity of the right hand and the left hand, or the nonidentity of oriented "regions of space"—is used to prove, first, that space is independent of the existence of any matter and, second, that space has a reality of its own as principle of the composition of all matter. A further conclusion reached by Kant in 1768 establishes that absolute space is not an object of external sensation but rather a "fundamental concept" that makes sensation possible.[34]

This latter claim leads to a crucial thesis of Kant's 1770 dissertation, "De mundi sensibilis atque intelligibilis forma et principiis."[35] Space is the absolute order in which all relations of things are inscribed. Yet now counter to Newton himself, Kant argues that the nature of space (and time) is not real but *ideal*. Space and time are pure intuitions that do not result from our perception of external objects but are rather the very conditions for all internal and external appearance.[36] Thereby Kant establishes the autonomy of both sensibility and understanding. This distinction was probably reached by 1769 and is related to the "great light" that opened a new path to his thought.[37] Kant distinguishes between intellectual and sensible cognition and places intellectual cognition in opposition to sensible cognition. In relation to the *cognitio intellectualis*, Kant further distinguishes a twofold employment of the understanding: a "real use" and a "logical use." In the first case, the understanding produces out of itself concepts of objects and their relations, whereas in the second case, it only works on already given concepts by performing on them the various logical operations (subordination, coordination, classification, comparison, etc.). The logical use of the understanding is proper to all sciences. By contrast, its real use is confined to metaphysics.

The concepts that the understanding uses in its real function are purely intellectual. They are *Ideae purae*[38] in the sense that their origin is to be located in the pure nature of understanding. They are neither abstracted from the activity of the

---

32. "Von dem ersten Grunde," AA, II, 378.

33. See Jill V. Buroker, *Space and Incongruence: The Origin of Kant's Idealism,* Dordrecht/London, Riedel, 1981.

34. "Von dem ersten Grunde," AA, II, 383.

35. AA, II, 385–419.

36. "De mundi," §§14–15.

37. Reflexion 5037, AA, XVIII, 69.

38. "De mundi," §9.

senses (they are "ideas"), nor do they entail any sensible component (they are "pure"). Kant is already in search of the a priori condition of knowledge and experience. In setting up his argument against the traditional view of the distinction between phenomena and noumena as one that concerns the degree of clarity and distinctness in our cognition, Kant provides a crucial example for these purely intellectual concepts. "Moral concepts are known not by experience but by the pure understanding itself."[39] Here, for the very first time, moral concepts are declared by Kant to be a priori concepts. In the *Dissertatio,* Kant associates the use of understanding in metaphysics with two very different types of concepts: the categories of understanding and the ideas of reason, to use the later terminology of the *Critique.*

Kant was not entirely satisfied with the conclusions of the *Dissertatio.* Moreover, the theory of the ideality of space and time did not persuade authoritative correspondents such as Lambert and Mendelssohn;[40] the idea of intellectual cognition was not really explained, nor was the charge of idealism easy to overcome. In the famous letter of February 21, 1772, to Marcus Herz, Kant writes that he is working on a book entitled *The Limits of Sensibility and Reason,*[41] divided into a theoretical part and a practical part. The first part would, in turn, contain two divisions: "1. Phenomenology in general. 2. Metaphysics—albeit only according to its name and method." The second part would be subdivided into "1. General principles of feeling, taste, and sensible desire. 2. The first grounds of morality." Kant faces problems left open by the *Dissertatio.* He raises the twofold problem of what the first *Critique* would call the transcendental deduction and the metaphysical deduction of the concepts of the understanding. Kant asks himself the famous question: "What is the ground of the relation of what is called representation in us to the object?" It would take Kant nine years to answer this question—one with a relatively easy answer in the case of empirical concepts but with an extremely complex solution for the a priori concepts of the understanding. Nonetheless, Kant wrote to Herz that he was confident that the work—a "critique of pure reason"—would be ready for publication in three months.

It was probably soon after this letter that Kant's reflections on Hume's skepticism[42] aroused him from his "dogmatic slumber," and allowed him to address the

---

39. "De mundi," §7.

40. See Kant's letter to Lambert, September 2, 1770; Lambert to Kant, October 13, 1770; and Mendelssohn to Kant, December 25, 1770.

41. This title was already announced in the letter to M. Herz of June 7, 1771.

42. Kant knew Hume's work since 1759 through Hamann's translations. The question of the ways in which Kant read Hume's work is still largely debated in the literature; see Frederick C. Beiser, *The Fate of Reason: German Philosophy from Kant to Fichte,* Cambridge, Cambridge University Press, 1987; I. Berlin, "David Hume and the Sources of German Anti-Rationalism," in *David Hume: Bicentenary Papers,* ed. by G.P. Morice, Edinburgh, Edinburgh University Press, 1977, 95–116. For the connection with Hamann, see

problem of metaphysics in a new way. In the years between the 1770 *Dissertatio* and the first edition of the *Critique of Pure Reason* in 1781, Kant did not publish anything on his theoretical philosophy.[43] The correspondence and the collection of manuscripts known as the *Duisburgischer Nachlass* are the only sources for the development of his thought in this period.[44] Around 1775, Kant abandoned the claim that understanding can have a "real" use that discloses the essence of things as they are in themselves. He started reflecting upon the idea of a logic that dealt with the constitution of the object and with the activity of synthesis proper to the understanding. The "transcendental" use of understanding inherits its "objectivity" from the previous "real use," while it owes its "formality" and the relation to sensibility to the previous "logical use." Only in 1778 did Kant seem to reach a solution to the problem of the "metaphysical deduction" of the categories. After 1778, he reflected on the role of the imagination and on the separation between understanding and reason. Among the most important influences on him were Hume, Newton, Leibniz, Aristotle for the table of the categories, Plato for the doctrine of ideas, Tetens for his psychology, and Lambert.[45]

3. *The* Critique of Pure Reason*:* *Early Polemics and Developments, 1781–1790*

The *Critique of Pure Reason* was published in Riga in the spring of 1781.[46] The appearance of this work was met with a general silence. Kant probably expected even worse reactions, for he had been planning to write a more popular and accessible excerpt of the book since the summer of the same year.[47] In January 1782 the *Göttingische Gelehrte Anzeigen* published an anonymous review of the *Cri-*

P. Merlan, "From Hume to Hamann," in *Kleine philosophische Schriften,* ed. by F. Merlan, Hildesheim/New York, DeGruyter, 1976, 506–518.

43 It is the so-called "silent decade." In 1771, Kant wrote the short review of Pietro Moscati, "Recension von Moscatis Schrift: Von dem körperlichen wesentlichen Unterschiede zwischen der Struktur der Thiere und Menschen," (AA, II, 421–425), an important document of his anthropological interests. In 1775, for his course on physical geography, he worked on "Von den verschiedenen Racen der Menschen" (On the Different Human Races; AA, II, 427–443), where he first attempted a classification of the different human races on the basis of final causes.

44. Th. Hearing, *Der Duisburg'sche Nachlass und Kants Kritizismus um 1775,* Tübingen, Hirschfeld, 1910; these texts are now in AA, XVII, 643–673 (*Reflexionen* 4674-4684); see P. Guyer, *Kant and the Claims of Knowledge,* Cambridge, Cambridge University Press, 1979, 25–70. On the evolution of Kant's thought toward the first *Critique* see also H.-J. DeVleeschauwer, *L'évolution de la pensée kantienne,* Paris, Alcan, 1939.

45. See H.-J. DeVleeschauwer, *La déduction transcendentale dans l'oeuvre de Kant,* I., Antwerpen-Paris, De Sikkel, 1934.

46. For a systematic explanation of the main concepts of the first *Critique,* see chapter 2.

47. See Kant's letter to Herder, August 1781.

tique that shows a radical incomprehension of Kant's main theses.[48] Driven by this unfavorable reception, Kant resolved to present a new exposition of his thought. The *Prolegomena to Any Future Metaphysics That Shall Come Forth as Science*[49] appeared in 1783. While the *Critique* is constructed according to a synthetic and progressive method, in the *Prolegomena* Kant proceeds according to an analytic and regressive method. Such a method allows him to start from "facts" generally accepted by common understanding and then to go back to the conditions of their possibility. Some of the major differences between the 1781 work and the 1783 work can be accounted for by the fact that Kant's intentions in the *Prolegomena* are chiefly epistemological.[50] In 1786, Kant began the revision for a second edition of the *Critique,* which appeared in Riga in the spring of 1787. In this edition, Kant builds the link to the idea of a "critique of practical reason."[51] At the end of the prefaces to both editions, he announces the project of a metaphysics of nature,[52] which in the second edition is accompanied by a metaphysics of morals in order to constitute the system of reason. Moreover, Kant suggests that these two metaphysics should confirm the correctness of the critiques of both speculative and practical reason. In 1786, Kant published the *First Metaphysical Principles of Natural Science,*[53] where he develops the project of a metaphysics of nature as an applied metaphysics according to the principles of the *Critique.* Herein he presents the principles of our a priori knowledge both of material, corporeal nature (*Körperlehre*) and of thinking nature (*Seelenlehre*) insofar as this nature is empirically given to us.

---

48. See the material in *Rezensionen zur Kantischen Philosophie 1781–87,* vol. I, Bebra, 1991.

49. *Prolegomena zu einer jeden künftigen Metaphysik, die als Wissenschaft soll auftreten können,* AA, IV, 253–383.

50. In the *Prolegomena,* Kant introduces the distinction between "judgments of perception" and "judgments of experience" (§§18–23). The distinction is taken up again in the second edition of the *Critique* (§19, KrV B 142); he does not dwell on the topic of ideas and their regulative function (but see §§44, 56); the moral perspective that animates the last part of the *Critique* is almost absent.

51. Cf. Kant's own remarks on the new edition in KrV B XXXVII ff. The most relevant changes regard the introduction of Bacon's motto in the frontispiece, a new preface, some additions to the introduction concerning synthetic a priori judgment that bring back to the experience of the *Prolegomena,* the division of the Aesthetic and Analytic of Concepts in 27 paragraphs, additions to the Aesthetics (in particular to §8), the complete revision of the transcendental deduction of the categories (§§15–27), the introduction of the "Refutation of Idealism" and of the "General Observation on the System of Principles," changes in chapter 2 of the Analytic of Principles and in the Paralogism chapter of the Dialectic, where a refutation of Mendelssohn's argument for the immortality of the soul is added. All modifications cease at A 405.

52. KrV A XXI, B XLIII.

53. *Metaphysische Anfangsgründe der Naturwissenschaft,* AA, IV, 465–565.

In 1790, Kant wrote a harsh polemical defense[54] of the *Critique of Pure Reason* against Johann August Eberhard's attacks that appeared in the *Philosophisches Magazin*. This defense was necessitated by the fact that Eberhard was pleading for a return to Wolffian metaphysics arguing against the major points of Kant's philosophy.

In the *Critique of Pure Reason*, Kant presents a "self-criticism" of pure reason, thereby indicating the a priori sources and the limits of human knowledge. The possibility of metaphysics as science hinges upon the assessment of the limits of a priori knowledge. The question that Kant raises in the introduction regards the possibility of "synthetic a priori judgments."[55] In the *Critique*, he makes a twofold discovery. On the one hand, the so-called Copernican Revolution allows for a radical transformation of the problem of knowledge—namely of the question already posed in the 1772 letter to Herz concerning the ground of the relation between our concepts of the object and the object itself. Taking up the examples of mathematics and natural science, the *Critique* starts out with the hypothesis that knowing is doing[56] that is, that we can know of things only what our understanding puts into them. Instead of assuming that our understanding should conform to the structure of reality in order to know objects, Kant suggests that the way in which something is first constituted as reality for us depends upon the structure and the functions of the understanding itself.[57] Transcendental knowledge is therefore that knowledge that "is concerned not with objects but rather with our cognition of objects insofar as it is possible a priori."[58] On the other hand, opposing the metaphysical tradition, Kant sees in sensibility and understanding two sources of human knowledge that are different in kind, not just in degree.[59]

The limits of human knowledge follow from its structure. "Possible experience" is limited to the realm of appearances or of things as they appear to us; that is, as they are given to our sensibility. No knowledge of "things in themselves" is possible to us, as no experience is possible where sensibility is lacking. Kant establishes these limits as the condition for the possibility of freedom. He claims that we cannot know freedom in the same way and according to the same laws that guide our knowledge of phenomena in natural science. Yet it is only because we cannot know freedom theoretically that freedom can be the object of *practical* reason.

The *Critique of Pure Reason* is divided into a "Transcendental Doctrine of Elements" and a "Transcendental Doctrine of Method." The first division, in turn,

---

54. "Über eine Entdeckung, nach der alle neue Kritik der reinen Vernunft durch eine ältere entbehrlich gemacht werden soll," AA, VIII, 185–251.

55. KrV B 19.

56. KrV B XI ff.

57. KrV B XVI ff.

58. KrV A 11 f./B 25.

59. KrV A 15/B 29.

has two parts—first, the "Transcendental Aesthetics," in which Kant presents his theory of the transcendental ideality of space and time as pure a priori forms of intuition; and second, the "Transcendental Logic." The first division of the logic develops an "Analytic of Concepts," in which Kant presents by means of a "metaphysical deduction" the complete table of all the concepts of the understanding (categories) obtained from the original functions of judgment; he then shows, by means of a "transcendental deduction," that those concepts have indeed "objective reality," or "validity"—can be applied to objects. The "Analytic of Concepts" is followed by an "Analytic of Principles," which shows how the world of mathematics and natural sciences is constructed by the collaboration of understanding and sensibility. The second division of the logic is the "Transcendental Dialectic," in which Kant presents the inevitable "antinomies" and the unavoidable "illusion" in which speculative reason falls once it tries to go beyond the limits of possible experience.

4. Philosophy of History and the Project of a Critical Ethics, 1784–1788

In the years 1784–86, Kant published a series of writings on the philosophy of history. In the 1784 "Idea for a Universal History with Cosmopolitan Intent,"[60] he outlines a teleological philosophy of history that complements his moral philosophy. He examines the question of whether the evil tendencies of human nature can be reconciled with the assumption of a natural purposiveness of history.[61] Assuming that the natural constitution of all creatures strives toward its complete development, and given that human life is too short to bring human nature to completion, Kant points to the life of the species as the subject of history. History is a causal mechanism that uses natural antagonisms and contradictions—the famous "unsociable sociability"[62]—in order to raise the human species to a higher level of culture. This progress affects, at the same time, both the juridical constitution of civil society and the relations among states. History moves toward the condition of perpetual peace. In 1785, with the "Determination of the Concept of Human Race,"[63] Kant went back to a topic already addressed in 1775–77 and further developed the idea of a teleological disposition of the natural faculties of the human being. In the notion of teleology, Kant's views of natural science, ethics, anthropology, and history ultimately meet.

In the 1784 article "Answer to the Question: What Is Enlightenment?"[64] Kant defines the principle of the Enlightenment. The concept was already at work in

60. "Idee einer allgemeinen Geschichte in weltbürgerlicher Absicht," AA, VIII, 15–31.

61. "Idee," AA, VIII, 17 f.

62. "Idee," AA, VIII, 20.

63. "Bestimmung des Begriffs einer Menschenrace," AA, VIII, 89–106.

64. "Beantwortung der Frage: Was ist Aufklarung?," AA, VIII, 33–42.

the first *Critique,* which pointedly defines it as the "age of the critique," as the self-liberation through which the human being finally reaches the age of its adulthood, maturity, and full moral responsibility learning how to think independent of any external authority. In its historical significance, enlightenment (*Aufklärung*) promotes the juridical order that will eventually lead humanity to abandon the state of subjection to power and to establish a cosmopolitan order of perpetual peace. A year later, Kant restated his argument against Herder's *Ideas on the Philosophy of History of Humanity.*[65] In the 1786 "Suppositions on the Beginning of Human History,"[66] Kant takes up the idea formulated in 1784 that history is the scene of a conciliation between nature and culture. In the two articles on history, however, Kant's view of the relation between history and morality changes. Inbetween, in 1785, the *Groundwork of the Metaphysics of Morals* had laid the foundation of Kant's critical ethics.

The *Groundwork of the Metaphysics of Morals*[67] is the first work on ethics from the standpoint of critical philosophy. The analytic method allows Kant to proceed from the common knowledge of morality to the philosophical knowledge of a metaphysics of morals in the formulation of the supreme principle of morality. The synthetic method brings us back from the examination of this principle through a critique of pure practical reason to the common knowledge in which the principle is applied.[68] In contrast to the tradition of British and Scottish empiricism and its theory of "moral sentiments," Kant argues that moral philosophy can be grounded only as "pure" moral philosophy, the sources of moral obligation being found in the a priori principles of reason and not in the empirical realm of feeling. From this revolution in moral philosophy follows that the concept of happiness as highest moral end and principle of action is abandoned in favor of a radical a priori foundation of ethics in pure practical reason alone. Kant's inquiry, which set out to discover the "highest principle of morality,"[69] leads to the notion of "good will." Nothing can be said to be good in itself, since only the will is able to make things good. Hence the only thing that can be considered good without qualification is a "good will," which is free from any contingent empirical determination.[70] The ground of its determination is reason itself. In the *Groundwork,* Kant gives three different formulations of the "categorical imperative" (i.e., the a

---

65. "Recensionen von J. G. Herders Ideen zur Philosophie der Geschichte der Menschheit," AA, VIII, 43–66.

66. "Muthmasslicher Anfang der Menschengeschichte," AA, VIII, 107–123.

67. *Grundlegung zur Metaphysik der Sitten,* AA, IV, 385–463.

68. *Grundlegung,* AA, IV, 392; see the titles of the three chapters of the book: 1. "Transition from Ordinary Rational Knowledge of Morality to Philosophical"; 2. "Transition from Popular Moral Philosophy to a Metaphysics of Morals"; 3. "Final Step from a Metaphysics of Morals to a Critique of Pure Reason."

69. Ibid.

70. *Grundlegung,* AA, IV, 393.

priori synthetic-practical proposition)[71] that constitutes the formal ground of the determination of the good will.

In 1786, Kant published the article "What Does It Mean: To Orient Oneself in Thought?"[72] in which he discusses rules and conditions necessary to guarantee freedom of thought. This short essay builds a bridge between speculative reason and practical reason.

Even if the *Groundwork* already announced a transition to a critique of pure practical reason, the composition of the *Critique of Practical Reason*[73] (published in 1788) did not follow from the 1785 work according to a clearly established plan.[74] As the first *Critique*, the *Critique of Practical Reason* also is divided into a "Doctrine of Elements" and a "Doctrine of Method." The first includes in turn an Analytic (in which, however, the exposition is reversed so that the principles precede the concepts, while the sensible impulses of pure practical reason are presented last)[75] and a Dialectic. Kant's aim is to show that pure reason can be practical and, as such, is the only motive that determines the will immediately and purely a priori. Unlike the *Groundwork*, the second *Critique* deduces the principle of practical reason from the moral law taken as *Faktum* of pure reason (i.e., as its most proper action, or *facere*). The moral law is the *ratio cognoscendi* of freedom, and freedom the *ratio essendi* of the moral law. Once stated that the pure will can only be determined *formally* by the moral law, Kant argues that the *object* of the will—the highest good—includes both the highest virtue and the happiness of each individual in relation to his/her merits. This leads Kant to the doctrine of the "postulates": freedom as condition for the possibility of moral action; the immortality of the soul as condition for the infinite perfectibility of the human being; and god's existence, god being the one who attributes merits according to virtue.

5. *The* Critique of Judgment: *Aesthetics, Teleology, and Religion, 1788–1794*

The 1788 article "On the Use of Teleological Principles in Philosophy,"[76] in which Kant discusses again the concept of race, can be considered as a prelude to the *Critique of Judgment*. Kant maintains that the concept of race does not simply

71. *Grundlegung,* AA, IV, 420.

72. "Was heisst: Sich im Denken orientieren?" AA, VIII, 131–147.

73. *Kritik der praktischen Vernunft,* AA, V, 1–164. For a systematic explanation of the main concepts of the second *Critique,* see chapter 3.

74. For the genesis of the *Critique of Practical Reason,* see P. Natorp's "Nachwort" to his edition in AA, V, 489–498, and K. Vorländer's introduction to his edition in *Kritik der praktischen Vernunft,* Hamburg, 1952, XI–XXVI.

75. KpV, (AA, V, 16, 42f., 89 ff.) A32.

76. "Über den Gebrauch teleologischer Principien in der Philosophie," AA, VIII, 157–184.

provide a systematic classification of beings according to their empirical similarities but rather orders those similarities according to the laws of the understanding. In other words, the concept of race is a regulative concept, not an objective one.[77] Moreover, in the study of races, the insufficiencies met by theory should necessarily be integrated by the principles of teleology. Kant distinguishes between "description of nature" and "history of nature," the latter being the specific field for the use of teleology.

The *Critique of Judgment*,[78] published in 1790, is the systematic conclusion of Kant's critical project. Its two parts are dedicated respectively to the analysis of the a priori principles of the judgment of taste and of teleological judgment. Kant became convinced only very late of the possibility of discovering an a priori principle for our faculty of judgment and of seeing in the notion of purposiveness the unifying principle for both an experience of beauty in nature and art and an enlarged scientific approach to nature.[79] Kant's suggestion in the third *Critique* is that human reason, despite the fundamental dualism of nature and freedom, works in a systematic and unitary way. The aim of the *Critique of Pure Reason* was to show the necessary limits of human theoretical knowledge. However, what in the first *Critique* appears as the necessary limitation of human knowledge (the fact that freedom escapes any attempt at scientific conceptualization), discloses the specific realm proper to pure practical reason, namely, the sphere of morality. In the *Critique of Practical Reason*, Kant elaborates the unlimited capacity of human free action in the world as opposed to our limited knowledge of it. It is only in the *Critique of Judgment*, however, that Kant reflects on the split that his previous work introduced into the life and the essence of the human being. In the first two *Critiques*, the human being was thought of as a citizen of two irreconcilable worlds—the natural world of science and the moral "kingdom" of freedom. On the one hand, human theoretical reason appeared as bound to the mechanism of nature, limited to and by it; on the other hand, practical activity was proclaimed unlimited because it strives beyond nature and follows exclusively the law of freedom. In the third *Critique*, Kant attempts to think of the "unity" of the human being—of its physical body and its moral soul—on the basis of the unitary way in which reason works in the aforementioned two spheres. He recognizes that reason tries to bring freedom into the realm of nature by relating to nature in ways that provide an alternative to natural science but are not purely moral. Reason discovers the two "logics" of beauty and life, or teleology, which are both free of any direct (constitutive) cognitive or moral aim and are both necessary if the system of reason is to be complete. Our feelings for the beauty of nature, art, and the human body, as well as the inscrutable phenomenon of life, are the new fields that Kant opens to investigation.

---

77. "Über den Gebrauch," AA, VIII, 163.

78. *Kritik der Urteilskraft,* AA, V, 165–485.

79. For a detailed exposition and discussion of all these topics both in a historical perspective and a systematic perspective, see chapter 4 and part III.

The analysis of the second part of the *Critique of Judgment* leads Kant to the idea of an ethical foundation of theology. Kant's ethical theology radically differs from both speculative theology and speculative teleology. This is the topic of the 1791 essay "On the Failure of all Philosophical Attempts at a Theodicy."[80]

In 1793, Kant started to work on the essay "What Is the Real Progress That Metaphysics Has Made in Germany Since the Time of Leibniz and Wolff?"[81] in response to the prize topic formulated by the Berlin Academy for the year 1791 and then deferred to 1795. The work remained unfinished and was published by Friedrich Theodor Rink in 1804. Here Kant reflects on the historical significance of the critical project viewed now as a systematic whole.

In *Religion Within the Limits of Reason Alone*[82] (1793), Kant addresses the topic of religion. He originally planned to print the four parts of the book as four successive articles in the *Berlinische Monatsschrift*. In 1792 appeared the first essay on "Radical Evil in Human Nature," but since a second one was rejected by Prussian censorship, Kant decided to publish the four articles together in book form. Kant's aim was to show that since the Christian religion entails the fundamental truths of a rational practical faith and the elements of a rational religion, it can be the object of critical and philosophical exposition. He interprets the doctrine of original sin as the radical evil in human nature from which we can be liberated only by a "revolution of spirit."[83] This revolution would enable us to put forth the original tendency toward the good that consists in the foundation of virtue on duty and the moral law.

6. Right, Politics, and Anthropology, 1793–1798

The close relation between Kant's doctrine of ethics, politics, and right is demonstrated by the essay "On the Old Saying: That May Be Right in Theory But Does Not Work in Practice"[84] (1793), where he argues against the separation between theory and praxis, showing that in the realm of morals only pure reason can be

---

80. *Über das Misslingen aller philosophischen Versuche in der Theodizee,* AA, VIII, 253–271.

81. "Welches sind die wirklichen Fortschritte, die die Metaphysik seit Leibnizens und Wolf's Zeiten in Deutschland gemacht hat?" XX, 253–351.

82. *Die Religion innerhalb der Grenzen der blossen Vernunft,* AA, VI, 1–202; a second edition of the *Religion* appears in 1794 with a new preface and new footnotes. See J. Bohatec, *Die Religionsphilosophie Kants in der "Religion innerhalb der Grenzen der bloßen Vernunft." Mit besonderer Berücksichtigung ihrer theologisch-dogmatischen Quellen,* Hamburg, Hoffmann u. Campe, 1938; T. M. Greene, *The Historical Context and Religious Significance of Kant's Religion, Introductory Essay to Religion Within the Limits of Reason Alone,* New York, Harper, 1960; A. W. Wood, *Kant's Moral Religion,* Ithaca, Cornell University Press, 1970.

83. *Religion,* AA, VI, 46 f.

84. "Über den Gemeinspruch: Das mag in der Theorie richtig sein, taugt aber nicht für die Praxis," AA, VIII, 273–313.

practical in an unconditioned way. Kant develops his argument in relation to morals in general (against Garve), to public right (against Hobbes), and to international right (against Mendelssohn).

In the 1795 (1796^2) essay "Toward Perpetual Peace,"[85] Kant outlines the idea of perpetual peace on the ground of his moral philosophy and his philosophy of history. Six preliminary articles concern the elimination of the obstacles against a future peaceful order, while three definitive articles set up the institutional conditions meant to guarantee that order. The definitive articles require, first, that the political constitution of all states should be a republic; second, that international law should be based upon a federation of free states; and third, that cosmopolitan right should be limited to the conditions of a universal hospitality.[86] In the appendix, Kant discusses the relation between politics and morals. He distinguishes two determinations of politics according to which the politician can be seen either as "moral politician" or "political moralist." In the first case, politics formulate a morals that specifically follows the interests of the state, whereas in the second case, the principles of politics are thought of as consistent with the principles of morals. Kant contends that politics must be critically supported and controlled by the "principle of publicity."[87]

In 1797, Kant published the definitive systematization of his political and juridical thought in the two volumes of the *Metaphysics of Morals.*[88] The *Metaphysical Principles of the Doctrine of Right* presents the a priori principles of natural right, while the *Metaphysical Principles of the Doctrine of Virtue* is a systematic exposition of the duties of virtue. Kant had been announcing a work with this title since 1765. Since the *Critique of Pure Reason*, he repeatedly pointed to a metaphysics of morals that, together with a metaphysics of nature,[89] was meant to complete the systematic task of his philosophy. As opposed to the *Groundwork* and the *Critique of Practical Reason*, the *Metaphysics of Morals* is an "applied ethics." It deals neither with the supreme principle of morality valid for all rational beings nor with a foundation of the metaphysics of morals. It is rather a systematization of duties as specifically *human* duties and an application of the categorical imperative to the *particular conditions of human* action. In the doctrine of right, "legality" is defined as the external accordance between action and

---

85. "Zum ewigen Frieden. Ein philosophischer Entwurf," AA, VIII, 341–86.

86. "Zum ewigen Frieden," respectively: AA, VIII, 351, 354, 357.

87. "Zum ewigen Frieden," AA, VIII, 381 ff.

88. *Die Metaphysik der Sitten,* AA, VI, 203–493. One of the best studies is Mary J. Gregor, *Laws of Freedom: A Study of Kant's Method of Applying the Categorical Imperative in the* Metaphysik der Sitten, Oxford, Oxford University Press, 1963. See also W. Kersting, *Wohlgeordnete Freiheit. Kants Rechts- und Staatphilosophie,* Frankfurt a.M., Suhrkamp, 1983; Susan M. Shell, *The Rights of Reason: A Study of Kant's Philosophy and Politics,* Toronto, University of Toronto Press, 1980.

89. See the already quoted KrV A XXI, B XLIII.

the law of reason. Kant translates the categorical imperative into the principle of right: "Act externally so that the free use of your will can subsist together with the freedom of everyone else according to a universal law."[90] Right is the external limitation of freedom by a universal law valid for everyone. Both private right and public right derive from the right to external freedom given by nature to every individual. From the obligation proper of the sphere of right, a transition is made to the obligation proper of ethical duties. The second part of the *Metaphysics of Morals* ("Doctrine of Virtue") deals with the systematic exposition of duties. Therein Kant follows the division already presented in the *Groundwork* (perfect and imperfect duties, duties toward oneself, toward others, and toward god).

In *The Conflict of the Faculties*[91] (1798), Kant turns his attention to the problem of the role of science in society and directly discusses the relation between the "highest faculties," namely theology, jurisprudence, and medicine, and the "lower faculty," namely philosophy. Kant argues that since the highest faculties depend both on external public legislation and on the internal legislation of reason (for the search of truth defines their very aim), they ultimately depend on philosophy, which is the faculty that assumes the self-legislation of reason as its only principle.

Appearing in the same year as the *Conflict of the Faculties*, the *Anthropology from a Pragmatic Point of View*[92] is the last work published by Kant. Both in the *Groundwork* and in the *Metaphysics of Morals*, he regarded "practical anthropology" as the empirical part of ethics as opposed to its rational part (i.e., to the metaphysics of morals proper). In that connection, the task of anthropology follows closely to the task of a moral pedagogy. Different, however, are the characters that Kant attributes to a "*pragmatic*" anthropology. For Kant, this is a form of "knowledge of the world" and specifically of the human being as citizen of the world (accordingly, Kant's pragmatic anthropology is neither a human psychology nor a human physiology). Its object is not the natural human being taken as a product of nature but the human being viewed as the product both of his/her own conscious activity and of social conditions and relations (i.e., as a product of culture).

7. Opus Postumum, *Lecture Courses, and* Reflexionen

Kant's correspondence of the nineties reveals his plan to write a book on the foundation of natural science and in particular on the problem of the "transition from the *Metaphysical Principles of Natural Science* to physics." Kant's purpose

---

90. *Metaphysik der Sitten,* AA, VI, 231.

91. *Der Streit der Fakultäten,* AA, VIII, 1–116.

92. *Anthropologie in pragmatischer Hinsicht,* AA, VII, 117–333. See F. van de Pitte, *Kant as Philosophical Anthropologist,* The Hague, Nijhoff, 1971, and the excellent edition by Mary J. Gregor of I. Kant, *Anthropology from a Pragmatic Point of View,* The Hague, Nijhoff, 1974.

is to definitively "fill the gaps still left open in the system of critical philosophy."[93] The analysis concentrates on the question of how transcendental principles of thought become concrete in the production of experience, bridging the gap between a priori structures and experience itself. While the principles established by the *Critique of Pure Reason* were valid for the realm of nature in general and not for nature in a particular determination, the *Metaphysical Principles of Natural Science* showed the specific principles of corporeal nature and its movement. Kant's 1786 work, however, left open the question of the possibility of an empirical physics. To this topic, Kant dedicated his later efforts. This work remained unfinished, in the status of preparatory sketches and drafts, notes, and sometimes fragments. This material was published for the first time in 1936 and 1938 in the *Gesammelte Schriften.*[94] The last developments of Kant's philosophy are known as the *Opus Postumum.*

As Kant discloses in the preface of the *Anthropology*, the text of his last published book was made up by the lecture-courses that he gave for years in the winter semester. In 1800, Gottlob Benjamin Jäsche, Kant's student and friend, published a compendium of the lectures that Kant held on logic since the winter semester of 1755–56.[95] In 1802 Friedrich Theodor Rink, another student of Kant's, published the lectures on physical geography[96] on the basis of Kant's manuscripts (some of them dating back to the sixties) as well as on his own notes. Rink is also responsible for the publication of Kant's lectures on pedagogy in 1803. However, because of the questionable criteria with which Jäsche and Rink at first, Karl Heinrich Ludwig Pölitz and Fr. Ch. Starke later, proceeded in publishing Kant's lectures (using different sources that dated back to different periods without editorial differentiation), Kant's first editors, Friedrich Wilhelm Schubert, Karl Rosenkranz, and Gustav Hartenstein, decided not to include the lecture-courses in their complete edition of Kant's works. Only after Max Heinze, at the end of the century, was finally able to date and analyze the philological problems of the metaphysics lectures edited by Pölitz, were the *Lectures* accepted in the plan of Kant's *Gesammelte Schriften* initiated in 1900 by Wilhelm Dilthey for the Berlin Academy.[97] Yet, the controversy on Kant's *Lectures* arose again and again, starting in the first decade of the twentieth century with Benno Erdmann's skeptical stance on the problem and Erich Adickes's edition of the physical geography lectures. In the twenties, however, the value of this material for the study of Kant's thought was restated in Paul Menzer's edition of an ethics course dating back to a few years before the 1781 edition of the *Critique of Pure Reason*; by Arnold

93. Kant's letter to Garve, September 21, 1798.

94. *Opus Postumum,* AA, XXI, XXII, ed. by G. Lehmann and A. Buchenau.

95. *Logik. Ein Handbuch zu Vorlesungen,* AA, IX, 1–150.

96. *Physische Geographie,* AA, IX, 151–436.

97. See Dilthey's announcement in the preface to the first volume, which appeared in 1902: AA, I, XIII f.

Kowalewski's edition of Kant's courses on anthropology, logic, and metaphysics during the years 1791–93; and later by Kurt Beyer's publication of the lectures on religion and Gerhard Lehmann's final edition for the *Gesammelte Schriften*. In recent years, new criticism has arisen of Lehmann's editorial work.[98] Reinhard Brandt is presently responsible for the publication of the last volumes of the *Lectures* (AA, XXV, XXVI). Together with Werner Stark, Brandt has instituted a *Kant-Archiv* at the University of Marburg for the Kant edition and the study of new material concerning Kant's life and work.[99]

Related to the philological questions opened by Kant's *Lectures* are the problems of Kant's *handschriftlicher Nachlass*—the manuscript material on different topics and of different periods that Kant left behind at the time of his death. A major part of this material is constituted by Kant's marginalia, observations, and reflections (the so-called *Reflexionen*) on the manuals that he used to comment on during his lectures. Schubert was the first to organize the material left in the library of Königsberg. In 1882, Erdmann published Kant's *Reflexionen* on Baumgarten's *Metaphysica*, followed in 1889 by R. Reicke's edition of the first *Lose Blätter* (loose sheets). A thorough work on the *Nachlass* is the life's work of Adickes, who carefully dated and edited all the manuscript materials now published in volumes XIV–XXII of the *Gesammelte Schriften*.[100]

98. See N. Hinske, "Die Kantausgabe der Preußischen Akademie der Wissenschaften und ihre Probleme," in *Il cannocchiale* 3, 1990, 229–54; W. Stark, "Probleme der Edition und Dokumentation," ibid., 255–61.

99. See R. Brandt, W. Stark, "Kant-Archiv Marburg," in *Information Philosophie*, 1983, 49–52.

100. The publication of the *Nachlass* was completed by G. Lehmann after Adickes's death.

Chapter 2

The Critique of Pure Reason: Sensibility, Understanding, and Reason

This chapter presents Kant's main division of the cognitive faculty (*Erkenntnisvermögen*) as it is developed in the *Critique of Pure Reason.*

1. The Problem of Knowledge: The A Priori of Knowledge and the Copernican Revolution

In the preface to the second edition of the *Critique of Pure Reason*, Kant presents the radical innovation of his critical project through the famous image of the Copernican Revolution. The problem that he outlines from the very beginning of the 1781 preface—the problem in which his revolution is inscribed—concerns the possibility of metaphysics as science or the possibility of metaphysical *knowledge*. The urgency of the question is dictated by the "peculiar destiny" of our human reason (i.e., our unavoidable natural disposition to get involved in the metaphysical quest).[1] The problem that Kant sets out to address in the *Critique* concerns what and how much understanding and reason can know under the twofold condition (i) of being considered apart from—and before all—experience (i.e., a priori), and (ii) of being constituted in such a way as to provide a form of knowledge "free of all experience," or *pure.*[2] The inquiry leads thereby to Kant's formulation of a new concept of experience. This concept will be opposed to the traditional view that sees experience as coextensive with sheer empirical data. Kant's transcendental notion of experience accounts precisely for the non-empirical a priori elements that first make experience possible for us. That is, it accounts for those elements that the understanding puts in experience by taking them out of its own essence and function.

A priori knowledge of reason is twofold according to the way in which the relation to the object is established. If the task is simply to "determine" the object and its concept, then knowledge is *theoretical*; if the task is also to "make the object real" according to concepts, then knowledge is *practical.*[3] Kant's question in the first *Critique* regards the sources and limits of pure a priori *theoretical* knowledge of reason. Yet the entire development of Kant's argument eventually institutes the relation between theoretical and practical knowledge, suggesting that the *Critique of Pure Reason* is only the beginning—indeed, the foundation—of a more extensive critical project. On this basis, critical philosophy ultimately opens

1. KrV A VII–IX.
2. KrV A XVII.
3. KrV B IX f.

up to the complete "system" of reason—or at least to the regulative ideal of such a system.

To explore whether metaphysics can be a science, Kant discusses the nature of the scientific knowledge embodied in the concrete procedures and results of mathematics and physics. Mathematics and physics are the two forms of "theoretical knowledge of reason"[4] that can determine their objects entirely a priori. That is, they do not imply any derivation from experience but rather make experience of their objects possible for the first time. Mathematics and physics do not find their respective object as an already constituted 'given.' They produce or construct it for the very first time. Only under this condition can the object be given at all as the object of a possible experience. In relation to the specific knowledge proper to these sciences, the problem of metaphysics receives a more precise determination. The history of mathematics shows how all successful work in this field rests on a crucial methodological premise. The mathematician Tales did not derive his proofs by observing the properties of the isosceles triangle, nor did he try to infer them from its concept. In sum, Kant suggests that mathematical knowledge is neither *empirical* knowledge (cognition that arises out of observation) nor *analytical* knowledge (cognition that only needs the concept of its object in order to formulate judgments). Mathematical knowledge results instead from "construction" (i.e. from the procedure that allows understanding to know a priori those components of the object that it put into the object itself in the process of its very generation).[5] An analogous methodological lesson can be found in natural science, where history teaches that scientists such as Galilei, Torricelli, and Stahl were able to reach their discoveries and carry on their experiments only because they did not accept the methodological device of simply following thc guidancc of nature. They were convinced that only by forcing nature to answer their questions could the path of truth be opened to reason. They understood that reason sees in things only what it derives from its own concepts, judgments, and principles.[6] True method—for mathematics as well as for physics—is therefore the discovery of the *legislative power of reason*. In this sense, the *Critique of Pure Reason* can truly be called a "treatise on method"[7] in relation to philosophy itself.

Following the suggestion of mathematics and natural science and referring to a well-established tradition that goes back at least to Gianbattista Vico and Thomas Hobbes, Kant proposes an idea of knowledge according to which knowing is doing,[8] producing, and constructing. Knowledge is an activity of understanding

---

4. KrV B X.
5. KrV B XI f.
6. KrV B XIII.
7. KrV B XXII—as opposed to the "system of science."
8. See M. Baum, "Erkennen und Machen in der *Kritik der reinen Vernunft,*" in: *Probleme der "Kritik der reinen Vernunft,"* ed. by B. Tuschling, Berlin, De Gruyter, 1984, 161–177, for the historical antcedents of this model and its development in the KrV.

and reason,[9] not the passive contemplation or the subsidiary description of a given object (either of an idea or of merely empirical data). From this model it follows that the general distinction between activity and passivity becomes insufficient to account for not only the separation between theoretical knowledge (or theoretical reason) and practical knowledge (or practical reason) but also for the differentiation among the elements and functions of knowledge itself. Hence, in order to ground this distinction Kant needs to address a different set of issues. The moment of understanding's active contribution to the process of cognition is what Kant calls the 'a priori' of knowledge. Assuming that "knowledge of experience" (*Erfahrungserkenntnis*)[10] is constituted of different elements, its a priori component is the specific "addition"[11] for which only our faculty of knowledge must be considered responsible. A priori knowledge is thereby opposed to empirical, or a posteriori, knowledge, which has its source not in understanding but in experience. The inquiry of the first *Critique* is dedicated to the investigation of this a priori discovered by Kant right at the heart of the knowledge of experience (and not beyond it as metaphysics wants).

Examples of mathematics and physics lead Kant's argument to a further conclusion. Certainly, the methodological move that allowed mathematicians as well as natural scientists to reach successful results in their respective fields had the historical significance of a "revolution"—a radical change that affected the very mode, or "way of thinking" (*Denkungsart*), proper to those sciences. If that revolution was made possible by the discovery that to understanding belongs a specific activity through which it constitutes and constructs its own object and without which nature itself could never guide us to truth, then it should be possible to extend the revolutionary method of thinking and knowing to philosophy and, in particular, to metaphysics. For metaphysics is the highest form of "rational knowledge."[12] Yet in the realm of metaphysics, history has been teaching a different lesson. Here revolution is yet to come,[13] since reality as the criterion of all truth has never been questioned. From this unquestioned assumption it follows that knowledge must consist in understanding's effort to conform to the structure of the object to be known.[14] This is precisely the claim that Kant rejects. Kant's Copernican Revolution is the methodological hypothesis that radically changes the direction in which the cognitive relation between subject and object is instituted. The given object is no longer the fixed center of the epistemological relation, but it rather has to comply with rules dictated only by the structures proper to the hu-

9. The difference between understanding and reason will be addressed later on in this chapter.

10. KrV B 1/A 2.

11. KrV B 2/A 2.

12. KrV B XVI.

13. KrV B XVI.

14. Kant strongly questioned this traditional claim in the letter to M. Herz, February 21, 1772. However, he did not have any answer for it at that time.

man cognitive faculty. This is the foremost condition that allows it to become an object of possible knowledge.

Because of the two terms involved in the cognitive relation, Kant's Copernican Revolution presents two sides, or takes place according to two steps, respectively (i) the side of our faculty of knowledge and (ii) that of the known object. The argument of the *Critique* will proceed developing the two sides in parallel, and showing how the constitution of knowledge through its functions is, at the same time, the transcendental construction of the object to be known.

(i) As far as the knowing subject is concerned, Kant draws a crucial distinction between intuition of objects and concepts thereof. If intuition had to conform to the structure of the reality already given to our senses—as has always been assumed in metaphysics—then no a priori of intuition would ever be possible, for prior to the act of intuiting the given object nothing at all would be meaningful. In this connection, a faculty of intuition in general could only be the topic of a psychological inquiry and ultimately would not differ from a collection of individual acts of intuiting. Yet Kant's *Critique* is set out in a radically anti-psychological perspective. Its inquiry is called "transcendental" as it regards neither the objects of knowledge nor the psychology of the subjective mechanism of cognition but rather our very mode of knowing objects *insofar as this knowledge is possible a priori.*[15] Hence, if traditional views of metaphysics make all a priori of intuition impossible, the contrary hypothesis has to be explored. We have to assume that it is the object that has to comply with the prescriptions given by our faculty of intuition (and not simply by the single act of intuiting) on the ground of its own transcendental constitution. In this case, and in this case only, the a priori of intuition—or an a priori intuition—indeed makes sense. Since the a priori is precisely that which allows something either to be represented/thought of at all or to be represented/thought of as an object, it must *precede* the object itself and consequently can rest exclusively on our cognitive faculty.

However, Kant argues that intuition should be regarded only as one moment in the process of cognition. Intuitions as such do not provide cognition yet. Properly speaking, at the level of intuition we cannot even say that what we intuit are objects. In order to do so, we need first to *relate* our intuitions—taken now as "representations" of something—to something taken as the "object" of those representations, and we need second to "*determine*" the object through "concepts."[16] Kant feels the need to restate the necessity of his methodological hypothesis for concepts as well since concepts belong to a radically different faculty than do intuitions. As was the case for intuitions, the a priori of concepts—or the possibility of a priori concepts—rests on the assumption that the objects to be known do not have an absolute reality (i.e., a reality in themselves that places them outside all possible rela-

15. KrV B 25/A 12.
16. KrV B XVII.

tion to our cognitive faculty). On the contrary, objects behave as objects only as they follow the rules prescribed a priori to them by our understanding.

(ii) While opening up the possibility for intuitions and concepts to relate a priori to the objective side of the cognitive relation, Kant's revolution progressively transforms the notion of the object of cognition. Accordingly, the first, indeterminate "something" of intuition is *determined* as "object" by the concept. However, the object of knowledge in a more proper and complete sense is called "experience,"[17] and is seen as the product of both intuition and concept—as their "synthesis." In sum, the Copernican Revolution amounts to the claim that experience is precisely the object produced by our cognitive faculty synthetically at work through its two functions of intuitions and concepts (or sensibility and understanding). Experience is not the source of our concepts and intuitions of reality; on the contrary, sensibility and understanding are the sources of that construction which is experience. This predicament is reflected in the famous statement that opens the 1787 introduction of the *Critique*: "Though all our knowledge begins with experience, it does not follow that it all arises out of experience."[18] Moreover, if experience is the general object of our knowledge, then all objects of knowledge are objects of a possible experience. This methodological move allows Kant a first answer to the problem of the possibility of metaphysics as science. Metaphysical knowledge is possible for Kant only as metaphysics of experience,[19] given the new meaning of the notion of experience.

Yet metaphysics makes claims that exceed the objective realm of experience, for reason can well think of objects that will never be met within a possible experience. In order to address the peculiar difficulty raised by metaphysics, Kant draws the crucial distinction between "knowing" an object and merely "thinking" of an object. This distinction is paralleled by a further transformation of the notion of object now seen either as "appearance"—as object of possible knowledge; or as "thing in itself"—as the unknowable object of mere thought. In order for an object to be *thinkable,* what is required is simply its "logical possibility" which is guaranteed by the principle of contradiction. But in order to *know* an object, its "real possibility" should be demonstrated, either empirically by experience of its reality or a priori by reason. In other words, if I can "think whatever I want insofar as I do not contradict myself,"[20] the mere thought of something does not allow me any inference about the objective reality (or the existence) of what I think. The transcendental inquiry of the *Critique of Pure Reason* rests on the delimitation, within the realm of objects, between what can respectively be known and be

---

17. KrV B XVII.

18. KrV B 1.

19. See N. H. J. Paton's book: *Kant's Metaphysics of Experience. A Commentary on the First Half of the Kritik der reinen Vernunft*, London, Allen & Unwin, 1936.

20. KrV B XXVI, Fn. See this important distinction at work, for example, in the conclusions of the transcendental deduction: B 165.

thought. Accordingly, all that can be known can also be thought, but not all that can be thought can be known. Counter to metaphysics, which has always mistaken the possibility of thinking things for the possibility of knowing them, the *Critique* establishes that the sphere of what can be thought is not coextensive with the realm of the knowable. The domain of pure thought is, in fact, far more extended than that of pure a priori knowledge. It includes speculative knowledge of reason, practical knowledge, and the teleology of reason. Hence, it is on the distinction between thinking and knowing that Kant ultimately grounds the peculiar relation between different uses of reason.

Objects that can be *known* through the combined activity (synthesis) of sensibility and understanding and thereby fall within the limits of a possible experience are called by Kant "appearances." Thereby he indicates the reality that is posited in relation to our faculty of knowledge: things as they appear to us and insofar as they appear to us (i.e., insofar as they constitute a reality for us). "Things in themselves" are instead those objects that can only be *thought* by reason as transcending the limits of a possible experience. They are "in themselves" since they have a reality that has no relation to us. They transcend both theoretical knowledge and sensibility and are thoroughly independent of our knowing faculty. Yet these objects are nonetheless real—albeit in a different way than are the objects of the senses. Reality for Kant cannot be coextensive with sensibility if freedom—and practical reason—is to be possible. For freedom, as we will see, is the foremost example of an object of thought that can never be known theoretically since it does not meet the conditions of our sensibility.[21] Yet freedom not only can be thought without contradiction but also can be practically known or be the object of practical knowledge. Kant's second answer to the problem of the possibility of metaphysics suggests therefore the possibility of a "metaphysics of morals," a metaphysics not of pure speculative reason but rather of practical reason.

2. The Theory of Sensibility: Intuition and Sensation

One of the most striking suggestions of the first *Critique* is the claim that sensibility along with reason and understanding is an activity that implies pure a priori structures. Kant's thesis stands thoroughly unprecedented. In the *Prolegomena* Kant himself recognizes that "it never occurred to anyone that the senses might intuit a priori." Even though Kant takes up the traditional language of receptivity and affection to indicate the specific way in which sensibility works, this receptivity, insofar as it qualifies the a priori forms of sensibility, is not sheer passivity. Kant suggests that the possibility for sensibility to be modified precedes a priori all its affections.[22] Moreover, the object by which the subject is affected is not the same object that results from the way in which the subject is affected. Properly speaking, the first object—the "something" that affects our receptivity—is not an

21. KrV B XXV.
22. See *Prolegomena*, §8.

object yet. For objects do not affect sensibility since objects exist for us only because sensibility is the subject's capacity of being affected. Sensibility comes before all knowledge of objects and is the necessary condition thereof. Thereby Kant suggests that there is an a priori of sensibility that precedes even the logical a priori of understanding and is thoroughly independent of it.

The whole metaphysical tradition, ending up in the Leibnizian-Wolffian systematization, used to consider the difference between understanding and sensibility—or concepts and intuitions—as one of degree in clarity and in distinctness. Accordingly, such a difference can always be bridged by appropriate procedures of clarification. The empiricist tradition, on the other hand, locating the source and origin of all knowledge in the supposedly empirical nature of sensibility falls directly into Hume's skepticism. Kant's notion of the a priori is the decisive answer both to the empty speculations of metaphysics and to Hume's skeptical objection against the empiricist attempts to provide a foundation of science. Kant concludes the introduction to the *Critique* with a general claim that radically breaks with both those traditions. He maintains that human knowledge originates out of two "branches": "sensibility," through which objects are *given* to us; and "understanding," through which, instead, objects are "*thought*."[23] These two branches, or functions, of human knowledge are different in kind (not just in degree), so that the possibility of a transition from one to the other is, in principle, impossible. Because of the fundamental heterogeneity that divides them, they produce a synthesis by working together. Yet along with the strong claim that separates sensibility and understanding, Kant opens up to the hypothesis ("perhaps") that these two functions might branch out of a "common, although to us unknown, root."[24] Thereby Kant is pointing to the possibility of bringing the differentiation of the functions of human knowledge back to a unitary source. He is suggesting the possibility of the unity of reason. To be sure, Kant strongly denies that this common root can ever be found *theoretically* as a metaphysical common origin of all our mental powers. Although this possibility must be ruled out by the critical inquiry, however, the thesis that theoretical reason is structurally identical with practical reason still stands in need of demonstration.[25] Kant's claim against Christian Wolff's attempt to reduce all the powers of the soul to a unity will be restated in the introduction to the *Critique of Judgment*.

Sensibility is generally defined by Kant as the capacity of producing representations through the way in which our senses are affected by objects. Sensibility is

---

23. KrV B 29/A 15; cf. B 74/A 50 and the "two original sources of the *Gemüt.*"

24. KrV B 29/A 15. This is the starting point of M. Heidegger's Kant interpretation in *Kant und das Problem der Metaphysik* (*Kant and the Problem of Metaphysics*, trans. by R. Taft, Bloomington, Indiana University Press, 1990); for a discussion of the problem raised by Kant's text in relation to Heidegger's interpretation, see D. Henrich, "On the Unity of Subjectivity," in *The Unity of Reason: Essays on Kant's Philosophy*, Cambridge, Mass., Harvard University Press, 1994, 17–54; see the commentary to KU E §§II–III in chapter 6.

25. See D. Henrich, *On the Unity of Subjectivity*, op. cit., 31.

a modality of our relation to objects. Thinking never relates to objects immediately; it relates to objects only through the mediation of sensibility and its representations. Kant's theory of sensibility recognizes two general forms of this relation, namely "intuition" and "sensation." Kant's purpose in his analysis of sensibility in §1 of the *Critique* (Transcendental Aesthetic) is to discern its different elements in order to "isolate"[26] the specific a priori components. Intuition is *immediate* relation to objects; it is also *singular* and concrete representation, as opposed to the generality and abstractness of the concept. For intuition to occur, the determinate affection of the *Gemüt* is required. In sum, through sensibility, objects are given from which empirical intuitions arise; intuitions are means and instruments that allow thinking to relate to objects and to determine them as objects. As a modality of sensibility, sensation is defined in an analogous way as the effect of an object on our faculty of representation. More precisely, however, sensation always expresses the *empirical* moment of sensibility while intuition can be either *empirical* or *pure*.

The object given to sensibility and affecting the *Gemüt* is "appearance": it is the object as it appears to our empirical intuition or sensation, which thereby constitutes their content. With regard to appearance, Kant distinguishes between "matter," which is empirically given in sensation, and "form," the structure of order in which different sensations are organized according to certain relations. Kant's further distinction regards "empirical" and "pure" representations of sensibility. It is at this point that the difference between sensation and intuition starts to reveal its force and *raison d'être*. A representation is called "pure" when it does not contain anything that belongs to sensation. From this definition it follows that sensation can never be pure. In the Transcendental Aesthetic, Kant always equates sensation with the empirical and material moment of sensibility. In intuition, he discovers instead the possibility of a formal and pure component of sensibility. Thus, from intuition as one of the forms of sensibility, Kant goes back to the "pure form of sensible intuitions in general" to be found a priori at the very heart of the *Gemüt*.[27] It is *in* this pure form that all acts of intuition of objects take place. "This pure form of sensibility is itself called *pure intuition*."[28] It should be stressed, however, that with regard to the *human* faculty of knowledge, pure intuition does not cease to always be "*sensible* intuition." Yet, for Kant, not all intuition is sensible intuition.[29] We can very well think of a form of "intellectual intuition"—even though human intuition will never work this way. Thus, the analysis of sensibility in the first section of the Transcendental Doctrine of Elements led Kant to differentiate between sensation, which seems to be always empirical and therefore a posteriori, and intuition, which on the contrary may also concern a

26. KrV B 36/A 22.
27. KrV B 34/A 20.
28. KrV B 34 f/A 20.
29. See, for example, KrV B 72, B 51/A 35.

formal and pure aspect of sensibility, and in this respect has to be given a priori. Sensible intuition can be either empirical and a posteriori (as sensation is) or pure and a priori.

At the beginning of the Transcendental Dialectic, introducing the notion of "idea" of reason, Kant presents a *Stufenleiter*—a ladder-like ascending structure —to guide us in the division of the genus representation (*repraesentatio*). Here sensation is defined as a *subjective* perception, namely as a perception that "relates only to the subject as a modification of its status." To *subjective* perception he opposes "*objective* perception," or "knowledge," which is in turn either "intuition" or "concept."[30] The distinction between sensation and intuition in the first division of *Critique* (Transcendental Aesthetic), served the purpose of discovering in sensible intuition the possibility of pure a priori forms, which in turn led to define the elements of theoretical knowledge in its objective validity. At the level of the Dialectic, Kant specifies that in relation to knowledge, sensation only provides the empirical material to be thought and therefore is merely subjective, whereas pure intuition participates together with concept in the constitution of objective knowledge.

In the *Critique of Judgment* (§3), Kant will further refine his theory of sensibility, this time showing how sensation can have another meaning in connection with a different faculty than the cognitive faculty, namely the feeling of pleasure and displeasure. While pure intuition is a merely theoretical function that relates to the cognitive faculty (understanding) alone, sensation can be found operative in connection with different faculties. "When a determination of the feeling of pleasure and displeasure is called sensation, this expression has a very different meaning than when I call sensation a representation of a thing (through the senses as a receptivity that belongs to the faculty of knowledge)." In relation to the cognitive faculty, the representation provided by sensation is referred to the object in order to produce cognition of it. By contrast, if set in relation to the feeling of pleasure and displeasure, sensation refers exclusively to the subject. In this case, however, no determinate cognition is provided. Kant adds, "not even the cognition through which the subject knows itself." By reading together the Dialectic-passage of the first *Critique* and §3 of the third *Critique*, we can conclude that sensation, if taken exclusively in relation to the cognitive faculty, should be viewed as an objective representation of the senses that yet represents of the object only that which modifies the status of the subject. Instead, that element of sensation that is irreducibly subjective and therefore can by no means serve as a representation of the object is called by Kant "feeling."

Kant's discovery of pure a priori forms of sensible intuition allows him to develop a specific "science of all the a priori principles of sensibility." This science, under the title of Transcendental Aesthetic, constitutes the first section of the *Critique of Pure Reason*. Given the important connection to the topic of the

30. KrV B 376/A 320.

third *Critique*, a brief reflection on this title is in order. *"Aesthetics,"* observes Kant in a footnote that comments on the aforementioned title,[31] is the name that the German language uses to indicate what is generally called "critique of taste."[32] Aesthetics means theory of sensation. The double meaning of aesthetics should not surprise us once we take into account the twofold use of the notion of sensation that has just been discussed. In 1781 and again in 1787, albeit now in a somehow more hesitant tone,[33] Kant is clearly convinced of the impossibility of following A. G. Baumgarten in trying to develop a critique of taste in scientific form, namely according to a priori principles.[34] Its rules can only be empirical and therefore can never serve as "a priori laws" (or as "*determinate* a priori laws" as Kant significantly adds in the 1787 edition)[35] for the use of our judgments of taste. Thus, what is left is only the possibility of understanding aesthetics according to the ancient division of knowledge in αἶσθητά and νοητά (the sensible and the intelligible), and developing a scientific "transcendental" theory of the a priori forms of sensibility—specifically of intuition—as first part of a theory of knowledge. Kant now views any other attempt to talk about sensibility as one destined to be empirical and therefore merely psychological. Consequently, a transcendental theory (or critique) of taste is for Kant thoroughly impossible.

In the Transcendental Aesthetic, Kant presents two pure a priori forms of sensible intuitions, or formal intuitions—space and time. Space is the necessary condition of all relations in which objects are intuited by me as *outside* of myself; time is the necessary condition of my intuition of myself and of my *inner state*. Throughout four arguments on space paralleled by and expanded in five arguments on time,[36] Kant discusses the specific nature of space and time as ob-

---

31. KrV B 35 f./A 21, fn.

32. It is interesting to observe that Kant sees the idea of "critique" as already incorporated into the notion of "aesthetics"—thereby recalling the origin of the term "*critique*" in the field of literary criticism (see R. Wellek, *A History of Modern Criticism: 1., The Later Eighteenth Century*, New Haven, Yale University Press, 1955).

33. To explain this hesitation we should be aware of the fact that in 1787 Kant was about to start working on the third *Critique*.

34. See A. G. Baumgarten, *Aesthetica*, Frankfurt an der Oder, 1750–58; Mary J. Gregor, "Baumgarten's Aesthetica," *Review of Metaphysics* 37 (1983–84), 357–385; A. Nuzzo, "Kant and Herder on Baumgarten's *Aesthetica*," *Journal of the History of Philosophy*, forthcoming.

35. A comparison of the two versions of this footnote in the two editions of the *Critique* is a *locus communis* in the literature: see for all W. Windelband, "Einleitung zur Kritik der Urtheilskraft," in AA, V, 512–527, here 514; H.-J. De Vleeschauwer, *L'évolution de la pensée kantienne*, Paris, Alcan, 1939, chap. 3, 3; P. Guyer, *Kant and the Claims of Taste*, Cambridge, Cambridge University Press, 1997^2, 26–27; L. Amoroso, *Kant et le nom de l'Esthétique*, in *Kants Ästhetik-Kant's Aesthetics-L'esthétique de Kant*, ed. by H. Parret, Berlin/New York, De Gruyter, 1998, 701–705.

36. The four arguments on space and time are, respectively, in KrV B 38/A 23–B 40/A 25, and B 46/A 30–B 48/A 32.

jects (as mere forms hypostatized to objects) or formal intuitions and concludes with the claim that space and time are pure forms of intuition.[37] The arguments on space and time are crucial for establishing the general and formal features of a priori sensible intuition. The first argument presents the *non-empirical* character of space and time, maintaining that space is an a priori condition of the possibility of outer experience, while time is the a priori condition of the possibility of inner experience. The second argument proves that space is an a priori intuition and as such is the necessary condition of the objects of outer experience (i.e., of the appearances of outer senses). We cannot intuit objects of outer senses without intuiting them in space. Time is an a priori intuition that refers to the objects of inner experience and the inner sense as their necessary condition. In the third argument, Kant shows that space is *one* and *individual* and that it is a *totum* and not a *compositum* (in it the whole precedes its parts and is the condition of their possibility and not vice versa). Correspondingly, time is one as well, as it has only one dimension (different times are not contemporary, but successive; different spaces are not one after another, but at the same time). It follows that space and time cannot be discursive concepts but are necessarily pure forms of sensible intuition. This is the conclusion of the fourth argument that discusses the incompatibility of the infinite character of space (as *quantum* of an infinite number of parts) and time[38] with the intension of a concept that, on the contrary, can never be infinite.

From the third and fourth arguments, Kant's conclusion follows that space and time can neither be properties of things in themselves nor express relations of things in themselves.[39] Space is rather the "form of all *appearance* of external sense"[40] while time is the "formal condition of *all appearance in general*."[41] If space and time were determinations of things in themselves, they would be concepts since things in themselves are *Gedankendinge* (objects that are simply thought by the understanding), which accordingly should be known only through concepts by the understanding. Thus, since space and time are pure forms of intuition, they cannot be determinations of things in themselves and their relations, but only forms of appearances (i.e., forms of things as they are given to our sensibility). Hence Kant argues for the "transcendental ideality" of space and time. Space and time do not exist outside of the subjective conditions of our sensible

---

37. For the details of Kant's arguments see M. Baum, "Kant on Pure Intuition," in *Minds, Ideas, and Objects*, ed. by Ph. D. Cummins, G. Zöller, Atascadero, Ridgeview, 1992, 303–316, who argues against P. Guyer's reconstruction of Kant's argument in *Kant and the Claims of Knowledge*, Cambridge, Cambridge University Press, 1987, 345 ff.

38. To the discussion of the infinite character of time is dedicated a fifth argument (KrV B 47 f./A 32).

39. See M. Baum, "Dinge an sich und Raum bei Kant," in *Akten der siebenten Internationalen Kant-Kongresses*, Bonn, Bouvier, 1991, 63–72.

40. KrV B 42/A 26.

41. KrV B 50/A 34.

intuition. In other words, they do not have "absolute reality" but only "empirical reality" as conditions of experience.[42]

Kant's theory of space and time as pure forms of intuition remains a milestone of the first *Critique*. It is destined to have far reaching consequences in the Transcendental Dialectic allowing for the possibility of "transcendental freedom" on the one hand and playing a crucial role in matters of natural theology[43] on the other. Moreover this theory should be seen as the real foundation of the critical project as a whole since the very possibility of freedom and of the practical use of reason rests precisely on the transcendental ideality of space and time, namely on their limited validity to appearances.

However, Kant's theory of sensibility is not yet completed by the Transcendental Aesthetic. Another important step is carried through by the Analytic of Principles. Therein Kant sets out to show in what sense and in which ways sensibility works together with understanding in order to produce knowledge of objects and, in particular, in order to produce the scientific knowledge of nature proper to mathematics and physics.[44] This is the task of the doctrine of the "schematism." In *Prolegomena* §36, while asking "How is nature itself possible," Kant refers back to the Transcendental Aesthetic as the place where he provided an answer concerning "nature in its material sense, namely according to intuition, as the complex of appearance." There the question regarded the general possibility of space, time, and that which "fills up both, namely the object of experience." The theory of the a priori forms of intuition—space and time—represents Kant's first answer to the problem. But what about the reference to "that which fills up both?" For what fills up space and time is nothing else but sensation that constitutes the matter of appearances and that, due to its assumed exclusively *empirical* character, cannot be dealt with in a transcendental inquiry dedicated to pure a priori principles. This is precisely what we find stated in §1 of the Transcendental Aesthetic. However, in the Analytic of Principles, in studying the ways in which the categories of understanding work together with sensibility in order to produce knowledge, Kant goes back to the topic of sensation. At this level, in the "Anticipations of Perception" he discovers an *a priori of sensation* itself, namely the "degree" (*Grad*). Kant characterizes sensation in a twofold way. First, sensation is "*modification* of our sensibility." Second, as "modification of our sensibility," sensation is "the only way in which objects are given to us."[45] It expresses the "reality," or the material element of something existing, and as "perception" (i.e., that which has in itself the modification or sensation) it represents the "only character of reality."[46] Thus, sensation reveals a peculiar a priori structure precisely in

42. See KrV §6 B 52/A 35 ff. and §§7–8.

43. This result is already anticipated in the Aesthetic KrV B71 f.

44. See for what follows L. Scaravelli, "La sensazione e il grado," in *Scritti kantiani*, Firenze, La Nuova Italia, 1968, 71–141.

45. KrV B 178/A 139.

46. KrV B 273/A 225.

constituting a synthesis with the category of reality. This structure could not be detected in the isolation in which it was taken at the level of the Transcendental Aesthetic.

In sum, sensibility consists for Kant in a *form* that is intuition and has its a priori forms in space and time and in a *content* that is sensation and is instead a posteriori. Sensation, however, when taken in connection with understanding, displays in turn a moment that can be known a priori.[47] This a priori of sensation is that which can be "anticipated" in all experience. When sensation is synthesized with the category of "reality," it reveals an a priori moment that is the "degree," or the "intensive magnitude," that belongs to all reality.[48] Kant's formulation of the Axioms of Intuition states that all appearances in their *form,* or *intuition,* have a magnitude that can be expressed in space and time. The Anticipations of Perception, on the other hand, state that all appearances in their *material content,* or *sensation,* have a magnitude that cannot be expressed in space and time but by its degree. Kant's purpose is to show that all appearances, both according to the form and content, can be constructed by mathematics. The second principle is crucial for physics since without sensation no object could be given in its *reality*, no reality would *exist*, and nature "in its material sense" would have no meaning at all.[49]

3. The Understanding: Judgment and Concepts

In Kant's system of the faculties, "understanding" is the second "original source of the *Gemüt.*" Understanding never relates to objects immediately but only through the mediation of representations of sensibility. Its task is to produce *knowledge* of them. While objects are *given* through sensibility, through understanding objects are *thought*. As opposed to sensibility—defined as the "*receptivity* of impressions"—understanding is defined by the "*spontaneity* of concepts."[50] Because of the parallelism and yet the radical heterogeneity that divides the two branches of the *Gemüt*, human intuition is always *sensible*, whereas human understanding is always *discursive* (i.e., such as to necessarily need concepts in order to think). As in the case of intuitions, Kant divides concepts into "pure" and "empirical." Pure concepts, or categories, entail only the "form of the thought of an object in general."[51] Only pure concepts (as only pure intuitions) are possible a priori. They constitute the topic of the second part of the Transcendental Doctrine of Elements. Kant calls "transcendental logic" that logic which instead of making

---

47. This explains why Kant could not deal with the a priori of sensation at the level of the isolated sensibility of the Transcendental Aesthetic, which in fact contains only the two a priori forms of intuition—space and time. The "degree" is instead a synthesis of sensation and the category of reality.

48. KrV B 209/A 167 f.

49. Kant will use the idea of "degree" again in the Dialectic's Paralogism chapter against Mendelssohn's proof of the immortality of the soul (KrV B 414).

50. KrV B 74/50.

51. KrV B 75/A 50.

abstraction from all content of thinking (as does formal or "general logic") is concerned precisely (i) with our *knowledge of objects in general*, (ii) with its sources insofar as they are not to be ascribed to the object but rather to the faculty of understanding, and (iii) with the limits of both its domain and its objective validity.[52] While general formal logic deals exclusively with the formal truth of thinking, transcendental logic investigates the conditions of objective truth proper to knowledge. Transcendental logic isolates understanding (as transcendental aesthetic isolates sensibility) from all other faculties and functions of the mind, and in knowledge considers only that part of thinking that has its origin exclusively in understanding.[53] As the source of both pure concepts and principles, understanding is pure understanding.

Kant's fundamental move in his analysis of understanding as a cognitive faculty that proceeds through concepts is to refer it back to the notion of "judgment" (*Urteil*). Judgment is the "function" on which all concepts as well as all "actions" of understanding ultimately rest. As sensible intuition rests on affections of our sensibility, concepts rest on functions that express the "unity of the action" through which understanding distinguishes, connects, and orders a manifold of different representations, bringing them under a common representation.[54] This unitary action is judgment. Judgment expresses the peculiar nature of the "spontaneity" of understanding. All actions of understanding can be brought back to the functions of judgments. Concepts are indeed nothing but "predicates of possible judgments."[55] Therein lies the ground of Kant's "metaphysical deduction" of the categories. The idea of bringing the activity of the understanding back to the functions of judgments (i.e., to the different forms of judgment) opens up the possibility of a derivation of the complete set of concepts proper to the understanding itself.[56]

However, since transcendental logic has to deal with knowledge of objects and not with mere formal thinking, another step is required for the metaphysical deduction to take place. As opposed to formal logic, which by making abstraction from all content of thought is merely analytical in its procedures, transcendental logic presupposes content given by pure a priori intuition as a manifold in space and time. Although Kant proceeds by isolating understanding and its spontaneity,

---

52. KrV B 81/A 57.
53. KrV B 87/A 62.
54. KrV B 93/A 68 ff.
55. KrV B 94/A 69.
56. For this classical problem of the Kant-interpretation, see K. Reich, *Die Vollständigkeit der Kantischen Urteilstafel*, Berlin, Schoetz, 1948 (*The Completeness of Kant's Table of Judgments*, trans. by J. Kneller and M. Losonsky, Stanford, Ca., 1992), and more recently M. Wolff, *Die Vollständigkeit der Kantischen Urteilstafel*, Frankfurt a.M., Klostermann, 1995; R. Brandt, *Die Urteilstafel. Kritik der reinen Vernunft A 67–76; B 92–101*, Hamburg, Meiner, 1991; B. Longuenesse, *Kant and the Capacity to Judge*, Princeton, Princeton University Press, 1998.

he maintains that the manifold of pure intuition "*always affects* the concept" of the understanding.[57] Since the act of the understanding arises out of its unity with the material given by sensibility, it is synthetic in its very origin. Moreover, the spontaneity of understanding needs to be set in motion by sensibility (intuition and sensation). Insofar as the task of transcendental logic is the study of the way in which concepts are applied to objects in order to produce knowledge, the function of judgment meets the activity of synthesis. Synthesis is the "action" through which the spontaneity of thinking refers to the manifold of intuition (either pure or empirical) elaborating, appropriating, and ordering it, and establishing different connections. The purpose of synthesis is to produce knowledge by grasping the manifold of different representation in one cognition.[58] Thus Kant defines the "concept of the understanding" both through the notion of judgment, as "predicate of a possible judgment," and through the notion of synthesis, as "pure synthesis."[59] The two functions of judgment and synthesis are ultimately brought back to the same understanding that operates with them. For "*the same function* that gives unity to different representations in one judgment gives unity to the mere synthesis of different representations in one intuition." This synthesis constitutes the "pure concept of the understanding."[60] It is precisely the *sameness* of the function at work that allows Kant to derive from the table of judgments the complete table of the categories with which transcendental logic will from now on operate. Kant will employ this table again and again both in the applied philosophy that follows the critique, and in the other *Critiques* that follow the *Critique of Pure Reason*.

The metaphysical deduction served the purpose of obtaining the complete set of a priori concepts of the understanding by anchoring it in logic (once again, against psychology). The metaphysical deduction is followed by a "transcendental deduction" where Kant provides a justification, or legitimization, of the "right" claimed by the understanding in using its pure a priori concepts to produce real knowledge of objects.[61] At stake in the transcendental deduction is the problem of the "objective validity" or the truth of the categories as well as their

57. KrV B 192/A 77.

58. KrV B 102 f./A 77.

59. KrV B 104/A 78.

60. KrV B 104 f./A 79.

61. For the crucial juridical meaning of the deduction-procedure, see D. Henrich, "Kant's Notion of a Deduction and the Methodological Background of the First Critique," in: *Kant's Transcendental Deductions*, ed. by E. Förster, Stanford, Stanford University Press, 1989, 29–47. The literature on the transcendental deduction is huge; see at least H.-J. DeVleeschauwer, *La déduction transcendentale dans l'oeuvre de Kant*, 3 vol., Antwerpern/ Paris, De Sikkel, 1934–37; D. Henrich, "The Proof-Structure of Kant's Transcendental Deduction," *Review of Metaphysics* 22 (1969), 640–659; M. Baum, *Deduktion und Beweis in Kants Transzendentalphilosophie. Untersuchungen zur "Kritik der reinen Vernunft,"* Königstein/Ts., Hain, 1986; P. Guyer, *Kant and the Claims of Knowledge*, op. cit. (part II).

meaningfulness.[62] Kant has to explain how a priori concepts can refer to objects. The very heart of Kant's extremely complex argument consists in the discovery that the "logical form of all judgments consists in the objective unity of the apperception of the concepts contained therein," as Kant entitles §19 of the 1787 transcendental deduction. The idea of synthesis led Kant to the notion of an "original synthetic unity of apperception" (§16) (i.e., to the act of the "I think" that unifies all representations and makes the unity of thinking possible). The turning point of Kant's argument is the relation between the original synthesis of apperception and the function of judgment. The transcendental unity of apperception synthetically unifies the manifold of the given representations into an objective unity, thereby constituting what Kant calls "experience." Thus, the form of experience is grounded a priori in the understanding. Experience is possible, however, only in relation to the manifold given by intuition. Consequently, the a priori constructions of the understanding exhibit a validity that is confined to the objects of possible experience (i.e., to appearances). Because of the nature of understanding (and of sensibility), knowledge is possible only of appearances and not of things in themselves.

Kant's transcendental logic follows the division of the "higher cognitive faculty" into understanding, judgment, and reason.[63] Thus, after having isolated the concepts of the understanding taken as the faculty of rules and having justified their use, Kant deals with the faculty of judgment as the capacity to subsume under those rules and to discern whether something falls under a certain rule.[64] The analysis of this faculty constitutes the Analytic of Principles, which discusses the *application* of the a priori rules of the understanding to appearances through judgment. This is the doctrine of the transcendental "schematism."

4. Reason: Ideas and System

Following sensibility and understanding, reason represents the accomplishment and the culmination of the cognitive faculty. Its function is to bring "under the highest unity of thinking"[65] what has already been worked out and appropriated by the understanding on the basis of sensibility. Kant recognizes both a "logical" and a "real" use of reason. As was the case for the treatment of understanding proper to formal logic, the *logical* use of reason makes abstraction from all content of knowledge and considers reason as the capacity of constructing syllogisms or drawing mediated consequences out of premises. In its *real* or *transcendental* use, on the contrary, reason is itself the source of original concepts and principles

---

62. See, for example, KrV B 116/A 84; Kant speaks repeatedly of *Sinn* and *Bedeutung*. In the present connection it is not my aim to provide a summary of Kant's complex transcendental deduction.

63. KrV B 169/A 130.

64. KrV B 171/A 132.

65. KrV B 355/A 298.

that it shares neither with sensibility nor with understanding. The idea of the fundamental independence and heterogeneity among the faculties of the mind is thereby restated. As opposed to understanding as the faculty of rules, reason is defined as the "faculty of principles."[66] "Knowledge out of principles"[67] distinguishes reason from understanding and designates rational knowledge in its more general form. If understanding refers to objects only through the mediation of sensibility's own representations, reason is characterized by an even higher form of mediation. Reason is "the faculty of the unity of the understanding's own rules under principles."[68] Consequently, reason never relates to experience, nor does it refer to any object taken in the sense established by the understanding (as object of possible experience). Reason relates rather to the complex of understanding's own cognition producing its unity under a priori concepts. As sensibility was the object of understanding, understanding is now an "object" for reason.[69]

Kant's question at the beginning of the Transcendental Dialectic regards the possibility of a synthetic a priori knowledge of reason, namely the possibility of a "synthesis out of concepts"[70] alone, a synthesis that the understanding can never produce. At this point, Kant introduces the crucial idea of the "unity of reason." In relation to the activity of the understanding whose unity was expressed by the idea of the a priori *synthesis* operating on the manifold of intuition, the unity (or synthesis) of pure reason is expressed by the idea of *system*, and implies both the completeness of its manifold elements and the systematicity of its structures. "System" is defined by Kant as the "unity of the manifold of knowledge under one idea."[71] On the basis of the body of scientific knowledge established by the understanding, reason strives toward its organization and *extension* to the form of the *complete system of human knowledge*.[72] However, Kant's unity of reason has also a second—indeed an objective and theoretically higher—meaning, which suggests that reason is a unique and unitary faculty that is capable of radically different uses. The unity of reason provides the concept whose division gives rise, in turn, to the particular analysis of the first *Critique*. In this sense, reason itself is, for Kant, a "system."[73]

---

66. KrV B 356/A 299.
67. KrV B 357 f./A 300 f.
68. KrV B 359/A 302.
69. KrV B 692/A 664.
70. KrV 357/A 301.
71. KrV B 860/A 832. For a detailed analysis of Kant's notion of system, see A. Nuzzo, *Logica e sistema. Sull'idea hegeliana di filosofia*, Genova, Pantograf, 1992; and *System*, Bielefeld, Transcript Verlag, 2003.
72. In this first sense, the genitive 'unity *of reason*' is a *subjective* genitive as it indicates the unity that reason itself tries to accomplish. This is the topic of P. Guyer, "The Unity of Reason: Pure Reason as Practical Reason in Kant's Early Conception of the Transcendental Dialectic," *The Monist* 72 (1989), 139–167; Guyer fails, however, to recognize the importance of the second meaning of that unity.
73. KrV B 765f/A 738.

Moreover, it is precisely this second sense of unity that brings the argument of the Transcendental Dialectic out of the strictly epistemological context and opens up to the issue of the *practical* use of reason, or to the problem of *practical reason.* It is important to stress that reason's unity does not simply describe the structure of this faculty or the way in which it functions—as did the synthesis for the understanding, for Kant expresses through it the most proper "need" of reason[74] (a need that reason properly "feels").[75]

Proceeding in an analogous way as with sensibility and understanding, Kant sets out to "isolate"[76] reason, and to investigate in what sense pure reason can be considered as an autonomous faculty with its own concepts and judgments, leading to a specific kind of knowledge of a specific kind of objects. The question that Kant addresses in the Transcendental Dialectic regards the possibility for reason, considered in itself as isolated (i.e., as *pure* reason), to entail "a priori synthetic principles and rules."[77] While the principles of understanding are immanent, referring to a merely empirical use within the limits of possible experience, reason's own principles are transcendent as they abolish those limits and aim directly at the "unconditioned." This transcendence produces the dialectical illusion proper to the nonempirical use of the concepts of the understanding. For when the concepts of the understanding are no longer considered as "keys"[78] to our cognition of appearances but are viewed as providing knowledge of things in themselves, the same dialectical illusion arises that characterizes the speculations of traditional metaphysics. In the Analytic, the transcendental deduction proved that concepts of the understanding have objective validity in the realm of appearances or for objects of a possible experience only. Concepts of reason, on the contrary, raise claim to a validity that extends far beyond those limits. Concepts of reason, or ideas, propose themselves as archetypes, or original models of the reality of things. Their truth does not need the confirmation of experience as they propose themselves as the model for all experience.

In the *Critique of Pure Reason*—as was already the case, and for the very first time, in the 1770 *Dissertatio*—Kant's discussion of the notions of "idea" and "ideal" goes back to Plato.[79] Plato observed that human reason "feels a higher need"[80] than to simply spell out appearances according to their synthetic unity. Reason strives naturally toward a kind of knowledge that cannot be given in any experience and yet is not imaginary. It is a kind of knowledge that has "its own

74. KrV B 365/A 309.
75. KrV B 370/A 314.
76. KrV B 362/A 305.
77. KrV B 363/A 306.
78. KrV B 370/A 313.
79. For Kant's notion of idea see A. Nuzzo, "'Idee' bei Kant und Hegel," in *Das Recht der Vernunft. Kant und Hegel über Denken, Erkennen und Handeln*, ed. by C. Fricke, P. König, and T. Petersen, Stuttgart, Frommann, 1995, 81–120.
80. KrV B 370/A 314.

reality" and is not just a "fiction of the brain."[81] However, Kant's agreement with Plato regards not so much the theoretical sense of the Platonic idea but rather its reference to a *practical* reality. "Plato found the chief instances of his ideas in the practical (i.e., in what is grounded on freedom), which in turn stays under a knowledge that is the peculiar product of reason."[82] It is in the realm of the practical or in relation to the notion of freedom that ideas find their proper and adequate reality and propose themselves as models for a possible experience (which, accordingly, is no longer experience in the theoretical sense). Ideas always express a "maximum,"[83] or a "perfection," in relation to their claim to reality. As examples, Kant presents the idea of virtue, which is nowhere to be met empirically in its accomplished perfection, and the idea of the Platonic republic, which is a perfect construction of reason that has its reality beyond all possible experience. Meeting the difference between idea and ideal (the ideal being an idea both *in concreto* and *in individuo*) and repeating almost literally the formulations of §9 and §25 of the *Dissertatio,* Kant states, "What for us is an ideal was in Plato's view an idea of the divine understanding, an individual object of its pure intuition, the most perfect of every kind of possible being."[84] Kant's Plato is here clearly not the historical Plato but rather the image of Plato developed by later Roman authors.[85] According to this tradition, Plato's ideas are nothing but the divine intellect itself taken in its full creative powers. The critical Kant places his own doctrine of ideas precisely against this conception by claiming that "human reason contains not only ideas but also ideals, which, although they do not have, like the Platonic ideas, creative power, yet have practical power. . . ."[86] In the Dialectic, Kant determines this practical power as the *legislative* function that reason manifests through ideas. There is a law-giving activity that is proper to reason already in its "speculative" use.[87] In sum, reason's own concepts are ideas whose reality is negatively defined as not being purely fictitious and is placed beyond all possible experience—alluding indeed to the realm of practical reality but not yet positively determining it as such. From the very beginning of the Transcendental Dialectic, the crucial question concerns the type of reality to be attributed to ideas. Since the object that corresponds to the idea cannot be known through understanding and its categories, we can form only a "problematic concept"[88] of it. In the language of the *Critique*, it is, once again, a problem of "deduction." Yet

---

81. KrV B 371/A 314.

82. KrV B 371/A 314 f.

83. KrV B 374/A 317.

84. KrV B 596/A 568.

85. See Cicero's use of the term *idea* in *De officiis,* in particular see Cicero's notion of the *vir bonus* in lib. III, cap. 19, §§ 76–77.

86. KrV B 597/A 569.

87. KrV B 373/A 316; see also B 576/A 548, where Kant sees in reason a faculty that, in its spontaneity (freedom) constructs "its own order according to ideas."

88. KrV B 397/A 339.

under the new conditions dictated by the structure of reason, a deduction as the one provided for the concepts of the understanding cannot be provided.[89] In addition, the specific problem raised by reason is now twofold. (i) On the one hand, the question needs to be answered regarding the nature of ideas as concepts of reason; more precisely, whether they are *conceptus ratiocinati* (i.e., concepts that result from a correct inference of reason) or *conceptus ratiocinantes* (i.e., concepts that result from a sophistic inference).[90] (ii) On the other hand, the question regards what kind of use reason can legitimately make of these concepts. For reason, as opposed to understanding, allows for more than an exclusively theoretical or speculative function. What is at stake are the two distinct but closely related issues of the *practical reality of ideas* on the one hand and of *the practical use of reason* on the other.

The reference to logic, according to which reason is the faculty of reaching mediated conclusions through syllogisms, allows Kant a complete derivation of the dialectical syllogisms of reason (transcendental paralogisms, antinomies of pure reason, and its ideal)[91] corresponding to the respective ideas of the immortality of the soul, the world, and god. In relation to the problem of the objective validity of reason's own concepts and procedures, on the other hand, Kant refuses to resolve it following Plato's shortcut of a "mystical deduction"[92] (i.e., by hypostatizing ideas into metaphysical entities). The deduction of ideas needs therefore take a more complex course. The transcendental deduction of the categories followed a juridical model according to which a "judge" had to decide on the right and the legitimacy of a certain possession and use, on this ground declaring the victory of one fighting party over the other (skepticism vs. pure understanding). As a result, the conditions for the truth of knowledge seen as its "objective validity" were established. The deduction of the ideas of reason imposes a change of model that complies with the image of a "legislation"[93] of reason rather than with that of the judge, and with the "certainty"[94] and the "interest"[95] of reason in its proper knowledge rather than with its logical truth. This new argument eventually coincides with the process through which Kant fulfills the task of the isolation of reason as an independent faculty of knowledge in its own right. Moreover, what

89. KrV B 805 f./A 777 f., B 691 f./A 663 f., B 697/A 669. See D. Henrich, *Kant's Notion of a Deduction*, op. cit. This does not mean, however, that a different deduction of the ideas cannot be provided.

90. KrV B 367/A 311.

91. KrV B 397 f./A 339 f.

92. KrV B 371/A 315 fn.

93. KrV B 358/A 301, for the opposition between *Kampfrichter* and *Gesetzgeber* see B 451 f./A 423 f.

94. KrV B 449/A 421.

95. KrV B 439/A 465.

Kant specifically calls deduction of ideas is seen as constituting the very "completion [*Vollendung*] of the critical task of pure reason."[96]

The first step of Kant's argument takes place in the Paralogisms chapter of the Transcendental Dialectic and establishes that ideas are unique "possessions"[97] of reason, for no synthetic judgment of the understanding can ever be successful in their realm. Kant's awareness of the importance of this step is well expressed in his suggestion that "a huge, actually the only stumbling-block [*Stein des Anstosses*] against our critique would be the possibility of demonstrating a priori that all thinking essence is in itself a simple substance."[98] If synthetic a priori propositions of rational psychology could be demonstrated by the understanding, then understanding would have no limits, and consequently reason would have neither a specific use nor a proper realm of its own. In this case, ideas would really be nothing but fictitious entities. The second step is undertaken in the Antinomies chapter. The third antinomy in particular shows that the "pure transcendental idea of freedom"[99] can have a *practical reality* since this claim does not contradict the necessity that reigns in the realm of nature and appearances (the highest good is *possible*). This was precisely the first objective of Kant's deduction of ideas. At this level, however, Kant has not yet established that reason can be practical (or that reason can make a practical use of the idea of freedom). This conclusion will result from Kant's argument in the Ideal of Pure Reason. In formulating his idea of a "moral theology," Kant shows that reason can be practical (or can make a practical use of its ideas) within the sphere of religion.[100] The idea of god is therefore presented as a "postulate" that is necessary if reason has to be practical (the highest good is *necessary*).

Explicitly providing a deduction of the ideas of reason as the conclusion of his critical task, Kant maintains that in the realm of theoretical knowledge ideas cannot have a constitutive function since they are not determinations of objects given in a possible experience. Ideas constitute neither objects (they do not have the creative power of the Neoplatonic mind of god) nor knowledge of objects (human discursive knowledge cannot go beyond the limits set by experience and sensibility). Yet ideas have a fundamental regulative function.[101] When an object is considered "in the idea,"[102] (i.e., in the dimension of the "unity of reason"), not for

---

96. KrV B 698/A 670.

97. KrV B 410; see also B 426: the "dialectical illusion in rational psychology rests upon the confusion [*Verwechselung*] that takes an idea of reason [the idea of a pure intelligence] for the concept, which is indeterminate in all its components, of a thinking being in general."

98. KrV B 409.

99. KrV B 561 ff./A 533 ff.

100. This argument is taken up again in the Canon of Pure Reason.

101. KrV B 699/A 671; ideas are "heuristic," not "ostensive" concepts (ibid.).

102. See Kant's expression in KrV B 698/A 670, the "Gegenstand in der Idee," as the result of the deduction.

the purpose of speculative knowledge but for the sake of the systematicity of human cognition, then we reach reason's own kind of knowledge. Through ideas, reason considers the reality of things—and nature as a whole—"as if" it were a totality ordered by a highest intelligence. In the sphere of theoretical knowledge, ideas have reality as schemas of a "regulative principle of the unity of all knowledge of nature."[103] It is in this function that reason relates to the knowledge attained by the understanding and even "opens up new ways that the understanding does not know"[104] allowing it to extend its research in infinite directions. Already in the first *Critique*, "*teleology*" is one of these new ways. Regulative principles open up radically new perspectives on the world of nature to reason, allowing it to consider natural things and events in connections ruled by "teleological laws" (in addition to the mechanical laws that constitute them). Thereby reason reaches the most extended "systematic unity" of nature.[105]

103. KrV B 702/A 674.
104. KrV B 708/A 680.
105. KrV B 715/A 687.

Chapter 3

The *Critique of Practical Reason*: Pure Reason—Speculative and Practical Reason

The present chapter follows Kant's idea of practical reason as developed in the second *Critique*. While my exposition will revolve around the crucial task that Kant puts at the center of this work—namely the thesis that pure reason is practical—the discussion will further pursue the approach presented in the previous chapter and will analyze the relation between pure practical reason and sensibility.

1. Critique of Pure Practical Reason and Critique of Practical Reason

In seventeenth and eighteenth century moral philosophy, it is a widespread view that human action cannot be motivated by reason but only by passions. Human will is moved to decision and action exclusively by the influence of inclinations, passions, and sentiments. The empirical affection of the will is considered as the only possible type of determination. The interplay of passions is represented as a mechanism whose elements are all homogeneous—namely the empirical affection exercised by the passions and the empirically affected will. Accordingly, the act of the will (deliberation or choice) is nothing but its mechanical response to the stimulation of the passions. The way to fight a set of bad inclinations consists therefore in replacing them with good inclinations. The task of moral philosophy is precisely to study how this mechanism functions as well as to devise different balancing strategies among the passions. It follows that in this tradition ethics is closely related to—if not mixed with—disciplines based upon the empirical observation of human nature, such as empirical psychology and anthropology. David Hume had drawn extreme consequences out of this consideration of moral philosophy, claiming that reason is thoroughly impotent if set against the mechanism of passions and sentiments. Reason is an exclusively theoretical faculty that by no means can exercise any kind of causality over the will. Reason, according to Hume, can never be practical. At most, it can be instrumental in relation to already set goals. Since morality is based upon a specific sentiment, namely "moral sentiment," it constitutes an empirical discipline to be developed entirely a posteriori. In the context of the rationalist tradition, on the other hand, Christian Wolff, moving from radically different premises, reached an analogous result by denying the autonomous value of practical reason in relation to theoretical reason. Wolff's monistic approach to the faculties of the mind reduces morality to theoretical knowledge by ultimately deducing the will from the understanding.

In the *Groundwork of the Metaphysics of Morals*, Kant already set out his theory against the conclusions of both the empiricist and the rationalist traditions. He argues that moral philosophy is possible only as *pure* moral philosophy (i.e., only on the ground of an a priori foundation of its first principle). This foundation, however, is feasible only under the condition that reason, as opposed to Hume's thesis, can really be *practical* as *pure* reason. Since reason is the one and only motive for action without requiring any additional influence from empirical motives, the project of a pure moral philosophy can succeed in finding an a priori principle entirely based upon reason itself if and only if reason can exercise an immediate causality over the will. In the *Groundwork*, however, Kant still regards the critical task of practical philosophy as being parallel to that of the *Critique of Pure Reason*. The *Groundwork* provides only the preliminary step toward a comprehensive "metaphysics of morals." Its task is to find out and to assure the first principle of morality. This would then be followed by a "critique of *pure* practical reason."[1] The object of criticism is, in this case as in that of theoretical reason, pure reason itself. Therefore, in 1785, "pure practical reason" seems to be both that which allows a transcendental foundation of moral philosophy by providing a first principle of morality, and that which needs to be criticized precisely in this function. Kant's distance from Wolff is not yet deep enough.

Kant opens the *Critique of Practical Reason* with a different—and indeed a clearer—position. He argues that the critique regards now "the *entire* practical faculty,"[2] whereas the question whether pure reason can be practical at all is set directly at the heart of the inquiry and gains thereby a decisive priority. The former idea of a criticism of pure reason is now made dispensable upon the previous fulfillment of the task of proving that pure reason can be practical. In other words, Kant argues that if we succeed in showing that pure reason is indeed practical, then a critique of *pure* practical reason is no longer required. What needs to be provided, rather, is a critique of the "*entire*" practical faculty; that is, of practical reason in general, or of practical reason insofar as its causality may also include the influence of empirical elements and hence be empirically conditioned. Thereby Kant makes his refutation of Hume's position even more articulated and effective. He does not simply oppose to Hume's empirical moral philosophy based upon moral sentiments an a priori foundation that being based on reason alone radically cuts out all empirical influence of passions by denying their effectiveness over the will. Kant's point is to recognize that if pure reason provides the "sufficient"[3] determination of the will, this is still not the only type of determination possible. Since the influence of feeling is both undeniable and unavoidable, Kant needs to show the only way in which the empirical affection of the will can be included in the project of a *pure* moral philosophy without jeopardizing its pure character. In its own right, a criticism of the "entire" practical faculty draws the limits of the legitimate use of practical reason showing, at the same time, the role played by the sensible affection of the will in the determination of action.

1. *Grundlegung*, AB XIII f.
2. KpV A 3.
3. KpV A 35.

Kant's suggestion is that sensibility should never be considered as motive but always as the matter of moral action itself. For the motive is always and necessarily formal. This line of thought grounds Kant's so-called moral formalism.

The programmatic aim of the 1788 *Critique*—namely to show that pure reason is practical—expresses clearly that the second *Critique* is not a continuation of the first. This continuity was still claimed in 1786 when the Jena journal, *Allgemeine Literaturzeitung,* announcing the second edition of the *Critique of Pure Reason* anticipated that this edition would entail a "critique of pure practical reason" as well.[4] Evidently, at some point during 1786, Kant realized that the two *Critiques* had indeed opposite tasks.[5] The first *Critique* criticizes the *speculative* use of reason because reason is transcendent—and therefore illegitimate in its theoretical use—when it is pure (i.e., when it raises claims of knowledge beyond all possible experience). The second *Critique*, on the contrary, criticizes reason when it is *empirically* conditioned because only in this case does its practical use become illegitimate by transcending its purity and giving in to the determination of pathological affections.

2. Pure Reason Is Practical

With the claim that opens the *Critique of Practical Reason*—the claim that pure reason is practical—Kant suggests that reason, insofar as it is pure (i.e., taken in its complete independence from sensibility) exercises an *immediate* and *effective* causality on the will.

(i) It is the category of *causality* that lends the first meaning to the practical use of reason. The third antinomy of the *Critique of Pure Reason* had already opened up to the possibility of a specific kind of causality exercised by reason, namely "causality *through* freedom" or "causality *from* freedom." The notion of "transcendental freedom" that expresses reason's causality, however, does not analytically imply that reason is effectively practical.[6] This is precisely the additional step that Kant needs to undertake in the second *Critique*. Moreover, Kant projects the importance of the thesis of the second *Critique* back on the results of the critique of speculative reason. By significantly reversing the order of the relation between practical and theoretical reason established by the first *Critique*, Kant maintains that practical reason creates an "unsolvable problem" to speculative reason with the concept of freedom.[7] Kant's suggestion is that if reason were not practical through the moral law, then there would be no escape from the third antinomy, and the concept of freedom could never be introduced in practical philosophy.[8]

---

4. *Allgemeine Literaturzeitung*, Jena, November 21, 1786.
5. Their "parallelism" being only illusory: KpV A 3 (*scheint*).
6. See the important passage KrV B 561/A 533.
7. KpV A 53.
8. KpV A 53–54.

(ii) Second, reason is practical insofar as the peculiar type of causality exercised by it, namely causality through freedom, is directed not towards objects but towards the *will.*[9] It is only through reason's free causality that objects are produced out of their representation. The causality of reason as pure practical reason consists in the *immediate determination of the will.* This distinction allows Kant to separate theoretical knowledge from "practical knowledge." In practical knowledge, knowledge itself is the ground of the existence of the object and is thereby opposed to theoretical knowledge that presupposes the object as given.[10] In both the published introduction and the so-called "First Introduction" to the *Critique of Judgment,* Kant will further develop this distinction. Kant presently argues that while theoretical reason is determined by the objective constitution of the objects in its knowledge of nature, in practical knowledge, reason is concerned only with the grounds of the determination of the will; therefore, being only in relation with the subject, reason is self-determined in its causality.[11] Pure reason is practical as it relates to the subject's "faculty of desire" (*Begehrungsvermögen, facultas appetitiva*) in the form of the "pure will." With this claim, Kant takes up the traditional Aristotelian—and successively Wolffian—terminology that opposes the faculty of desire to the theoretical faculty, but he does so only in order to radically change the meaning of that *facultas appetitiva.* Kant's suggestion is that since it is pure reason that relates to the faculty of desire, this faculty, in the form of the pure will, proves itself to be a *faculty that does not (only) desire.*[12] For if it could *only* desire, it would be, as it is in the tradition, a merely empirical faculty. On the contrary, Kant's claim that pure reason is practical amounts to the suggestion that there is a pure motive—which is not an empirical desire—through which the faculty of desire is determined to action.

Kant's solution of the problem consists in showing that pure practical reason determines the will in an exclusively *formal* way through the moral law. In order to arrive at this solution, however, Kant needs to establish, against Wolff's distinction between a lower and a higher *facultas appetitiva,* the only sense in which practical reason can legitimately be called a "higher faculty of desire." The first step in the demonstration that pure reason is practical consists therefore in establishing what counts, on the contrary, as the *empirical* determination of the will. Wolff maintained that while the lower faculty of desire is determined by merely empirical representations (i.e., by representations that have their origin in the senses), the higher faculty is determined by intellectual representations (i.e., by representations that have their origin in the understanding). In both cases, however, what moves the will is a representation conjoined with a "feeling of pleasure or displeasure." Kant's argument here runs parallel to the one that, at

---

9. See KpV A 32; 96.

10. KpV A 80–81

11. KpV A 36.

12. See S. Landucci, *La "Critica della ragion pratica" di Kant. Introduzione alla lettura*, Roma, La Nuova Italia Scientifica, 1993, 41.

the beginning of the first *Critique*, drew a radical distinction between sensibility and understanding. In the practical sphere, however, Kant's claim seems to present the opposite direction than in the theoretical sphere. This is due precisely to the above discussed difference between the respective tasks of the two *Critiques*. In the *Critique of Pure Reason*, Kant argues against the traditional view according to which the difference between concepts and (sensible) intuitions is only a difference *in degree* of clarity and distinctness of our representations. His move was to establish a radical separation *in type* between the two branches of our knowledge. In the *Critique of Practical Reason,*[13] Kant maintains that the mere difference in the *origin* of our representations cannot justify the internal distinction within the faculty of desire in a higher and a lower faculty. For if we assume that the only thing that the faculty of desire can do is to desire according to a feeling of pleasure, and given that all desires and feelings of pleasure are empirical, then the different origin of our representations of what is desirable (i.e., of an object) would not make any real difference in the type of motive that moves this faculty. In other words, as long as the will is determined by a representation *of the object*—namely by the representation of the pleasure or displeasure that the subject can expect from it—the determination of the faculty of desire is material and empirical, no matter what the origin of that representation (the senses or the understanding). In this case, Kant argues, the different origin of our representations of what is pleasurable amounts only to a difference of "degree,"[14] not to a difference in the type of force that moves the will. The radical difference that justifies a real separation between higher and lower faculty of desire can only be grounded by *the way in which* the will is determined (i.e., by the difference between a *material* and a purely *formal* determination). Therefore the possibility for pure reason to be the higher faculty of desire depends upon the possibility that pure reason determines the will through a "*purely formal* law."[15] This law is a "fundamental law," namely the "moral law" or, in the terminology of the *Groundwork*, the "categorical imperative." Kant sees clearly that, at this point, his argument has opened up an alternative. Since the principle of one's own happiness—no matter what its origin—contains only an empirical determination of the will and is therefore to be ascribed only to the lower faculty of desire, the alternative presented by Kant is that "either no higher faculty of desire exists or *pure reason* must be in itself alone practical" (i.e., reason must be practical directly and immediately without presupposing any kind of feeling). Thence the conclusion: pure reason is practical in determining the will through the "*mere form* of the practical rule." This means that pure reason is practical insofar as it is legislative reason.[16]

---

13. See §3 Remark I (A 41 ff.).
14. KpV A 42.
15. KpV A 41.
16. KpV A 44–45.

(iii) Kant's argument leads thereby to the crucial reciprocal relation between *pure practical reason* (i.e., the form of the moral law) and the *freedom* of a will determined by it.[17] Once the opening claim that pure reason is practical has been satisfied by the formality of the determination of the will through the moral law (free will), Kant needs to address the other formulation of the same programmatic claim, equally anticipated at the beginning of the preface. The *Critique of Practical Reason*, Kant argued in its very first page, "has simply to prove *that pure practical reason exists*"—or that *there is* practical reason.[18] What needs to be proved seems therefore a simple fact. Yet, in the same opening passage, Kant suggested that this peculiar fact can only be proved by the very "act" of pure reason itself. *Factum* is what *factum est* (i.e., it is the result of an action, of reason's own action).[19] Kant's doctrine of the *Faktum der Vernunft*—the *factum* of reason—is nothing but the most advanced formulation of the central issue of the second *Critique.*[20] "If reason as pure reason is actually practical, then it will prove its own reality and the reality of its concept *through action*, and all disputations to prove its impossibility will be in vain."[21] It is precisely this additional step—or rather this specific formulation of the question—that allows Kant to overcome the impasse where the *Groundwork* had left the relation between categorical imperative and freedom.

In the *Groundwork* Kant's deduction moved from the freedom of the will to a justification of the categorical imperative. This procedure came up against the problem of reconciling the result of the deduction with the conclusions of the first *Critique*. The dialectic of speculative reason reached only the possibility of transcendental freedom—or only its compatibility (non-contradiction) with the necessity of nature. This result therefore allowed only for a hypothetical assumption of freedom and consequently only for a hypothetical assumption of the moral law. In the practical sphere, however, this conclusion could hardly be seen as satisfactory. In the second *Critique*, Kant's argument is still developed in the form of a deduction. The "*factum* of reason," as the consciousness of the moral law, now grounds the idea of freedom. In the *Critique of Practical Reason* Kant grants the moral law the status of a *factum* that does not need to be deduced since its objective reality is immediately proved through the action of pure reason itself (an action that has always already been accomplished and exists as the *factum* of its own result). Now the deduction sets out to demonstrate the unity between the *factum* of reason and the consciousness of the freedom of the will.[22]

---

17. KpV A 52 f.

18. KpV A 3: "Sie soll bloß dartun, *daß es reine praktische Vernunft gebe*."

19. *Factum* has the same relation to *facere* that the German *Wirken* has to *Wirklichkeit*. In the practical sphere, the proof of the reality of a concept is provided by the action that produces it.

20. See D. Henrich, *Der Begriff der sittlichen Einsicht und Kants Lehre vom Faktum der Vernunft*, in: *Die Gegenwart der Griechen im neueren Denken*, Festschrift f. H. G. Gadamer, Tübingen, Mohr, 1960, 75–115.

21. KpV A 3.

22. KpV A 72.

As in the first *Critique*, Kant's model for his deduction is a juridical one. In the legal vocabulary of Kant's time, a *factum* is the action committed by someone on which legal judgment is to be passed. The *factum* is, as such, the basis of the deduction. The "objective reality" of the *factum* of reason is not a sensible one, for it is not a *datum* that can be presented in a sensible intuition and known by theoretical reason. The reality of the *factum* is, for Kant, the supersensible or intelligible reality of the practical—a reality that cannot be conceived through the conditions of space and time and yet is so apodictically certain as to "be firmly established for itself."[23] "When it comes to the law of our intelligible existence (the moral law) *reason recognizes no temporal distinctions, and the only thing it asks is whether the event belongs to me as an act.*"[24] This model of moral accountability is used for the first time by reason itself with regard to its own action (i.e., in relation to the *factum* as the ground for a deduction of the freedom of the will). Moving from the *Faktum der Vernunft*, the deduction proves that the subject accountable for that action is pure reason itself or a pure will determined solely and immediately by the formality of the moral law. This determination is the act of freedom. Thus, Kant's doctrine of the *Faktum der Vernunft* establishes the central thesis that pure reason is indeed practical.

3. Pure Practical Reason and the Influence of Sensibility

Kant's proof that pure reason is practical and therefore able to determine the will formally through the moral law without recurring to an object given in the feeling of pleasure or displeasure already entails a response to an objection previously raised against the *Groundwork*. This objection regarded the inversion operated by Kant in presenting the highest principle of morality *before* the concept of the good (and even before the notion of a faculty of desire).[25] In confronting both the method and structure of the *Critique of Pure Reason* with those of the *Critique of Practical Reason*, Kant underlines the inversion that needs to take place in the order of the exposition proper to the Analytic of Practical Reason. Here we begin with the *principle* of morality that constitutes the only guarantee for the possibility of the present critical task. The principle is followed by the *concepts* of the objects of practical reason, namely the concepts of good and evil, whereas the last part is more problematically[26] indicated by Kant as a transition to sensibility. The order of the first *Critique* was exactly the opposite, starting out with sensibility, moving on to the concepts of the understanding, and ending with an Analytic of Principles. The reason for this inversion is precisely the above discussed nature of pure practical reason, namely both the condition for its being effectively practical and its relating

23. KpV A 82.
24. KpV A 177.
25. KpV A 15, 16 Anm.
26. KpV A 31–32, see A 32: in the *Critique of Practical Reason* "we begin with principles and move on to concepts and from these, for the first time, *where possible*, to the senses."

to the will and not to objects. What needs to be presently explained is the role played by sensibility with regard to practical reason. As we already argued in presenting Kant's opening of the first *Critique*, Kant distinguishes two branches of sensibility, namely intuition and sensation. In the *Critique of Practical Reason*, sensible intuition still has for Kant an exclusively theoretical use in relation to the faculty of knowledge (understanding as faculty of concepts). Sensation, on the contrary, allows for a differentiated use in relation to different faculties of the *Gemüt*. Kant's discussion of sensibility in the second *Critique* shows accordingly (i) a repeated insistence on the radical exclusion of intuition (any form of intuition, i.e., both sensible and intellectual) from the realm of the practical on the one hand, and (ii) the practical transformation of the materiality of sensation into feeling on the other. In the *Critique of Judgment*, Kant's theory of sensibility would be carried a step further. Here Kant would strengthen the connection between sensation and feeling while allowing for a use of intuition without determinate concepts according to which imagination connects it to the feeling of pleasure and displeasure.

(i) Kant refers to the methodological difference between the two *Critiques* as a "curious contrast"[27] between them and even as the "paradox of the method of a critique of practical reason."[28] In the case of theoretical reason the beginning was made by the first "datum" given to cognition—namely with "sensible intuition (space and time)."[29] In the case of pure practical reason, on the contrary, first comes the *factum* of reason itself in the form of a principle (i.e., the law). That this *factum* is not, in turn, a *datum* is due precisely to the impossibility of its being given or presented in any sensible intuition. The action of pure practical reason belongs to the intelligible world whose events cannot be grasped, exhibited, or given in any intuition—neither sensible nor intelligible. (a) The claim that the activity of practical reason is determined by sensible intuition amounts, for Kant, to the positions of determinism, fatalism, and Spinozism[30] (i.e., to the sheer negation of freedom). (b) The attempt to introduce intellectual intuition into the realm of the practical leads instead to the position of "enthusiasm" that Kant opposes in each of its forms.

(a) At the beginning of the first *Critique* Kant established the crucial thesis that the transcendental ideality of space and time is the condition of the possibility of freedom; he took this thesis up again in the discussion of the third antinomy in the Dialectic. In the "Critical Elucidation of the Analytic of Pure Practical Reason,"[31] Kant addresses the problem of the free causality of an agent that belongs, at the

27. KpV A 73.

28. KpV A 110—here Kant takes up again, albeit implicitly, his refutation of the argument of his opponent in relation to the *Groundwork*.

29. KpV A 73.

30. KpV A 182–183.

31. KpV A 159 ff.

same time, to the sensible and to the intelligible worlds. To affirm that moral actions are affected by time (and space)—or, as Kant puts it, that time is a property of things in themselves and not simply of appearances—means to regard every action as necessarily determined by a previous occurrence in time. In this situation, freedom is utterly impossible and its concept is void and self-contradictory.[32] The only possible form of causality would be the necessary causality of nature,[33] which would reduce actions to mechanism and agents to marionettes or automata.[34] The only way to save "transcendental freedom" (not just "psychological freedom")[35] is therefore to recognize its radical independence from the empirical condition of time. It is only under the condition that time determines the natural necessity of appearances but does not affect the reality of the noumena that moral freedom and natural necessity can be thought together without implying contradiction.

To this conclusion, already reached in the first *Critique*, the Critical Elucidation adds an important yet highly problematic dimension. In the second *Critique*, Kant needs to address the question of the "application" of that solution to the case of a subject whose action manifests the unity of both natural necessity and causality through freedom in one and the same occurrence. The consideration of the effective action of practical freedom in the sensible world viewed through the perspective of the finite agent is the very problem that presents "great difficulties, which seem to make such a unification impossible."[36] Kant's suggestion is that the subject, as a part of nature or appearance, is thoroughly determined by natural necessity. This necessity posits the conditions of her own causality (namely her own character as well as the whole history of her past deeds) in a past moment of time that necessarily exceeds her own powers to control and determine. That same subject, however, is conscious of her existence as a thing in itself, or is conscious of her noumenal character. This *consciousness*, in the form of the *Gewissen*,[37] allows for the possibility of regarding one's own action in a totally different perspective, namely one in which there is no time-determination and where only agency itself is relevant. "For reason, when it comes down to the law of our intelligible existence (the moral law), *recognizes no temporal distinctions, and the only thing it asks is whether the event belongs to me as an act.*"[38] This conclusion is a further implication of the *factum* of reason that was established in its identity with the consciousness of the moral law. This consciousness now grounds on the side of the subject the awareness of her twofold existence as a part of nature on the one hand and as free agent on the other. In particular, it grounds the possibil-

---

32. KpV A 170.
33. KpV A 169 ff.
34. KpV A 182.
35. KpV A 173.
36. KpV A 170–171.
37. KpV A 175.
38. KpV A 177.

ity for the subject to consider her existence as an existence not affected by time and therefore as an existence that lies completely in her own power to shape and to determine according to the law of reason. In this perspective (i.e., to the consciousness of one's noumenal existence), every action as well as every determination of the inner sense and one's whole existence as a sensible being is not a consequence of a previous determination or action in time. Every action belongs instead to a single determination of the subject's character, "which he himself creates, and according to which he imputes to himself, as a cause independent of all sensibility, the causality of those same appearances."[39] The consciousness of the moral law eventually lends a concrete meaning to the noumenal existence, which came to the fore already in the first *Critique*. In this way, moral consciousness allows for a return to the world of the phenomena by presenting its own causality within this world as independent of time.

With this crucial argument, Kant renders the meaning of his idea of freedom as autonomy extremely concrete for the life of the particular individual subject. This subject, in her physical and natural existence, now struggles in order to find the space of a freedom that radically exceeds the realm of natural determinism. Kant's ethical formalism is, to be sure, a highly concrete argument in favor of a "supersensible" meaning of human existence that is grounded precisely in our own *consciousness* of freedom. The essential condition for Kant's concept of autonomy, however, is the elimination of reason's reference to sensibility—not only its dependence upon sensation and feeling but also its reference to sensible intuition (i.e., to the conditions of space and time). This move follows precisely from Kant's suggestion that pure practical reason refers to the will and not to desired objects. For only objects can be given in space and time or produce the sensation of a feeling of pleasure or displeasure. What needs to be determined in practical knowledge is, on the contrary, the pure form of the will itself or pure practical reason as will. The *immediacy* and *formality* of this self-determination excludes the possibility for both intuition and feeling to intervene.

(b) If, in the second *Critique*, Kant ultimately leaves the task of radically excluding sensible intuition from the realm of practical knowledge to the principle of the *factum* of reason and to its identity with the consciousness of freedom, the same principle also provides him with a strong argument for banishing even "intellectual intuition" from practical knowledge as such. Against the claim that only "if we were capable of an intellectual intuition" of the acting subject "we would then discover that the entire chain of appearances, with reference to that which concerns only the moral law, depends upon the spontaneity of the subject as a thing in itself," Kant argues that we do not really need to appeal to an unreachable intellectual intuition as we have consciousness of the moral law.[40] In other words, we do not need to assume that human freedom can be explained only from god's

39. KpV A 175.
40. KpV A 178.

perspective—or generally from a perspective that is by definition not a human one—since the *factum* of reason provides us with the immediate consciousness of that freedom. Moreover, to claim an intellectual or a "supersensible intuition" as taking place in the realm of the practical can only lead, according to Kant, to fanaticism and enthusiasm.[41] This claim thus cancels the distinction between theoretical and practical reason and ultimately makes the very existence of practical reason impossible.

(ii) By terminologically distinguishing between intuition and sensation, the *Critique of Pure Reason* already made clear that while the pure a priori forms of intuition were always working in conjunction with the faculty of knowledge,[42] the material side of sensibility, namely sensation, could provide different uses according to the different faculty of the *Gemüt* involved. In particular, and according to a long tradition, sensation in conjunction with the will would provide a feeling of pleasure or displeasure and lead thereby to action. As I have argued above, Kant's fundamental move in the second *Critique* is to radically separate the "faculty of desire" from the "feeling of pleasure and displeasure," pointing to the immediate and formal determination of the will through pure reason alone. In this way, Kant separates the realm of the *practical stricto sensu* as that which belongs to freedom from the *pathological* sphere that defines the realm of the empirical determination of the will. It is precisely in this latter sphere that sensation as *Gefühl,* or feeling, enters Kant's critique of the "entire" practical faculty.[43] Moreover, the distinction between two meanings of the practical, namely practical according to freedom and practical as merely technical, will become a central systematic issue in the third *Critique*.

The *immediate* determination of the will through pure reason or the moral law defines "morality." If, however, the determination of the will occurs according to the moral law and yet is not immediate but requires the *mediation* of a presupposed feeling, what we have is "legality." This distinction regards the *Triebfeder*—the *elater animi,* or springing motive (drive)—of the will in its determination to action. Because of the general alternative that Kant opens up as a choice between pure reason and empirical feeling, the issue regards from the very outset the "subjective determining ground" of a will that, like the human and unlike the "holy" divine one, can be subject to sensuous impulses (i.e., a will that is not necessarily determined, on the ground of its very nature, in accordance with the moral law).[44] Therefore, Kant's problem is to show a priori "the way in which the moral law becomes the springing motive" for the will and to show "what happens to the human faculty of desire"[45] as a consequence of the effect that the moral law has

---

41. KpV A 244–245; also A 125, where Kant mentions "mysticism."
42. KrV B 66/A 49.
43. KpV A 3.
44. KpV A 126–127.
45. KpV A 128.

on it as its springing motive. In other words, Kant's problem regards the possibility of bringing into his project of a critical ethics an a priori presentation of feeling or the a priori determination of a "moral feeling." Kant's suggestion is that whereas feeling needed to be excluded as *grounding motive* or *determining ground* of the will in order for morality to be possible, it can now be reintroduced in relation to the moral law as its very peculiar *effect* or *consequence*.

The first a priori determinable effect of the moral law upon feeling is a merely negative one. By determining the will immediately, the moral law rejects and thwarts all inclinations, thereby producing a feeling of pain. "Here we have the first, and perhaps the only case in which we can determine a priori out of concepts the relation between a cognition (here a cognition of pure practical reason) to the feeling of pleasure and displeasure."[46] However, since the moral law is the form of an intellectual causality, namely causality through freedom, it is in itself something "positive." As such, it is at the same time "an object of respect" that humiliates our self-conceit. By imposing itself as object of the highest respect, the moral law is "the ground of a positive feeling that does not have an empirical origin, and can be known a priori." This feeling is "respect for the moral law." Moreover, "this feeling is the only one that we can know completely a priori and the necessity of which we can discern."[47] This feeling is, according to Kant, the only "*moral feeling*."[48]

Such a feeling does not *precede* the moral law as its motive or determining ground but rather *follows* from it as its effect. Herein a further reason for Kant's methodological inversion in the division of the second *Critique* in relation to the first becomes apparent. While in the *Critique* of theoretical knowledge sensibility comes first because of the immediacy with which it relates to objects, in the *Critique* of practical reason it is pure reason that determines the will immediately and that produces, as an effect of this determination, a specific form of practical sensibility, which is the moral feeling of reverence for the law. Paradoxically, sensibility is not a first and given moment but rather a *produced* consequence of pure practical reason itself. From this follows Kant's peculiar qualification of the reverence for the law as a moral feeling. As opposed to all feeling in general, which is "pathological" (i.e., derives empirically from other feelings and inclinations), the feeling of reverence (and negatively that of humiliation) in front of the law is the effect of an intelligible causality and is therefore qualified as a "moral," (i.e., genuinely *practical*) feeling. As a feeling, reverence is necessarily sensible and therefore can never be the ground for a determination of the will. Yet, having its origin in pure practical reason this "sensation . . . is not pathological, but must be said *practically produced*."[49] In other words, reverence is a feeling or a sensation

46. KpV A 129.
47. KpV A 130.
48. KpV A 133.
49. KpV A 134.

that is not suffered by the subject but practically produced and experienced precisely in this productive and active form.[50]

Kant's awareness of the peculiar character of the moral feeling as feeling or sensation is revealed by his need for a careful qualification of the ways in which it works (one may even suspect that respect for the law might be something that *functions as* a feeling rather than a feeling proper). "Respect for the law is not springing motive for morality but is morality itself"[51] only taken in its subjective meaning; it is neither a principle for judging actions[52] nor properly a "feeling of pleasure."[53]

In sum, Kant views the moral law as a determining ground of the will on different levels. Through pure practical reason it represents a "*formal* determining ground of action." Through the notions of "good and evil" it provides the "*material* though purely *objective*" determination of the objects of action. Finally, through the moral feeling of reverence, it also generates a "*subjective*" motive for the will.[54]

4. Speculative Reason and Pure Practical Reason: Their Unity and Their Different Employment

Kant concludes the Dialectic of the *Critique of Practical Reason* taking up the conclusions of the *Critique of Pure Reason* and inserting them in a teleological presentation of the faculties of the mind. To be sure, Kant never stops reminding us of this relation throughout the whole development of the second *Critique*. It is *one and the same reason* that is shown in its twofold use as producing two different types of knowledge (different and yet still forms of knowledge referred to "one cognitive faculty").[55] Thus, insofar as reason is concerned, these two critical parts of Kant's transcendental philosophy refer to the underlying "unity of the whole faculty of pure reason,"[56] a unity on which the third *Critique* will further elaborate. If the task of the *Critique of Judgment* is commonly seen as that of bridging the gap between two radically separate parts of Kant's system of reason, we can start to recognize that the problem is even more complicated. For in this regard, the problem of the unity of reason is already strongly outlined in the second *Critique*.

---

50. The distinction between "action" and "sensation" becomes crucial in the Dialectic of Practical Reason. Herein the antinomy arises precisely as the effect of an "optical illusion" from the confusion between "what one does" and "what one feels" (KpV A 210).

51. KpV A 134.

52. KpV A 135.

53. KpV A 137.

54. KpV A 133.

55. KpV A 159.

56. KpV A 162: "Einheit des ganzen reinen Vernünftvermögens (des theoretischen sowohl als praktischen)."

At the end of the Dialectic, Kant shows how the limitation of *speculative* reason is functional to the *practical* determination of reason itself and thereby to the "extension" of pure reason as such. Theoretical knowledge needs to be limited if pure reason ought to be practical. The relevance of this inference, once the crucial thesis of the practical import of pure reason has been established, is brought back to the moral "determination" of human nature. In relation to this issue, the system of the faculties of the mind (the *Gemüt*) ultimately reveals its *teleological* orientation. If human nature is *"determined"* (or "called upon") to strive toward the highest good, then "the measure of its cognitive faculties and especially their relation to one another *must* be assumed to be suitable to this end."[57] From the very beginning of the work, Kant has presented the reciprocal relation between speculative and practical reason by stressing their radical independence on the ground of a common striving toward the solution of the same problem, namely the problem of freedom. In other words, this independence was argued on the basis of their *common interest*, not as the result of the separate spheres in which their principles or concepts respectively find objective validity.

The notion of pure reason is presented from the very outset as the "ground" for its differential employment both as speculative and as practical reason, as well as for the systematic proper to each of them.[58] After the reciprocal implication between the idea of freedom and the unconditioned moral law and consequently the equivalence between pure practical reason and the positive concept of freedom has been established, Kant finally rectifies the "true order" of our concepts. He contends that even though the problem of freedom emerged for the first time as result of the dialectic of speculative reason in the idea of "transcendental freedom," it is "morality that first reveals the concept of freedom to us and therefore it is *practical reason* that first posits, with this concept, the insolvable problem to speculative reason."[59] This is the ground of the "primacy" of practical reason over speculative reason. This primacy is due not only to the solution provided but rather, in the first place, to the question addressed as *the* very problem of reason as such. The notion of the "*Primat*" is closely related to that of an "extension" of reason's own knowledge. If the Dialectic of the first *Critique* showed how speculative reason is destined to fail in its—albeit natural—attempt to enlarge the field of its cognition through concepts into a territory that cannot be explored by experience, Kant will concede to practical reason a *potestas*—a right—to enlarge its use in ways that were impossible to speculative reason.[60] However, the primacy

57. KpV A 263.

58. KpV A 31.

59. KpV A 53.

60. See the title of the second section of the chapter on the "Principles of Pure Practical Reason" (Analytic): "2. On the Right [*Befügnis*] of Pure Reason to an Extension in Its Practical Use which is not Possible to It in Its Speculative Use."

that practical reason thereby attains can only be gained, according to Kant, "*in connection*" with speculative reason.[61]

Kant's doctrine of the "postulates"[62] of pure practical reason defines the status of the ideas of freedom, immortality of the soul, and existence of god in the context of moral philosophy. This doctrine goes back to the deduction of the ideas of pure reason attempted by Kant already in the *Critique of Pure Reason*. However, since those ideas do not have an objective validity for speculative reason, the first *Critique* could not provide a deduction in the form of a demonstration of objective reality. It is precisely this demonstration that is reached in the doctrine of the postulates. Such doctrine emends on the one hand the "impotence of speculative reason," while on the other hand, it establishes a relation between morality and religion.[63] The postulates proceed out of the "principle of morality, which is not a postulate but a law." While the law is a *practical* proposition (the only practical proposition) the postulates are *theoretical* propositions[64] that concern the possibility of an action given that the *conditions* of its possibility are satisfied. A postulate has therefore the following form: It is possible that action x will reach the end of the good since the conditions of the possibility of that action are satisfied. More specifically, the conditions are satisfied by the assumption of the existence of god, freedom, and the immortality of the soul. These postulates, argues Kant, "are not theoretical dogmas but presuppositions of necessarily practical import; thus, *while they do not extend speculative knowledge, they give objective reality to the ideas of speculative reason in general* (by means of their relation to the practical), and justify speculative reason in holding to concepts whose possibility it could not otherwise venture to affirm."[65]

---

61. See the title of the third section of the chapter on the Dialectic of Pure Reason in Defining the Concept of the Highest Good (Dialectic): "III. On the Primacy of Pure Practical Reason in its Connection with Speculative Reason."

62. The notion of "postulate" is particularily important to Kant. He uses "postulates" in the *Critique of Pure Reason* both in the Analytic (the "Postulates of empirical thinking") and in the Dialectic (KrV B 673/A 645: the idea of a system of knowledge "postulates the complete unity of understanding's knowledge"); in the present context of the *Critique of Practical Reason*; and in the *Metaphysical Principles of a Doctrine of Right* (the "Juridical Postulate of Practical Reason"). For an extensive analysis see P. König, "Kants Postulate der Vernunft und Hegels 'Verstellung der Sache,'" in *Das Recht der Vernunft. Kant und Hegel über Denken, Erkennen und Handeln*, ed. by Ch. Fricke, P. König, Th. Petersen, Stuttgart, Frommann, 1995, 121–155. The notion of the postulate becomes extremely important for Schelling, who reinterprets as "practical propositions" what for Kant, on the contrary, is always a theoretical proposition.

63. KpV A 221. This is the ground of Kant's "moral theology" and theory of "rational faith (*Vernunftglaube*)" in favor of which Kant argued—albeit with different grounds—already in the Canon of the first *Critique*.

64. KpV A 221.

65. KpV A 238.

The "objective reality" that the postulates claim for the ideas of "speculative reason *in general*" is not a phenomenical reality in space and time but an intelligible *practical* reality. Kant stresses that the "enlargement" or "extension" of theoretical reason that thereby takes place "is not an extension of speculation itself," namely is not an extension of reason in the "theoretical respect." The discovery of a practical use of pure reason does not remove speculation's own limitations but makes them even deeper. For those speculatively unattainable ideas do have now an objective reality and yet speculative reason can still make no positive use of them.[66] Therefore the extension that the postulates allow for is not an extension of reason's knowledge *of objects* but rather an enlargement of reason's knowledge *of "reason in general"*[67] (i.e., of reason's self-knowledge). The postulates disclose to reason the dimension of the "supersensible." The *Übersinnliches*, however, is not an object of theoretical knowledge. The postulates allow reason to *practically* know the supersensible meaning of its own practical determination. In this way they reveal to pure reason the supersensible dimension of its own nature as practical reason.[68]

66. KpV A 242.
67. KpV A 243.
68. See KpV A 244.

Chapter 4

The *Critique of Judgment:* A Preliminary Investigation

The previous two chapters have provided an indirect introduction to the problematic of the *Critique of Judgment.* They implicitly position Kant's 1790 work within the development of his critical philosophy. The present chapter gives a preliminary introduction to the third *Critique.* It moves along historical lines in order to address three different sets of issues. First, it presents a critical confrontation with the methodological strategies generally employed in the interpretation of this work; second, it briefly follows the emergence of the problematic of the third *Critique* in Kant's philosophical development; and third, it addresses the question of the internal genesis of the text.

1. *"Tout est dit" and the* Critique of Judgment

Viewed from the standpoint of the enormous amount of literature that the *Critique of Judgment* has produced since its publication in 1790, Kant's third *Critique* seems to escape any definition. Two crucial preliminary questions— what is the specific content or topic of Kant's last *Critique?* and how should this work be read and interpreted?—have been answered in an astonishing variety of ways. If a conclusion had to be drawn on the basis of all these interpretations, it would be the admission that the *Critique of Judgment* contains everything along with its opposite. In 1968, Luigi Scaravelli began an important essay on Kant's third *Critique* with a claim that today can only be reinforced:[1] "The famous *tout est dit* with which La Bruyère begins his *Caractères* could very well be extended to every new work on the *Critique of Judgment* . . . What novelty can one hope to find—or imagine to find—in a book that at this point has been studied again and again in all its problems and disassembled again and again in each single part?"[2] Indeed, Scaravelli's claim had an openly ironic intention.

Kant's last enterprise in critical philosophy has been interpreted, among other things, both as the final chapter of the history of eighteenth century aesthetics and as the "first manifesto"[3] of Romantic aesthetics—as the very beginning and source of the philosophy of German Idealism. On the one hand, it has been

---

1. Scaravelli's claim has been recently reinforced by E. Garroni and H. Hohenegger in the introduction to their new Italian translation of the third *Critique*, *Critica della facoltà di giudizio*, a cura di E. Garroni, H. Hohenegger, Torino, Einaudi, 1999, see xii.

2. L. Scaravelli, "Osservazioni sulla Critica del giudizio," in *Scritti kantiani*, Firenze, La Nuova Italia, 1968, 336–528, 341.

3. L. Pareyson, *L'estetica di Kant. Lettura della "Critica del giudizio,"* Milano, Mursia, 1984, 9.

viewed as a chaotic assemblage of heterogeneous material, as a book that precisely for its excessive richness served as inspiration for the generation to come. On the other hand, attempts have been made to see the *Critique of Judgment* as the triumph of a systematic spirit that allegedly took hold of Kant in his late years. According to this view, Kant brought together in the extrinsic form of a third *Critique* topics that do not have anything in common, such as the contemplation of works of art and the explanation of organized beings. From this perspective, the idea of unifying aesthetic and teleological judgment in the form of the "reflective faculty of judgment" has been seen as a forceful move due exclusively to the spirit of the system. Contrary to this position, however, it has also been claimed that the connection between aesthetics and teleology was already present in the tradition, that Kant simply took up and repeated a conventional idea, and that precisely for this reason his contemporaries easily accepted this part of his doctrine without ever questioning it.[4]

Correspondingly, in looking for a methodological key to the heart of Kant's third *Critique*, all kinds of interpretive approaches have been tested. (i) The most frequent reaction to the heterogeneity of topics that occupy Kant in his 1790 work consists in dismembering this work by focusing exclusively on one of those topics. In this way, and more generally, the Critique of the Aesthetic Faculty of Judgment and the Critique of the Teleological Faculty of Judgment are studied as independent parts without any necessary connection to each other.[5] Moreover, the fact that Kant did bring up the need to integrate these two parts into a unitary theory—which is precisely the thought that brought him from the idea of a "critique of *taste*"[6] to the idea of a "critique of the *faculty of judgment*"—and to consider them as two forms of the "reflective faculty of judgment" is sometimes viewed as a source of confusion, as the disturbing intrusion of a theory that even distorts Kant's critique of taste, and eventually condemns it to failure.[7] (ii) The so-called question of the genesis of the text has been another methodological response to the suggestion that Kant merges a number of unrelated topics into the ultimately disorganized body of his 1790 work. This approach brings the internal tensions of the *Critique of Judgment* back to their different chronological emergence in Kant's work. (iii) The attempt of a systematic reconstruction of the third *Critique*

---

4. H.-J. De Vleeschauwer, *L'évolution de la pensée kantienne*, Paris, Alcan, 1939, 140 (*The Development of Kantian Thought*, trans. by A. R. C. Duncan, Edinburgh, 1962). De Vleeschauwer's position has been recently repeated by, among others, D. Dumouchel, "Genèse de la troisième Critique: le role de l'esthétique dans l'achèvement du système critique," in *Kants Ästhetik/Kant's Aesthetics/L'esthétique de Kant,* ed. by H. Parret, Berlin/New York, De Gruyter, 1998, 18–40, 28.

5. Already, for example, E. v. Hartmann, *Die deutsche Aesthetik seit Kant*, Leipzig, Friedrich, 1886, 10.

6. P. Guyer, *Kant and the Claims of Taste*, Cambridge, Cambridge University Press, 1997[2], 30–31; see also D. Dumouchel, "Genèse de la troisième Critique," op. cit., 38 ff.

7. J. Kulenkampff, *Kants Logik des asthetischen Urteils*, Frankfurt a.M., Klostermann, 1978, 32 ff.

achieves an analogous result as does the apparently conflicting genetic approach. It imposes a forceful unity on the text and explains its inconsistencies by bringing its composition back to different times and phases, to different and successive twists and turns[8] in Kant's thought that, however, have been maintained next to each other in spite of their incompatibility. Herein, the leading assumption is that there cannot be any internal contradiction in the systematic of the third *Critique*. Since the text does display contradictions, they need to be explained as belonging to different periods in the composition of the work. This argument is reinforced by the claim that postulates successive turns in Kant's convictions. By inserting the condition of time, the principle of noncontradiction is respected and the coherence of the whole is saved. In both these perspectives—the genetic and the systematic—pieces of information belonging to the external history of the text are given an exclusive value and transformed into constitutive elements (and even key elements) in understanding its philosophical content. Although the historical perspective underlying both these approaches does indeed provide important clues to an interpretation of Kant's last *Critique*, it is only the discovery of the "theoretical heart"[9] of this work that allows a philosophical reconstruction of its true unity. Furthermore, what needs to be addressed in a more convincing way is the epistemological meaning of the notion of system, as well as its relation to the entire critical project. As the history of the formation of the third *Critique* sufficiently proves, the idea of a system of three critiques is certainly not a plan that Kant has been following from the very beginning.[10] If Kant's transcendental philosophy is a system, it is a system constantly *in fieri*, a system that constantly defines—and redefines—its conditions within the process of its very construction.

What is inevitably lost in the aforementioned interpretive approaches is the more profound significance of the unity that is at work in the *Critique of Judgment*, a unity of effort toward a systematic comprehension of the world of human experience. In this effort, and in line with the thinking introduced for the first time by the *Critique of Pure Reason*, Kant's critical philosophy still works toward a new definition of the concept of experience. Kant's task reveals therein the most peculiar and authentic character of his philosophy,[11] the nature of critical thinking as an enterprise open to the experience of philosophizing. Philosophizing, in turn,

---

8. See J. H. Zammito, *The Genesis of Kant's Critique of Judgment*, Chicago, University of Chicago Press, 1992; Zammito explains the genesis of the third *Critique* as a succession of three "turns."

9. Following Scaravelli's suggestion, my starting point and the center of my interpretation is still the "luogo teoretico" that he has disclosed (*Osservazioni sulla Critica del giudizio*, op. cit., 348).

10. Initially, Kant viewed the *Critique of Pure Reason* as the whole of transcendental philosophy including in it both his theoretical and his practical philosophy.

11. This line of interpretation is suggested by E. Garroni and H. Hohenegger, see "Introduzione," op. cit., xiv f.; see also N. Hinske, *Kants Weg zur Transzendentalphilosophie. Der dreißigjährige Kant*, Stuttgart, Kohlhammer, 1970, 133, for the difference between Kant's critical and pre-critical positions.

is regarded as the process of reason's own self-questioning, as its inevitable tendency toward a constant self-transcendence and self-redefinition. The internal tensions of the third *Critique* are precisely a consequence of Kant's way of practicing philosophy. At the end of the whole critical project, the 1790 *Critique* displays this practice in its fullest meaning.

This conclusion suggests that the necessary interpretive move of putting the *Critique of Judgment* into its proper philosophical and theoretical context is one that sees it in relation to the crucial issues and discoveries of both the *Critique of Pure Reason* and the *Critique of Practical Reason.*[12] This *internal* contextualization of the third *Critique* will prove indispensable to a correct understanding of the peculiar character of its systematic unity. (iv) This implies, however, that the method of interpreting Kant's third *Critique* exclusively by reconstructing its historical background and the net of its historical influences (*a parte ante,* as well as *a parte post*) must be recognized as a tool that is indeed necessary but certainly not sufficient in order to disclose the philosophical meaning of this work. An ironic radicalization of the results of such an interpretive strategy can be found, once again, in Scaravelli's remarks. *Tout est dit* on each single part into which the third *Critique* has been successively dismembered. The original idea of each single part has been traced back to a particular German, Swiss, French, British or Scottish author.[13]

> So that—not to mention Kant's more relevant debt towards Hume, Leibniz, and Wolff—the notions of creative imagination and the originality of genius are ascribed to Addison; the systematic of aesthetic problems, the parallelism between aesthetics and logic, etc., to Baumgarten; the distinctions between beautiful and sublime and between pleasure and taste, as well as the separation between perfection and beauty to Burke; the distinction between genius and *ingenium*, the definition of genius as balance of imagination and judgment, and genius' direct relation to taste, to Gerard; the subjective character of aesthetic judgment in its necessity and universality, and the notion of "purposiveness without purpose" to Hutcheson; the distinction between "faculty of approval" and cognitive faculty on the one hand and faculty of desire on the other, to Mendelssohn; the idea of freedom as condition to life, the link between aesthetic and moral feelings, and the view of art as contemplation without desires,

---

12. To which I should add the relation to the *Opus postumum:* see V. Mathieu, "Opus postumum e Critica del Giudizio," in *La filosofia trascendentale e l' "Opus postumum" di Kant*, Torino, Edizioni di Filosofia, 1958, 149–160.

13. See the two classical studies, one by O. Schlapp, *Kants Lehre vom Genie und die Entstehung der "Kritik der Urteilskraft,"* Göttingen, Vandenhoeck & Ruprecht, 1901, that underlines the influence of British and Scottish aesthetic theories on Kant; and the other by A. Baeumler, *Das Irrationalitätsproblem in der Ästhetik und Logik des 18. Jahrhunderts bis zur Kritik der Urteilskraft*, Darmstadt, Wissenschaftliche Buchgesellschaft, 1967, which insists instead on the influence of German and French aesthetics.

> to Shaftesbury; the notion of "agreeable," the idea of *Geist*, and the necessity of taste for the genius, to Sulzer; the distinction—or better the new value and specific importance attributed to the already accepted distinction—between objectivity of representations and subjectivity of feelings, to Tetens; allegory, the theory of aesthetic attributes, and the doctrine of the ideal, to Winckelmann; the opposition between genius and spirit of imitation, and the idea of genius as source of rules, to Young.[14]

The list of Kant's debts could easily be made even longer. It can also be paralleled by a reconstruction of the anticipation of all those ideas in Kant's own writings during the precritical period, starting from 1764—and even from 1755. Yet, the recounting of the "genealogy" of Kant's concepts and terms can be multiplied *ad libitum* without disclosing the internal "miracle"[15] of this work. In other words, the *Critique of Judgment* is not the end result or the sum total of all these historical influences together with their critical transformation. All the notions that these manifold traditions offered Kant were also offered to Feder or Garve. Hence, what a convincing and complete reconstruction of the third *Critique* needs to assume as guiding principle is rather the theoretical principle, or "critical point,"[16] that effected those transformations, bringing them together precisely in Kant's *Critique of Judgment.*

While the second and third parts of this study will explore this crucial issue in detail, I will briefly present, in what follows and by way of introduction, the historical steps that led Kant to the composition of the third *Critique.*

2. The Genesis of the Critique of Judgment: *Problematic and Text*

In setting out to retrace the *Entstehungsgeschichte*—the history of the formation —of the *Critique of Judgment*, it is important to distinguish two different issues. (2.1.) The first issue regards the presence of the topics that will eventually converge in the *Critique of Judgment* in Kant's thought from approximately 1755 to 1790. In relation to this point, I will follow the development of both the theme of aesthetics and that of teleology along parallel lines. (2.2.) The second issue concerns the internal development of the text of the third *Critique*; that is, the history of the composition of its different parts between the end of 1787 and the end of March 1790.[17] In relation to this point, I will schematically present one of the traditional solutions of the problem of this development.

---

14. L. Scaravelli, "Osservazioni sulla Critica del giudizio," op. cit., 341 f. (my translation).

15. E. Cassirer, *Kants Leben und Lehre*, Berlin, Bruno Cassirer, 1918, 291.

16. L. Scaravelli, *Osservazioni sulla Critica del giudizio*, op. cit., 348.

17. Among the numerous studies on both these—obviously connected—topics, I will only mention here those contributions that every new study must necessarily confront. The first to inaugurate the way of an "archeological investigation into the genesis of the third

2.1. The Problematic

We can now return to the opposition between historical reconstruction of the text and its philosophical understanding on the basis of a theoretical key point. The real turning point in the *Entstehungsgeschichte* of the *Critique of Judgment* is the idea that the problems of art and the beautiful on the one hand and those of organic life on the other necessarily belong together and therefore should be treated together under one and the same transcendental principle. Taken separately, the two topics—the beautiful and life—occupied Kant almost constantly from early on. Their development has been equally constant and slow. The convergence of the two series of problems, on the contrary, occurred suddenly and unexpectedly. The discovery of a common principle that allowed Kant to consider those issues as occupying a new part of transcendental philosophy was totally unpredictable to

---

Critique" (J. H. Zammito, *The Genesis of Kant's Critique of Judgment*, op. cit., 4 f.) has been M. Souriau, *Le jugement réflechissant dans la philosophie critique de Kant*, Paris, Alcan, 1926, followed by G. Tonelli's two studies, *Dall'estetica metafisica all'estetica psicoempirica. Studi sulla genesi del criticismo*, Torino, Memorie dell'Accademia delle Scienze di Torino, 1955, and "La formazione del testo della Kritik der Urteilskraft," in *Revue Internationale de Philosophie*, 30, (1954), 423–449 (the first deals mainly with the issue of the genesis of Kant's aesthetic problematic, while the second addresses the question of the internal formation of the text of the third *Critique*). Both Souriau and Tonelli assume the idea of "reflective judgment" as the key for their reconstruction. In addition to these works, very informative is W. Windelband's *Einleitung* (introduction) to the *Akademie* edition of the third *Critique*: *Einleitung*, in AA, V, 512-527. See also H.-J. De Vleeschauwer, *L'évolution de la pensée kantienne*, op. cit.; P. Menzer, *Kants Aesthetik in ihrer Entwicklung*, Berlin, Abhandlungen der deutschen Akademie der Wissenschaften, 1952; J. C., Meredith, "Last Stages of the Development of Kant's Critique of Taste," in *Kant's Critique of Aesthetic Judgment: Translated with Seven Introductory Essays, Notes, and Analytical Index*, Oxford, Oxford University Press, 1911; O. Schlapp, *Kants Lehre vom Genie und die Enstehung der "Kritik der Urteilskraft,"* op. cit.; A. Baeumler, *Das Irrationalitätsproblem*, op. cit. More recently, see chapter 1 of P. Guyer's *Kant and the Claims of Taste*, op. cit.; the comprehensive study by J. H. Zammito, *The Genesis of Kant's Critique of Judgment*, op. cit.; and the different articles by D. Dumouchel, "La découverte de la faculté de juger réfléchissante. Le role heuristique de la "Critique du gout" dans la formation de la Critique de la faculté de juger," in *Kant Studien* 85, (1994), 419–442; "L'ésthétique pré-critique de Kant. Genèse de la théorie du 'gout' et du beau," in *Archives de Philosophie* 60 (1997), 59–86; "Genèse de la troisième Critique: le role de l'esthétique dans l'achèvement du système critique," in *Kant's Aesthetics/Kants Aesthetik/L'esthétique de Kant*, op. cit.; M. Frank, "Kants 'Reflexionen zur Ästhetik.' Zur Werkgeschichte der 'Kritik der ästehtischen Urteilskraft,'" in *Revue Internationale de Philosophie* 4 (1990), 552–580. Both in the case of Zammito's book and in the case of Dumouchel's articles, however, the insufficiencies of the historical reconstruction discussed above can clearly be felt (for a similar criticism see also E.Garroni/H. Hohenegger, introduzione, op. cit., xiii–xvi).

Kant himself.[18] Hence, if the thematic material of the third *Critique* allows for a historical reconstruction, the very central idea around which the *Critique* is constructed is without a proper development and consequently asks for a thoroughly different kind of interpretation.

The topic of teleology was widely present in the scientific, philosophical, and theological discussions of the eighteenth century. Both in the observation of nature and in cosmological inquiry, it represented the *pendant*—the theoretical alternative and limit-concept—to the dominant ideas of mechanism. Kant already started concerning himself with these ideas in the 1755 *Universal History of Nature and Theory of the Heavens, or, an Essay on the Constitution and Mechanical Origins of the Entire Cosmic Edifice, Treated in Accordance with Newtonian Principles*, where he recognizes that "the formation of celestial bodies, the cause of their movement, in short, the very origin of the entire present constitution of the cosmic edifice, will be discovered before one can clearly and completely explain, on the basis of mechanical causes, the production of a single blade of grass or of a worm."[19] Although with this generic opposition between mechanism and organic life Kant seems to already be setting the limits of the mechanistic explanation of nature, it is only in the first *Critique*, in the appendix to the Transcendental Dialectic, that he reaches a more precise awareness of the important "regulative" and not constitutive use that reason can make of the idea of *Zweckmäßigkeit,* or purposiveness. This idea opens up to a *systematic* view of nature as a whole. *Zweckmäßigkeit* is closely connected to the notion of "system." However, Kant is not yet clear about the kind of principle that purposiveness should represent, since it is certainly not a transcendental principle at this time. Consequently, his discussion of the topic is still relegated to an appendix of the Dialectic.

The idea of teleology, or purposiveness, takes up further significance in connection with Kant's philosophy of history, anthropology, and practical philosophy in general. In the series of writings on history[20] inaugurated by the 1784 "Idea for a Universal History with Cosmopolitan Intent," Kant sees in teleology nature's own purposiveness with regard to the human being and its species. Teleology is

---

18. See W. Windelband's introduction, op. cit., AA, V, 512. The awareness of this important difference (ideas cannot be reduced to history even though they do have a history) is difficult to find in the interpreters. P. Guyer opposes this position (see *Kant and the Claims of Taste*, op. cit., 25–27) considering an already made theory of taste that Kant would have unnecessarily complicated and even distorted by "submerging the problem of taste into a larger problem of finding principles for a faculty of reflective judgment" (ibid., 27).

19. AA, I, 230 (my translation). An account of the development of Kant's teleology can be found in J. H. Tufts, *The Sources and Development of Kant's Teleology*, Chicago, 1892—a work, however, which in 1954 Tonelli considered "completely outdated" (*La formazione del testo della Kritik der Urteilskraft*, op. cit., 432 n.).

20. See chapter 1 for more details on these writings. These writings are chronologically placed between the two editions of the first *Critique*.

the law that allows the philosopher to transform the scattered and fortuitous manifold of human actions and events into the coherent development of the whole of history. It is important to stress that the subject of teleology is for Kant nature as a whole, not the individual human agent as such. World history is for Kant an "idea" whose philosophical reconstruction takes place according to an a priori "guiding-thread."[21] First in the 1785 *Determination of the Concept of Human Race* that goes back to a topic already discussed in a group of essays of 1775–77 and then in the essay "On the Use of Teleological Principles in Philosophy" (1788) written at the completion of the second *Critique*, Kant further develops the idea of a *heuristic* use of teleology in the philosophical understanding of the human being.[22] In all these writings, however, Kant seems to see in the notion of *Zweckmäßigkeit* neither a principle that requires a separate—transcendental or critical—theorization nor a concept in some ways problematic. Moreover, no hints are given for an explicit connection between teleology and aesthetics, or at least, this connection cannot be read as easily from the stance of teleology as it can from the stance of aesthetics.[23] For, in relation to the topic of aesthetics, the idea of a "harmony" of the faculties of the mind as well as the notion of the "accordance" or attunement between the constitution of the object and the feeling of the subject was already established by the Leibnizian-Wolffian tradition.

In a crucial letter to K. L. Reinhold of December 28 and 31, 1787, Kant reveals that he is working on a "Critique of taste" for which he found a new, unexpected realm of a priori principles. As immediate consequence, the very physiognomy of philosophy is for him transformed. He now recognizes "three parts of philosophy, each of which has its own a priori principles . . . theoretical philosophy, teleology, and practical philosophy." Kant does not specify what he understands under "teleology;" he suggests, however, that one will find this intermediary part of philosophy to be the poorest with regard to a priori determinations.

I turn now to the development of Kant's interests in aesthetics, taste, and the beautiful.[24] These topics are connected from the very beginning with issues as different as logic, gnoseology, psychology, anthropology, and morals, and therefore cover the same wide range of issues as the topic of teleology. Early on, Kant's treatment of aesthetics plays itself out between two main connections: a

21. AA, VIII, 30.

22. For the discussion of the topic of teleology in Kant's writings, see J. D., McFarland, *Kant's Concept of Teleology*, Edinburgh, University of Edinburgh Press, 1970.

23. See the already mentioned suggestion of De Vleeschauwer that the connection between the beautiful and teleology was a *locus communis* in the eighteenth-century philosophical debate (*L'évolution de la pensée kantienne*, op. cit., 140).

24. I will provide an exclusively chronological listing of the places and works in which Kant is concerned with the topic of aesthetics before the *Critique of Judgment* without getting into the issue, common in the literature, of distinguishing different phases in Kant's precritical theory of taste. For a discussion of the philosophical issues at stake in this early theory, see section 3 in the present chapter.

gnoseological one where aesthetics, in the tradition of Baumgarten's and Meier's rationalism, intersects with logic, and a more generally practical one, closer to the British and Scottish tradition and influenced by Rousseau, where aesthetics connects with issues of anthropology, psychology, and morals. Kant's first presentation of aesthetic material is given in the *Observations on the Feeling of the Beautiful and Sublime* of 1764. Already in the 1750s, however, Meier's *Auszug aus der Vernunftlehre* (1752) drew Kant's attention to the topic of *Geschmack* (taste)[25] and to the connection between taste and "aesthetic perfection." "A sensible consideration of perfection is taste. A cognition is called aesthetic, when it is considered perfect by sensible judgment." *Geschmacklehre*, a "doctrine of taste" is in charge of determining "what taste is."[26] Even before the *Observations*, the *Inquiry into the Clarity of the Principles of Natural Theology and Morals* (1764) shows Kant's confrontation with the notion of *Gefühl* (Kant mentions here Hutcheson's "moral feeling").[27] In the 1764 *Observations*, Kant's theory of taste displays a psychological and empirical character that develops into an anthropological rather than a gnoseological connection as was, instead, the case of the *Reflections* of the mid-1750s. It has been observed that in 1764 Kant's theory already entailed, at least "materially," almost all the notions that would later appear in the third *Critique*, namely the notions of "taste" and "genius" common to the contemporary discussion; the ideas of "form," "harmony" and "play" of the faculties of the mind (imagination and understanding in particular); the accordance with the purposiveness of nature; the notion of "feeling of pleasure and displeasure."[28] As it appears from the presentation of Kant's lectures in the winter semester 1765–1766, the topic of taste—this time under the title of a "*critique* of taste, i.e., aesthetics" (and not of "*doctrine* of taste")—has become one of the topics of Kant's teaching activity. Moreover, the "critique of taste" is set here in relation to a "critique of reason,"[29] (i.e., in relation to logic), on which Kant lectures from Meier's *Vernunftlehre.*[30]

After the 1770 *Dissertatio* that led him to a new theory of sensibility, in his letter of June 7, 1771, Kant writes to Marcus Herz that he is working on a book entitled "The limits of sensibility and reason." In it he presents "the relation be-

---

25. See the group of *Reflexionen* of these years on G. Fr. Meier, *Auszug aus der Vernunftlehre*, Halle, J. J. Gebauer, 1752, published by E. Adickes in AA, XVI.

26. R 1748 (1755–1756), AA, XVI, 100.

27. *Versuch*, AA, II, 298–300; see also II, 280, "Gefühl des Erhabenen, des Schönen."

28. E. Garroni/H. Hohenegger, "Introduzione," op. cit., xxii; also D. Henrich, "Kant's Explanation of Aesthetic Judgment," in *Aesthetic Judgment and the Moral Image of the World: Studies in Kant*, Stanford, Stanford University Press, 1992, 29–56, 33, 35.

29. "Nachricht von der Einrichtung seiner Vorlesungen in dem Winterhalbenjahre von 1765–1766," in AA, II, 303–314, here 311.

30. For the important relation between Kant's aesthetics and Meier's logic on the one hand and Baumgarten's *psychologia empirica* on the other, see D. Henrich, *Kant's Explanation of Aesthetic Judgment*, op. cit., 32 ff.

tween the fundamental concepts and the laws of the sensible world along with the plan of what constitutes the nature of a doctrine of taste, metaphysics, and moral." Despite the fact that Kant uses here the term "*doctrine*" instead of "*critique*," a theory of taste is for him an utterly empirical discipline. In the famous letter of February 21, 1772, Kant further describes to Herz the plan of his work on "The limits of sensibility and reason," which he divides into a theoretical part and a practical part. The first part entails, in turn, two divisions: "1. Phenomenology in general. 2. Metaphysics—albeit only according to its name and method." The second part is further divided into "1. General principles of feeling, taste, and sensible desire. 2. The first grounds of morality."[31] Taste is here just one of the topics that are concerned with the forms of our sensible response to objects. At this point, Kant does not seem to need a particular discipline for it—be it doctrine or critique. During the nine "years of silence" that led Kant to the first edition of the *Critique of Pure Reason*, only the rich material of the *Reflections* provides us with hints for the development of Kant's thought on the matter of aesthetics and taste. Kant's work is dedicated now to the transcendental foundation of subjectivity. His interests revolve around the link between the new theory of sensibility and the notion of feeling and taste, thus pointing to the problem of the rules of taste.[32]

The two editions of the *Critique of Pure Reason*, with the important changes in the footnote of the Transcendental Aesthetic regarding the meaning of the German word *Aesthetik* as opposed to *Kritik des Geschmacks*[33] and its correct use in philosophy, mark an important moment in the development of Kant's theory. The 1781 edition radically rejects Baumgarten's efforts of promoting a theory of taste in the scientific form of a discipline called "aesthetics." Kant reserves this title to "transcendental aesthetic," namely to the theory of space and time as a priori forms of intuition. In the 1787 edition, however, when Kant is about to start his work on the *Critique of Judgment*, he revises those claims. *Aesthetics* is now a term permitted not only for a transcendental but also for a psychological inquiry (a concession to Baumgarten). Moreover, the claim that rules and criteria of taste, on the ground of their sources, can only be empirical and never serve as a priori principles, is now corrected by the specification that rules of taste, being of empirical nature because of their "*principal*" source, can never serve as "*determinate* laws a priori." In another footnote in the Canon of Pure Reason of the Transcendental Doctrine of Method, Kant excludes all the concepts that refer to objects of our feeling from the realm of transcendental philosophy. He maintains that these concepts, insofar as they relate to "pleasure and displeasure," belong to the sphere of the practical.[34]

---

31. Letter to M. Herz February 21, 1772.
32. See section 3 below.
33. KrV B 35/A 20:21; see the discussion in chapter 2 above.
34. KrV B 829/A 801.

Kant's letters from the years 1787–1789 witness the difficulties in defining the systematic place that his work on the topic of taste will occupy in his philosophy. Hence, the indecision on the title of the work itself. Johann Bering's letter to Kant of May 28, 1787, reveals that the catalogue of the Easter book fair of that year was announcing Kant's "Grundlegung zur Kritik des Geschmacks." Kant's letter to Ch. G. Schütz of June 25, 1787, repeats an analogous title. Therein Kant announces that the *Critique of Practical Reason* is ready for publication and that he has no time to review Herder's third part of the *Ideen* as he has to rush back to work on his "Grundlage der Kritik des Geschmacks." The expression *Grundlegung/Grundlage zur Kritik* (groundwork/foundation) obviously repeats the relation that Kant already established in his moral philosophy between the *Groundwork of the Metaphysics of Morals* and the *Critique of Practical Reason.*[35] The important difference, however, is that in the former we have a "*critique*" of taste, while in the latter the groundwork refers to a "*metaphysics*" of moral. That a theory of taste cannot be a "doctrine" or a "metaphysics," has been clear to Kant since the 1760s.[36] In the 1760s, however, Kant had been using the term "*critique*" under the influence of Lord Kames's empiricism.[37] It is only in the summer of 1787 that Kant sees the critique of taste as a part of transcendental philosophy proper and hence as belonging to the project of a critique of reason. The term "*critique,*" whose origin as a philosophical term goes back precisely to the sphere of taste (as literary criticism), once appropriated by Kant's transcendental project, is turned back to designate the possibility of a new theory of taste carried out under transcendental principles.

The letter to L. H. Jakob of September 11, 1787, sees Kant at work on his "Kritik des Geschmacks," which is meant to "conclude the critical task" and to allow him to pass to the "dogmatic task" of his philosophy. Kant hopes to see the "Critique of Taste" in print right before Easter.[38] Yet, he would still have to struggle for a few years before seeing the conclusion of his critical project. In his letter to K. L. Reinhold of December 28–31, 1787, Kant reveals that the work on the "Kritik des Geschmacks" brought him to a crucial discovery from which the entire systematic of philosophy had to be reformulated. In this letter, Kant dis-

35. Hence B. Erdmann's hypothesis, favored by W. Windelband, that Kant had thought for a while of having a "Groundwork to the Critique of Taste" precede the "Critique of Taste" in the same way as the *Groundwork of the Metaphysics of Morals* preceded the *Critique of Practical Reason*. Windelband, however, concludes with a certain reservation regarding the possibility of ever verifying this hypothesis; see Windelband, *Einleitung*, op. cit., 515.

36. Kant's very last claim concerning this issue is at the end of the preface of the *Critique of Judgment* (X, AA V, 170, 24).

37. H. Home, (Lord Kames), *Elements of Criticism*, printed for A. Miller, London, and A. Kincaid & J. Bell, Edinburgh, 1762 (the German translation appears in 1763).

38. See also the letter to M. Herz, December 24, 1787, in which Kant declares his hopes to soon see the "conclusion" of his philosophical plan.

closes to Reinhold the secret of his research method. When he is exploring a new territory and is indecisive as to which direction to take, he only has to appeal to the general characters of the "elements of knowledge and of the corresponding forces of the *Gemüt*" in order to progress. Following this method in his work on the "Critique of Taste," Kant discovered a "new type of a priori principles." However, he does not reveal what the discovered a priori principles are. As in the case of the previous two *Critiques,* he seems to delegate to the immanent development of the *Critique* itself the determination of what these principles are and what their use is. He provides, instead, some hints as to the direction of his thoughts on the matter. The faculties of the *Gemüt,* Kant explains, are three: the faculty of knowledge, the feeling of pleasure and displeasure, and the faculty of desire. The first faculty was the object of the "critique of pure (theoretical) reason" while the third was the object of the "critique of practical reason." These *Critiques* discovered the a priori principles of the respective faculties. Kant suggests that it is a "systematic" consideration of the second faculty of the *Gemüt* that has convinced him of the possibility, long denied, of finding specific a priori principles for the feeling of pleasure and displeasure. These principles will determine the third, intermediary part of philosophy next to theoretical and practical philosophy, namely "Teleology." In this letter, the crucial link is established between the idea of possible a priori principles for taste (and for teleology as a philosophical discipline) and the feeling of pleasure and displeasure.

On January 6, 1788, the publisher J. F. Hartknoch wrote to Kant asking news about both his critique of practical reason and the "critique of beautiful taste [Kritik des schönen Geschmacks]." Certainly, his work on the *Critique of Practical Reason* (1788)[39] helped Kant shed light on the new direction that his critique of taste was going to take. For it is the second *Critique* that brought Kant to the radical distinction between the feeling of pleasure and displeasure and the faculty of desire. It is only after having freed the faculty of desire of all connections to the feeling of pleasure and displeasure that the peculiar sphere proper to this last activity can emerge in its own right. To be sure, a passage at the end of the second *Critique* is already significant for the direction of Kant's reflection in these crucial years. At the end of the Doctrine of Method, Kant distinguishes a peculiar "activity of the faculty of judgment that makes us feel our own cognitive faculties" and that is not yet "interest in actions and their morality itself." This activity of judgment lends rather the "form of beauty" to virtue itself as well as to the attitude of the mind according to moral laws. This form of beauty "is admired but not yet sought. . . . It is the same with everything whose contemplation produces subjectively a consciousness of the harmony of our powers of representation by which we feel our entire cognitive faculty (understanding and imagination) strengthened; it produces satisfaction that can be communicated to

39. The manuscript of the second *Critique* was finished in the summer of 1787.

others, but the existence of its object remains indifferent to us."[40] This passage clearly reveals Kant's parallel occupation with the problematic of the *Critique of Judgment.*[41]

The last important turn in Kant's reflection on the systematic place and character of his work on taste takes place in early 1789 (or in the second half of 1788).[42] After the publication of the *Critique of Practical Reason*, the "Critique of Taste" was transformed into a "Critique of Judgment." The title *Kritik der Urteilskraft* appears for the very first time in Kant's letter to K. L. Reinhold of May 12, 1789. Kant recognizes therein that the "Kritik des Geschmacks" is a "part" of his "Kritik der Urteilskraft." In the letter to M. Herz of May 26, 1789, the *Critique of Judgment* is considered, in turn, as the "last part of the critique" of reason to which the "system of a metaphysics of nature and morals" should follow. In the notion of *Urteilskraft*—judgment, or "faculty," or "capacity" to judge[43]—Kant finally attained the unification of the aesthetic and teleological problem. Once Kant managed to reach this point, the completion of the work proceeded relatively quickly and without surprises.

2.2. The Text

The attempt to reconstruct the internal development of the text of the *Critique of Judgment* is closely connected to the previously sketched *Entwicklungsgeschichte* of its problems.[44] Lacking any additional objective element, however, all efforts remain therein necessarily hypothetical. Since Giorgio Tonelli's reconstruction can still be found at the basis of the most recent interpretations,[45] I will mainly draw on his chronological schema. Tonelli's analysis has a fundamentally "philological basis" and tries to avoid all appeal to "dubious 'internal grounds'."[46] Its interpretive principle is the notion of reflective judgment, which Tonelli main-

---

40. KpV A 285–286.

41. For the editorial history of the third *Critique*, and the history of its successive editions, see W. Windelband's detailed account in *Einleitung*, op. cit., 522–527; see also G. Tonelli, *La formazione del testo della Kritik der Urteilskraft*, op. cit., 429 f. During Kant's life three editions of the *Critik der Urtheilskraft* appeared: the first, in Berlin und Libau, bey Lagarde und Friedrich, 1790; the second, in Berlin, bey F. T. Lagarde, 1793; and the third, in Berlin, bey F. T. Lagarde, 1799 (generally indicated as A, B, and C editions). These three editions do not differ significantly from each other.

42. See G. Tonelli, *La formazione*, op. cit., 446 f.

43. For the difficulties in rendering *Urteilskraft* in translation, see the note to the translation of the preface.

44. See G. Tonelli's two classical works, the first dedicated to the development of Kant's aesthetic, the second dedicated to the internal formation of the text.

45. As the ones already mentioned by Zammito and Dumouchel, which I am here using along with Tonelli's work.

46. G. Tonelli, *La formazione del testo della Kritik der Urteilskraft*, op. cit., 426.

tains Kant did not discover until the composition of the "First Introduction" dated by him before May 1789.[47]

A first phase of the composition goes from the end of September 1787 to the summer of 1788. The Analytic of the Beautiful (§§1–22 of the *Critique of Judgment*), along with §§31–40 of the Deduction of Aesthetic Judgment, represents the core of the originally planned "Critique of Taste," which was thought of as a mere "exposition of taste" and which excluded the topic of the sublime. Additional material from the first part of the third *Critique*, namely §§41–54 and the Dialectic of Aesthetic Judgment (§§55–60, excluding §58) is considered as preceding Kant's focus on the faculty of judgment and is hence ascribed to the year 1788.

A second phase runs from the summer of 1788 to January 1790. Kant changes the title of the work from "Critique of Taste" to "Critique of Judgment." The later §§58, 23, and 30 belong to this period. The Analytic of the Sublime (§§23–30) was written, according to Tonelli, in line with the "First Introduction" and immediately after it and then added to the original plan of a "Critique of Taste." The Critique of Teleological Judgment, as second part of the third *Critique*, became possible for Kant only after the discovery of the unifying principle of the reflective faculty of judgment; its composition is therefore dated after May 1789. (iii) The latest parts of the book are represented by the final (January–March or March 1790)[48] and the preface, both sent to the publisher on March 22, 1790.

3. Taste, Feeling, and Sensibility before Aesthetic Judgment

In Kant's philosophy the term *Aesthetik* never takes on the meaning of "*doctrine* of art and beauty."[49] With this in mind, I analyze now a few thematic elements in Kant's reflection on the problem of taste, bringing them back to the general issue of the internal organization and definition of the sphere of sensibility before the *Critique of Judgment* (more precisely, in the precritical period). In doing this, I pursue the same aim as in the previous two chapters.[50]

---

47. See the above discussed letters to Reinhold and Herz of May 1789; see, however, Tonelli's correction of his own hypothesis in his review of N. Hinske et alii's edition of Kant's *Erste Einleitung in der Kritik der Urteilskraft*, Stuttgart, Frommann, 1965, in *Philosophy and History*, 1968, 167–172. Tonelli's terminological analysis follows Kant's different employment of terms such as *Geschmack*, *Urteilskraft*, *Urteil*, *Reflexion*, and *Zweckmäßigkeit* in order to discover the different chronological layers of the text of the third *Critique*. For example: the use of *Geschmacksurteil*—or judgment of taste—is the sign of an older conception, while the use of *ästhetisches Urtheil*—aesthetic judgment—more frequent starting from the Analytic of the Sublime, discloses a later view.

48. The introduction was composed in the period between January and March 1790, according to Bueck and Hinske; in the short period between March 7 and 22, 1790, according to Lehmann. For this discussion see chapter 5.

49. See E. Garroni/H. Hohenegger, *Introduzione*, op. cit., xvii.

50. In this last section of the chapter, my aim is neither a chronological reconstruction of the development of Kant's theory of taste nor a complete account of his precritical aesthetics. Rather, following the line opened with my discussion of the problem of sensibility in

Since its first appearance in the Spanish language in the work of Gracian[51] in the second half of the seventeenth century, the term *gusto* (taste) shows an inner connection to the empirical universality of an intersubjective agreement. In Gracian's terminology, however, *gusto* refers more to the sphere of moral and political dispositions than to aesthetic experience. It designates the ability to make the right choice; that is, a choice that is always accompanied by universal consensus. Taste not only applies to man in society; it is also the source of all sociability, culture, and social development. Gracian was most influential in France. Through French authors, however, Gracian's work was introduced in Germany by Christian Thomasius. Gracian's "man of taste"—the *discreto*—becomes Thomasius's *politicus*, the man who knows the rules of correct behavior in court. Yet the practical disposition expressed by the term *taste* was so foreign to German culture that Thomasius did not yet dare to translate the word——or, better, to coin a new term for it—in the German language.[52] Instead, he rendered Gracian's maxims in French. In his 1687 program on the "imitation of the French people"[53] we find a formulation that Kant will repeat and comment on in his early *Reflections.* Thomasius's rendering of Gracian's sixty-seventh maxim is: "le gout universel d'autrui . . . est la vrai méthode de choisir." Along the same lines, Kant will consider *Geschmack* as "*Vermögen zu wählen*"—the capacity or faculty to choose not what pleases the individual in her private subjectivity but what meets general or public approval.[54]

This historical reference sheds light on the twofold connection that taste manifests from the very beginning in Kant's thought. On the one hand, taste is related to judgment; on the other, it implies universality and intersubjectivity (and therefore also communicability). One of the achievements of eighteenth-century aesthetics is the subjective (anti-Platonic) turn that brings the judgments on the beautiful back to the subject's own sensibility. Whether "sensible evaluation" (Kant himself talks of *sinnliche Urtheilskraft* and *sinnliche Beurtheilung*) takes place

---

the first and second *Critiques*, and having the *Critique of Judgment* in view, I want to provide a few elements of reflection that will prove essential in the reading of this last work.

51. For this analysis, see A. Bäumler, *Das Irrationalitätsproblem*, op. cit., 18 ff.; see in particular R. Hildebrand, *Geschmack in Anwendung auf das Schöne*, in *Beiträge zum deutschen Unterricht*, 1897, 314.

52. See A. Bäumler, *Das Irrationalitätsproblem*, op. cit., 21–22.

53. Ch. Thomasius, "Welcher Gestalt mandenen Frantzosen in gemeinem Leben und Wandel nachahmen solle? ein Collegium über Gratians Grund-Reguln, vernünftig, klug und artig zu leben," in *Deutsche Literaturdenkmale* 51, 1687.

54. Bäumler develops the interesting point that the birthplace of Kant's aesthetics is not "high in the library" but "far under in the kitchen" (see the group of *Reflections* quoted by him, *Das Irrationalitätsproblem*, op. cit., 265). Thomasius's passage goes on with the following statement: "le gout universel d'autrui, qui est la vrai méthode de choisir. Car il en est comme d'un festin, ou les viandes ne s'appretent pas du gout des cuisiniers, mais à celuy du convivez." Kant writes in R 2040: "malim convivis quam placuisse cocis," probably quoting Martial who, in turn, was also Gracian's source (AA, XVI, 209).

without understanding[55]—and as its alternative—or understanding itself operates as a sensible power in this type of evaluation,[56] taste is considered a *feeling* for the beautiful. The sphere of taste is the sphere of sensibility, and this in turn is further specified as the realm of feeling. Moreover, feeling is directed both to the realm of the beautiful (and sublime) and to the realm of the practical. For along with the "feeling for the beautiful," we also have "moral feelings." However, by establishing this important parallel or analogy between the two families of feelings—the aesthetic and the moral—the empiricist tradition was complicating Kant's route toward an understanding of the specificity of *Gefühl*. Kant first has to understand that morality cannot be grounded upon feeling in order to recognize that the independence of the feeling of pleasure and displeasure rests on a new specific kind of a priori principles. Early on, Kant's theory of taste follows from his attempt to determine the role of feeling in relation to the other faculties of the mind. *Gefühl* seems from the outset an intermediary faculty at play between the cognitive faculty and the faculty of desire.[57]

From the very beginning, Kant's theory of taste plays itself out between two different issues. The *Critique of Judgment* will arise only when the two issues eventually meet. (i) On the one hand, Kant firmly determines the realm of taste as the realm of *sensibility*. Consequently, up until the second edition of the *Critique of Pure Reason,* he would strenuously oppose any attempt to ground aesthetics on a priori rules. (ii) On the other hand, however, Kant seems determined to save the whole sphere of sensibility (namely not only the theoretical function of sensibility, although theoretical sensibility will be saved first) from the fate to which the empiricist tradition had confined it.[58] The *Critique of Judgment* is the latest result of Kant's life-long philosophical experimentation on the topic of sensibility. Taste and the feeling of the beautiful are the spheres in which this experimentation starts and the theoretical place in which this experimentation ends. Given that sensibility (as intuition, perception, feeling, drive, etc.) permeates human existence in all its manifestations, Kant's effort is to find the a priori of the forms of sensibility respectively implicated in the activity of the different faculties of the

---

55. As for Hume, Home, Burke, Hutcheson.

56. As for Gottsched, Bodmer, Breitinger.

57. In relation to this problem, Kant is indebted both to Mendelssohn—who recognizes as a third faculty the "faculty of approving" (*das Billigen*), which is contemplation of beauty, and to Tetens, who sees in the *Gefühl* a third and autonomous faculty next to the cognitive and the practical one.

58. Accordingly, I propose to substitute this distinction, which regards the internal configuration of the sphere of sensibility (*Sinnlichkeit* is the sphere of materiality, giveness, passivity, etc., yet there are areas within the sphere of sensibility that show the character of formality, spontaneity, etc.), to Guyer's claim that Kant's precritical theory of taste (and to a certain extent still the theory of the third *Critique*) is based upon a confusion between aesthetic *response*, i.e., our *pleasure* in the beautiful, and aesthetic *judgment*, i.e., the *claim to universal validity* inherent in a judgment of taste (*Kant and the Claims of Taste*, op. cit., 13–32).

mind. Viewed from the late perspective of the *Critique of Judgment*, Kant's 1771 title: "*The Limits of Sensibility and Reason*" was already accurately outlining the program of the entire critical philosophy. The first *Critique* (and already the *Dissertatio*) proved that a peculiar form of spontaneity belongs to intuition; that is, to sensibility in relation to the theoretical faculty of the understanding. The second *Critique* provided the negative proof that *pure* practical reason, not sensibility, is the source of moral determination; yet the pure feeling of "reverence" for the law appeared as a unique example of a pure practical feeling. The last stage of this itinerary is reached once Kant sees the possibility of finding a priori principles related to feeling as an independent third faculty of the mind by means of the activity of the faculty of judgment.

Since taste relates to the subject's own sensibility, the "perfection" that characterizes the beautiful is different in principle from logical perfection. In Meier's definition, which Kant comments on in a variety of ways, the notion of "perfection of cognition" already implies both teleological orientation and organic constitution: "When the manifold in cognition agrees toward an intent or entails the sufficient ground for it: therein consists *perfection of cognition* [*perfectio cognitionis*]. Perfections of cognition are to be found in it either insofar as cognition is clear or insofar as it is unclear. The former is *logical perfection of cognition* [*perfectio cognitionis logica*], the latter is *its beauty* [*pulchritudo et perfectio aesthetica cognitionis*]."[59] Kant's early recognition[60] that sensibility has its own "lawfulness" (in whichever way this lawfulness might still be thought) leads him to follow Baumgarten's and Meier's suggestion that attributes a particular kind of perfection to sensibility. Yet, this perfection is still determined in a sort of subsidiary way in relation to the understanding's own cognition. Accordingly, taste is defined as the faculty that presents abstract concepts in a sensible individual intuition.[61] Taste is a preparation for the "clear" cognition of the understanding. What is important to stress is the close relation that early on links Kant's reflection on taste and the beautiful on the one hand and epistemological issues of logic and theory of knowledge on the other—a relation that remains crucial to the *Critique of Judgment.*

Kant's notes on Meier's quoted passage reinforce the distinction, within the notion of perfection, between an aesthetic and a logical perfection. Yet, Kant insists on specifying beauty's relation to the subject and does so by inserting a series of further oppositions that are interesting in light of his developing theory of sensibility. Kant's move can be seen as an attempt to combine rationalist and empiricist traditions in order to find precisely that universality—or lawfulness—of sensibility on which alone a theory of taste could be grounded. "Logical perfections relate to the *object*, beauty to the *subject*. (The *matter* of cognition in rela-

59. G. Fr. Meier, *Auszug aus der Vernunftlehre*, op. cit., §22.

60. To be dated back to the years 1769–70.

61. See, for example, R 1794 (dated 1769–70), AA, XVI, 118; also R 1799 (dated 1769–75), AA, XVI, 119.

tion to the *subject* is *sensation*. The *form* of cognition in relation to the *subject* is called *appearance*)." That which pleases always discloses an "agreement." If this is an agreement within the subject, we have feeling or taste. If the agreement is objective, then it is also universally valid.[62] Aesthetic perfection is not the agreement or correspondence of the object with its concept—which would be logical "truth"[63]—but rather the agreement of the object with the law or form of sensibility, an agreement that takes place not in the materiality of sensation but in the formality of appearance and intuition. What specifies aesthetic perfection against logical perfection, for Kant, is not its unclearness but the *relation to the subject.* Moreover, this reference to the subject becomes for Kant the starting point for an important series of oppositions that are placed right within the sphere of sensibility itself. As far as cognition is concerned, on the ground of its relation to the subject we can distinguish a matter and a form. Here, matter is (as it would be later in the first *Critique*) that mode of sensibility called sensation; form is instead appearance— "the feeling of the form is taste."[64]

By locating both "feeling" and "taste" in "appearance" thereby providing the conditions for aesthetic perfection, Kant further specifies the difference between sensation and appearance in the following way: "Appearance is distinguished from sensation in that sensation is that element within sensibility that constitutes a part of the subject's own condition; appearance, instead, is an *effective action of the cognitive faculty* that moves toward the object and is the cause of this sensation."[65] There are two components of sensibility: a thoroughly passive and material one that reveals the status of the subject, which is sensation, and a decidedly active and formal one, which is appearance (and is the *cause* of sensation itself).

Beauty is perfection in sensibility;[66] beauty is more exactly the "exterior side of perfection." As perfection is a form of agreement, Kant does not hesitate to relate it to the form of *Zweckmäßigkeit.*[67] Beauty is the "internal perfection"[68] of a thing that manifests itself in external form and thereby becomes sensible.

The other side of Kant's reflection on the problem of feeling, taste, and beauty regards the possibility of rules and the type of rules that can be ascribed to taste. Kant's attack on Baumgarten in the famous footnote of the Transcendental Aesthetic of the first *Critique* was meant to rule out the possibility of raising aesthetics as theory of taste to the level of a science because of the necessarily empirical nature of its principles. Yet Kant has been strenuously looking for a way of grant-

---

62. R 1780 (dated either 1764–68 or 1769), AA, XVI, 112. It is a Reflection on Meier's *Auszug*, §22.

63. See R 1794, op. cit.

64. Among the many Reflections on this topic see R 1795 (1769–73/75), AA, XVI, 118.

65. R 1791 (dated 1769–70), AA, XVI, 116.

66. R 1799, op. cit.

67. R 696 (dated 1770), AA XV, 309.

68. R 628 (dated 1769), AA XV, 273.

ing to taste and beauty a kind of universality and formality that, despite its being merely empirical, could nonetheless be distinguished from the materiality of sensation. The aforementioned distinction between two elements, or components, of sensibility was precisely the condition for this. If sensibility were for Kant only sensation, he would not even have felt the need of including that note in the two editions of the *Critique of Pure Reason*. What makes the later remark so dramatic is the fact that it applies not only to Baumgarten but to Kant's own research during the second half of 1760 and throughout the 1770s.

I have already suggested that both the idea of an intersubjective, public dimension of consensus and the notion of taste as judgment were constitutive of taste since the very introduction of the term in the philosophical vocabulary. It is therefore perfectly comprehensible that Kant had been viewing his theory of taste in this context from the outset. Yet how can the "universal validity" of taste and feeling be justified if taste is confined to the subjective realm of sensibility? Kant is aware that there can be neither an "a priori doctrine"[69] of taste nor a "theory of taste"[70] or a "science of the beautiful."[71] Yet there can very well be a "critique of taste." "Our judgments of taste follow not a rule, but intuition,"[72] so that there are "aesthetic observations"[73] and not *dogmata*. If with the title of a "critique of taste" Kant explicitly follows Home's designation,[74] he is nonetheless developing it out of a very different theory of sensibility. Kant attempts to specify the type of rules that belong to taste's proper way of evaluation and judgment. The general question therein is "Whether taste has fixed and universal rules," to which Kant answers: "Yet not rules to know a priori [*in abstracto*], but to know *in concreto*. [Taste] is a sensible judgment that is valid for everyone."[75]

Thus, a critique of taste should be based upon—and account for—the *empirical* universality of aesthetic agreement. However, given Kant's suggestion that the empirical sphere of sensibility displays a differential composition (i.e., that there are "sensible" representations, "even more sensible" ones, and those that are "sensible in highest degree),"[76] the question to be raised now concerns the particular kind of sensibility that belongs to judgments of taste. "The evaluation of

---

69. R 1821 (dated 1771–75), AA XVI, 128.

70. R 1585 (dated 1760–79), AA, XVI, 26.

71. R 1588 (dated 1772–75), AA, XVI, 27; also R 622 (dated 1769), AA, XV, 269; and the later R 1892 (dated 1776–78), AA, XVI, 150: "There is no science [*Wissenschaft*] of the beautiful, but only art [*Kunst*]."

72. R 1823 (dated 1772–75), AA, XVI, 129.

73. R 1585, op. cit.—hence the title of Kant's 1764 work *Observations on the Feeling of the Beautiful and Sublime.*

74. R 1588, op. cit.

75. R 1851 (dated ca. 1771), AA, XVI, 137; see also the interesting suggestion of R 875 (dated 1776–78), AA, XV, 384: "all cases in which rules cannot be drawn from objective grounds but only from subjective ones: taste, feeling—belong to *anthropology*."

76. R 646 (dated 1769–70), AA, XV, 284.

an object through sensation is not universally valid; the evaluation through true taste is valid for all human beings—both are subjective. . . . If the object agrees with the feeling of the subject according to *matter*, is agreeable and charms as well as moves; if it agrees with the feeling according to *form*, it is beautiful."[77] It is precisely the distinction between a form and a matter of sensibility, between sensation and appearance, that grounds the legitimacy of the universality of taste. For in the case of taste and feeling, universality lies in formality, intuition, and appearance.

In a period in which Kant is developing his aesthetic doctrine of space and time as a priori forms of intuition, this same doctrine seems to have some influence on the issue of the other aesthetics, which concerns taste and feeling.[78] At this point, Kant seems to distinguish even three levels of sensibility (that eventually intersect with each other). "A representation is *sensible* if in it is the form of space and time; it is *even more sensible* if it is accompanied by a sensation (color); it is *sensible in the highest degree*: if it is attributed to the observer precisely as it is observed by others. Beautiful objects are those objects whose order pleases according to the laws of intuition."[79] Hence the definition of taste as the capacity of choosing what sensibly pleases in accordance to others. However, the agreement on which the universality of taste is based cannot be grounded on *sensation* because "in sensation the agreement *is not as necessary* as it is in appearance."[80] Kant is not only appealing to the criterion of universality but also to that of necessity. Since the agreement that leads to a judgment of taste is not based on sensation, it must be grounded in *appearance*. Now, "taste in appearance is grounded upon the relations of space and time . . . and upon the rules of reflection."[81] "That which in an object pleases and we regard as one of its properties must consist in what is valid for everyone. The relations of space and time are valid for everyone, whatever the sensation one might have. Accordingly, in all appearance the form is valid for everyone." This form is known by the logical rule of coordination. "Hence that which is in agreement with the rule of coordination in space and time pleases *necessarily* everyone and is beautiful."[82]

Kant's attempt to justify the universal agreement of taste through the universality and necessity proper to the relations of space and time will prove, in this form, to be unsuccessful. For what meaning could the reference to the forms of

---

77. R 1796 (dated 1769–70), AA XVI, 118–119.

78. The two aesthetics remain radically separated for Kant in the years of the *Dissertatio*—contrary to D. Dumouchel (*L'esthétique pré-critique de Kant*, op. cit., 68), who sees them as merging into each other; Kant's theory of space and time, however, does manifest an influence on the theory of taste, contrary to P. Guyer's claim (*Kant and the Claims of Taste*, op. cit., 26).

79. R 646, op. cit.

80. R 647 (dated 1769-1770), AA, XV, 284.

81. R 648 (dated 1769–70), AA, XV, 284.

82. R 672 (dated 1769–70), AA, XV, 298.

space and time ever have for a judgment of the beautiful? Yet this attempt is significant in order to understand both Kant's uneasiness with the empiricist notion of "universal validity" as referred to taste and his striving toward a more articulate definition of sensibility. Moreover, Kant's shift toward the formality of space and time establishes a crucial point of intersection between the two aesthetics that, in its further critical development, will be ultimately responsible for Kant's so-called "formalism."[83] Furthermore, the reference to the first aesthetics—or, better, to the formal intuitions of space and time as conditions of our perception of objects—accounts for the fact that in Kant's later theory of taste the work of art is not the only object that occasions aesthetic pleasure. For all objects given by intuition in space and time (both natural objects and objects produced by technique) can occasion aesthetic pleasure.[84] Kant's solution of the problem points to the way in which imagination and understanding work together in their "harmonious play" in a process of "exhibition" that instantiates the universal concept in a spatial and temporal individual shape.

---

83. This point is carefully discussed in part III.

84. See D. Henrich, "Kant's Explanation of Aesthetic Judgment," op. cit., 35: Kant's temptation to justify the universal validity of the aesthetic form through the a priori forms of space and time still has an influence in the argument of §14 of the *Critique of Judgment*.

Part II

The Introduction to the *Critique of Judgment*

Chapter 5

The Text

This chapter will approach the text of the published introduction to the *Critique of Judgment* as a whole by discussing both the history of its composition and the general lines of its argument.[1] The text is reprinted, newly translated, and commented on in the following three chapters. Given the theoretical and stylistic density of the introduction, an overview of the whole argument is necessary before addressing its more particular issues. I will outline the structure of the problem of the third *Critique* in terms of the problem presented by Kant in the preface and introduction.

1. "First Introduction," Introduction, and Preface: The History

The complicated history of the text of the third *Critique* finds its last chapter in Kant's decision to replace the long introduction he had been working on, probably since April–May 1789, with the new, shorter, and conceptually different introduction that accompanies the 1790 published book. Kant worked on the first text, generally known as the "First Introduction" to the *Critique of Judgment,* for the last time in the months of December 1789–January 1790.[2] Both theoretical and formal reasons led Kant to write a new introduction for his book. According to Tonelli, the composition of the "First Introduction" precedes the Analytic of the Sublime as well as the Critique of Teleological Judgment. Hence, by rewriting the introduction, Kant probably meant to present an argument that could reflect the results of the whole book in its final form. In addition, the first text was, in Kant's view, "disproportionally extended"[3] to aptly serve as an introduction.

However, Kant does not reject the "First Introduction" in its philosophical content. He recognizes that "it still contains something that can contribute to a more complete understanding of the concept of a purposiveness of nature."[4] With these words Kant promises to send his former student Jakob Sigismund Beck the manuscript of the discarded introduction.[5] Beck's intention was to use Kant's text in the second volume of his own publication on Kant's critical philosophy, *Erläuternder*

1. With regard to the relation between the so-called "First Introduction" and the published introduction, I will only briefly engage in the questions of the history of the texts and the comparison of their respective content. A discussion of some of the crucial passages of the "First Introduction" will follow from the analysis of the published introduction.

2. According to Lehmann, instead, the "First Introduction" was not finished until the beginning of March 1790; see G. Lehmann's *Anhang* to AA, XX, 475–479, here 476.

3. Letter to J. S. Beck, December 4, 1792.

4. Ibid.

5. The manuscript was sent on August 1793; see Kant's letter to Beck, August 18, 1793, and Beck's letter to Kant, April 30, 1793.

Auszug aus den critischen Schriften des Herrn Prof. Kant auf Anrathen desselben.[6] Kant supports Beck's work as a possible weapon in his ongoing polemic against the Wolffians. In sending him the manuscript, Kant suggested that the "First Introduction" could still serve one as a key for entering the complicated world of the third *Critique.*[7] In 1794 Beck published excerpts of Kant's manuscript with the title *Anmerkungen zur Einleitung in die Critik der Urtheilskraft.*[8] In 1833 Beck's text is taken up in F. Ch. Starke's collection of Kant's short writings and published with the title *Über die Philosophie überhaupt und über die Kritik der Urteilskraft insbesondere (1794).*[9] In 1889 the manuscript used by Beck was found by W. Dilthey in the Rostock University library; it was published in 1914 by O. Bueck in E. Cassirer's edition of Kant's works as *Erste Einleitung in die Kritik der Urteilskraft.*[10]

The draft of the published introduction occupies Kant in the short period between March 7 and 22, 1790, according to some interpreters (G. Lehmann) or in the period between January and March 1790 according to others (O. Bueck, N. Hinske).[11] In his letters to the editor Lagarde in the months approaching the publication of the third *Critique,* Kant expresses his doubts on the "First Introduction," viewing it as still needing the "effort" of further work. Kant sees his task as one of "shortening" it, while making it more concise and dense in briefly presenting the "concept of the work's content."[12] Despite Kant's indications, however, the pub-

---

6. The first volume on the critique of speculative and practical reason appeared in 1793.

7. Kant's letter to Beck, August 18, 1793.

8. As appendix in J. S. Beck, *Erläuternder Auszug aus den critischen Schriften des Herrn Prof. Kant auf Anrathen desselben, Zweyter Band, welcher die Critik der Urtheilskraft und die metaphysischen Anfangsgründe der Naturwissenschaft enthält,* Riga, bey Johann Friedrich Hartknoch, 1794.

9. The text would appear with the same title in G. Hartenstein's and K. Rosenkranz's editions. The title indicates that the introductory function of Kant's text is no longer maintained. In 1880 B. Erdmann in his edition of the third *Critique* presents the "First Introduction" as "Auszug aus Kant's ursprünglichem Entwurf der Einleitung in die Kritik der Urteilskraft 1789, 1797."

10. The text has been edited again by G. Lehmann (1927, 1942, in the *Akademie Ausgabe*) and by N. Hinske, W. Müller-Lauter, and M. Theunissen in a facsimile edition (1965). For a detailed history of the "First Introduction" see the facsimile edition, *Erste Einleitung in die Kritik der Urteilskraft. Faksimile und Transkription,* hrsg. v. N. Hinske, W. Müller-Lauter, M. Theunissen, Stuttgart, Frommann, 1965; and in particular Hinske's appendix, "Zur Geschichte des Texts" (III–XII); see also G. Lehmann's *Anhang* to AA, XX, 475–479, and introduction to I. Kant, *Erste Einleitung in die Kritik der Urteilskraft,* Leipzig, Meiner, 1927; and the thorough work by H. Mertens, *Kommentar zur ersten Einleitung in Kants Kritik der Urteilskraft. Zur systematischen Funktion der Kritik der Urteilskraft für das System der Philosophie,* München, Berchmans Verlag, 1975 (235 ff.).

11. See the works cited in the previous footnote.

12. Kant's letter to Lagarde, March 9, 1790; in the letter to Lagarde, February 9, 1790, Kant announces a "dense introduction [*starke Einleitung*]."

lished introduction is not just a shorter version of the "First Introduction." Hence, if Kant's intention was originally to shorten the overextended "First Introduction,"[13] he soon abandoned the project in order to completely rewrite and reelaborate it into a thoroughly new text.

Kant's decision to replace the "First Introduction" mirrors the many difficulties he encountered in presenting the third *Critique* to the general public—and in particular to the philosophical public. He was well aware that the third *Critique* deals with a "presupposition of our reason," which he does not hesitate to define as "*peculiar and strange*."[14] Human reason presupposes the principle of a unity of nature, or its formal purposiveness. However, we presuppose this principle and use it with legitimacy "not because we know this purposiveness as necessary in itself but only because we are in need of it."[15] The "peculiar and strange" presupposition is therefore only subjectively necessary for our human reason and is subjectively necessary *because reason needs it.* Indeed, both reason's presupposition and its justification could sound strange.

Along the same lines, the preface to the book—the very last part written by Kant just before publication—ends by summing up his perplexities in the form of an apology. The topic of the book is the very peculiar "*Phänomen* der Urteilskraft."[16] Kant recognizes that the way this phenomenon has been derived from its principle "may fall short of the clarity we are entitled to demand elsewhere, namely where we deal with cognition according to concepts." This lack of clarity is especially disturbing in the first part of the book in relation to the aesthetic faculty of judgment. Excusing himself, Kant appeals to the extreme difficulty of solving a "problem that nature itself has rendered so involved"[17] by placing a real enigma at the heart of it.[18] Thereby, Kant implicitly provides an account of why a critical and transcendental solution to the problem of taste has come only at this point in his philosophical career and has taken the shape of a 'Critique of Judgment.'

2. The Problem of the Introduction as the Problem of the Third Critique

As is often the case with the introductory writings of major philosophical works of German Idealism, the introduction to the *Critique of Judgment* is not really an introduction *stricto sensu.* In its intention, it is much more than a simple invitation to the text; to be sure, because of its incredibly dense style and conceptually ar-

---

13. See also Kant's explicit formulation in his letter to Kiesewetter, March 25, 1790: "I shortened the introduction that you copied some time ago."

14. Kant's letter to J. S. Beck, August 18, 1793: the "First Introduction" deals with a "*besondere und seltsame* Voraussetzung unserer Vernunft . . ."—(my emphasis).

15. Ibid.

16. Preface X (AA, V, 170, 16).

17. Preface IX–X (AA, V, 170,12–14).

18. Preface IX (AA, V, 169, 36).

duous pace, it can hardly be seen as an invitation at all. The introduction is rather the conclusion of both the third *Critique* and of the critical project as a whole. Kant was well aware of this, and similar considerations led him to replace the "First Introduction" with the published one.[19] Yet, the introduction does not provide a résumé of the book—neither of its content nor of the unfolding of its arguments; nor does it simply anticipate what will receive a full explanation in the course of the book. In §§I–VI, for example, Kant discusses crucial issues that will often be mentioned and recalled again in the development of the *Critique of Judgment* but will never again be taken up systematically. The introduction constitutes an integral part of the third *Critique*. Along with the preface, it puts forth the hypothesis on which the third *Critique* is constructed and then provides the "deduction" of the transcendental principle of judgment. Hence, it is only after the introduction that the Analytic of the Beautiful can begin. Viewed in this perspective, the introduction is not the quasi-independent treatise that the "First Introduction" might represent.

The introduction provides the *methodological key* that allows one to follow the whole development of the *Critique of Judgment*. The introduction is the methodological key to the peculiar and much discussed unity of the third *Critique*, and its true *raison d'être*. Kant's aim in this text is to clearly and synthetically outline the unitary topic of the *Critique of Judgment* once the manifold developments of its presentation have been carried through. Therefore, the introduction logically precedes all the analyses that follow. Both in the preface and in the introduction, Kant addresses the unitary topic of the *Critique of Judgment* in the form of the peculiar "problem"[20] that still faces the transcendental inquiry after the results of the first and second *Critique*. Accordingly, he indicates the lines along which a transcendental research has to solve its new problem. This consideration allows us a first general conclusion: the unitary topic of the third *Critique* is not, in the first place, a particular thesis or content to be presented or demonstrated nor the solution or ultimate answer given to a problem but rather the problem itself along with the research-itinerary to be carried through in the framework of transcendental philosophy. As we will have the opportunity to observe along our textual analysis, the stylistic quality of Kant's writing—especially in §§I–V of the introduction—mirrors the advancement of a search that progresses through hypotheses and analogies and programmatically chooses to comply with the imperative necessity that leads to explore certain paths instead of others. Hence the first interpretive task will be to precisely outline the terms of the *problem* that re-

---

19. In the "First Introduction" Kant is primarily concerned with the problem of a teleology of nature while he dedicates less attention to aesthetic judgment. This can be historically explained by Tonelli's suggestion that at the time Kant set out to write the "First Introduction" he had just finished the Analytic of the Beautiful and was reflecting precisely on the problem of teleology.

20. Preface IX (AA, V, 170,12).

quired Kant to develop the search-process set up in the form of a *Critique of Judgment*.

The introduction contains Kant's recapitulation and final reflection on transcendental philosophy. Kant's standpoint is placed therein in the perspective of the "*system*" of philosophy. The system, which the first *Critique* was still presenting as a merely regulative (although indispensable) idea for all scientific enterprise, now shows a much more approachable reality, being ultimately the perspective proper to the faculty of judgment. Within the framework of the system, Kant reconsiders the results of both the *Critique of Pure Reason* and the *Critique of Practical Reason* and, as a consequence, sheds an unexpected new light on the meaning of the theoretical as well as the practical dimensions of reason. In this connection, the crucial question that we will have to address regards the meaning of Kant's notion of system.

As already suggested, the third *Critique* is Kant's most clear, self-conscious, and thematic *practice* of transcendental philosophy. This practice, in the form of a most sophisticated philosophical research, opens up the idea of system to the infinite variety of human experience. The introduction presents the generative core of that infinitely diversified experience and looks for the unifying function that grounds human experience precisely in the multiplicity of its forms by only existing in and through the infinite variety of its forms. This unity is provided by Kant's new notion of "reflective judgment." What is at stake therein is the new meaning of 'transcendental,' once reflective judgment is recognized as the force responsible for the meaningfulness of what is empirical, particular, irreducible, and sheerly contingent in human experience. Only through that meaningfulness does experience as a coherent system become possible for the first time.[21] In relation to the first *Critique*, Kant's task is now to ground an enlarged notion of *experience* transcendentally (i.e., the experience of the empirical laws of nature as opposed to the universal laws of nature as well as the experience of individual events). Judgment becomes the faculty that first allows one to speak in a meaningful way of the system of experience, of the system of the faculties, and of the system of philosophy itself. Hence *Urteilskraft* cannot be just another faculty next to understanding and reason but will almost appear as a "meta-faculty" or the "critical faculty par excellence";[22] judgment is the faculty used and practiced by critical philosophy itself. Consequently, this new faculty will require a reflection on what has been previously thematized both under the functions of understanding and reason, and under the titles of theoretical and practical.

One of the problems of the introduction (and the preface) is to locate the new faculty of reflective judgment within the system—the system of philosophy, the

---

21. See the title of "First Introduction" (=EE) §IV: "Of Experience as a System for the Faculty of Judgment."

22. See E. Garroni and H. Hohenegger in the introduction to I. Kant, *Critica della facoltà di giudizio,* a cura di E. Garroni, H. Hohenegger, Torino, Einaudi, 1999, 31.

system of the faculties of the mind, and the system of human experience.[23] The system is ultimately constructed "*for* the faculty of judgment"[24] and by it. The notion of system has a meaning *for* reflective judgment and through it.[25] Kant's suggestion is that judgment occupy the place of a *Mittelglied*—a term that is at the same time intermediary and mediating. The nature of the faculty of judgment is to be both intermediary and mediating; at the same time, it is the object of the third *Critique* and its acting subject. Reflective judgment is both the solution to the problem and the problem itself, the tool that guides Kant's research along the many different paths of the third *Critique*, and the transcendental function that directly engages in that search.

The systematic perspective implies a preoccupation with completeness.[26] In order to complete its task, transcendental philosophy must address the question posed by the faculty of judgment as an independent faculty of the mind and must find its peculiar transcendental a priori principle. Yet to present Kant's systematic problem merely in terms of a demand for numerical completeness that would require judgment to be thematized next to theoretical reason and practical reason (or between them) would be to miss the very nature of Kant's problem at the time of the *Critique of Judgment.* Certainly in his letter to Reinhold of December 28–31, 1787, Kant is the first to suggest that it is precisely a systematic consideration that led him to discover a "new type of a priori principles." These principles disclose the new territory of teleology and parallel those proper to understanding and reason by referring to the feeling of pleasure and displeasure. Yet in this letter, nothing more is said about the nature of that new type of a priori principles. Moreover, teleology seems to gain so much priority as to appear as a third part of philosophy next to theoretical and practical philosophy. In 1790 Kant's position changes due, among other things, to the peculiar nature of judgment's own principle, namely to the way in which the notion of a formal purposiveness of nature relates to the feeling of pleasure and displeasure bringing together under a same

---

23. This progression is particularly relevant and explicit in the "First Introduction." See the titles of §§ I–IV: "I. Von der Philosophie als einem System" (Of Philosophy as a System); "II. Von dem System der obern Erkenntnisvermögen . . ." (Of the System of the Higher Cognitive Faculties); "III. Von dem System aller Vermögen des menschlichen Gemüts" (Of the System of all Faculties of the Human Mind); "IV. Von der Erfahrung als einem System für die Urteilskraft" (Of Experience as a System for the Faculty of Judgment); see also the title of §§ VI, XI.

24. See EE §IV: "Von der Erfahrung als einem System *für die Urteilskraft.*" Windelband observes that neither in the first nor in the published introduction is the notion of "purposiveness" related to aesthetic questions or to the question of living organisms. Purposiveness has rather to do with the "problem of the unity of nature as a system of experience" (W. Windelband, *Einleitung,* in AA, V, 512–527, 520 f.).

25. In relation to the first *Critique* and the idea of system therein presented, we can say that reflective judgment is able to provide a meaning for this notion that is qualitatively and methodologically different from the meaning provided for it by the understanding.

26. See preface VI (AA, V, 168, 23).

function of judgment the issues of taste and teleology. Hence, neither taste nor teleology alone can constitute the topic of a third Critique. Kant argues that a critique of the faculty of judgment needs to find a place in "a critique of pure reason" (in the enlarged sense attributed to it at the beginning of the preface) as a "special part" of it.[27] Yet in the "system of pure philosophy" the principles of the faculty of judgment do not constitute any "special part between theoretical and practical philosophy."[28]

To be sure, *Urteilskraft* has already been operating next to the understanding in the first *Critique* and next to reason in the second *Critique*. In both cases, however, its role was that of applying rules already given by other faculties.[29] It is only through the specific function of reflective judgment—and more precisely through a particular form of it, namely aesthetic judgment—that Kant discovers that *Urteilskraft* still needs to be thematized as an independent cognitive faculty of the mind (*Erkenntnisvermögen*) along with understanding and reason. This implies that the faculty of judgment has an a priori principle of its own. Because of the nature of *Urteilskraft*, however, the search for this principle is announced from the very outset as full of great difficulties and perplexities,[30] encountered particularly with relation to "aesthetic" judgments—namely in those evaluations where judgment confronts issues of the beautiful and the sublime both in nature and art. Accordingly, in a critique of this faculty, the inquiry into its a priori principle represents the "most important"—but also the most difficult—part of the research.[31] Kant observes how aesthetic evaluations do not contribute to any cognition of their object but bring the cognitive faculty in an "*immediate relation* . . . to the feeling of pleasure and displeasure."[32] In the preface, Kant is still making room for the main argument to be presented in the introduction. The relation between the faculty of judgment, its a priori principle, and the feeling of pleasure and displeasure is outlined in a merely negative—and even paradoxical—way. The principle of aesthetic judgment relates to the feeling of pleasure and displeasure *but not* to that same pleasure that is connected to the faculty of desire; in this activity, judgment belongs to the cognitive faculties *but not* in order to provide a cognition of things.[33] What is then the pleasure or displeasure that accompanies these judgments, and what do these judgments say about things in a cognitive and yet not really cognitive way?

The problem becomes even more complicated as Kant draws an apparent parallelism with the first *Critique* and sees a "*logical* evaluation of nature" to follow

---

27. Preface VI (AA, V, 168, 26); see also EE §I, AA, XX, 195, 5–10.
28. Preface VI (AA, V, 168, 27–28).
29. See, for example, KrV B 171/A, 132 ff.: "*Urteilskraft* is the power of *subsuming* under rules, i.e., of distinguishing whether something does or does not stand under a given rule."
30. See preface VII (AA, V, 169,1–4; 169, 15).
31. Preface VII–VIII (AA, V, 169, 15–20); see also E L (AA, V, 193, 25).
32. Preface VIII (AA, V, 169, 22–23), my emphasis.
33. See preface VIII (AA, V, 169, 20–26).

the "*aesthetic*" one.[34] Thereby two forms of reflective judgment are introduced. In a very important way, Kant is playing again with an ambiguity of the term *aesthetic* that has been well known to us since the 1781 and 1787 versions of the footnote to the Transcendental Aesthetic of the *Critique of Pure Reason*.[35] The third *Critique* is divided into an aesthetic of (reflective) judgment and a logic of (reflective) judgment. In the logical consideration of nature as opposed to the merely aesthetic one, in certain cases where experience manifests a lawfulness that the understanding cannot sufficiently explain by way of its notion of the "sensible" (*Sinnliches*), judgment is the faculty that brings in the "principle of a relation between natural things and the unknowable supersensible" in order to produce, once again, a special kind of cognition. This cognition, to be sure, relates more to practical reason than to theoretical reason, at least insofar as it opens up perspectives advantageous to practical reason. To acknowledge a discrepancy that divides understanding from experience represents Kant's crucial step toward the problem of the third *Critique*. There is a lawfulness (*Gesetzmäßigkeit*) that, essential to experience, cannot be explained in terms of the universal laws of the understanding: What kind of lawfulness is it? As opposed to aesthetic reflection, logical reflection on nature does not display any "*immediate relation* to the feeling of pleasure and displeasure."[36] Indeed, Kant's enigmatic way of presenting the problem of judgment already reveals this much in the preface: the problem consists in the relation between the faculty of judgment as cognitive faculty, its transcendental principle, and the feeling of pleasure and displeasure. What judgment evaluates—aesthetically or logically—are sensible things in nature and art. The problem is first (i) to establish what kind of relation—whether "immediate" or not —takes place to the feeling of pleasure and displeasure in these cases and then (ii) to ascertain what peculiar kind of cognition is gained respectively in these cases. The division of the *Critique of Judgment* will follow from these considerations. The outline of Kant's problematic given in the preface makes clear from the very outset that an *epistemological* question marks the essential step toward the discovery of the transcendental principle of the faculty of judgment—a principle that is not cognitive but aesthetic. It is only after this principle has been established that teleological judgment follows. For only aesthetic judgment is a "special faculty," while teleological judgment is "only reflective judgment in general."[37] Significantly, the grounding place for Kant's epistemological reflection in the third *Critique* is not teleological judgment but aesthetic judgment.

---

34. Preface VIII (AA, V, 169, 26): Rosenkranz's edition reads "teleological" instead of "logical"; see EE §XII, AA, XX, 249 and E §VII, "Von der *ästhetischen* Vorstellung der Zweckmäßigkeit der Natur" (On the *Aesthetic* Representation of the Purposiveness of Nature); §VIII, "Von der *logischen* Vorstellung der Zweckmäßigkeit der Natur" (On the *Logical* Representation of the Purposiveness of Nature).

35. KrV B 34f./A 20 f. fn.

36. Preface VIII–IX (AA, V, 169, 26–35).

37. E §VIII, LII (AA, V, 194, 23–25).

As has been already observed, the preface addresses the problem of the third *Critique* in terms of the search for a *Mittelglied*[38] between theoretical and practical reason, and between the two worlds that reason determines in its different uses. To be sure, the introduction makes clear that the crucial problem regards the *relation* between those terms (i.e., in the first place, the very possibility of a relation). Thereby the mediating principle is announced from the very outset as a relational principle that is not part of the system but is that which keeps the parts together in order for the unity of the system to be possible. The system is not only completed *with* the faculty of judgment (objectively) but is completed, first and foremost, *by* the faculty of judgment itself (subjectively).[39] Introduction §II sharpens the problem posed by that mediating function as it highlights the "immeasurable abyss"[40] that separates the realm of nature from that of freedom. To be in the middle, between terms separated by an abyss, is to be nowhere. To occupy this position requires the capacity to establish a *dynamic* relation of transition—the movement of an impossible *Übergang;* it requires the capacity to bridge heterogeneous worlds even without having any solid ground to sustain this bridge. The faculty of judgment will not make theoretical reason and practical reason any closer, nor will it cancel the abyss or fill the gap between the two worlds of reason's respective legislations. Kant never repeals the separation between theoretical and practical; he only sharpens it: "it is not possible to throw a bridge from one domain to the other"[41]—he repeats at the end of the introduction. Nonetheless, judgment will be able to displace the objective "abyss" in a subjective territory, thereby establishing a relation between the two terms in a third one.

The relation that links the faculty of judgment to understanding and reason and the peculiar nature of its principle already anticipate both the different role that Kant attributes to the *Critique of Judgment* in relation to the other *Critiques* (the third *Critique* will not be followed by a corresponding doctrinal part), and the different structure that the *Critique of Judgment* presents in its internal division. For the principle of the faculty of judgment does not legislate in the domain of a world. Moreover, only the principle of aesthetic judgment has a constitutive function and hence requires a "deduction" (its function, however, is constitutive not in relation to objects but in relation to the subject's feeling of pleasure and displeasure). Instead, the principle of teleological judgment is merely regulative and needs only an "exposition," not a "deduction."[42]

---

38. Preface V (AA, V, 168, 15; 168, 19).

39. See E. Garroni and Hohenegger, op. cit., XXXI.

40. E §II, XIX (AA, V, 175, 36).

41. E §IX, LIV (AA, V, 195, 15–16).

42. This important distinction in the way in which the principle of the faculty of judgment works respectively in the cases of aesthetic and teleological judgment was not drawn yet in the "First Introduction." Here Kant still sees the *Critique of Judgment* as divided into four books (critique of taste or judgment of the beautiful; judgment of the sublime; judgment of the internal purposiveness of things; judgment of the relative purposiveness of

Considering the issue of systematic completeness with regard to the application of the faculties' respective principles to different realms of objects, many interpreters have drawn the conclusion that the topic of the third *Critique* arises out of Kant's need to finally include in the framework of transcendental philosophy issues that could find a place neither in the world of scientific cognition of the first *Critique* nor in the moral world of the second *Critique*. Residual topics such as taste, the beautiful and sublime, and the teleology of organisms must now become parts of a third 'critique.' Once again, to address the problem of the content of the *Critique of Judgment* in this way is to miss the very nature of Kant's problem.

Kant's reflection in the introductory writings revolves around one crucial question: Is there a necessary relation that links transcendentally the following three terms: the *faculty of judgment* to the *principle of purposiveness* and to the *feeling of pleasure and displeasure*? Why is this connection transcendentally necessary? And what has this connection to do with the beautiful in nature and art, the sublime, and the teleology of organic life? The development of the *Critique of Judgment* in its two parts—the Critique of Aesthetic Judgment and the Critique of Teleological Judgment—is nothing but Kant's argument for the necessity of this connection. This is the unitary "problem"—the "enigma" (*das Rätselhafte*)[43]—of the third *Critique*. "Whether the *faculty of judgment* which in the order of our cognitive faculties constitutes a mediating link [*Mittelglied*] between understanding and reason also has a priori principles of its own; whether these principles are constitutive or merely regulative (in which case they would not prove a domain of its own); and whether the faculty of judgment gives the rule a priori to the feeling of pleasure and displeasure as the mediating link between the cognitive faculty and the faculty of desire . . . : this is what occupies the present critique of judgment."[44] The task is to draw the limits of the sphere of experience that belongs to reflective judgment on the one hand and to provide the transcendental foundation or justification for this sphere on the other. The commitment to showing that the "content" of this new realm of experience is the beautiful, the sublime, and life is a necessary part of Kant's problem, not the final and more or less forceful systematization of residual topics of his reflection.

3. The Structure of the Introduction

The introduction ends with a table containing an "overview of all the higher faculties in their systematic unity." The table is preceded by an important footnote in which Kant describes a general methodological procedure proper to his critical

---

things), each having an Analytic and a Dialectic, each Analytic in turn being divided into an "Exposition" and a "Deduction of the concept of a purposiveness of nature" (EE §XII, AA, XX, 251).

43. See Preface IX (AA, V, 169, 36).

44. Preface V–VI (AA, V, 168, 14–22).

philosophy. This footnote, along with the table of the faculties, will be assumed as a guide in our commentary on the text.[45]

> It has been considered suspicious that my partitions [*Einteilungen*] in pure philosophy come out almost always as tripartite. But this lies in the nature of the matter itself. If a partition is to be made a priori, then it will be either *analytic* according to the principle of contradiction; and in this case it is always bipartite (quodlibet ens est aut A aut non A). Or else it will be *synthetic*, and, if in this case it is to be made from a priori *concepts* (and not, as in mathematics, from the intuition that corresponds a priori to the concept), then the partition must be necessarily a trichotomy on the ground of that which is required for the synthetic unity in general, namely: 1. condition, 2. a conditioned, 3. the concept that arises from the unification [*Vereinigung*] of the conditioned with its condition.[46]

As Kant indicates, the necessity of the "suspicious" "trichotomy" lies in the *Sache selbst* (i.e., in the subject matter itself). A priori analytic divisions or partitions according to the principle of contradiction occur when abstraction is made from all content of cognition, and hence only the *logical form* is taken into account. In this case, the division contemplates only two possibilities: "an entity is either A or not A"; every concept is determined either by a predicate or by its contradictory opposite. Instead, in transcendental philosophy (and, I would argue, even more so in the third *Critique*), the content of cognition is taken into account; for this content must become the given object of experience. This is why in transcendental philosophy a priori divisions take place synthetically. The principle of contradiction is here insufficient to draw the partition. What is divided is a unity—an analytic unity in the case of purely logical partitions, a synthetic unity in the case of transcendental partitions. Analytic unity is the unity of what is common to different terms. Synthetic unity is the unity of what is different in one. As Kant suggests, to synthetic unity in general three elements are required: (1) the condition, (2) the conditioned, and (3) the concept that constitutes the unification of the previous two terms. In transcendental philosophy, one must provide the *condition* that allows a given *conditioned* to be possible and must then examine their *union*. Hence, in transcendental philosophy divisions from a priori concepts are tripartite. The *Critique of Pure Reason* has shown how understanding and speculative reason respectively proceed in their quest for synthetic unity. The *Critique of Judgment* sets out to show how the faculty of judgment constructs its

---

45. I follow here the indications found in Garroni/Hohenegger, introduzione, op. cit. XXVII ff., and the appendix to E. Garroni, *Senso e paradosso. L'estetica filosofia non speciale,* Bari, Laterza, 1986, 283–296. P. Guyer, on the contrary, never takes Kant's trichotomies too seriously and sees them rather as Kant's obsession with architectonic (*Kant and the Claims of Taste,* Cambridge, Cambridge University Press, 1992).

46. E §IX, LVIII (AA, V, 197, 18–27); see also the important Reflexion 3030 (AA XVI, 622–623).

own immanent partition. The synthetic unity that the last *Critique* attempts to establish is the "system of experience."

It should be observed that the trichotomic method that Kant presents in the quoted footnote as typical of "pure philosophy" mirrors Kant's general way of reasoning from a given conditioned to its condition of possibility. The unifying term expresses the synthetic moment of a reflection that brings the two previous terms back to their relation. Insofar as this is the rhythm of Kant's trichotomies, all temptation to conflate this method with anything like (post-Kantian or Hegelian) dialectic should be avoided. In particular, the meaning of transcendental *Vereinigung* must be explored with extreme caution. Moreover, the trichotomic method of transcendental philosophy should not be viewed as the dogmatic and extrinsic schema according to which an arbitrarily given content must be arranged. Instead, it is the way in which the special problem of the third *Critique* is both generated and solved. In addition, it is important to notice that the triadic rhythm is proper to the faculty of judgment (*Urteilskraft*) as such. Formal logic's definition of judgment (*Urteil*) already makes this point clear. Judgment is the act through which we represent two terms—namely first a thing and then something that belongs or does not belong to it. And then we either connect those two terms with each other or separate them from each other, so that we have three concepts.

The introduction is clearly structured according to a trichotomic synthetic partition. It is divided into nine sections that form three groups, each of which in turn consists again of three terms. The condition of the main trichotomy is presented in §§I–III; the conditioned made possible by that condition is introduced in §§IV–VI; and the concept of the unity of condition and conditioned is finally achieved in §§VII–IX.[47] Similarly, each term of the major trichotomy is constituted by a condition (§§I, IV, VII), a conditioned (§§II, V, VIII), and their unification (§§III, VI, IX). §III, §VI, and §IX, as third terms of each minor trichotomy, respectively mention in their title a moment or a function of unification (*Verbindungsmittel, Verbindung, Verknüpfung*). We must stress by way of introduction the importance of Kant's repetition of the trichotomy in all of its three terms.

The titles of the sections of the introduction read as follows:

(i):

I. On the Partition of Philosophy
II. On the Domain of Philosophy in General
III. On the Critique of Judgment as a *Means to Connect* [*Verbindungsmittel*] the Two Parts of Philosophy into a Whole

(ii):

IV. On the Faculty of Judgment as a Faculty That Legislates A Priori
V. The Principle of Formal Purposiveness of Nature Is a Transcendental Principle of the Faculty of Judgment

47. The condition will be the topic of chapter 6; the conditioned will be the topic of chapter 7; and their unification will be the topic of chapter 8.

VI. On the *Conjunction* [*Verbindung*] of the Feeling of Pleasure with the Concept of the Purposiveness of Nature

(iii):
VII. On the Aesthetic Representation of the Purposiveness of Nature
VIII. On the Logical Representation of the Purposiveness of Nature
IX. On the *Connection* [*Verknüpfung*] between the Legislations of the Understanding and Reason Through the Faculty of Judgment

(i) The condition of the main trichotomy (§§I–III) regards the idea of philosophy. Kant discusses therein the condition under which alone the new conditioned presented in (ii) §§IV–VI can be thought. The new conditioned is the problem of empirical knowledge, namely of the lawfulness of an experience for which the understanding cannot account. It concerns the realm of nature as a manifold of empirical laws (i.e., the possibility for nature to be experienced as a coherent system of particular events and empirical laws). (iii) The union of the major condition and conditioned leads to reflective judgment's principle of the formal purposiveness of nature in its aesthetic and teleological functions (§§VII, VIII) and thereby to the possibility of connecting the two legislations of understanding and reason (§IX). To sum up the argument of the introduction, we can say that viewed in the perspective of the transcendental system of the faculties established by the third *Critique* (iii), the system of philosophy completed by the faculty of judgment (i) allows Kant to think of the system of experience as possible (ii).

(i) The first term of the first trichotomy expresses a condition. In §I, Kant presents the results of both the *Critique of Pure Reason* (the concepts of nature) and the *Critique of Practical Reason* (the concept of freedom)—as the ground for the division of philosophy into two parts only, namely theoretical and practical. §II introduces the realm of objects to which the first condition refers. This is the conditioned of the world of nature in general and of the world of freedom respectively. In relating those concepts (of nature and freedom) to these objects and asking about the relations between the legislations of understanding and reason, Kant opens up to the new problematic of the third *Critique* (i.e., to the need for the third term of the first trichotomy): the *Critique of Judgment* as *Verbindungsmittel* of the two parts of philosophy into a whole. Understanding and reason established their different legislations "on one and the same territory of experience."[48] Yet their separation is measured by an immeasurable "abyss." In order to solve the problem thereby construed by the two *Critiques*, §III introduces the faculty of judgment as a "mediating link" between understanding and reason. In addressing the first two titles of the table found at the end of the introduction, Kant introduces judgment as a third cognitive faculty (*Erkenntnisvermögen*, reads the final table) and the feeling of pleasure and displeasure as a third faculty of the *Gemüt*

48. E§II, XVIII (AA, V, 175,6).

(*Gesammte Vermögen des Gemüts*). This move complicates the dichotomic structure of the first two sections. However, Kant is cautious in the introduction of this third term; the unification accomplished at this point is weak. His argument is dictated only by a possible analogy. The analogy with understanding and reason allows him to infer that judgment may have its own a priori principle as well as, at least, a territory in which to be valid. Kant proceeds in a hypothetical and analogical manner up until §V, where the transcendental foundation of the a priori principle of judgment follows.

(ii) The idea of transcendental philosophy is the sole condition under which the new conditioned represented by the realm of "empirical knowledge in general" (§V) can be explored. Within this new conditioned, Kant presents in turn a condition, a conditioned, and their unification. In §IV, reflective judgment emerges as the condition of the possibility of thinking nature, in the manifold of its empirical laws, as a coherent system; §V entails the deduction of the principle of formal purposiveness as the transcendental principle of reflective judgment. For nature as a manifold of empirical laws to become the object of a coherent experience, reflective judgment "must" consider it according to the subjective principle of purposiveness. Kant's hypothetical and analogical argument yields to the necessity implied by the deduction of judgment's own principle. §V provides a conditioned. Therein Kant deals with the *application* of the principle to experience, namely to that which is made possible by that principle and by that principle alone as its own "territory." Formal purposiveness of nature, on the other hand, makes sense only under the condition of reflective judgment (i.e., neither understanding nor reason can make use of it in their legislations). §VI shows how the principle of formal purposiveness relates a priori to the feeling of pleasure and displeasure. Formal purposiveness, however, is not yet related to aesthetic evaluation of beautiful objects or to teleological evaluation of particular beings.

(iii) The last three conclusive sections give the critical specification of the principle of judgment with regard to the particular realm of objects (i.e., the particular conditioned) to which it is applied. It is at this point that Kant addresses the question of the specific domain proper to that principle (see the first trichotomy, §II). This discloses the sense in which the last trichotomy represents the unification of the preceding two. Thus the relation between reflective judgment, formal purposiveness, and the topics of the beautiful, sublime, and living organisms directly takes up the issue of *Erfahrungserkenntnis überhaupt* (empirical knowledge in general). §VII explores the a priori principle of aesthetic judgment as a condition that does not, however, objectively constitute any realm of objects. As was the case with the second term of both previous trichotomies (§II and §V), in expressing a conditioned, §VIII deals with the *application* of the principle of purposiveness to a particular realm of objects, namely organisms. Read in relation to the methodological distinction of condition and conditioned, Kant's presentation of an "aesthetic representation of the purposiveness of nature" (§VII) and a "logical representation of the purposiveness of nature" (§VIII) does not simply entail a distinction between two principles or two forms of the principle of reflective judgment. The distinction between aesthetic and teleological applies rather to the specific conditioned to which the same principle is applied. Both terms of the last minor trichotomy are conjoined in §IX. It is only at the very end of the introduction, once the transcendental principle has been deduced and grounded in its employment on a twofold realm, that the faculty of judgment can be presented as a moment of *Verknüpfung* between theoretical and practical. The commentary to the text will further discuss the nature of that *Verknüpfung* as well as the sense in which it can be said to represent a kind of unification. Therefore Kant, in the same conclusive section, both claims and denies the possibility of a unification. Against all dialectical temptation, the question to be raised here regards the relation between the bond—or *Verknüpfung*—claimed by the title of the section, and the unification—or *Vereinigung*—that Kant presents as the conclusive moment of "synthetic unity in general."

AA171

|XI Einleitung

I. Von der Einteilung der Philosophie

Wenn man die Philosophie, sofern sie Prinzipien der Vernunfterkenntnis der Dinge (nicht bloß, wie die Logik, Prinzipien der Form des Denkens überhaupt, ohne Unterschied der Objekte) durch Begriffe enthält, wie gewöhnlich in die *theoretische* und *praktische* einteilt: so verfährt man ganz recht. Aber alsdann müssen auch die Begriffe, welche den Prinzipien dieser Vernunfterkenntnis ihr Objekt anweisen, spezifisch verschieden sein, weil sie sonst zu keiner Einteilung berechtigen würden, welche jederzeit eine Entgegensetzung der Prinzipien, der zu den verschiedenen Teilen einer Wissenschaft gehörigen Vernunfterkenntnis, voraussetzt.

Es sind aber nur zweierlei Begriffe, welche eben so viel verschiedene Prinzipien der Möglichkeit ihrer Gegenstände zulassen: nämlich die *Naturbegriffe* und der *Freiheitsbegriff*. Da nun die ersteren ein *theo* | XII *retisches* Erkenntnis nach Prinzipien a priori möglich machen, der zweite aber in Ansehung derselben nur ein negatives Prinzip (der bloßen Entgegensetzung) schon in seinem Begriffe bei sich führt, dagegen für die Willensbestimmung erweiternde Grundsätze, welche darum praktisch heißen, errichtet: so wird die Philosophie in zwei, den Prinzipien nach ganz verschiedene, Teile, in die theoretische als *Naturphilosophie*, und die praktische als *Moralphilosophie* (denn so wird die praktische Gesetzgebung der Vernunft nach dem Freiheitsbegriffe genannt) mit Recht eingeteilt. Es hat aber bisher ein großer Mißbrauch mit diesen Ausdrücken zur Einteilung der verschiedenen Prinzipien, und mit ihnen auch der Philosophie, geherrscht: indem man das Praktische nach Naturbegriffen mit dem Praktischen nach dem Freiheitsbegriffe für einerlei
AA172 nahm, und so, || unter denselben Benennungen einer theoretischen und praktischen Philosophie, eine Einteilung machte, durch welche (da beide Teile einerlei Prinzipien haben konnten) in der Tat nichts eingeteilt war.

Der Wille, als Begehrungsvermögen, ist nämlich eine von den mancherlei Natururasachen in der Welt, nämlich diejenige, welche nach Begriffen wirkt; und alles, was als durch einen Willen möglich (oder notwendig) vor-

Chapter 6

Introduction §§I–III: The Idea of Philosophy and the *Critique of Judgment*

Text

XI Introduction

I. On the Partition of Philosophy

To draw the partition of philosophy, insofar as it contains principles [*Prinzipien*] of the rational cognition of things through concepts (not simply, as logic does, principles of the form of thinking in general, without distinction of objects), as it is customary, into *theoretical* and *practical* philosophy, is to proceed in an entirely correct way. But then the concepts that assign to the principles of this rational knowledge their respective objects must be specifically different as well. Otherwise, they would not justify a partition, as a partition always presupposes mutual opposition of the principles of rational cognition belonging to the different parts of a science.

However, there are only two types of concepts that allow for two different principles concerning the possibility of their objects, i.e., the *concepts of nature* and the *concept of freedom*. Now, if concepts of nature make possible XII theoretical knowledge according to a priori principles, freedom contains already in its very concept only a negative principle (of mere opposition) in relation to that knowledge, and establishes instead extensive principles [*erweiternde Grundsätze*] for the determination of the will, which are therefore called practical. Hence philosophy is correctly divided into two parts that are thoroughly different in their principles, i.e., into theoretical philosophy as *philosophy of nature*, and practical philosophy as *moral philosophy* (*moral* is called the practical legislation of reason according to the concept of freedom). Yet, up until now, these terms have been badly misused in the partition of the different principles, and consequently also in the partition of philosophy. The practical [*das Praktische*] according to concepts of nature has been taken as one with the practical according to the concept of freedom, with the result that under the same denomination of theoretical and practical philosophy a division has been made through which, in fact, nothing has been divided (since the two parts might have the same principles).

The will, as faculty of desire, is precisely one of the many natural causes in the world, namely the one that acts according to concepts; and whatever is gestellt wird, heißt praktisch-möglich (oder notwendig): zum Unterschiede von der physischen Möglichkeit oder Notwendigkeit einer Wirkung, wozu die | XIII Ursache nicht durch Begriffe (sondern, wie bei der leblosen Materie, durch Mechanism, und bei Tieren, durch Instinkt) zur Kausalität bestimmt wird. —Hier wird nun in Ansehung des Praktischen unbestimmt gelassen: ob der Begriff, der der Kausalität des Willens die Regel gibt, ein Naturbegriff, oder ein Freiheitsbegriff sei.

Der letztere Unterschied aber ist wesentlich. Denn, ist der die Kausalität bestimmende Begriff ein Naturbegriff, so sind die Prinzipien *technisch-praktisch*; ist er aber ein Freiheitsbegriff, so sind diese *moralisch-praktisch*: und weil es in der Einteilung einer Vernunftwissenschaft gänzlich auf diejenige Verschiedenheit der Gegenstände ankommt, deren Erkenntnis verschiedener Prinzipien bedarf, so werden die ersteren zur theoretischen Philosophie (als Naturlehre) gehören, die andern aber ganz allein den zweiten Teil, nämlich (als Sittenlehre) die praktische Philosophie, ausmachen.

Alle technisch-praktische Regeln (d. i. die der Kunst und Geschicklichkeit überhaupt, oder auch der Klugheit, als einer Geschicklichkeit auf Menschen und ihren Willen Einfluß zu haben), so fern ihre Prinzipien auf Begriffen beruhen, müssen nur als Korollarien zur theoretischen Philosophie gezählt werden. Denn sie betreffen nur die Möglichkeit der Dinge nach Naturbegriffen, wozu nicht allein die Mittel, die in der Natur dazu anzutreffen sind, sondern selbst der Wille (als Begehrungs-, mithin als Naturvermögen) gehört, sofern er durch Trieb | XIV federn der Natur jenen Regeln gemäß bestimmt werden kann. Doch heißen dergleichen praktische Regeln nicht Gesetze (etwa so wie physische), sondern nur Vorschriften: und zwar darum, weil der Wille nicht bloß unter dem Naturbegriffe, sondern auch unter dem Freiheitsbegriffe steht, in Beziehung auf welchen die Prinzipien desselben Gesetze heißen, und, mit ihren Folgerungen, den zweiten Teil der Philosophie, nämlich den praktischen, allein ausmachen.

AA173 So wenig also die Auflösung der Probleme der reinen Geometrie zu || einem besonderen Teile derselben gehört, oder die Feldmeßkunst den Namen einer praktischen Geometrie, zum Unterschiede von der reinen, als ein zweiter Teil der Geometrie überhaupt verdient: so und noch weniger, darf die mechanische oder chemische Kunst der Experimente oder der Beobachtungen für einen praktischen Teil der Naturlehre, endlich die Haus- Land- Staatswirtschaft, die Kunst des Umganges, die Vorschrift der Diätetik, selbst nicht die allgemeine Glückseligkeitslehre, sogar nicht einmal die Bezähmung der Neigungen und Bändigung der Affekten zum Behuf der letzteren, zur praktischen Philosophie gezählt werden, oder die letzteren wohl gar den zweiten Teil der Philosophie überhaupt ausmachen weil sie insgesamt nur Regeln der Geschicklichkeit, die mithin nur technisch-praktisch sind, enthalten, um eine Wirkung hervorzubringen, die nach Naturbegriffen der Ursachen und Wirkungen mög | XV lich ist, welche, da sie zur theoretischen Philosophie gehören, jenen Vorschriften als bloßen Korollarien aus derselben (der Naturwissenschaft) unterworfen sind, und also keine Stelle in einer represented as possible (or necessary) through a will is called practically-possible (or necessary). This distinguishes it from the physical possibility or necessity of an effect, whose XIII cause is not determined to causality through concepts (but rather, through mechanism, as in the case of lifeless matter, and through instinct, as in the case of animals).—Therefore here, in relation to the practical, what is left undetermined is whether the concept that gives the rule to the causality of the will is a concept of nature or a concept of freedom.

Yet the latter distinction is essential. For if the concept that determines the causality is a concept of nature, then the principles are *technical-practical*, but if it is a concept of freedom, the principles are *moral-practical*. And since in the partition of a rational science everything depends upon that difference of objects whose knowledge requires different principles, the technical-practical principles will belong to theoretical philosophy (as doctrine of nature), while the other principles, and they alone, will constitute the second part of philosophy, namely practical philosophy (as doctrine of morals [*Sittenlehre*]).

All technical-practical rules (i.e., the rules of art and of skill in general, or also of prudence as a skill in influencing people and their will), insofar as their principles rest on concepts, must be counted only among the corollaries of theoretical philosophy. For they concern only the possibility of things according to concepts of nature; and to this belong not only the means that can be found in nature to that aim [*dazu*], but even the will (as faculty of desire and hence as natural faculty) insofar as it can be determined through XIV natural drives in accordance to those rules. However, such practical rules are not called laws (as are, e.g., physical laws), but only precepts. This is certainly due to the fact that the will stays not only under the concept of nature but also under the concept of freedom, and in relation to freedom its principles are called laws. These laws—and these laws only—along with what follows from them, constitute the second part of philosophy, namely practical philosophy.

Thus, as the solution of the problems of pure geometry does not belong to a special part of geometry, nor does the art of land surveying deserve the name of practical geometry as a second part of geometry in general, distinguished from pure geometry, so just as little, and even less, the mechanical or chemical art of experimentation or observation deserves to be considered as a practical part of natural science. Finally, in the same way, all disciplines like domestic, agricultural, or political economy, the art of social relations, the precepts of dietetics, even the general doctrine of how to reach happiness, indeed even the art of refraining and taming the passions for the sake of happiness—all these disciplines should not be included in practical philosophy, nor should the last mentioned disciplines be considered as constituting the second part of philosophy in general. For all these arts contain only rules of skill, which are consequently merely technical-practical, for producing an effect XV that is possible according to the concepts of nature concerning causes and effects. And since these concepts belong to theoretical philosophy, they are subject to those precepts as mere corollaries derived from it (from the science of nature), and therefore cannot claim any place in a spebesonderen Philosophie, die praktische genannt, verlangen können. Dagegen machen die moralisch-praktischen Vorschriften, die sich gänzlich auf dem Freiheitsbegriffe, mit völliger Ausschließung der Bestimmungsgründe des Willens aus der Natur, gründen, eine ganz besondere Art von Vorschriften aus: welche auch, gleich den Regeln, welchen die Natur gehorcht, schlechthin Gesetze heißen, aber nicht, wie diese, auf sinnlichen Bedingungen, sondern auf einem übersinnlichen Prinzip beruhen, und, neben dem theoretischen Teile der Philosophie, für sich ganz allein, einen anderen Teil, unter dem Namen der praktischen Philosophie, fordern.

Man siehet hieraus, daß ein Inbegriff praktischer Vorschriften, welche die Philosophie gibt, nicht einen besonderen, dem theoretischen zur Seite gesetzten, Teil derselben darum ausmache, weil sie praktisch sind; denn das könnten sie sein, wenn ihre Prinzipien gleich gänzlich aus der theoretischen Erkenntnis der Natur hergenommen wären (als technisch-praktische Regeln); sondern, weil und wenn ihr Prinzip gar nicht vom Naturbegriffe, der jederzeit sinnlich bedingt ist, entlehnt ist, mithin auf dem übersinnlichen, welches der Freiheitsbegriff allein durch formale Gesetze kennbar macht, be | XVI ruht, und sie also moralisch-praktisch, d. i. nicht bloß Vorschriften und Regeln in dieser oder jener Absicht, sondern, ohne vorgehendes Bezugnehmung auf
AA174 Zwecke und Absichten, Gesetze sind. ||

II. Vom Gebiete der Philosophie überhaupt

So weit Begriffe a priori ihre Anwendung haben, so weit reicht der Gebrauch unseres Erkenntnisvermögens nach Prinzipien, und mit ihm die Philosophie.

Der Inbegriff aller Gegenstände aber, worauf jene Begriffe bezogen werden, und, wo möglich, ein Erkenntnis derselben zustande zu bringen, kann, nach der verschiedenen Zulänglichkeit oder Unzulänglichkeit unserer Vermögen zu dieser Absicht, eingeteilt werden.

Begriffe, sofern sie auf Gegenstände bezogen werden, unangesehen, ob ein Erkenntnis derselben möglich sei oder nicht, haben ihr Feld, welches bloß nach dem Verhältnisse, das ihr Objekt zu unserem Erkenntnisvermögen überhaupt hat, bestimmt wird.—Der Teil dieses Feldes, worin für uns Erkenntnis möglich ist, ist ein Boden (*territorium*) für diese Begriffe und das dazu erforderliche Erkenntnisvermögen. Der Teil des Bodens, worauf diese gesetzgebend sind, ist das Gebiet (*ditio*) dieser Begriffe und der ihnen zustehenden Erkenntnisvermögen. Erfahrungsbegriffe haben also | XVII zwar ihren Boden in der Natur, als dem Inbegriffe aller Gegenstände der Sinne, aber kein Gebiet (sondern nur ihren Aufenthalt, *domicilium*); weil sie zwar gesetzlich erzeugt werden, aber nicht gesetzgebend sind, sondern die auf sie gegründeten Regeln empirisch, mithin zufällig, sind.

Unser gesamtes Erkenntnisvermögen hat zwei Gebiete, das der Naturbegriffe, und das des Freiheitsbegriffs; denn durch beide ist es a priori gesetzgebend. Die Philosophie teilt sich nun auch, diesem gemäß, in die theoretische und die praktische. Aber der Boden, auf welchem ihr Gebiet errichtet, cial philosophy called practical. Moral-practical precepts, on the contrary, which are grounded entirely on the concept of freedom, and completely exclude all principles of determination of the will derived from nature, constitute a very special kind of precepts. These are called simply laws, just as are the rules that nature obeys. Yet they do not rest on sensible conditions as natural laws do. Rather, practical laws rest on a supersensible principle and claim for themselves alone another part of philosophy next to theoretical philosophy, a part that is called practical philosophy.

It is evident from the above that a complex [*Inbegriff*] of practical precepts provided by philosophy does not constitute a special part of philosophy next to the theoretical part merely because those rules are practical. For they could be practical even if their principles were taken entirely from theoretical knowledge of nature (as technical-practical rules). Instead, they are practical only when and if their principle is by no means borrowed from the concept of nature, which is always dependent upon a sensible condition, but
XVI rest on the supersensible that only the concept of freedom allows us to know [*kennbar*] through formal laws. These precepts are therefore moral-practical, i.e., they are not simply precepts and rules in relation to this or that intention, but are rather laws without presupposing any reference to ends and intentions.

II. On the Domain of Philosophy in General

The use of our cognitive faculty according to principles, and with it philosophy, extends as far as concepts a priori have their application.

But the complex of all the objects to which we refer those concepts in order to produce cognition of them—where this is possible—can be divided according to the way in which our faculties are sufficient or insufficient to this aim.

Insofar as we refer concepts to objects, without considering whether or not knowledge of these objects is possible, they have their field. This field is determined merely by the relation that the object of these concepts has with our cognitive faculty in general.—The part of this field in which cognition is possible for us is a territory (*territorium*) for these concepts and for the cognitive faculty required for such cognition. The part of the territory over which these concepts legislate is the domain (*ditio*) of these concepts and the respective cognitive faculties. Therefore, concepts of experience do have XVII
their territory in nature, viewed as complex of all objects of the senses, and yet they do not have any domain in it (rather, only their residence, *domicilium*). For although they are produced according to law, they are not themselves legislative; rather, the rules that are based upon them are empirical and hence contingent.

Our entire cognitive faculty has two domains, that of the concepts of nature and that of the concept of freedom; for this faculty legislates a priori through both types of concepts. Philosophy too is divided according to our cognitive faculty into theoretical and practical. However, the territory on und ihre Gesetzgebung *ausgeübt* wird, ist immer doch nur der Inbegriff der Gegenstände aller möglichen Erfahrung, sofern sie für nichts mehr als bloße Erscheinungen genommen werden; denn ohnedas würde keine Gesetzgebung des Verstandes in Ansehung derselben gedacht werden können.

Die Gesetzgebung durch Naturbegriffe geschieht durch den Verstand, und ist theoretisch. Die Gesetzgebung durch den Freiheitsbegriff geschieht von der Vernunft, und ist bloß praktisch. Nur allein im Praktischen kann die Vernunft gesetzgebend sein; in Ansehung des theoretischen Erkenntnisses
AA175 (der Natur) kann sie nur (als gesetzkundig, vermittelst des Verstan || des) aus gegebenen Gesetzen durch Schlüsse Folgerungen ziehen, die doch immer nur bei der Natur stehen bleiben. Umgekehrt aber, wo Regeln praktisch sind, ist die Vernunft | XVIII nicht darum sofort *gesetzgebend*, weil sie auch technisch-praktisch sein können.

Verstand und Vernunft haben also zwei verschiedene Gesetzgebungen auf einem und demselben Boden der Erfahrung, ohne daß eine der anderen Eintrag tun darf. Denn so wenig der Naturbegriff auf die Gesetzgebung durch den Freiheitsbegriff Einfluß hat, ebensowenig stört dieser die Gesetzgebung der Natur.—Die Möglichkeit, das Zusammenbestehen beider Gesetzgebungen und der dazu gehörigen Vermögen in demselben Subjekt sich wenigstens ohne Widerspruch zu denken, bewies die Kritik der reinen Vernunft, indem sie die Einwürfe dawider durch Aufdeckung des dialektischen Scheins in denselben vernichtete.

Aber, daß diese zwei verschiedenen Gebiete, die sich zwar nicht in ihrer Gesetzgebung, aber doch in ihren Wirkungen in der Sinnenwelt unaufhörlich einschränken, nicht *eines* ausmachen, kommt daher: daß der Naturbegriff zwar seine Gegenstände in der Anschauung, aber nicht als Dinge an sich selbst, sondern als bloße Erscheinungen, der Freiheitsbegriff dagegen in seinem Objekte zwar ein Ding an sich selbst, aber nicht in der Anschauung vorstellig machen, mithin keiner von beiden ein theoretisches Erkenntnis von seinem Objekte (und selbst dem denkenden Subjekte) als Dinge an sich verschaffen kann, welches das Übersinnliche sein würde, wovon man die Idee zwar der Möglichkeit aller jener | XIX Gegenstände der Erfahrung unterlegen muß, sie selbst aber niemals zu einem Erkenntnisse erheben und erweitern kann.

Es gibt also ein unbegrenztes, aber auch unzugängliches Feld für unser gesamtes Erkenntnisvermögen, nämlich das Feld des Übersinnlichen, worin wir keinen Boden für uns finden, also auf demselben weder für die Verstandes- noch Vernunftbegriffe ein Gebiet zum theoretischen Erkenntnis haben können; ein Feld, welches wir zwar zum Behuf des theoretischen sowohl als praktischen Gebrauchs der Vernunft mit Ideen besetzen müssen, denen wir aber in Beziehung auf die Gesetze aus dem Freiheitsbegriffe, keine andere als praktische Realität verschaffen können, wodurch demnach unser theoretisches Erkenntnis nicht im mindesten zu dem Übersinnlichen erweitert wird.

Ob nun zwar eine unübersehbare Kluft zwischen dem Gebiete des Natur-
AA176 begriffs, als dem Sinnlichen, und dem Gebiete des Freiheits || begriffs, als

which philosophy establishes its domain and *exercises* its legislation is still always only the complex of the objects of all possible experience insofar as they are taken for nothing more than sheer appearances. For otherwise no legislation of the understanding in relation to them could ever be conceivable.

Legislation through concepts of nature takes place through the understanding and is theoretical. Legislation through the concept of freedom takes place through reason and is merely practical. Reason can be legislative only and exclusively in the practical sphere; with regard to theoretical knowledge (of nature), reason can only draw conclusions through syllogisms out of given laws (of which it is informed by the understanding). These conclusions, however, remain always within nature. On the contrary, however, if rules are practical, XVIII that does not yet make reason *legislative*, since they might be also technical-practical.

Hence understanding and reason have two different legislations on one and the same territory of experience. Yet these legislations should not interfere with each other. For as the concept of nature has no influence on the legislation through the concept of freedom, so the concept of freedom does not disturb the legislation of nature.—The *Critique of Pure Reason* proved that it is possible at least to think, without contradiction, that these two legislations together with the faculties belonging to them can coexist in the same subject. For the *Critique* destroyed the objections against this possibility by revealing in them the dialectical illusion.

But the fact that these two different domains—that do not limit each other in their legislation and yet do limit each other constantly in their effects in the sensible world—do not constitute *one* domain—this fact is due to the following reason: the concept of nature can indeed make its objects [*Gegenstände*] representable in intuition but only as appearances, not as things in themselves; the concept of freedom, on the contrary, can indeed make representable in its object [*Objekte*] a thing in itself but not in intuition. Hence, neither concept can provide theoretical cognition of its object (not even of the thinking subject) as thing in itself, which would be the supersensible. Indeed, we must assume the idea of the supersensible as the ground of the possibility of all those XIX objects [*Gegenstände*] of experience, although we can never raise the idea itself to cognition nor extend it to cognition.

Hence, there is a field that is unlimited but also inaccessible to our entire cognitive faculty, namely the field of the supersensible. Therein, we cannot find for ourselves any territory on which to establish a domain of theoretical cognition, whether for concepts of the understanding or for concepts of reason. We must indeed occupy this field with ideas that can help us in both the theoretical and the practical use of reason, and yet, in relation to the laws that derive from the concept of freedom, we cannot produce any other reality for those ideas but a practical one. Consequently, this practical reality does not in the least extend our theoretical cognition to the supersensible.

Now, although an immense abyss indeed stays fixed between the domain of the concept of nature as the sensible and the domain of the concept dem Übersinnlichen, befestigt ist, so daß von dem ersteren zum anderen (also vermittelst des theoretischen Gebrauchs der Vernunft) kein Übergang möglich ist, gleich als ob es so viel verschiedene Welten wären, deren erste auf die zweite keinen Einfluß haben kann: so *soll* doch diese auf jene einen Einfluß haben, nämlich der Freiheitsbegriff soll den durch seine Gesetze aufgegebenen Zweck in der Sinnenwelt wirklich machen; und die Natur muß folg | XX lich auch so gedacht werden können, daß die Gesetzmäßigkeit ihrer Form wenigstens zur Möglichkeit der in ihr zu bewirkenden Zwecke nach Freiheitsgesetzen zusammenstimme.—Also muß es doch einen Grund der *Einheit* des Übersinnlichen, welches der Natur zum Grunde liegt, mit dem was der Freiheitsbegriff praktisch enthält, geben, wovon der Begriff, wenn er gleich weder theoretisch noch praktisch zu einem Erkenntnisse desselben gelangt, mithin kein eigentümliches Gebiet hat, dennoch den Übergang von der Denkungsart nach den Prinzipien der einen, zu der nach Prinzipien der anderen, möglich macht.

III. Von der Kritik der Urteilskraft, als einem Verbindungsmittel der zwei Teile der Philosophie zu einem Ganzen

Die Kritik der Erkenntnisvermögen in Ansehung dessen, was sie a priori leisten können, hat eigentlich kein Gebiet in Ansehung der Objekte; weil sie keine Doktrin ist, sondern nur, ob und wie, nach der Bewandtnis, die es mit unseren Vermögen hat, eine Doktrin durch sie möglich sei, zu untersuchen hat. Ihr Feld erstreckt sich auf alle Anmaßungen derselben, um sie in die Grenzen ihrer Rechtmäßigkeit zu setzen. Was aber nicht in die Einteilung der Philosophie kommen kann, | XXI das kann doch, als ein Hauptteil, in die Kritik des reinen Erkenntnisvermögens überhaupt kommen, wenn es nämlich Prinzipien enthält, die für sich weder zum theoretischen noch praktischen Gebrauche tauglich sind.

Die Naturbegriffe, welche den Grund zu allem theoretischen Erkenntnis a priori enthalten, beruheten auf der Gesetzgebung des Verstandes.—Der Freiheitsbegriff, der den Grund zu allen sinnlich-unbedingten praktischen Vorschriften a priori enthielt, beruhete auf der Gesetzgebung der Vernunft. Beide Vermögen also haben, außer dem, daß sie der logischen Form nach auf Prinzipien, welchen Ursprungs sie auch sein mögen, angewandt werden
AA177 können, überdem noch jedes seine eigene Gesetzgebung || dem Inhalte nach, über die es keine andere (a priori) gibt, und die daher die Einteilung der Philosophie in die theoretische und praktische rechtfertigt.

Allein in der Familie der oberen Erkenntnisvermögen gibt es doch noch ein Mittelglied zwischen dem Verstande und der Vernunft. Dieses ist die *Urteilskraft*, von welcher man Ursache hat, nach der Analogie zu vermuten, daß sie ebensowohl, wenn gleich nicht eine eigene Gesetzgebung, doch ein ihr eigenes Prinzip nach Gesetzen zu suchen, allenfalls ein bloß subjektives a priori, in sich enthalten dürfte; welches, wenn ihm gleich kein Feld der Gegenstände als sein Gebiet zustände, doch irgendeinen Boden haben kann, of freedom as the supersensible so that no transition is possible from the first to the second (i.e., by means of the theoretical use of reason), just as if these domains were two different worlds, the first of which cannot have any influence over the second, yet the second *ought to* have an influence over the first, namely the concept of freedom ought to actualize in the sensible world the purpose assigned by its laws. Consequently, it must be possible XX to think of nature also as being such that the lawfulness of its form agrees with at least the possibility for purposes to be achieved in nature, to be actualized according to the laws of freedom.—But then there must be a ground for the *unity* of the supersensible that underlies nature and the supersensible that the concept of freedom contains practically. Even though the concept of this ground cannot reach a cognition of the supersensible either theoretically or practically and hence does not have its own peculiar domain, it makes nonetheless possible the transition from the way of thinking according to the principles of nature to the way of thinking according to the principles of freedom.

III. On the Critique of Judgment as a Means to Connect the Two Parts of Philosophy into a Whole

The critique of the cognitive faculties with regard to what these faculties can accomplish a priori has properly no domain with regard to objects. The reason for this is that it is not a doctrine: it only has to investigate whether and how, given the nature of our faculties, a doctrine is possible through them. Its field extends to all pretensions held by those faculties in order to establish them within the limits of their legitimacy. However, what cannot be included in the partition of philosophy, XXI can still have a place as a principal part in the critique of the pure cognitive faculty in general, namely, if it contains principles that considered in themselves are not suitable for either theoretical or practical use.

The concepts of nature, which contain the ground for all theoretical knowledge a priori, were found to rest on the legislation of the understanding.—The concept of freedom, which contains the ground for all practical precepts a priori that are not conditioned by sensibility, was found to rest on the legislation of reason. Therefore, both faculties, in addition to their applicability to principles of whatever origin according to the logical form, have also, each of them, their own peculiar legislation according to the content. As there can be no other legislation (a priori) above this one, the partition of philosophy in theoretical and practical philosophy is justified.

And yet, in the family of the higher cognitive faculties there is also a middle term between understanding and reason. This is the *faculty of judgment*. We have good reasons to suppose, by analogy, that the faculty of judgment may likewise contain in itself—if not its own legislation, at least a principle of its own by which to search for laws—in any case, a merely subjective principle a priori. Even though such a principle is not entitled to a field of objects as its own domain, it can nonetheless have a territory of some und eine gewisse | XXII Beschaffenheit desselben, wofür gerade nur dieses Prinzip geltend sein möchte.

Hierzu kommt aber noch (nach der Analogie zu urteilen) ein neuer Grund, die Urteilskraft mit einer anderen Ordnung unserer Vorstellungskräfte in Verknüpfung zu bringen, welche von noch größerer Wichtigkeit zu sein scheint, als die der Verwandtschaft mit der Familie der Erkenntnisvermögen. Denn alle Seelenvermögen, oder Fähigkeiten, können auf die drei zurückgeführt werden, welche sich nicht ferner aus einem gemeinschaftlichen Grunde ableiten lassen: das *Erkenntnisvermögen*, das *Gefühl der Lust und Unlust*,
AA178 und das *Begehrungsvermögen.**) || Für | XXIII das Erkenntnisvermögen ist allein der Verstand gesetzgebend, wenn jenes (wie es auch geschehen muß, wenn es | XXIV für sich, ohne Vermischung mit dem Begehrungsvermögen, betrachtet wird) als Vermögen eines *theoretischen Erkenntnisses* auf die Natur

---

*Es ist von Nutzen: zu Begriffen, welche man als empirische Prinzipien braucht, wenn man Ursache hat zu vermuten, daß sie mit dem reinen Erkenntnisvermögen a priori in Verwandtschaft stehen, dieser Beziehung wegen, eine transzendentale Definition zu versuchen: nämlich durch rein Kategorien, sofern diese allein schon den Unterschied des vorliegenden Begriffs von anderen hinreichend angeben. Man folgt hierin dem Beispiel des Mathematikers, der die empirischen Data seiner Aufgabe unbestimmt läßt, und nur ihr Verhältnis in der reinen Synthesis derselben unter die Begriffe der reinen Arithmetik bringt und sich dadurch die Auflösung derselben verallgemeinert.—Man hat mir aus einem ähnlichen Verfahren (Krit. der prakt. V., S. 16 der Vorrede) einen Vorwurf gemacht und die Definition des Begehrungsvermögens, als Vermögens, durch seine Vorstellungen Ursache von der Wirklichkeit der Gegenstände dieser Vorstellungen zu sein, getadelt: weil | XXIV bloße Wünsche doch auch Begehrungen wären, von denen sich doch jeder bescheidet, daß er durch dieselben allein ihr Objekt nicht hervorbringen könne.—Dieses aber beweiset nichts weiter, als daß es auch Begehrungen im Menschen gebe, wodurch derselbe mit sich selbst im Widerspruche steht: indem er durch seine Vorstellung allein zur Hervorbringung des Objekts hinwirkt, von der er doch keinen Erfolg erwarten kann, weil er sich bewußt ist, daß seine mechanischen Kräfte (wenn ich
AA179 die nicht psychologischen so nennen soll), die durch jene Vorstellung || bestimmt werden müßten, um das Objekt (mithin mittelbar) zu bewirken, entweder nicht zulänglich sind, oder gar auf etwas Unmögliches gehen, z. B. das Geschehene ungeschehen zu machen (O mihi praeteritos, etc.), oder im ungeduldigen Harren die Zwischenzeit bis zum herbeigewünschten Augenblick, vernichten zu können.—Ob wir uns gleich in solchen phantastischen Begehrungen der Unzulänglichkeit unserer Vorstellungen (oder gar ihrer Untauglichkeit), Ursache ihrer Gegenstände zu sein, bewußt sind; so ist doch die Beziehung derselben als Ursache, mithin die Vorstellung ihrer Kausalität, in jedem Wunsche enthalten, und vornehmlich alsdann sichtbar, wenn dieser ein Affekt, nämlich Sehnsucht, ist. Denn diese beweisen dadurch, daß sie das Herz ausdehnen und welk machen und so die Kräfte erschöpfen, daß die Kräfte durch Vorstellungen wiederholentlich angespannt werden, aber das Gemüt bei der Rücksicht auf die Unmöglichkeit unaufhörlich wiederum in Ermattung zurücksinken lassen. Selbst die Gebete um Abwendung großer und so viel man einsieht, unvermeidlicher Übel, und manche abergläubische Mittel zu Erreichung natürlicherweise unmöglicher Zwecke, beweisen die Kausalbeziehung der Vorstellungen auf ihre Objekte, die sogar durch das Bewußtsein ihrer Unzulänglichkeit zum Effekt von der Bestrebung dazu nicht abgehalten werden

kind; and this territory might be so XXII constituted as to allow only for this principle to be valid in it.

But in addition to this (to judge by the analogy), a new reason leads us to connect judgment with another order of our powers of representation. This order seems to be even more important than that of the kinship with the family of the cognitive faculties. For all of the faculties or capacities of the soul can be brought back to three faculties that cannot be derived further from a common ground: the *cognitive faculty*, the *feeling of pleasure and displeasure*, and the *faculty of desire*.*) For XXIII the cognitive faculty, the understanding alone is legislative when this faculty relates to nature as a faculty of *theoretical cognition* (as indeed should happen when it is considered XXIV for itself, without being mingled with the faculty of desire). It is

---

*When concepts are used as empirical principles and we have reason to assume that they have some affinity with the pure cognitive faculty a priori, then it is useful to attempt, on account of this affinity, a transcendental definition of them, i.e., a definition by means of pure categories insofar as these are already sufficient to differentiate the given concept from others. This procedure follows the example of the mathematician, who leaves the empirical data of his problem undetermined and only brings their relation in their pure synthesis under the concepts of pure arithmetics, thereby generalizing his solution.—I have been reproached for having adopted a similar procedure (*Critique of Practical Reason*, p. 16 preface), and for having defined the faculty of desire as a *faculty of being the cause of the actuality of the objects of one's representations through these very representations.* This definition has been criticized with the argument that XXIII mere *wishes* would be desires too, and yet everyone agrees on the impossibility of producing their object through wishes alone.—This argument, however, only goes as far as proving that the human being has also desires that put him in contradiction with himself. For he aims at the production of the object by means of its representation *alone*, although he cannot expect any success from it. This happens because he is conscious that his mechanical forces (if I may so call the forces that are not psychological), which would have to be determined by that representation in order to actualize the object (therefore mediately), are either insufficient or even directed to something impossible, such as, for example, to make that what has happened has not happened (*O mihi praeteritos*, etc.) or as being able, as we are impatiently waiting for some wished-for moment, to eliminate the interval of time that divides us from it.—Even if in these fanciful desires we are indeed conscious that our representations are insufficient (or even unfit) to be the *cause* of their objects, the relation of these representations as causes—hence the representation of their *causality*—is still contained in every *wish*, and is especially visible where the wish is an affection, namely *longing*. For these desires, since they expand the heart and render it languid thus exhausting its forces, prove that these forces are repeatedly tensed by representations, but again and again they allow the *Gemüt* to relapse into weariness as it faces the impossibility. Even prayers meant to deflect some great and, as far as we can see, unavoidable evil, as well as many superstitious means to attain purposes otherwise unattainable by ways of nature, prove the causal relation of these representations to their objects. Not even the awareness of the insufficiency of this causality to produce the effect can keep it from striving toward it.—But the question of why an inclination to-bezogen wird, in Ansehung deren allein (als Erscheinung) es uns möglich ist, durch Naturbegriffe a priori, welche eigentlich reine Verstandesbegriffe sind, Gesetze zu geben.—Für das Begehrungsvermögen, als ein oberes Vermögen nach dem Freiheitsbegriffe, ist allein die Vernunft (in der allein dieser Begriff statthat) a priori gesetzgebend.—Nun ist zwischen dem Erkenntnis- und dem Begehrungsvermögen das Gefühl der Lust, so wie zwischen dem Verstande und der Vernunft die Urteilskraft, enthalten. Es ist also wenigstens vorläufig zu vermuten, daß die Urteilskraft eben so wohl für sich ein Prinzip a priori enthalte, und, da mit dem Begehrungsvermögen notwendig Lust oder Unlust verbunden ist (es sei daß sie, | XXV wie beim unteren, vor dem Prin- AA179 zip desselben vorhergehe, oder, wie beim || oberen, nur aus der Bestimmung desselben durch das moralische Gesetz folge), ebensowohl einen Übergang vom reinen Erkenntnisvermögen, d. i. vom Gebiete der Naturbegriffe zum Gebiete des Freiheitsbegriffs, bewirken werde, als sie im logischen Gebrauche den Übergang vom Verstande zur Vernunft möglich macht.

Wenn also gleich die Philosophie nur in zwei Hauptteile, die theoretische und die praktische, eingeteilt werden kann; wenn gleich alles, was wir von den eignen Prinzipien der Urteilskraft zu sagen haben möchten, in ihr zum theoretischen Teile, d. i. dem Vernunfterkenntnis nach Naturbegriffen, gezählt werden müßte; so besteht doch die Kritik der reinen Vernunft, die alles dieses vor der Unternehmung jenes Systems, zum Behuf der Möglichkeit desselben, ausmachen muß, aus drei Teilen: der Kritik des reinen Verstandes, der reinen Urteilskraft und der reinen Vernunft, welche Vermögen darum rein genannt werden, weil sie a priori gesetzgebend sind.

---

kann.—Warum aber in unsere Natur der Hang zu mit Bewußtsein leeren Begehrungen gelegt worden, das ist eine anthropologisch-teleologische Frage. Es scheint: daß, sollten wir nicht eher, als bis wir uns von der Zulänglichkeit unseres Vermögens zu Hervorbringung eines Objekts versichert hätten, zur Kraftanwendung bestimmt werden, diese großenteils unbenutzt bleiben würde. Denn gemeiniglich lernen wir unsere Kräfte nur dadurch allererst kennen, daß wir sie versuchen. Diese Täuschung in leeren Wünschen ist also nur die Folge von einer wohltätigen Anordnung in unserer Natur.

only with respect to nature (as appearance) that it is possible for us to give laws by means of a priori concepts of nature that are properly pure concepts of the understanding.—For the faculty of desire, as higher faculty according to the concept of freedom, only reason (in which alone this concept can be met) is a priori legislative.—Now between the cognitive faculty and the faculty of desire lies the feeling of pleasure, just as judgment lies between understanding and reason. Hence we must suppose, at least provisionally, that judgment as well contains an a priori principle of its own and that, since pleasure or displeasure is necessarily connected to the faculty of desire (whether XXV it precedes the principle of this faculty, as with the lower faculty of desire or, as with the higher faculty of desire, only follows from its determination through the moral law), judgment would produce a transition from the pure cognitive faculty, i.e., from the domain of the concepts of nature, to the domain of the concept of freedom just as, in its logical use, judgment makes possible the transition from understanding to reason.

Hence, even if philosophy can be divided only into two main parts, theoretical and practical, and even if all we may have to say of the faculty of judgment's own principles must be ascribed to the theoretical part of philosophy, namely to rational knowledge according to concepts of nature, yet the critique of pure reason, which has to establish all of this for the possibility of that system before its actual construction, consists of three parts: the critique of pure understanding, of pure judgment, and of pure reason. These faculties are called pure because they legislate a priori.

---

ward desires of whose emptiness we are aware has been set in our nature is an anthropological and teleological question. It seems that if we had to reassure ourselves that we can in fact produce the object before we could be determined to apply our force, then our force would remain to a large extent unused. For generally we get to know our forces only as we try them out in the first place. Therefore this deceit of empty wishes is only the consequence of a beneficent disposition of our nature.

Commentary

The present chapter opens our commentary to the text of the introduction. The structure of the commentary is provided by the methodological notion of "trichotomy" that Kant presents in the footnote at the very end of §IX. I will offer a brief synopsis of each section followed by a close analysis of Kant's text.

1. Synopsis: §I, On the Partition of Philosophy

The problem of the system of philosophy that Kant puts in the foreground in the "First Introduction" and discusses again in the preface to the *Critique of Judgment* is addressed in the first section of the introduction from the different perspective of the "partition" (or "division"—*Einteilung*) of philosophy. While accepting the traditional division of philosophy into theoretical and practical philosophy, Kant questions the way in which this partition has generally been drawn. Traditionally, the notions of theoretical and practical have been so abused as to cancel all distinction between the concepts as well as the objects that fall respectively under these two parts of philosophy. Thus Kant sets out to show the specific and essential difference that requires the separation between theoretical and practical philosophy as its only two distinct and irreducible "parts." The chief source of ambiguity lies in the notion of the practical. Kant distinguishes the "technical-practical" from the "moral-practical" meaning of the term. It is this distinction that allows him to claim that only the moral-practical requires and justifies a "special part" of philosophy, which is practical or moral philosophy. All "applied" disciplines, on the contrary, belong to theoretical philosophy as mere "corollaries." Only theoretical philosophy and practical (moral) philosophy deal with "laws," of nature and freedom respectively; technical disciplines, on the contrary, deal with merely technical or pragmatic precepts or rules. Yet, while the laws of nature of theoretical philosophy rest on sensible conditions, the practical law rests on the "supersensible."

Kant's argument in the first section builds on the results of the first two *Critiques* in order to address the question of the position of the *Critique of Judgment* in the system of philosophy. The partition of philosophy can yield two parts and two parts only. Yet the notion of "technic," or "technical-practical," if used in the analogical way already suggested by Kant at the end of §I of the "First Introduction," opens up to a new realm of inquiry.[1] Hence, to think the partition of philosophy according to what Kant indicates in this opening section becomes the

1. EE §I, AA, XX, 201, 3.

condition for the possibility of thinking the particular domain of objects that constitutes the specific "conditioned" of the third *Critique*. This leads to the exposition of §II.

1.1. §I Commentary: Theoretical, Technical-Practical, and Moral-Practical Spheres of Philosophy

It is common to many of Kant's works to start out with a discussion of the partition of philosophy in order to place within it the discipline that will be developed. The first section of the "First Introduction," focusing on the notion of a "*system* of rational cognition through concepts," again attempts a partition of the system. The first section of the introduction does not simply repeat the argument of the unpublished text. Kant's starting point is no longer the system of philosophy from which the partition seems to be analytically obtained. §I makes rather clear that the system results, synthetically, from the way in which the partition is drawn. Hence, in the introduction, philosophy will be construed "to a whole" (§III) as the result of the first trichotomy (§§I–III), the starting point being the question of the partition itself (§I). Since in the "First Introduction" Kant's starting point is instead the system of philosophy (§I), in the two following sections of this text he has to address the question of its constitutive elements: namely in §II the "system of the higher cognitive faculties," and in §III the "system of all the faculties of the human *Gemüt*." But if philosophy as system is no longer the starting point, as is the case in the introduction, then neither the notion of a "system of the higher faculties" nor the notion of the "complex of all the faculties of the *Gemüt*" can be derived from the idea of philosophy. What follows is the new methodological structure of the first trichotomy.

Kant's argument in the opening section of the "First Introduction" closely follows the opening of the preface to the *Groundwork of the Metaphysics of Morals*. As in the 1786 text, Kant distinguishes a "formal" from a "material" part of philosophy. The formal part is concerned exclusively with the "form of thinking in a system of rules" and makes abstraction from all reference to objects. The material part, on the contrary, is concerned with objects insofar as rational cognition from concepts is possible of them.[2] The formal part of philosophy is logic (more precisely, what was traditionally called "general logic"). The material, or "real part," is, in turn, twofold. In the *Groundwork*, Kant indicates these material parts as a "doctrine of nature" and a "doctrine of morals." Together with logic, these disciplines reproduce the traditional Greek partition of philosophy in "physics, ethics, and logic."[3] Kant's aim in the preface to the *Groundwork* is to draw a radical distinction between the empirical and the rational parts of science, and to show that practical philosophy can only be structured as *pure* moral philosophy, and hence as *metaphysics* of morals. The "First Introduction" instead attains the distinction

2. EE §I, AA, XX, 201, 10–15.
3. *Groundwork*, preface, BA III.

between "philosophy of nature" and "moral philosophy" by means of the distinction between "theoretical and practical philosophy." Similarly, in introduction §I, Kant's focus is, from the very outset, the issue of the specific separation between theoretical and practical. It is this distinction that now grounds the partition of philosophy. Thus, in our text, philosophy is implicitly taken according to the real, or material (and rational) meaning illustrated by the other texts. Philosophy is rational cognition *of things* through concepts, and is thereby distinguished from formal logic, which contains only principles of the form of thinking without distinction of objects. Moreover, in the *Groundwork*, Kant presents a further specification. He suggests that philosophy, insofar as it is developed on the ground of experience, is "empirical"; insofar as it is construed "exclusively from a priori principles," is "pure."[4] Pure formal philosophy is logic; pure philosophy that relates to determinate objects as "rational *cognition of things*" is metaphysics. Kant's formulations in both introductions to the *Critique of Judgment* depart significantly from those analogous reflections of the *Groundwork* (or, later on, of the *Metaphysics of Morals*) insofar as the specific problem of metaphysics—a metaphysics of nature and a metaphysics of morals—is not directly raised, and the term *metaphysics* is not even used. We know that "a system of a priori cognition from mere concepts" is metaphysics.[5] However, Kant has already clarified in the preface that in the case of the third *Critique* no doctrinal part and no metaphysics will follow the critical task.[6]

The confrontation between our text and analogous discussions on the partition of philosophy with which Kant opens both the critique of speculative reason and the critique of practical reason, sheds light on an important feature of Kant's procedure of partition in the third *Critique*. In light of Kant's concluding remarks in the footnote to introduction §IX, we can observe that while the "*system* of pure philosophy," or metaphysics, entails *two parts* only, the partition of the "*critique* of pure reason" requires the *three parts* of a trichotomy.[7] In the first and second *Critiques*, Kant is concerned with the first problem—that is, with the relation between critique and metaphysics as well as between critique and system.[8] In the introduction to the *Critique of Judgment*, he focuses clearly, and for the very first time, on the second issue: a "meta"-critical reflection on the very idea of a "critique of pure reason" broadly understood in its internal articulation. The first section, in particular, sets up the scene for the transition from the dichotomy between theoretical and practical spheres to the necessary introduction of a third term—namely the faculty of judgment and its critique (§§II–III).

---

4. *Groundwork*, preface, BA V.

5. See, for example, *Metaphysics of Morals*, AA, VI, 216; *Groundwork*, preface, BA V f., and KU preface, VI (AA, V, 168, 30–31).

6. As announced at the very end of the preface, X (AA, V, 170, 23–27).

7. See the passage of the preface (VI, AA, V, 168, 23–27) discussed in the previous chapter.

8. For the first *Critique*, see KrV BXLIII.

As was the case in the opening of the *Groundwork*, the first section of the introduction takes up again the traditional division of philosophy. Kant considers its "customary" partition in theoretical and practical philosophy as "entirely correct." His task, however, is to provide a transcendental justification for this division. Kant contends that the traditional division, being drawn upon an incorrect understanding of the meaning of the practical, is ultimately a division in which, in fact, nothing is really divided (XII, 171, 26–172, 3). Kant's argument leads, therefore, from the correct custom of dividing philosophy into theoretical and practical to the transcendental justification of such a custom.[9]

Philosophy as "rational cognition of things from concepts" (XI, 171, 4–5)

On what basis must partition be performed? As Kant already contended in the *Groundwork*'s preface, the task of the transcendental philosopher is to provide the "principle" of the partition. Interestingly enough, the problem of *Einteilung* opens and closes the text of the introduction. What is at stake in the opening section is the partition of philosophy, while the closing footnote addresses the issue of philosophical a priori partition as such. To address the issue of the principle of partition, Kant starts with a general definition of philosophy. Philosophy contains the principles of "rational cognition of things through concepts" (XI, 171, 4–6). *Vernunfterkenntnis* is for Kant cognition that arises—both subjectively and objectively—exclusively "from [*aus*] human reason."[10] Both philosophy and mathematics qualify for this definition. However, while mathematical cognition takes place "from the construction of concepts" and hence implies intuition, philosophical cognition takes place specifically "through concepts" (or, also "from concepts") alone.[11] The essential difference between philosophical and mathematical *Vernunfterkenntnis* is ultimately a distinction in their objects.[12] In the first *Critique*, Kant explains that in the case of "cognition from principles" "the particular is apprehended in the universal through concepts"[13] (and not through intuition). Since principles, in the proper sense of the term, are themselves "synthetic cognition from concepts," understanding can never supply any such cognition.[14] Cognition from principles is therefore typical of reason.

---

9. From: "is to proceed in an entirely correct way" (XI, 171, 8) to "hence philosophy is *correctly* divided into two parts . . ." (XII, 171, 20–24).

10. KrV B 864/A 836: the opposition is here twofold. On the one hand, *Vernunfterkenntnis* refers to the *origin* of cognition, which in this case arises from reason and not from experience; on the other hand, it refers to "rational" cognition as opposed to "historical" cognition. *Vernunfterkenntnis* means both rational cognition and cognition of reason (subjectively and objectively).

11. KrV B 740 f./A 712 f.; B 865/A 837.

12. KrV B 742 f./A 714 f.

13. KrV B 356 f./A 300.

14. KrV B 357 f./A 301; note, however, that in the same passage Kant distinguishes two meanings of the term *Prinzip*, one of which also applies to the understanding. In this case, however, we talk of principles not "absolutely" but only "comparatively."

The Partition of Philosophy (XI, 171, 5–15)

Kant's view of the way in which partition should be obtained follows from this definition of philosophy. Two conditions are provided. (i) First, theoretical and practical philosophy can legitimately constitute two parts of philosophy if and only if "the *concepts* that indicate to the *principles* of this rational knowledge their respective *objects*" are also "specifically different" (XI, 171, 8–10). Kant establishes a relation between three terms: *concepts*, *principles*, and *objects*—whereby concepts constitute the realm of objects, and principles allow for their a priori rational cognition. This distinction is extremely important and should be kept in mind as it constitutes the internal structure that supports Kant's argument throughout the text. This same structure will emerge in the table of the faculties that concludes the introduction and summarizes its entire argument. Different faculties of the mind, which are the source of different types of concepts, are ruled by different principles, which in turn apply to different objective realms. Since *concepts* assign to *principles* the realm of *objects* that can thereby be known, the partition of a rational science "depends upon that difference of objects whose knowledge requires different principles" (XIII, 172, 17–19). In other words, those so-called "practical" propositions that differ from theoretical propositions only in the way in which they address the will by presenting the possibility of things as laying in its causality rather than in the things themselves[15] (but do not differ from them in their content, which still regards only how things are, and not how they ought to be) cannot be legitimately said to be distinct in kind from theoretical propositions and to belong to practical philosophy.

(ii) Second, a sufficient ground for the partition of philosophy into theoretical and practical can be provided, according to Kant, only by a specific, or "essential difference" (XIII, 172, 14) in the concepts so that a "mutual opposition" (XI, 171, 11; XII, 171, 18) of the principles of the two parts of philosophy is generated. It is only on the ground of such an opposition of principles that theoretical and practical can be said to constitute two "specifically" (XI, 171, 9) and "completely different" (XII, 171, 21) parts of philosophy.[16] This is, to be sure, a typical way of thinking for Kant. He always argues from the position of separation, so that the task becomes one of synthetically constituting a whole, or a system or a unity out of parts that are different in kind (and not just different in degree or form, as the tradition generally has it).[17] The systematic problem of the third *Critique* is thereby posited in its very first section.

---

15. EE §I, AA, XX, 196, 4; 196, 31–32).

16. See, once again, the footnote to §IX on Kant's general procedure of "partition."

17. The problem of the first *Critique* can be summarized in the following questions: How are synthetic a priori judgments possible? How is knowledge possible starting from two radically heterogeneous elements of cognition (intuition and concepts), i.e., how is synthesis possible?

It is only in the published introduction, however, that Kant is able to present the sharp separation between theoretical and practical philosophy in such a clear-cut way. The two aforementioned conditions for partition—the specific difference of concepts and the mutual opposition of principles—are in charge of that separation. In the "First Introduction," §I, Kant is still comparing theoretical and practical propositions with regard to "form" and "content," noticing the insufficient ground for their traditional distinction. Hence the need for the long remark in which the argument is further developed in terms of "principles" and "consequences."[18]

Concepts of Nature and the Concept of Freedom (XII, 171, 15–XIII, 172, 22)

Given the two conditions for a partition of philosophy, Kant's problem is to find those two *concepts* that can generate two *objective realms* whose cognitive *principles* are mutually opposed. This will be the only ground and justification for the twofold partition of philosophy. Thus, there are only two types of concepts that allow for two mutually opposed principles of the possibility of their objects. These are the concepts of nature whose principle is nature's causality, and the (unique) concept of freedom whose principle is causality through/from freedom. What is at stake is the relation between concepts and a priori cognition of the respective objects. The Transcendental Analytic of the first *Critique* has demonstrated that concepts of nature allow for a priori *theoretical* cognition. Moreover, the Transcendental Dialectic has shown that if the concept of freedom raises claim to this same type of cognition, an "opposition" in its concept is immediately produced (XII, 171, 18). The concept of freedom does not determine any object of theoretical cognition (i.e., is neither a synthetic cognitive principle nor an object of theoretical cognition); it is, rather, transcendent in relation to all theoretical knowledge. Freedom can be inferred neither from experience nor from a description of how things are. Freedom is, in its negative determination, what is not subjected to nature's causal laws. To this extent, it is a "negative" and merely regulative principle of speculative reason.[19] With regard to the immediate determination of the will, on the contrary, the concept of freedom provides "extensive principles" (XII, 171, 19). As opposed to "explicative" judgments, which are analytic, "extensive" judgments are synthetic.[20] Propositions that are *synthetic* and can be principles of the will's own *determination* are, for Kant, genuinely "practical." This distinction yields the partition into "theoretical philosophy as philosophy of nature," and "practical philosophy as moral philosophy." These two parts are "thoroughly different" on the ground of their mutually opposed principles (XII, 171, 20–22). Traditional divisions of philosophy fall short of recognizing the need for a distinction of *principles* (and not simply of the proposition's form or formulation) as the ground for a definition of what is properly practical. In the

18. EE §I, AA, XX, 197, 16–17.
19. See *Metaphysics of Morals*, AA, VI, 221.
20. KrV B 11/A 7.

1787 preface to the first *Critique*, we are offered a definition of theoretical and practical *Vernunfterkenntnis*. Kant contends that in the sciences we find that reason's a priori knowledge is related to its object in two possible ways: "either as merely *determining* it and its concept . . . or as also *making it actual*. The former is *theoretical*; the latter is *practical cognition* of reason."[21] This important distinction is further emended in the present connection.

Kant detects a crucial ambiguity in the notion of practical. The ambiguity is brought back to the twofold use of the notion of causality. Kant argues that to attribute a certain effect to the will's causality is not sufficient to specifically define the practical sphere. This remark will play a crucial role in the second part of the *Critique of Judgment*. The will exercises causality as "faculty of desire" (XII, 172, 4), which is still a merely "natural faculty" (XIV, 172, 29–30). The will is just one of the many causes to be found in nature. It can also, in turn, be affected by natural causes, namely by passions and desires. Its peculiarity consists only in "acting according to concepts" (XII, 172, 5–6).[22] The practical possibility or necessity of an effect due to the causality of the will is thereby distinguished from the merely "physical possibility or necessity" (XII, 172, 7–8) of an effect that results either from the mechanism of matter or from the blind force of instinct, neither of which acts according to concepts. However, all this is still not enough to qualify the will as practical in the proper sense that Kant wants to claim for the term (i.e., to distinguish its causality as different in kind from merely natural causality). Kant suggests that the only way of raising the activity of the will out of the sphere of nature, and hence of defining the specificity of the practical, is to qualify the "concept" that determines the causality of the will either as a concept of nature or as the concept of freedom. Only this move can provide the "essential difference" Kant is after (XIII, 172, 14). The will, as faculty of desire, is a natural cause among many natural causes. Yet, if (and only if) the concept that gives the "rule" for its action is not a concept of nature but the concept of freedom, the will sets itself out against the natural chain of causes, and acts *morally*. In this case, the will's causality is not determined by natural laws but is a causality from and through freedom. The will is immediately and exclusively determined by the moral law.[23] This repeats the doctrine of the second *Critique*. In the present connection, however, Kant introduces a terminological specification in order to appropriately qualify the term "*practical*." Concepts of nature provide "technical-practical" principles, while the concept of freedom provides "moral-practical" principles (XIII, 172, 15–17). This difference grounds the partition of philosophy

21. KrV B IX f.; for the meaning of "practical cognition" see also KpV A 80.

22. See the definition of the "faculty of desire" in KpV A 16 fn.; "*Begehrungsvermögen*" is the capacity of "being the cause, through one's representations, of the objects of these representations." This faculty can be determined either by laws of nature or by the moral law.

23. See KrV B 560 ff./A 532 ff.

into two doctrinal or metaphysical parts: a "doctrine of nature" and a "doctrine of morals" (XIII, 172, 20–21).[24]

"Technical-Practical" and "Moral-Practical" (XIII, 172, 15–XVI, 173, 36)

Kant sets out to define the technical-practical sphere. He denies, however, that the technical-practical, in its proper sense, could raise claim to any independence or specificity in the system of philosophy. All rules, whose principles are not merely empirical but rest on concepts,[25] and regard the possibility of things according to concepts of nature, are inferences or consequences of theory, and hence theoretical propositions themselves. They are nothing but "corollaries" of the theory (XIII, 172, 26). For, those concepts provide everything that is needed to produce those objects as means to an end—the will as a natural faculty being just one of the means. Technical rules that prescribe how to produce certain things or effects are inferences out of theoretical knowledge of those things and effects. What is "practical" in them is exclusively the fact that they address the will, and that they require an application of the theory. These rules do not have the force of "laws" but are mere "prescriptions" (XIV, 172, 31–32), or suggestions, that relate to skill or art and are valid only under the hypothetical assumption that one wants certain results. Hence these rules do not have anything to do with the moral law, which alone can ground a second, "special" part of philosophy (XV, 173, 16).[26] Thus the realm of all technical-practical rules is characterized as a set of inferences from the natural laws of nature, and represents the technical and applicative aspect of our scientific knowledge of nature. Accordingly, Kant reviews a series of disciplines that being merely applicative and technical-practical constitute neither independent sciences nor independent parts of philosophy. Moral-practical precepts, on the contrary, derive entirely from the concept of freedom. They entail a ground for the determination of the will to action that *extends* beyond nature so as to completely *exclude* any sensible determination of the will. While technical-practical rules establish an analytic relation between theoretical knowledge and action within nature, moral-practical rules are synthetic principles that transcend (extend beyond) the sphere of nature. Moral-practical rules or precepts have the force of law. They are "simply," "most properly," and "absolutely" laws (XV, 173, 11) since they do not require any previous intention or particular aim to ground

---

24. See KpV A165, for the distinction between "doctrine of morals" and "doctrine of happiness." In the section we are presently analyzing, the doctrine of happiness falls under the merely technical-practical disciplines.

25. This is the difference between the technical-practical consequences drawn from the a priori principles of mathematics and the consequences drawn from the a posteriori principles of the natural sciences.

26. Correspondingly, in the KpV Kant observes that a "postulate" of pure practical reason is a "theoretical proposition" that is an inseparable corollary of the one and only practical law (KpV A 220).

their validity (XVI, 172, 35–36).[27] These alone are the rules that constitute a special part of philosophy, namely practical, or moral, philosophy.

Thus the technical-practical sphere covers for Kant a middle ground that includes two kinds of propositions. It designates both what is merely technical in theoretical knowledge of nature, namely the realm of the applicative branches of natural sciences (as mechanics, applied geometry, practical psychology, and so forth [XIV, 171–172]);[28] and what is theoretical in practical knowledge, namely the sphere of "hypothetical imperatives" (rules of skill and prudence as well as the "general doctrine of happiness," XIII, 172, 23–25; XIV, 173, 7)—in other words, those maxims and rules that neither obligate with the categorical force of a law nor determine the will through freedom, but determine the will to action simply by means of a theoretical representation of the object. This last aspect of the technical-practical is already outlined in the *Groundwork*.[29] Here Kant employs the term "*technical*" to designate a particular type of hypothetical imperatives, namely the imperatives of skill.[30] In our text, the technical-practical sphere covers that which the *Groundwork* distinguishes as the two kinds of "hypothetical" imperatives, namely imperatives of skill (technical) and imperatives of prudence (pragmatic).

By means of the distinction between technical-practical and moral-practical rules, Kant finds that the two conditions for a complete partition of philosophy are eventually fulfilled. Philosophy has only two parts: theoretical and practical. They both deal with laws (and not simply with rules, subjective maxims, or precepts). In order to belong to practical philosophy, however, a rule must prove its principle to be unconditioned—not to rest upon concepts of nature, which are always conditioned (dependent upon the condition of a sensible intuition). Practical rules as laws lay in the "supersensible" disclosed by the concept of freedom (XV, 173, 32–33; XIV, 173, 22).

The concepts of nature and the concept of freedom ground not only the radical separation between two parts of philosophy but also the radical separation between two "worlds" (i.e., the two objective realms in which those concepts are constitutive of objects). Thereby a transition is provided from the "condition" of the first section to the "conditioned" of the second section of the introduction.

---

27. See *Groundwork*, BA 44.

28. Similarly, we find "*technic*" and "*technical*" used in the *Logic* (AA, IX, 18) in Kant's discussion of the traditional division of logic in "theoretical and practical logic."

29. *Groundwork*, BA 41 (AA, IV, 415).

30. *Groundwork*, BA 44 (AA, IV, 416). In a footnote of the remark to EE §I, Kant 'corrects' the *Groundwork*'s classification of imperatives by claiming that what he there called "hypothetical imperatives" should rather have been called "technical imperatives, i.e., imperatives of art" (AA, XX, 200, 15–16). Kant uses the term *technisch* also in KpV A 46 fn. with regard to propositions of mathematics and natural science.

Note on the Term "Technik"

The distinction between a technical and a moral meaning of the practical will prove of great momentum in the *Critique of Judgment*. To be sure, Kant seems to reproduce a distinction well known since Aristotle. Plato still employs the terms τεχνη (techne), ποιησις (poiesis), and πραξις (praxis) without a clear conceptual differentiation.[31] According to Plato, τεχνη is knowledge of the ground of existence of things as well as of causal connections;[32] the epistemic dimension of τεχνη opposes it to εμπειρια (empeiria), which is activity that proceeds with no knowledge of why one acts in a certain way instead of another.[33] This opposition is crucial for Aristotle as well. Plato defines ποιησις as "whatever is the cause of the transition of something from not-being into being"[34] and includes both that which is produced by nature and that which is produced by human activity (including art). Moreover, by way of analogy, Plato extends the ways of human (technical and poietic) production to the gods.[35] Practical activity is mimetic activity that reproduces the forms of ideal reality. Following Socrates, Plato qualifies πραξις, in the ethical sense of ευ πραττειν (eu prattein), as the highest form of human activity. More generally, however, the term designates all technical-poietic activity, which, being well performed, leads to successful results (as in medical art, agriculture, and mostly in politics). Plato proposes a division of sciences in πρακτικαι (practicai) and γνωστικαι (gnosticai).[36] It is relevant to observe that in the tradition of Platonism, the terminological distinction is programmatically lost. In the *Septuaginta*, ποιησις translates the act of god's creation, thereby setting an important standard for the later employment of the term. According to Plotinus the eternal One "creates/produces itself [ποιει]" as well as everything else. Since any kind of production outside the One is incompatible with its monistic structure, every production must take place within the One in a complete identity between theory and activity. Along with the distinction theory/practice, Plotinus also eliminates the Aristotelian distinction between ποιησις and πραξις.

Aristotle is the first to introduce a technical distinction in the terminology of practical philosophy. Ποιησις is a specifically human form of activity connected with and grounded on τεχνη (technic and art) that proceeds knowing the causes and producing objects (artifacts). Πραξις instead, in its most proper, ethical-anthropological significance, designates an activity connected with and grounded

---

31. Only in *Charmides*, 163 a–e Plato attempts a distinction between ποιησις and πραξις.

32. See *Gorgias*, 465 a.

33. See in particular *Gorgias*, 462 b ff., 500 a ff.; see also H. Holzhey, *Kants Erfahrungsbegriff*, Basel/Stuttgart, Schwabe, 1970, 50 ff.

34. *Symposion*, 205 b 8 f.; *Sophistes*, 265 b 8–10.

35. See *Sophistes*, 265 e 3–6.

36. See *Politeia*, 258 e 5, 259 d 1.

on virtue. Aristotle radically separates natural production from technical and poietic activity.[37] For natural beings have their τελος (i.e., the principle of development), in themselves, whereas the product of ποιησις and art has its principle in something else, namely in the artist or human agent that produces it.[38] The notion of πραξις, on the other hand, besides the more specific, anthropological and ethical meaning, has for Aristotle almost universal applicability. He attributes πραξις to the gods, the first heaven, stars, plants, animals, human beings, the body politic. In its cosmological meaning, πραξις is movement and life, and indicates the cause of movement. In the biological context, the term is synonym with life. Πραξις relates both to the living being as a whole and to its organs (in plants and animals), designating the specific function of each particular organ. In all its applications, the term for Aristotle is clearly connected with the issue of teleology.

While Aristotle excluded τεχνη and ποιησις from the realm of nature, expressing with these terms a typically human form of activity, Kant's aim is to draw a distinction within the practical sphere in order to preserve the specificity of what is moral. Thereby he suggests that an alliance between technic and nature—the natural will but also nature as such—is somehow possible.[39] With regard to the notion of πραξις, Kant does not see in Aristotle's connotation of the term sufficient ground for its strictly moral employment. For he opposes, from very early on, all forms of eudaimonistic ethic. Moreover, because of its close relation to the notion of teleology, πραξις had, for Aristotle, an extremely extended and unspecific applicability. In the light of this ancient employment of the term, Kant's program can be seen as a deconstruction of the notion of the practical in order to attribute to the moral-practical the narrowest and most specific meaning possible. A new notion of nature's teleology allows him to recuperate for nature the vocabulary of technic, poiesis, and art hitherto restricted to human activity.

Kant's move has at least two major consequences. On the one hand, it calls for a new definition of nature. For, the nature that can be viewed as acting in a technical way or according to a technic is certainly not the same mechanistic "nature in general" explored in the first *Critique*. On the other hand, a new inquiry is needed that looks at the way of thinking and knowing of a nature that acts *in analogy* to human technic and purposive activity. For neither understanding nor

---

37. With regard to our topic, see O. Kristeller, "The Modern System of the Arts," in *Renaissance Thought and the Arts: Collected Essays*, Princeton, Princeton University Press, 1990, 163–228, 166.

38. This distinction will play an important role in the Analytic of the Teleological Faculty of Judgment with regard to Kant's distinction between external and internal purposiveness of nature.

39. This consequence is already drawn by Kant in the remark to the "First Introduction," §I (AA, XX, 200, 7 ff.); for a later example see *On Perpetual Peace*, AA, VIII, 417, where the laws of nature's mechanism are called "technical-practical."

practical reason can claim any access to this realm. It is clear from this presentation of the problem that the first section of the introduction only lays the condition for thinking about the issue of what Kant will later call "technic of nature." Further steps are needed in order to justify the employment and the meaning of this expression. In the "First Introduction," on the contrary, Kant introduces a new use of "technic" at the end of the first section. He simply contrasts it to the hitherto discussed notion of the "technical-practical" by adding the following explanation: the term *technical* is predicated on "objects of nature" in relation to our *evaluation* of them. In this perspective, the predicate indicates something about their origin: we evaluate them "*as if* their possibility were grounded in art."[40] However, judgment neither constitutes nor determines its objects; it only indicates, "by way of analogy with art,"[41] not objectively but only subjectively, the way in which nature would have produced those objects. What is "technical," therein, is judgment, and, according to judgment, nature.

2. Synopsis: §II, On the Domain of Philosophy in General

The question of the conditioned that we think of under the condition exposed in §I, regards the object that we think or know according to concepts and principles of reason. In Kant's transcendental philosophy the object is not (empirically or metaphysically) given, but construed as a function of our cognitive faculty and its a priori principles. Accordingly, in §II Kant sets out to articulate the objective realm in which our "entire cognitive faculty" extends in its differential activity. The question of the employment, or exercise, of this faculty is therein addressed. Kant's attention is brought to the "mental space," or "field of competence," within which this faculty can be successfully and legitimately employed. The result is a map that portrays a mental geography in which the *Critiques* of speculative and practical reason find their place. In addition, this map allows us, first, to locate the blank spots that the two *Critiques* opened up but could not account for as parts of this mental geography. Second, it offers us an overview of our cognitive faculty as a whole. Finally, it address the relations among the different regions including the geographical hindrances that divide them. In this way, at the end of the section, Kant opens up to the new region that the *Critique of Judgment* is in charge of exploring. Kant's argument aims at providing the systematic necessity of the *Mittelglied* between theoretical and practical philosophy at which he already hinted in the preface. While Kant radically excludes all possibility of a mediation or "transition" between the two worlds of nature and freedom, he suggests the possibility of a transition or mediation between two "ways of thinking" human experience. This will be the function of a third faculty, *Urteilskraft*.

40. EE §I, AA, XX, 200, 8–10—emphasis in the text.
41. EE §I, AA, XX, 201, 3.

2.1. §II Commentary: A Geography of the Cognitive Faculty

Concepts and Objects (XVI/XVII, 174, 22)

At the beginning of §II, Kant again takes up both the definition of philosophy provided in §I (philosophy is rational cognition from concepts), and the relation between concepts, principles, and objects that structures rational cognition as such. It is immediately clear that the partition of philosophy is still the issue. Kant establishes a direct relation between the applicability and application of a priori concepts and the "employment" (XVI, 174, 3–4) of the cognitive faculty according to principles, thereby determining the limits within which philosophy extends. The use of our cognitive faculty in its principles depends upon the range of applicability of a priori concepts, and is coextensive with it. This claim confirms what was discussed in §I; there, the partition of philosophy in its principles followed from the distinction of two kinds of a priori concepts (concepts of nature and concept of freedom).

When objects are brought into the picture, the partition of philosophy again becomes an issue. While the division of philosophy as rational cognition of things was the topic of §I, in §II Kant directly addresses the partition of the "complex [*Inbegriff*] of all the objects" (XVI, 174, 6–7) to which concepts refer. The new perspective is mediated by the role played by different faculties in cognition (XVI, 174, 8–9).[42] Cognition arises when a priori concepts refer to objects. Kant intimates, however, that cognition is not always possible. This means both that cognition is not possible *for all objects*, and that cognition is not possible *for all faculties* that attempt to refer concepts to objects. What Kant calls object in §II is to be taken in the most general sense provided by his definition of transcendental philosophy: "I entitle transcendental all knowledge that is occupied not so much with objects as with the mode of our knowledge of objects insofar as this mode of knowledge is to be possible a priori"[43]—clarified Kant in the introduction to the *Critique of Pure Reason*. When "the way in which something can be an object of cognition *for us*" is at stake, then "concepts are not compared with objects but merely with our cognitive faculty and the use that . . . this faculty can make of the given representation."[44] Accordingly, the topological division of the objective realm becomes a function of the relation that objects have to concepts in order to produce a priori knowledge.

What Kant presents in the opening of this section is a "geography" of human reason in its thinking and knowing of objects. Kant maps out this geography in a progression that tightens together, in a more and more specific way, the relation between cognitive faculties and objects of cognition. Thereby Kant brings to-

42. Clearly EE §II shifts from the "partition of a philosophy" to the partition of "our higher cognitive faculty" (AA, XX, 201, 14–15).

43. KrV B 25/A 11–12.

44. KU §91 (454, AA 467, 4–9).

gether two metaphoric fields often encountered in critical philosophy, namely geographic and juridical metaphors.[45] The division is drawn this time according to a twofold criterion. On the one hand, objects are compared to concepts through the relation that they have to our cognitive faculties and their use. This provides a specific meaning for expressions such as "concepts *of nature*" and "concept *of freedom*" already employed in §I. On the other hand, the question in relation to which each geographical region is defined looks at whether cognition is possible of those objects, and what type of cognition is possible of them.

(i) The most extended region in Kant's geography is the "field." The field of a concept indicates the objective range of application and applicability of an a priori concept when the question of the possibility of our cognition of objects is suspended (XVI, 174, 10–11) and the cognitive faculty in relation to which the object is taken is not further specified (i.e., is just our "cognitive faculty in general") (XVI, 174, 12–13). (ii) Kant's geographical partition individuates in the "territory" (*Boden, territorium*) of the concepts and the respective faculties, that part of the field in which "knowledge is possible for us" (XVI, 174, 14–15). (iii) Proceeding within the territory, that part of the territory in which concepts exercise a right of jurisdiction due to their legislative function toward objects is the "domain" (*Gebiet, ditio*) of those concepts and faculties. It is this notion of a domain that Kant mentions in the title of §II, where he signals his search for the objective realm within which philosophical cognition "in general" is not only possible but also legislative with regard to its objects. (iv) Negatively defined, the other part of the territory, complementary to the domain, in which concepts are not legislative and yet do provide a certain cognition of objects, is their "residence" (*Aufenthalt, domicilium*). In this geography, all regions are enclosed by limits that structurally imply a within and a without. Kant will argue, however, that the field is for us unlimited. Moreover, while the notion of field encompasses that of territory, and this in turn includes both domain and domicilium, the latter notions lay one next to the other in a relation of mutual exclusion.

The Territory of Experience (XVII, 174, 26–XVIII, 175, 4)

In §I, the twofold partition of philosophy followed from the fact that "there are only two types of concepts that allow for two different principles concerning the possibility of their objects, i.e., the *concepts of nature* and the *concept of freedom*" (XI, 171, 13–15). Now, on the ground of this topology, Kant again takes up the same issue with regard to our cognitive faculty and its objective realm. The partition of philosophy is the division of its domains. Our *entire* cognitive faculty[46] has two domains but only one territory. Its domains are respectively the domain in which concepts of nature are a priori legislative (theoretical philoso-

45. See H. Holzhey, *Kants Erfahrungsbegriff*, op. cit.

46. Note Kant's specifications: here the cognitive faculty is qualified as "*gesamtes*," in other occurrences as "*überhaupt*."

phy) and the domain of freedom's own a priori legislation (practical philosophy) (XVII, 174, 25–26).

Now applying these topological distinctions regressively to the notion of philosophy, Kant argues that the *territory* (the region in which knowledge is possible for us) on which philosophy establishes its twofold domain can only be constituted by "the complex [*Inbegriff*] of the objects of all possible experience" taken as mere appearances (XVII, 174, 28–29). To define the territory of our cognitive faculty as an *Inbegriff* is to determine it as the structured context in which experience is possible for us. Experience is the realm within which all appearances are located.[47] This important limitation is imposed on our cognitive faculty as a whole by the nature of the understanding, which can legislate a priori only if placed on the territory of experience (XVII, 174, 29–31). Since the territory on which our cognitive faculty operates can only be one (for the "subject" of that faculty is one, XVIII, 175, 11), it is on the territory of experience that philosophy "*exercises its legislation*" (XVII, 174, 27; XVI, 174, 3–5). This is also the reason why the *Critique of Pure Reason* had to be the first step of Kant's critical enterprise. Interestingly, Kant's aim is not to separate understanding from practical reason on this issue. He does not claim that the understanding is confined to the realm of appearances while practical reason extends beyond it to the noumena. He maintains, rather, that the *one and only* territory of the *one and only* human experience[48] is the same for both faculties, and he intimates that this territory is experience viewed as the sensible world of appearances (this territory, however, might be experienced in a different way by different faculties). Reason, as opposed to understanding, gives the law only to itself as a noumenon. Yet, the only access we have to a knowledge of reason in its determination and real activity is through and in experience. In this respect, we recognize that practical reason does belong to the complex of all experience.

The map of our entire cognitive faculty allows Kant to qualify more specifically the type of objects and hence the type of concepts to which cognition refers, thereby approaching the new range of problems proper to the third *Critique*. The question regards the kind of objects that we encounter in surveying the different regions of the map. "Concepts of experience" (XVI/XVII, 174, 17–18) are located within the territory of nature, which is defined, accordingly, as the "complex of all objects of the senses" (XVII, 174, 18–19).[49] This territory, however, is

47. For this terminology see H. Holzhey, *Kants Erfahrungsbegriff*, op. cit., 247; for the meaning of the claim that experience is for us territory, see 250–252; for the term *Inbegriff* see J. C. Adelung, *Grammatisch-kritisches Wörterbuch der hochdeutschen Mundart*, 2, Leipzig, 1796. Generally, *Inbegriff* is translated as "sum-total." Kant himself, however, in his *Reflexionen* renders it with the Latin *complexus*.

48. For the topic of the "singularity" of experience see H. Holzhey, *Kants Erfahrungsbegriff*, op. cit., 244 ff.

49. This definition parallels the one just discussed of the territory as "the complex of the objects of all possible experience" taken as mere appearances (XVII, 174, 28–29).

for those concepts only domicilium, not domain (i.e., the juridical status that justifies the presence of concepts of experience on the territory of nature is provided by the residence, not the domain). With this suggestion Kant sheds light on the way in which laws operate in theoretical philosophy (§I), thereby addressing with a new question the world of the first *Critique*. In the same territory of nature, we find not only a priori concepts of the understanding but also a posteriori concepts of experience (*Erfahrungsbegriffe* and *empirische Begriffe*). Through its a priori concepts, the understanding legislates on "nature in general," establishing its domain therein.[50] Concepts of experience, on the contrary, are not directly legislative over nature considered as the complex of all objects of the senses. They are only "produced according to law"—they are "lawful" (XVII, 174, 20) insofar as they can refer to objects in general on the ground of both understanding's a priori concepts and pure forms of sensible intuition. Hence the rules of theoretical knowledge, insofar as they regard concepts of experience and their objects, are empirical and contingent and do not guarantee objective (universal and necessary) knowledge.[51] In other words, from the legislative function of the universal and necessary concepts of the understanding, it does not follow that empirical knowledge of contingent natural objects is itself possible. Evidently while the first *Critique* established the domain of its legislation by inspecting the territory of theoretical cognition, it also left the domicilium of the concepts of experience still unexplored. It is this region that the third *Critique* sets out to investigate. The third *Critique* poses the question of whether in the sphere of an experience apparently dominated by contingency an order and a peculiar type of lawfulness could still be detected that is not the order and lawfulness of the understanding. Accordingly, Kant is also suggesting a new and more articulate meaning for the notion of experience. Experience encompasses both the theoretical and the practical, both that which belongs to a domain and that which belongs to a domicilium.

Since the partition of philosophy follows from the division of our cognitive faculty, Kant suggests that the theoretical legislation through concepts of nature is the work of understanding while reason is alone responsible for the practical legislation through freedom. As the Transcendental Dialectic of the first *Critique* has shown, there is indeed a theoretical use of reason (in nature), which, however, establishes no legislation of its own.[52] In its theoretical employment, reason takes its wisdom concerning laws from the understanding. Reason's function is to construct syllogisms and draw conclusions from laws already given by the understanding. These conclusions remain in the territory of nature and do not constitute an independent domain. Reason's domain is limited to the (moral-)practical sphere of freedom. We know from §I that from the simple occurrence of practical rules, we cannot infer the legislative function of reason. For reason may be here at work in its merely technical-practical employment (XVIII, 175, 2–4). This conclusion is

50. See, for example, KrV B 165.

51. For example: KrV B 218 ff./ A 176 ff.; see also B 64/A 47, B 148 f.

52. See the whole introduction to the Transcendental Dialectic of the first *Critique*.

important and parallels the one drawn with relation to the use of the understanding. Playing with the complex meaning of experience (already in the first *Critique* the term indicates both the construction of the understanding and the realm of the sheer empirical), Kant suggests that understanding's a priori concepts are a guarantee of the meaningfulness of experience, while empirical concepts do not ensure universal and necessary theoretical cognition. This asymmetry characterizes the domicilium of empirical concepts on the territory of a merely contingent experience as opposed to the domain of the concepts of nature on the territory of the necessary and universal experience that they constitute for the first time.

Two Domains on the Same Territory, Two Legislations in the Same Subject (XVIII, 175, 5–25)

The territory of philosophy is one and unique while its domain is twofold. The *territory* common to understanding and reason is constituted by the world of possible experience. The *domain* of theoretical philosophy is determined by the legislation of the understanding through its a priori concepts, while its adjacent *domicilium* is occupied by empirical concepts. The *domain* of practical philosophy is constituted by reason's legislation through the concept of freedom while its adjacent *domicilium* is represented by the realm of its technical-practical use. While understanding and reason share one and "the same territory of experience" (XVIII, 175, 5–6), their respective legislations are radically separated. Their domicilia intersect each other.

Drawing from elements present already in the first and second *Critiques*, §II introduces two parallel lines of thought that are indeed new in Kant's reflection. They open up to specific problems that a new "conditioned" poses to his critical reflection. The new conditioned is represented by the two domicilia of empirical concepts and the technical-practical use of reason. In both regions, neither understanding nor reason legislates, so that neither strict necessity and universality nor unconditioned and categorical validity is possible therein. Both regions belong, however, to the common territory of human experience. In addition, the third *Critique* will give an account of another unexplored region of this geography, namely the field of the supersensible. Kant introduces this issue in the remainder of §II.

Two crucial questions of the *Critique of Judgment* appear for the first time in this argument. On the one hand, the redefinition of the complex domain of philosophy in general requires a new notion of experience as the territory on which that domain can be successfully established. On the other hand, Kant holds on to the important idea of the uniqueness of the territory of experience for the subject, despite the new problems that the tension between that unique territory and the dualism of its domains immediately reveals. The issue of the "abyss" that separates theoretical and practical, and the problem of the "supersensible" are the new controversial regions that Kant's geography of the cognitive faculty now needs to accommodate. Kant's problem in this section is to define the complex set of *relations* that bind and at the same time separate two radically heterogeneous terms or domains of our experience. The conclusion opens up to a new "field" of inquiry. Since neither theoretical nor practical reason is any longer sufficient to account for it, a third cognitive faculty will be called into the picture (§III). This argument does not appear in the "First Introduction." Since herein the issue is the completeness of the system's partition, which is exhausted by theoretical and practical philosophy, the faculty of judgment is introduced in a merely hypothetical and analogical way.[53]

The question of how and under which conditions two opposed and incompatible legislations in one and the same territory are possible, occupies Kant again after the merely negative solution provided by the Transcendental Dialectic of the first *Critique*. There Kant demonstrated that it is at least possible "to think without contradiction" that the two legislations along with their respective faculties coexist in one and the same subject (XVIII, 175, 9–12).[54] Now the radical separation of the two domains guarantees that understanding's and reason's respective legislations "do not interfere with each other" (XVIII, 175, 6–9). However, the "effects" of those legislations "in the sensible world" do conflict and limit each other all the time (XVIII, 175, 15–16). Kant's awareness of the difficulties raised by this situation was voiced already in the second *Critique*. There reason's legislation was enacted by the subject taken as "sensuous being (*Sinnenwesen*)" through the moral law and thereby translated in the world of appearances.[55] The territory of experience, previously defined as "the complex of the objects of all possible experience" as sheer appearances (XVII, 174, 28–29), now gains the shape of a "world."[56] Our territory is the "sensible world"; only in it is experience possible. It is on this common territory that both legislations (not the understanding's alone) are exercised and concretely manifest their effects (XVII, 174, 27; XVI, 174, 3–5). Having set both legislations on the same territory of the sensible world, Kant is now concerned with saving the results of the two *Critiques* by reinforcing the reason that after all prevents the two domains from merging into one (XVIII, 175, 16). What hinders such a merge is the impossibility of a theoretical access to the thing in itself or to the "supersensible" (XVIII, 175, 22). In arguing for this impossibility, Kant implicitly sets both domains in relation to the same problem of the thing-in-itself. Paradoxically, that which separates the two domains also unites them.

The Field of the Supersensible (XIX, 175, 22–34)

At stake is, once again, the relation between concepts and objects respectively in the theoretical and practical domain. Since concepts of nature need intuition in order to produce *knowledge* of their objects—as *Gegenstände*—these objects can

53. See EE §II, AA, XX, 202.

54. See Kant's conclusion in KrV B 586/A 558.

55. See KpV A 170 ff.; see chapter 3.

56. See KrV B 446 f./A 418 f. for the terminological distinction between "nature" and "world."

only be appearances and never things in themselves. The concept of freedom, on the other hand, does represent in its object—as *Objekt*—a thing in itself; yet lacking all intuition, this representation cannot provide theoretical cognition. Hence, in neither case is theoretical knowledge of objects (or even of the thinking subject, as claimed by rational psychology) possible as things in themselves. An object (*Objekt*) known as *Ding an sich* would be the "supersensible" (not only an object that is placed ontologically beyond or above the sensible world, but one whose theoretical cognition does not require the contribution of intuition). Kant now makes the important admission that we must assume the supersensible as an "idea" in order to ground the possibility of the territory of experience on which both domains establish their legislation (XVIII/XIX, 175, 23–24). While the legislation of the understanding must assume the supersensible as that which underlies the very possibility of experience (as a regulative idea), the legislation of practical reason has the supersensible as its object (it gives practical reality to that idea). This different relation to a third term, namely the supersensible, grounds the separation of the two domains by relocating them within the broader region of a new field.

For our cognitive faculty, the supersensible constitutes the "field" (XIX, 175, 26) within which the territory of experience is placed. In all its extension, the territory can never cover this field (XIX, 175, 24–25). The condition of the possibility of all experience cannot itself be an experience. As opposed to the other regions of Kant's mental geography, this field is for us "unlimited" (it is itself the limit of the territory of the sensible world) and also "inaccessible" to our cognitive faculty (XIX, 175, 26). For us, the field of the supersensible will never acquire the familiarity of a territory on which to build the edifice of a doctrine; neither understanding nor reason will ever establish a domain for theoretical knowledge in the field of the supersensible. Yet that field is necessary for us in order to orient and locate reason both in its theoretical and practical use. The field of the supersensible is the ideal place from which the territory of experience is laid out for us. What kind of objects occupy the field of the supersensible? Kant assigns to this field the ideas of reason.[57] As the second *Critique* demonstrated, the practical legislation of reason provides only "*practical* reality" for these ideas (XIX, 175, 33). Theoretical cognition of the supersensible instead remains thoroughly impossible.

The "Abyss" Between Nature and Freedom (XIX, 175, 35–XX, 176, 9)

With the introduction of the supersensible, the domains of understanding and practical reason gain a new qualification. The domain of the concepts of nature is the "sensible," while the domain of the concept of freedom is the "supersensible" (XIX, 175, 37–176, 1). Both domains are rooted in the sensible territory of experience. Their separation is radical: between them an immense and immeasurable "abyss" lies fixed (XIX, 175, 36), which makes utterly impossible all "transi-

---

57. Note that the supersensible was assumed as a necessary "idea" that grounds the possibility of experience (XVIII/XIX, 175, 23).

tion" from the realm of nature to the realm of freedom by means of a theoretical use of reason (XIX, 175, 1–3). We know that the effects of both legislations meet in the same sensible world (XVIII, 175, 15–16) and that both legislations have to be rooted in the field of the supersensible in order to be possible (XVIII/XIX, 176, 22–24). Yet the abyss that divides the two legislations makes them appear so far apart from each other as if they belonged to two different worlds. Thereby, Kant is taking on the perspective of a human subject who—finally disposing of a map to orient herself—can locate for the very first time the abyss that divides two regions of her experience. To be sure, the presence of that gulf had been sensed already in different occasions. It is only here, however, that Kant is able to track it down for the very first time. Facing the impossibility of bridging the abyss, this subject comes to the conclusion that the two regions lay opposed to each other "as if they were two different worlds" (XX, 176, 3).[58]

The separation is an asymmetric relation that works differently if approached from the two different banks of the abyss. Kant resolutely denies that the world of nature can exercise any influence on the world of freedom (XIX, 176, 4). This would imply an extension of theoretical cognition to the supersensible. The Dialectic of the first *Critique* has proved this extension illusory; while the second *Critique*, by showing the way in which reason is practical, has further denied the possibility of any "influence" of the world of nature upon reason. The opposite influence, however, is not only possible but is emphatically presented by Kant in the form of the (practical) necessity of an "*ought to*" (XIX, 176, 4). The concept of freedom *ought to* exercise an influence over the world of nature. Freedom must see its ends actualized in the sensible world, even though it cannot prescribe laws to the *Sinnenwelt* but only raise claim to nature's accordance with freedom's own law. At this point, Kant's insistence in placing both domains on the same territory of experience and in locating the effects of their legislations in the same sensible world, reveals its necessity. Kant's present concern is not so much to underline the access that practical reason has to the supersensible but rather to stress its efficacy in the sensible realm of human experience. Kant carries this argument a step further and suggests that freedom's efficacy in the sensible world would be impossible (and impossible to think of) were nature not constituted by its own laws so as to harmonize with the ends proper to freedom's law (even though the two legislations are thoroughly independent of each other). How does the world of nature appear if considered under the condition of this necessary efficacy or influence exercised on it by freedom? Given that freedom must see the purpose assigned by its law actualized in the world of nature, nature itself, at least as far as the "*form* of its lawfulness" (XX, 176, 8) is concerned, must be thought of as compatible with the possibility for freedom to realize its purposes within it. This view opens clearly a new perspective on the consideration of nature. Thus, even if the immense abyss that separates the sensible from the supersensible world makes

58. Note here the first occurrence of an "*als . . . ob*"—"as . . . if"—construction.

any transition from nature to freedom impossible, nature must be thought of as allowing in its form an accordance (*Zusammenstimmung*) with freedom's purposes. What Kant previously hinted at as the *reciprocal hindrance* that nature and freedom exercise over each other in their effects in the sensible world, is complemented now by the possibility of a *reciprocal harmony* between them. This argument will be at the center of the Methodology of the Critique of the teleological faculty of judgment.

The "Concept" of the Supersensible: Mittelglied *and* Denkungsart *(XX, 176, 9–15)*

The impossibility of a cognitive access to the supersensible allowed Kant to maintain the necessary separation between nature's and freedom's domains, and to disclose, at the same time, the field of the supersensible as the region on which the whole territory of experience in its two domains is ultimately grounded. Now it is precisely this field that constitutes both the *unitary ground* and the "*ground for the unity*" (XX, 176, 10) underlying nature and freedom. According to Kant's topology of the cognitive faculty, the "concept" (XX, 176, 12) of this unitary ground belongs neither to the concepts of nature nor to the concept of freedom. For if it were a concept of nature, the harmony between the two legislations would be grounded on the law of the understanding, and freedom would have to follow this law—which is a contradiction (freedom would be impossible). But if the concept of the supersensible belonged to the realm of freedom, then nature itself would have to be subsumed under this law—which is also a contradiction (mechanism would be impossible). As it cannot provide any knowledge, such a concept is not legislative on a domain of its own. Hence it also does not constitute a world of its own. With this concept, Kant introduces for the first time an irreducible third term, which the preface called, problematically, the *Mittelglied* between theoretical and practical. To be sure, Kant still maintains—and even stresses—the impossibility of a "transition" from one domain to the other: no bridge can be thrown over the abyss; the ontological separation can only be reinforced. Yet what the *Critique of Judgment* starts disclosing as its own field of competence is the possibility of another type of transition. Such transition takes place on a metacritical level and allows one to rethink the map of the cognitive faculty so that the "abyss" is nothing but one of its regions. Kant's move suggests the possibility of a switch in the "way of thinking" and experiencing the gap between theoretical and practical, and with it, the supersensible. It is on the middle-ground thereby instituted that the transition "from the way of thinking [*Denkungsart*] according to the principles of nature to the way of thinking according to the principles of freedom" takes place (XX, 176, 14–15).

What Kant is looking for in this section is a way of relating the supersensible to the realm of experience, a new way—or an "extended" way—of thinking and experiencing the common ground underlying the domains of nature and freedom. The impossibility of gaining theoretical knowledge of the supersensible revealed the practical reality of freedom. Yet freedom itself belongs—at least in its effects or in our actions—to the sensible world as the only possible world of experience. The possibility of locating the supersensible on the map of the cognitive faculties as a field in its own right and not, as was still the case in the first *Critique*, as that which lays beyond the "field of experience,"[59] the possibility of seeing in the supersensible that which defines the farthest limits of experience and its ultimate ground, and finally the possibility of arguing that a "concept" of the supersensible is possible for us (although neither as a theoretical nor as a practical concept that can legislate on a domain)—these all suggest that there is a "thought-way," or "way of thinking" (*Denkungsart*), that not being confined to any particular region of this mental geography is precisely the condition that allows us to construct such a geography in the first place. This *Denkungsart* allows us if not a transition between the two separate worlds of nature and freedom at least a transition between two ways of thinking and living our human condition of beings that participate in both the sensible and the intelligible world.

There is no "common although to us unknown root" to which, "perhaps," the different branches of human cognition go back as to their origin.[60] In the third *Critique* Kant vigorously restates the claim that in the first *Critique* he played against Wolff's attempt to reduce all faculties of the soul to a metaphysical unity. The possibility of a "point of unification"[61] between the sensible and the supersensible remains theoretically unknown and necessarily unknowable to us. Yet it is possible for us to think—in a unifying and unified way—of the constitution of both the natural and the moral worlds, thereby "bringing reason into harmony with itself."[62] This possibility is disclosed by the *Denkungsart* that construes a new world of human experience in another way (i.e., not through the a priori legislation of the understanding or reason). Given the separation of the two worlds, the "ground for the unity" of the supersensible, which underlies nature and is the practical object of freedom, can have only the critical force of a new way of thinking (not the force of a law).

It is important to stress that the new field of competence proper to the third *Critique* is disclosed by the problem of the possibility of conceiving of the constitution of the world of nature as compatible with (and not simply, as the first *Cri-*

---

59. For a list of the occurrences of this expression in KrV see H. Holzhey, *Kants Erfahrungsbegriff*, op. cit., 248–249, n. 15.

60. KrVB 29/A 15; Kant will further develop this point in KU introduction §III, XXII AA, V, 177, 18–19. The passage from the first *Critique* is the starting point of M. Heidegger's Kant interpretation in *Kant und das Problem der Metaphysik* (*Kant and the Problem of Metaphysics*, trans. by R. Taft, Bloomington, Indiana University Press, 1990); for a discussion of the problem in relation to Heidegger's interpretation, see D. Henrich, "On the Unity of Subjectivity," in *The Unity of Reason: Essays on Kant's Philosophy*, Cambridge, Mass., Harvard University Press, 1994, 17–54.

61. KU § 57, 239, AA 341, 30–31.

62. KU § 57, 239, AA 341, 32–33.

tique maintained, not contradictory to) the necessity for freedom to actualize its law in it. The crucial point, however, consists in Kant's contention that the solution of this problem cannot take place along the same lines as in the previous *Critiques*. There can be only two parts of philosophy and only two types of concepts: concepts of nature and the concept of freedom. Hence the *Critique of Judgment* has to argue in a way that is hitherto unknown to critical philosophy. As already suggested, the third *Critique* is a metacritical discourse that does not address a concept analogous to the concepts of nature or freedom but rather addresses a thought-way under which, in turn, both nature and freedom become possible.

In the preface to the *Critique of Pure Reason*, Kant indicates, with the term *Denkungsart*, the realm in which "revolution" in science takes place. Revolutions in science—including the revolution brought in philosophy by the first *Critique*—are radical transformations of the *Denkart*, are transformations in the way in which science has been practiced up until that point.[63] The significance of the term is close to what Thomas Kuhn calls a scientific "paradigm." *Denkungsart* designates both the methodological structure of inquiry and the general mode, or way of proceeding in the inquiry. Moreover, *Denkungsart,* or *Denkart,* means for Kant, as for the Enlightenment in general, *Weltanschauung*; it indicates the rational approach to the world and to life proper to our common human understanding. In §40 of the *Critique of Judgment*, Kant presents the "maxims of the common human understanding" as an important integration and explanation of the principles of the critique of taste. Such maxims directly regard our *Denkungsart*. They are (i) the maxim of thinking for oneself, (i.e., the maxim of an "unprejudiced *Denkungsart*"); (ii) the maxim of thinking from the standpoint of everyone else (i.e., the maxim of a "broadened *Denkungsart*"); and (iii) the maxim of always thinking consistently (i.e., the idea of a "consistent *Denkungsart*").[64] *Denkungsart* is the capacity of employing one's own faculties in a purposive (and this means, among other things, self-conscious and significant) way.[65] In this sense, Kant's *Denkungsart* comes close to what Gregory Bateson designates as "thought-way," a term that translates *eidos* for him and expresses the very nature of a culture.[66]

3. *Synopsis: §III, On the* Critique of Judgment *as a Means to Connect the Two Parts of Philosophy into a Whole*

The third member of the first trichotomy provides the connection between the conditions for cognition that define the realm of philosophy in general (§I), and

---

63. See KrV B XI ff.: "*Revolution der Denkart*," B XVI "*Umänderung der Denkart*." The term is of relatively new introduction in the German language, since it starts being used in the second half of the eighteenth century (see J. Grimm/W. Grimm, *Deutsches Wörterbuch*, vol. 2, Leipzig, Verlag von S. Hirzel, 1860, art. "Denkart," "Denkungsart").

64. KU §40, 158 f., V, 294 f.

65. KU §40, 159, V, 295, 7.

66. G. Bateson, *Steps to an Ecology of Mind*, San Francisco, Chandler, 1972.

the new questions opened up by the conditioned that is being thought of under those conditions (§II). In §III, Kant introduces the "faculty of judgment" for the first time. This faculty is initially presented in a merely hypothetical and analogical way. Initially, the faculty of judgment parallels understanding and reason and claims a principle of its own only hypothetically. It is, however, clear from the outset that the faculty of judgment reveals a critical status that is different from both understanding and reason. The task of the second trichotomy is to provide the transcendental justification of this assumption.

The section begins with a shift from the partition of philosophy to the partition of critique and ends with a shift from the system of the "cognitive faculties"—understanding, judgment, and reason—to the system of the "faculties of the soul"—cognitive faculty, feeling of pleasure and displeasure, and faculty of desire. In Kant's view, the cognitive faculties provide the a priori principles that guide the respective faculties of the soul in their endeavors.[67] Already in the title, Kant formulates the problem that arises out of the question of the division of philosophy. Given its dualistic structure, philosophy can be constituted "to a whole" only by means of a third term that mediates between its parts, thereby connecting them into a totality. This third term, however, is not itself a doctrinal part of philosophy but can be only a third critique. Hence, while philosophy admits only two parts, critique is necessarily tripartite.

3.1. §III Commentary: Urtheilskraft *and Its Critique*

Two Doctrines But Three Critiques (XX, 176, 19–XXII, 177, 12)

Kant opens the section with the distinction between "doctrine" and "critique." He takes up again with more clarity the argument of the introduction to the *Critique of Pure Reason,* where the distinctions between "critique," "transcendental philosophy," "metaphysics," and "system of pure reason" were at stake.[68] Critique, as opposed to doctrine (or metaphysics), is merely "*propaedeutic* to the system of pure reason."[69] As "*transcendental* critique,"[70] it relates not to objects but to the possibility of our a priori cognition of them. Critique investigates the limits within which our cognitive faculty can legitimately work; it does not claim the extension of our cognition of objects beyond those limits (XX, 176, 19–22). Hence critique "has properly no domain with regard to objects" (XX, 176, 20). A critique of our cognitive faculties establishes instead the possibility of a doctrine based upon those faculties. Thereby the "field" proper to critique is marked out (XX, 176, 23–24): it

---

67. See the title of EE §II: "On the System of the Higher Cognitive Faculties *That Ground Philosophy*."

68. See KrV B 24/A 10 ff.

69. KrV B 25/A 11.

70. KrV B 26/A 12; for the distinction between "transcendental philosophy" and "critique" see B 27/A 13 f.

is a field that concerns faculties and their activity and applications, not a field *of objects*. As the *critique* of pure theoretical reason grounded the possibility of a *doctrine,* or metaphysics, of nature, the *critique* of practical reason grounded the possibility of a *doctrine,* or metaphysics, of morals.[71] Therefore, as far as the partition of philosophy in theoretical and practical is concerned, critique and doctrine correspond to each other so that a division of its critical parts, which is analogous to the division of its doctrinal parts, can be claimed.[72] However, this correspondence does not allow one to infer that critique and doctrine are coextensive so that, the partition of philosophy in theoretical and practical being complete, the critical task would also have to be declared exhausted by the correspondent two critical branches.

In the first two sections of the introduction, Kant has painstakingly drawn the partition of philosophy, the respective domains of its parts, and has shown what needs to be left out of this principal division since it cannot claim an objective domain of its own. Accordingly, the realm of the technical-practical was denied the independence of a part of philosophy in its own right (§I), while the field of the supersensible was denied the possibility of ever becoming territory for us and domain for theoretical cognition (§II). In §III Kant contends that "what cannot be included in the partition of philosophy can still have a place as a principal part in the critique of the pure cognitive faculty in general" (XX/XXI, 176, 24–27). In the conclusion of §II, Kant opened up the domain of philosophy to the field of the supersensible. The supersensible, however, as the unitary ground that underlies both nature and freedom and makes both theoretical and practical philosophy possible, falls neither under concepts of nature nor under the concept of freedom and hence belongs neither to theoretical nor to practical philosophy as an independent domain. Now Kant suggests that this field can indeed be relocated as a part—even a "principal part"—in the "critique of the pure cognitive faculty in general." In the preface, Kant indicated under the general title of "critique of pure reason" (VI, 168, 23), the task of critical philosophy as a whole. What he presently calls "critique of the pure cognitive faculty in general" corresponds to that title. There is no third doctrinal part of philosophy, but there *might be* a third critique. The only requisite for being included in the partition of critical philosophy is to contain a priori principles, which in this case, "*considered in themselves* are not suitable for either theoretical or practical use" (XXI, 176, 27–28) and yet are necessary principles. They are the only principles that can give an account of a certain territory of human experience (XXI, 177, 11–12). The task of §III is precisely to justify on this basis the possibility of a third critique.

---

71. See, for example, *Grundlegung*, BA XIII; KrV preface B XLIV reverses the relation between critique and metaphysics and presents "the metaphysics of nature as well as the metaphysics of morals as confirmation of the correctness of both the critique of speculative reason and the critique of practical reason."

72. See the end of the preface, X, 170, 23–27.

It is important to underline that Kant calls attention to principles that belong neither to theoretical nor to practical philosophy *if considered in themselves* (i.e., if taken as *isolated* from the context in which they usually occur combined with other principles). These principles can claim to belong to the "*pure*" cognitive faculty in general only as isolated. Kant has been following the procedure of isolation already when in search for pure a priori forms of sensibility in the Transcendental Aesthetic of the first *Critique*. Therein, the methodological device was to "*isolate* sensibility." This procedure was carried out through a twofold move, the first implying isolation from other sources of knowledge, the second implying the individuation of a pure component of sensibility. First, sensibility is isolated "by taking away from it everything that the understanding thinks through its concepts so that nothing may be left save empirical intuition." Secondly, sensibility is isolated by separating from it "everything that belongs to sensation, so that nothing may remain save pure intuition and the mere form of appearances, which is all that sensibility can supply a priori."[73] This reductive method was enacted again in the Transcendental Logic, where the task was to "isolate the understanding," "separating out from our knowledge that part of thought which has its origin solely in the understanding," getting thereby to "pure cognition."[74] A similar reduction was essential to Kant's notion of practical reason in the second *Critique* (XXIV, 178, 2–3). Finally, an analogous procedure guides Kant in his presentation of the third faculty, to which refer principles that are neither theoretical nor practical (XXI, 176, 27). We can also suggest that Kant's own path toward a third *Critique* has been affected by the intrinsic difficulty of isolating a faculty that, for its very nature, is an intermediary function constantly at work together with other faculties and under other principles. The possibility of a *Critique of Judgment* arises as soon as the faculty of judgment is isolated and finally considered "in itself."

"Cognitive Faculties" and "Faculties of the Soul": The Faculty of Judgment (XXII, 177, 13–XXV, 179, 15)

Kant again takes up the argument that in §§I–II led him to the partition of philosophy into theoretical and practical. Thereby, he shows that the necessity for a third part of critique must be argued for along different lines. Kant needs to broaden his consideration and call into the picture the "faculties of the soul" to which, in turn, our "cognitive faculties" must be brought back (XXII, 177, 17). Moreover, Kant's argument will no longer maintain the assertive character that was hitherto justified by the possibility of referring to the results of the two previous *Critiques*. From now on, Kant ventures into a new territory. It follows that until a transcendental justification is provided, he can raise claims only in an analogical, merely hypothetical, and provisional way. Kant invites us to participate in a searching process which is even more interesting considering that what he is

73. KrV B 35/A 21.
74. KrV B 87/A 62.

looking for is precisely the searching faculty *par excellence*.[75] Moreover, if Kant can talk of this new faculty only in an analogical way, we will soon discover that it is precisely the faculty of judgment that makes use of the peculiar instrument of analogy as its heuristic principle.[76]

Dealing only with our cognitive faculties in general, Kant has found that concepts of nature ground all theoretical philosophy and rest on the understanding's legislation, while the concept of freedom grounds all pure practical philosophy and rests on reason's legislation. These two faculties, considered in their "logical form," can be applied, as it were, to all sort of principles, whatever their origin. In addition, they establish their own legislation and hence their domain "according to the content" (XXI, 176, 33–177, 1); that is, they legislate over a world by constituting it. In this regard, they are the ultimate source of principles so that no higher legislation over them is possible. Their providing the ultimate source of legislation justifies the complete partition of philosophy into theoretical and practical.

However, the higher cognitive faculty on which this partition of philosophy is drawn does not include only understanding and reason. "In the family of the higher *Erkenntnisvermögen*" (XXI, 177, 4) there is a third cognitive faculty that functions as a "*Mittelglied*"[77] (i.e., both as a middle-term and mediating link between understanding and reason). This faculty is *Urteilskraft*—the "faculty of judgment."[78] Kant provides two arguments, both constructed "by analogy," in favor of the attribution to the faculty of judgment of an a priori principle of its own.[79] While Kant inherits the system of the higher cognitive faculties from the tradition, he sees the specific aim of a critique as that of providing the transcendental principles that justify their empirical employment.

(i) The first argument constructs an analogy between the faculty of judgment on the one hand and understanding and reason on the other on the basis of their

75. See KrV A XV for the difference between the present assumption of hypotheses as an essential methodological moment of the critical research and Kant's rejection of hypotheses as "prohibited merchandise" in science. See also KrV B 797/A 769, where Kant invokes a discipline of pure reason with regard to hypotheses. See AA, XXIV, 737, *Logik Dohna-Wundlacken*: *iudicium praevium* is that judgment that precedes the research. It is an insufficiently grounded judgment but consciously so. See KU §90, 447, AA 463.

76. See E. Garroni/H. Hohenegger, "Introduction" to I. Kant, *Critica della facoltà di giudizio*, a cura di E. Garroni, H. Hohenegger, Torino, Einaudi, 1999.

77. See in EE §III, AA, XX, 207, 24: "ein mittleres Vermögen."

78. In his philosophy Kant often refers to this traditional division of the "higher cognitive faculty"; see KrV B 169/A 130.

79. Kant's expressions are: "nach der Analogie zu vermuten" (XXI, 177, 6–7); "nach der Analogie zu urteilen" (XXII, 177, 13); "wenigstens vorläufig zu vermuten" (XXIV, 178, 12); also "so ist doch nach der Analogie zu erwarten" (EE §II, AA, XX, 202, 8–9). Compare to the passage of EE §III, AA, XX, 207, 26–208, 1, which avoids the analogical way, and more problematically formulates a supposition on the mere ground of its coming "naturally" to us: "What is more natural than to suppose . . ."

common belonging to the family of higher cognitive faculties. On the ground of their kinship, Kant suggests, one has "good reasons *to suppose, by analogy*" (XXI, 177, 6–7) that the faculty of judgment as well may contain in itself a "principle of its own" (XXI, 177, 8). However, this would be a very peculiar principle, since the realm of principles that legislates over objects has already been exhausted by understanding and reason. Hence we can be sure that judgment's own principle will not have a legislation of its own—will not legislate over the domain of a world, as do understanding and reason. If not a principle by which to *give laws*, this could be nonetheless a principle "by which to *search for laws*" (XXII, 177, 8). The faculty of judgment appears from the very outset as a *searching* faculty. Moreover, since this principle does not constitute a legislation over objects, it will be a "merely *subjective* principle a priori" (XXI, 177, 9). Finally, even if no "field *of objects*" (XXI, 177, 10) (not just no field as such) can be ascribed to judgment as a domain, it will nonetheless occupy "a territory of some kind" (XXII, 177, 11) and consequently will ground a type of experience of its own. Such a territory will be so constituted as to admit the faculty of judgment's principle—and this principle alone—as valid within its limits.

(ii) The second argument is even more relevant. Kant still argues by way of analogy with understanding and reason (XXII, 177, 13). This time, however, he places the faculty of judgment in connection with yet another, higher "order of our powers of representation" (XXII, 177, 14–16). All faculties are now brought back to those three "faculties or capacities of the soul" (XXII, 177, 17) that Kant recognizes as irreducible and original (for they cannot be further derived from a common ground).[80] In the light of the "First Introduction," in which Kant does not refrain from a polemical tone, this claim is clearly played against Leibniz's and Wolff's reduction of all faculties to the cognitive one (to the *vis repraesentativa* and to the criterion of intellectual clarity and distinction).[81] If the notion of a system of the faculties of the mind well describes one of the objectives of the

---

80. This threefold division of the faculties of the soul, mentioned in this same order, appears for the first time in Kant's letter to Reinhold, December 28, 1787.

81. For this irreducibility see the argument developed in the commentary to §II with regard to the impossibility of a transition between sensible and intelligible world (see KrV B 29/A 15). See the formulation of EE §III, AA, XX, 206, 1–5. Wolff's reduction of all faculties to the *vis repraesentativa* was formulated under the influence of Leibniz's notion of substance as representative force. Kant rejects this argument by claiming that force is not inherent to substance but to its accidents so that a simple substance, as the soul, can very well have manifold accidents. Against dogmatic metaphysics Kant does not hypostatize the "forces" or "faculties" of the soul but sees them as "functions that are dynamically actualized" (see H. Mertens, *Kommentar zur ersten Einleitung in Kants Kritik der Urteilskraft. Zur systematischen Funktion der Kritik der Urteilskraft für das System der Philosophie*, München, Berchmans Verlag, 1975, 65); see D. Henrich, "On the Unity of Subjectivity," op. cit., 20–27.

third *Critique*, Kant denies that Wolff's *reductio ad unum* could ever be the way of achieving it. In the "First Introduction," Kant elliptically refers to the most recent results of contemporary German aesthetics and psychology, which, against Wolff, already claimed the impossibility of reducing feeling to the cognitive faculty.[82] The names of Rüdiger, Crusius, Sulzer, Tetens, and Mendelssohn must be mentioned in this connection.[83]

By introducing the three original faculties of the soul, Kant shifts the focus of his argument and points to a new section of the table that concludes the introduction. This table displays the way in which, from the connection with (i) the "entire faculties of the *Gemüt*," (ii) the specifically "cognitive faculties" are able to exhibit (iii) their own "a priori principles" that legislate over those faculties of the soul in order for them (iv) to be "applied" to respective realms of objects. According to this new distribution of the "faculties of the *Gemüt*," the cognitive faculties appear as the first title only. Next to them, as middle-term and mediating link, Kant puts the "feeling of pleasure and displeasure," placing the "faculty of desire" (XXII, 177, 19–20) as the third term. In light of this new "order," the whole issue of a division of *critical* philosophy is now reconsidered.

The higher cognitive faculties do not relate to the faculties of the soul in a merely accidental way. They provide the transcendental principle of determination for the powers of the *Gemüt*. Understanding provides the principle for the cognitive faculty, as does reason for the appetitive faculty. Among the cognitive faculties, the understanding alone is capable of a priori legislation. Only the inquiry of the first *Critique*, which isolates this faculty from its mingling with the faculty of desire, is able to discover how understanding can be the source of a priori theoretical cognition when referred to nature taken as appearance. We can legislate over appearances only through the understanding's pure a priori concepts that gain the validity of laws for nature. With regard to the faculty of desire, the second *Critique* already opposed the traditional Wolffian distinction between a lower and a higher *facultas appetitiva* (XXV, 178, 15–179, 1).[84] According to Kant, only reason, being the source of the concept of freedom, can be considered the "higher" faculty of desire, capable of a legislation of its own. Finally, the introduction of the feeling of pleasure and displeasure placed "between" (XXIV, 178, 9) the cognitive faculty and the faculty of desire allows Kant to explain in what sense we must "suppose, at least provisionally" (XXIV, 177, 19–20), that judgment may work as a mediating faculty between understanding and reason with its

82. See EE §III, AA, XX, 206, 7–8: the task of "bringing unity in this multiplicity of faculties is futile."

83. The importance of Crusius is stressed by D. Henrich, *On the Unity of Subjectivity*, op. cit.; see also H. Heimsoeth, "Metaphysik und Kritik bei Ch. A. Crusius," in *Studien zur Philosophie Immanuel Kants: Metaphysische Ursprünge und ontologische Grundlagen*, Köln, Kölner Universitätsverlag, 1956, 125–188.

84. See chapter 3 above.

own a priori principle. Such principle, according to the analogy, will be the *somehow* legislative principle for the feeling of pleasure and displeasure. How then is this mediating connection established?

Kant draws a parallel between judgment's function within the family of the cognitive faculties and its function within the higher order of the faculties of the soul. With regard to the first connection, the *Critique of Pure Reason* showed how the "logical use" of the faculty of judgment mediates between understanding and reason thereby producing a "transition" between them (XXV, 179, 4–5). Already "general logic is constructed upon a ground-plan that exactly coincides with the partition of the higher cognitive faculties. These are *understanding, judgment, and reason*,"[85] observed Kant at the beginning of the Analytic of Principles. Transcendental logic differs from general logic insofar as it does not take those faculties in their merely formal use but refers them to a determinate content. Accordingly, the use of reason does not belong to the Analytic and to transcendental logic as "logic of truth." Since it generates a "logic of illusion," it belongs to the Dialectic.[86] For Kant's present purposes, however, the Analytic of Principles or Transcendental Doctrine of Judgment can still be said to occupy the middle ground between the Analytic of the Concepts and the Transcendental Dialectic and hence to produce a transition between understanding and reason. Moreover, and even more significantly, the faculty of judgment builds a bridge from the theoretical legislation of the understanding to which it can be said to belong, to reason, which is responsible for the only possible practical legislation.

What is the role of the faculty of judgment within the "order" that includes the cognitive faculties, the feeling of pleasure and displeasure, and the faculty of desire? The faculty of judgment builds a bridge from the side of practical reason, to which it also somehow belongs. For "pleasure and displeasure is necessarily connected to the faculty of desire" (XXIV/XXV, 178, 14–15).[87] Against the tradition of eudaimonism, the *Critique of Practical Reason* has shown that this connection can take place in two ways. Not only can pleasure and displeasure be the ground of the determination of the will, in which case we only have the lower faculty of desire, which is merely empirical and thoroughly unable to legislate. Kant demonstrated that when pure practical reason immediately determines the will through the moral law a peculiar feeling of pleasure arises as a consequence. This is the crucial connection between the faculty of desire and the feeling of pleasure and displeasure. It is in this connection, that the faculty of judgment and its alleged principle can be said to effect the "transition from the pure cognitive faculty, i.e., from the domain of the concepts of nature, to the domain of the concept of freedom" (XXV, 179, 2–4). For the feeling of pleasure that follows from the will's

85. KrV B 169/A 130.

86. KrV B 170 f./A 131 f.

87. See the whole connection displayed: the cognitive faculty is *vermischt* with the faculty of desire, the faculty of desire is *verbunden* with pleasure (are we allowed the conclusion, hence pleasure is *somehow* connected with the cognitive faculty?).

determination through the moral law mediates between our sensible and our noumenal existence and hence between the world of nature and the world of freedom. It is already clear that the faculty of judgment, because of its mediating role, does not operate as a static structure but has rather a highly dynamic function.

It is apparent that what Kant's analogical and provisional argument has yet to prove is precisely the *crucial connection between faculty of judgment and feeling of pleasure and displeasure*. How do the two middle terms of the two different orders (or titles of the final table) relate to each other? At least for now, the introduction of a third faculty (not simply as *Mittelglied* but as *Verbindungsmittel,* §III, title) to make the transition between the domain of the concepts of nature and the domain of the concept of freedom, is considered sufficient to draw a conclusion. Even if philosophy can have *two* parts only, namely theoretical and practical (§I) (for "all we may have to say of the faculty of judgment's own principles must be ascribed to the theoretical part of philosophy," XXV, 179, 6–9), the "critique of pure reason" consists of *three* parts: "the critique of pure understanding, of pure judgment, and of pure reason" (XXV, 179, 12–14). Such a tripartite critique is in turn necessary in order to assess the possibility of the "system" of philosophy (XXV, 179, 11).

Kant's concluding line in this section seems to advance a step further. He makes an important claim with regard to the alleged principle of the faculty of judgment. Kant clarifies that the critique takes its respective faculties each time as "pure" indicating in this way the fact that "they legislate a priori" (XXV, 179, 14–15). To be sure, what has hitherto been suggested about the faculty of judgment's relation to law is only that it cannot possibly be the function of *giving* law, as was the case for understanding and reason, but it may rather be the function of *searching* for a law (XXI, 177, 7–8). Now Kant discloses that a legislation for judgment is *somehow* possible, as the faculty of judgment can be indeed isolated and taken for itself as *pure* in its own principle. This claim leads to the topic of the first member of the second trichotomy: "IV. On the Faculty of Judgment as a Faculty that Legislates A Priori."

The Faculties of the Soul: Psychology and Transcendental Philosophy

Kant inherits the notion of a tripartite system of all the *Gemüt* faculties from the rational psychology of contemporary German scholasticism.[88] However, here as in other occurrences, he distances himself radically from that tradition. Kant's account of the three original and irreducible "faculties or capacities of the soul"—the cognitive faculty, the feeling of pleasure and displeasure, and the faculty of desire—is followed by a long footnote[89] in which he defends, once again, the treatment that a central topic both of empirical and rational psychology and of

---

88. See M. Dessoir, *Geschichte der neueren deutschen Psychologie*, Berlin, Duncker, 1902. See also the discussion in relation to the "First Introduction," in H. Mertens, *Kommentar zur ersten Einleitung*, op. cit., 63 ff.

89. This footnote is added in B.

traditional practical philosophy must receive in transcendental philosophy. Kant's project is to bring those faculties, which are empirically given in consciousness, back to their transcendental conditions. The task is to find the transcendental a priori principle that legislates over those faculties and thereby guarantees their universal validity and necessity.

Kant's claim in this footnote corresponds to the openly polemical argument developed in §III of the "First Introduction." In our section, Kant explicitly refers to the preface of the *Critique of Practical Reason,* where a contested definition of the faculty of desire is discussed.[90] The faculty of desire is the "capacity of being the cause of the actuality of the objects of one's representations through these very representations." Kant suggests that for those concepts that relate to a pure cognitive faculty a priori, because of their being susceptible to employment as empirical principles as well, a "transcendental definition" through "pure categories" is in order. One needs to distinguish the pure use of a concept from the empirical (i.e., psychological and "anthropological-teleological," XXIV, 178, 33–34) questions that it raises. One needs to distinguish when a concept is referred to a transcendental faculty as opposed to being merely borrowed from psychology.

Moreover, Kant's aim is to establish the difference in kind that divides three types of "representations": those that refer respectively to the cognitive faculty, to the faculty of desire, and to the feeling of pleasure and displeasure.[91] In the footnote to §III, Kant discusses the relation between the "causality" exercised by our representations and their objects. At stake is the way in which the faculty of desire on the one hand, and empirical affections on the other, can exercise this causality (i.e., can make objects actual or real). While the cognitive faculty and the faculty of desire relate their representations to and exercise their causality over objects, *the feeling of pleasure refers only to the subject.* In the *Critique of Practical Reason* the issue is the relation between faculty of desire and feeling of pleasure and displeasure (i.e., the very possibility for pure reason to be practical) so that pleasure is conceived as the effect, not the cause of the determination of the will. At stake in the third *Critique* is precisely the other side of the same problem, namely on the one hand the possibility for the feeling of pleasure to have its own a priori principle independently of the relation both with practical and theoretical reason and, on the other hand, the possibility for the feeling of pleasure to be connected to the other faculties according to an a priori principle and not on merely empirical grounds. It is only under these conditions that a "system" of the faculties and hence the "idea of philosophy as a system" becomes possible.[92]

---

90. KpV A 16.
91. EE §III, AA, XX, 206, 8–17.
92 . EE §III, AA, XX, 207, 16–17.

IV. Von der Urteilskraft, als einem a priori gesetzgebenden Vermögen

Urteilskraft überhaupt ist das Vermögen, das Besondere als enthalten unter dem Allgemeinen zu denken. | XXVI Ist das Allgemeine (die Regel, das Prinzip, das Gesetz) gegeben, so ist die Urteilskraft, welche das Besondere darunter subsumiert (auch, wenn sie, als transzendentale Urteilskraft, a priori die Bedingungen angibt, welchen gemäß allein unter jenem Allgemeinen subsumiert werden kann) *bestimmend*. Ist aber nur das Besondere gegeben, wozu sie das Allgemeine finden soll, so ist die Urteilskraft bloß *reflektierend*.

Die bestimmende Urteilskraft unter allgemeinen transzendentalen Gesetzen, die der Verstand gibt, ist nur subsumierend; das Gesetz ist ihr a priori vorgezeichnet, und sie hat also nicht nötig, für sich selbst auf ein Gesetz zu denken, um das Besondere in der Natur dem Allgemeinen unterordnen zu können. Allein es sind so mannigfaltige Formen der Natur, gleichsam so viele Modifikationen der allgemeinen transzendentalen Naturbegriffe, die durch jene Gesetze, welche der reine Verstand a priori gibt, weil dieselben nur auf die Möglichkeit einer Natur (als Gegenstandes der Sinne) überhaupt
AA180 gehen, unbestimmt gelassen werden, daß dafür doch || auch Gesetze sein müssen, die zwar, als empirische, nach *unserer* Verstandeseinsicht zufällig sein mögen, die aber doch, wenn sie Gesetze heißen sollen (wie es auch der Begriff einer Natur erfordert) aus einem, wenngleich uns unbekannten, Prinzip der Einheit des Mannigfaltigen, als notwendig angesehen werden müssen.— Die reflektierende Urteilskraft, die von dem Besondern in der | XXVII Natur zum Allgemeinen aufzusteigen die Obliegenheit hat, bedarf also eines Prinzips, welches sie nicht von der Erfahrung entlehnen kann, weil es eben die Einheit aller empirischen Prinzipien unter gleichfalls empirischen, aber höheren Prinzipien, und also die Möglichkeit der systematischen Unterordnung derselben unter einander, begründen soll. Ein solches transzendentales Prinzip kann also die reflektierende Urteilskraft sich nur selbst als Gesetz geben, nicht anderwärts hernehmen (weil sie sonst bestimmende Urteilskraft sein würde), noch der Natur vorschreiben; weil die Reflexion über die Gesetze der Natur sich nach der Natur, und diese sich nicht nach den Bedingungen richtet, nach welchen wir einen in Ansehung dieser ganz zufälligen Begriff von ihr zu erwerben trachten.

Chapter 7

Introduction §§IV–VI: Reflective Faculty of Judgment and Formal Purposiveness of Nature

Text

IV. On the Faculty of Judgment as a Faculty that Legislates A Priori

The faculty of judgment in general is the faculty of thinking the particular as contained under the universal. XXVI If the universal (the rule, principle, law) is given, then the faculty of judgment which subsumes the particular under it is *determinant* (even though, as transcendental faculty of judgment, it provides a priori the conditions in conformity with which alone the subsumption under that universal can take place). If, however, only the particular is given for which judgment must find the universal, then the faculty of judgment is merely *reflective*.

The determinant faculty of judgment, which operates under the universal transcendental laws given by the understanding, is subsumptive only. Since the law is marked out for it a priori, the faculty of judgment has no need to think for itself of a law that allows it to subordinate the particular in nature to the universal.—But there are such manifold forms of nature, so many modifications as it were of the universal transcendental concepts of nature left indeterminate by those laws given a priori by the understanding since those laws concern only the possibility of a nature (as object of sense) in general—that there must be also laws for this manifold of forms and modifications. Since these laws are empirical, they may indeed be contingent as far as *our* understanding can see; and yet, if they are to be called laws (as the concept of a nature does require), then they must be considered as necessary on the ground of a principle of the unity of the manifold, although this principle is unknown to us.—The reflective faculty of judgment, which has the obligation of ascending from the particular in XXVII nature to the universal, stands, therefore, in need of a principle that it cannot borrow from experience precisely because it must ground the unity of all empirical principles under likewise empirical, but higher, principles and hence must ground the possibility of the systematic subordination of those principles to one another. Therefore, the reflective faculty of judgment can give only to itself this transcendental principle as law; it cannot take it from somewhere else (otherwise it would be determinant faculty of judgment) nor can it prescribe this principle to nature, because our reflection on the laws of nature depends on nature, not nature on the conditions according to which we try to obtain a concept of nature that is quite contingent with respect to those conditions.

Nun kann dieses Prinzip kein anderes sein, als: daß, da allgemeine Naturgesetze ihren Grund in unserem Verstande haben, der sie der Natur (obzwar nur nach dem allgemeinen Begriffe von ihr als Natur) vorschreibt, die besondern, empirischen Gesetze in Ansehung dessen, was in ihnen durch jene unbestimmt gelassen ist, nach einer solchen Einheit betrachtet werden müssen, als ob gleichfalls ein Verstand (wenngleich nicht der unsrige) sie zum Behuf unserer Erkenntnisvermögen, um ein System der Erfahrung nach besonderen Naturgesetzen möglich zu machen, gegeben hätte. Nicht, als wenn auf diese Art wirklich ein solcher Verstand angenommen werden müßte (denn es ist nur die reflektierende Urteilskraft, der diese | XXVIII Idee zum Prinzip dient, zum Reflektieren, nicht zum Bestimmen); sondern dieses Vermögen gibt sich dadurch nur selbst, und nicht der Natur, ein Gesetz.

Weil nun der Begriff von einem Objekt, sofern er zugleich den Grund der Wirklichkeit dieses Objekts enthält, der *Zweck* und die Übereinstimmung eines Dinges mit derjenigen Beschaffenheit der Dinge, die nur nach Zwecken möglich ist, die *Zweckmäßigkeit* der Form desselben heißt: so ist das Prinzip der Urteilskraft, in Ansehung der Form der Dinge der Natur unter empirischen Gesetzen überhaupt, die *Zweckmäßigkeit der Natur* in ihrer Mannigfaltigkeit.
AA181 D. i. die Natur wird durch diesen Be||griff so vorgestellt, als ob ein Verstand den Grund der Einheit des Mannigfaltigen ihrer empirischen Gesetze enthalte.

Die Zweckmäßigkeit der Natur ist also ein besonderer Begriff a priori, der lediglich in der reflektierenden Urteilskraft seinen Ursprung hat. Denn den Naturprodukten kann man so etwas, als Beziehung der Natur an ihnen auf Zwecke, nicht beilegen, sondern diesen Begriff nur brauchen, um über sie in Ansehung der Verknüpfung der Erscheinungen in ihr, die nach empirischen Gesetzen gegeben ist, zu reflektieren. Auch ist dieser Begriff von der praktischen Zweckmäßigkeit (der menschlichen Kunst oder auch der Sitten) ganz unterschieden, ob er zwar nach einer Analogie mit derselben gedacht wird.

V. Das Prinzip der formalen Zweckmäßigkeit der Natur ist ein transzendentales Prinzip der Urteilskraft

Ein transzendentales Prinzip ist dasjenige, durch welches die allgemeine Bedingung a priori vorgestellt wird, unter der allein Dinge Objekte unserer Erkenntnis überhaupt werden können. Dagegen heißt ein Prinzip metaphysisch, wenn es die Bedingung a priori vorstellt, unter der allein Objekte, deren Begriff empirisch gegeben sein muß, a priori weiter bestimmet werden können. So ist das Prinzip der Erkenntnis der Körper, als Substanzen und als veränderlicher Substanzen, transzendental, wenn dadurch gesagt wird, daß ihre Veränderung eine Ursache haben müsse; es ist aber metaphysisch, wenn dadurch gesagt wird, ihre Veränderung müsse eine *äußere* Ursache haben: weil im ersteren Falle der Körper nur durch ontologische Prädikate (reine Verstandesbegriffe), z. B. als Substanz, gedacht werden darf, um den Satz a priori zu erkennen; im zweiten aber der empirische Begriff eines Körpers (als eines beweglichen Dinges im Raum) diesem Satze zum Grunde gelegt werden

Now this principle can be no other than the following: since universal laws of nature have their foundation in our understanding, which prescribes them to nature (though only according to its universal concept as a nature), the particular empirical laws, as regards what is left undetermined in them by those universal laws, must be considered according to such a unity as they would have if an understanding (even though not ours) had given them also to the advantage of our cognitive faculties, so as to make possible a system of experience according to particular laws. This does not mean that such an understanding must be actually assumed (for this idea XXVIII serves as a principle only to the reflective faculty of judgment in order to reflect, not to determine); rather, in this way, this faculty gives a law only to itself, and not to nature.

Now, the concept of an object insofar as it contains, at the same time, the ground for the actuality of this object, is called *purpose*, and the accordance of a thing with that constitution of things that is possible only through purposes is called the *purposiveness* of its form. Accordingly, the principle of the faculty of judgment with respect to the form that things of nature have under empirical laws in general is the *purposiveness of nature* in its manifold. In other words, this concept represents nature as if an understanding contained the ground for the unity of the manifold of its empirical laws.

Hence the purposiveness of nature is a special concept a priori that has its origin exclusively in the reflective faculty of judgment. For we cannot ascribe to natural products anything like nature's relation to purposes in them; rather, we can only use this concept in order to reflect on nature as regards the connection of appearances in it—a connection that is given according to empirical laws. This concept is also quite different from practical purposiveness (proper to human art or also to morals), even though we do think of it by analogy with practical purposiveness.

XXIX V. The Principle of Formal Purposiveness of Nature Is a Transcendental Principle of the Faculty of Judgment

A transcendental principle is one by which we represent the universal a priori condition under which alone things can become objects of our cognition in general. On the other hand, a principle is called metaphysical if it represents the a priori condition under which alone objects, whose concept must be given empirically, can be further determined a priori. Thus, the principle of our cognition of bodies as substances and as changeable substances is transcendental if it says that change in bodies must have a cause; but it is a metaphysical principle if it says that their change must have an *external* cause. For, in the first case, the body needs only to be thought through ontological predicates (pure concepts of the understanding), e.g., as substance, in order for us to know a priori the proposition, but in the second case, the empirical concept of a body (as a movable thing in space) must ground this proposition, although after this it can be seen entirely a muß, alsdann aber, daß dem Körper das letztere Prädikat (der Bewegung nur durch äußere Ursache) zukomme, völlig a priori eingesehen werden kann.—So ist, wie ich sogleich zeigen werde, das Prinzip der | XXX Zweckmäßigkeit der Natur (in der Mannigfaltigkeit ihrer empirischen Gesetze) ein transzendentales Prinzip. Denn der Begriff von den Objekten, sofern sie als unter diesem Prinzip stehend gedacht werden, ist nur der reine Begriff AA182 von Gegenständen des möglichen Erfahrungserkennt||nisses überhaupt, und enthält nichts Empirisches. Dagegen wäre das Prinzip der praktischen Zweckmäßigkeit, die in der Idee der *Bestimmung* eines freien *Willens* gedacht werden muß, ein metaphysisches Prinzip; weil der Begriff eines Begehrungsvermögens als eines Willens doch empirisch gegeben werden muß (nicht zu den transzendentalen Prädikaten gehört). Beide Prinzipien aber sind dennoch nicht empirisch, sondern Prinzipien a priori: weil es zur Verbindung des Prädikats mit dem empirischen Begriffe des Subjekts ihrer Urteile keiner weiteren Erfahrung bedarf, sondern jene völlig a priori eingesehen werden kann.

Daß der Begriff einer Zweckmäßigkeit der Natur zu den transzendentalen Prinzipien gehöre, kann man aus den Maximen der Urteilskraft, die der Nachforschung der Natur a priori zum Grunde gelegt werden, und die dennoch auf nichts, als die Möglichkeit der Erfahrung, mithin der Erkenntnis der Natur, aber nicht bloß als Natur überhaupt, sondern als durch eine Mannigfaltigkeit besonderer Gesetze bestimmten Natur, gehen, hinreichend ersehen. —Sie kommen, als Sentenzen der metaphysischen Weisheit, bei Gelegenheit mancher Re | XXXI geln, deren Notwendigkeit man nicht aus Begriffen dartun kann, im Laufe dieser Wissenschaft oft genug, aber nur zerstreut vor. "Die Natur nimmt den kürzesten Weg (*lex parsimoniae*); sie tut gleichwohl keinen Sprung, weder in der Folge ihrer Veränderungen, noch der Zusammenstellung spezifisch verschiedener Formen (*lex continui in natura*); ihre große Mannigfaltigkeit in empirischen Gesetzen ist gleichwohl Einheit unter wenigen Prinzipien (*principia praeter necessitatem non sunt multiplicanda*);" u. dgl. m.

Wenn man aber von diesen Grundsätzen den Ursprung anzugeben denkt, und es auf dem psychologischen Wege versucht, so ist dies dem Sinne derselben gänzlich zuwider. Denn sie sagen nicht, was geschieht, d. i. nach welcher Regel unsere Erkenntniskräfte ihr Spiel wirklich treiben, und wie geurteilt wird, sondern wie geurteilt werden soll; und da kommt diese logische objektive Notwendigkeit nicht heraus, wenn die Prinzipien bloß empirisch sind. Also ist die Zweckmäßigkeit der Natur für unsere Erkenntnisvermögen und ihren Gebrauch, welche offenbar aus ihnen hervorleuchtet, ein transzendentales Prinzip der Urteile und bedarf also auch einer transzendentalen Deduktion, vermittelst deren der Grund so zu urteilen in den Erkenntnisquellen a priori aufgesucht werden muß.

AA183 Wir finden nämlich in den Gründen der Möglichkeit einer Er||fahrung zuerst freilich etwas Notwendiges, | XXXII nämlich die allgemeinen Gesetze, ohne welche Natur überhaupt (als Gegenstand der Sinne) nicht gedacht werden kann; und diese beruhen auf den Kategorien, angewandt auf die formalen Bedingungen aller uns möglichen Anschauung, sofern sie gleichfalls a priori gegeben ist. Unter diesen Gesetzen nun ist die Urteilskraft bestimmend; denn priori that the latter predicate (of motion only through an external cause) applies to the body.—Accordingly, as I shall presently show, the principle of the XXX purposiveness of nature (in the manifold of its empirical laws) is a transcendental principle. For the concept of objects [*Objekte*], insofar as they are thought as subject to this principle, is only the pure concept of the objects [*Gegenstände*] of our possible knowledge through experience in general and contains nothing empirical. On the other hand, the principle of practical purposiveness that must be thought in the idea of the *determination* of a free *will*, would be a metaphysical principle because the concept of a faculty of desire considered as a will does indeed have to be given empirically (it does not belong to the transcendental predicates). Still, both principles are nonetheless not empirical but a priori because the conjunction of the predicate with the empirical concept of the subject of their judgments does not need any other experience but can be seen completely a priori.

It is sufficiently evident from the maxims of the faculty of judgment that the concept of a purposiveness of nature belongs to the transcendental principles. Such maxims are laid as an a priori ground for our investigation of nature, and yet they regard nothing else but the possibility of experience and hence of cognition of nature—but nature considered not merely as nature in general, but rather as nature determined through a manifold of particular laws.—These maxims occur as pronouncements of metaphysical wisdom frequently enough—although only sporadically—in the course of this science, in occasion of certain XXXI rules whose necessity cannot be demonstrated from concepts. "Nature takes the shortest way (*lex parsimoniae*); yet it makes no leap, either in the sequence of its changes or in the juxtaposition of specifically different forms (*lex continui in natura*); its great variety in empirical laws is nonetheless a unity under few principles (*principia praeter necessitatem non sunt multiplicanda*);" and so forth.

But if we think of indicating the origin of these principles and attempt to do so in a psychological way, then we go completely against their meaning. For they do not say what happens, i.e., according to what rules our cognitive powers actually play their role, and how we judge; they rather say how we ought to judge; and we cannot obtain this logical objective necessity if the principles are merely empirical. Therefore, the purposiveness of nature for our cognitive faculties and their use, which manifestly shines forth from those principles, is a transcendental principle of judgments, and hence it too needs a transcendental deduction, by means of which the ground for such judging must be found a priori in the sources of cognition.

In the grounds of the possibility of experience we find admittedly, in the first place, something necessary, XXXII namely the universal laws without which nature in general (as object of sense) cannot be thought, and these laws rest on the categories applied to the formal conditions of all intuition that is possible to us insofar as this intuition is likewise given a priori. Now, under these laws the faculty of judgment is determinant; for all it has to do is

sie hat nichts zu tun, als unter gegebenen Gesetzen zu subsumieren. Z. B. der Verstand sagt: Alle Veränderung hat ihre Ursache (allgemeines Naturgesetz); die transzendentale Urteilskraft hat nun nichts weiter zu tun, als die Bedingung der Subsumtion unter dem vorgelegten Verstandesbegriff a priori anzugeben: und das ist die Sukzession der Bestimmungen eines und desselben Dinges. Für die Natur nun überhaupt (als Gegenstand möglicher Erfahrung) wird jenes Gesetz als schlechterdings notwendig erkannt.—Nun sind aber die Gegenstände der empirischen Erkenntnis, außer jener formalen Zeitbedingung, noch auf mancherlei Art bestimmt, oder, so viel man a priori urteilen kann, bestimmbar, so daß spezifisch-verschiedene Naturen, außer dem, was sie, als zur Natur überhaupt gehörig, gemein haben, noch auf unendlich mannigfaltige Weise Ursachen sein können; und eine jede dieser Arten muß (nach dem Begriffe einer Ursache überhaupt) ihre Regel haben, die Gesetz ist, mithin Notwendigkeit bei sich führt: ob wir gleich nach der Beschaffenheit und den Schranken unserer Erkenntnisvermögen diese Notwendigkeit gar | XXXIII nicht einsehen. Also müssen wir in der Natur, in Ansehung ihrer bloß empirischen Gesetze, eine Möglichkeit unendlich mannigfaltiger empirischer Gesetze denken, die für unsere Einsicht dennoch zufällig sind (a priori nicht erkannt werden können); und in deren Ansehung beurteilen wir die Natureinheit nach empirischen Gesetzen, und die Möglichkeit der Einheit der Erfahrung (als Systems nach empirischen Gesetzen), als zufällig. Weil aber doch eine solche Einheit notwendig vorausgesetzt und angenommen werden muß, da sonst kein durchgängiger Zusammenhang empirischer Erkenntnisse zu einem Ganzen der Erfahrung stattfinden würde, indem die allgemeinen Naturgesetze zwar einen solchen Zusammenhang unter den Dingen ihrer Gattung nach, als Naturdinge überhaupt, aber nicht spezifisch, als solche besondere Naturwesen, an die Hand geben: so muß die Urteilskraft für ihren eigenen Gebrauch es als Prinzip a priori annehmen, daß das für die menschliche Einsicht Zufällige in den besonderen (empirischen) Naturgesetzen dennoch eine, für uns zwar nicht
AA184 zu ergründende aber doch || denkbare, gesetzliche Einheit, in der Verbindung ihres Mannigfaltigen zu einer an sich möglichen Erfahrung, enthalte. Folglich, weil die gesetzliche Einheit in einer Verbindung, die wir zwar einer notwendigen Absicht (einem Bedürfnis) des Verstandes gemäß, aber zugleich doch als an sich zufällig Erkennen, als Zweckmäßigkeit der Objekte (hier der | XXXIV Natur) vorgestellt wird: so muß die Urteilskraft, die, in Ansehung der Dinge unter möglichen (noch zu entdeckenden) empirischen Gesetzen, bloß reflektierend ist, die Natur in Ansehung der letzteren nach einem *Prinzip der Zweckmäßigkeit* für unser Erkenntnisvermögen denken, welches dann in obigen Maximen der Urteilskraft ausgedrückt wird. Dieser transzendentale Begriff einer Zweckmäßigkeit der Natur ist nun weder ein Naturbegriff, noch ein Freiheitsbegriff, weil er gar nichts dem Objekte (der Natur) beilegt, sondern nur die einzige Art, wie wir in der Reflexion über die Gegenstände der Natur in Absicht auf eine durchgängig zusammenhängende Erfahrung verfahren müssen, vorstellt, folglich ein subjektives Prinzip (Maxime) der

to subsume under given laws. For example, the understanding says: All change has its cause (universal law of nature); now the transcendental faculty of judgment has nothing else to do but to provide a priori the condition of the subsumption under the concept of the understanding that is at hand. This condition is the succession of the determinations of one and the same thing. Now for nature in general (as object of possible experience) that law is cognized as absolutely necessary.—But besides that formal condition of time, objects of empirical cognition are further determined in a multiplicity of ways or, as far as we can judge a priori, are determinable in a multiplicity of ways so that specifically different natures, apart from what they have in common as belonging to nature in general, can still be causes in an infinite variety of ways. Each of these ways must (in accordance with the concept of a cause in general) have its rule, and this rule is a law that consequently carries necessity with itself, even though we are thoroughly XXXIII unable to see this necessity because of the constitution and limits of our cognitive faculties. Hence we must think in nature, as regards its merely empirical laws, a possibility of an infinite multiplicity of empirical laws that are nonetheless contingent (cannot be known a priori) as far as our insight goes, and in respect to this possibility we judge the unity of nature according to empirical laws, as well as the possibility of the unity of experience (as system according to empirical laws) to be contingent. Yet, such a unity must necessarily be presupposed and assumed; otherwise there would not be a thoroughgoing interconnection of our empirical cognitions into a whole of experience; for the universal laws of nature provide indeed such a connection among things taken in their genus as things of nature in general but not amongst things taken in their specificity as the particular natural beings that they are. Hence the faculty of judgment must assume as an a priori principle for its own use that what to human insight is contingent in the particular (empirical) laws of nature does nonetheless contain a lawful unity—unfathomable, although still thinkable for us—in the connection of its manifold into an experience that is in itself possible. Consequently, since the lawful unity in a conjunction that we cognize as in accordance with a necessary aim (a need) of the understanding and yet, at the same time, as contingent in itself, is represented as purposiveness of the objects (here: of XXXIV nature), so the faculty of judgment, which as regards things under possible (still to be discovered) empirical laws is merely reflective, must think of nature as regards these laws according to a *principle of purposiveness* for our cognitive faculty; this principle is then expressed in the above mentioned maxims of the faculty of judgment. Now, this transcendental concept of a purposiveness of nature is neither a concept of nature nor a concept of freedom, for it attributes nothing whatsoever to the object [*Objekt*] (of nature). This transcendental concept represents only the unique way in which we must proceed in our reflection on the objects [*Gegenstände*] of nature, if our aim is a thoroughgoing interconnected experience. Therefore, it is a subjective principle (maxim) of the faculty of judgment. This explains

Urteilskraft; daher wir auch, gleich als ob es ein glücklicher unsre Absicht begünstigender Zufall wäre, erfreuet (eigentlich eines Bedürfnisses entledigt) werden, wenn wir eine solche systematische Einheit unter bloß empirischen Gesetzen antreffen: ob wir gleich notwendig annehmen mußten, es sei eine solche Einheit, ohne daß wir sie doch einzusehen und zu beweisen vermochten.

Um sich von der Richtigkeit dieser Deduktion des vorliegenden Begriffs, und der Notwendigkeit, ihn als transzendentales Erkenntnisprinzip anzunehmen, zu überzeugen, bedenke man nur die Größe der Aufgabe: aus gegebenen Wahrnehmungen einer allenfalls unendliche Mannigfaltigkeit empirischer Gesetze enthaltenden | XXXV Natur eine zusammenhängende Erfahrung zu machen, welche Aufgabe a priori in unserm Verstande liegt. Der Verstand ist zwar a priori im Besitze allgemeiner Gesetze der Natur, ohne welche sie gar kein Gegenstand einer Erfahrung sein könnte: aber er bedarf doch auch überdem noch einer gewissen Ordnung der Natur, in den besonderen Regeln derselben, die ihm nur empirisch bekannt werden können, und die in Ansehung seiner zufällig sind. Diese Regeln, ohne welche kein Fortgang von der allgemeinen Analogie einer möglichen Erfahrung überhaupt zur besonderen stattfinden würde, muß er sich als Gesetze (d. i. als notwendig) denken: weil sie sonst keine Naturordnung ausmachen würden, ob er gleich ihre Notwendigkeit nicht erkennt, oder jemals einsehen könnte. Ob er also
AA185 gleich in Ansehung der||selben (Objekte) a priori nichts bestimmen kann, so muß er doch, um diesen empirischen sogenannten Gesetzen nachzugehen, ein Prinzip a priori, daß nämlich nach ihnen eine erkennbare Ordnung der Natur möglich sei, aller Reflexion über dieselbe zum Grunde legen, dergleichen Prinzip nachfolgende Sätze ausdrücken: daß es in ihr eine für uns faßliche Unterordnung von Gattungen und Arten gebe; daß jene sich einander wiederum nach einem gemeinschaftlichen Prinzip nähern, damit ein Übergang von einer zu der anderen, und dadurch zu einer höheren Gattung möglich sei; daß, da für die spezifische Verschiedenheit der Naturwirkungen ebensoviel verschiedene Arten der | XXXVI Kausalität annehmen zu müssen, unserem Verstande anfänglich unvermeidlich scheint, sie dennoch unter einer geringen Zahl von Prinzipien stehen mögen, mit deren Aufsuchung wir uns zu beschäftigen haben, usw. Diese Zusammenstimmung der Natur zu unserem Erkenntnisvermögen wird von der Urteilskraft, zum Behuf ihrer Reflexion über dieselbe, nach ihren empirischen Gesetzen, a priori vorausgesetzt; indem sie der Verstand zugleich objektiv als zufällig anerkennt, und bloß die Urteilskraft sie der Natur als transzendentale Zweckmäßigkeit (in Beziehung auf das Erkenntnisvermögen des Subjekts) beilegt: weil wir ohne diese vorauszusetzen, keine Ordnung der Natur nach empirischen Gesetzen, mithin keinen Leitfaden für eine mit diesen nach aller ihrer Mannigfaltigkeitanzustellende Erfahrung und Nachforschung derselben haben würden.

Denn es läßt sich wohl denken: daß, ungeachtet aller der Gleichförmigkeit der Naturdinge nach den allgemeinen Gesetzen, ohne welche die Form eines Erfahrungserkenntnisses überhaupt gar nicht stattfinden würde, die spezifische Verschiedenheit der empirischen Gesetze der Natur, samt ihren Wirkungen, why we also rejoice (actually we are relieved of a need) just as if it were a lucky chance that favors our intentions when we meet such a systematic unity under merely empirical laws: although we necessarily had to assume that there is such unity even though we have no insight into it and cannot prove it.

In order to convince ourselves of the correctness of this deduction of the concept in question and of the necessity of assuming it as a transcendental principle of cognition, we need only consider the magnitude of the task: we have to constitute an interconnected experience out of given perceptions of a XXXV nature containing a perhaps infinite multiplicity of empirical laws. This task lies a priori in our understanding. The understanding is, no doubt, a priori in possession of universal laws of nature, without which nature could not become an object of experience at all. Yet, in addition to these universal laws, the understanding needs also a certain order of nature in its particular rules, which the understanding can come to know only empirically and are, as far as this is concerned, contingent. Since without these rules no advancement from the universal analogy of a possible experience in general to a particular one would take place, the understanding must think of those rules as laws (i.e., as necessary) even if it does not recognize their necessity or could never come to an insight into it. For otherwise these rules would not constitute an order of nature. Thus, although the understanding cannot determine anything a priori with regard to them (objects), nonetheless it must, in order to investigate these empirical so-called laws, lay as the ground of all reflection on nature an a priori principle—the principle, namely, that a knowable a priori order of nature is possible according to those laws. Such a principle is expressed in the following propositions: that there is in nature a subordination of genera and species comprehensible by us; that genera in turn approach one another according to a common principle, so that a transition may be possible from one to the other and thereby to a higher genus; that although to our understanding it seems initially unavoidable to assume as many different types of XXXVI causality as there are specific differences in natural effects, they may nevertheless fall under a small number of principles whose discovery becomes our task, etc. This attunement of nature to our cognitive faculty is presupposed a priori by the faculty of judgment in view of its reflection on nature according to empirical laws, while at the same time, the understanding recognizes that attunement as objectively contingent, and only the faculty of judgment attributes it to nature as transcendental purposiveness (in relation to the subject's cognitive faculty). For were we not presupposing it, we would have no order of nature according to empirical laws and consequently no guiding thread both for an experience to be had according to those laws in all their multiplicity and for an investigation of them.

For it is quite conceivable that despite all the uniformity of natural things in terms of universal laws, without which the form of a knowledge of experience in general would not occur at all, the specific differences in the empirical laws of nature, along with their effects, might still be so great as to dennoch so groß sein könnte, daß es für unseren Verstand unmöglich wäre, in ihr eine faßliche Ordnung zu entdecken, ihre Produkte in Gattungen und Arten einzuteilen, um die Prinzipien der Erklärung und des Verständnisses des einen auch zur Erklärung und Begreifung des an | XXXVII dern zu gebrauchen, und aus einem für uns so verworrenen (eigentlich nur unendlich mannigfaltigen, unserer Fassungskraft nicht angemessenen) Stoffe eine zusammenhängende Erfahrung zu machen.

Die Urteilskraft hat also auch ein Prinzip a priori für die Möglichkeit der Natur, aber nur in subjektiver Rücksicht, in sich, wodurch sie, nicht der AA186 *Natur (als Autonomie),* sondern ihr selbst (als Heautonomie) || für die Reflexion über jene, ein Gesetz vorschreibt, welches man das *Gesetz der Spezifikation der Natur* in Ansehung ihrer empirischen Gesetze nennen könnte, das sie a priori an ihr nicht erkennt, sondern zum Behuf einer für unseren Verstand erkennbaren Ordnung derselben in der Einteilung, die sie von ihren allgemeinen Gesetzen macht, annimmt, wenn sie diesen eine Mannigfaltigkeit der besondern unterordnen will. Wenn man also sagt: die Natur spezifiziert ihre allgemeinen Gesetze nach dem Prinzip der Zweckmäßigkeit für unser Erkenntnisvermögen, d. i. zur Angemessenheit mit dem menschlichen Verstande in seinem notwendigen Geschäfte: zum Besonderen, welches ihm die Wahrnehmung darbietet, das Allgemeine, und zum Verschiedenen (für jede Spezies zwar Allgemeinen) wiederum Verknüpfung in der Einheit des Prinzips zu finden; so schreibt man dadurch weder der Natur ein Gesetz vor, noch lernt man eines von ihr durch Beobachtung (obzwar jenes Prinzip durch diese bestätigt werden kann). Denn es ist nicht ein Prinzip der | XXXVIII bestimmenden, sondern bloß der reflektierenden Urteilskraft; man will nur, daß man, die Natur mag ihren allgemeinen Gesetzen nach eingerichtet sein wie sie wolle, durchaus nach jenem Prinzip und den sich darauf gründenden Maximen ihren empirischen Gesetzen nachspüren müsse, weil wir, nur so weit als jenes stattfindet, mit dem Gebrauche unseres Verstandes in der Erfahrung fortkommen und Erkenntnis erwerben können.

VI. Von der Verbindung des Gefühls der Lust mit dem Begriffe der Zweckmäßigkeit der Natur

Die gedachte Übereinstimmung der Natur in der Mannigfaltigkeit ihrer besonderen Gesetze zu unserem Bedürfnisse, Allgemeinheit der Prinzipien für sie aufzufinden, muß nach aller unserer Einsicht, als zufällig beurteilt werden, gleichwohl aber doch, für unser Verstandesbedürfnis, als unentbehrlich, mithin als Zweckmäßigkeit, wodurch die Natur mit unserer, aber nur auf Erkenntnis gerichteten, Absicht übereinstimmt.—Die allgemeinen Gesetze des Verstandes, welche zugleich Gesetze der Natur sind, sind derselben ebenso notwendig (obgleich aus Spontaneität entsprungen), als die Bewegungsgesetze der Materie; und ihre Erzeugung setzt keine Absicht mit unseren Erkenntnisvermögen voraus, weil wir nur durch dieselben von dem, was Erkenntnis der | XXXIX Dinge (der Natur) sei, make impossible for our understanding to discover in it a comprehensible order; impossible to divide nature's products in genera and species so as to use the principles for explaining and understanding one thing also to explain and grasp the | XXXVII other; and impossible to make an interconnected experience out of a material that appears to us so confused (properly speaking: only infinitely manifold and not appropriate to our power of comprehending it).

Therefore the faculty of judgment also has in itself an a priori principle for the possibility of nature but such only in a subjective respect. Through this principle the faculty of judgment prescribes a law not to nature (as autonomy) but to itself (as heautonomy) for the reflection on nature. This law could be called the *law of specification of nature* with regard to its empirical laws. It is a law that the faculty of judgment does not know a priori in nature, but rather assumes in view of an order of nature, knowable to the understanding, when it divides the universal laws of nature so as to subordinate to them the manifold of particular laws. So if we say that nature specifies its universal laws according to the principle of purposiveness for our cognitive faculty—i.e., in a way adequate to the human understanding in its necessary activity of finding the universal for the particular offered to it by perception, and furthermore of finding connection in the unity of the principle for what is different (though universal within each species)—then, in that way, we are neither prescribing a law to nature nor learning a law from nature by observation (although that principle can be confirmed by observation). For this is not a principle of XXXVIII the determinant faculty of judgment but merely of the reflective faculty of judgment. All that is intended is that however nature may be arranged in its universal laws we must search for its empirical laws throughout following that principle as well as the maxims grounded upon it, because only to the extent that this principle applies can we make progress in experience with the use of our understanding and gain knowledge.

VI. On the Conjunction of the Feeling of Pleasure with the Concept of Purposiveness of Nature

The agreement, so conceived, of nature in the manifold of its particular laws with our need to find for it universality of principles must be judged, as far as all our insight goes, as contingent yet as also indispensable for the need of our understanding and hence as the purposiveness through which nature agrees with our aim but only insofar as this is directed to knowledge.—The universal laws of the understanding, which are at the same time laws of nature, are just as necessary for nature (even if they arise from spontaneity) as are the laws of motion concerning matter. The production of these laws does not presuppose any aim with regard to our cognitive faculties because it is only through such laws that we first gain a concept of what knowledge of XXXIX things (of nature) is and because these laws apply with necessity to nature as object of our

AA187 zu||erst einen Begriff erhalten, und sie der Natur, als Objekt unserer Erkenntnis überhaupt, notwendig zukommen. Allein, daß die Ordnung der Natur nach ihren besonderen Gesetzen, bei aller unsere Fassungskraft übersteigenden wenigstens möglichen Mannigfaltigkeit und Ungleichartigkeit, doch dieser wirklich angemessen sei, ist, soviel wir einsehen können, zufällig; und die Auffindung derselben ist ein Geschäft des Verstandes, welches mit Absicht zu einem notwendigen Zwecke desselben, nämlich Einheit der Prinzipien in sie hineinzubringen, geführt wird: welchen Zweck dann die Urteilskraft der Natur beilegen muß, weil der Verstand ihr hierüber kein Gesetz vorschreiben kann.

Die Erreichung jeder Absicht ist mit dem Gefühle der Lust verbunden; und, ist die Bedingung der erstern eine Vorstellung a priori, wie hier ein Prinzip für die reflektierende Urteilskraft überhaupt, so ist das Gefühl der Lust auch durch einen Grund a priori und für jedermann gültig bestimmt: und zwar bloß durch die Beziehung des Objekts auf das Erkenntnisvermögen, ohne daß der Begriff der Zweckmäßigkeit hier im mindesten auf das Begehrungsvermögen Rücksicht nimmt, und sich also von aller praktischen Zweckmäßigkeit der Natur gänzlich unterscheidet.

In der Tat, da wir von dem Zusammentreffen der Wahrnehmungen mit den Gesetzen nach allgemeinen Naturbegriffen (den Kategorien) nicht die mindeste | XL Wirkung auf das Gefühl der Lust in uns antreffen, auch nicht antreffen können, weil der Verstand damit unabsichtlich nach seiner Natur notwendig verfährt: so ist andrerseits die entdeckte Vereinbarkeit zweier oder mehrerer empirischen heterogenen Naturgesetze unter einem sie beide befassenden Prinzip der Grund einer sehr merklichen Lust, oft sogar einer Bewunderung, selbst einer solchen, die nicht aufhört, ob man schon mit dem Gegenstande derselben genug bekannt ist. Zwar spüren wir an der Faßlichkeit der Natur, und ihrer Einheit der Abteilung in Gattungen und Arten, wodurch allein empirische Begriffe möglich sind, durch welche wir sie nach ihren besonderen Gesetzen erkennen, keine merkliche Lust mehr: aber sie ist gewiß zu ihrer Zeit gewesen, und nur weil die gemeinste Erfahrung ohne sie nicht möglich sein würde, ist sie allmählich mit dem bloßen Erkenntnisse vermischt, und nicht mehr besonders bemerkt worden.—Es gehört also etwas, das in der Beurteilung der Natur auf die Zweckmäßigkeit derselben für unsern Verstand aufmerksam macht, ein Studium: ungleichartige Gesetze derselben, wo möglich, unter höhere, obwohl immer noch empirische, zu bringen, dazu,
AA188 || um, wenn es gelingt, an dieser Einstimmung derselben für unser Erkenntnisvermögen, die wir als bloß zufällig ansehen, Lust zu empfinden. Dagegen würde uns eine Vorstellung der Natur durchaus mißfallen, durch welche man uns voraussagte, daß, bei der min | XLI desten Nachforschung über die gemeinste Erfahrung hinaus, wir auf eine Heterogeneität ihrer Gesetze stoßen würden, welche die Vereinigung ihrer besonderen Gesetze unter allgemeinen empirischen für unseren Verstand unmöglich machte; weil dies dem Prinzip der subjektiv-zweckmäßigen Spezifikation der Natur in ihren Gattungen,

cognition in general. But as far as we can see, it is contingent that the order of nature in its particular laws with all their—at least possible—multiplicity and heterogeneity that exceed our capacity of comprehension should nonetheless be actually commensurate with that capacity. Moreover, the discovery of these laws is an occupation of the understanding that aims, in performing this task, to a necessary purpose of its own—namely to bring in them [*in sie*][1] unity of principles. The faculty of judgment must then attribute such a purpose to nature since the understanding in this regard cannot prescribe to it any law.

The attainment of every aim is connected to a feeling of pleasure, and if the condition of this attainment is an a priori representation, as here it is a principle for the reflective faculty of judgment in general, then the feeling of pleasure also is determined through a ground that is a priori and valid for everyone. This determination takes place simply as the object is related to the cognitive faculty. For in this case the concept of purposiveness does not take in the least into account the faculty of desire and hence distinguishes itself entirely from any practical purposiveness of nature.

As a matter of fact, we do not find—and cannot find—that the concurrence of our perceptions with the laws according to universal concepts of nature (the categories) has the slightest | XL effect in ourselves upon the feeling of pleasure. For the understanding proceeds therein necessarily without aim according to its own nature. On the other hand, the discovery of a possible unification of two or more different heterogeneous empirical laws of nature under one principle that encompasses them both is the ground of a quite noticeable pleasure, frequently even of admiration, even of an admiration that does not cease when we have become familiar enough with its object. It is true that we no longer feel a noticeable pleasure arising from the possibility of comprehending nature and its unity in the division of genera and species that alone makes possible the empirical concepts through which we know nature in its particular laws. But that pleasure was certainly there once, and it is only because the most common experience would not be possible without it that pleasure has been progressively mixed with our simple knowledge and has no longer been noticed.—What is needed is therefore something that in our judgments of nature would call our attention to its purposiveness for our understanding—an endeavor to bring, where possible, nature's heterogeneous laws under higher although still empirical laws. So that when this endeavor meets with success, we feel pleasure for nature's unison with our cognitive faculty—a unison that we regard as merely contingent. By contrast, a representation of nature would altogether cause us displeasure were it to foresee for us that in the | LXI least investigation of nature carried beyond the most common experience we would come up against such a heterogeneity among nature's laws that would make thoroughly impossible for our understanding to unify its particular laws under universal empirical laws. For this conflicts with the principle of the subjectively purposive specification of na-

1. In the manifold of empirical laws, not in nature itself. The latter is the aim of the faculty of judgment [A.N.].

und unserer reflektierenden Urteilskraft in der Absicht der letzteren, widerstreitet.

Diese Voraussetzung der Urteilskraft ist gleichwohl darüber so unbestimmt: wie weit jene idealische Zweckmäßigkeit der Natur für unser Erkenntnisvermögen ausgedehnt werden solle, daß, wenn man uns sagt, eine tiefere oder ausgebreitetere Kenntnis der Natur durch Beobachtung müsse zuletzt auf eine Mannigfaltigkeit von Gesetzen stoßen, die kein menschlicher Verstand auf ein Prinzip zurückführen kann, wir es auch zufrieden sind, ob wir es gleich lieber hören, wenn andere uns Hoffnung geben: daß, je mehr wir die Natur im Inneren kennen würden, oder mit äußeren uns für jetzt unbekannten Gliedern vergleichen könnten, wir sie in ihren Prinzipien um desto einfacher, und, bei der scheinbaren Heterogeneität ihrer empirischen Gesetze, einhelliger finden würden, je weiter unsere Erfahrung fortschritte. Denn es ist ein Geheiß unserer Urteilskraft, nach dem Prinzip der Angemessenheit der Natur zu unserem Erkenntnisvermögen zu verfahren, so weit es reicht, ohne (weil es keine bestimmende Urteilskraft ist, die uns diese Regel gibt) | XLII auszumachen, ob es irgendwo seine Grenzen habe, oder nicht; weil wir zwar in Ansehung des rationalen Gebrauchs unserer Erkenntnisvermögen Grenzen bestimmen können, im empirischen Felde aber keine Grenzbestimmung möglich ist.

ture in its genera as well as with our reflective faculty of judgment in respect thereof.

Yet this presupposition of the faculty of judgment is so indeterminate on the question of how far that ideal purposiveness of nature for our cognitive faculty should be extended that if we are told that a deeper or more extended knowledge of nature reached through observation must eventually come up against a manifold of laws that no human understanding can bring back to one principle, then we would be content with this thought too. But we would still prefer to listen to others giving us hope that the closer we could get to an insight into the interior of nature or compare it with external parts still unknown to us, the simpler would we find nature in its principles, and the farther our experience progresses, the more harmonious would we find it in the apparent heterogeneity of its empirical laws. For our faculty of judgment commands us to proceed according to the principle of nature's conformity to our cognitive faculty as far as this faculty extends, leaving undecided (since it is not a determinant faculty of judgment that gives us this rule) | XLII whether or not it meets somewhere its limits. For if we are able to determine the limit with regard to the rational use of our cognitive faculty, in the empirical realm no determination of limit is possible.

Commentary

In addressing the critical and systematic problem of philosophy, the first trichotomy of §§I–III introduced the faculty of judgment as a mediating and connecting term between understanding and reason. However, the unification of the parts of philosophy into a whole announced by §III is still more the enunciation of a programmatic task than a concrete accomplishment. The introduction of the faculty of judgment poses a new set of issues. First is the justification of its status as an independent cognitive faculty, an independence that hitherto could only be assumed by way of analogy. Second, Kant has to present the transcendental a priori principle of judgment and to provide its "deduction." This occupies §§IV–V. §VI shows the connection between the principle of purposiveness and the feeling of pleasure and displeasure, thereby taking up again the argument first endorsed in §III and opening up to the developments of the third and last trichotomy.

The central sections of the introduction are among the most dense and complex of our text. Herein Kant outlines the crucial problem of the *Critique of Judgment*, the essential *epistemological* question to which both parts of the book provide an answer. The objective realm of the beautiful and that of organic life are the fundamental instances of that problem. Two general points need to be made from the outset. First, these sections show how the essentially *cognitive* problem of the first *Critique* yields to the *epistemological* problem of the third *Critique*. Kant's task in the *Critique of Pure Reason* was to demonstrate that the universal laws of the understanding are at the same time universal laws of nature, necessary with regard to it as nature in general. The *Critique of Judgment* deals instead with the possibility of empirical science and our both cognitive and noncognitive approach to empirically given particulars and contingent cases. Second, it is important to recognize from the outset that this problem occupies the center of the third *Critique*. It represents the common ground motivating Kant's discourse on aesthetics as well as teleology. Thus the epistemological problem raised in these sections can be viewed as the ongoing thread and the key—the *Leitfaden*—to the entire *Critique of Judgment*. It is precisely in this sense that the thread is taken up by §§VII–IX.

1. Synopsis: §IV, On the Faculty of Judgment as a Faculty That Legislates A Priori

The first trichotomy has only proved that in order to set foot on the territory disclosed by a necessary third critique further conditions are required than those provided by the critique of speculative and practical reason. §IV sets out to show the further conditions that allow one to think the new conditioned of nature's manifold empirical forms. It is in §V that the new conditioned proper to the faculty of judgment is fleshed out in its most concrete features. The chief question of the third *Critique* is clearly indicated in the problem of the possibility of *empirical knowledge*. Empirical knowledge ultimately comprehends scientific knowledge, scientific induction, judgments of taste, and teleological judgments; that is, all our attempts to reflect upon empirically given, contingent individual cases and to attribute sense and meaning to them. This becomes possible, according to Kant, only once we are able to think those particulars as inscribed, despite their contingency, within a certain lawful order. In presenting this problem, Kant reconsiders the results of the first *Critique* and complements them with a new notion of "nature" as well as a new notion of "experience." The world of the third *Critique* is neither "nature *in general*" nor the world ruled by *universal* laws of nature only. It is rather the seemingly chaotic "labyrinth" of an infinite multiplicity of empirical "forms" for which only particular, empirical laws can be formulated. Hence the dramatic questions that Kant raises in these sections: how can we orient ourselves in this labyrinth; how is a coherent and unitary (and systematic) experience possible in—and of—the manifold of nature's empirical and contingent forms? The answer is suggested by the *reflective* faculty of judgment and its principle of formal purposiveness. In §§IV–V Kant clearly isolates the question that in the "First Introduction" could not yet have found its legitimate place having already been raised in a footnote of §II even before the notion of reflective judgment had been introduced and the issue of the "system according to empirical laws" raised.

In the following commentary, I will present the development of Kant's argument in §IV. In addition, I will briefly discuss the relation between Kant's presentations of *Urteilskraft* in the *Critique of Pure Reason* and the *Critique of Judgment* in order to underline the novelty of the idea of "reflective" faculty of judgment. The crucial issue posed by the manifold forms of nature and its empirical laws will be discussed in connection with §V.

Kant's argument in §IV proceeds in three steps. First, Kant provides a definition, or presentation, of *Urteilskraft* by distinguishing between "determinant" and "reflective" faculty of judgment (XXV–XXVI, 179, 19–26). Then he outlines the specific problem posed by the uncontrollable manifold forms of nature as the *epistemological* problem that only the *reflective* faculty of judgment can face. In relation to this problem, it becomes necessary to appeal to a new principle (we *must* do so, contends Kant, if an experience of those empirical forms of nature should be possible at all, XXVI, 179, 27–XXVIII, 180, 31). Finally, he gives a formulation of this principle as the principle of the "purposiveness of nature in its manifold" (XXVIII, 180, 31–181, 11).

1.1. §IV Commentary: Reflective and Determinant Faculty of Judgment

The Faculty of Judgment: Determinant and Reflective (XXV–XXVI, 179, 19–26)

In the conclusion of §III, Kant suggested that "all we may have to say of the faculty of judgment's own principles must be ascribed to the theoretical part of philosophy" (XXV, 179, 7–9). The faculty of judgment "in general" is now defined as the "faculty of thinking the particular as contained under the universal" (XXV, 179, 19–20). The faculty of judgment, taken in its more general function, establishes a relation between particular and universal—the particular being a case or instance and the universal being the concept, rule or principle, law or maxim. *Urteilskraft überhaupt* connects particular cases to the general laws that relate to those cases and connects universal laws with particular cases.

This connection can take place in two different ways. If the universal law, rule or principle "is given" by the understanding as faculty of principles, then the faculty of judgment's own task is simply—and exclusively—that of "subsuming" the particular case under the given universal. To be sure, in this situation, what is given to the faculty of judgment is not only the rule but also the case. The particular instance is thereby brought back to the universal *under which* it is contained. The particular is thought of precisely as an instance of that law. Kant names the faculty of judgment thus employed "determinant" (*bestimmende*). The general concept is determined by the particular case as the rule for that instance.[1] "*Determination,*" explains Kant in the first *Critique*, "is a predicate that is added to the concept of the subject and extends it."[2] This definition, contends Kant, applies also to the "transcendental faculty of judgment" at work in the first *Critique*. This is the faculty that "provides a priori the conditions" that justify the subsumption under the given law (XXVI, 179, 23–24).[3]

But if on the contrary "*only* the particular is given" (and not, as in the case of the determinant faculty of judgment *both* particular *and* universal), then the faculty of judgment must first of all "find" the universal for that particular instance—that is, the universal concept "made possible" by that particular instance.[4] This move must obviously precede all further operation of this faculty and becomes its most proper task. In this case, no determination of objects takes place but only "reflection." The faculty of judgment is accordingly "merely reflective" (XXVI, 179, 19–26). The "First Introduction" explains this reflection with the term *Überlegen*, namely with the act of deliberating and considering. A form of

---

1. More clearly EE §V, AA, XX, 211, 12: here the faculty of judgment determines the "concept that forms the basis through a given empirical representation."
2. KrV B 626/A 598.
3. See KrV B 174/A 135: Transcendental philosophy (specifically transcendental logic) provides not just the rule but the "universal condition to rules."
4. See the formulation of EE §V, AA, XX, 211, 9.

reflection—albeit a merely instinctive one—must be presupposed in animals as well.[5] To reflect "is to hold given representations up to and to compare them with either other representations or one's cognitive faculty with relation to a concept that is thereby made possible."[6] This definition echoes the terminology of reflection commonly employed by Wolff and his school. In this tradition, reflection along with attention is one of the basic functions of the understanding.[7] It consists in a form of elemental cognition that accompanies all processes of the mind at all times, without effort from our part and even without awareness. Reflection makes possible a comparison of different representations and operations of the mind that are otherwise intertwined and confused with each other. Thereby *reflexio* (*Überlegen*) is the necessary preparation for *examinatio* (*Untersuchen*) or investigation.[8] Kant's notion of reflective faculty of judgment needs to be kept distinct from this activity of "reflection" employed by the understanding in the process of concept formation.[9]

Überlegung, or *reflectio*, explains Kant at the beginning of the "Amphiboly" chapter of the first *Critique,* "is not concerned with objects themselves so as to derive concepts from them directly but is rather that state of the *Gemüt* in which we first set ourselves *to discover* the subjective conditions under which we are able to arrive at concepts. It is the consciousness of the relation of given representations to our different sources of knowledge, and only by way of such consciousness can the relation of the sources of knowledge to one another be rightly determined."[10] While this definition clearly entails a reference to the traditional use of the concept, reflection shows also some of the traits proper to the reflective

---

5. EE §V, AA XX, 211, 19–20.

6. EE §V, AA XX, 211, 14–18.

7. See, for example, Ch. Wolff, *Psychologia empirica*, Fracofurti & Lipsiae, in officina libraria Rengeriana, 1738, §257.

8. KrV B 316/A 261. See D. Henrich, "Kant's Explanation of Aesthetic Judgment," in *Aesthetic Judgment and the Moral Image of the World*, Stanford, Stanford University Press, 1992, 29–58, 39. For the relation between "reflection" and "investigation" and "reflection" and "deduction," see his "Kant's Notion of a Deduction and the Methodological Background of the First *Critique*," in *Kant's Transcendental Deductions*, ed. by E. Förster, Stanford, Stanford University Press, 1989, 29–46, 42 ff.; see also B. Longuenesse, *Kant and the Capacity to Judge*, Princeton, Princeton University Press, 1998.

9. A. Model suggests that the expression *reflektierende Urteilskraft* was probably invented by Kant himself (A. Model, "Zur Bedeutung und Ursprung der 'reflektierenden Urteilskraft' bei Kant," in *Akten des Siebenten Internationalen Kant-Kongresses, 1990*, ed. by G. Funke, Bonn, Bouvier, 1991, 135–141, 139).

10. See KrV B316 ff./A 260 ff. An additional set of meanings related to the notion of reflection is disclosed by Kant's relation to Leibniz in the "Amphiboly" chapter of the first *Critique*. This relation is discussed by A. Model, *Metaphysik und reflektierende Urteilskraft bei Kant*, Frankfurt a.M., Athenaeum, 1987; I do not accept Model's main thesis according to which the reflection implied by the notion of reflective faculty of judgment is modeled after Leibniz's monad as "mirror of the universe."

faculty of judgment investigated by the third *Critique*. Reflection is presented as a status of the mind that is merely concerned with the subjective conditions to concepts rather than with the direct determination of objects. In this activity of self-consideration we need to find those conditions by sorting out their belonging to different faculties. More specifically, Kant defines "transcendental reflection" (*Überlegung*) as the complex relational act that confronts *relations* between faculties and representations (not just faculties and representations but relations among them). Thereby reflection almost steps out and above the very act of cognition in order to bring the focus on the subject itself. Transcendental reflection is the "act by which I confront the comparison of representations in general with the cognitive faculty in which the comparison is effected."[11] Through this act I distinguish to which faculty my representations respectively belong. Reflection is a transcendental (not a psychological) activity of discovery that the subject exercises upon itself. It displays two distinct components. On the one hand it is an act of *Zusammenhalten*—an act of confronting two heterogeneous terms such as cognitive faculties and representations by "keeping them together," one in front of the other. On the other hand it is a critical act of *Unterscheiden,* or distinguishing, which implies a selection and attribution of determinate representations to their respective faculty.

The distinction between determinant and reflective *Urteilskraft* is the distinction between application and acquisition of concepts or general rules. We must recall that in §III, Kant described the faculty of judgment's peculiar type of relation to law as "searching for laws" (XXI, 177, 8) as opposed to understanding's and reason's "legislation," which is the act of giving law. Now the task of "finding" the law becomes, more precisely, the specific activity of the *reflective* faculty of judgment. This connection to law reveals already that it is the *reflective* faculty of judgment that must interest Kant specifically in the third *Critique* as an autonomous cognitive faculty.[12] It is also clear that determinant and reflective faculties of judgment do not stand to each other as simply parallel functions of a faculty of judgment in general. In the opening passage of the section, it becomes clear why the *Urteilskraft* that occupies the third *Critique* can only be the *reflective* faculty of judgment. In the first place, the meaning of the "givenness" respectively of the rule and the instance with which judgment operates is different in the case of determinant and reflective *Urteilskraft* because different is the source from which they are given. For determinant judgment, the fact that the rule is given means that the faculty of judgment simply has to execute or apply an a priori rule whose source is the understanding. For reflective judgment, instead, the givenness of the particular has an exclusively empirical meaning. It is only experience that can provide a posteriori the specific case—and this is also all reflective judgment can count on (for only the particular is given to it). The reflective faculty of judg-

11. KrV B 317/A 261.
12. Compare the titles of §III and §IV.

ment has its necessary starting point in experience. Hence, for reflective judgment the crucial issue is not so much thinking the particular as contained under the universal but rather *finding* the universal for a specific given particular. This is, in fact, quite a complicated task never before addressed by Kant. First, a universal must be found, but second, this cannot be a universal whatsoever but must be precisely the rule *required by that specific given case*. Consequently, only the reflective faculty of judgment has a somehow original relation to the universal as law or rule. As far as the determinant faculty of judgment is concerned, it simply has to apply a rule that is already prescribed by the understanding. In this respect, determinant judgment is a sort of continuation of the activity of the understanding.

Urteil *and* Urteilskraft

At this point, a terminological clarification is in order. One of the first problems that any translation of Kant's text (in any language) has to face is the way to render the term *Urteilskraft*. This term needs to be somehow distinguished from *Urteil*. While *Urteil* is "judgment" as the product of the activity of *Urteilen* (judging), *Urteilskraft* is the faculty, capacity, ability, or power that judges and pronounces judgments. E. Weil even proposes to render it with *faculté judiciaire*.[13] Kant's definition of *Urteilskraft überhaupt* provided at the beginning of our section—"the faculty of judgment in general is the faculty of thinking the particular as contained under the universal"—can be compared with the *Logic*'s explanation of what an *Urteil überhaupt* is: "A judgment is the representation of the unity of the consciousness of different representations or the representation of their relation insofar as they constitute a concept."[14] This definition sheds light on the way in which judgment relates to the understanding (as faculty of concepts but also as faculty to judge).[15] As the *Critique of Pure Reason* demonstrates, the table of the categories as concepts of the understanding derives from the table of judgments (metaphysical deduction of the concepts of the understanding). Concepts are "predicates of possible judgments."[16] In addition, we should note that while Kant's terminology attributes the notions of determinant and reflective both to *Urteilskraft* and to *Urteil*, the occurrences of the latter are extremely rare.[17] The distinction between determinant and reflective indicates a differentiation of the *faculty* of judgment itself (not of the product of this ability).

Within the *Critique of Judgment*, the designation determinant/reflective faculty of judgment does not occur at all in the Analytic of the Beautiful; it is men-

13. E. Weil, *Problèmes kantiens*, Paris, Vrin, 1970, 62.

14. *Logic*, §17 (AA, IX, 101).

15. KrV B 94/A 69: Verstand is "ein *Vermögen zu urteilen*."

16. KrV B 94/A 69.

17. So much so that Eisler in his *Kant-Lexicon* (Hildesheim, Olms, 1964), registers the distinction *bestimmende/reflektierende* only for *Urteilskraft*, not for *Urteil* (see E. Garroni, *Estetica ed epistemologia. Riflessioni sulla "Critica del giudizio,"* Roma, Bulzoni, 1976, 38. Moreover, in the case of reflective as attributed to judgment, Kant prefers the expression *Reflexionsurteil*.

tioned only in two passages in the Deduction of Pure Aesthetic Judgments and once in the Dialectic of the Aesthetic Faculty of Judgment.[18] Kant probably comes to draw this distinction within the notion of *Urteilskraft* only at the end or after the composition of the Analytic of the Beautiful. It is also significant that after the *Critique of Judgment*, the terminus *reflective faculty of judgment* is no longer employed.[19]

The Determinant Faculty of Judgment and the Employment of the Understanding (XXVI, 179, 27–31)

In the first *Critique* Kant explored at length not only the issue of the possibility of a priori synthetic judgments but also the way in which the "transcendental faculty of judgment" functions in the construction of pure a priori cognition.[20] Therein he defines *Urteilskraft überhaupt* as the "faculty of *subsuming* under rules, i.e., of distinguishing whether something does or does not stand under a given rule (*casus datae legis*)."[21] The rule is given by the understanding as "faculty of rules."[22] The faculty of judgment is in charge of distinguishing whether the given rule applies to the case at hand. Subsumption is the faculty of judgment's own procedure. It is the act of bringing the particular under the universal or the representation of an object under a concept. At the very outset, however, Kant identifies the crucial problem proper to this faculty: *Urteilskraft* is the faculty of subsuming under rules, and yet there is no rule for subsuming. The understanding gives the rule under which to subsume, but there is no objective rule that can teach the faculty of judgment how to perform the subsumption correctly.

Kant distinguishes the role of the faculty of judgment in formal or general logic from its function in transcendental logic. "General logic contains, and can contain, no rules for the faculty of judgment."[23] Making abstraction from all content of knowledge, general logic is a merely analytical exposition of the forms of thinking: concepts, judgments (*Urteile*), and syllogisms. In this consists "all employment of the understanding." The faculty of judgment is thereby considered only insofar as formal employment of the understanding is concerned. General logic, however, cannot give any prescription or rule as to how to operate the subsumption (for this would require yet another rule, and so forth in a *regressus ad*

---

18. KU §40, AA 161; §44, AA 179; §57, AA 238.

19. The only two exceptions are the *Logik*, §§81–84, which is not, however, a text edited by Kant himself (only approved), and a passage in the *Opus Postumum*, AA XXIII, 484. For a discussion thereof, see A. Model, *Zur Bedeutung und Ursprung der "reflektierenden Urteilskraft" bei Kant*, op. cit.

20. KrV see the introductory section, On the Transcendental Faculty of Judgment in General, B 171 ff./A 132 ff.

21. See KrV B 171/A 132.

22. See KrV A 126 for the various definitions of *Verstand,* among which "faculty of rules" is seen as "more fruitful" and such as to approximate more to the nature of the understanding.

23. KrV B 171/A 132.

infinitum).[24] The only two ways out of this problem are either to declare that the faculty of judgment is a peculiar "natural talent" that cannot be taught but only practiced[25] or to declare that the faculty of judgment is an a priori faculty that finds in itself (or gives to itself) its own a priori principle or rule. The *Critique of Pure Reason* suggests the first solution; the *Critique of Judgment* follows the second.

The problem that arises is, Kant suggests, no less than the problem of "stupidity" as lack of "natural judgment."[26] From the fact that one may lack judgment yet not understanding (and even doctrine), it follows that the two faculties are not completely reducible to one. Kant presents the example of a physician, a judge, or a ruler who might very well know the universal rules and master all the concepts of the particular discipline yet might still not be able to *apply* them correctly to particular and concrete cases. Most importantly, this person might lack the ability of distinguishing "whether a case *in concreto* belongs" to the universal *in abstracto* expressed by the rule; that is, the person might not be able *to judge* of which rule a particular case is in fact a case. This is precisely all that judgment is about. The faculty of judgment deals with the "*application*" of the rule. To *subsume* under a rule means nothing else than to *apply* the rule to given cases.[27]

If general logic can offer no suggestion as to how to emend the faculty of judgment (i.e., how to avoid stupidity by providing an objective rule for subsumption), it seems that transcendental logic, which deals instead with the content of knowledge, may have something to say with regard to the present issue. Transcendental logic "would seem to have as its peculiar task to correct and secure the faculty of judgment by means of determinate rules in the use of pure understanding."[28] For "transcendental philosophy has the peculiarity that besides the rule (or rather the universal condition of rules), which is given in the pure concept of the understanding, *it can also specify a priori the instance to which the rule is to be applied*."[29] Does this claim solve the problem of judgment? The transcendental faculty of judgment provides the a priori conditions under which objects can be given as instances of the rule. These conditions are space, time, and schematism. What results from this doctrine are the "synthetic judgments that under these conditions follow a priori from pure concepts of the understanding."[30] In this case, the universal rule is provided by the category of the understanding. But since the particular is specified *a priori* as an instance of the rule, it cannot be the empirically given particular. In fact, Kant designates it with the expression "appearances in general."[31] The particular to which the category is applied as a rule is sensible

24. See also KU preface, VII, 169,10–14.
25. KrV B 172/A 133; B 173/A 134; see also B 173/A 134: *natürliche Urteilskraft.*
26. See KrV B 172 f./A 133 f. fn.
27. KrV B 173/A 134, see fn.; B 176/A 137.
28. KrV B 174/A 135.
29. KrV B 174 f./A 135.
30. KrV B 175/A 136.
31. KrV B 177/A 138.

intuition insofar as it is schematized a priori through the transcendental determination of time. It follows that the synthetic a priori judgments or principles of the understanding formulated by the Transcendental Doctrine of Judgment (or Analytic of Principles) are not those same judgments that the physician, the judge, and the ruler need to correctly pronounce when facing concrete cases. Rather, the synthetic a priori judgments of the understanding are universal laws of nature and contain in themselves no rule or principle as to how the faculty of judgment should effect subsumptions *of empirically given cases*. With regard to the issue that was troubling the physician, the judge, and the ruler (*casus datae legis*), transcendental logic is no substantial advance over merely formal logic. In transcendental logic, however, their problem does not even subsist. The a priori synthetic judgments of the understanding do not, after all, require the faculty of judgment as an independent faculty for their formulation.

The Transcendental Doctrine of Judgment of the first *Critique* is concerned with understanding as a faculty of principles and its use in providing pure a priori cognition of nature in general. In the first *Critique*, the particular empirical instance has not yet come to the fore. Accordingly, the activity of subsuming given empirical cases under concepts does not yet need to be carried out. The chief problem of the *Critique of Pure Reason*, namely the problem of the transcendental laws of nature, does not yet require empirical subsumption. Thus, the first *Critique* provides exclusively the pure a priori conditions for all possible subsumption under a priori universal rules (XXVI, 179, 23–24; KrV B 174/A 135). In the third *Critique*, Kant logically recognizes the procedure of the "transcendental faculty of judgment" at work in the Analytic of Principles as the procedure proper to the *determinant* faculty of judgment. Note that in the statement that defines the determinant faculty of judgment, no specification is given of the nature of particular that is subsumed under the universal.[32] Here, the particular can be either appearance in general as the a priori instance specified by the understanding, or the empirically given case. Although transcendental and determinant *Urteilskraft* are not identical, the two cases can be discussed together at this point since in both instances the faculty of judgment does not pose a problem of principles of its own.[33] "The determinant faculty of judgment, which operates under the universal transcendental laws given by the understanding, is subsumptive *only*" (XXVI, 179, 27–28). With this claim, Kant recognizes that determinant judgment as such does not raise any specific problem of its own. For the "only" task it has to perform is to subsume under the rule provided to it by the understanding—with no regard to the question of *what* must be subsumed (i.e., with no regard to the question of whether a particular case *in concreto* falls under the universal *in abstracto*). In this case, the faculty of judgment would need a particular "talent" (in the language of the first *Critique*) or an a priori "principle" (in the language of the

32. Not so EE §V, AA XX, 211, 12: here the faculty of judgment determines the "concept that forms the basis through *a given empirical representation*."

33. Compare E §IV, XXVI, 179, 28–29 with EE §V, AA, XX, 212, 7–16.

third *Critique*) to search for the universal and would then be reflective, not determinant, judgment. But since the universal is already marked out for it a priori, "the faculty of judgment has no need for thinking by itself of a law" (XXVI, 179, 28–29) nor has it a need for discriminating whether that universal is the right universal for that specific particular.

At this point, we need to return briefly to the important issue of the difference between determinant faculty of judgment and the judgment that is at work in the first *Critique*. The synthetic a priori judgments of the Analytic of Principles are pure conditions for all possible subsumption. They do not deal with empirically given cases but with appearances in general as instances that can be specified a priori. Insofar as the principles of the understanding imply a "subsumption"[34] of sensible intuition under a pure concept by means of a schema, they can be said to proceed as determinant. Yet, since this subsumption, which is simply the work of the understanding, does not require judgment as an independent cognitive faculty, Kant does not need to raise the question of determinant judgment in the first *Critique*. In the third *Critique*, at the beginning of §IV of the Introduction, Kant has moved a step forward. He is now addressing the *epistemological* question left open by the understanding and its principles. Herein, retrospectively, the "transcendental faculty of judgment" of the first *Critique* appears to work as determinant as well, albeit on a different level; that is, on the level of transcendental laws of nature in general as opposed to the general laws of sciences such as mathematics or physics. A priori synthetic judgments are products of understanding; they are transcendental laws of nature. Mathematical and physical judgments differ from the a priori synthetic judgments. They are products of the determinant faculty of judgment and, strictly speaking, find no place in the first *Critique* (the first *Critique* provides only the conditions thereof).[35] Mathematical propositions, if compared to a priori synthetic judgments or *universal* laws of nature, are indeed *synthetic*; yet they are only *particular* propositions as shown by the famous case of 7 + 5 = 12.[36] On the other hand, Kant holds that physics cannot entail a priori synthetic judgments only, which constitute its necessary conditions. Judgments of physics are synthetic a posteriori judgments. We can conclude by saying that the transcendental and determinant faculties of judgment are not identical. They are both subsumptive and they both relate to understanding as faculty of rules. However, if it is correct to say that transcendental judgment works as determinant judgment, the reverse is not the case. Determinant judgment is more comprehensive than transcendental judgment. Determinant judgment, as opposed to transcendental judgment, deals also with the particular.

---

34. KrV B 176/A 137.

35. See L. Scaravelli, *Scritti kantiani*, Firenze, La Nuova Italia, 1968, 379 fn.

36. See KrV B 205/A 164, in which Kant declares the judgment 7 + 5 = 12 to be "indeed a synthetic and yet still only a singular proposition."

The Reflective Faculty of Judgment (XXVI, 179, 31–XXVIII, 180, 30)

Once the distinction within the notion of faculty of judgment in general has been drawn, the second step in Kant's argument is to show the limits of the use of determinant judgment and to demonstrate that reflective judgment alone can intervene where determinant judgment fails. This is the case whenever our starting points are empirically given objects and where applicable general concepts are lacking.

The world of nature in general established by the first *Critique*, as well as the procedure of subsumption proper to the determinant faculty of judgment, still leaves a whole realm out of the reach of experience. Transcendental "laws given a priori by the understanding" guarantee the "possibility of a nature (as object of sense) *in general*" but still leave undetermined the great variety of possible applications ("modifications") of those "universal transcendental concepts of nature" (XXVI, 179, 31–33). In this perspective, no account can be given of the manifold, particular forms that nature concretely displays. Thereby Kant opposes the "manifold forms" of nature that are expressed by the infinite variety of possible particular applications of the transcendental universal laws to the legal order of the understanding; that is, to those universal laws that constitute "nature in general." Kant discloses the existence of *another* nature for which the principles of the first *Critique* no longer provide sufficient explanation. There is *another* nature within the realm of nature in general that cannot simply be deduced from it (does not follow analytically from it). This is the world that the third *Critique* will animate with particular objects and new forms of experience—the experience of beauty and life.

What is the epistemological problem that the *Critique of Pure Reason* left open to Kant's notion of an independent, *reflective* faculty of judgment? According to the Analytic of Principles, understanding gives, for example, the transcendental law according to which all events can be measured. This law does not teach anything with regard to the specific issue of how the particular appearance that one has to measure must be compared with a given measurement standard. The Analytic proves that all appearance and all intuition can be determined quantitatively. Yet, on the ground of this principle alone, no single given appearance or intuition can be quantitatively determined. Similarly, in the case of the principle that every event has a cause, transcendental logic does not say *what* this cause is or *which* among the many possible causes is the real cause in the specific case.[37] Yet this is precisely the point of interest in natural science. The task of the first *Critique* was exclusively to establish the objective validity of the physical world. Since the understanding's a priori synthetic judgments or universal laws of nature *leave undetermined* all the infinite cases that can be counted under those laws, it follows that in addition to the understanding a particular faculty is needed that can

37. See for this L. Scaravelli's illuminating observations in *Scritti kantiani*, op. cit., 405.

effectively *determine* those particular cases. This faculty will be able to connect general laws with particular cases and particular cases to their general laws. This is the faculty of judgment that comes to the fore in the third *Critique*. Since determinant judgment by simply executing understanding's rule "is only subsumptive," it can provide no real determination for those manifold, empirical forms of nature that are left, as it were, thoroughly "indeterminate." It is at this point that Kant presents the specific function of the *reflective* faculty of judgment.

It should be noted that the realm of nature's manifold manifestations is introduced at first only in an oblique way. It is the task of the following §V to develop its features in a full-fledged way. Presently, Kant's aim is to disclose the necessity of a new principle that grounds the use of an independent *reflective* faculty of judgment. This principle is presented as the only condition under which we can possibly think and have experience of the manifold forms of nature left out of the first *Critique*. This is the conceptual reason for the long consecutive clause in which the opposition between nature in general and manifold forms of nature is inserted. Kant's main point in this statement is to introduce—with the necessity of a "must"—our need to appeal to a new principle. "*But there are such manifold forms* of nature, *so many modifications* as it were of the universal transcendental concepts of nature left indeterminate by those laws . . . *that there must be also laws for this manifold of forms and modifications*" (XXVI, 179, 31–180, 1). Strictly speaking, what Kant is deducing or inferring with this consecutive clause is not empirical laws of nature, which are simply *given* to our understanding ("*there are* such manifold forms"). He rather holds that since a manifold of empirical laws actually exists, they must be laws on the ground of an a priori necessary principle (this is an inference from the very notion of law). However, the understanding that legislates over "nature in general," is no longer legislative in "the labyrinth of the manifold of possible particular laws." In this sphere, understanding is suddenly dumb: "it cannot say anything"[38] concerning them, confesses Kant in the "First Introduction." The very "concept of a system according to these (empirical) laws is thoroughly alien to the understanding."[39] Particular empirical laws cannot be deduced from the transcendental laws of nature in a merely analytical way. Particular laws are called "modifications" (XXVI, 179, 32) of the universal concepts of nature (as their applications), but the transition from the universal to the particular is a problem that understanding cannot solve. There is no deductive transition from experience in general to a system of empirical laws. Hence, in the perspective of the understanding, a gap of legislation seems to threaten the world of nature. Yet, empirical laws are still there as *laws of nature*. We must keep in mind that nature, for Kant, always designates a system of phenomena regulated by laws; it is never a sum of merely empirically given events. Accordingly, empirical laws must be *somehow* necessary even though "*our* un-

38. EE §V, AA, XX, 214, 5–8.
39. EE §II, AA, XX, 203, 9–11.

derstanding" cannot but regard them as "contingent" (XXVI, 180, 1–2). From the facts that nature is present to us in its manifold manifestations and that neither understanding nor determinant faculty of judgment can provide us with rules to think of those manifold forms, it follows that we "must" assume that the empirical laws that determine those forms owe their "necessity" to a *different* "principle of the unity of the manifold." We must assume "this principle" even though, at this point, it still remains "unknown to us" (XXVI, 180, 4–5). So far, however, Kant has already disclosed that this principle must be the principle of the *unity* of an empirical manifold (i.e., a principle that guarantees the *systematicity* of the empirical and particular component of our experience of nature).

Kant is thereby addressing the problem of scientific induction. What is needed in this situation is the reflective faculty of judgment as the only faculty that is capable of finding out the universal rule for a particular empirical case. Since this faculty cannot be reduced to understanding and its laws, it will need its own principle. Accordingly, the still unknown principle of the unity of the empirical manifold must be a principle for the reflective faculty of judgment and for this faculty only. Once this relation is established, Kant has to address two further issues. (i) The first regards the origin and nature of this principle; (ii) the second regards the addressee of the legislation that arises out of that principle. In the case of reflective judgment the two questions will converge in one and the same answer.

(i) Experience cannot be the source of the principle. Ultimately, reflective judgment must ground the "possibility of the systematic subordination" (XXVII, 180, 10) of all empirical principles according to their ascending generality, which is precisely what makes possible our experience of the manifold forms of nature. But the principle that first makes experience possible cannot in turn be an empirical principle. Hence it must be a "transcendental principle" (XXVII, 180, 11).[40] The total system of experience cannot be grounded upon a principle that is itself empirical since the notion of a systematic unity is not possible by way of a posteriori inference. Moreover, the reflective faculty of judgment cannot take its principle from another faculty (be it understanding or reason) because, in this case, it would be reduced precisely to the function of determinant judgment (XXVII, 180, 12–13). Kant concludes that the source of the principle can only be the reflective faculty of judgment itself.

(ii) Reflective judgment cannot prescribe "such transcendental principle as law" to nature but only to itself (XXVII, 180, 11–12). Its function is not to determine the object for cognition but only to reflect on the particular in order to produce the general order of its lawfulness. Since "reflection" is bound to an empirical and particular starting point, we must assume that it is judgment that "depends on nature, not nature" (XXVII, 180, 14–17) on the merely contingent concept that we

40. Being a "transcendental principle," it will need a "deduction"; this will be the topic of §V.

can obtain for it. In the realm of the manifold manifestations of nature—as opposed to the world of nature in general proper to mathematics and (Newtonian) physics, no Copernican revolution seems possible. A distinctive type of lawfulness, however, can still be established therein by reflection. Kant calls this peculiar form of legislation "heautonomy." Since judgment can raise claim to an a priori legislation of its own, it does have an "autonomy." This legislation, however, is not "objective" as are the legislations of understanding and reason. These refer to concepts of objects or possible actions and first constitute them as what they are (as objects of possible knowledge or free actions). Instead, reflective judgment's legislation is only "subjective," namely valid for the faculty of judgment insofar as its activity is grounded on a principle a priori. The faculty of judgment gives the law neither to nature nor to freedom but only to itself.[41] This is judgment's heautonomy.

The Principle of Formal Purposiveness of Nature (XXVIII, 180, 31–181, 11)

Kant formulates the principle of the reflective faculty of judgment in the light of the previous considerations. Thereby he also clarifies what it means for the reflective faculty of judgment to be both source and addressee of a new transcendental principle. This is the only principle that makes it possible for us to think of the chaotic labyrinth of the manifold forms of nature as a coherent system of thoroughly interconnected empirical laws or as the unity of a "system of experience" (XXVII, 180, 24–25). Since this unity cannot be derived directly from our understanding's legislation (i.e., from universal laws of nature in general) as this leaves those manifold forms "indeterminate," we can make sense of such an order only in a reflected way. We must evaluate or judge this unity "as if" it had been established by "an understanding (even though not ours)" (XXVII, 180, 23–24) that would have given coherence to a manifold of empirical laws to the advantage of our cognitive faculties; that is, in order for us to have actual experience in a world in which our understanding cannot legislate and where, as a result, all experience seems to be utterly impossible. This said, Kant immediately opposes his as-if clause to what we must "actually" think (XXVII, 180, 23–24). Against all metaphysical temptations, Kant restates that the *status* of this alleged non-human understanding is only the *status* of an "idea" (XXVIII, 180, 28) that is necessary only subjectively for reflection, not for determination of objects. In other words, it is a regulative, not a constitutive, idea for our faculty of judgment; it is a rule that judgment gives only to itself in order to reflect upon nature, not to nature in order to determine it as an object of knowledge.[42] The understanding that we must assume in an *als-ob* hypothetical statement would arrange nature with the aim of producing the possibility of our experience of it. Neither our understanding nor an-

41. See EE §VIII, AA, XX, 225, 20–28 and §IX, 234, 23–24.

42. We can draw the difference by comparing the following expressions: in the present case, we evaluate or judge nature "as if it were . . ."; the understanding instead determines and knows appearances "as they are"; practical reason knows things "as they ought to be."

other understanding can give law to nature considered in the variety of its empirical forms; it is rather the reflective faculty of judgment that gives a rule to itself in order to think of nature as a coherent system of experience. It is important to stress that the indirect as-if procedure that authorizes us to formulate the transcendental principle of reflection is precisely that same heuristic procedure through which the reflective faculty of judgment operates (we must employ reflection in order to critically think about and to present the nature of the reflective faculty of judgment).

In Kant's view, the notion of system, or the lawful unity of a manifold of empirical laws to which the reflective faculty of judgment resolves, leads directly to the notions of *Zweck* and *Zweckmäßigkeit*—purpose and purposiveness. Understanding's legislation establishes the existence of objects in the sensible world with no concern for the purposes to which that existence may refer. Moreover, the unity of the system of experience that both transcendental and determinant judgment are able to construct is the product of mere subsumption under given laws and is not the unity of a final purpose. Practical reason, on the other hand, does recognize the notion of purpose as essential; yet for practical reason, purpose is ultimately identical with the very idea of freedom. Instead, for the reflective faculty of judgment, purpose becomes the constitutive notion that defines its transcendental specificity as an independent cognitive faculty.

In the concluding passages of the section, Kant presents two crucial ideas: in the first place, the notion of *Zweck,* which he defines as "the concept of an object insofar as it contains, at the same time, the ground for the actuality of this object" (XXVIII, 180, 31–32). The definition of *Zweckmäßigkeit* follows: "The accordance of a thing with that constitution of things that is possible only through purposes" is the purposiveness of its "form" (XXVIII, 180, 34–33). In the light of these notions, Kant can reformulate the principle of the faculty of judgment as the principle of the *formal purposiveness of nature* in its manifold (XXVIII, 180, 36–37).[43] Reflective judgment does not assume any (objective) purpose of nature; it rather formulates, as a condition for the possibility of an experience of nature in its manifold, the maxim according to which things in nature can be considered as in harmony with an order of things that would be possible only according to purposes. This harmony, or accordance (*Übereinstimmung*), is expressed by Kant's notion of "formal purposiveness." From the mere *form* of the purposiveness of a thing, no inference is allowed to the existence of a *real* purpose. For real purpose, as opposed to merely formal purposiveness, always presupposes the existence of a rational (or intelligent) cause that judgment is not authorized to infer. Yet the notion of formal purposiveness still represents nature "as if an understanding (al-

---

43. In the "First Introduction," Kant still uses the notion of "technic of nature" as synonym of purposiveness of nature, meaning both purposiveness of nature with regard to our cognitive faculties and nature's own purposive formations (see, for example, EE §V, AA XX, 213–214). In the introduction and throughout the third *Critique*, the expression "technic of nature" is employed only in the second meaning.

beit not a determinant understanding) contained the ground for the unity of the manifold of its empirical laws" (XXVIII, 181,1–2). By means of this principle, the reflective faculty of judgment is able to constitute the chaotic manifold of nature's forms into a *system* of empirical laws in general.

The notion of formal purposiveness appears as the a priori condition for all possible particular purpose. The notion of purpose is an empirical concept that can make sense, transcendentally, only on the ground of the specific a priori principle of formal purposiveness. Formal purposiveness cannot, in turn, be identified with any particular purpose (we know that reflective judgment's principle cannot be taken from experience). Formal purposiveness is a particular and "*special* [*besonderer*] concept a priori" (XXVIII, 181, 3–4) (not a *universal* law of nature) that can have its source only in the reflective faculty of judgment. As already suggested, since the notion of purpose can neither be constitutive of natural objects as such nor provide knowledge of things, it does not belong to understanding's legislation, even though it concerns the sensible world of nature. It is a notion used to reflect upon nature and to represent the possibility of a thoroughgoing connection of its empirical laws. The faculty of judgment's principle differs also from "practical purposiveness (proper to human art or also to morals), even though we do think of it by analogy with practical purposiveness" (XXVIII, 181, 9–11). The analogic way of representing nature's purposiveness is the first occurrence of the notion of a technical consideration of nature, which Kant disclosed already in §I of the "First Introduction."[44] Thereby Kant suggests that analogy is somehow constitutive of reflective judgment's own principle and procedure. In this connection, the notions of purpose and purposiveness already reveal the intermediary and mediating character proper to the faculty of judgment's principle. This principle is a rule that functions in analogy with practical reason. While it regards the possibility of an object's reality in the sensible world, it also connects *somehow* this sensible reality to the supersensible proper to practical reason.

Apodeictic and Regulative Use of Reason and the Determinant/Reflective Distinction

In the appendix to the Transcendental Dialectic of the first *Critique*, Kant offers a discussion of concepts and procedures of scientific reasoning that seems to anticipate the topic of the third *Critique* as formulated, in its first occurrence, in §§IV–V of the introduction.[45] In particular, he draws a distinction between the "constitutive," or "apodeictic," use of reason and its ideas, and its "regulative," or "hypothetical," employment—a distinction in which we can find the conceptual antece-

---

44. See, Kant's *On the Use of Teleological Principles in Philosophy*, AA VIII, 181.

45. See the general remarks by M. Friedman, "Kant on Laws of Nature and the Foundations of Newtonian Science," in *Proceedings: Sixth International Kant Congress*, ed. by G. Funke, Th. Seebohm, Washington D.C., University Press of America, 97–107, here 97 f; see also his "Regulative and Constitutive," in *The Southern Journal of Philosophy,* 1991, 30, Supplement, 73–101.

dent of the distinction between determinant and reflective faculty of judgment.[46] In this appendix, Kant raises numerous issues that he will be taking up again in the third *Critique*. At stake is the possibility of a systematic unity of all cognition reached through understanding: that is, a systematic unity of experience. With regard to this issue, Kant introduces the notions of purposiveness, systematicity, heuristic principles in science, the affinity of natural phenomena, the classification of phenomena in genera and species, the maxims of homogeneity, specification, and continuity of natural forms. However, it is important to observe that at the end of the first *Critique*, Kant saw the only legitimate place for this discussion to be a mere appendix to the Dialectic. This indicates that in 1781–1787, the problem of the possibility of a system of experience (i.e., the issue of a unification of the manifold empirical laws of nature) does not yet present the urgency of a critical or transcendental problem for Kant. It is certainly not a problem concerning a specific cognitive faculty and involving a specific a priori principle.[47]

In a statement that seems to be constructed as a parallel to the opening of §IV of our text, Kant claims that "if reason is a faculty of deducing the particular from the universal," two cases are possible. "Either the universal is already certain in itself and given, and only *Urteilskraft* is required to execute the process of subsumption, and the particular is thereby determined in a necessary manner. This I shall entitle the apodeictic use of reason. Or the universal is admitted as *problematic* only, and is a mere idea; the particular is certain, but the universality of the rule of which it is a consequence is still a problem. Several particular instances, which are all certain, are scrutinized in view of the rule, to see whether they follow from it," namely to see whether they are instances of precisely that rule. "This I shall entitle the hypothetical employment of reason."[48] The hypothetical employment of reason is not

---

46. For a discussion of the relation between this appendix and the deduction of the principle of purposiveness in the third *Critique*, see W. Bartuschat, *Zum systematischen Ort von Kants Kritik der Urteilskraft*, Frankfurt a.M., Klostermann, 1972, 39–53; R. P. Horstmann, "Why Must There Be a Transcendental Deduction in the Third Critique?" in *Kant's Transcendental Deductions*, ed. by E. Förster, Stanford, Stanford University Press, 1989, 157–177, 165, 168. For Horstmann there is a contradiction between the notion of a *logical* principle of purposiveness presented in the first *Critique* and the *transcendental* principle of purposiveness that he offers in the third *Critique*. Different is the position held by R. Brandt, *The Deductions in the Critique of Judgment: Comments on Hampshire and Horstmann*, in *Kant's Transcendental Deductions,* op. cit., 177–190.

47. For a discussion of this section of the first *Critique*, see chapter 4. See L. Scaravelli, *Scritti kantiani*, op. cit., 387 ff. It is interesting to note that all passages that in the first *Critique* bear some relation to the notion of reflection formulated in the *Critique of Judgment* are to be found in appendixes, not in the body of the main argument (namely the appendix on the Amphiboly of *Reflexionsbegriffe* and the appendix on the Regulative Employment of the Ideals of Pure Reason).

48. KrV B 674 f./A 646 f. For the relation between regulative use of ideas and the *principia convenientiae* that Kant formulates already in the *Dissertatio* of 1770 (§30, AA, II, 418), see R. Brandt, *The Deductions in the Critique of Judgment*, op. cit., 181; and N.

constitutive of objects but is a fundamental regulative tool that reason provides to the understanding's work in science. Kant draws this distinction while presenting the need of our reason to proceed in search of the unifying principle of all cognition proper to the understanding. This search displays the ascending structure that leads to the construction of a system of experience based upon the progressive subordination of particulars under more general rules (the notions of genus and species).[49]

The "highest formal unity" that reason produces in its endeavor toward systematicity is the "*purposive* unity of things."[50] Such a unity allows for the most extended systematic view of the connection of things according to "teleological laws."[51] In the first *Critique*, Kant provides no justification for the possibility of this notion of purposiveness and teleology. He does not even feel the need for such a justification. The regulative use of reason is simply juxtaposed to other functions of both understanding and theoretical reason and does not demand any particular a priori principle. Consequently, its discussion pertains only to an appendix. It would take Kant almost ten years to recognize in the regulative use of reason with regard to the highest unity of appearances and their laws the activity of the reflective faculty of judgment in need for an a priori principle of its own.

2. Synopsis: §V, The Principle of Formal Purposiveness of Nature Is a Transcendental Principle of the Faculty of Judgment

The conclusion of §IV presented the notion of formal purposiveness as reflective judgment's "special" principle a priori. The task is now to show that this purposiveness differs *in principle* both from technical-practical (i.e., theoretical purposiveness) and from moral-practical purposiveness. In addition, reflective judgment's principle is now assessed as a "transcendental principle" whose legitimacy is accordingly in need of a preliminary "deduction." In §V, Kant presents the world of the third *Critique* in its general traits. The section is articulated in three major steps. First Kant has to show that the principle of formal purposiveness of nature for our cognitive faculties is an a priori "transcendental principle" of our reflective faculty of judgment (XXIX, 181,15–XXXI, 182, 25). Then, he has to provide a "transcendental deduction" of this principle (XXXI, 182, 26–XXXIV, 184, 21). Finally, he has to establish this principle as specific to the reflective faculty of judgment in an investigation of nature in its empirical forms that extends beyond what the a priori laws of the understanding would allow us to know (XXXIV, 184, 22–XXXVIII, 186, 21).

Kemp-Smith, *A Commentary to Kant's Critique of Pure Reason*, London, Macmillan, 1918, 548.

49. KrV B 683/A 655.
50. KrV B 714/A 686.
51. KrV B 715/A 687.

2.1. §V Commentary: Nature in General and Nature in Its Manifold Empirical Forms—Transcendental Laws and Empirical Laws

What kind of principle is the special principle of the reflective faculty of judgment? In the "First Introduction," Kant designates this principle in a variety of ways. He refers to it as "principle for evaluating and investigating nature," a "maxim" for the faculty of judgment, a "mere idea" for researching nature, a "heuristic principle in the evaluation of empirical laws," a "transcendental presupposition" (*transcendentale Voraussetzung*), and a "transcendental principle."[52] Through all these designations, Kant pursues a twofold aim. On the one hand, he points to the stage of the research in which such a presupposition, maxim, or idea is to be encountered; on the other, he refers to the place occupied by such a principle in the system of the faculties.

Transcendental and Metaphysical Principles (XXIX, 181,15–XXXI, 182,36)

At the beginning of §V, Kant draws a twofold distinction. On the one hand, he distinguishes a "transcendental" from a "metaphysical" principle (XXIX, 181, 15–20). On the other, he separates empirical principles from principles a priori (XXX, 182, 6–9). Kant contends that the principle of formal purposiveness of nature is a transcendental a priori principle of the reflective faculty of judgment. He reaches this conclusion through a series of steps in which he proves that (i) formal purposiveness is not a metaphysical but a transcendental principle; (ii) it is a rule that grounds our evaluation of nature and yet can be provided neither by understanding as legislator over nature in general nor by reason in its moral or speculative (regulative) employment but only by reflection; (iii) its logical necessity cannot be justified in a psychological or empirical way but is to be proved only by a transcendental deduction.

(i) A transcendental principle provides the a priori universal condition under which alone things can become objects (*Objekte*) of our "cognition in general" (XXIX, 181,17).[53] A metaphysical principle "represents the only a priori condition under which objects whose concept must be given empirically can be further determined a priori" (XXIX, 181, 18–20). In both cases, the principle provides an a priori condition, but while a transcendental principle first institutes the possibility of ever thinking or knowing objects as such, a metaphysical principle requires the empirical concept of an object as its starting point. Both transcendental and metaphysical principles are a priori, for in neither case does the determination of the subject through the predicate require reference to experience. Kant exemplifies this difference by comparing two propositions concerning our cognition of bodies as changeable substances. "Change in bodies must have a cause" (XXIX,

52. See in order EE §II 204, 7; 205, 3; 205,7; 205, 12; §IV 209, 3; §V 223, 34.

53. See R. P. Horstmann, "Why Must There Be a Transcendental Deduction," op. cit., 168, 170 for the "shift" in the meaning of "*transcendental*" that he claims would take place between the first and the third *Critique*.

181, 22–23) is a transcendental proposition that we can know a priori by simply assuming the concept "body" as determined through a category or *pure* concept of the understanding (for example, substance). "Change must have an *external* cause" (XXIX, 181, 24) is, on the contrary, a metaphysical proposition whose starting point must be the *empirical* concept of a body (viewed as a thing in space subject to movement) if we want its further determination through the predicate "*external* cause" to follow a priori (and hence the judgment to be an a priori and not a merely empirical judgment). Referring back to the discussion of §IV, Kant contends that the principle of formal purposiveness of nature in its manifold empirical laws is transcendental. The concept of the object that is thought of "under" this principle (i.e., as belonging to an order of nature that is in accordance with our cognitive faculties) is not an empirical concept but rather the "pure concept of the objects [*Gegenstände*] of our possible knowledge through experience in general" (XXX, 181, 34–182, 1). As we have argued, formal purposiveness is not identical with real purpose, which is an empirical concept. It is rather the only a priori condition under which the manifold forms of nature can become for us the object of a coherent experience in general. This distinction allows Kant to separate the notion of formal purposiveness from practical purposiveness. The principle of practical purposiveness implied by the determination of the free will is a metaphysical principle as it must assume the empirical notion of a will as its starting point.

In §74, while discussing the notion of *Naturzweck* and its status, Kant presents the difference between "dogmatic" and "critical" procedures of reason.[54] The dogmatic procedure is metaphysical and is followed by the determinant faculty of judgment; the critical procedure is transcendental and is followed by the reflective faculty of judgment. To treat a concept (even if its origin is empirical) "dogmatically" is to think of it as "contained under another concept of the object that constitutes a principle of reason" and to determine it according to this principle. This procedure "has the force of law" (is "*gesetzmäßig*") for determinant judgment in all its subsumptions. On the contrary, "we treat a concept merely *critically* if we consider it only in relation to our cognitive faculty, and hence in relation to the subjective conditions under which we think of it, without venturing to decide anything about its object."[55] The critical and transcendental procedure of reason is *gesetzmäßig* for the reflective faculty of judgment. The concept of a thing as "natural purpose" is a concept whose objective reality cannot be proved. Therefore, no determination of objects is possible through it except in a dogmatic and metaphysical way. The concept, however, can be used by the reflective faculty of judgment in order to critically and transcendentally reflect upon the relation between the object and our cognitive faculties.

---

54. In this connection Kant discusses the lack of "objective reality" proper to the concept of real purpose: §74, 330, 331, AA 396,12–13; 397, 2–3.

55. §74, 329, AA 395, 30–32; see also §91, 454, AA 467, 4–9.

(ii) The "maxims of the faculty of judgment" that are used as the a priori ground for our investigation of nature provide an example of how the transcendental principle of nature's purposiveness is at work in scientific thinking. We stand in need of these maxims when the question is not merely the possibility of our knowledge of "nature in general" (a question answered by the first *Critique* along with mathematics' and physics' a priori propositions), but rather when the question concerns the possibility of our experience of nature as "determined through a manifold of particular laws" (XXX, 182, 14–16). Kant presents under these maxims those traditional formulations, which were made into a trend[56] by Linnaeus in the taxonomy and systematic of eighteenth-century natural sciences. They occur in metaphysics as well, where they have the status of rules that cannot be demonstrated from concepts. Among such formulae, Kant mentions the *lex parsimoniae*, the *lex continui in naturae*, the rule *principia praeter necessitatem non sunt multiplicanda*, and so forth.[57] These paradigmatic propositions make sense only in relation to particular experiences as well as to a corpus of actual scientific knowledge. The laws thus expressed are attempts at a systematization of nature in its manifold empirical forms, attempts to think of a unitary order within which the chaotic labyrinth of natural forms could make sense and be grasped by our cognitive faculty. These maxims are nothing but instances of the principle of formal purposiveness whose source is neither understanding nor reason (not even in its regulative employment as still suggested in the appendix to the Transcendental Dialectic of the first *Critique*)[58] nor the determinant faculty of judgment but the *reflective* faculty of judgment only. They do not express any objective constitution of things in nature (they are not rules to determine nature) but merely provide a tool for our subjective reflection upon nature. By their means, the reflective faculty of judgment institutes a relation between the manifold empirical forms of nature and our cognitive faculties in order to be able to ascend from the particular and empirical case to a general—even though still empirical—rule under which the particular can be thought of.

(iii) What is the ground, or the source, of the *Grundsätze* expressed in those formulas? The source cannot be identified in a psychological way, warns Kant. For empirical psychology would trace them back to a merely empirical source (XXXI, 182, 26–27). But their nonempirical origin, according to Kant, is clearly imprinted in them as we can easily recognize if only we focus on what these maxims

56. See EE §IV, 210, 20 ff.

57. See also KrV B 685 ff./A 657 ff., where the principles of "homogeneity, specification, and continuity" of nature's forms are mentioned. See, for the general topic represented by these laws, A. Lovejoy, *The Great Chain of Being*, New York/London, Harper & Row, 1936, here 240 f. It is worth noticing that Lovejoy does not mention the *Critique of Judgment* at all and only refers to Kant's formulations in the appendix to the Transcendental Dialectic of the first *Critique*.

58. EE §IV, 210, 26–28; see KrV B 679 f./A 651 f.

really mean (XXXI, 182, 33–34). For they do not describe what happens, according to what rule our cognitive processes take place and how we do formulate our judgments, which could still be a matter of psychology. They rather prescribe how we "ought to judge" in order to make sense of the particular empirical constitution of nature. Thus, these rules claim a "logical objective necessity" that no empirical source and no empirical consideration can justify (XXXI, 182,31). As Kant contended in §IV, if empirical laws of nature should indeed be called "laws," they must be able to claim a necessity that only an a priori principle can grant to them (XXVI, 182, 2–3).

From these considerations, Kant's conclusion follows. Given that the principle of "formal purposiveness of nature for our cognitive faculties and their use" is neither a metaphysical principle of reason nor an empirical principle of psychology, it must be recognized as "a transcendental principle of judgments [*Urteile*]" (XXXI, 182, 32–34). As such, it "needs a transcendental deduction by means of which the ground for such judging must be found a priori in the sources of cognition" (XXXI, 182, 34–36). A deduction has to prove that without that principle, experience of nature in its manifold empirical forms would be utterly impossible for us.

Deduction of the Principle of Formal Purposiveness of Nature: Nature in General and Specifically Different Natures (XXXI, 182, 37–XXXII, 183, 13)

Kant opposes the world of nature in general established by the *Critique of Pure Reason* to the manifold forms of nature and their empirical laws whose possible experience is now the issue at stake. The whole section is built on the relation and opposition between pairs of terms: nature in general/manifold forms of nature, universal and transcendental laws/particular and empirical laws, possible experience in general/empirical cognition. The problem of the third *Critique* arises out of the impossibility of an analytical and deductive transition from the laws of the understanding to empirical concepts. Reflective judgment is the power that allows Kant to account for the possibility of empirical concepts and their meaningfulness for our cognitive faculty.

The world of nature in general is the world governed by the transcendental laws of the understanding explored in the first *Critique*. It is a world of appearances in general, of objects in space and time made possible for us by the synthesis in the unity of the "I think" and by a priori principles such as those of substance, causality, and community. These principles are established independently of experience by applying the categories of the understanding to the pure a priori forms of intuition by means of the schematism and are strictly necessary (XXXII, 183, 1–5, 13). They make experience first possible for us, for without them nature as a complex of all objects of the senses would not be even thinkable (XXXII, 183, 2–3).

Within the homogeneous generality of this world, Kant places the determinant faculty of judgment. Kant has already shown that under the understanding's legislation the faculty of judgment is *only* determinant. Its exclusive job is to subsume given cases (which can be cases given empirically as well as a priori) under those general laws and principles (XXXII, 183, 5–7). Understanding, for example, gives the "universal law of nature": "all change has its cause"—which is the principle expressed by the second "analogy of experience."[59] This law determines for the first time what appearances *in general* or objects *in general* are for us, and hence it is valid for all objects as possible objects of experience. "The transcendental faculty of judgment" now has the task of *applying* this principle. To this aim, it has "nothing else to do but to provide a priori the condition of the subsumption under the concept of the understanding that is at hand. This condition is the succession of the determinations of one and the same thing" (XXXII, 183, 7–12). The faculty of judgment, which is here determinant, has only to indicate the condition under which subsumption under the given concept can take place. In our case, judgment has to check whether the condition of the succession of determinations in one and the same thing is fulfilled, which is the a priori determination of change. If there is change, then it must have its cause. "Experience itself —in other words, empirical knowledge of appearances—is possible only insofar as we subject the succession of appearances, and therefore all alteration, to the law of causality."[60]

All this holds for the world of nature in general, in which universal laws of nature define the realm of what is for us "possible experience" (XXXII, 183, 12–13). Besides this sphere, however, we find the vast, yet unexplored realm of particular objects of "empirical cognition" (XXXII, 183,14). The problem that this realm poses to us is not sufficiently answered (properly, is not even addressed) by the claim that if there is change, then it must have its cause, for the question is now, *What* is the specific cause of *this* specific change? What we have to account for in this world of particular events is not simply the way in which the category of causality is commonly shared by a manifold of empirical causes. We must account for a manifold of different causes that differ precisely in the specific way in which they are cause. How does the world of nature in general relate to our particular empirical cognitions; how does the unity of experience in general relate to the manifold of our 'empirical experiences'?[61]

A passage of the 1781 edition of the Transcendental Deduction shows Kant's awareness of the issue at stake already at that time. Yet in this same passage, Kant clearly states that the task of the first *Critique* is exclusively that of establishing the transcendental laws of nature according to which and under which the manifold of nature's empirical laws becomes possible—even though these empirical laws cannot be derived from understanding itself.

59. See KrV B 232 ff./A 189 ff.

60. KrV B 234/A 189.

61. The expression *empirical experience* seems a tautological reiteration of one and the same concept. However, in the case of the confrontation between the first and the third *Critique* it aptly expresses the development of Kant's problem of experience.

> However exaggerated and absurd it may sound, to say that understanding is itself the source of the laws of nature, and so of its formal unity, such an assertion in nonetheless correct and is in keeping with the object to which it refers, namely experience. Certainly, *empirical laws*, as such, *can never derive their origin from pure understanding*. That is as little possible as to understanding completely the inexhaustible multiplicity of appearances merely by reference to the pure form of sensible intuition. But *all empirical laws are only special determinations of the pure laws of the understanding, under which, and according to the norm of which, they first become possible.*[62]

In an extraordinary footnote to §II of the "First Introduction," Kant presents in a dramatic way the problem opened by the first *Critique*. This problem is now the crucial issue brought to the fore by the new critical framework of the third *Critique*.

> The possibility of an experience in general is the possibility of empirical cognitions as synthetic judgments. Hence this possibility cannot be derived *analytically* from a mere comparison of perceptions . . . for the connection of two different perceptions in the concept of an object (to yield a cognition of it) is a *synthesis*, and the only way in which this synthesis makes empirical cognition, i.e., experience, possible is through principles [*Prinzipien*] of the synthetic unity of appearances, i.e., through principles [*Grundsätze*] by which they are brought under the categories. Now these empirical cognitions do form an *analytic unity of all experience according to that which they necessarily have in common (namely those transcendental laws of nature), but they do not form that synthetic unity of experience as a system that connects the empirical laws even according to that in which they differ (and where their diversity can be infinite) . . .*[63]

This footnote has not been included in the published introduction even though its content is integrally maintained in §V. It has been rightly suggested that one of the reasons for not including this passage in the final text was probably the striking contrast with the main thesis of the first *Critique* generated by the claim that the *synthetic* principles of the understanding form, as it were, nothing more than a merely *analytic* unity and have, after all the first *Critique* tried to demonstrate, a merely *analytical* function.[64]

A priori principles and judgments ground the possibility of experience insofar as—and precisely because—they are *synthetic*. This is the crucial issue raised by the first *Critique*, namely the possibility of a priori *synthetic* judgments. Now Kant contends that synthetic a priori principles entail that which all our empirical cognitions "*have necessarily in common.*" Therefore, on the ground of synthetic a priori

62. KrV A 127 f.; see also KrV B 165 for the relation between the lawfulness of "nature in general" and "particular laws" that concern "empirically determined appearances."

63. EE §II, AA, XX, 203–204 fn.

64. See L. Scaravelli, *Scritti kantiani*, op. cit. 349 ff.

principles (transcendental laws of nature), "the *analytic* unity of all experience" first becomes possible. Yet, quite paradoxically, Kant has to admit that synthetic a priori principles still do not make possible "that *synthetic* unity of experience as a system that connects under one principle empirical laws *also according to that in which they differ* . . ." It is evident that in this footnote Kant presents as analytic what in the first *Critique* was claimed instead to be synthetic. Those same transcendental principles that the first *Critique* demonstrated to be synthetic have here, with regard to the empirical difference of phenomena, a merely analytic function. Although logically their synthetic nature is certainly not repealed, Kant is now interested in stressing their transcendental role within the process of our *empirical* cognition of nature. With regard to this further problem, they do provide the analytic unity of experience in general by expressing that which all experiences have in common. Yet, since they cannot say anything concerning how different empirical laws actually differ from each other, they cannot ground the synthetic unity of empirical cognitions or the system of empirical laws of nature.[65] Both the work of the understanding and the work of determinant judgment take place in a realm where all phenomena and objects are viewed as completely *homogeneous*. This is the world of nature in general. Through its laws we know what empirical objects have necessarily in common but nothing more than that. Understanding's synthetic a priori principles provide us with no access to how empirical things in their specificity differ as they cannot account for a world whose composition is essentially *heterogeneous*. To be sure, on the ground of those principles alone we would not even be able to distinguish one object from the other as a specifically and empirically determined object (and not just as appearance in general). A star, a volcano, a beam of light, a stone are homogeneous things insofar as they are all appearances in space and time, all have a degree, are in reciprocal connection, and so on. All these features, however, by simply constituting the necessary conditions of the possibility of these objects as phenomena of nature—and hence the necessary conditions of their being, for us, possible objects of experience—are only conditions that all objects have necessarily in common. These conditions are indeed necessary in order to qualify those objects as objects of nature in general, but they do not specify them in their empirical difference (i.e., precisely as a star, a volcano, a beam of light, a stone [even less as *this* star, stone, etc.]). Hence, by subsuming under understanding's laws, we can by no means know objects in their heterogeneity. This is, however, the essential additional step in all natural sciences and in all empirical cognition.

The issue of what makes the *specific difference* of our empirical cognitions of things in nature—the problem of the *synthetic* unity of experience and empirical laws insofar as they are different (and not insofar as they have something in common)—is the special problem raised by the reflective faculty of judgment and its "special" a priori principle in the third *Critique*. In light of this new problem of

---

65. In what sense does Newton's law of gravitation—$F = Gm_1m_2$—differ from Coulomb's law: $F = -kg_1g_2$?

'synthesis,' nature in its manifold forms raises new questions for us. If the "succession of the determinations of one and the same thing" (change) is the condition that guarantees the possibility of subsuming a given case under the universal law of causality, and if our transcendental judgment is supposed to determine our object for us in this way, then we can easily voice our dissatisfaction with this determination. We can easily recognize that "besides that formal condition of time, objects of empirical cognition are further determined in a multiplicity of ways, or as far as we can judge a priori, are determinable in a multiplicity of ways so that *specifically different natures, apart from what they have in common as belonging to nature in general, can still be causes in an infinite variety of ways*" (XXXII, 183, 14–18). There is a point in all scientific inquiry in which what we want to know is the specific cause of a certain specific effect. When facing this problem, we can certainly not be satisfied by the general claim that all change has a cause. There is a whole realm of possible determination, or determinability, that both understanding with its universal laws and determinant judgment in its application of them cannot but leave completely indeterminate.

Kant grants that we can already see so much by way of mere a priori consideration, which deals with nature in general and not with specifically different natures to which only empirical cognition has access. Even though understanding has no access to the realm of "possible determination" that constitutes the specificity of each particular case of experience, and precisely because determinant judgment falls short in its effort to determine it, understanding is led to suspect that a vast sphere of determinability must extend beyond its own domain. Understanding must recognize a priori that it is at least *possible* that objects of experience stay under an infinite number of empirical rules besides the transcendental laws of nature. While experience in general is predicated upon the condition that "we subject the succession of appearances and therefore all alteration, to the law of causality,"[66] empirical cognition is concerned precisely with the *different ways* in which causality can be attributed to different objects and even to one and the same object in varying (empirical and experimental) situations.

Deduction of the Principle of Formal Purposiveness of Nature.
Empirical Laws of Nature: Contingency and Necessity (XXXII, 183, 14–XXXIV, 184, 21)

What can we establish with regard to the relation between transcendental laws of nature and empirical laws? We have already noticed that in the understanding's perspective (i.e., "as far as we can judge a priori"), empirical laws in their manifold cannot be analytically derived, deduced, or inferred exclusively from universal laws. Their possibility, however, is still recognized a priori by the understanding. In spite of the impossibility of providing a strict necessity for empirical laws analogous to the absolute necessity proper to transcendental laws of nature, Kant's argument will proceed from now on through a series of "musts" (XXXII, 183,19; XXXIII, 183, 23, 29, 34; XXXIV, 184, 6, 15) that mark a crucial transi-

66. KrV B 234/A 189.

tion in the argument of the introduction from the hypothetical procedure that characterized §§I–IV to the result of the deduction of reflective judgment's own principle in its necessity.

Kant argues in terms of a dialectic that plays itself out between our thinking of empirical laws in their *manifold* and our thinking of them in their *unity*. What is at stake in this dialectic is the relation between *contingency* and *necessity*. In the "First Introduction" Kant adds the opposition between "aggregate" and "system"[67]—an opposition that becomes relevant in the present connection. The crucial question can be formulated as follows: what is it that allows us to think of the infinite multiplicity and heterogeneity of nature's laws as unified in a coherent *system* of experience rather than assembled randomly together to form an incoherent *aggregate*? While the problem of the *Critique of Pure Reason* was to establish the conditions of the possibility of experience *in general*; the task of the third *Critique* is to establish the conditions for the possibility of a *systematic* experience. The crucial point is that from the absolute necessity of the former the necessity of the latter cannot be inferred. Kant's argument can be summarized as follows: empirical *laws* of nature enjoy the necessity of laws; however, being *empirical* laws, their necessity for us is not an a priori necessity, and in this respect they must be considered as contingent. Contingency leads us to assume that empirical laws must be *infinite* in their heterogeneity (and therefore ungraspable by a finite understanding). Accordingly, the *unity* of this manifold is also judged by us as contingent. Yet we *must* necessarily assume the systematic unity of experience. Otherwise no experience of nature in its infinite variety of forms would be possible for us, and we would be condemned to think and live in the chaos of a totally disconnected and meaningless aggregate of perceptions. The principle that grounds the assumption of the systematic unity of experience is reflective judgment's principle of the formal purposiveness of nature.

Kant's first step in this preliminary deduction is to establish the necessity proper to empirical laws. As he already suggested in §IV (XXVI, 180, 2–3), if every mode in which a thing can be a cause describes (or instantiates) a particular kind of causality (i.e., can still refer to the notion of causality in general [XXXII, 183, 19–20]) (as it actually is the case in natural science) even though it cannot be deduced from it in its specificity, then each one of the different ways in which causality works "*must* . . . have its rule, and this rule is a law that consequently carries *necessity* with itself" (XXXII, 183, 20–21). Yet we can only infer this distributive necessity (the necessity of each particular rule) in an indirect way. We cannot prove it a priori. This is due to the limitation of our cognitive faculties and in particular of our understanding and its legislation.

Moreover, precisely because of the limitation of our cognitive faculties, we must infer an *unlimited* manifold of empirical laws; we must think of the *manifold*

---

67. EE §IV, AA XX, 209, 17. For the difference between system and aggregate, see A. Nuzzo, *System,* Bielefeld, Transcript Verlag, 2003.

of nature's empirical laws as potentially *infinite* and contingent. "We *must* think in nature, as regards its *merely empirical laws*, a possibility of an *infinite multiplicity of empirical laws* that are nonetheless contingent (cannot be known a priori) so far as our insight goes" (XXXIII, 183, 22–26). Kant's careful sketch of the geography of the human mind in §II defined a topography of closed, limited regions (field, territory, and domain). The necessary limitation of our cognitive faculties amounts to the necessarily limited and finite extension of their respective domains as well as to the limited and finite number of a priori universal laws that exercise legislation therein (both in the theoretical and in the practical domain). On the contrary, the new territory of the reflective faculty of judgment is announced from the outset as unlimited and infinite in its empirical manifold.[68] Being an infinite realm, it will not be mastered by any finite set of a priori objective laws but will display a necessarily infinite variety of empirical laws.

We must regard such multiplicity of empirical laws as contingent (i.e., not determinable a priori), although the very possibility of this multiplicity can be stated a priori. In addition, we evaluate as contingent *their unity* as well as the *possibility of a systematic unity of our experience.* With regard to the infinite variety of empirical laws "we judge the *unity of nature according to empirical laws*, as well as the *possibility of the unity of experience* (as system according to empirical laws) to be contingent" (XXXIII, 183, 26–28). There is no objective a priori necessity that can ground our claim to a systematic experience of an infinite number of empirical laws, even though each of those empirical laws must be necessary in order for it to be a law. This means that our experience of the manifold forms of nature could very well be the nonexperience of a chaos, the devastating encounter with a "crude chaotic aggregate without the slightest trace of a system,"[69] the situation of a "labyrinth of manifold possible particular laws"[70] with no possibility of orientation in it or even a way out from it.

It is at this point that Kant introduces a crucial "must" in the argument of the deduction.[71] Upon this must, namely, upon the necessity of assuming a way out of the "labyrinth" of experience toward a "system" of it, depends the legitimacy of the problem of the third *Critique.* Even though we do judge the possibility of a systematic unity of experience to be contingent, the manifold of empirical laws *viewed as a whole must* have a certain peculiar type of necessity so that "such a unity *must necessarily* be presupposed and assumed; otherwise . . ." (XXXIII, 183, 29). As the construction of Kant's argument suggests, the necessity of this presupposition is one that can be reached only by an *ad absurdum* reasoning (i.e., indirectly, under the threatening menace of an untenable "otherwise" that would immediately follow). We do judge the unity of empirical laws as (objectively)

---

68. See E §VI, LXII, 188, 26–29.

69. EE §IV, AA XX, 209, 17.

70. EE §V, AA XX, 214,7-8.

71. See also EE §IV, AA XX, 208, 27: "Eben darum *muß* auch die Erfahrung . . . ," 209, 24–25.

contingent and yet we must necessarily assume this unity; that is, we must assume the system of experience as a necessary presupposition (note that Kant is not saying that we must judge this unity to be *objectively* necessary, for objectively this unity is thoroughly contingent—experience constantly reminds us of this, and understanding judges it accordingly; the necessity of our assumption is rather a merely *subjective* necessity). Doing "otherwise" would immediately lead us to the impossibility of having any coherent experience of the whole of nature in the heterogeneity of its empirical laws. The consequence, in point of fact, would be that "our empirical cognitions would not cohere to form the thoroughgoing interconnection of a whole of experience" (XXXIII, 183, 30–31). In this case, to be sure, no empirical cognition would be possible at all.

Kant's explanation of this impossibility is relevant as it brings us back to the footnote to §II of the "First Introduction" previously discussed. The possibility for us to connect empirical cognitions into a meaningful whole of experience necessarily depends upon our assumption of the possibility of a system of experience since this whole cannot be grounded upon "the universal laws of nature" established by the understanding. The possibility of empirical cognition as experience is not guaranteed by the possibility of experience in general, for the *synthetic unity* of empirical cognition cannot be grounded upon or deduced from the *analytic unity* of experience in general. The world of nature in general could still appear to us as totally disconnected from the empirical world of nature, and no experience would be possible in this situation. "The universal laws of nature provide indeed such a connection among things taken in their genus as things of nature in general but not among things taken in their specificity as the particular natural beings that they are" (XXXIII, 183, 32–34).

At this point, Kant reveals the subject of all these "musts."[72] It is only the faculty of judgment that can—and therefore also must—necessarily assume the possibility of a systematic unity of nature in its manifold empirical laws. For understanding, as we have already seen, "cannot say anything" with regard to the labyrinth of nature's particular laws.[73] Hence, the reflective faculty of judgment must intervene by assuming the a priori principle of formal purposiveness of nature as the necessary presupposition for its own reflective employment (the task is *to find* the universal for the particular empirically given case since the empirically given case cannot be subsumed under any of the given universals or—which is the same—since no universal is given for the empirical case at hand). Such principle assumes the system of experience as necessary with regard to our cognitive faculties (i.e., as *subjectively* necessary). It says that what in particular empirical laws is merely contingent from the perspective of our *human* insight contains a lawful unity of the manifold, albeit a unity of which we can have no insight and can give no objective justification. "The faculty of judgment *must* assume as an a

72. See also EE §IV, AA XX, 210, 11.
73. EE §V, AA XX, 214, 5.

priori principle for its own use that what to human insight is contingent in the particular (empirical) laws of nature, does nonetheless contain a lawful unity—unfathomable although still thinkable for us—in the connection of its manifold into an experience that is in itself possible" (XXXIII, 183, 34–184, 2). In this perspective, the contingency of the particular laws is not denied but simply ordered within the whole of experience, which is in itself objectively possible and subjectively necessary. The principle of reflective judgment provides, as Kant suggests, the "lawfulness of the contingent as such."[74]

In the light of the definition of purposiveness provided at the end of §IV, Kant suggests that to represent an object as ordered according to a lawful unity that responds to the "*necessary* aim (a need) of the understanding" (XXXIII, 184, 3–4) and yet is in itself merely *contingent* is to represent the object according to the form of purposiveness. Purposive is that which is conducive to a certain aim and nonetheless is in itself contingent. Understanding *needs* to think that experience of nature is possible not only in its analytic but also in its synthetic unity (i.e., also in the heterogeneity of its empirical forms). Understanding, however, falls short before this heterogeneity. In the appendix to the Transcendental Dialectic of the first *Critique*, Kant suggested that speculative reason might work as a possible ally to the understanding in this task. Yet no transcendental justification could be provided for this claim nor any a priori principle formulated. Now it is clear that not speculative reason but only the reflective faculty of judgment can help the understanding in its representation of a systematic experience of nature in all its forms. Thereby, the reflective faculty of judgment is instituted as a mediating function with regard to the understanding. What is needed is the a priori principle of formal purposiveness. This principle is not an objective principle through which objects are determined but a merely subjective device (i.e., a maxim, XXXIV, 184, 15–16)[75] in our reflection upon nature. Formal purposiveness is neither a concept of the understanding (i.e., a concept of nature), nor an idea of reason (i.e., a concept of freedom). It is instead the independent transcendental principle of reflective judgment (XXXIV, 184, 10–13). We "must" think in the way expressed by this principle—and by this principle only—if a coherent systematic experience of nature is to be possible at all (XXXIV, 184, 13–15).

Kant presents the situation of natural science in its ongoing search for laws, order, and classifications in our experience of nature. There is a whole realm of possible empirical laws still to be discovered. This is the realm proper to our reflection and investigation of nature. Therein, "the faculty of judgment, which as regards things under possible (still to be discovered) empirical laws is merely reflective, *must* think of nature as regards these laws according to a *principle of purposiveness* for our cognitive faculty—this principle being then expressed in the above mentioned maxims of the faculty of judgment" (XXXIV, 184, 6–10). In

74. EE §VI, AA XX, 217, 28.
75. See EE §II, AA XX, 205,3; KrV B 708/A 680; B 699/A 671.

other words, the *lex parsimoniae*, *lex continui in naturae,* and the rule *principia praeter necessitatem non sunt multiplicanda* are not objective principles of the constitution of nature but simply regulative, heuristic principles (or maxims) by which our reflection upon nature leads us to organize in a coherent way our experience of an otherwise ungraspable infinite variety of natural forms. Most importantly, these maxims do not refer to a closed, finite body of wisdom. Rather, they guide us in our continuous efforts to extend our knowledge of nature, thereby underlining the unfinished and open character of science and scientific research.

The principle of purposiveness sets an accord between the infinite variety of nature's forms and empirical laws on the one hand and our cognitive faculties on the other. Thereby it also explains our psychological reaction when scientific endeavors are rewarded with success (hence, as Kant contended, it is not psychology that can justify the transcendental principle but rather this principle that accounts for certain psychological events). It "explains why we . . . rejoice (actually we are relieved of a need), just as if it were a lucky chance that favors our intentions, when we meet such a systematic unity under merely empirical laws" (XXXIV, 184, 16–19). The systematic unity of experience is merely assumed as a regulative principle for our research. Understanding, in all its efforts, will never be able to prove this principle as objective and constitutive of nature itself. The sensible world of nature meets us with particular cases of objects for which applicable general concepts are lacking. These cases seem to throw both understanding and determinant judgment into despair but are viewed by the reflective faculty of judgment as extremely fortunate cases. Reflection judges as if the constitution of those objects were attuned to our cognitive faculties; as if those objects were meeting a need or an aim proper to our cognitive powers; as if those objects were made by an understanding like ours (although not ours) in order to meet the demand of a meaningful experience. The encounter with such cases is obviously merely contingent—it is, as Kant puts it, a "lucky chance." In these occurrences we are presented with a formal purposiveness of nature. A feeling of pleasure—a rejoicing—arises here for the first time. It is the task of the following §VI to justify the a priori and necessary character of the connection between purposiveness and feeling of pleasure, namely the fact that such connection is not merely psychological. Herein lies also the difference between reflection's formal purposiveness and merely technical-practical purposiveness. In a technical-practical judgment, the correspondence between the aim of technic and its product by no means constitutes a specific problem since the accordance simply results from the application of empirical rules inferred from our knowledge. The claim that a natural object—and nature in its manifestations—is in accord with our cognitive faculties constitutes instead a specifically new problem. For, in this case, the accordance is thoroughly contingent. This problem is brought to light precisely by those particularly fortunate occurrences in which objects appear as if they were constituted—despite their contingency—so that we might be able to make sense of them.

The Deduction of the Principle of Formal Purposiveness of Nature: The Principle of Reflection as Heuristic Principle of Science (XXXIV, 184, 22–XXXVI, 185, 22)

The deduction of the principle proper to the reflective faculty of judgment is presented as the deduction of the "transcendental principle of cognition" (XXXIV, 184, 23–24). Herein the argument seems to have come to a turning point. Kant restates the importance and the magnitude of the problem posed by the third *Critique*. This leads to a renewed confrontation with the first *Critique*. Kant further states the *necessity* of the principle and the relation between the faculty of judgment and the understanding. Thereby the mediating role attributed to *Urteilskraft* is confirmed. The general problem receives the following formulation: "we have to constitute an interconnected experience out of given perceptions of a nature containing a perhaps infinite multiplicity of empirical laws" (XXXIV/XXXV, 184, 25–27). The formulation could have been taken from the first *Critique* if it were not for the fact that we are dealing here with "*empirical*" (as opposed to universal) laws. Once again, at stake is clearly a problem of synthesis. This problem, Kant adds, "lies a priori in our understanding" (XXXV, 184, 27–28). And if it lies a priori in our understanding, it is a *necessary* problem for Kant. However, in the "First Introduction," Kant has been stressing in a particularly emphatic way that the present problem is "totally alien" to the understanding to the point that this faculty cannot have anything to say about that which appears to it only as a chaotic labyrinth without order.[76] The crucial point is that this problem lies only in part in the understanding and hence cannot be solved by the understanding alone. This is why the deduction of the transcendental principle could be effected only by means of an *ad absurdum* argument (i.e., indirectly). As we have seen, the necessary assumption of a coherent system of empirical cognitions and empirical laws of nature cannot be derived from the understanding and its universal laws but needs to be established by an a priori principle proper to a different faculty, namely the reflective faculty of judgment.

For experience to be possible, two conditions are required: first, "universal laws of nature" provided a priori by the understanding (without them "nature could not become an object of experience at all," XXXV, 184, 28–30); second, "in addition to these universal laws, the understanding also needs a *certain order of nature in its particular rules*" (XXXV, 184, 30–31). Understanding "needs" this order but cannot impose it on nature (it cannot legislate over nature in its empirical laws). Accordingly, universal laws are indeed necessary, and yet still not sufficient to establish an "order *of* nature" that could account for the particulars *in* nature (i.e., for particular laws, particular natural forms, and particular experiences and knowledge). For the particular as such can only be known by the understanding *empirically* and is consequently *contingent* (XXXV, 184, 31–32). What is at stake is precisely the possibility of a transition "from the *universal*

76. See the passages already commented upon: EE §II, AA XX, 203, 10; §V, AA XX, 214, 5–7.

analogy of a possible experience in general, to a *particular* one" (XXXV, 184, 33–34). Since the understanding cannot legislate over nature in its particular and empirical forms, and yet needs a "*certain order of nature in its particular rules*" as a necessary condition to experience, it follows that the understanding must think of these rules as having the force of law—as being as necessary as the universal laws with which it legislates (albeit following a different kind of necessity)—even though it will never be able to prove this necessity or gain any insight into it.

In this way, Kant presents the necessity for the understanding to presuppose the a priori principle of the reflective faculty of judgment as a regulative principle in its own investigation of nature. Expressed in the perspective of the understanding, the principle now takes the following form: "a knowable a priori order of nature is possible" according to *empirical* laws (XXXV, 185, 3) and not only according to the *universal* transcendental laws that result from the first *Critique*. This principle grounds all reflection upon nature and provides the heuristic maxims that lead us to discoveries and advancement in science. It grounds the very possibility of thinking of nature according to the order expressed, for example, by the rule of the subordination of genera and species and by the common principle that allows one to envisage a possible transition from one genus to another and to a yet higher genus. Still arguing *ad absurdum*, Kant suggests that were we not presupposing this principle, "we would have no *order of nature according to empirical laws* and consequently no guiding-thread both for an experience to be had according to those laws in all their multiplicity and for an investigation of them" (XXXVI, 185, 19–22). Moreover, the a priori principle of reflection, by assuming the possibility of a systematic unity of our experience, also justifies the need of scicntific thinking to reduce the infinite heterogeneity of forms and laws in nature to the smallest number possible, thereby achieving the highest degree of simplicity (XXXVI, 185, 9–13). Thus, by means of the faculty of judgment, the employment of understanding has indeed reached an extension unimaginable in the world of transcendental laws of nature.

How is the "attunement" (*Zusammenstimmung*) (XXXVI, 185, 13) between nature and our cognitive faculties viewed respectively by understanding and faculty of judgment? This question is relevant to Kant at this point in order to show, once again, that even if the principle of formal purposiveness is somehow required by the understanding (it responds to a problem that lies a priori in this faculty), only reflective judgment can establish it as a *necessary transcendental principle a priori*. While understanding views this harmony as "objectively contingent" (XXXVI, 185, 16–17), for the faculty of judgment it constitutes an a priori presupposition that is subjectively valid in order to make possible a reflection upon nature in its empirical laws. Consequently, it is only the faculty of judgment that can attribute this harmony "to nature as transcendental purposiveness (in relation to the subject's cognitive faculty)" (XXXVI, 185, 17–19).

Chaos in Nature and the Need for the Principle of Formal Purposiveness (XXXVI, 185, 23–XXXVIII, 186, 21)

The *necessity* of the principle of formal purposiveness is grounded in a dreadful possibility that Kant has been considering all through §V and eventually comes to express in all its clarity toward the conclusion of the section. At issue still remains the impossibility of deducing particular empirical laws from universal transcendental principles of nature, empirical cognitions from universal concepts, heterogeneity from homogeneity. "It is quite conceivable," he contends, that we could master the world of nature in general in its universal laws and still have no clue whatsoever as to how to provide a meaningful explanation of the specific differences we encounter in our experience of nature. Experience, properly speaking, would be utterly impossible for us. Given that this is the situation in which we would find ourselves if we did we not endorse the principle of purposiveness, we have to underline that in this case, contrary to any strict *ad absurdum* logic, Kant does not present the opposite case as contradictory but as very well conceivable. Hence the peculiar status of the problem of the third *Critique.* What we would have were we not appealing to the principle of reflection is a world in which the specific differences among natural things would be so numerous as to be ungraspable; no order would be possible at all and hence no comprehension; heterogeneity would be infinite and hence irreducible to a finite number of rules so that any attempt at subordination of genera and species would necessarily fail. In this world, *despite the retained and recognized validity of the first Critique and its laws*, everything would appear in a state of confusion and chaos. Hence, in order for empirical heterogeneity to be conceivable, systematicity must be assumed. Systematicity carries with itself the issue of *Zweckmäßigkeit.*

In a footnote to §V of the "First Introduction," Kant presents the relation between the heterogeneity of nature's forms and their interconnection into a systematic unity as an essential presupposition for science. "One may wonder whether Linnaeus ever could have hoped to design a system of nature if he had had to worry that a stone that he found and that he called granite might differ in its inner character from any other stone even if it looked the same, so that all he could ever hope to find would be single things—isolated, as it were, for the understanding—but never a class of them that could be brought under concepts of genera and species."[77] Empirical sciences do not aim only at providing analytical classifications of objects according to their homogeneity. They also need to establish laws that allow one to unify classes of objects according to their specific differences.

The situation that Kant faces in the deduction of reflective judgment's own principle can be compared to the one that grounds the need for a transcendental deduction of the categories in the *Critique of Pure Reason.* Kant argues in this latter case that since "the categories of the understanding . . . do not represent the conditions under which objects are given in intuition," the world of sensibility

77. EE §V, AA XX, 215, 34–216, 27–31.

could very well be thought of as completely disconnected from the world of the understanding. In this case, "objects would still appear to us without their having to be necessarily related to the functions of the understanding."[78] Hence, the necessity of a transcendental deduction of the categories that was not required for the forms of intuition. For

> appearances might very well be so constituted that the understanding should not find them to be in accordance with the conditions of its unity. *Everything might be in such confusion* that, for instance, in the series of appearances nothing presented itself that might yield a rule of synthesis and so answer to the concept of cause and effect. This concept would then be altogether empty, null, and meaningless. But since intuition stands in no need whatsoever of the functions of thought, appearances would nonetheless present objects to our intuition.[79]

No experience would be possible in this "confusion," but only a rhapsody of perceptions. The situation of introduction §V is somehow parallel to the one just examined. It is, however, placed on a different level of experience. If we did not assume the possible unity of a system of experience, every perception would subsist separately from all others with no possibility of relating them to one another. Each perception would account for a world of its own. In this world, Linnaeus never would have been able to recognize and construct an ordered system of nature. A unitary communicable experience would be utterly impossible.

It is important to notice that in the third *Critique* the possibility that the empirical manifold of nature's forms was disconnected from the world ruled by the understanding's legislation, and hence the possibility of conceiving experience to be utterly impossible is not raised as the basis for a deduction, as was the case in the transcendental deduction of the categories as objectively constitutive concepts of cognition. As far as the principle of formal purposiveness is concerned, the still persisting possibility of conceiving a chaotic world restates the validity of a principle that is only regulative, heuristic, and subjectively necessary, employed for reflection and not determination of objects. The threat of meaninglessness is always there. Accordingly, the demand for meaningfulness remains a constant thread that runs throughout the *Critique of Judgment*. This thread is taken up and restated in different ways and on different occasions as the work develops.

At this point the deduction is concluded, and Kant proceeds to summarize its results. The faculty of judgment has proved to have its own a priori transcendental principle and hence to be an independent cognitive faculty next to understanding and reason. This is a principle for the "possibility of nature" (XXXVII, 185, 35–36). Its validity, however, is only subjective; it applies only insofar as nature is considered in relation to the subject and its cognitive powers. Therefore, it is a principle that does not legislate over nature (it is not an objective a priori law of

78. KrV B 122/A 89.
79. KrV B 123/A 90 f.

nature)—which is the function that Kant calls "autonomy." Rather, it provides a rule for the faculty of judgment itself whereby "heautonomy" is expressed (XXXVII, 185, 37).[80] This principle is now stated as the "*law of specification of nature* with regard to its empirical laws" (XXXVII, 186, 1–3).[81] It is a law that the faculty of judgment formulates in view of a sort of collaboration and integration with the activity of the understanding. "It is a law that the faculty of judgment does not know a priori in nature but rather assumes in view of an order of nature knowable to the understanding when it divides the universal laws of nature so as to subordinate to them the manifold of particular laws" (XXXVII, 186, 3–7). At this point, as a result of the deduction and in force of the principle of nature's specification, the two orders of law (the order of *universal* laws of nature and the order of *particular* empirical laws) no longer appear as merely parallel and disconnected from each other. Through its transcendental principle of purposiveness, the faculty of judgment eventually manages to connect the two orders. Accordingly, a partition is drawn within the universal legislation so as to create the order of the empirical particulars. It is here that reflection sees the possibility of discovering the problematic infinite "modifications" of the universal concepts of nature (§IV, XXVI, 179, 32).

Following the newly discovered principle, we can now assume that "nature specifies its universal laws according to the principle of purposiveness for our cognitive faculty" (XXXVII, 186, 7–8). We can assume that heterogeneity is generated according to an order fully comprehensible to the human cognitive faculties. Thus, it becomes possible to find the universal for a particular empirically given in perception—a problem that neither the understanding nor the determinant faculty of judgment ever could hope to solve. Furthermore, it becomes possible to establish connections among what is different in experience and hence to arrange our empirical cognitions in the coherent unity of a system. This is the work of the *reflective* faculty of judgment. Its principle defines the limits of all our searching endeavors with regard to nature's empirical laws. Science is possible only insofar as the principle of purposiveness of nature as well as the "maxims grounded upon it" (XXXVIII, 186, 18–19)—namely *lex parsimoniae*, *lex continui in naturae*, the rule *principia praeter necessitatem non sunt multiplicanda*, and so forth—are assumed as guiding principles in our research. The conclusion follows: "Only so far as that principle applies can we make progress in experience with the use of our understanding and gain knowledge" (XXXVIII, 186, 20–21).

3. *Synopsis: §VI, On the Conjunction of the Feeling of Pleasure with the Concept of Purposiveness of Nature*

As was the case with the third term of the first trichotomy (§III: On the Critique of Judgment as a *Means to Connect* the Two Parts of Philosophy into a Whole),

80. See EE §VIII, AA XX, 225, 20–32.
81. See EE §V, AA XX, 215, 1–13.

§VI is presented as *Verbindung* of the two previous terms. The unification that thereby takes place opens up new questions for the *Critique of Judgment.*

In §III, Kant introduced the faculty of judgment as an independent faculty next to understanding and reason by framing the problem of a possible third cognitive faculty within the higher order of the powers of the soul represented by cognitive faculty, feeling of pleasure and displeasure, and faculty of desire. In §VI Kant takes up that same connection. The task is now to show the necessary relation between faculty of judgment and feeling of pleasure by means of the relation between feeling of pleasure and the concept of purposiveness of nature, which has just been deduced as the special a priori principle of the faculty of judgment. It is clear from the connection of §§V–VI that the issue of a formal purposiveness of nature is meant to respond to a twofold problem. On the one hand it provides the answer to the question of the *Übergang* from the way of thinking according to principles of nature to the way of thinking according to principles of freedom (§II). On the other hand, reflective judgment's own principle responds to the problem of the possibility of a systematic experience of nature in its manifold—that is, to the issue of the possibility of empirical concepts, empirical science, and scientific induction. In this way, §VI as third term of the second trichotomy brings together not only the results of §§IV and V but also the issues raised more generally by the two conditioned respectively of §II and §V.

Kant's argument develops along the following steps. He first raises the problem of the way in which the faculties involved in the task of "cognition in general"—namely understanding and reflective faculty of judgment—can be said to work in an intentional way. The question regards whether or not understanding and judgment need to presuppose an "*Absicht*" in carrying out their function. Then the argument moves on to determine what this "aim" is respectively for the two cognitive faculties (XXXVIII, 186, 25–XXXIX, 187, 10). Feeling of pleasure is the feeling that always accompanies the achievement of one's aims. Kant's crucial claim is that an aim that is grounded a priori must necessarily lead to a feeling that has an a priori ground (XXXIX, 187, 11–18). The possibility of an a priori of feeling is the crucial discovery of the third *Critique*. Once the connection between purposiveness and feeling is established, Kant reviews the results of §V in light of the constitutive openness of empirical science (XXXIX, 187, 19–XLII, 188, 29).

3.1. §VI Commentary: The Aim of Reflection and the Feeling of Pleasure and Displeasure

Cognition and the "Aim" of Understanding and Reflective Faculty of Judgment (XXXVIII, 186, 25–XXXIX, 187, 10)

The section opens with a recapitulation of the argument of the previous deduction, which is taken up again with a further goal in view. Kant clarifies, in the first place, the nature of the necessity proper to the faculty of judgment's transcendental principle. Kant's argument still proceeds through the apodeitic "must" disclosed in §V. Moreover, it is important to stress that while the principle of purposiveness is restricted in its employment to a cognitive function (XXXVIII, 186, 30), the vocabulary that Kant uses to describe this function is specific to the epistemological problem of the third *Critique.* Kant presents us with issues of *needs, intentions,* and *hopes* proper to our cognitive faculties, which were unknown to the first *Critique.*[82] The context is no longer that of a corpus of knowledge fully determined and concluded in its possibility, but it is rather defined by the open space of an ongoing open-ended inquiry. As has been stated throughout the second trichotomy, the cognitive task proper to the reflective faculty of judgment is not legislation but a search for law and order whose actual occurrence in nature is thoroughly contingent.

The function of the reflective faculty of judgment is to find the universal principle for a manifold of empirical laws. This function is grounded upon a "need" of our cognitive faculties for order and systematicity (XXXVIII, 186, 26, 28). Now, we *must* judge the accordance and agreement between the world of nature in the manifold of its particular laws, and "our need" of finding the universal for those particular given cases as contingent. For "as far as all our insight goes" (XXXVIII, 186, 27), no matter how deeply we investigate, we will never see a priori the necessity of this agreement. Yet, since this agreement is "indispensable" to our need, it displays its own subjective necessity. The harmony between nature and our faculties, however, is indispensable only when *cognition* is at stake, warns Kant, in order to clearly differentiate reflective judgment's principle from all practical purposiveness that is not inscribed into nature (XXXVIII, 186, 30). *Zweckmäßigkeit* is, once again, the subjective, functional necessity according to which the contingency of what is given agrees with our *cognitive* intention. Kant adds that purposiveness relates to the specific intentionality of our faculties; it is always related to a cognitive "*Absicht.*" Thereby the "analogy" to (technical-) practical purposiveness announced at the end of §IV starts revealing its meaning (XXVIII, 181, 10).[83]

While both understanding and reflective judgment are cognitive faculties, they do not both necessarily imply an "aim." The notion of *Absicht* refers to the pursuit of an object or situation whose opposite can be thought as possible. We can set ourselves the goal of remaining healthy, of becoming wise; yet no one would set him/herself the goal of breathing as long as s/he lives, since the opposite is impossible. Thus, understanding's universal legislation takes place with no *Absicht,* because it is impossible for us to imagine a world where these laws would not be valid. Universal laws of nature owe their absolute necessity to the understanding. Even though this legislation arises out of the "spontaneity" (autonomy)

82. In the first *Critique* we encountered the "need" of speculative reason; the vocabulary of need and intention is closer to the realm of the practical.

83. See also §22, General Remark, 70, 242 for the notion of *Absicht;* see, however, §VII, XLIV, 190, 4, 8 for the "unintentional" and noncognitive use of the reflective faculty of judgment in the *aesthetic* representation of purposiveness.

of the understanding, universal laws are rigorously deterministic. They are as necessary as are laws of motion for matter. Universal laws are *objectively* constitutive of nature and are so regardless of the subject's faculties. Hence, for the formulation of those laws, the understanding does not have to take into account a need of our cognitive faculties; no aim or intention is required with respect to them. Knowledge of things would be utterly impossible without understanding's laws simply because no object would be there for us to know and nothing would appear to us, not even a nature in general. *The Critique of Pure Reason* has shown that the order of the understanding is the same as the order of nature ("the universal laws of the understanding, which are at the same time laws of nature," XXXVIII, 186, 31), this identity cutting off all problem of a possible purposive relation between the two terms. The order of the understanding is constitutive, objectively necessary, and closed; that is, determined by a finite number of principles derived according to the table of the categories. The opposite of this order or another order would imply the impossibility of human knowledge as such.

The order of the reflective faculty of judgment, on the contrary, is regulative, subjectively necessary, merely provisional, and essentially open. Its opposite is very well possible at all times. Herein lawfulness is present in an infinite variety of forms and instances that cannot be derived from higher a priori principles. It is in this context that purposiveness—a regard toward our cognitive faculties—is at work. With regard to the manifold of nature's empirical laws, there is no objective necessity for the empirical world to be constituted so as to be graspable and comprehensible for us. Nature's agreement with our cognitive faculties is merely contingent. Kant reiterates that we speak from the perspective of our consideration of nature: "as far as all our insight goes" (XXXIII, 186, 27) and "as far as we can see" (XXXIX, 187, 5), "it is contingent that the order of nature in its particular laws, with all their—at least possible—multiplicity and heterogeneity exceeding our capacity of comprehension, should nonetheless be *actually* commensurate with that capacity" (XXXIX, 187, 2–6). As Kant contended in §V, we can very well see a priori the *possibility* of an infinite heterogeneity of empirical forms and laws in nature. Yet the *actuality* of the only order in which this infinite heterogeneity can be graspable is utterly contingent. It is quite possible that a manifold of empirical laws would not be reducible to the unity of a common principle or that nature would show no regularities that allow us to draw divisions and classifications of genera and species. This is, to be sure, a highly antianthropocentric and antiteleological point. There is no objective necessity that authorizes us to conclude that the world of nature in its infinite variety of forms must be comprehensible for the human being. The world of nature in general must be graspable by us simply because it is the world that our understanding constructs with its a priori legislation. On the contrary, we have no possible control over the manifold of empirical laws, which might very well be laid out in a chaos totally inaccessible to us. This is also the reason why the reflective faculty of judgment needs to proceed with an *Absicht* if it wants to discover intelligible regularities in nature.

Thus, if understanding is aimless (*keine Absicht,* XXXVIII, 186, 34; "*unabsichtlich,*" XL, 187, 22) in its universal legislation, it does indeed have an aim when searching for empirical laws ("*mit Absicht,*" XXXIX, 187, 7). The task of discovering nature's empirical laws requires the purposive employment of the understanding. For the understanding would not be able to discover empirical laws if it did not have a "necessary purpose of its own" (XXXIX, 187, 7). Such purpose is the idea of bringing a scattered manifold of laws under the unity of a principle. The regulative idea of the system is, as it were, necessarily presupposed to the discovery of its parts. It does not arise out of its parts as in the case of the aggregate. Yet, even though it proceeds with an aim, the understanding still does not show any concern toward our faculties. This is the case instead with judgment. Given the work of the understanding, reflective judgment "*must* then attribute such a purpose to nature" (XXXIX, 187, 9). Since understanding cannot legislate over nature in its empirical manifold, it is the faculty of judgment that now takes over a quasi-legislative task. What judgment imposes on nature, however, is not a law but a purpose (a purpose shared by the understanding).

Feeling of Pleasure and Principle of Purposiveness (XXXIX, 187, 11–LX, 187, 34)

Once Kant has established in what sense and under which conditions understanding and faculty of judgment proceed in an intentional way in order to produce knowledge, he can discuss the relation to the middle term of the "faculties of the soul," the feeling of pleasure and displeasure. What is the connection between faculty of judgment, formal purposiveness, and feeling of pleasure? The general indisputable statement that opens Kant's argument reads as follows: "the attainment of every aim is connected to a feeling of pleasure" (XXXIX, 187, 11–12).[84] We have to remember that the feeling of pleasure has traditionally been counted among the lower appetitive faculties. Kant's task in the *Critique of Practical Reason* was to show that reason, as higher appetitive faculty, is truly practical (i.e., moral) if and only if it is not determined by feeling. Being empirical and merely subjective,[85] feeling can neither provide the a priori ground for practical determination nor be universally valid. On the other hand, the connection that the present section is trying to establish has carefully limited the employment of the notion of purposiveness to a specific kind of *cognitive* endeavors (i.e., not to the cognitive function of the understanding in its universal legislation but to a reflective search for laws). Along these lines Kant has been making room for a specific a priori connection between purposiveness and feeling that is not theoretical and yet is somehow cognitive; nor is it practical as it relates neither to the lower nor to the

---

84. E. Garroni/H. Hohenegger, introduction to I. Kant, *Critica della facoltà di giudizio*, a cura di E. Garroni, H. Hohenegger, Torino, Einaudi, 1999, xl, suggest as a possible source for Kant's claim *Christian Wolffens Meinungen . . . und A. Rüdigers Gegen-Meinungen*, Leipzig, 1727, 229.

85. See also Kant's position in the first *Critique:* KrV B 28 f./A 15.

higher appetitive faculty and yet presents an analogy with practical purposiveness.[86]

From the aforementioned general statement, Kant draws the following conclusion: if the condition that allows us to achieve a certain aim is an a priori condition, then the feeling of pleasure that arises from the attainment of our aim is determined through an a priori ground (XXXIX, 187, 12–14). In our case, the a priori condition is the principle of formal purposiveness of nature. Our cognitive aim of finding out a variety of empirical laws that is intelligible because it is placed within the systematic unity of experience depends upon the assumption that nature is constituted as if in agreement with our faculties in their cognitive endeavor. Since it has been shown that this assumption is the a priori condition of our reflection upon nature (§V), then we can conclude that the feeling of pleasure that arises when our inquiry is crowned with success is a peculiar feeling that has an a priori ground. We have to underline that, at this point (i.e., when getting to the *Verbindung* between feeling of pleasure and faculty of judgment by means of its a priori principle), Kant is talking of "reflective faculty of judgment *in general*" (XXXIX, 187, 13). We know that two different types of connection—aesthetic and teleological—will be established in the following sections.

But what does it mean for feeling to be determined by an a priori ground? Kant's long-standing uneasiness with the notion of feeling, both in relation to the problem of eudaimonistic practical philosophy and in relation to the issue of taste, was due to the impossibility of attributing shared universality and necessity to the propositions built upon it. In short, the difficulties arise from the merely empirical and subjective validity of feeling. Being occasioned by the different affection of the lower faculty of desire, feeling seemed to be condemned to be necessarily a posteriori and limited to one's individual experience. Now, on the contrary, Kant introduces for the first time a feeling that rests on an a priori condition and hence (i) has an a priori *necessary* ground, and (ii) displays *universal validity*. It is a feeling that "is valid for everyone" (XXXIX, 187, 14–15).[87] Kant underlines the novelty of this connection between feeling and purposiveness by distinguishing it from the purposiveness that relates to the faculty of desire. In our case, the determination of feeling "takes place simply as the object is related to the *cognitive* faculty," not to the faculty of desire (XXXIX, 187, 15–16). Since what is at stake is purposiveness *of nature*, what we are dealing with is certainly not a "*practical* purposiveness of nature" (XXXIX, 187, 18). Once again, purposiveness that constitutes the a priori ground for feeling is neither technical-practical nor moral-practical purposiveness (*Zweckmäßigkeit* is not a moral law). It seems as if we were imposing practical purposiveness on nature, but in fact we are dealing with a

86. See EE §VIII, AA, XX, 230, 8–231, 2 for a transcendental definition of the "feeling of pleasure."

87. See P. Guyer's objection (*Kant and the Claims of Taste*, Cambridge, Cambridge University Press, 1992, 64–65), according to which universal validity does not follow from apriority (this objection will be discussed in Part III).

purposiveness of its own kind that relates neither to understanding nor to reason, neither to the cognitive faculty (strictly defined) nor to the faculty of desire but to a faculty in the middle.

Accordingly, the task is now to show that the connection between purposiveness and feeling can only be established in the case of the faculty of judgment. We know from the second *Critique* that no feeling of pleasure can be combined with practical reason as its determining ground. We should know it so well at this point that Kant does not even consider this possibility in order to exclude it. He contends that since understanding in its universal legislation "proceeds necessarily, without aim" and according to its own nature (XL, 187, 22–23), no feeling of pleasure arises—nor ever can arise—from the accordance of our perceptions with those universal laws. In other words, the condition of the possibility of experience disclosed by the first *Critique*, not being related to an aim of the understanding, has also nothing to do with feeling of pleasure and displeasure. Moreover, since this condition is set once and for all, no chance is left of ever seeing a connection to feeling established in the further development of our knowledge.

The perspective of a science *in fieri* is endorsed instead by the activity of reflection that constantly looks for unification of heterogeneous empirical laws and phenomena under more comprehensive principles. It is in the course of this process, when the goal meets with success, that a feeling of pleasure may arise. Kant underlines the peculiar character of this feeling, which borders on "admiration," amazement, and wonder.[88] It is a feeling that occurs unexpectedly upon encounter with utterly contingent cases (recall the rejoicing upon the "lucky chance" of finding certain individual cases that meet our generalizations [XXXIV, 184, 17]). We do not cease to be filled with wonder and admiration, observes Kant, even when we become familiar with the objects that caused this feeling. For what is at stake is not so much the admiration that arises out of the novelty or exotic character of single objects but rather the pleasure that is produced by the fulfillment of our aim for systematicity and is occasioned by the very possibility of establishing relations among heterogeneous phenomena. In other words, it is not so much the pleasure in the object itself but rather the pleasure produced by scientific discovery as such. The crucial component of this feeling of pleasure is the recognition of the *contingency* of the event. Kant takes into account that habit can dim this original feeling once discovery has been accepted and integrated into our normal view of nature. In this case, we see as necessary what is instead merely contingent. By losing sight of the essential contingency of the harmony between nature and our faculties, we lose the feeling of pleasure as well. Thus, we "no longer feel a perceptible pleasure" in contemplating the division of natural forms in genera and species (XL, 187, 28–31). But this only happens because we take a purely contingent possibility disclosed by our scientific engagement to be a natural necessity. Yet "that pleasure was certainly there once, and it is only because the

88. See KU §62, 274, AA 363, 36–364, 2.

most common experience *would not be possible without it* that it has been progressively mixed with our simple knowledge and has no longer been noticed" (XL, 187, 31–34). Kant certainly does not mean to say that the most common experience would not be possible without pleasure, but that the condition that makes experience possible is originally and transcendentally connected to pleasure.[89] The possibility of organizing experiences in genera and species, Kant contends, is crucial to the task of forming empirical concepts, and this in turn is essential to empirical cognition. It is precisely because "the most common experience would not be possible" without the unity from which that pleasure necessarily and originally arises that we have become used to it and no longer perceive it as pleasure (XL, 187, 32). The world of nature in its empirical laws tends to conform to—and to be structured by analogy with—the world of nature in general.

Feeling of Pleasure and Possibility of Displeasure (LX, 187, 34–XLII, 189, 29)

Kant concludes that only the intentional set up of our cognitive faculties (i.e., our explicit "endeavor," or aim, to a systematization of nature in its empirical forms) can call our attention to "nature's purposiveness for our understanding" (XL, 187, 35). Pleasure is the result of a successful endeavor. What we feel pleasure in is, in this case, the very contingent accordance, harmony, or "suitability"—the *Einstimmung, Überein-stimmung, Zusammen-stimmung*—between nature and those faculties of the mind that made success possible. What we feel pleasure in is the possibility of attributing meaning to the world of experience. The opposite feeling—namely a feeling of displeasure—arises, on the contrary, when we find ourselves in a world that appears to us as meaningless. Kant warns us that the search for meaning is not necessarily successful ("*wenn es gelingt,*" XL, 188, 1) and that a chaotic manifold of forms with no regularity is a possibility of which we can very well conceive and can never completely rule out (XXXVI, 185, 23). The threat of the "labyrinth" with no way out mentioned by the "First Introduction" is always an open chance (it is, this time, an unlucky chance). Such representation of nature, holds Kant, would "cause us displeasure" (XL, 188, 3). It is important to underline that the "connection" that this section establishes between the principle of nature's purposiveness and the faculty of feeling—*Gefühl*—is a connection that always leaves open the alternative between feeling of *pleasure* and feeling of *displeasure*. The duality of feelings is constitutive of this faculty precisely because of the contingency proper to the order in which it is inscribed. While pleasure arises out of the accordance and harmony between our cognitive faculties and nature's order, displeasure is the result of a conflict (*widerstreiten*; XLI, 188, 10) between nature's disorder and irreducible heterogeneity of forms and reflective judgment's quest for meaning. The alternative possibility of meaning and lack of meaning pervades the whole development of the third *Critique*.

---

89. See E. Garroni/H. Hohenegger, introduction to I. Kant, *Critica della facoltà di giudizio*, op. cit., xli.

To be sure, the alternative between feeling of pleasure and feeling of displeasure rests on the very function of the faculty of judgment. While understanding's and reason's legislations fully *determine* the respective realms so that no employment of their principles is allowed beyond the limits of their domains, the faculty of judgment's "presupposition" is "*indeterminate*" precisely with regard to the limits of applicability of the "ideal purposiveness of nature for our cognitive faculty" (XLI, 188, 12–13).[90] "For if we are able to determine the limit with regard to the rational use of our cognitive faculty, *in the empirical realm no determination of limit is possible*" (XLII, 188,26–29). No determination of limit is possible in the empirical world of nature, which constitutes the *domicilium* of the reflective faculty of judgment. Consequently no limit is determinately set for empirical science. The function of the maxims of judgment is indeterminate in the same sense as are reason's regulative ideas. Given the specific function of the *reflective* faculty of judgment, it is not even possible to ascertain whether we will ever meet a limit in our efforts of classification and systematization. No ultimate universal is given for subsumption. Reflection is a progressive task of acquisition of meaning that needs to maintain the ideal of a purposiveness of nature with regard to our cognitive powers as well as its hopes for success as its ongoing and necessary presupposition. Yet it is not possible to foresee how far we will be able to extend our empirical cognition of nature. The system of experience is an incomplete (and never to be completed) task. If the major task of Kant's critical project in the first two *Critiques* is that of drawing the limits of the legitimacy of a certain employment of our faculties, it is evident that in the case of the faculty of judgment, critique encounters an essential complication of its meaning. What shall a critique of the faculty of judgment accomplish if no limit to the extension of its ideal principle can be assigned? A third *Critique* is possible only as the critique of the faculty of feeling of pleasure and displeasure, and this is possible in turn only on the ground of its a priori principle, which is the faculty of judgment's own principle.

90. For this indeterminacy, see P. Guyer, *Kant and the Claims of Taste*, op. cit., 45 f.

VII. Von der ästhetischen Vorstellung der Zweckmäßigkeit der Natur

Was an der Vorstellung eines Objekts bloß subjektiv ist, d. i. Ihre Beziehung auf das Subjekt, nicht auf den Gegenstand ausmacht, ist die ästhetische AA189 Beschaffenheit derselben; was aber an ihr zur Bestimmung || des Gegenstandes (zum Erkenntnisse) dient, oder gebraucht werden kann, ist ihre logische Gültigkeit. In dem Erkenntnisse eines Gegenstandes der Sinne kommen beide Beziehungen zusammen vor. In der Sinnenvorstellung der Dinge außer mir ist die Qualität des Raums, worin wir sie anschauen, das bloß Subjektive meiner Vorstellung derselben (wodurch, was sie als Objekte an sich sein mögen, unausgemacht bleibt), um welcher Beziehung willen der Gegenstand auch dadurch bloß als Erscheinung gedacht wird; der Raum ist aber, seiner bloß subjektiven Qualität ungeachtet, gleichwohl doch ein Erkenntnisstück der Dinge als Erscheinungen. *Empfindung* (hier die äußere) drückt ebensowohl das bloß Subjektive unserer Vorstel | XLIII lungen der Dinge außer uns aus, aber eigentlich das Materielle (Reale) derselben (wodurch etwas Existierendes gegeben wird), so wie der Raum die bloße Form a priori der Möglichkeit ihrer Anschauung; und gleichwohl wird jene auch zum Erkenntnis der Objekte außer uns gebraucht.

Dasjenige Subjektive aber an einer Vorstellung, *was gar kein Erkenntnisstück werden kann*, ist die mit ihr verbundene *Lust* oder *Unlust*; denn durch sie erkenne ich nichts an dem Gegenstande der Vorstellung, obgleich sie wohl die Wirkung irgendeiner Erkenntnis sein kann. Nun ist die Zweckmäßigkeit eines Dinges, sofern sie in der Wahrnehmung vorgestellt wird, auch keine Beschaffenheit des Objekts selbst (denn eine solche kann nicht wahrgenommen werden), ob sie gleich aus einem Erkenntnisse der Dinge gefolgert werden kann. Die Zweckmäßigkeit also, die vor dem Erkenntnisse eines Objekts vorhergeht, ja sogar, ohne die Vorstellung desselben zu einem Erkenntnis brauchen zu wollen, gleichwohl mit ihr unmittelbar verbunden wird, ist das Subjektive derselben, was gar kein Erkenntnisstück werden kann. Also wird der Gegenstand alsdann nur darum zweckmäßig genannt, weil seine Vorstellung unmittelbar mit dem Gefühle der Lust verbunden ist; und diese Vorstellung selbst ist eine ästhetische Vorstellung der Zweck | LXIV

Chapter 8

Introduction §§VII–IX: A Critique of the Faculty of Judgment—Aesthetic and Teleological

Text

VII. On the Aesthetic Representation of the Purposiveness of Nature

What is merely subjective in the representation of an object [*Objekt*], i.e., what constitutes its relation to the subject and not to the object [*Gegenstand*], is its aesthetic quality. But what in it serves, or can be used to determine the object (for cognition) is its logical validity. In the cognition of an object of the senses, these two references occur together. In the sensible representation of things outside of me, the quality of the space in which we intuit them is the merely subjective component of my representation of them (by which it remains undecided what things may be as objects in themselves), and because of this subjective reference we also think of the object merely as appearance. But despite its merely subjective quality, space is still a constitutive element in the cognition of things as appearances. *Sensation* (here outer sensation) also expresses what is merely subjective in our XLIII representations of things outside us, but properly it expresses what is material (real) in them (that through which something existent is given), just as space expresses the mere a priori form of the possibility of intuition of things; and yet sensation is also employed for cognition of objects outside us.

But that subjective component in a representation, *which cannot at all become an element of cognition,* is the *pleasure* or *displeasure* connected with it. For through pleasure I do not know anything in the object of the representation, although it may very well be the effect of some cognition. Now, the purposiveness of a thing, insofar as it is represented in perception, is also not a quality of the object itself (since such quality cannot be perceived), even though it can be inferred from a cognition of things. Therefore, the purposiveness that precedes the cognition of an object and that is even immediately connected with it—even if we do not want to use its representation for cognition—, is the subjective component of the representation, i.e., that which cannot at all become an element of cognition. Hence, in this case, the object is called purposive only because its representation is immediately connected with the feeling of pleasure; and this representation itself is an aesthetic representation of purposiveness XLIV.—

mäßigkeit.—Es fragt sich nur, ob es überhaupt eine solche Vorstellung der Zweckmäßigkeit gebe.

Wenn mit der bloßen Auffassung (*apprehensio*) der Form eines Gegenstandes der Anschauung, ohne Beziehung derselben auf einen Begriff zu einem bestimmten Erkenntnis, Lust verbunden ist: so wird die Vorstellung dadurch nicht auf das Objekt, sondern lediglich auf das Subjekt bezogen; und die Lust kann nichts anders als die Angemessenheit desselben zu den Erkenntnisver-
AA190 mögen, die in der reflektierenden Urteils || kraft im Spiel sind, und sofern sie darin sind, also bloß eine subjektive formale Zweckmäßigkeit des Objekts ausdrücken. Denn jene Auffassung der Formen in die Einbildungskraft kann niemals geschehen, ohne daß die reflektierende Urteilskraft, auch unabsichtlich, sie wenigstens mit ihrem Vermögen, Anschauungen auf Begriffe zu beziehen, vergliche. Wenn nun in dieser Vergleichung die Einbildungskraft (als Vermögen der Anschauungen a priori) zum Verstande (als Vermögen der Begriffe) durch eine gegebene Vorstellung unabsichtlich in Einstimmung versetzt und dadurch ein Gefühl der Lust erweckt wird, so muß der Gegenstand alsdann als zweckmäßig für die reflektierende Urteilskraft angesehen werden. Ein solches Urteil ist ein ästhetisches Urteil über die Zweckmäßigkeit des Objekts, welches sich auf keinem vorhandenen Begriffe vom Gegenstande gründet, und keinen von ihm verschafft. Wessen Gegenstandes Form (nicht das | XLV Materielle seiner Vorstellung, als Empfindung) in der bloßen Reflexion über dieselbe (ohne Absicht auf einen von ihm zu erwerbenden Begriff) als der Grund einer Lust an der Vorstellung eines solchen Objekts beurteilt wird; mit dessen Vorstellung wird diese Lust auch als notwendig verbunden geurteilt, folglich als nicht bloß für das Subjekt, welches diese Form auffaßt, sondern für jeden Urteilenden überhaupt. Der Gegenstand heißt alsdann schön; und das Vermögen, durch eine solche Lust (folglich auch allgemeingültig) zu urteilen, der Geschmack. Denn da der Grund der Lust bloß in der Form des Gegenstandes für die Reflexion überhaupt, mithin in keiner Empfindung des Gegenstandes, und auch ohne Beziehung auf einen Begriff, der irgendeine Absicht enthielte, gesetzt wird: so ist es allein die Gesetzmäßigkeit im empirischen Gebrauche der Urteilskraft überhaupt (Einheit der Einbildungskraft mit dem Verstande) in dem Subjekte, mit der die Vorstellung des Objekts in der Reflexion, deren Bedingungen a priori allgemein gelten, zusammenstimmt; und, da diese Zusammenstimmung des Gegenstandes mit den Vermögen des Subjekts zufällig ist, so bewirkt sie die Vorstellung einer Zweckmäßigkeit desselben in Ansehung der Erkenntnisvermögen des Subjekts.

Hier ist nun eine Lust, die, wie alle Lust oder Unlust, welche nicht durch den Freiheitsbegriff (d. i. durch die vorhergehende Bestimmung des oberen Begehrungsver | XLI mögens durch reine Vernunft) gewirkt wird, niemals aus Begriffen als mit der Vorstellung eines Gegenstandes notwendig verbunden,
AA191 eingesehen werden kann, sondern jederzeit nur durch || reflektierte Wahrnehmung als mit dieser verknüpft erkannt werden muß, folglich, wie alle empirische Urteile, keine objektive Notwendigkeit ankündigen und auf Gültigkeit a priori Anspruch machen kann. Aber, das Geschmacksurteil macht auch nur Anspruch,

The only question is whether there is such a representation of purposiveness at all.

If pleasure is connected with the mere apprehension (*apprehensio*) of the form of an object of intuition, without referring it to a concept in view of a determinate cognition, then in that way the representation is not related to the object but solely to the subject, and the pleasure cannot express anything else but the conformity of the object to the cognitive faculties that are at play in the reflective faculty of judgment and insofar as they are at play therein. Hence it simply expresses a subjective formal purposiveness of the object. For that apprehension of the forms in the imagination can never occur unless the reflective faculty of judgment at least compares it [*sie*],[1] even unintentionally, with its faculty of relating intuitions to concepts. Now, if in this comparison the imagination (as faculty of a priori intuitions) is unintentionally brought into unison with the understanding (as faculty of concepts) through a given representation, and in this way a feeling of pleasure arises, then the object must be regarded as purposive for the reflective faculty of judgment. A judgment of this kind is an aesthetic judgment on the purposiveness of the object. This judgment is not grounded on any available concept of the object, nor does it provide one. When the form of an object (not what is XLV material in its representation, as sensation), in the mere reflection on this form (with no aim at acquiring any concept of it), is judged to be the ground of a pleasure in the representation of such an object, then this pleasure is also judged as necessarily connected with its representation, and hence not simply for the subject apprehending this form but for every judging subject in general. The object is then called beautiful, and the faculty of judging by such a pleasure (hence also with universal validity) is called taste. Since the ground for the pleasure is posited merely in the form of the object for reflection in general, and hence not in a sensation of the object nor in relation to a concept that would contain a certain aim, then in the subject the representation of the object in the reflection, whose conditions are a priori universally valid, is attuned only with the lawfulness in the empirical use of the faculty of judgment in general (unity between imagination and understanding). And since this attunement of the object with the faculties of the subject is contingent, it produces the representation of a purposiveness of the object with regard to the cognitive faculties of the subject.

Here, then, is a pleasure that, like all pleasure or displeasure that is not brought about by the concept of freedom (i.e., by the prior determination of the higher faculty of desire XLVI through pure reason), no concept would ever allow us to see as necessarily conjoined [*verbunden*] with the representation of an object; rather, it must always be recognized as connected [*verknüpft*] with that representation only through reflected perception. Hence, like all empirical judgments, it cannot announce any objective necessity nor lay claim to a priori validity. But then the judgment of taste, as any other

1. I translate *sie* as the "apprehension"—the faculty of judgment "compares the apprehension"—following here Garroni and Philonenko. Pluhar and Meredith refer *sie* to "forms" [A.N.].

wie jedes andere empirische Urteil, für jedermann zu gelten, welches, ungeachtet der inneren Zufälligkeit desselben, immer möglich ist. Das Befremdende und Abweichende liegt nur darin: daß es nicht ein empirischer Begriff, sondern ein Gefühl der Lust (folglich gar kein Begriff) ist, welches doch durch das Geschmacksurteil, gleich als ob es ein mit dem Erkenntnisse des Objekts verbundenes Prädikat wäre, jedermann zugemutet und mit der Vorstellung desselben verknüpft werden soll.

Ein einzelnes Erfahrungsurteil, z. B. von dem, der in einem Bergkristall einen beweglichen Tropfen Wasser wahrnimmt, verlangt mit Recht, daß ein jeder andere es ebenso finden müsse, weil er dieses Urteil, nach den allgemeinen Bedingungen der bestimmenden Urteilskraft, unter den Gesetzen einer möglichen Erfahrung überhaupt gefället hat. Ebenso macht derjenige, welcher in der bloßen Reflexion über die Form eines Gegenstandes, ohne Rücksicht auf einen Begriff, Lust empfindet, obzwar | XLII dieses Urteil empirisch und ein einzelnes Urteil ist, mit Recht Anspruch auf jedermanns Beistimmung; weil der Grund zu dieser Lust in der allgemeinen obzwar subjektiven Bedingung der reflektierenden Urteile, nämlich der zweckmäßigen Übereinstimmung eines Gegenstandes (er sei Produkt der Natur oder der Kunst) mit dem Verhältnis der Erkenntnisvermögen unter sich, die zu jedem empirischen Erkenntnis erfordert werden (der Einbildungskraft und des Verstandes), angetroffen wird. Die Lust ist also im Geschmacksurteile zwar von einer empirischen Vorstellung abhängig, und kann a priori mit keinem Begriffe verbunden werden (man kann a priori nicht bestimmen, welcher Gegenstand dem Geschmacke gemäß sein werde, oder nicht, man muß ihn versuchen); aber sie ist doch der Bestimmungsgrund dieses Urteils nur dadurch, daß man sich bewußt ist, sie beruhe bloß auf der Reflexion und den allgemeinen, obwohl nur subjektiven, Bedingungen der Übereinstimmung derselben zum Erkenntnis der Objekte überhaupt, für welche die Form des Objekts zweckmäßig ist.

Das ist die Ursache, warum die Urteile des Geschmacks ihrer Möglichkeit nach, weil diese ein Prinzip a priori voraussetzt, auch einer Kritik unterworfen
AA192 sind, obgleich dieses Prinzip weder ein Erkenntnisprinzip || für den Verstand, noch ein praktisches für den Willen, und also a priori gar nicht bestimmend ist.

| XLIII Die Empfänglichkeit einer Lust aus der Reflexion über die Formen der Sachen (der Natur sowohl als der Kunst) bezeichnet aber nicht allein eine Zweckmäßigkeit der Objekte im Verhältnis auf die reflektierende Urteilskraft, gemäß dem Naturbegriffe am Subjekt, sondern auch umgekehrt des Subjekts in Ansehung der Gegenstände ihrer Form, ja selbst ihrer Unform nach, zufolge dem Freiheitsbegriffe; und dadurch geschieht es: daß das ästhetische Urteil, nicht bloß als Geschmacksurteil, auf das Schöne, sondern auch, als aus einem Geistesgefühl entsprungenes, auf das *Erhabene* bezogen wird, und so jene Kritik der ästhetischen Urteilskraft in zwei diesen gemäße Hauptteile zerfallen muß.

empirical judgment, claims only to be valid for everyone, and this is always possible despite its inner contingency. What is strange and peculiar about this is that it is not an empirical concept but a feeling of pleasure (hence no concept at all) that through the judgment of taste must nonetheless be attributed to everyone and connected with the representation of the object as if it were a predicate connected with the cognition of the object.

A singular judgment of experience, as for example the judgment of someone who perceives a moving drop of water in a crystal rock, rightly demands that anyone else must find things as stated because this judgment was made according to the universal conditions of the determinant faculty of judgment under the laws of a possible experience in general. In the same way, someone who feels pleasure in the mere reflection on the form of an object, without consideration of a concept, rightly lays claim to everyone's assent even though XLVII this judgment is an empirical and singular judgment. For the ground of this pleasure is found in the universal, although subjective, condition of reflective judgments, namely, in the purposive agreement of an object (be it a product of nature or of art) with the mutual relation of the cognitive faculties (of the imagination and the understanding), which are required for every empirical cognition. Therefore in the judgment of taste the pleasure is indeed dependent on an empirical representation and cannot be conjoined a priori with any concept (it cannot be determined a priori which object will or will not be in accordance with taste; one must try it out). Yet the pleasure is still the determining ground of this judgment only because we are conscious that the pleasure rests merely on reflection and on the universal though only subjective conditions of the agreement of that reflection for a cognition of objects in general, an agreement for which the form of the object is purposive.

This is the reason why judgments of taste are also subject to a critique with respect to their possibility. For their possibility presupposes an a priori principle, even though this principle is neither a cognitive principle for the understanding nor a practical principle for the will, and consequently is not at all determinant a priori.

XLVIII However, the receptivity to a pleasure that arises from our reflection on the forms of things [*Sachen*] (both of nature and of art) indicates not only a purposiveness of objects in relation to the reflective faculty of judgment in the subject, according to the concept of nature. It indicates also, conversely, a purposiveness of the subject with regard to objects in their forms—and even their lack of form [*Unform*]—according to the concept of freedom. In this way, it happens that aesthetic judgment is referred not only to the beautiful as judgment of taste, but also to the *sublime* as a judgment that arises from a feeling of spirit [*Geistesgefühl*]. Hence this critique of the aesthetic faculty of judgment must be divided, correspondingly, in two main parts.

VIII. Von der logischen Vorstellung der Zweckmäßigkeit der Natur

An einem in der Erfahrung gegebenen Gegenstande kann Zweckmäßigkeit vorgestellt werden: entweder aus einem bloß subjektiven Grunde, als Übereinstimmung seiner Form, in der *Auffassung* (*apprehensio*) desselben vor allem Begriffe, mit den Erkenntnisvermögen, um die Anschauung mit Begriffen zu einem Erkenntnis überhaupt zu vereinigen; oder aus einem objektiven, als Übereinstimmung seiner Form mit der Möglichkeit des Dinges selbst, nach einem Begriffe von ihm, der | XLIX vorhergeht und den Grund dieser Form enthält. Wir haben gesehen: daß die Vorstellung der Zweckmäßigkeit der ersteren Art auf der unmittelbaren Lust an der Form des Gegenstandes in der bloßen Reflexion über sie beruhe; die also von der Zweckmäßigkeit der zweiten Art, da sie die Form des Objekts nicht auf die Erkenntnisvermögen des Subjekts in der Auffassung derselben, sondern auf ein bestimmtes Erkenntnis des Gegenstandes unter einem gegebenen Begriffe bezieht, hat nichts mit einem Gefühle der Lust an den Dingen, sondern mit dem Verstande in Beurteilung derselben zu tun. Wenn der Begriff von einem Gegenstande gegeben ist, so besteht das Geschäft der Urteilskraft im Gebrauche desselben zum Erkenntnis in der *Darstellung* (*exhibitio*), d. i. darin, dem Begriffe eine korrespondierende Anschauung zur Seite zu stellen: es sei, daß dieses
AA193 durch unsere eigene Einbildungskraft geschehe, wie in der Kunst, || wenn wir einen vorhergefaßten Begriff von einem Gegenstande, der für uns Zweck ist, realisieren, oder durch die Natur, in der Technik derselben (wie bei organisierten Körpern), wenn wir ihr unseren Begriff vom Zweck zur Beurteilung ihres Produkts unterlegen; in welchem Falle nicht bloß *Zweckmäßigkeit* der Natur in der Form des Dinges, sondern dieses ihr Produkt als *Naturzweck* vorgestellt wird.—Obzwar unser Begriff von einer subjektiven Zweckmäßigkeit der Natur in ihren Formen, nach empirischen Gesetzen, gar kein Begriff vom Objekt | L ist, sondern nur ein Prinzip der Urteilskraft sich in dieser ihrer übergroßen Mannigfaltigkeit Begriffe zu verschaffen (in ihr orientieren zu können): so legen wir ihr doch hiedurch gleichsam eine Rücksicht auf unser Erkenntnisvermögen nach der Analogie eines Zwecks bei; und so können wir die *Naturschönheit* als *Darstellung* des Begriffs der formalen (bloß subjektiven), und die *Naturzwecke* als Darstellung des Begriffs einer realen (objektiven) Zweckmäßigkeit ansehen, deren eine wir durch Geschmack (ästhetisch, vermittelst des Gefühls der Lust), die andere durch Verstand und Vernunft (logisch, nach Begriffen) beurteilen.

Hierauf gründet sich die Einteilung der Kritik der Urteilskraft in die der *ästhetischen* und *teleologischen*; indem unter der ersteren das Vermögen, die formale Zweckmäßigkeit (sonst auch subjektive genannt) durch das Gefühl der Lust oder Unlust; unter der zweiten das Vermögen, die reale Zweckmäßigkeit (objektive) der Natur durch Verstand und Vernunft zu beurteilen, verstanden wird.

In einer Kritik der Urteilskraft ist der Teil, welcher die ästhetische Urteils-

VIII. On the Logical Representation of the Purposiveness of Nature

In an object given in experience, purposiveness can be represented either on a merely subjective ground as agreement of the form of the object, in its *apprehension* (*apprehensio*) prior to any concept, with the cognitive faculties in order to unify the intuition with concepts in a cognition in general. Or it can be represented on an objective ground as agreement of the form of the object with the possibility of the thing itself according to a concept of it that XLIX precedes, and contains the ground of this form. We have seen that the representation of the first kind of purposiveness rests on the immediate pleasure we feel from the form of the object in the mere reflection on that form. Therefore, since the representation of the second form of purposiveness relates the form of the object not to the cognitive faculties of the subject in the apprehension of this form but to a determinate cognition of the object under a given concept, the representation of this purposiveness has nothing to do with a feeling of pleasure in things but has rather to do with the understanding in our judging of them. If the concept of an object is given, then the task of the faculty of judgment in its employment of that concept for cognition consists in *exhibition* (*exhibitio*), i.e., in placing beside the concept an intuition corresponding to it. It may be that this exhibition occurs by means of our own imagination, as is the case in art, when we make real a concept that we have already formed of an object that is a purpose for us. Or it may occur through nature, in its technic (as in the case of organized bodies), when we attribute to nature our concept of a purpose in order to judge its product. In that case, we represent not just *purposiveness* of nature in the form of the thing, but we represent this product itself as a *natural purpose*.—Although our concept of a subjective purposiveness of nature in its forms with regard to empirical laws is not at all a concept of an object L, but is only a principle of the faculty of judgment by which this faculty provides itself with concepts in nature's immense variety (so that it can orient itself in it), in this way we are still attributing to nature, in analogy to a purpose, a certain concern for our cognitive faculty. Therefore we may regard *natural beauty* as *exhibition* of the concept of formal (merely subjective) purposiveness and *natural purposes* as exhibition of the concept of a real (objective) purposiveness. The former of these we judge by taste (aesthetically, by means of the feeling of pleasure) and the latter by understanding and reason (logically, according to concepts).

This is the ground for the partition of the critique of the faculty of judgment into critique of *aesthetic* and critique of *teleological* faculty of judgment. By the first, we understand the faculty of judging the formal purposiveness (otherwise also called subjective purposiveness) by the feeling of pleasure or displeasure; by the second, we understand the faculty of judging the real (objective) purposiveness of nature by understanding and reason.

In a critique of the faculty of judgment, the part that deals with the aes-

kraft enthält, ihr wesentlich angehörig, weil diese allein ein Prinzip enthält, welches die Urteilskraft völlig a priori ihrer Reflexion über die Natur zum Grunde legt, nämlich das einer formalen Zweckmäßigkeit der Natur nach ihren besonderen (empirischen) Gesetzen für unser Erkenntnisvermögen, ohne | LI welche sich der Verstand in sie nicht finden könnte: anstatt daß gar kein Grund a priori angegeben werden kann, ja nicht einmal die Möglichkeit davon aus dem Begriffe einer Natur, als Gegenstande der Erfahrung im allgemeinen sowohl, als im besonderen, erhellet, daß es objektive Zwecke der Natur, d. i. Dinge die nur als Naturzwecke möglich sind, geben müsse; sondern nur die Urteilskraft, ohne ein Prinzip dazu a priori in sich zu enthalten, in vorkommenden Fällen (gewisser Produkte), um zum Behuf der Vernunft von dem Begriffe der Zwecke Gebrauch zu machen, die Regel enthält; nachdem
AA194 jenes transzendentale || Prinzip schon den Begriff eines Zwecks (wenigstens der Form nach) auf die Natur anzuwenden den Verstand vorbereitet hat.

Der transzendentale Grundsatz aber, sich eine Zweckmäßigkeit der Natur in subjektiver Beziehung auf unser Erkenntnisvermögen an der Form eines Dinges als ein Prinzip der Beurteilung derselben vorzustellen, läßt es gänzlich unbestimmt, wo und in welchen Fällen ich die Beurteilung, als die eines Produkts nach einem Prinzip der Zweckmäßigkeit, und nicht vielmehr bloß nach allgemeinen Naturgesetzen anzustellen habe, und überläßt es der *ästhetischen* Urteilskraft, im Geschmacke die Angemessenheit desselben (seiner Form) zu unseren Erkenntnisvermögen (sofern diese nicht durch Übereinstimmung mit Begriffen, sondern durch das Gefühl entscheidet) auszumachen. Dagegen gibt die teleologisch-gebrauchte | LII Urteilskraft die Bedingungen bestimmt an, unter denen etwas (z. B. ein organisierter Körper) nach der Idee eines Zwecks der Natur zu beurteilen sei; kann aber keinen Grundsatz aus dem Begriffe der Natur, als Gegenstandes der Erfahrung, für die Befugnis anführen, ihr eine Beziehung auf Zwecke a priori beizulegen, und auch nur unbestimmt dergleichen von der wirklichen Erfahrung an solchen Produkten anzunehmen: wovon der Grund ist, daß viele besondere Erfahrungen angestellt und unter der Einheit ihres Prinzips betrachtet werden müssen, um eine objektive Zweckmäßigkeit an einem gewissen Gegenstande nur empirisch erkennen zu können.—Die ästhetische Urteilskraft ist also ein besonderes Vermögen, Dinge nach einer Regel, aber nicht nach Begriffen, zu beurteilen. Die teleologische ist kein besonderes Vermögen, sondern nur die reflektierende Urteilskraft überhaupt, sofern sie, wie überall im theoretischen Erkenntnisse, nach Begriffen, aber in Ansehung gewisser Gegenstände der Natur nach besonderen Prinzipien, nämlich einer bloß reflektierenden, nicht Objekte bestimmenden Urteilskraft, verfährt, also ihrer Anwendung nach zum theoretischen Teile der Philosophie gehöret, und der besonderen Prinzipien wegen, die nicht, wie es in einer Doktrin sein muß, bestimmend sind, auch einen besonderen Teil der Kritik ausmachen muß; anstatt daß die ästhetische Urteilskraft zum Erkenntnis ihrer Gegenstände nichts beiträgt, und also *nur* zur Kritik des urteilenden Subjekts und der | LIII Erkenntnisvermögen desselben, sofern sie der Prinzipien thetic faculty of judgment belongs to it essentially, because this faculty alone contains a principle that the faculty of judgment lays completely a priori at the ground of its reflection on nature, namely the principle of a formal purposiveness of nature in terms of its particular (empirical) laws, for our cognitive faculty. Without LI this principle, the understanding would not be able to find its way about in nature. By contrast, it is clear that no a priori ground at all can be provided for the claim that there must be objective purposes of nature, i.e., things that are possible only as natural purposes; not even the possibility of such a ground can be obtained from the concept of nature as object of experience in general as well as in particular. Instead, it is only the faculty of judgment that, without containing in itself an a priori principle for that aim, contains in certain cases (of certain products) the rule that allows it to make use of the concept of a purpose to the advantage of reason after the former transcendental principle has already prepared the understanding to apply the concept of a purpose (at least with regard to the form) to nature.

But the transcendental principle of representing in the form of a thing a purposiveness of nature, subjectively, with regard to our cognitive faculty, as a principle for judging of the form itself, leaves it wholly indeterminate where and in what cases I would have to judge as if I were judging of a product according to a principle of purposiveness and not rather simply according to universal laws of nature. The principle leaves it to the *aesthetic* faculty of judgment to ascertain by taste whether that product (its form) is commensurate with our cognitive faculties (as far as this faculty decides not by an agreement with concepts but by feeling). On the contrary, the LII faculty of judgment, employed teleologically, provides determinately the conditions under which something (e.g., an organized body) is to be judged according to the idea of a purpose of nature. But it cannot adduce any principle from the concept of nature as object of experience so as to be entitled to ascribe a priori to nature a reference to purposes or to be entitled to assume anything of this sort on the basis of our actual experience of such products, not even only indeterminately. The reason for this is that, in order to know only empirically an objective purposiveness in a certain object, many particular experiences must be made and considered under the unity of their principle.—Therefore, the aesthetic faculty of judgment is a special faculty of judging things according to a rule but not according to concepts. The teleological faculty of judgment is not a special faculty, but is only the faculty of judgment in general proceeding according to concepts, as is always the case in theoretical cognition, but proceeding, with regard to certain objects of nature, according to special principles, namely the principles of a merely reflective faculty of judgment, not of a judgment that determines objects. Hence, considered in its application, the teleological faculty of judgment belongs to the theoretical part of philosophy, and because of its special principles, which are not determinant, as principles must be in a doctrine, it must also constitute a special part of the critique. The aesthetic faculty of judgment, instead, contributes nothing to the cognition of its objects and therefore must be ascribed *only* to the critique of the judging subject and his LIII cognitive facul-

a priori fähig sind, von welchem Gebrauche (dem theoretischen oder praktischen) diese übrigens auch sein mögen, gezählt werden muß, welche
AA195 die Propädeutik aller Philosophie ist.||

IX. Von der Verknüpfung der Gesetzgebungen des Verstandes und der Vernunft durch die Urteilskraft

Der Verstand ist a priori gesetzgebend für die Natur als Objekt der Sinne, zu einem theoretischen Erkenntnis derselben in einer möglichen Erfahrung. Die Vernunft ist a priori gesetzgebend für die Freiheit und ihre eigene Kausalität, als das Übersinnliche in dem Subjekte, zu einem unbedingt-praktischen Erkenntnis. Das Gebiet des Naturbegriffs, unter der einen, und das des Freiheitsbegriffs unter der anderen Gesetzgebung, sind gegen allen wechselseitigen Einfluß, den sie für sich (ein jedes nach seinen Grundgesetzen) aufeinander haben könnten, durch die große Kluft, welche das Übersinnliche von den Erscheinungen trennt, gänzlich abgesondert. Der Freiheitsbegriff bestimmt nichts in Ansehung der theoretischen Erkenntnis der Natur; der Naturbegriff ebensowohl nichts in Ansehung der praktischen Gesetze der Freiheit: und es ist insofern nicht | LIV möglich, eine Brücke von einem Gebiete zu dem andern hinüberzuschlagen.—Allein wenn die Bestimmungsgründe der Kausalität nach dem Freiheitsbegriffe (und der praktischen Regel die er enthält) gleich nicht in der Natur belegen sind, und das Sinnliche das übersinnliche im Subjekte nicht bestimmen kann; so ist dieses doch umgekehrt (zwar nicht in Ansehung des Erkenntnisses der Natur, aber doch der Folgen aus dem ersteren auf die letztere) möglich und schon in dem Begriffe einer Kausalität durch Freiheit enthalten, deren *Wirkung* diesen ihren formalen Gesetzen gemäß in der Welt geschehen soll, obzwar das Wort *Ursache*, von dem Übersinnlichen gebraucht, nur den *Grund* bedeutet, die Kausalität der Naturdinge zu einer Wirkung, gemäß ihren eigenen Naturgesetzen, zugleich aber doch auch mit dem formalen Prinzip der Vernunftgesetze einhellig, zu bestimmen, wovon die Möglichkeit zwar nicht eingesehen, aber der Einwurf von einem vorgeblichen Widerspruch, der sich darin fände, hinreichend widerlegt werden kann.*) —Die Wirkung nach dem | LV Frei-

---

* Einer von den verschiedenen vermeinten Widersprüchen in dieser gänzlichen Unterscheidung der Naturkausalität von der durch Freiheit ist der, da man ihr den Vorwurf macht: daß, wenn ich von *Hindernissen*, die die Natur der Kausalität nach Freiheitsgesetzen (den moralischen) legt, oder ihre *Beförderung* durch dieselbe rede,
AA196 ich doch der ersteren auf die letztere einen *Einfluß* einräume. Aber, wenn || man das Gesagte nur verstehen will, so ist die Mißdeutung | LV sehr leicht zu verhüten. Der Widerstand, oder die Beförderung, ist nicht zwischen der Natur und der Freiheit, sondern der ersteren als Erscheinung und den *Wirkungen* der letztern als Erscheinungen in der Sinnenwelt; und selbst die *Kausalität* der Freiheit (der reinen und praktischen Vernunft) ist die *Kausalität* einer jener untergeordneten Naturursache (des Subjekts, als Mensch, folglich als Erscheinung betrachtet), von deren *Bestimmung* das Intelligible, welches unter der Freiheit gedacht wird, auf eine übrigens (ebenso wie ebendasselbe, was das übersinnliche Substrat der Natur ausmacht) unerklärliche Art, den Grund enthält.

ties, insofar as these are capable of possessing a priori principles, no matter what their use may be (theoretical or practical). This critique is the propaedeutic to all philosophy.

IX. On the Connection Between the Legislations of the Understanding and Reason Through the Faculty of Judgment

The understanding legislates a priori for nature, as object of the senses, in order to produce a theoretical cognition of nature in a possible experience. Reason legislates a priori for freedom and for freedom's own causality, as the supersensible in the subject, in order to produce an unconditioned practical cognition. The domain of the concept of nature under the one legislation and the domain of the concept of freedom under the other are completely cut off from all reciprocal influence that they for themselves might have on each other (each according to its fundamental laws) by the great abyss that separates the supersensible from appearances. The concept of freedom determines nothing with regard to our theoretical cognition of nature, just as the concept of nature determines nothing with regard to the practical laws of freedom; and to this extent it is not LIV possible to throw a bridge from one domain to the other.—Yet, although nature does not provide evidence for the determining grounds of the causality according to the concept of freedom (and to the practical rule contained in this concept), and although the sensible cannot determine the supersensible in the subject, yet the reverse is possible (not, indeed, in respect to our cognition of nature but still in respect to the consequences that the concept of freedom can have on nature), and this possibility is already contained in the concept of a causality through freedom, whose *effect* is to take place in the world in conformity to its formal laws. The term *cause*, however, if used for the supersensible, signifies only the *ground* that determines the causality of natural things to an effect in conformity to their own natural laws and yet, at the same time, also in accordance with the formal principle of the laws of reason. Although we have no insight into the possibility of all this, yet the charge of an alleged contradiction to be found therein can be adequately refuted.*) (The effect according

---

* One of the various supposed contradictions in this complete distinction of the causality of nature from the causality through freedom is expressed in the following objection. It is held that when I speak of *hindrances* opposed by nature to the causality according to laws of freedom (the moral laws), or of nature *furthering* freedom, I do, after all, admit an influence of the first over the second. But the misinterpretation LV is easily avoided if only one tries to understand what I just said. The resistance or furtherance is not between nature and freedom but between nature as appearance and the *effects* of freedom as appearances in the sensible world; and the *causality* of freedom itself (of pure and practical reason) is the *causality* of a natural cause subordinated to nature (of the subject considered as human being, and hence as appearance). The *determination* of this causality is grounded in the intelligible, which is thought under freedom, in a manner not otherwise explicable (just as in the case of the intelligible that is the supersensible substrate of nature).

AA196 heitsbegriffe ist der || Endzweck, der (oder dessen Erscheinung in der Sinnenwelt) existieren soll, wozu die Bedingung der Möglichkeit desselben in der Natur (des Subjekts als Sinnenwesens, nämlich als Mensch) vorausgesetzt wird. Das, was diese a priori und ohne Rücksicht auf das Praktische voraussetzt, die Urteilskraft, gibt den vermittelnden Begriff zwischen den Naturbegriffen und dem Freiheitsbegriffe, der den Übergang von der reinen theoretischen zur reinen praktischen, von der Gesetzmäßigkeit nach der ersten zum Endzwecke nach dem letzten möglich macht, in dem Begriffe einer *Zweckmäßigkeit* der Natur an die Hand; denn dadurch wird die Möglichkeit des Endzwecks, der allein in der Natur und mit Einstimmung ihrer Gesetze wirklich werden kann, erkannt.

Der Verstand gibt, durch die Möglichkeit seiner Gesetze a priori für die Natur, einen Beweis davon, | LVI daß diese von uns nur als Erscheinung erkannt werde, mithin zugleich Anzeige auf ein übersinnliches Substrat derselben; aber läßt dieses gänzlich *unbestimmt*. Die Urteilskraft verschafft durch ihr Prinzip a priori der Beurteilung der Natur, nach möglichen besonderen Gesetzen derselben, ihrem übersinnlichen Substrat (in uns sowohl als außer uns) *Bestimmbarkeit durch das intellektuelle Vermögen*. Die Vernunft aber gibt eben demselben durch ihr praktisches Gesetz a priori die *Bestimmung*; und so macht die Urteilskraft den Übergang vom Gebiete des Naturbegriffs zu dem des Freiheitsbegriffs möglich.

In Ansehung der Seelenvermögen überhaupt, sofern sie als obere, d. i. Als solche, die eine Autonomie enthalten, betrachtet werden, ist für das *Erkenntnisvermögen* (das theoretische der Natur) der Verstand dasjenige, welches die *konstitutiven* Prinzipien a priori enthält; für das *Gefühl der Lust und Unlust* ist es die Urteilskraft, unabhängig von Begriffen und Emp-
AA197 findungen, die sich auf Bestimmung des Begeh || rungsvermögens beziehen und dadurch unmittelbar praktisch sein könnten; für das *Begehrungsvermögen* die Vernunft, welche ohne Vermittelung irgendeiner Lust, woher sie auch komme, praktisch ist, und demselben, als oberes Vermögen, den Endzweck bestimmt, der zugleich das reine intellektuelle Wohlgefallen am Objekte mit sich führt.—Der Begriff der Urteilskraft von | LVII einer Zweckmäßigkeit der Natur ist noch zu den Naturbegriffen gehörig, aber nur als regulatives Prinzip des Erkenntnisvermögens; obzwar das ästhetische Urteil über gewisse Gegenstände (der Natur oder der Kunst), welches ihn veranlasset, in Ansehung des Gefühls der Lust oder Unlust ein konstitutives Prinzip ist. Die Spontaneität im Spiele der Erkenntnisvermögen, deren Zusammenstimmung den Grund dieser Lust enthält, macht den gedachten Begriff zur Vermittelung der Verknüpfung der Gebiete des Naturbegriffs mit dem Freiheitsbegriffe in ihren Folgen tauglich, indem diese zugleich die Empfänglichkeit des Gemüts für

to LV the concept of freedom is the final purpose, which (or its appearance in the sensible world) ought to exist; and for this its condition of possibility is presupposed in nature (in the nature of the subject as sensible being, namely as human being). It is the faculty of judgment that presupposes this condition a priori and without regard to the practical. With the concept of a *purposiveness* of nature, the faculty of judgment provides us with the concept that mediates between the concepts of nature and the concept of freedom and makes possible the transition from the pure theoretical to the pure practical lawfulness,[2] from the lawfulness according to the concepts of nature to the final purpose according to the concept of freedom. For, in this way. we recognize the possibility of the final purpose, which can only become actual in nature and in accordance with its laws.

The understanding, through the possibility of its giving laws a priori to nature, proves LVI that we can know nature only as appearance, and hence it points, at the same time, to its supersensible substrate. Yet it leaves this substrate entirely *indeterminate*. The faculty of judgment, through its a priori principle for judging of nature in its possible particular laws, provides its supersensible substrate (in us as well as outside of us) with *determinability through the intellectual faculty*. But reason, through its a priori practical law, provides this supersensible substrate with *determination*. Thus, the faculty of judgment makes possible the transition from the domain of the concept of nature to the domain of the concept of freedom.

With regard to the faculties of the soul in general, insofar as they are considered as higher faculties, i.e., as containing an autonomy: for the *cognitive faculty* (theoretical cognition of nature) the faculty that contains the *constitutive* principles a priori is the understanding; for the *feeling of pleasure and displeasure* is the faculty of judgment, independent of concepts and sensations, which may refer to the determination of the faculty of desire and hence be immediately practical; for the *faculty of desire* is reason, which is practical without the mediation of any pleasure whatsoever, regardless of origin, and which determines the final purpose for the faculty of desire as higher faculty. This final purpose carries with itself, at the same time, pure intellectual liking for its object.—The faculty of judgment's concept of LVII a purposiveness of nature still belongs to the concepts of nature, but only as a regulative principle of the cognitive faculty, even though the aesthetic faculty of judgment on certain objects (of nature or of art) occasioning that concept is a constitutive principle with regard to the feeling of pleasure or displeasure. The spontaneity in the play of the cognitive faculties, whose attunement contains the ground of this pleasure, makes that concept suitable as mediation of the connection of the domain of nature with the domain of freedom in its consequences and also promotes at the same time the recep-

2. Vorländer suggests, instead, that "Vernunft" is the implied reference in both cases, so that the translation would be: "from pure theoretical reason to pure practical reason" [A.N.].

das moralische Gefühl befördert.—Folgende Tafel kann die Übersicht aller oberen Vermögen ihrer systematischen Einheit nach erleichtern.**

Gesamte Vermögen des Gemüts	Erkenntnisvermögen	Prinzipien a priori	Anwendung auf
Erkenntnisvermögen	Verstand	Gesetzmäßigkeit	Natur
Gefühl der Lust und Unlust	Urteilskraft	Zweckmäßigkeit	Kunst
Begehrungsvermögen	Vernunft	Endzweck	Freiheit

** Man hat es bedenklich gefunden, daß meine Einteilungen in der reinen Philosophie fast immer dreiteilig ausfallen. Das liegt aber in der Natur der Sache. Soll eine Einteilung a priori geschehen, so wird sie entweder *analytisch* sein, nach dem Satze des Widerspruchs; und da ist sie jederzeit zweiteilig (quodlibet ens est aut A aut non A). Oder sie ist *synthetisch*; und, wenn sie in diesem Falle aus *Begriffen* a priori (nicht, wie in der Mathematik, aus der a priori dem Begriffe korrespondierenden Anschauung) soll geführt werden, so muß, nach demjenigen, was zu der synthetischen Einheit überhaupt erforderlich ist, nämlich 1) Bedingung, 2) ein Bedingtes, 3) der Begriff, der aus der Vereinigung des Bedingten mit seiner Bedingung entspringt, die Einteilung notwendig Trichotomie sein.

tivity of the *Gemüt* to moral feeling.—The following table can facilitate an overview of all the higher faculties in their systematic unity.**

All the Faculties of the *Gemüt*	Cognitive Faculties	A Priori Principles	Application to
Cognitive Faculty	Understanding	Lawfulness	Nature
Feeling of Pleasure and Displeasure	Faculty of Judgment	Purposiveness	Art
Faculty of Desire	Reason	Final Purpose	Freedom

** It has been considered suspicious that my partitions in pure philosophy come out almost always as tripartite. But this lies in the nature of the matter itself. If a partition is to be made a priori, then it will be either *analytic*, according to the principle of contradiction, and in this case it is always bipartite (*quodlibet ens est aut A aut non A*). Or else it will be *synthetic*, and if in this case it is to be made from a priori *concepts* (and not, as in mathematics, from the intuition that corresponds a priori to the concept), then the partition must be necessarily a trichotomy on the ground of that which is required for the synthetic unity in general, namely: 1. condition, 2. a conditioned, 3. the concept that arises from the unification of the conditioned with its condition.

Commentary

In §§I–VI Kant has presented an argument for the necessity of a third *Critique* based upon the critical necessity of its central epistemological question. The last trichotomy of the introduction develops that central question, thereby addressing the issue of the conceptual division of the *Critique of Judgment* into Critique of Aesthetic Judgment, Critique of Teleological Judgment, and Methodology of Teleological Judgment. The third trichotomy can be read as the conclusive union, or the final connection, that arises out of the problems discussed in the first two trichotomies (as "condition" and "conditioned" of the entire *Critique*), placing them in the light of a new *critical* development.

1. Synopsis: §VII, On the Aesthetic Representation of the Purposiveness of Nature

§VII determines the subjective principle of purposiveness as constitutive "aesthetic" principle of *Urteilskraft überhaupt*—of the faculty of judgment *in general* in its different uses. In §VII, Kant provides the critical foundation of the problem of experience in general that was addressed in the previous trichotomy. Kant's aim in this section is to show, in the aftermath of §VI, the grounding relationship between feeling of pleasure, principle of purposiveness, and faculty of judgment, and to present this relation as the new *critical problem*. The "*aesthetic* representation of the purposiveness of nature" qualifies the specific, noncognitive activity of the reflective faculty of judgment that is immediately connected (i.e., not mediated by a concept) to the feeling of pleasure. Both a "critique" of our "judgments of taste" or of the aesthetic faculty of judgment and the internal division of this critique follow from the necessity and universal validity that we must ascribe to judgments of taste. Thus, this section provides the real introduction to Kant's theory of taste.[1]

As transcendental principle of the faculty of judgment, purposiveness plays a role in cognition insofar as it represents the *regulative* principle for the possibility of a systematic unity of experience. Purposiveness, however, is not only a regulative but also a *constitutive* principle. It is the constitutive a priori principle of the (faculty of) feeling of pleasure and displeasure. Thereby the possibility of a critique of feeling is first disclosed. In this connection, purposiveness has nothing to do with conceptual cognition. Kant's task is to show the sense in which a critique

1. For this position see P. Guyer, *Kant and the Claims of Taste*, Cambridge, Cambridge University Press, 1992, 54.

of taste has to be structured as a critique of judgment. His first move in this section is to clarify the nature of the subjectivity proper to the principle of purposiveness (XLII, 188, 33–XLIII, 189, 23). Thereby a crucial argument for the relation between feeling of pleasure and purposiveness is provided (XLIII, 189, 23–190, 13) and the issue of the necessity and universal validity of aesthetic judgments addressed (XLV, 190, 13–XLVIII, 191, 34).

1.1. §VII Commentary: Another Aesthetic

Aesthetic and "das Subjektive" in the Representation of Things (XLII, 188, 33–XLIII, 189, 23)

In presenting and deducing the faculty of judgment's own principle, Kant has repeatedly underlined—but not yet explicitly discussed—its subjective character. Formal purposiveness was indeed recognized as the "subjective principle (maxim)" for the faculty of judgment (§V, XXXIV, 184, 15–16), which in addition only relates to the cognitive faculties of the subject and does not constitute or determine objects for cognition (§V, XXXVI, 185, 18–19; also §VI, XLI, 188, 8). A subjective character of some kind was also disclosed by its being the principle of judgment's "heautonomy" (§V, XXXVII, 185, 36). The issue of what constitutes the specific subjective element proper to our representation of nature (i.e., of objects of the senses) is now thematically addressed at the beginning of §VII. *Das Subjektive* is therein specified with regard to two issues. (i) On the one hand, its character is decided by the question of whether the subjective element plays a role in our cognition of objects or can never be used for cognition. (ii) On the other hand, the issue is raised of whether the subjective element is related to the representation of the object in a material or formal way. Kant takes up again the problem discussed in the first *Critique* regarding the role of sensibility in our cognition of things and institutes the first important relation between two aesthetics; that is, between the aesthetic nature of intuition and the aesthetic nature of feeling.

What is it that should be called "subjective"—and more precisely "merely subjective"—in the representation of an object (*Objekt*) (XLII, 188, 33)? This is presently Kant's general question. If *Vorstellung* (*repraesentatio*) establishes the relation between subject and object, we can say in the most general way that our task is to qualify the element that constitutes the "relation to the subject and not to the object [*Gegenstand*]" (XLII, 188, 34). Kant examines the following possible candidates: pure sensible intuition, sensation, pleasure and displeasure, and the representation of purposiveness. He will soon show that the latter two terms constitute two sides of one and the same issue and can eventually be considered as identical.[2] In the most general way, the subjective component of our representation of an object is defined as "its aesthetic quality" (XLII, 188, 35). It is immediately apparent that

2. See EE §XII, AA, XX, 249, 2–3: the feeling of pleasure is *einerlei* with the "representation of the subjective purposiveness."

this subjective component indicates also the side that regards *sensibility* in general —this is precisely what aesthetic in its etymological significance (*aistheta*) is all about.[3] The "aesthetic quality" of a representation is opposed to its "logical validity" (XLII, 189, 2), i.e., to that element in our representation that serves to determine the object and thereby to produce cognition. In point of fact, in our cognition of objects of the senses, the two sides necessarily occur together: when knowledge is the result of a synthesis of pure form of intuition and category, we have a priori cognition; when it results from sensation and the activity of understanding, we have a posteriori cognition. Evidently, the distinction between aesthetic quality and logical validity is the same general distinction that grounds the division of the *Critique of Pure Reason* in transcendental aesthetic and transcendental logic. The distinction between aesthetic and teleological faculty of judgment will reproduce the same opposition. While aesthetic judgment refers to the aesthetic quality, teleological judgment implies the logical validity of the object. In the formulation of the "First Introduction," which is rendered less explicit and more nuanced in the published one, the third *Critique* is divided into an *Ästhetik* of the reflective faculty of judgment and a *Logik* of the same faculty, which is "Teleology."[4]

Intuition (XLII, 189, 2–10)

The first instance of the aesthetic or subjective quality of our representation is provided by *intuition*. Kant refers to a "sensible representation of things outside of me" (XLII, 189, 3–4), which is made possible by space as pure form of intuition. Space designates the "formal constitution" of the subject, its disposition to being affected by external objects.[5] We know from the first *Critique* that space represents things merely as they appear to us, leaving undecided what they might be in themselves. Through space, things are represented, and then they are thought of as appearances. The "merely subjective" character of space is precisely its subjective reality or transcendental ideality. Despite its subjectivity, however, space is still a constitutive element of cognition and gains thereby its objective validity (and hence something analogous to a logical validity). In the *Critique of Pure Reason*, Kant presented a *Stufenleiter*—a ladder-like ascending structure—to guide us in the division of the genus "representation (*repraesentatio*)." Herein intuition appears along with "concept" as "*objective* perception" or "knowledge (*cognitio*)."[6] In sum, the subjectivity of intuition is, according to Kant, merely *formal* and is an indispensable ingredient in our cognition of things.

Sensation (XLII–XLIII, 189, 10–15)

The same passage of the first *Critique*, in perfect agreement with the position of §VII of the third *Critique*, opposes intuition to "sensation," which is defined as

---

3. See KrV B 35/A 21 fn.
4. EE §XII, AA, XX, 249, 9–11.
5. KrV B 41/A 26.
6. KrV B 376/A 320; see also *Prolegomena*, §20, AA, IV, 300.

subjective perception. Sensation is perception that "relates only to the subject as a modification of its status." Since we deal with objects of the outer senses, Kant specifically analyzes "outer sensation." As is the case with intuition, sensation "also expresses what is merely subjective in our representations of things outside us" (XLII–XLIII, 189, 10–11). Yet sensation refers to what is *material* in given objects, which are thereby represented as real or existent. Sensation is employed in *empirical* cognition of external objects. Kant analyzes this function of sensation in the postulates of empirical thinking of the Analytic of Principles. "Reality" is only provided by "sensation as matter of experience."[7] While pure intuition constitutes the form of appearances, sensation constitutes its matter, which is always given a posteriori.[8] Both intuition and sensation are *aesthetic* components of our cognition of things if we take aesthetic as meaning *aistheta* in general. The first *Critique* has shown that since there is an a priori of sensible intuition a *transcendental* aesthetic is possible, but because of the materiality of sensation, no a priori science of sensation is possible (and hence sensation does not belong to a transcendental aesthetic). However, insofar as sensation is still a fundamental ingredient of empirical knowledge, Kant attributes to it an objective validity of some kind. §3 of the third *Critique* will further distinguish a twofold meaning of sensation—namely an "objective sensation" that relates to the perception of an object of the senses and a "subjective sensation" that considers the object as object of our "liking" (§3, 9, AA 206, 26–36).

Feeling of Pleasure or Displeasure (XLIII, 189, 16–19)

While both intuition and sensation, despite their subjectivity, are employed in cognition of things as appearances (a priori or a posteriori synthetic judgments), the third candidate to qualify for the "aesthetic quality" of our representation excludes all possible contribution to cognition. "*But*, that subjective component in a representation *that cannot at all become an element of cognition* is the *pleasure* or *displeasure* connected with it" (XLIII, 189, 16–18). Kant clearly constructs the pleasure or displeasure that accompanies our representation of things and cannot be reduced to a function of cognition in antithesis to intuition and sensation ("But..."). Since both intuition and sensation are elements of cognition, they still somehow participate in its objectivity or logical validity. Pleasure and displeasure, on the contrary, can by no means be employed in a cognitive function. Therefore, they are even more truly subjective—they are "*merely* subjective" in the proper sense.[9] As Kant mentioned in §VI, pleasure might very well arise out of cognition (XL, 187, 25) but is certainly not its cause. As opposed to intuition (which says that the object is intuited in space) and sensation (which says, at the very least, that the object is perceived as real or existent), pleasure does not say anything about the repre-

7. KrV B 270/A 223.
8. See KrV B34/A 20.
9. See KrV B 66/A 49: both feeling and the will are excluded from cognition.

sented object. It merely expresses something about the subject that represents the object. It still remains to decide whether this pleasure that is "connected" to a representation of objects of the senses is material or formal. This is, to be sure, a crucial point. For only under the condition that an a priori of the faculty of feeling be provided does a critique of this faculty become possible.

Interestingly, starting from the *Critique of Pure Reason* up to the *Critique of Judgment*, Kant progressively shifts the meanings of the subjectivity and objectivity proper to the different forms of sensibility. This move is related to the fundamental issue of what is aesthetic in transcendental philosophy. When the only possible transcendental aesthetic is the doctrine of the pure forms of sensible intuition, these forms alone are seen as objectively valid, while all other expressions of sensibility (sensation, desires, feelings) are seen as merely subjective and hence not as a possible object of a transcendental theory of cognition. But as soon as Kant sees the possibility of a second aesthetic—or, better, of a "critique of the aesthetic faculty of judgment"[10]—as the first division of the third *Critique*, the subjectivity of sensibility needs to be recognized as a possible candidate for transcendental philosophy on the one hand and to be restricted to the faculty of feeling alone on the other hand. For the only way of claiming the independence of feeling, and hence the possibility for this faculty of displaying an a priori principle of its own, is to deny it any cognitive (objective) validity.[11]

In §VIII, Remark, of the "First Introduction," Kant gives a transcendental *Erklärung* (definition, explanation) of the feeling of pleasure considered in general terms, "without considering the distinction as to whether it accompanies sensation produced from the senses, reflection, or the determination of the will." The explanation reads as follows: "Pleasure is a state of the *Gemüt*, in which a representation is in accordance with itself as ground either for merely preserving this state itself . . . or for producing the object of this representation."[12] It is important to stress that feeling's transcendental ambiguity rests on the fact that it may "accompany" *all* the faculties of the soul. Kant mentions the three different cases of sensible pleasure, pleasure that arises in reflection, and pleasure connected to the faculty of desire. The task of §VII of the final introduction is to clarify these differences.

The general definition of feeling quoted above from the "First Introduction" addresses two issues. On the one hand, pleasure is connected to the notion of harmony, or self-accordance of a set of representations; on the other hand, this feeling is the ground for a twofold response: either for a contemplating furtherance of the status of the *Gemüt* (reflection) or for the production of the object (faculty of desire). With regard to this latter alternative, Kant distinguishes the "aesthetic judgment of reflection" from the "aesthetic-pathological or aesthetic practical

---

10. See EE §XI, AA, XX, 247, 7–8.

11. It should also be noted that while the focus of §VII is the notion of subjectivity, the starting point of the corresponding §VIII of the "First Introduction" is an explanation of the expression "aesthetic."

12. EE §VIII, AA, XX, 230, 8–232, 1.

judgment."[13] The argument of §VII of the final introduction takes a different route. It proceeds to a progressive restriction of the subjectivity proper to the functions of sensibility so that the only remaining candidate for a purely aesthetic judgment is the feeling of pleasure and displeasure. Thus, against all other forms of sensibility (E §VII)—and hence of pleasure connected to different faculties of the soul (EE §VIII)—the feeling of pleasure is the only term that fulfills both conditions of pure aesthetic validity and irreducible subjectivity.

Formal Purposiveness (XLIII, 189, 20–27)

For the moment, Kant seems to leave unsettled the question of the formality vs. materiality of the feeling of pleasure. He moves on to identify a fourth instance of that initial subjective element of our representation of objects. "Purposiveness of a thing, insofar as it is represented in perception, is also not a quality of the object itself (since such quality cannot be perceived)" (XLIII, 189, 20–22). Purposiveness is merely subjective. However, its belonging to sensibility, hence its aesthetic character (in the etymological sense), is merely formal. Purposiveness depends upon the perception of the object and yet is related only to the form of the object. It is apparent that Kant constructs the two cases of pleasure/displeasure and purposiveness in a parallel way. In both cases it holds true that they do not constitute cognition of the object and yet can arise out of cognition (pleasure) or can be inferred from cognition (purposiveness). A purposiveness, which logically *precedes* our cognition of things (even a cognition that we might already have) and, as demonstrated in §§IV–V, makes empirical cognition of nature possible without constituting objects as such, is the "subjective component" of our representation of objects (i.e., "that which cannot at all become an element of cognition," XLIII, 189, 26–27), even though is immediately connected with such a representation. The crucial point of Kant's argument is to show that feeling of pleasure and purposive representation of the object are not two different things but rather two aspects of the same relation to the subject (as relation, respectively, to the faculty of feeling and to the faculty of judgment). We can also claim that the feeling of pleasure or displeasure is that which gives meaning to (or schematizes) the principle of purposiveness; feeling is the subjective representation of the purposiveness of the object. Purposiveness is a meaningful notion only insofar as it can be exhibited in and by a feeling; it then becomes a principle for the faculty of judgment when it comes to be applied through the pure feeling of pleasure (as its schema).[14]

Aesthetic Representation of Purposiveness, Pleasure, and the Judgment of Taste (XLIII, 189, 23–190, 13)

What then allows us to call an object purposive if purposiveness does not provide in itself cognition of the object and either precedes our cognition or follows from it? Kant's answer makes a conclusive point. "In this case, the object *is called* pur-

13. EE §VIII, AA, XX, 230, 8–232, 1.

14. See E. Garroni, *Estetica ed epistemologia*, Roma, Bulzoni, 1976, 69.

posive *only because* its representation is *immediately* connected with the feeling of pleasure, and this representation itself is an *aesthetic* representation of purposiveness" (XLIII–XLIV, 189, 27–30). While judgments in which intuition or sensation play a role are judgments that say what objects *are* (i.e., how they appear to us; they say that objects *are* in space, *are* real, etc.), in the case in point, Kant stresses that the object "*is called*" purposive (no claim is made as to what the thing objectively is). Moreover, the *only reason* why an object is called purposive is that its representation *immediately* produces pleasure in the subject.[15] Purposiveness does not express anything about the object's constitution. It rather presents a subjective mode of apprehending the object. It voices the suitability of the object's representation to the subject's faculties whereby pleasure is immediately produced. This means that the pleasure that is connected to the representation of the object's purposiveness is referred to the *form* of the object. For purposiveness is not a material feature of the object itself. The representation is called, in this case, "*aesthetic* representation of purposiveness" and simply expresses a "*subjective formal* purposiveness of the object" (XLIV, 190, 1–2).

To confirm the initial definition of the subjective component of our representation as that which refers merely to the subject, Kant reconstructs the situation in which a judgment regarding the purposiveness of an object is formulated. The situation regards a specific modality of apprehending (*Auffassung*, *apprehensio*) the form of an object given in intuition by means of imagination. Apprehension is the imagination's act of recollecting a manifold of empirical intuitions in the unity of a synthesis in order to produce perception.[16] When the object is given and its form apprehended, we can either bring its intuition under a concept in view of "*determinate* cognition" (XLIV, 189, 34)—and this is what happens in cognition (in the use of understanding and determinant faculty of judgment or in the quasi-cognition of the teleological faculty of judgment §VIII, XLIX, 192, 28–29)—or we can bypass the cognitive reference to the concept and, in this case, the representation of the object may be "connected" instead with pleasure (or displeasure). We know, on the other hand, that no universal concept is given to the reflective faculty of judgment, so that this latter case specifically requires the intervention of the reflective faculty of judgment. In this case, the representation "is not related to the object but solely to the subject" (XLIV, 189, 35–36), which confirms the initial assumption. Pleasure expresses the purposiveness of the object, the *Angemessenheit*, or "conformity" of its form "to the cognitive faculties that are at play in the reflective faculty of judgment and insofar as they are at play therein" (XLIV, 189, 36–37/190, 1). It is now clear that *"pleasure"* is another word for *"purposiveness"* when the relation to the subject is taken as the relation to its faculty of *Gefühl* rather than to the faculty of reflective judgment.

---

15. For the immediacy of the relation, see also preface, VIII, 169, 22.
16. See, for example, KrV B 160 ff.

What Kant has established so far is that *if* a representation of purposiveness *precedes* our cognition of the represented object, since the representation of the object is connected, in this case, neither to the cognitive faculty nor to the faculty of desire, then purposiveness can be related to neither of those faculties, and hence the object can be called purposive only because its representation is immediately connected with a feeling of pleasure. It is clear that "the only question is whether there is such a representation of purposiveness at all" (XLIV, 189, 30–31). Evidently, this is a conclusive question if compared to the developments of the first two trichotomies. It is obviously not so much a factual question but a question of possibility. Is such a representation of purposiveness (i.e., a purely formal feeling) possible at all? In §§I–III Kant has proposed the notion of an independent faculty of judgment in a merely hypothetical and analogical way, while in §§IV–VI, he has given the deduction of the a priori principle of this faculty thereby providing transcendental plausibility to that initial assumption. However, the definitive foundation of the problem of the third *Critique* can be reached only once the present question—"whether there is such a representation of purposiveness at all"—has been conclusively answered. From this question depends the possibility of a third *Critique* (XLIV, 189, 30–3; see XLVII, 191, 35–37); that is, the possibility of judgments of taste and their a priori principle. Kant's argument sets out to prove precisely that there is indeed such a representation (or that such a representation is indeed possible).

In order to establish how the harmony between the form of the object and our faculties can arise, Kant has to indicate, first, which faculties are at play in the act of reflection upon the object and, second, how the harmony plays itself out in the act of reflection. In §IV, Kant has suggested that the determinant faculty of judgment is at work with understanding (and as understanding), but no mention is made of the functions required for the exercise of the reflective faculty of judgment. Kant now introduces the work of imagination, which apprehends the form of the object given in sensible intuition. What the reflective faculty of judgment effects at this point is an act of "comparison" between imagination and understanding—a comparison that can remain in some sense "unintentional" (i.e. referred to no practical aim) (XLIV, 190, 4, 8). As established already in the first *Critique*, reflection is the act that brings back to a consideration of the subject's own faculties by comparing and combining given representations with these faculties. The reflective faculty of judgment compares the apprehension of the form of the object with the faculty that is delegated to that apprehension, namely imagination, which in turn relates intuitions to concepts.[17] At this point, we can encounter the fortunate case of a representation in which the comparison of imagination and understanding produces *Einstimmung*—unison and harmony—in an immediate and unintentional way. We can easily see that, even though no constitutive

17. See the different reconstruction suggested in EE §VII, AA, XX, 220–221, where the crucial difference lies in the function ascribed to the faculty of judgment; see also 223, 9–10 and 225, 31.

reference to a concept is made, reflection deals with nothing else but "cognition in general" and with relations among cognitive faculties (also XLIV, 189, 36–37/190, 1). What follows in the subject is a feeling of pleasure. In this case, we certainly do not come to know but indeed we *feel* the internal relation between our faculties; we feel (and become aware of) the whole status of our mind—our *Gemützustand.*[18] It is precisely when this complex situation takes place that we "must" regard the form of the object as purposive for the reflective faculty of judgment. The judgment that we thereby pronounce is an "aesthetic judgment" (*Urteil*) (XLIV, 190, 5–11). In this judgment, no cognition of the object takes place. If a concept (i.e., understanding) is involved, it is neither as the ground of the judgment itself nor as its product. The only point that aesthetic judgment makes is that the object's form in its apprehension meets with an accordance of imagination and understanding.

This complicated reconstruction of the occurrence of aesthetic judgment offers a first answer to the initial problem of "whether there is such a representation of purposiveness at all" (XLIV, 189, 30–3). Kant's contention is that the representation of an aesthetic purposiveness does indeed exist—and is therefore possible—precisely because it results from a simple reflection upon the relation between imagination and understanding—a relation that grounds the very possibility of experience in general and cognition in general. This explains why the formulation of the aesthetic principle of the faculty of judgment depends upon the formulation of the crucial *epistemological* problem that occupies the second trichotomy of the introduction (§§IV–VI).[19] Formal purposiveness, feeling of pleasure (as representation of the purposiveness of the object), harmony of the cognitive faculties, and empirical cognition in general are but different modes to express the same *epistemological* situation.[20] Even though the aesthetic principle of the faculty of judgment does not produce determinate knowledge of things, it still refers to the necessary conditions of an *Erkenntnis überhaupt* (i.e., to the conditions for the unity of a manifold without which no knowledge would be possible). Moreover, the relation between aesthetic faculty of judgment and cognition in general grounds the methodological need for developing the critical exposition of judgments of taste according to the four moments (quality, quantity, relation, modality) corresponding to the table of the categories. This is the structure that articulates the Analytic of the Beautiful.

---

18. See EE § VII, AA, XX, 223, 15–16.

19. See the passage commented upon in the previous chapter: §VI, XL, 187, 31–34.

20. See for this argument E. Garroni/H. Hohenegger, introduction to I. Kant, *Critica della facoltà di giudizio*, a cura di E. Garroni, H. Hohenegger, Torino, Einaudi, 1999, XLII. The opposite interpretive position is held by P. Guyer, *Kant and the Claims of Taste*, op. cit., chapter 2, who concludes, for example, that "Kant's association of the problem of taste with that of the systematicity of nature leads to a deeply misleading suggestion about the actual content of the a priori principle of taste" (57).

Necessity and Universal Validity of Aesthetic Judgment (XLV, 190, 13–32)

Kant's further step is to argue for the specific modality—the necessity and universal validity—of aesthetic judgments.[21] In order for a critique of the aesthetic faculty of judgment to be possible, Kant has to show that the aesthetic faculty of judgment has an a priori ground (i.e., that the pleasure connected to the representation of the object's formal purposiveness is *somehow a pure form of sensibility*). While the *logical* validity of our cognitive judgments amounts to objective necessity and universality (*Allgemeinheit*), the aesthetic quality proper to our purposive representation of things or to our aesthetic judgments allows only for subjective necessity and universal—or intersubjective—validity (*Allgemeingültigkeit*). In the context of the first *Critique*, with regard to cognitive judgments, the issue of intersubjective validity did not appear to Kant as an issue separate from that of judgments' objective validity and necessity. In the *Prolegomena*, Kant even holds that "objective validity and necessary universality (for everybody) are equivalent terms."[22] In the third *Critique* instead, where aesthetic judgments, lacking any cognitive reference to concepts, do not at all address the question of objective validity, the issue of intersubjective or universal validity comes to the fore as an independent issue, namely as the specific form of universality proper to judgments of taste. Herein intersubjective validity refers to the communicability of aesthetic judgments. A critique of the aesthetic faculty of judgment is possible only if Kant can argue that aesthetic judgments are intersubjectively valid and hence do enjoy a specific kind of universality even though they are not objectively valid (i.e., constitutive of objects). On the other hand, the universality of judgments of taste must also be distinguished from the universality proper to the moral law as the universality that arises out of the universalizability of the subjective maxim in the test of the categorical imperative. For both in the case of understanding's principles and in the case of reason's moral law, *Allgemeinheit* is the universality of a *law*. It is precisely this universality that is not accessible to the faculty of judgment's own principle (which is not a law).

If in reflecting upon the *form* of an object we judge that the mere apprehension of this form, not the material content of our sensation, *grounds* a pleasure in the representation of such an object, then this pleasure "is judged as *necessarily* connected with its representation, and hence not simply for the subject apprehending this form but *for every judging subject in general*" (XLIV–XLV, 190, 13–20). In this case, the object *is called* beautiful, and "the faculty of judging by such a pleasure . . . is called taste" (XLV, 190, 20–21). Both the *necessity* and the intersubjective universal validity of judgments of taste are grounded upon the formal nature of the pleasure that arises out of the representation of objects. Its necessity is the necessary relation between the formality of the purposive repre-

---

21. This problem occupies Kant in the second and fourth moment of the judgment of taste in the Analytic of the Beautiful (see the discussion in part III).

22. *Prolegomena*, §19, AA, IV, 298.

sentation and pleasure. Pleasure is not produced by this or that sensation of an object but by the mere apprehension of a form and by the act of reflecting upon it (see §VIII, 192, 24–25). While the noncognitive subjectivity of pleasure was previously opposed to the cognitive validity of space and time, now pleasure, on the ground of its formality, is lined up with intuition and opposed to the materiality of sensation. The subjectivity of such a pleasure (as the subjectivity of space and time) does not imply the private validity of the feeling, which would be the case if the pleasure had material origin in sensation. Thus subjectivity reveals *universal validity*: we assume that our judgment would be endorsed by "every judging subject in general."

Once again, the fact that the activity of the reflective faculty of judgment is inscribed within the a priori conditions of cognition in general proves itself crucial (therein Kant carries on the analogy with cognition in general). Kant repeats that in reflecting upon the form of the object, no cognition is involved and no practical aim is presupposed; we are dealing with a specific activity of the mind that can be reduced neither to the theoretical nor to the practical use of our faculties. If we ask with what precisely the representation of the object upon which we reflect is in accordance or harmony, Kant's answer is "with the *lawfulness* in the *empirical use* of the *faculty of judgment in general* (unity between imagination and understanding)" (XLV, 190, 25–26). The general character of this answer is important. *Whenever* the *empirical* use of the faculty of judgment in general establishes *Gesetzmäßigkeit*, this lawfulness allows for a special feeling of pleasure that can claim universal validity. This is the case, in the first place, for the cognitive use of the reflective faculty of judgment that was discussed in sections §§IV–VI. We must recall that the "First Introduction" defined purposiveness as "a lawfulness of the contingent as such."[23] The issue at stake in §§IV–VI was precisely the problem of the possibility of empirical cognition insofar as this cognition depends upon the possibility of a lawfulness of the empirical manifold of natural forms. Kant's present argument moves along the same lines and develops in analogy with the epistemological problem of empirical cognition in general. The unity of imagination and understanding is the agreement that reflection ascertains in the act of apprehending the object's form. Moreover, while the relation between representation of the object and feeling of pleasure is necessary upon occurrence of the attunement or harmony between the object's form and our mental faculties, the occurrence of this *Zusammenstimmung* is merely contingent. Such contingency (as opposed to the deterministic necessity with which cognition takes place) is the ground for the representation of the purposiveness of the object with regard to the subject's cognitive faculties. No object would in fact be represented as purposive—and hence judged beautiful—were its relation to the cognitive faculties a necessary one (see §VI, XXXVIII, 186, 31–XXXIX, 187, 2).

---

23. EE §VI, AA, XX, 217, 28; see also §XI, 243, 5–6.

Aesthetic Pleasure and Aesthetic Judgment (XLVI, 190, 33–191, 11)

In §VI, Kant mentioned the quite peculiar character of the feeling of pleasure that arises once the harmonious relation among the cognitive faculties at play in the act of reflection takes place (XL, 187, 25). What is this peculiarity? We need to recall a distinction between three types of pleasure. First, we have the pleasure that arises in connection with the lower faculty of desire, namely the merely empirical and material response to agreeable sensations. This type of pleasure cannot be connected to the representation of purposiveness because of its *materiality*. Secondly, the only instance of a formal pleasure that is universally valid and necessary is the pleasure brought about by the concept of freedom (i.e., by the *prior* determination of the higher faculty of desire by pure reason) (XLV/XLVI, 190, 34–35). Since it is produced by a *concept* (the moral law), this pure pleasure cannot be ascribed to the reflective faculty of judgment but relates only to pure practical reason. Finally, we have a pleasure that no concept can present as being necessarily connected to a representation of an object precisely because it is not produced by any concept and yet is also not produced by any material sensation. This is the case of *aesthetic* pleasure.

To say that a given object is beautiful means, first, to institute a necessary relation between the representation of the object and a feeling of pleasure occurring in the subject and, second, to assume that any judging subject would agree with my judgment. The point is that only "reflected perception" (i.e., the act of apprehending the object's form along with the reflection on this act) (XLVI, 191, 1), not a concept, can allow us to recognize the connection between the representation of the object and the feeling of pleasure. I do not *know* of this connection through a concept, and I certainly do not know of it a priori since I cannot determine a priori which object is going to be in accordance with my taste; I must first try out and experience the object itself (XLVII, 191, 28–29). Yet I *feel* this connection directly. In this case, a *formal* relation between pleasure and the representation of the object is instituted. Yet since this relation is not a conceptual a priori relation, it cannot claim the same type of "objective necessity" and "a priori validity" that is proper of purely cognitive or purely practical judgments. I certainly cannot oblige someone else to agree with my aesthetic judgment on the ground of an a priori concept that everyone must recognize as logically valid (e.g., a standard of taste). And yet I assume that everyone else, in experiencing a certain object in perception, would be prompted to pronounce the same judgment that I pronounce.

In this respect, aesthetic judgments behave rather as empirical judgments, which cannot claim any constitutive function with regard to objectivity (they have a domicilium but not a domain).[24] In spite of their purity (which only concerns the determining ground of the judgment), aesthetic judgments are still empirical judgments.[25] "But then the judgment of taste, as any other empirical judgment, claims

---

24. See §II on "concepts of experience" (XVI/XVII, 174, 17–18).

25. For the purity of aesthetic judgments, see §14, which distinguishes between pure and empirical aesthetic judgments addressing the topic of sensation; see also EE§XII, 248, 33.

only to be valid for everyone, and this is always possible despite its inner contingency" (XLVI, 191, 3–6). There is an ongoing analogy between noncognitive aesthetic judgments and empirical judgments of cognition. The only pretension of a judgment of taste is that it be valid for every judging subject; this is still recognized as a possibility in spite of the contingency that affects the relation between the representation of the object and the representation of its purposiveness. What makes for the "strangeness and peculiarity" (XLVI, 191, 6–7) of judgments of taste is that herein the feeling of pleasure takes the place that the empirical concept has in empirical judgments. Judgments of taste raise a claim to universal validity that is not grounded upon a concept—neither pure nor empirical. In aesthetic judgment, purposiveness is "represented in perception" (XLIII, 189, 20–21)—although it cannot be itself perceived—and hence logically precedes all concept. Aesthetic judgment connects a predicate to a subject by means of a feeling of pleasure (the ground of the statement "This object is beautiful" is a feeling in the subject, not an empirical concept of the object). It does so "*as if* it were a predicate connected with the cognition of the object" (XLVI, 191, 7–11). On the basis of this analogical predication, we assume that the judgment of taste can be endorsed by everyone. Aesthetic judgment is not a cognitive judgment and yet is constructed and formulated in analogy to a cognitive judgment, as if cognition were implied.

Judgments of Experience and Judgments of Taste (XLVI/XLVII, 191, 12–34)

What is the difference between a singular judgment of experience regarding, for example, the perception of a moving drop of water in a crystal rock, and an aesthetic judgment regarding the beauty of a specific given individual object (*this* is beautiful)? The former judgment is an empirical judgment based on perception, which under the universal conditions of "experience in general" established by understanding becomes, according to the doctrine of the *Prolegomena*, a judgment of experience with universal validity.[26] It is formulated "according to the universal conditions of the determinant faculty of judgment under the laws of a possible experience in general" (XLVI, 191, 15–16). On this basis, it demands universal validity—in this case, *universality*. Kant holds that "in the same way" (XLVI, 191, 17), in pronouncing a judgment of taste regarding the beauty of a given object, what we are expressing is that we feel pleasure "in the mere reflection on the form of an object"—and hence we attribute the predicate *beautiful* to the object without taking any concept into account. On the other hand, however, our judgment is indeed empirical since it is occasioned by the perception of a singular given object. Yet our pleasure is still pure and formal since it does not derive from sensation but from reflection upon the object's form. It is important to stress that aesthetic judgment always refers to a *singular* feeling whereby the singularity expresses not so much

26. See *Prolegomena*, §20, AA, IV, 300 f. For the general issue of judgments of experience, see B. Longuenesse, *Kant and the Capacity to Judge,* Princeton, Princeton University Press, 1998, chapter 7.

that the feeling belongs to a singular individual subject but rather the impossibility of considering this feeling as an instance of a class to which a concept could be referred as the universal under which the particular could then be subsumed. Hence Kant contends that even though the judgment of taste is a nonconceptual, empirical, and always necessarily singular judgment, we do have the right to lay claim "to everyone's assent" (XLVII, 191, 20). The ground of this right is a parallelism between the conditions for the use of the determinant faculty of judgment and the conditions for the use of the reflective faculty of judgment. Whereas the empirical judgment of perception is pronounced according to the universal objective conditions of a possible experience in general (i.e., to the transcendental laws that understanding gives to nature in general), a judgment of taste is pronounced according to the universal subjective condition of the reflective faculty of judgment (i.e., to the principle of formal purposiveness of the object with regard to our cognitive faculties [imagination and understanding]) (XLVII, 191, 20–26). In §§IV–VI, the object—or the conditioned—whose possible cognition was allowed only by the principle of purposiveness, was nature in the manifold of its empirical forms. In the present connection, Kant suggests that the object whose purposiveness for the cognitive faculties is expressed by a judgment of taste is either "a product of nature or of art" (XLVII, 191, 23; again XLVIII, 192, 4). Henceforth the problem will be addressed according to this more inclusive formulation. Nonetheless, the titles of both §VII and §VIII concern the "representation of the purposiveness *of nature*."

The twofold relation (i) between feeling of pleasure in the form of the object and reflection and (ii) between reflection and conditions of experience in general allows Kant to give a critical foundation to the problem of the third *Critique*. Given that in the judgment of taste pleasure depends upon an empirical representation and hence has empirical (yet not material) origin, and given that the relationship of this pleasure to the object cannot be determined a priori through a concept (it is merely contingent), *it is only through the crucial relation between aesthetic faculty of judgment and conditions of experience in general* that Kant can conclude that such a pleasure still constitutes the *Bestimmungsgrund* of judgment. This is, first, because we "are conscious" that this pleasure is merely *formal* (i.e., that it does not arise from sensation but from our reflection upon the form of the object). We are conscious of the effect of the principle (not of the principle itself) aesthetically through a feeling, not intellectually through a concept.[27] Second, this pleasure rests on the universal—although merely subjective—"conditions of the *agreement of that reflection for a cognition of objects in general*" (XLVII, 191, 32–34). This *Übereinstimmung* makes us judge the form of the object as purposive.

It is relevant that Kant formulates the crucial issue in terms of the *Bestimmungsgrund* of judgment of taste as such, not in terms of actual, individual judgments of taste.[28] What is at stake is only the principle, or ground, of determina-

27. See also §1 and §9.

28. See §1.

tion—and legitimization—of aesthetic judgment; that is, the principle according to which such a judgment (and all aesthetic judgments), if possible, is precisely and specifically an *aesthetic* judgment. Only after this principle has been identified can one further discuss whether this or that actual judgment of taste does or does not depend upon that principle and is really a judgment of taste in Kant's sense.[29] It is important to stress that the issue of the *Bestimmungsgrund* comes to the fore as a crucial issue only in the *Critique of Practical Reason* and in the *Critique of Judgment*. For it is only in the cases of practical judgments and aesthetic judgments, as opposed to logical judgments, that the determining ground cannot be revealed by an analysis of the external form of the judgment itself.[30]

Critique of Taste and Critique of the Aesthetic Faculty of Judgment (XLVII/XLVIII, 191, 35–192, 12)

The previous argument justifies the need for a critique of the judgments of taste. With regard to the question raised at the beginning of the section (XLIV, 189, 30–31), Kant has shown that the possibility of a judgment of taste presupposes an a priori principle. This principle, however, being neither cognitive nor practical must be a principle of the *reflective* faculty of judgment as *Urteilskraft überhaupt*. Hence a critique of taste must be a critique of the reflective faculty of judgment. Once the necessity of a critique of the faculty of judgment is established, Kant takes up again, in a conclusive albeit still merely hypothetical way, the issue of the *Mittelglied* that occupied the first trichotomy. The faculty of judgment has been proposed as the intermediary and mediating faculty that would allow for a transition from the *Denkungsart* according to principles of nature to a *Denkungsart* according to freedom. At the end of §VII, Kant can finally show how this mediation takes place. This argument presents, at the same time, the internal division of the "critique of the aesthetic faculty of judgment" into its two main parts (XLVIII, 191, 11–12).

Once the notion of a purposiveness of the forms of *Sachen*—both products of nature and art—has been established with regard to the faculty of judgment and the subject's "receptivity" to pleasure (i.e. its sensibility), Kant suggests a reverse way to look at the purposive relation between subject and object. This time, purposiveness is not ascribed to the form of the object but to the subject itself with regard to the form—and even to "the lack of form" (*Unform*) (XLVIII, 191, 7–8)—of the object. In this connection, the form or *Unform* of the object would correspond to the feeling of pleasure or displeasure in the subject. While the first type of relationship is inscribed within the framework of the concepts of nature

29. See §8.

30. See E. Garroni/H. Hohenegger, introduction to I. Kant, *Critica della facoltà di giudizio*, op. cit., LVI. Moreover, given the peculiarity of the judgment of taste, *Bestimmungsgrund*, which is a principle and at the same time a feeling, also could be translated as "motivation" in order to underline the relation between the faculty of judgment and the natural talent and common sense mentioned by Kant already in the first *Critique*.

where "taste" prompts aesthetic judgments of the *beautiful*, the second type of relationship is determined by the concept of freedom and prompts aesthetic judgments of the *sublime*. The latter arise "from a feeling of spirit" (XLVIII, 191, 10). In the case of the sublime, no purposiveness seems to be contained in the form of the object itself. The fact that the object displays a lack of form seems to speak against the very possibility of regarding the object as purposive at all. In this case, however, the representation of the object can be set in relation to a purposiveness that rests instead *in the subject*. Purposiveness speaks this time to the *Geistesgefühl*, which the "First Introduction" explains as being the "supersensible determination of the subject's *Gemütskräfte*."[31]

2. Synopsis: §VIII, On the Logical Representation of the Purposiveness of Nature

Kant seems to formulate the title of §VIII as a parallel to §VII. In both cases, at stake is our representation of nature's purposiveness, which is qualified in §VII as "aesthetic" and §VIII as "logical." Kant provided the ground for this distinction right at the beginning of §VII. Now the distinction between "aesthetic quality" and "logical validity" is discussed in relation to the difference between the subjective and objective character of the representation. However, by following the methodological suggestion implied by the trichotomic architecture of the introduction, we must reject the easy dichotomic parallelism of the two cases and move in another direction. The two sections do not mirror each other because the sequence in which they are constructed cannot be reversed (the two terms are not perfectly symmetric). While §VII has the status of a "condition," §VIII gives the "conditioned" that can be thought only under that condition. In other words, in §VIII Kant is neither presenting another, alternative principle of purposiveness nor arguing for another use of this principle (an objective-logical one rather than a subjective-aesthetic one). Instead, he is introducing *another conditioned* in relation to which the *aesthetic* principle of the faculty of judgment can be employed. At issue now is a special application of the aesthetic principle, which regards objects, has a quasi-cognitive value, and does not involve feeling of pleasure or displeasure. Moreover, while §VII relates back to the general condition of the faculty of reflective judgment presented in §IV, §VIII is constructed on the central epistemological topic addressed in §V that leads to the deduction of the transcendental principle of this faculty.

Kant's argument provides, first, a discussion of the difference between our subjective and objective grounds for the representation of an object's purposiveness (XLVIII/XLIX, 192, 16–31); then it takes up again the notion of "technic" (§I) and argues for its use both in relation to our own technical activity and to nature's productivity (XLIX, 192, 31–193, 6). Finally, it draws the distinction between aes-

31 EE §XII, 250, 1–2.

thetic and teleological faculty of judgment and shows their relation within a "critique" of the faculty of judgment (XLIX/L, 193, 6–LIII, 194, 37).

2.1. §VIII Commentary: Aesthetic and Teleological Faculty of Judgment

Subjective and Objective Grounds for the Representation of Purposiveness (XLVIII/XLIX, 192, 16–31)

With regard to an object given in experience, and hence to the senses, we can have a twofold "ground" for coming up with a representation of purposiveness. (i) We know that purposiveness is predicated upon a certain "agreement" and that this agreement regards, on the one hand, the "form of the object." As Kant has shown in the previous section, when the form of the object apprehended in the imagination produces a harmony among our cognitive faculties independently of (prior to) any concept that we might have of the object, we have a "*merely subjective* ground" (XLVIII, 192, 17) for representing the object's purposiveness. In this case, even though no cognition of the object is reached, the form of the object suits the assignment of our cognitive faculties—namely to "unify the intuition with concepts in a *cognition in general*" (XLVIII, 192, 19–20)—and is seen as purposive with regard to this task.[32] The form of the object is represented as functional with respect to the necessary conditions for "cognition in general." In this case, the representation of purposiveness is grounded upon a pleasure that is "immediate" (XLIX, 192, 24) and hence merely *subjective* as it arises only out of "mere reflection" on the form of the object (XLIX, 192, 25).[33]

(ii) On the other hand, we have an "*objective* ground" for a representation of purposiveness when the form of the given object is represented as in agreement with a concept that grounds the very possibility of the thing itself in its form. In this case, as is obvious, the concept must "precede" our reflection upon the object's form as its condition of possibility (XLIX, 192, 22–23). The form of the object is not set in relation to the subject's faculties in view of "cognition *in general*," which is implied in its apprehension. Rather, it is set in relation to a "*determinate* cognition of the object under a given concept" (XLIX, 192, 28–29). However, since Kant is talking about reflective, not determinant, faculty of judgment, we

---

32. One of the meanings of the German word *Zweckmäßigkeit* is "seiner Bestimmung gut angepaßt, geeignet, nützlich, passend" (Wilhelm and Jakob Grimm, *Deutsches Wörterbuch*, Leipzig, Hirzel Verlag, 1897). *Zweckmäßigkeit* means adequate or conformity to one's own constitution or function, proper, suitable, fit, apt. In this sense the strictly purposive terminology yields a meaning directly bound to utility.

33. It is important to stress Kant's wording: the aesthetic representation of purposiveness rests on the "immediate pleasure we feel from the form of the object in the mere reflection on that form" (XLIX, 192, 24–25). Kant does not just say: the pleasure we feel when we reflect on the form of the object. Kant's wording implies here two acts: the reflection on the form and the feeling of pleasure in it. The pleasure is produced by the form of the object on which we reflect. In this sense, judgments of taste do engage in a relation to the object.

must assume that the concept is not used to determine the object but only to reflect upon it.[34] Thus, the representation of purposiveness is now mediated by a concept and has nothing to do with a "feeling of pleasure *in things*" or, as Kant put it in the Preface, "has *no immediate relation* to the feeling of pleasure and displeasure."[35] In this case, the faculty involved is understanding in its judging things. To be sure, what Kant is denying in this passage is not any kind of relationship with the feeling of pleasure but only the "*immediate* relation" that applied to aesthetic judgments on the one hand and the practical or pathological relation of "pleasure *in things*" on the other.

In sum, two possibilities are at hand: a reflection that *precedes all concept* and relates the object's form to the *subject*'s faculties according to the conditions of *cognition in general*; and a reflection that *follows a concept* and relates the object's form to the concept that grounds the *object*'s own possibility in view of a *determinate cognition* of the object.

Darstellung *and Technic of Nature (XLIX, 192, 31–193, 6)*

While the beginning of the section lays out the situation in which an *object* is given in order to determine the two ways in which one can represent the object's purposiveness, now Kant moves on to determine the specific assignment of the faculty of judgment when that which is given is "the *concept* of an object" (XLIX, 192, 31–32). This is the situation to which the second notion of purposiveness led. The faculty of judgment is now concerned with the new task of the "employment of that concept for cognition" (XLIX, 192, 32–33). To this aim, the concept must be exhibited *in concreto* in a corresponding sensible intuition. The faculty of *Darstellung* is imagination (XLIX, 192, 35; §17, 55, AA 232, 25).[36] Kant presents a twofold possibility for the exhibition of a given concept, which he constructs through an alternative. Exhibition can occur either *through our imagination*, as is the case in art when we "realize" a previously conceived concept (when we make it real and sensible by putting it into existence); or "it may occur *through nature*" in its technic, as is made clear in the case of organized bodies and living organisms as natural

34. See §61, 270, AA 361, 5–6.

35. See KU Preface, IX, 169, 35.

36. In the "First Introduction" (§VII, AA, XX, 220, 14–22) Kant distinguishes three actions in the formation of empirical concepts: the function of imagination is *apprehensio* of the manifold of intuition; the function of understanding is *apperceptio comprehensiva* (i.e., the act of synthesis of the manifold of consciousness in the concept of the object); finally, the task of the faculty of judgment is *exhibitio,* or *Darstellung*, namely the exhibition or presentation in intuition of the object that corresponds to the concept. Kant claims that "when the given concept is an empirical concept, exhibition is the work of the determinant faculty of judgment." Thereby he displays a notion of determinant judgment quite different from the one presented in the published introduction. Accordingly, also the notion of reflective faculty of judgment in its relation to the determinant faculty of judgment is different in the "First Introduction." In the later text, exhibition is not a function of the faculty of judgment but of the imagination.

products. Thus, the alternative exhibition is either by art through imagination or by nature's technic through nature's own causality or productivity.

At this point the question arises: what is the condition for our judging of the two cases respectively of art products and beautiful forms of nature on the one hand and natural living organisms on the other? If compared to the distinction between subjective and objective ground for the attribution of purposiveness to given objects (XLVIII/XLIX, 192, 16–31), the present argument operates a shift in the employment of the notion of purposiveness. Hitherto purposiveness has indicated the suitability of the form of the object (or of nature in its manifold empirical forms or laws) either to our cognitive faculties for cognition in general or to a previously given concept for determinate cognition. Kant is now addressing the idea that there may be certain objects in nature (or art) that are not simply things or objects but "products" (XLIX, 193, 4)—that in themselves exhibit a purposive form with regard to their own constitution (i.e., are themselves represented as purposes of nature) (XLIX, 193, 6). The notion of *Zweckmäßigkeit* of nature yields to the notion of natural *Zweck*.[37] Kant shifts from the indeterminate representation of things as "purposive forms of nature" to the problem of a representation of things as "natural purposes."[38]

The issue that Kant is raising regards the principle, or rule, according to which we ought to judge nature's products in the case of organisms or beings whose internal constitution is that of systems as opposed to aggregates. The notion of "natural purpose" is an "idea." The "particular representation of a whole that precedes the possibility of the parts is a mere idea, and when this idea is seen as the ground of causality, it is called purpose."[39] Kant's general answer points to our need to "attribute to nature . . . *our* concept of a purpose" in order for judgment to be possible at all (XLIX, 193, 3–4). Thereby Kant's claim is not simply that we need to attribute a purpose to nature but that we need to attribute to nature "*our* purpose." We can judge certain objects only by representing them as natural purposes; that is, only by judging as if nature had produced them according to a technic, or art, which is analogous to the way in which we work when we put into existence the object of a previously conceived idea. We can explain the organized systematic constitution of a natural being only on the ground of a concept that makes possible that systematic form as the concrete exhibition in reality of that very concept. The notion of nature's art or technic is construed in analogy to human art and human purposive activity.

In the "First Introduction," Kant gives the notion of a "technic of nature" much more emphasis than in the published one.

> In saying that certain natural forms have an *absolute purposiveness*, I mean that their external figure or inner structure is of such a character

37. See §IV, XXVIII, 31–37 for the distinction *Zweckmäßigkeit/Zweck*.
38. EE §VII, AA, XX, 221, 15–16.
39. EE §IX, AA, XX, 236, 4–7.

> that we must, in our faculty of judgment, base their possibility on an *idea*. . . . Insofar as nature's products are aggregates, nature proceeds *mechanically, as mere nature*; but insofar as its products are systems, i.e., crystal formations, various figures of flowers, or the inner structure of plants and animals—nature proceeds *technically*, i.e., proceeds at the same time as *art*. The distinction between these two ways of judging natural beings is made merely by the *reflective* faculty of judgment.[40]

In §IX of the "First Introduction," Kant presents a complex partition of the notion of technic of nature that we do not find in the published introduction and that will be taken up again in a somehow similar way only in the second part of the *Critique of Judgment*. Kant distinguishes a "*formal*" from a "*real*" technic of nature. The former presents our faculty of judgment with "purposive *figures*"[41] whereby the faculty of judgment is *aesthetic* and the technic of nature is "*figürliche* Technik" or *technica speciosa*.[42] The "real" technic of nature, on the contrary, refers to "the concept of *things* as natural purposes"[43] whereby the faculty of judgment is *teleological* and the technic of nature is "*organische* Technik."[44]

Faculty of Judgment: Aesthetic and Teleological (XLIX, 193, 6-LIII, 194, 37)

It is apparent that Kant's task at this point is to relate the notion of nature's technic to the principle of formal purposiveness of nature that occupied the previous trichotomy (§IV–VI) and to show how from that principle, applied to the new conditioned, the division of the third *Critique* can eventually be derived. To this aim, Kant goes back to the central issue of §V (i.e., the "conditioned" of the previous trichotomy). The new conditioned is nature considered in an analogical way, namely nature as a system of beautiful forms and natural purposes. The notion of formal purposiveness deduced in §V appears now (according to §§VII–VIII: XLVIII/XLIX, 192, 16–31) as the "concept of *subjective* purposiveness of nature" (XLIX, 193, 7–8). It is not the constitutive concept of an object but a regulative notion or a principle for the reflective faculty of judgment. This subjective principle makes it possible for us to form empirical concepts (L, 193, 10). Thereby it allows us to orient ourselves in the infinite labyrinth of natural forms and empirical laws that would be otherwise thoroughly inaccessible. For were it not for the guidance of the reflective faculty of judgment's own principle, understanding would be disoriented and hence unable to find a way out of this labyrinth (L/LI, 193, 29).[45]

---

40. EE §VI, AA, XX, 217, 24–218, 2.
41. EE §IX, AA, XX, 232, 9–12.
42. EE §IX, AA, XX, 233, 36–234, 2.
43. EE §IX, AA, XX, 232, 14–17.
44. EE §IX, AA, XX, 234, 9.
45. For this important notion of "orientation" and *sich orientieren*, see Kant's essay "What Does It Mean: To Orient Oneself in Thought," AA, VIII, 134 ff. For Kant the notion of *sich orientieren* is based upon a "feeling."

Therein lies the necessity of the principle. Even though our concept of purposiveness is in this sense merely subjective, Kant suggests that this concept still implies the gesture of "attributing to nature, *in analogy to a purpose*, a certain concern for our cognitive faculty" (L, 193, 10–12). We reflect upon nature judging as if nature had set for itself as a purpose a special consideration for our cognitive faculties. Kant's formulation is cautious. What we attribute to nature is not really (i.e., not objectively) a purpose but rather the analogy to (our) purpose. On the ground of this analogy, we may regard "*natural beauty* as *exhibition* of the concept of formal (merely subjective) purposiveness, and *natural purposes* as exhibition of the concept of a real (objective) purposiveness" (L, 193, 12–15). Nature is judged either as acting with a special consideration for our cognitive faculties or as acting technically like an artist that translates her own ideas into existence. Therein Kant applies the distinction between subjective or formal and objective or real representation of purposiveness and considers the given object as natural object or natural product. Accordingly, we have two different judgments of reflection that concern two different predicates of objects. We judge natural things as beautiful by means of taste (i.e., aesthetically establishing an immediate relation to the feeling of pleasure), while we judge natural organized beings as purposes by means of understanding and reason (i.e., logically according to concepts) (L, 193, 15–17). Understanding is here at stake as faculty of concepts, while the reference to reason is justified by the necessary assumption of the idea of the systematicity of nature. In §67 Kant will suggest that the concept of natural purpose "leads us necessarily to the *idea* of the whole of nature as a system according to the rule of purposes" and that "*we must subordinate the mechanism of nature to this idea according to principles of reason* (at least to test nature's appearance against this idea)" (§67, 301, AA 379, 1–4).

These considerations justify the partition of the critique of the faculty of judgment into "*aesthetic* and *teleological* faculty of judgment" (L, 193, 19). The aesthetic faculty of judgment is responsible for judgments regarding formal and subjective purposiveness, i.e., beauty of objects, pronounced by means of the feeling of pleasure and displeasure; the teleological faculty of judgment is responsible for the real and objective representation of purposiveness of natural products; that is, for the representation of objects as natural purposes by means of understanding and reason.

At this point, Kant introduces his main argument concerning the different ranking of the two parts of the critique of the faculty of judgment—an argument already anticipated in the preface (VIII, 169, 19). It is now clear in what sense aesthetic and teleological representation of purposiveness are not just two parallel cases to be attributed to two parallel faculties of judgment. Kant intimates that the "most important part" (VIII, 169, 19) of a critique of the faculty of judgment, or the part that belongs to it "essentially" as a critique is the part that concerns the *aesthetic* faculty of judgment (L, 193, 25). For in this case—and in this case only—the faculty of judgment displays an a priori principle of its own, justified by a transcendental deduction and hence endorsed with the same necessity and universality pertaining to all the transcendental a priori principles proper to the other cognitive faculties for which a critique was in order.[46] In other words, Kant finds that the initial hypothesis of an independent faculty of judgment, which has been introduced for the first time in the first trichotomy (§§I–III) and then has been proved plausible in the second trichotomy by means of a deduction (§§IV–VI), is finally and conclusively verified in this section. However, we also find out that only the *aesthetic* faculty of judgment—not the teleological faculty of judgment—can really fulfill the conditions for the initial hypothesis, for the proof of a deduction can apply to it alone. It is only the *aesthetic* faculty of judgment that contains a principle laid entirely a priori to the ground of our reflection upon nature. Accordingly, only in the case of aesthetic judgments will Kant feel the need of providing a transcendental deduction.

In a formulation that echoes the very first introduction of the principle (§III XXVIII, 180, 36–37), we are dealing with "the principle of a formal purposiveness of nature according to its particular (empirical) laws, for our cognitive faculty" (L, 193, 27–28). This is, as it were, the only necessary principle for an experience of nature in its manifold empirical forms. It is a necessary principle, argues Kant, thereby summarizing the whole deduction of §V, because without it understanding "would not be able to find its way about in nature" (LI, 193, 29). We know that were it not for the a priori principle of reflection, nature would be a meaningless chaotic labyrinth and understanding would find no orientation in it. However, Kant has shown that this principle of formal purposiveness has an essential aesthetic character (i.e., has no relation to a concept) and is therefore the subjective principle of the *aesthetic* faculty of judgment (§VII). With regard to nature as object of the senses, the *teleological* faculty of judgment allows us to further explain natural products according to the *concept* of natural purpose. This is a logical employment of the faculty of judgment, which differs, as we have seen, in an essential way from the aesthetic one (XLVIII, 192, 16–L, 193, 23). Hitherto, Kant has been formulating this difference in terms of an opposition: while the aesthetic faculty of judgment is noncognitive and relates to feeling, the teleological faculty of judgment is quasi-cognitive (refers to a given concept) and relates to understanding and reason. Both operate by means of the representation of purposiveness—a subjective and formal one in the former case, an objective and real one in the latter. Now Kant sharpens the opposition so as to exclude, for the teleological faculty of judgment, the possibility of an independent a priori principle. Thus, he shows that the representation of an objective real purposiveness of nature is not an a priori principle of the faculty of judgment and allows for no deduction of an alleged necessity of its own.

§VII has argued for the possibility of an a priori condition for the existence of the representation of an aesthetic purposiveness in the object's form (the condi-

46. See the table of the faculties at the end of the introduction.

tion of experience in general), thereby solving the decisive problem of "whether there is such a representation of purposiveness at all" (§VII, XLIV, 189, 30–31). In the present case, Kant contends that "it is clear that no a priori ground at all can be provided for the claim that there must be objective purposes of nature, i.e., things that are possible only as natural purposes" (LI, 193, 30–31). Kant holds that not even the possibility of the existence of things as natural purposes can be inferred "from the concept of a nature as object of experience in general as well as in particular" (LI, 193, 30–32). Neither the world of nature in general, which is grounded upon understanding's transcendental laws, nor the world of nature in its manifold empirical forms, which is the object of our particular experience on the ground of the principle of formal purposiveness, allows us to infer even the *possibility* of objective purposes of nature (i.e., of natural beings whose existence is possible only as natural purposes). The existence of purposes can neither be deduced from the transcendental laws of the understanding nor perceived directly in a particular experience. "The universal idea of nature as the complex of sense objects gives us no basis whatever for assuming that things of nature serve one another as means to purposes, and that even their possibility cannot be adequately understood except through a causality in terms of purposes" (§61, 267/268, AA 359, 14–17). It is only the faculty of judgment that can make a regulative use of the concept of natural purpose. Yet as opposed to the concept of formal purposiveness for the aesthetic faculty of judgment, which is an a priori "*principle*," the teleological faculty of judgment cannot count on any a priori principle for this use but, at the most, only on a "*rule*." It is under occurrence of certain cases (i.e., of specific natural products), that the teleological faculty of judgment can adopt the concept of a purpose as a rule for judging them.

The employment of this rule—namely the real or objective purposiveness of nature—is predicated upon three conditions. First, the faculty of judgment depends upon the contingent occurrence of specific natural products (organisms); second, its use of the regulative rule is meant to be advantageous for reason, thereby pointing to a collaboration between faculty of judgment and reason. It is this collaboration that discloses the possibility of a relation to the supersensible hinted at in the preface. Since in its "logical" consideration of nature the faculty of judgment can refer the lawfulness of those particular natural things neither to understanding's legislation nor to feeling—being based upon a previously given concept—it must explain this lawfulness with regard "to the unknowable supersensible" provided by reason (preface, VIII, 169, 30). The third condition is a preliminary and preparatory employment of the transcendental principle of formal purposiveness (the transcendental a priori principle of the reflective faculty of judgment in general) under which alone understanding as faculty of concepts can make use of the teleological rule with regard to nature. The transcendental principle of purposiveness prepares the understanding to the application of the concept of a natural purpose—at least, Kant suggests, "with regard to the form" (LI, 194, 1). What we judge as a natural purpose is not the "existence" of the object (for which we would need to know the final purpose—*Endzweck*—of nature), but only its "intrinsic form" (§67, 299, AA 378, 12–13). Thus, the aesthetic faculty of judgment offers a sort of aesthetic preparation on whose ground empirical cognition becomes possible. It guarantees the possibility of our orientation in the world of experience. This is why the critique of the aesthetic faculty of judgment is the most important part of a critique of the faculty of judgment. In other words, the teleological faculty of judgment functions in analogy to the aesthetic faculty of judgment ("we can make nature comprehensible *in analogy* with a subjective ground of the connection of representations in us" (§61, 268, AA 360, 3–4), and depends upon its a priori aesthetic principle, which it employs objectively. Thus, Kant establishes a systematic priority of the aesthetic faculty of judgment over the teleological on the basis of the transcendentally grounding function of the principle of aesthetic formal purposiveness.

At this point, however, Kant goes back to the discussion of the intrinsic *indeterminacy* proper to the "transcendental principle" (LI, 194, 3) of formal purposiveness of nature that was mentioned for the first time at the end of §VI (XLI, 188, 11–12). Thereby he brings to the fore the crucial epistemological problem that requires the use of reflective judgment in general. Kant recapitulates a threefold occurrence of the principle of purposiveness: (i) as general principle of systematicity for our experience of nature in the manifold of its empirical laws, (ii) as principle for the aesthetic faculty of judgment which expresses the accordance of a natural object's form with our cognitive faculties, and finally (iii) as rule for the teleological faculty of judgment that judges something (e.g., an organized body) "according to the idea of a purpose of nature" (LII, 194, 14–15).

(i) The "First Introduction" distinguished two ways in which nature operates, namely, *mechanically* under the universal legislation of the understanding and *technically* as art. In our passage at the end of §VIII, Kant poses the crucial epistemological problem that concerns our judging of that alternative. How do we know when and with regard to which objects we have to judge according to the principle of purposiveness? How do we know "where and in which cases" (LI, 194, 6) we would have to judge nature as if we were judging nature's technical activity and not simply its strictly mechanical laws?[47] In this alternative consists the indeterminacy left open by the transcendental principle of nature's formal purposiveness. Thereby Kant points to the real problem proper to the faculty of judgment as *facultas dijudicandi.*[48] Judgment has to decide which cases *in concreto* are cases for a certain rule (*casus datae legis*), and there is no rule for how to make this decision.

---

47. This becomes a central question in the second part of the *Critique of Judgment*. See in particular Kant's distinction between internal and external purposiveness in §67, 301 f., AA379, 10 ff., and §68, 306 f., AA 382, 16 ff.

48. See chapter 7, both for the discussion of this problem in the first *Critique* and for a first explanation of the indeterminacy of the transcendental principle of the faculty of judgment.

(ii) It is precisely this indeterminacy that the transcendental principle "leaves to" the *aesthetic* faculty of judgment's own decision (LI, 194, 9). Only *taste* can solve the problem of judgment as *facultas dijudicandi* in a conclusive way. Taste immediately "decides" (LI, 194, 12) whether a given individual case does or does not fulfill the condition of the accordance between the object's form and our cognitive faculties. Taste needs only feeling in order to meet the decision, not a rule or a concept. Thereby the indeterminacy of the principle of the faculty of judgment is settled through a form of determination that happens through taste and feeling and does not appeal to any concept or rule.

(iii) The faculty of judgment "employed teleologically" (LI/LII, 194, 12–13)[49] is presented, once again, in opposition to the aesthetic faculty of judgment ("on the contrary," LI, 194, 12). Teleological judgment is working on the same indeterminacy left open by the transcendental principle of nature's purposiveness. Yet it suggests a different solution to the indeterminacy question. This time, determination comes from a determinate particular *concept*. "The faculty of judgment, employed teleologically, provides *determinately* the conditions under which something (e.g., an organized body) is to be judged according to the *idea* of a purpose of nature" (LI/LII, 194, 13–15). If an object as natural product (i.e., as organism or system as opposed to mechanism or aggregate) satisfies the definition of *Zweck*, then it can be judged as if it were a purpose of nature. However, no a priori principle allows for the inference from the concept of nature as object of experience to an alleged purpose of nature. Consequently, we have no a priori ground for ascribing to nature a reference to purposes (i.e., to determine a natural object as a real purpose of nature). Since no "actual experience" and no perception (LII, 194, 18) reveals to us—or ever will be able to reveal to us—the existence of something like a purpose of nature, we are not even allowed to assume in a merely indeterminate way the existence of such products. The reason for this impossibility is the nonempirical character of the concept—or better the "*idea*"—of "natural purpose" that describes a given object as an organism or a system. The "idea of a purpose of nature" is not constitutive of our experience. It is rather a regulative and still subjective device that allows us merely to reflect on our experience of nature. In addition, in order to know empirically that something *is* an objective or real purpose of nature, we would have to gather an infinite number of particular experiences and conceive of their unity under a principle (LII, 194, 19–22). This procedure describes what the first *Critique* defines as a system (system is "the unity of manifold cognitions under an idea")[50] and the "First Introduction" assumes as guideline for the general problem of the third *Critique*. Yet, since ideas can neither derive from experience nor be adequately exhibited in reality, the former task can only be fulfilled in an analogical and indirect way. In addition, in the manifold particular ex-

49. Note Kant's formulation: the teleological faculty of judgment is the faculty of judgment in general employed teleologically—"*die teleologisch-gebrauchte Urteilskraft.*"

50. KrV B 860/A 832.

periences needed to formulate a judgment on a single individual object, the individuality of the empirical case is necessarily lost. The concept of a natural purpose cannot be exhibited in a singular intuition; hence it provides only an *indirect* exhibition of the concept of formal purposiveness (L, 193, 12–15). This requisite must be contrasted to the immediate and unique apprehension of the individual object that takes place, instead, in the case of aesthetic judgments.

From these considerations, Kant concludes that only the aesthetic faculty of judgment is "a *special* [*besonderes*] faculty of judging things" since it has an a priori principle of its own. The teleological faculty of judgment, on the contrary, "is not a special faculty but is only the *faculty of judgment in general*" (LII, 194, 22–25). Looking back to the initial hypothetical assumption of a special faculty that could work as *Mittelglied* between understanding and reason, we have to conclude that only the *aesthetic* faculty of judgment satisfies the requisite of being indeed a "special faculty" with an a priori principle of its own. For aesthetic judgments are formulated "according to a rule, but not according to concepts" (LII, 194, 23). Instead, teleological judgments are based upon concepts and hence are instances of theoretical cognition in general. However, the teleological faculty of judgment is not a form of determinant judgment (i.e., does not use concepts to determine objects for cognition). It depends upon the empirical and contingent occurrence of a particular kind of objects in nature—these are the empirically given cases for which, as *reflective* faculty of judgment, it has to find the universal under which to operate the subsumption. Even though the teleological faculty of judgment is not a special faculty, nonetheless it has "special principles" according to which it reflects upon certain objects of nature because it is still *reflective* judgment (LII, 194, 27, 30). The teleological faculty of judgment is *Urteilskraft überhaupt* insofar as it works according to the aesthetic principle of purposiveness and, in addition, is subjected to a further restriction. Such restriction is due both to the kind of particular objects that are given to it (organisms), and to the "special principles" that it follows, which are analogically grounded on the aesthetic principle of purposiveness.

From this argument follows Kant's presentation of the internal structure of the *Critique of Judgment*. Since the teleological faculty of judgment works with concepts and concerns existing objects, it refers to understanding and reason and hence belongs to *theoretical* philosophy. Yet since these concepts are not constitutive of objects, the teleological faculty of judgment cannot belong to the *doctrinal* part of philosophy but only to the new *critique* of the reflective faculty of judgment (to which no doctrinal part follows).[51] The teleological faculty of judgment "considered in its application belongs to the theoretical part of philosophy" (LII, 194, 29–30) and is therefore denied the privilege of occupying the third part of philosophy between theoretical and practical that Kant still envisaged for it in the letter to Reinhold, December 28 and 31, 1787. In addition, Kant strongly de-

51. Kant dedicates to this topic a discussion in the *Methodology of Teleological Judgment*.

nies that teleology will ever ground a science of its own (not just a part of transcendental philosophy but also empirical natural science): "teleology . . . does not constitute a special part of the theoretical science of nature" (§68, 309, AA 383, 28–29). Yet "because of its special principles, which are not determinant, as principles must be in a doctrine, it must also constitute a special part of the *critique*" (LII, 194, 30–32). The case for the aesthetic faculty of judgment is different. Such faculty neither yields cognition of objects nor requires direct reference to concepts. Kant claims that this faculty, as true *Mittelglied*, "must be ascribed *only* to the critique of the judging subject and his cognitive faculties, insofar as these are capable of possessing a priori principles, no matter what their employment (theoretical or practical) may be" (LII/LIII, 194, 32–37). Finally, the crucial importance that Kant attributes to this critique with regard to philosophy in general is expressed in its presentation as "the propaedeutic to all philosophy" (LIII, 194, 37).

3. Synopsis: §IX, On the Connection Between the Legislations of Understanding and Reason Through the Faculty of Judgment

The idea of trichotomic partition exposed at the very end of the last section of the introduction, suggests that this section needs to be read as the *Vereinigung* (LVII, 197, 26), or "unification," that arises out of the two preceding "concepts." This is true in a twofold sense. §IX displays, first, the union of §§VII–VIII, while on a higher level, it is also the conclusive unification of the two preceding trichotomies. The analysis of this section reveals that rather than a true *Vereinigung*, what Kant's argument accomplishes here is only a *Verknüpfung* as the title puts it. The task of §IX is to show that the link between the legislation of understanding and the legislation of reason can be established only "*through*" the faculty of judgment. Thereby the issue of the analogical unity between the sensible and the supersensible is introduced. Analogy is, for us, the only possible way of making sense of the relation (or peculiar nonrelation) between the sensible and the supersensible, nature and freedom. Retrospectively, we can now say that only the faculty of judgment allows us at all to pose the question of the relation between the sensible and the supersensible.

While §III saw in the reflective faculty of judgment the *Verbindungsmittel* of the two parts of philosophy "*into* a whole" and §VI provided the *Verbindung* of feeling "*with* the concept of the purposiveness of nature," §IX effects a "*Verknüpfung*"—namely, establishes a connection "between" two legislations—"*through*" the faculty of judgment. In Kant's terminology, *Verbindung* (*conjunctio*) is a stronger bond that brings two terms together conjoining one with the other. *Verknüpfung* (*nexus*),[52] on the other hand, brings a link to the fore yet still maintains

52. See KrV B 129 ff./A 130 ff.; B 200/A 162 fn. defines *Verknüpfung* as a type of *Verbindung*: "All *Verbindung (conjunctio)* is either composition (*compositio*) or *Verknüpfung (nexus)*." The passage opposes *Verknüpfung*—where the relation of the parts that constitute the unity is necessary, to mere composition—where the relation of the parts is merely contingent.

the two terms as separated by an "in-between." Thus, the title of the section already warns us on the kind of "unification" that we should expect to take place at this point. Precisely for this reason, the crucial emphasis of the title should be not so much on the *Verknüpfung* but on the means *through which* (*durch*) that connection is established (i.e., "*through* the faculty of judgment"). It is only when the link is provided by the faculty of judgment that the connection can be grounded on an a priori principle. On the other hand, however, since ultimately all *Verknüpfung* is *synthesis*, the faculty of judgment reveals itself as the synthetic faculty par excellence. This final section entails Kant's strong claim that qualifies the aesthetic faculty of judgment and its a priori *constitutive* principle of formal purposiveness as the ground for the possibility of our experience in general.

The last section of the introduction provides three new expositions of the argument of the first trichotomy from the standpoint of the *aesthetic* faculty of judgment regarded as the mediating faculty between the sensible and the supersensible in the subject. By means of the notion of formal purposiveness, the faculty of judgment mediates between understanding's and reason's legislation (LIII, 195, 4–LV, 196, 11); in the context of our cognitive faculties, then, it determines the supersensible as determinable (LV/LVI, 196, 11–22); and finally within the context of the higher faculties of the soul, as aesthetic faculty of judgment, it displays a constitutive a priori principle for the feeling of pleasure and displeasure (LVI, 196, 23–LVII, 197, 17). At this point, the faculty of judgment is no longer a mere assumption. It is now a faculty whose a priori transcendental principle has been proved and whose principle, at the end of the section is further determined as a *constitutive* principle for reflection in general.

3.1. §IX Commentary: A Constitutive Aesthetic Principle for Experience in General

The Abyss Restated (LIII/LIV, 195, 4–16)

The opening of §IX confirms the diagnosis of §II regarding the dichotomic partition of philosophy based upon a twofold parallel legislation taking place on a twofold domain. Understanding legislates a priori over nature as world of appearances in order to produce theoretical cognition in a possible experience. Thereby it institutes its "domain" over nature viewed as mechanism and as the complex of all objects of the senses. Reason legislates a priori for freedom and its free causality; it produces a practical cognition that does not depend upon any previously given condition in the sensible world. Thereby it discloses the realm of the unconditioned that is now presented as "the supersensible in the subject" (LIII, 195, 7); that is, not just as a sphere that transcends human activity as such but as the peculiar supersensible character proper to the subject itself. The parallel constitution of the two domains implies that they are "completely cut off" (LIII, 195, 12–

13)[53] from each other so that all reciprocal influence is utterly excluded. Thus, the "great abyss" (LIII, 195, 11) that separates the domain of the concepts of nature from the domain of the concept of freedom (i.e., the sensible from the supersensible), which Kant first addressed in §II (XIX, 175, 36), is now confirmed. No reciprocal determination between the two realms is possible. Neither can the concept of freedom determine objects for our theoretical cognition of things, nor can the concept of nature determine anything with regard to the practical laws of freedom (understanding provides no determination for the will to action). "*To this extent*" (LIV, 195, 15), concludes Kant (i.e., if we aim only at discovering a reciprocal influence or determination between the two legislations), "it is not possible to throw a bridge from one domain to the other" (LIII/LIV, 195, 15–16). Consequently, in this perspective, no transition between the two domains is possible for us (restating §II, XIX, 176, 3). With the limitation of this *insofern* Kant suggests there may be yet another direction that we have to explore if we want to find a different kind of link (not properly a bridge) between the two legislations. On the contrary, *to the extent* that we limit our search to the aforementioned perspective, it is as if nothing had happened between the first trichotomy and the point at which we presently stand with regard to the gap that now lays open, as it were, as dramatically as before between the sensible and the supersensible. Concerning the problem of bringing the two sides of the abyss closer together, we stand now where we stood in §II. This suggests that Kant's main preoccupation in the sections that we have been analyzing has not been the issue of bridging the gap between understanding and reason. Kant defends the dualism of understanding and reason in the third *Critique* no less than in the first or in the second *Critique*. For the two legislations ought to be separated and protected from all reciprocal influence if they are to have the force of legislations on their respective domains. In point of fact, the problem of a *Verknüpfung* between the legislation of the understanding and that of reason arises precisely because no homology can be discovered between the two terms. Thereby Kant formulates the issue of synthesis again on a new level. It follows that the real task of the *Critique of Judgment* with regard to the relation between the sensible and the supersensible must be described differently than as a search for a "bridge" between the two legislations.

The Asymmetry between Nature and Freedom and the Principle of Purposiveness (LIV, 195, 17–LV, 196, 11)

The new direction of the search for a solution of the problem is hinted at by the asymmetry that Kant discovers in the relation between the sensible and the "supersensible in the subject." Thereby Kant introduces a new perspective that breaks the *impasse* of the perfect parallelism between the two worlds. He con-

53. Compare this "*gänzlich* abgesondert" to the following "*gänzliche[n]* Unterscheidung" between nature's causality and the causality through freedom at the beginning of Kant's footnote (LV, 195, 31–32).

tends that while we would find no evidence in nature of the "*determining grounds*" (LIV, 195, 17) of freedom's causality, we might instead be able to detect the *effects,* or "*consequences*" (LIV, 195, 21), of freedom in the sensible world. Kant argues that while the sensible nature of the subject can by no means influence the supersensible in it, the reverse relation stands indeed as a possibility worthy of further exploration. What kind of reverse relationship does Kant thereby suggest? He observes that by raising the question we would not gain anything with regard to our *cognition* of nature. Yet by asking about the practical "consequences" that the supersensible has on the sensible world or that the concept of freedom has on nature, a crucial *practical* issue is addressed. To be sure, the relation implied by this question is not just a possibility. Rather, it is presented as a necessary implication already entailed in the very concept of a "causality through freedom" (LIV, 195, 22–23). Freedom is granted an influence not on the *legislation* of nature as such but rather on the *objects* of this legislation, one of which is the (human) subject as moral agent. The "efficacy" of freedom's causality ought to take place and be manifested in the sensible world according to its formal laws. In other words, in the sensible world there are effects that follow from the purely formal legislation of practical reason. The Transcendental Dialectic of the first *Critique* has shown that there is neither conflict nor contradiction in thinking of a coexistence between the two legislations (already in §II, XVIII, 175, 11–13). Kant now adds that there might be cases in which one and the same sensible effect should be theoretically known exclusively in terms of the transcendental laws of nature as mechanism yet must *also and at the same time* be accounted for with regard to the sensible consequences of the supersensible legislation of reason and, hence, in the moral-practical perspective, must be explained as a sensible effect of the formal law of freedom. Given Kant's definition of the faculty of judgment in §III, it must be clear that the previous formulation already implies a use of this faculty. The formulation of this problem offers a concrete explanation of what is at stake in the issue of the connecting link between the two legislations. The faculty of judgment is the only faculty that allows us to comprehend the way in which freedom is present in the world of appearances. It is the faculty of judgment that produces a kind of synthesis at the level of the subjective conditions for the possibility of representing the way in which the principles of the moral world are manifested in the sensible realm of appearances. This is the function of judgment's principle of formal purposiveness. However, in order to introduce the necessary term of the faculty of judgment, Kant has to first show that neither understanding nor reason can be of any help in solving the problem.

In this passage, Kant's notion of causality is ambiguously played between two connections, namely the connection cause-effect (*Ursache-Wirkung*) on the one hand and the connection ground-consequence (*Grund-Folge*) on the other. Kant clarifies that in the case of the supersensible to be cause (*Ursache*) means only to be the "ground [*Grund*] that determines the causality of natural things to an effect [*Wirkung*] in conformity to their own natural laws yet, *at the same time, also* in accordance with the formal principle of the laws of reason" (LIV, 195, 24–28). Natural things are mechanistically determined according to their own natural laws yet "at the same time," they are "also" determined so as to be in accordance with the order of freedom. The ground of this accordance is the supersensible. Thereby Kant is introducing an idea of *accordance, harmony,* or *congruence* between two orders of legislation—an idea with which we are, at this point, familiar enough. This is the new idea that replaces the notion of "*influence*" (LIII, 195, 10; LV, 195, 35) as a means to think of the relation between nature and freedom. For the idea of a reciprocal influence between the two legislations only denies the possibility of bridging their separation. It should be clear at this point that Kant could formulate this argument only at the very end of his presentation, after the principle of formal purposiveness had been first hypothetically introduced, then transcendentally deduced, and finally completely justified in its different applications (§§VII–VIII). However, Kant is still extremely cautious in presenting his thought. He goes so far as to deny that we can have an insight even into the very possibility of this accordance. Yet in a footnote he provides an argument sufficient to reject the claim of its impossibility. Thus, all we can count on, *as long as we argue in terms of understanding and reason,* is that the notion of an accordance between the sensible and the supersensible cannot be proved as possible and also cannot be proved as impossible.

In the footnote, Kant responds to an objection still formulated in the vocabulary of "influence" between nature and freedom. To claim that nature sets obstacles to freedom's causality or that nature furthers freedom's efforts means, according to the objection, to assume a possible influence of nature over freedom that Kant instead denies. In other words, the contradiction is placed between Kant's attempt to maintain nature and freedom completely separated and his claim that freedom's causality, and only freedom's, has an import on nature's own causality. Kant clarifies that the vocabulary of "hindrances" to freedom or "furthering" of freedom does not establish any relation between nature and freedom as such. It only describes a relationship among appearances (i.e., the relation between natural appearances and the appearance of freedom's effects in the sensible world). In Kant's answer to the objection, the important relation to the human subject comes to the fore. The only reason why the problem of an *impossible influence*—and yet the *possibility of an accordance* between the two legislations—is ever raised is that it concerns the subject as "human being" (LV, 196, 34), as a being that acts according to its sensible nature and *also*, *and at the same time*, according to the supersensible nature in him/herself. The human being is the 'middle-ground' on which nature's and freedom's paths intersect. The human being as natural being or appearance is a "natural cause" that works in a strictly mechanistic way; the "determination" of his/her free causality, however, even though it takes place in the world of appearance, "is grounded in the intelligible that is thought of under freedom in a manner not otherwise explicable." This claim, valid initially for the human being, is extended then to nature as a whole.

Nature as well can be said to have a "supersensible substrate" (LV, 196, 33–37; then LVI, 196, 17–18). Thereby Kant raises the issue of the foundation of our human experience in the supersensible and the ways that we have of becoming aware of this foundation. For if we cannot explain, or *know*, this relation through understanding and reason, we may still perhaps *feel* it and *judge* it according to some analogy to what we can indeed know.

How then can we come to think of this *accordance* between the two legislations? Kant reformulates the claim of the asymmetric relation between freedom and nature in terms of the family of notions that has been occupying the central sections of the introduction—the vocabulary of purposiveness. The "effect" that follows from the law of freedom is the "final purpose," or *Endzweck*. Freedom's effect *ought to* come to existence and be actualized in the sensible world. This final purpose is a moral demand ("existieren *soll,*" LV, 196, 1; also §II, XIX, 176, 4). Its "condition of possibility is presupposed in nature" (i.e., in the human being as "subject") (LV, 196, 2–3).[54] We must assume that nature proceeds as if it were producing its forms technically, precisely because we are ourselves beings who belong to nature and who are able to act in a purposive way. If causality through freedom takes place in the world of nature, then nature must be so constituted as to make it possible for this causality to take place within it. Now causality through freedom is the causality of the human being as moral agent. Free causality can only take place in the sensible world (i.e., can only have sensible effects). Its agent as sensible being belongs to nature. It follows that nature must be conceived as to allow free causality to take place in it.

At this point, we can no longer delay the question of which faculty allows us to come to that condition of possibility by providing it a priori. It is only through that condition that it becomes possible for the first time to think of a relation that could not be otherwise articulated either in terms of understanding's concepts or in terms of reason's concepts. Kant's answer leads to the third cognitive faculty, the faculty of judgment that, with no need of appealing to the practical, "presupposes this condition a priori." "With the concept of a *purposiveness* of nature, the faculty of judgment provides us with the concept that mediates between the concepts of nature and the concept of freedom" (LV, 196, 4–7). It is only *by means* of the concept of purposiveness[55] that we can recognize the possibility of the final purpose. Thereby we effect a "transition" from the "lawfulness" of nature to that of freedom. We know that purposiveness is also a form of lawfulness (i.e., is the lawfulness of the contingent as such). In the General Remark to the Exposition of the Aesthetic Faculty of Judgment, Kant maintains that "aesthetic purposiveness is the lawfulness of the faculty of judgment in its freedom" (General Remark, 119, AA 270, 33–34).

---

54. See KpV A 74 (AA V, 43).

55. Recall our stress on *durch* in the title of §IX; see above, p. 249.

To be sure, at this point we have not constructed a bridge over the abyss that divides nature from freedom. Instead, we have undertaken the transcendental move of making explicit the conditions under which alone we can think of the way in which the two lawful orders of understanding and reason work—and precisely the way in which they work as separate orders that fulfill nonetheless the demand of being enacted (differently constructed and experienced) by the same human subject on the same territory of experience. Thus, there is no contradiction between the initial claim of the section according to which no bridge can be thrown over the abyss and the present contention that the faculty of judgment allows us to accomplish the "transition" between the two orders of nature and freedom. As mentioned above, the introduction of the faculty of judgment is the result of a new way of asking the question of the relation between the two parts of philosophy, a new question (and a new *Denkungsart*) that only the previous development of the introduction made possible.

Thus, it is in terms of "purposiveness" (or accordance), not in terms of reciprocal "influence," that we have to structure the relationship between nature and freedom. The concept of purposiveness enables us to recognize the "possibility of the final purpose," a possibility that was previously denied both to understanding and to practical reason (which could only postulate the actualization of freedom). Now we judge that the final purpose "can only become actual in nature and in accordance with its laws" (LV, 196, 9–11). Kant does not ask how the actualization of the final purpose is possible; rather, he asks *how we can know* the possibility of the final purpose as actualized in accordance with nature's laws. He asks *how* we are able to recognize that possibility—*by means (durch) of which faculty and by means of which concept*. Once again, the faculty of judgment is Kant's answer to an *epistemological* question. The question was left open in §II, where the faculty of judgment could be assumed, at the most, only hypothetically (XIX, 176, 4–9). In the light of these considerations, we can also begin to understand the sense of the mediating function that Kant attributes to the faculty of judgment and to its a priori principle as *Mittelglied* and *Verbindungsmittel* between the two parts of philosophy. Kant's ethico-theology developed in the Methodology of Teleological Judgment follows precisely from these considerations.

The Supersensible: Undetermined, Determinable, Determined (LV/LVI, 196, 12–22)

Having gained entrance into the relation between the two orders of legislation, Kant can now address for the first time in a direct way the question of the supersensible, or the "supersensible substrate (in us as well as outside us)" (LVI, 196, 17–18)—that is, the supersensible substrate in the human subject and in nature. With regard to the supersensible, the faculty of judgment mediates the transition from one order to the other or, as §II aptly puts it, from a *Denkungsart* according to principles of nature to a *Denkungsart* according to the principle of freedom (XX, 176, 14–15). Kant presents us with the three ways that our cognitive faculty has of approaching the supersensible: through understanding, faculty of judgment, and reason.

(i) The possibility of understanding's a priori legislation on nature is the "proof" that our knowledge is limited to nature as appearance. This same limitation, however, hints at something beyond appearances, namely at nature's "supersensible substrate" (LV/LVI, 196, 12–14). Supersensible things (i.e., things as noumena) mark the limit of cognition, thereby bringing it back to the conditions of sensibility.[56] Understanding cannot but leave the supersensible "entirely *indeterminate*" (LVI, 196, 15); for it is, we should add, entirely *indeterminable* through it: in the perspective of the understanding and by means of its concepts and principles, nothing can be said or determined of the supersensible substrate of nature.

(ii) It is the faculty of judgment that makes the supersensible determinable for the first time through our intellectual faculty. By means of the a priori principle of nature's formal purposiveness, the faculty of judgment makes possible our experience of nature not as a mechanism but as a system of *possible* particular empirical laws and forms. This idea makes possible the "*determinability*" of the supersensible substrate, both in us and outside of us (LVI, 196, 17–19). The faculty of judgment does not provide any strict determination of the substrate (it is the *aesthetic and reflective,* not the determinant, faculty of judgment that displays an a priori principle of its own). It opens up an access for reflecting upon the supersensible and for determining it analogically. *Determinability* is a disposition that the supersensible gains through our *aesthetic* faculty of judgment; it is judgment's own way of bridging the gap between the sensible and the supersensible; it is the open-ended task that involves our entire "intellectual faculty" by invoking the collaboration of understanding, imagination, reason, and intuition as the open range of different possibilities at play. Determinability is the analogical way that we have to think of the supersensible in us and outside of us *as if it were sensible for us*.

(iii) Only reason is able to practically determine the supersensible substrate. Thus, reason determines "through its a priori practical law" (LVI, 196, 19–20) the determinability opened by the reflective faculty of judgment. The only possible determination of the supersensible is practical determination through the moral law. Yet this practical determination works precisely on the determinability disclosed by the faculty of judgment through the noncognitive and nonpractical work of our intellectual faculties. In this way, the "transition from the domain of the concept of nature to the domain of the concept of freedom" eventually takes place (LVI, 196, 20–22). While any way of making sense of the supersensible other than merely *thinking* of it in its complete indeterminateness was forbidden to the understanding, the faculty of judgment is able to concretely make sense of it through

56. See the inference drawn in KrV B XXVI f. with regard to the relation appearance-thing in itself.

analogy, *imagination*, and *feeling*. There are things in nature and in us of which we can—and must—be able to talk meaningfully even though we cannot know them. We must be able to talk and communicate meaningfully about them even before raising the question of whether we can know them at all and even independently of this question and its answer. Through the faculty of judgment, the realm of the supersensible becomes accessible to us as a realm that does not lay beyond the sensible in an alleged transcendence but as the realm to which we are led in and by our experience of the sensible world. Within the space opened by a mere determinability, we can understand the special freedom ("spontaneity," LVII, 197, 10) that our cognitive faculties enjoy while at play in the act of reflection (herein there is no condition for determination that needs to be respected and no moral duty to respond to). Placed within this space, the supersensible is that which in its determinability receives a nonconceptual determination by means of reflection.

A Constitutive Principle for the Aesthetic Faculty of Judgment (LVI, 196, 23–LVII, 197, 17)

Following the line of Kant's argument in §III, the consideration of the three cognitive faculties' respective relation to the supersensible is supplemented by the consideration of the corresponding higher "faculties of the soul in general" (LVI, 196, 23; §III, XXII, 177, 13 ff.). This time, however, the faculty of judgment, which occupies the middle ground, represents not just a hypothetical and analogical assumption. It is rather the very condition that allows us to raise the question of a "systematic unity" of the faculties and to construct its synoptic table (LVII, 197, 16). The aesthetic faculty of judgment becomes the only faculty in terms of which a critical discourse on the system of the faculties can be framed at all.

Kant turns to the *Seelenvermögen* considered transcendentally to the extent in which they display a priori principles within themselves (i.e., an "autonomy" of legislation as higher faculties, LVI, 196, 24). (i) With regard to the *cognitive faculty*, understanding contains the a priori principles of our theoretical knowledge of nature. These principles are "*constitutive*" of our knowledge of objects, for it is under these principles (as conditions) alone that nature can become an object for cognition (LVI, 196, 25–26). (ii) The faculty of judgment provides the a priori principle for the *feeling of pleasure and displeasure*. In this case, the faculty of judgment relates *immediately* to the feeling of pleasure and displeasure whereby it is said to be independent of "concepts and sensations that may refer to the determination of the faculty of desire and hence be immediately practical" (LVI, 196, 26–197, 1). The feeling of pleasure grounded in the a priori principle of judgment is neither a pathological-practical nor a moral-practical feeling as it derives neither from empirical sensations nor from intellectual concepts. (iii) Reason provides the a priori principle for the *faculty of desire* by *immediately* determining this faculty through the moral law without appealing to the mediation of any pleasure whatsoever. Thereby reason determines the "final purpose" for the faculty of desire. This determination is followed, in turn, by a "pure intellectual liking" (LVI, 197, 4–5) for the object that is the ground of all moral interest. Reason's a priori principle is constitutive in the practical domain for the faculty of desire as understanding's laws are constitutive in the theoretical domain for the cognitive faculty.

What is the *status* of the a priori principle of the faculty of judgment for the feeling of pleasure with regard to the constitutive vs. regulative issue? Order here reveals that the reflective faculty of judgment functioning as *Mittelglied,* or agent, for the *Verknüpfung* between sensible and supersensible is specifically the *aesthetic* faculty of judgment. To solve the problem of the status of judgment's own principle, Kant asks, where does the concept of a purposiveness of nature belong? He recognizes that it still belongs to the concepts of nature, although not as a constitutive principle (in which case the faculty of judgment would be determinant and lack a principle of its own) but only as a "*regulative* principle of the cognitive faculty" (LVII, 197, 7–8). We must know by now that the notion of nature's formal purposiveness is a maxim, or subjective rule, for our reflection upon the whole of nature in its empirical manifold. Yet, in the case of the *aesthetic* faculty of judgment, Kant discovers the *constitutive status of the principle with regard to the feeling of pleasure and displeasure.* Thereby it becomes clear why Kant insists in relating the cognitive faculties to the respective powers of the soul by means of each faculty's a priori principle. For if the a priori principle of the faculty of judgment is not constitutive with regard to a realm of objects, it is indeed constitutive with regard to the corresponding power of the soul, namely the feeling of pleasure and displeasure. Our aesthetic judgment on certain specific and contingent products of nature or art, which prompts the concept of formal purposiveness (as harmony between the object's form and our faculties), is a constitutive principle for the feeling of pleasure because this feeling is grounded a priori on that principle (such feeling does not arise from our perception of the object but from our reflection on the apprehension of the object's form).

It is precisely this *constitutive* status of the principle with regard to the *aesthetic* faculty of judgment that explains why, in the previous section, Kant could claim that only the aesthetic and not the teleological faculty of judgment is a "special faculty" (§VIII, LII, 194, 22–23). The ground for the feeling of pleasure is the harmony or attunement (LVII, 197, 11) of the cognitive faculties in the free play in which they spontaneously engage once they are set free of the strict conditions under which they work under understanding's cognitive legislation as well as under reason's practical order. In this respect, the 'free play' of the cognitive faculties from which aesthetic pleasure arises is the *pendant* to the asset that the same faculties display in the cognitive situation. On the other hand, with regard to reason and the practical sphere, Kant contends that the freedom and "spontaneity" proper to the cognitive faculties at play in aesthetic reflection make the concept of purposiveness "suitable as mediation of the connection of the domain of nature with the domain of freedom in its consequences, and also promotes, at the same time, the receptivity of the *Gemüt* to moral feeling" (LVII, 197, 10–15). The aesthetic faculty of judgment is at work in the realm of the sensible, yet through its constitutive principle of purposiveness, this faculty discovers within the sensible the traces of the supersensible—it discovers *within nature* the consequences of freedom's final end. Aesthetic feeling is independent of moral feeling yet, belonging to the same family of pure feelings, is considered by Kant as preparing and facilitating our receptivity to moral feeling.[57] Aesthetic reflection allows us to experience a type of freedom different from moral freedom. However, since moral freedom cannot be—properly speaking—experienced by us, the "spontaneity" in the "free play of our cognitive faculties" opens up the only *experience* of freedom that we may have. Through the free play of the faculties that produces aesthetic pleasure, we experience, by way of analogy, moral freedom in the sensible world and gain a premonition of our intelligible determination. This is the aesthetic faculty of judgment's mediating function in the world of the third *Critique*.

57. See the Methodology of the Aesthetic Faculty of Judgment, §60.

Part III

The World of Experience: Beauty and Life

Chapter 9

The Analytic of the Aesthetic Faculty of Judgment (§§1–29): The Beautiful and the Sublime

This chapter opens the last section of the book. Herein I analyze the unfolding of the *Critique of Judgment* along its different divisions. As a general methodological device, I adhere to the line of Kant's argument. My aim is to present a synthesis of Kant's arguments by focusing on the main questions addressed. The present chapter provides an outline of the two books of the first division of the *Critique of Judgment*: the Analytic of the Beautiful and the Analytic of the Sublime. These two parts constitute the Analytic of the Aesthetic Faculty of Judgment. My opening remarks discuss the "partition of the whole work" that Kant places immediately after §IX of the introduction. These remarks link the observations concerning the division of the third *Critique* that we find in the final sections of the introduction to the actual development of the work. A reconstruction follows of the main argument developed in the four moments of the Analytic of the Beautiful (§§1–22) and the Analytic of the Sublime (§§23–27).[1]

1. The "Partition" of the Critique of Judgment

Kant concludes the "First Introduction" with a section dedicated to the "Partition of the Critique of Judgment" that we do not find in the published introduction. As we have seen, the latter ends with a footnote in which Kant explains the trichotomic nature of all partitions of pure philosophy. A table follows displaying the "systematic unity" (LVII, 197, 16) of the higher faculties (LVIII, 198) and the index of the whole work (LIX, 199). Therein the division of the third *Critique* appears always as dichotomic and is drawn according to the same general lines along which the previous two *Critiques* were structured. However, from the peculiar character of the faculty of judgment (as opposed to understanding and reason), it follows that within the common structure of a critical and transcendental inquiry, the third *Critique* will present a development of its own.

§XII of the "First Introduction" concludes the discussion of the systematic function of the third *Critique* that has guided Kant throughout this unpublished essay. The "partition" of the work follows immediately from its *systematic* structure.

1. A good collection of essays on the first division of the *Critique of Judgment* is *Kants Ästhetik/Kant's Aesthetics/L'esthétique de Kant*, ed. by H. Parret, Berlin, New York, de Gruyter, 1998. A comprehensive study of this part of the third *Critique* is P. Guyer, *Kant and the Claims of Taste*, Cambridge, Cambridge University Press, 1997; see also H.W. Cassirer, *A Commentary on Kant's Critique of Judgment*, London, Methuen, 1836.

Since the whole is a system and not an aggregate, its partition must be guided by an idea presupposed as the "principle" on which the division is "scientifically" drawn.[2] The general task of the partition is to articulate the domain or territory proper to the a priori faculty to which cognition refers. The faculty of judgment, however, only yields the whole of a "critique," not the system of a "doctrine." In the unpublished text, Kant summarizes in the following way the demonstrative thread of the introduction, which provides at the same time the ground for the partition. The faculty of judgment displays an a priori principle of its own only as *reflective*, not as determinant faculty of judgment; the reflective faculty of judgment proceeds according to the "principle of a technic of nature" (i.e., according to the notion of purposiveness).[3] This principle is *only subjective*, yet it also carries with itself "the concept of a possible objective purposiveness, i.e., the lawfulness of natural things as natural purposes."[4] To claim that the principle of purposiveness is a subjective principle for the faculty of judgment is to say that it does not and cannot imply a concept, for in this case, judgment would be determinant. It rather implies a "feeling of pleasure and displeasure," whereby the faculty of judgment is "aesthetic." Kant intimates that the "feeling of pleasure is one with the representation of subjective purposiveness,"[5] and this is also "the only way to judge aesthetically."[6] This argument, which summarizes what the published introduction presents in §VIII, grounds the general partition of the *Critique of Judgment* into "aesthetic"[7] and "logic," or "teleology," of the reflective faculty of judgment. In both parts, nature is regarded as "technical," or purposive, in its products. The aesthetic develops the principle of *subjective* purposiveness with regard to the subject's cognitive faculties. The form of purposiveness makes an object's "beauty"; beauty is judged by "taste." In addition, Kant suggests that all purposiveness can be regarded either as "internal" or as "relative" to its use. In the case of subjective purposiveness, we judge an object *beautiful* when its form is perceived as intrinsically purposive for reflective judgment (i.e., for all those cognitive faculties that are engaged in the act of judging). When, instead, the object has nothing purposive in its form for our reflection, but its representation is applied to a purposiveness resting a priori in the subject, the object is judged as *sublime*. Hence, the aesthetic of the faculty of judgment—or *Geschmackslehre* (doctrine of taste)—is divided into a theory of the beautiful and a theory of the sublime. The teleology of the faculty of judgment as the second division of the *Critique of Judgment* regards *objective* purposiveness in relation to the possibility of the object itself; purposiveness is

2. EE §XII, AA XX, 247, 24–35.
3. EE §XII, AA XX, 248, 20.
4. EE §XII, AA XX, 248, 24–26.
5. EE §XII, AA XX, 249, 2–3.
6. EE §XII, AA XX, 248, 30–31.
7. In the *Critique of Judgment*, Kant will no longer use the term *aesthetic* to designate any part of the work. He is extremely careful to avoid this designation throughout the Critique of the Aesthetic Faculty of Judgment.

here addressed as objective purpose, and the teleology of the faculty of judgment is accordingly a *physische Zweckslehre* (physical doctrine of purposes).[8] Its internal division is drawn, once again, with regard to the "internal" vs. "relative" character of objective purposiveness. In the first case, natural objects are judged according to their "internal possibility" ("perfection"), while in the second case they are judged according to "the relative possibility" of their external consequences ("utility").[9]

Being the two parts of a critique of the faculty of judgment, aesthetic and teleology follow the division according to which Kant structures all his critical works. A "doctrine of the elements" (a title that does not appear in the third *Critique*) is followed by a "doctrine of method" (a title that applies only improperly to a critique of taste—see §60, 262, AA 354, 34–355, 3). In addition, both the critique of the aesthetic and the critique of the teleological faculty of judgment are structured according to an analytic and a dialectic—the analytic of the aesthetic faculty of judgment being divided, for the reasons we have seen, into Analytic of the Beautiful and Analytic of the Sublime. However, by claiming that each analytic must be further articulated into an exposition and a deduction of the concepts in order, the "First Introduction" proposes a division that Kant will abandon in the actual development of the *Critique of Judgment.*[10] In the Critique of the Aesthetic Faculty of Judgment, it is only the notion of the beautiful that allows for the division into exposition and deduction. There is no deduction for the sublime for which, as Kant will claim, the exposition coincides with the deduction.[11] In addition, as the introduction already made clear, in the case of the Critique of the Teleological Faculty of Judgment, no deduction is properly required since teleological judgment does not follow an a priori principle of its own, independent of aesthetic judgment.

Moreover, if we compare Kant's different treatment of these divisions in the two parts of the book, we can observe that in the case of the aesthetic faculty of judgment the analytic takes up the central role; the dialectic only articulates what is already presented in the analytic; and the methodology has the merely negative function of showing that there can be no method for a critique of taste. In the case of the teleological faculty of judgment, on the contrary, the dialectic takes up a central role, and for the methodology, which aims at locating teleology within the whole system of philosophy, is recognized a crucial function (and yet still the function of an appendix).

---

8. EE §XII, AA XX, 249, 9–22.

9. EE §XII, AA XX, 250, 19–30.

10. EE §XII, AA XX, 251, 21–36. As shown in chapter 4, this discrepancy between the "First Introduction" and the published introduction has been used by different interpreters in order to provide a chronology of the composition of the third *Critique*.

11. See KU §§24, 30.

2. The Analytic of the Beautiful: The Task of a Transcendental Critique of Taste

It is important to make clear from the outset the perspective endorsed by Kant's argument in the Analytic of the Beautiful and the general questions addressed in this first book of the Analytic of the Aesthetic Faculty of Judgment. This perspective sets the tone for the development of the entire *Critique of Judgment.* At the end of the preface, against the aims generally attributed to contemporary aesthetic theories, Kant declares that the present "inquiry into the faculty of taste as aesthetic faculty of judgment is not meant to form and cultivate taste but has a *transcendental* aim" (preface, IX, 170, 5–8). To say that the traditional critique of *taste* is transformed into a critique of the *aesthetic faculty of judgment* means to claim the *transcendental* nature of the inquiry. Such an inquiry will concern not beautiful objects as such but our subjective way of judging something as beautiful; it will not address the question of what makes an object beautiful but rather the question of what we say *about ourselves* by judging something as beautiful. Kant addresses the issue of the "transcendental exposition of aesthetic judgment" in the General Remark to the First Division of the Analytic by opposing it to the "physiological" and merely empirical exposition attempted, among others, by Burke (General Remark to the First Division of the Analytic, 128, AA 277, 2 ff.).[12] This transcendental perspective is responsible, in the first place, for the peculiar structure of Kant's inquiry into our judgments on the beautiful.

Kant maintains that there is no objective criterion or rule for taste since no general criterion can define by determinate concepts what ought to be called beautiful (§17, 53, AA 231, 27–29). Hence it is only in a subjective way that a "critique of taste" is philosophically possible. Kant contends that there is only an empirical criterion for taste—a very weak one indeed—which has, however, a *transcendental origin.* The task of Kant's critique of taste is to bring to light this transcendental origin that lies "deeply hidden" in a "ground common to all human beings" (§17, 53, AA 232, 4–5). Thus, it is clear from the outset that to renounce the objectivity of taste does not mean, for Kant, to give up the claim to a universal validity of our aesthetic judgments. Their universal validity is, in fact, only subjective. In this case, *subjective* means that the critique will regard only the mode in which the representation by which an object is given to us relates to the subject's cognitive faculties. Taste is the expression of judgment, which implies, as §VIII of the introduction made clear, the participation of imagination and understanding. Hence, more precisely, such a critique is "the art or science of finding rules for the reciprocal relation of the understanding and the imagination in the given representation. . . . It is *art* if it shows this only through examples; it is *science* if it derives the possibility of such judging from the nature of these faculties as cognitive faculties in general."

12. Burke's physiological exposition goes only as far as producing an "empirical anthropology" (General Remark, 129, AA 277, 24).

Kant states that "it is with the latter alone as *transcendental critique* that we are here concerned throughout. Its aim is to develop and justify the subjective principle of taste as an a priori principle of the faculty of judgment" (§34, 144, AA 286, 11–23). Kant's transcendental critique is indeed a science and yet is not the scientific aesthetic parallel to logic that Baumgarten envisaged because it can claim no objective validity for its propositions.

In an important way, a critique of the aesthetic faculty of judgment is not concerned, for Kant, with the problem of "how we do judge" in matters of taste. This would make of the critique of taste a merely empirical or psychological inquiry (Burke is here the example). A transcendental critique, on the contrary, despite the lack of objective rules for taste, must address the problem of "how we ought to judge" (General Remark on the Exposition, 130, AA 278, 25–27). This perspective is made possible only by an a priori principle that can be discovered by going back to the subjective transcendental condition of all our factual judgments. This subjective condition is the faculty of judgment itself (§35, 145, AA 287, 6–7). The notion of an objective criterion of taste yields to the notion of an a priori principle of the faculty of judgment. Thus, in the Analytic of the Beautiful, Kant does not analyze concrete aesthetic judgments but only the a priori subjective conditions on which rests judging as such or judgment as an independent faculty of the mind. In a similar way, in the *Critique of Pure Reason* Kant did not analyze specific scientific cognitions but the transcendental conditions thereof. The perspective of the Analytic will change in the Deduction of Pure Aesthetic Judgment, namely in the sections dedicated to art, genius, and aesthetic ideas where Kant's analysis shifts from the issue of aesthetic appreciation to the issue of artistic production.

In the framework of Kant's transcendental critique, to ask for the origin of a judgment or to ask for the subjective condition of all our factual judgments concerning the beautiful is to ask for the *Bestimmungsgrund* of the judgment (i.e., for the ground or principle that *determines* the very formulation of aesthetic judgments). The question of the *Bestimmungsgrund* of a judgment of taste as aesthetic judgment is the main question that Kant raises throughout the Analytic of the Beautiful. It is only after the principle of a pure aesthetic judgment has been identified that it becomes possible to decide which of our factual judgments of taste are *pure* aesthetic judgments or to decide in which cases the subsumption of a particular instance under the notion of beautiful has been correctly effected. In this sense, the Analytic still retains its function of being a "logic of truth." As has already been noted, the issue of the *Bestimmungsgrund*, which appears for the first time in the discussion of §VII of the introduction,[13] becomes relevant only in the cases of aesthetic and moral judgments. For, in these cases, the external form of judgment does not allow one to infer the principle upon which judging rests. In the case of aesthetic judgment, however, the problem is even more crucial since

13. See the commentary to §VII in Chapter 8.

its principle turns out to be the very principle of the reflective faculty of judgment in general.

How does Kant structure this search for the "determining principle," or "determining ground," of our aesthetic judgments? The Analytic of the Beautiful articulates the four "moments" of the judgment of taste according to the four general titles under which the first *Critique* groups the categories of the understanding. It is common among Kant's interpreters to manifest discontent toward the forceful move that led Kant first to divide his inquiry into an analytic and a dialectic and then to structure the analytic according to the four titles of the understanding's categories: quality, quantity, relation, and modality. This move is generally seen as dictated by Kant's strict architectonic systematic but is hardly seen as helpful or as adequate to the material to be presented. The involvement of the understanding in the formulation of aesthetic judgments is cited as the more plausible justification for Kant's appeal to the table of the categories. Kant himself refers to the "relation to the understanding" in judgments of taste (§1 fn., 4, AA 203, 23–24) in order to explain the heuristic procedure of finding out the moments of the judgment of taste under the guidance of the categories as "logical functions of judging."

Yet nowhere to be found in the literature is the more important suggestion that Kant has been led precisely by the analysis of the faculty of judgment as such (i.e., in the form in which it manifests itself as a really independent cognitive faculty) to take up the table of the categories. It ought not to be forgotten that in the *Critique of Pure Reason* the table of the categories was metaphysically deduced from the table of judgments. The latter table presented the "moments" in which the "logical function" of the understanding in judging is articulated.[14] As concepts of the understanding, the categories are nothing but "predicates of possible judgments."[15] Hence, we can argue that the Analytic of the Beautiful must be structured according to the four moments of the judgment of taste because what is here at stake is the most original and independent function of judging. Thus, far from being forcefully dictated by an external need of uniformity with the other *Critiques*, the development of the four moments of the judgment of taste responds to an intrinsic need of the inquiry itself. Moreover, Kant observes that in the case of aesthetic judgments of the beautiful, quality is that to which judgment refers in the first place so that the succession of the moments must follow the precedence of quality over quantity (accordingly, quality is followed by quantity, relation, and modality).

With regard to the present issue, we can raise the more general question concerning the function of the categories in relation to the three cognitive faculties respectively. As far as understanding is concerned, the categories are logical predicates of possible judgments that, combined with sensible intuitions, allow for knowledge of objects as appearances. While categories cannot yield knowl-

---

14. KrV B 95/A 70: see also KU §1 fn., 4, AA 203, 22.
15. KrV B 94/A 69.

edge independently of sensible conditions, they still retain a purely logical value in relation to nonsensible objects. It is this (formal) logical validity that allows practical reason to take up the table of the categories in the Analytic of the *Critique of Practical Reason,* thereby constructing the table of the "categories of freedom."[16] In this case, the categories of freedom follow from the list of the categories of the understanding only because freedom manifests its effects in the world of appearances. In this table, Kant suggests, freedom "relates to the categories of its own natural possibility."[17] In the Analytic of the Beautiful, the logical functions of judgments are taken up under the condition that objects are not to be determined with regard to knowledge. The functions of judgment are rather analyzed in a purely subjective way (i.e., only with regard to the subjective ground for judging). Accordingly, the "logical functions to judge" regard judgment's relation to the subject and not to the object (§1 fn., 4, AA 203, 22). The succession of the four moments of the judgment of taste provides different entrances into the general problem of the *Bestimmungsgrund* of aesthetic judgment. The *Bestimmungsgrund* itself is not deduced from these functions but presented only in its fundamental characteristics.

The central problem of the determining principle of aesthetic judgment is discussed by Kant as the topic of an analytic; that is, it is addressed *analytically* from the standpoint of the faculty of judgment itself. In both the first and the third *Critiques*, the analytic entails a *Zergliederung* of the cognitive faculty (understanding and faculty of judgment respectively) with regard to its a priori components.[18] The key to understanding Kant's procedure is to be found at the very end of the last section of the Analytic of the Beautiful. "For the present," Kant argues, "our task is only to analyze the faculty of taste in its elements and to unite them ultimately in the idea of a common sense [*Gemeinsinn*]" (§22, 68, AA 240, 14–15). Facing a series of crucial questions arising out of the status of judgment's a priori principle (constitutive or regulative?) and concerning the very nature of taste as cognitive faculty (is taste a natural and original ability, or is it rather an ability to be acquired, developed, and exercised?), Kant limits the task of the analytic to a twofold aim. On the one hand, the faculty of taste must be analyzed in its constitutive elements, while on the other, these elements must be brought to unity in the idea of a *Gemeinsinn.* This is the approach followed by the argument of the Analytic of the Beautiful. The four moments of the judgment of taste are both the elements in which the aesthetic faculty of judgment is analytically divided and the elements that we will eventually find unified in the common sense as "idea" (last moment according to relation). It is only after this exposition has been provided that the issue of the possibility of pure a priori judgments of taste can be raised as

---

16. KpV A 116 ff.

17. KpV A 118.

18. KrV B 89/A 64; KU §8, 21, AA 213, 33; General Remark to the First Division of the Analytic, 68, AA 240, 21.

the principal problem of a "deduction" of the principle of taste (§§30–38). In turn, it is only after the deduction has transcendentally legitimated taste's claims to universality and necessity that the question of the status of the aesthetic faculty of judgment can be addressed (§§39–40).

What does Kant's analytic procedure imply with regard to the constitutive elements of the judgment of taste? The general method proper to Kant's transcendental inquiry sets out to *isolate* the specific faculty of the mind in order to find its pure components and its pure employment. In the *Critique of Pure Reason,* sensibility had first to be "isolated" from all contribution of understanding as well as from all reference to sensation. The result is the Transcendental Aesthetic that deals with space and time as pure a priori forms of our sensible intuition (i.e., with those components of our knowledge that are neither intellectual nor materially empirical).[19] Kant describes the task of the Transcendental Logic in analogous methodological terms. Herein we have to isolate the understanding and focus on that part of our thinking activity that has its origin exclusively in the understanding.[20] In the analysis of the four moments of the judgment of taste, Kant follows the same procedure. Since "beauty is nothing in itself" and is rather defined exclusively "in relation to the subject's feeling" (§9, 30, AA 218, 22–23), the task is to *isolate* (*Absonderung*, §8, 26, AA 216, 23) that which belongs solely to the subject's aesthetic feeling of pleasure, so that any mingling either with the understanding's concepts or with the faculty of desire is excluded. The pleasure in the beautiful is therefore isolated both from the merely empirical pleasure that arises from the "agreeable" and from the practical pleasure that arises in connection with the good. In order to become conscious of what belongs to the beautiful in its specificity, one must "separate whatever belongs to the agreeable and the good from the liking that remains to him after that" (§8, 26, AA 216, 22–25).

The difficulties faced by the procedure of isolation in the case of pure aesthetic judgments speak to the difficulties in grappling with the main issue of a critique of taste conceived as a critique of the faculty of judgment that Kant encounters along the different stages of the composition of the third *Critique*. The guiding thread in Kant's presentation of the four moments of the Analytic of the Beautiful is precisely the isolation of that which belongs to a pure aesthetic judgment (i.e., that which constitutes the formal "determining principle" for the attribution of the predicate beautiful, as opposed to agreeable or good). It is only by way of this analytical procedure of isolation of moments that the specific difference that distinguishes aesthetic judgments both from cognitive and practical judgments will be identified. In the fourth moment of the Analytic of the Beautiful, the question of the determining ground becomes explicitly the question of the "principle" of our judgments of taste, which is the idea of "common sense" (§20, 64, AA 238, 6). In this idea, the different specific elements of the faculty of taste are eventually unified.

---

19. KrV B 36/A 22.
20. KrV B 87/A 62.

The question of the *Bestimmungsgrund* is, to be sure, the preliminary question that must be addressed in order to formulate the crucial problem that the *Critique of Judgment* raises in parallel with the previous *Critiques*. The issue of the *Bestimmungsgrund* discussed in the exposition of the Analytic of the Beautiful prepares for the problem raised in the Deduction of Pure Aesthetic Judgments—namely whether and how are *pure aesthetic judgments a priori* possible? (§8, 30, AA 218, 24–25; §36, 148, 288, 21–22).[21] In the *Critique of Pure Reason*, the question of the possibility of synthetic judgments a priori involved the issue of the universality and necessity of our cognition. In the first book of the Analytic of the Aesthetic Faculty of Judgment, the issue of universality (second moment) and necessity (fourth moment) is taken up in order to show the "peculiarity" that these moments exhibit in the case of the aesthetic faculty of judgment. By demonstrating that the ground of our aesthetic judgments cannot be empirical (like sensation, charm, or emotion, §14) but must be a formal ground, and by showing in addition that only the feeling of the subject and not a concept of the object constitutes the determining ground (§17, 53, AA 231, 29–30), Kant lays out the conditions to answer the question of the possibility of pure aesthetic judgments a priori.

3. *The Four Moments of the Judgment of Taste (§§1–22)*

In assuming the table of the categories as a guiding thread for the analysis of the constitutive moments of our judgments of taste, Kant stresses the "peculiarity" and even "strangeness" that we discover once we ask for the significance of these moments in our attribution of the predicate beautiful to objects.[22] We have already noticed the precedence of quality over quantity that Kant announces from the very beginning of the Analytic of the Beautiful. We have also underlined the two crucial and related questions that structure this development: its exposition will provide an answer to the question of (i) what is the *Bestimmungsgrund* of our judgments of taste? thereby preparing for the question of the Deduction: (ii) are pure aesthetic judgments a priori possible and, if so, how? The four moments of the judgment of taste are interrelated and interconnected on the ground of those two questions, so that the successive moments often refer back to the previous ones and provide a different perspective on the same theoretical issue.

The four moments provide four different "explanations" of the notion of the beautiful: beautiful is (i) what we like in a disinterested way (first moment: quality, §§1–5); (ii) what has universality as "universal validity" without any concept being involved (second moment: quantity, §§6–9); (iii) what we like according to a purposiveness without purpose (third moment: relation, §§10–17); and (iv) what we recognize as the object of a necessary liking according to a subjective, exem-

21. See §36, 148, 288, 21–22: "How are judgments of taste possible?"—a question that is paralleled by a reference to the problem of the first *Critique:* "How are synthetic cognitive judgments a priori possible?" (§36, 147, AA 288, 7–8).

22. See in particular the second moment (universality) and the fourth (necessity).

plary necessity (fourth moment: modality, §§18–22). Kant's task in the exposition of the Analytic of the Beautiful is to present the *Mittelglied*-function of the aesthetic faculty of judgment, namely, its independent position between cognitive faculty and faculty of desire. Paradoxically, pure aesthetic judgment is a form of cognition that is not really cognition (does not refer to concepts of objects), is based upon a form of purposiveness that has no practical character (is purposiveness without a purpose), and implies a feeling of pleasure that has no reference either to the lower or higher faculty of desire. This is the reason for Kant's repeated efforts to differentiate pure judgments of taste from both cognitive judgments (both sensible and intellectual) and practical judgments (both pathological and pure).

The First Moment (Quality): The Judgment of Taste Is Disinterested, §§1–5

In the first moment of the judgment of taste in which beauty is defined according to quality, Kant shows what it means for the judgment of taste to be properly "aesthetic" (§1). In the case of taste and the beautiful, our judgment is guided by a "liking or disliking" that is totally *disinterested* (16, AA 211, 3). The reference to a purely subjective feeling that is not grounded upon an interest in the object's existence is the "quality" proper to aesthetic judgments. Kant's argument takes up the crucial move of §VII of the introduction, whose task was to define the specifically aesthetic, subjective nature of certain representations with reference to the subject's feeling of pleasure and displeasure. The peculiar nature of such feeling defines the aesthetic quality of the judgment of taste distinguishing it from the features proper both to cognitive (§1) and to practical judgments (§§2, 3). Kant's opening question is the following: how do we distinguish something beautiful from something that is not beautiful, i.e., how do we decide (judge) whether something can be called beautiful or not, and what do we mean by such judgment? This question provides a clear paradigmatic case for the use of the *reflective* faculty of judgment since thereby the issue is raised of what kind of predicate is expressed by the notion of beautiful. Kant claims that when we assess something as beautiful, the representation of the object is not referred to the object itself by means of understanding and its concepts so as to provide cognition. Instead, the representation is related to the subject's feeling of pleasure and displeasure by means of the imagination. As argued above, herein Kant's problem regards the *Bestimmungsgrund* of our judgment (§1, 4, AA 203, 14–15). The judgment of taste is aesthetic (as opposed to logical or cognitive) since its grounding principle is that which "cannot be other than subjective" (§1, 4, AA 203, 15). This irreducible subjectivity is the feeling of pleasure or displeasure with which the subject "feels itself." It is the subject's "feeling of life" (§1, 4, AA 204, 3; 204, 8). Yet this subjective feeling has also no reference to the faculty of desire.

What do we want to know by posing the initial question of whether something is beautiful? We want to know whether in reflecting upon a given object its representation is accompanied by a certain "liking." At this point, Kant needs to mark out the specificity of aesthetic judgment in relation to practical judgment since both involve feeling. Kant argues that in the case of the judgment of taste what matters is only what I do with the representation of the object "within myself" (§2, 6, AA 205, 10–11), whereby the intentional and purposive production of the object (its existence), which takes place when the feeling is related to the faculty of desire, is excluded. Hence, if the judgment of taste, being grounded upon a particular subjective feeling, does not imply any cognitive reference to the object (§1), it is also radically devoid of any reference to the practical faculty of desire. For the "liking" that "*determines* the judgment of taste" (§2, title), as opposed to the liking that refers to the faculty of desire, is not prompted by any "interest" in the existence of the object (although it can indeed produce an interest, §2, 7, AA 205, 32–33). The subjectivity of the feeling involved in a judgment of taste is not, in turn, grounded upon the existence of the object that causes that liking. A "pure judgment of taste" is neither "partial" (*parteilich*) nor "interested" (§2, 6, AA 205, 14–15) since the existence of the object plays no role in determining it (is not the judgment's "determining ground"). Hence, a pure judgment of taste is merely "contemplative" (§5, 14, AA 209, 23), and the liking that determines it is a "disinterested and free liking" (§5, 15–16, AA 210, 20–21); it does not depend upon a concept and does not show a further need to be fulfilled (§5, 15–16, AA 210, 20–21).

However, in order to demonstrate the aesthetic feeling of pleasure's independence of all practical reference, Kant needs to go a step further. Since the faculty of desire can be involved in our judging either in its pathological or in its purely practical determination, Kant further distinguishes three types of "liking" according to their reference to the notion of the "agreeable" (§3), the "good" (§4), or the "beautiful" (§5). As opposed to the disinterested character of the beautiful, both the agreeable and the good imply an interest in their respective objects—be it pathological or purely practical.

The Second Moment (Quantity): The Judgment of Taste Has Universal Validity, §§6–9

The second moment of the judgment of taste provides the explanation of the beautiful according to quantity. This moment follows immediately from the first, namely from the lack of any interest that characterizes aesthetic evaluations (as opposed to cognitive or practical ones). In §2, Kant already suggested that disinterestedness implies, in this case, that the judgment of taste has no *private validity* (i.e., is not *parteilich*). Yet while the *Bestimmungsgrund* of a purely aesthetic judgment is merely subjective, the subjectivity involved is not the private, empirical subjectivity of my sensations; it is rather a peculiarly universal subjectivity. Kant discusses the *universality* of the judgment of taste announcing its very remarkable, even strange, characteristics (*Merkwürdigkeit*, §8, 21, AA 213, 29–30; *befremdlich,* §8, 22, AA 214, 15). To be sure, the kind of universality that Kant sets out to present is "remarkable" only in the perspective of a transcendental analysis of the faculty of judgment, not so much in the perspective of logic.

Along with necessity, universality is for the transcendental philosopher a sign of the a priori character of judgment's own principle. In logic, a judgment that is "universally valid *objectively*" is also at the same time universally valid *subjectively* (§8, 23, AA 215, 3–6). In this case, the objective universality of a cognitive judgment can be considered identical with its subjective universal validity. This is how Kant considers the two notions in the first *Critique* and in the *Prolegomena*.[23] In cognitive judgments, the identity of objective universality and subjective universal validity is grounded upon the reference to the object's concept: a judgment is universally valid *objectively* when it is valid for all the instances that fall under the concept (the concept's extension). Consequently, an objectively universal judgment must also be valid *subjectively* for everyone who represents to herself an object by means of that concept. In the face of the objective validity of cognitive judgment, the issue of its subjective validity is not a separate issue, and taken separately it is certainly an immaterial point (the possibility for a cognitive judgment to be endorsed by all subjects is immaterial to its aims and logical structure). In the case of aesthetic judgments, however, due to the lack of any constitutive reference to a concept (in which case the faculty of judgment would be determinant and the judgment itself cognitive), the inference from subjective universality to logical universality is impossible. Hence the task of a transcendental critique of taste is to show how a merely subjective universality independent of any concept can still be the grounding feature of a priori aesthetic judgments—a feature radically different from empirical generality. The universality of aesthetic judgment is a subjective *aesthetic* universality (§8, 25, AA 215, 32–33); it is the "universal validity" that refers to a feeling of pleasure and displeasure. The universal validity of a judgment of taste constitutes the *public* dimension of its reach or its intrinsic "pluralistic" (as opposed to "egoistic") nature (General Remark to the First Division of the Analytic, 130, AA 278, 18–20). Universality applies, in this case, not to the domain of *objects* that fall under a concept (aesthetic judgments, as far as logical quantity is concerned, are always "singular judgments")[24] but to the sphere of the judging subjects that are expected to endorse my judgment of taste (§8, 24, AA 214, 11–13). No concept is thereby involved but only an immediate (§8, 24, AA 215, 15–16), shared reference to a feeling of pleasure and displeasure.

The ongoing issue that Kant is addressing concerns the "ground for the liking" (§6, 17, AA 211, 14–15, 19) from which the judgment of taste is pronounced. Since aesthetic judgment is free of all interest and inclination (first moment), and is grounded neither upon merely "private conditions" (§6, 17, AA 211, 19) nor upon

---

23. See *Prolegomena*, §19, AA IV, 298: Kant holds that "objective validity and necessary universality (for everybody) are equivalent terms."

24. "This rose is beautiful" is an aesthetic judgment that is singular with regard to its "logical quantity" (§8, 24, AA 215, 15) (it concerns an individual object) and is "universally valid" with regard to its "aesthetic quantity" (§8, 25, AA 215, 28–29). Instead, "roses in general are beautiful" is a "logical judgment based on an aesthetic one" (§8, 24, AA 215, 23–24).

a "private feeling" (§7, 18, AA 212, 17), the judging subject assumes that the liking she feels "*must* entail a ground" that holds for everyone. The moment of universality is common both to aesthetic and to logical judgments. This shared feature makes the judgment of taste appear similar to a logical and cognitive judgment. Accordingly, in our aesthetic judgments we speak indeed "*as if* beauty were a property of the object" (§6, 18, AA 211, 123–24; §7, 19–20, AA 212, 20–22; §9, 30, AA 218, 20) and our liking depended merely upon objective sensation (§8, 25, AA 216, 3–4). We have to be aware, on the contrary, that the predicate beautiful, indicating only the relation of the object's representation to the subject, says nothing about the object's constitution and only voices the subject's mental state and feeling. This feeling, however, is not the "objective sensation" through which I relate to objects in order to produce empirical cognition (§3, 9, AA 206, 31–32). Thus, because of this deceiving appearance produced in the form of the judgment itself, Kant's efforts are directed to show the peculiarity of taste's subjective universality (as opposed to logical universality) by inquiring into the *source* of judgment's own universality. The question is: where does the universality of aesthetic judgment come from? Kant's crucial point is that since judgment of taste refers to the subject's feeling and no transition from concepts to feeling is possible (the only case is the practical law, which, however, always presupposes an interest), its universality cannot be justified by concepts. Universal validity is not referred to the object through a concept but only to the subject through feeling.

The subjective universality proper to the judgment of taste is expressed by the "claim" or even the "demand" that the judging subject puts forward as the ground for her own judging in matters of taste. While with regard to the "agreeable," which is based on a "private feeling" or sensation, the notion holds true that everyone has her own taste; with regard to the beautiful a claim is made to public universal assent (§7). In pronouncing a judgment of taste, we do not simply count on other people to agree with us; we rather "demand" their agreement so that we deny their having taste in case they disagree with us (and yet we also demand as a universal condition that they *should* have taste, §7, 20, AA 213, 2–3). We need to recall that Kant is developing a transcendental inquiry that departs from any attempt to explain taste in psychological, physiological, sociological, or merely cultural terms. Accordingly, what Kant is thereby addressing is not the "generality" of empirical rules that may be valid for all members of a certain epoch, class, culture, or community (this could hold true for the agreeable, which is merely "empirical taste," but not for the beautiful, which is "taste of reflection," §8, 22, AA 214, 10–11). On the contrary, Kant is presenting a form of "universality" that must *constitute the ground* of our judgments of taste as condition for their very possibility. Hence, this condition must be presupposed by any empirical (or historical or cultural) inquiry into taste. Such universality is similar to the universal validity of the good, although no reference to a concept is made (§7, 21, AA 213, 20–24).

What is then the subjective, aesthetic universality of the judgment of taste? Kant suggests that it is the universality of the "universal voice" (§8, 25, AA 216, 5) with which the judging subject pronounces her judgments in matters of taste. In our aesthetic evaluations, we do not judge as isolated private individuals but as members of a public sphere, as members of the sphere of a judging humanity in whose voice we speak. Thereby, Kant introduces the crucial notion of "exemplarity" of the judgment of taste that we will encounter in the fourth moment in discussing the peculiar necessity proper to aesthetic judgments. With regard to the transcendental question that occupies the Analytic of the Beautiful, Kant claims that the "universal voice" is the condition for the "possibility of an aesthetic judgment" in its universal validity (§8, 25–26, AA 216, 11–12). What is the status of such a universal voice? Kant contends that the universal voice is only an "idea" (§8, 26, AA 216, 20). To be sure, what we assume—or, better, "postulate" (§8, 26, AA 216, 10)—with this idea is not a factual universal accord but only its possibility. Kant will take up this issue again in the fourth moment in presenting the very peculiar necessity of aesthetic judgment.

Once the universality of the judgment of taste has been assessed as *allgemeine Stimme*, Kant's argument proceeds to link this intersubjective voice to the "universal communicability" that must find its place under the conditions of aesthetic judgment (§9, 27, AA 217, 1). The universal voice communicates universally; it is everyone's voice that must reach everyone else. But what is it that this universal voice communicates, and what allows us to assume that this universal voice can really communicate in a universal way? What confers universal communicability to the logically singular content that we express in our aesthetic judgments? Kant has established that by attributing beauty to a particular object we take the responsibility of a universal voice upon ourselves; he has also argued that the universality of this voice is not based upon a concept but is rather related to a feeling of pleasure and displeasure. At this point, the following question must be raised: what exactly is the relation between our feeling of pleasure and displeasure and the universal communicability that grounds the judgment formulated by the universal voice? Kant formulates this problem as the question of whether in a judgment of taste the feeling of pleasure precedes our judging of the object or our judgment precedes the pleasure (§9, title). Kant considers this issue so crucial to his inquiry as to be the very "key to the critique of taste" (§9, 27, AA 216, 33–34). To be sure, this is yet another way of formulating the problem of the "determining ground" of the judgment of taste. With this question, Kant is asking whether our judgment is based upon a feeling of pleasure and displeasure, or whether instead it is the universal communicability that constitutes the ground for our aesthetic pleasure. With regard to this central problem, it is important to further ask, what is the content of the universal communicability, and in what do we feel pleasure by pronouncing our aesthetic judgments?

Kant immediately denies that the feeling of pleasure "in the given object" can come first, as if the task of the judgment of taste "were to attribute only the pleasure's universal communicability to the representation of the object" (§9, 27, AA 216, 35–217, 2). By saying that something is beautiful we do not mean to say that we feel pleasure in that object and to say, in addition, that this pleasure can be communicated in a universal way. For if a feeling of pleasure were to *precede* the judgment, then that pleasure would only be one of agreeable private sensations and the judgment could by no means claim universal validity. In this case, the judgment would be made dependent upon the existence of the object—a move that would contradict the essential feature that distinguishes a pure aesthetic judgment from a merely empirical pathological judgment (first moment). Hence, if the pleasure cannot precede the judgment without leading us into contradiction, then the question posed by the title of §9 is already decided by the very opening passage of the section: it is the "universal communicability of the mental state [*Gemützustand*]" produced by the representation of the object that must precede (both logically and temporally) and ground the judgment of taste as its "subjective condition" so that a feeling of pleasure "in the object" must follow (§9, 27, AA 217, 8–11). However, at this point Kant's task becomes rather complicated.[25] Moreover, the consequences of his statement of the problem are far-reaching. It is clear from the outset that if the feeling of pleasure must follow from the universal communicability of the subject's mental state, then our judgment of taste—as pure a priori aesthetic judgment—can be *neither a judgment about our feeling nor a judgment about our pleasure in the object* (which would obviously have to precede in order to be communicated). *What* is it then that we communicate in a universal voice if not a feeling of pleasure in the object that we call beautiful?

Kant's formulation of the problem of §9 reproduces the similar crucial problem that he was raising with regard to the faculty of desire in the *Critique of Practical Reason* and is articulated in analogy to it. In Theorem I (§2) of the second *Critique*, Kant addresses the issue of the *Bestimmungsgrund* of the will in its following practical principles. He contends that all practical principles, which must presuppose an object of the faculty of desire in order to determine the will, are without exception empirical and can hand down no practical law. This means that when the "desire for the object"—namely an expected "pleasure in the actuality of the object" itself—"*precedes* the practical rule" and is the condition under which the latter gains the force of a principle, then this principle is always empirical. If it were always the case that a desire—and hence an expectation of pleasure in the object—had to precede the practical rule as condition for the will's determination, then practical reason as "higher faculty of desire" could not be admitted, and *pure* practical philosophy would be utterly impossible.[26] An a priori pure practical proposition (the moral law) would be impossible under the condition that all prac-

25. For the many readings and misreadings that this moment of Kant's Analytic of the Beautiful has occasioned, see M. Baum, "Subjektivität, Allgemeingültigkeit und Apriorität des Geschmacksurteils bei Kant," in *Deutsche Zeitschrift für Philosophie*, 39, 3 (1991), 272–284. Baum argues both against P. Guyer, *Kant and the Claims of Taste*, Cambridge, Harvard University Press, 1979; and R. Meerbote, "Reflection on Beauty," in *Essays in Kant's Aesthetics*, ed. by T. Cohen, P. Guyer, Chicago, University of Chicago Press, 1982, 55–86.

26. KpV A 41.

tical principles, in order to be endorsed by the will (i.e., in order to function as its determining ground), have to be based upon the subject's capacity of feeling pleasure or displeasure. Neither universality nor necessity follow from that condition.

The same considerations regarding the precedence of the feeling of pleasure hold true for the critique of the aesthetic faculty of judgment. Such a critique would be impossible if the pleasure in the represented object always preceded our judging it as beautiful. In this case, no difference would separate the agreeable from the beautiful; all judgment of taste would be empirical and private; and no transcendental critique of taste would be possible. Moreover, both in the case of practical and aesthetic judgment, "we cannot know a priori from the representation of any object, *whatever the nature of this representation*, whether it will be associated with pleasure or displeasure or will be merely indifferent."[27] In this sense, the question posed by §9 of the Analytic of the Beautiful is really the "key" to Kant's critique of taste.

Once the possibility that the feeling of pleasure precedes our judgment (be it aesthetic or practical) has been excluded, the following questions must be addressed: what are aesthetic judgments about, and what is it that can be communicated universally and can produce pleasure as a "consequence"? (§9, 27, AA 217, 11). Kant contends that only "cognition" can be universally communicated. Representations can be communicated in a universal way only if they belong to cognition. *Erkenntnis* alone can provide the objective "universal reference point" with which everyone's cognitive faculties must also subjectively harmonize. Accordingly, Kant's claim that the judgment of taste has universal validity can be based only upon its relation to cognition, even though any proper cognitive value has been denied to aesthetic judgment from the outset. Kant solves this apparent contradiction by showing that the reference to cognition as the ground of the universal communicability of our representations opens up two different possibilities.

The first case is offered by objective, determinate cognition of objects through concepts. Evidently, this case does not apply to aesthetic judgment because of its employment of concepts. In this situation, imagination follows the lead taken by the understanding (and its concepts) so that the interplay of cognitive faculties is constrained by the employment of concepts and their application (the transcendental schematism of the first *Critique*) with a determinate cognitive aim in view. A second possibility is offered when the *Bestimmungsgrund* of the judgment that claims universal validity is not an objective concept but merely the subjective "mental state that is met in the relation of the powers of representation to each other insofar as they refer a given representation to *cognition in general*" (§9, 28, AA 217, 18–20). According to the distinction of the twofold use of the faculty of judgment in introduction §IV, a given representation can be used either to determine (know) objects or to reflect upon them. In the latter case, since nothing in the object is known and no given concept is employed by the understanding, the balance between the two cognitive faculties—imagination and understanding—is

---

27. KpV A 40.

even, and neither one takes the lead over the other as no particular cognitive aim needs to be reached. Imagination and understanding are in a "free play," in "harmony," or in a "*proportionierte Stimmung*."[28] This relation among the faculties is a sufficient subjective condition for cognition in general and hence is the ground of judgment's universal communicability. When the interplay of imagination and understanding in reflecting upon the object's representation meet the necessary subjective conditions for "cognition in general" (i.e., not a "determinate cognition" [§9, 29, AA 218, 6] nor objective conceptual cognition of objects), then this simple fulfillment of the subjective conditions for cognition in general is sufficient to ground and to justify the universal communicability of aesthetic judgment.

Thus, the necessary and sufficient subjective condition for cognition in general is the "free play" that characterizes our cognitive faculties in their *reflection* upon the represented object. This condition answers the question of the ground of our judgment's universal communicability. Universal communicability is not justified by a *content* but by the merely *formal* condition to *Erkenntnis überhaupt.* At this point, however, Kant still needs to address the issues of what is communicated in our judgment and of how a feeling of pleasure or displeasure is produced in this process. The answer is provided by the *reflective* character of aesthetic judgment. Aesthetic judgments communicate in a universal way the act of self-reflection that an object intuited and apprehended by means of imagination and understanding induces in the subject. Aesthetic judgments are judgments about objects of our intuition insofar as an act of self-reflection is involved in the apprehension of the object's representation. It is the universal communicability of this self-reflection that produces pleasure in us. Since the way in which the object is apprehended and synthesized by imagination and understanding sets these faculties in a free play (as opposed to constraining them in the asset required by the production of knowledge), the minimal condition for "subjective universal communicability" is fulfilled (§9, 29, AA 217, 35). Consequently, the subject, in reflecting upon her state of mind in judging the object beautiful, expresses the possibility of a universalization of her self-reflection from which a feeling of pleasure follows. As Kant states in the opening of §9, pleasure must follow the aesthetic evaluation of the object in which we feel pleasure (§9, 27, AA 217, 10–11; 29, AA 218, 8). Since pleasure in the object follows the universal communicability that takes place in the judgment of taste as its "ground," this mediation (or foundation) is responsible for the shift according to which the "pleasure *in the object*" (§9, 27, AA 217, 10–11) becomes the "pleasure *in the harmony of the cognitive faculties*" involved in my reflection upon it (§9, 29, AA 218, 8). Thus, aesthetic judgments are neither judgments about our pleasure nor judgments

28. See D. Henrich, "Kant's Explanation of Aesthetic Judgment," in *Aesthetic Judgment and the Moral Image of the World: Studies in Kant*, Stanford, Stanford University Press, 1992, 29–56, who focuses on the critical transformation of the notion of "harmonious play" of imagination and understanding as key to understand the notion of aesthetic judgment in the *Critique of Judgment.*

about our feelings—be it pleasure in the object or even in the harmonious state of our faculties (for in all these cases, pleasure would have to come first). They are judgments about those individual objects that induce in the subject a self-reflection in which the *Gemützustand*, due to the fulfillment of the necessary subjective condition of cognition in general (the "free play," or harmony, of imagination and understanding), is universally communicable. It is this complex situation that generates the specifically *aesthetic* pleasure in what I call beautiful. Thus, "beautiful is what, without a concept, is liked universally" (32, AA 219, 25).

The Third Moment (Relation): Purposiveness Without Purpose of the Pure Judgment of Taste, §§10–17

By establishing that the feeling of pleasure can only *follow* our aesthetic judgment as consequence or effect, the second moment leads to the third moment. Herein, the title of the categories ("relation") suggests an explanation of the specific type of causality through which the feeling of pleasure and displeasure can be said to follow from our representation of the object that we call beautiful. Taking up the analogy with practical reason, the third moment of the judgment of taste further determines the peculiar nature of the aesthetic feeling of pleasure bringing in the notions of "purposiveness" and "purpose." The crucial question of the *Bestimmungsgrund* of the judgment of taste receives further determination, so that *pure a priori* judgments of taste (§§12, 13) are clearly distinguished both from empirical judgments based upon sensation, charm, and emotion, and from intellectual judgments based upon interest, utility, and the notion of perfection (§§13–17).

The notion of "pleasure" leads Kant to the concepts of "purpose" and "purposiveness" (§10). Purpose is defined as "the object of a concept insofar as we regard this concept as the object's cause" or as the "real ground of its possibility" (§10, 32, AA 220, 1–3). The will is the faculty of desire that operates according to the representation of purposes. The representation of the effect is here the *Bestimmungsgrund* of its cause and precedes it. Pleasure is the relation of the desired object to the subject's state.[29] Purposiveness—or *forma finalis*—is the causality of a concept with regard to its object (§10, 32, AA 220, 3–4). As already suggested in the introduction, *Zweckmäßigkeit* is the "form" that exhibits the thing's harmony with a "constitution of things" possible only according to purposes.[30] Since a purpose always implies an interest in the existence of the object, a judgment of taste can be grounded neither in a subjective nor in an objective purpose (§11). This confirms the results of §9: the pleasure of a merely agreeable sensation cannot be the ground for the determination of the judgment of taste (§11, 35,

---

29. Or, in a somehow more convoluted formulation, pleasure is "the consciousness of a representation's causality with regard to the subject's state so as to keep the subject in that state" (§10, 33, AA 220, 9–11).

30. See introduction §IV, XXVIII, 180, 31–37. Purposiveness is defined as "the accordance of a thing with that constitution of things that is possible only through purposes" (XXVIII, 180, 34–33).

AA 221, 19–21). Yet, since purposiveness can indeed be thought of without reference to a purpose (namely without reference to the practical causality of a will and to the existence of a real purpose), the form of purposiveness or the very notion of a "purposiveness without a purpose" becomes the key to explaining the idea of beauty according to the moment of relation. In the case of aesthetic judgment, the notion of purposiveness is assumed in a merely "subjective" and "formal" sense as pertaining to the relation between the representation of the object and the subject's cognitive faculties. The notion of a "purposiveness without a purpose" allows Kant to explain the *relation* between the representation of the object that we call beautiful and the disposition of our cognitive faculties to each other (the free play of imagination and understanding) in the judgment of taste, from which the peculiar feeling of pleasure and displeasure arises.[31]

Kant claims that since formal subjective purposiveness without purpose constitutes the "*Bestimmungsgrund* of the judgment of taste" (§11, 35, AA 221, 27) such a judgment rests on an a priori ground (§12). The argument that supports this claim runs, once again, in analogy to the argument with which the *Critique of Practical Reason* explores the relation between the feeling of reverence for the moral law and the idea of the moral law itself. At this juncture, we see in what sense the two issues of the determining ground of the judgment of taste and its a priori character are related to each other. In §9, Kant has shown that the feeling of pleasure cannot precede our aesthetic judgment as its ground but must follow from it. In §§11–12, he makes clear that the feeling of pleasure cannot be the "effect" of a representation as a purpose, for in this case, the *Bestimmungsgrund* of the judgment would be empirical. The crucial point is directly parallel to the situation of the *Critique of Practical Reason.* The "connection" between the feeling of pleasure or displeasure as "effect" and a certain representation as its "cause" can never be established a priori. For, this type of causal relation can only be recognized a posteriori (i.e., empirically). I have already quoted the parallel passage of the second *Critique:* "we cannot know a priori from the representation of any object, whatever the nature of this representation, whether it will be associated with pleasure or displeasure or will be merely indifferent."[32] The question that Kant now addresses, is the following: what kind of pleasure is exactly "the pleasure in aesthetic judgments?" (§12, 36, AA 222, 18). To this question Kant responds in an analogous manner to the way in which the second *Critique* argued for the peculiar nature of the feeling of respect for the moral law. In both cases, the strategy is to deny that the feeling of pleasure properly follows from the representation of the beautiful object or from the idea of the moral law—as it can be neither deduced from it nor caused by it. In the latter case, Kant contends that the immediate consequence of the moral law is not the feeling itself but the determination of the will. The *Gemützustand* of the willing subject is in itself "identical"

31. For this argument see introduction §VII.
32. KpV A 40.

with a feeling of pleasure, and hence pleasure is properly not a consequence derived from the moral law. This identity guarantees that the determination of the will by means of the moral law is "immediate" (i.e., excludes any intervention of feeling).[33] This argument also grounds the peculiar pure a priori character of the moral feeling. The feeling of pleasure or displeasure is nothing but the state of mind of the subject that determines herself according to the law.

Kant contends that in the case of the peculiar pleasure in aesthetic judgments the situation is "similar" (§12, 36, AA 222, 18). Pleasure is here *identical* with the "consciousness of the merely formal purposiveness" of the object's representation for the subject's faculties (§12, 36–37, AA 222, 20–21); pleasure is not a consequence that follows the object's representation as its cause (in which case the relation would only be a posteriori) but is identical with that very moment of consciousness or self-reflection by which the subject relates the object's representation to the free play of her cognitive faculties. Thus, the feeling of pleasure that we experience in aesthetic judgments is grounded upon the formal purposiveness through which the representation of the object is related to the free play of imagination and understanding. The notion of formal purposiveness is the notion of an "internal causality" that fulfills the merely formal condition of "cognition in general" without leading to any determinate cognition of objects (§12, 38, AA 222, 25–27) and without implying any kind of practical causality. However, the notion of formal purposiveness still exercises a causality of its own in maintaining the mental state of a free play of imagination and understanding without any aim to be pursued (neither theoretical nor practical) nor further interest nor desire to be satisfied. Pleasure in the beautiful is a pure contemplative pleasure: "We *linger* in our contemplation of the beautiful because this contemplation reinforces and reproduces itself" (§12, 38, AA 222, 33–37). The *Bestimmungsgrund* of our aesthetic judgment is therefore the a priori notion of formal purposiveness as the principle of a "*pure* judgment of taste" (§13, 38, AA 223, 25).

A "pure judgment of taste" recognizes as its *only* determining ground the a priori principle of formal purposiveness—namely, a purposiveness without a purpose. This is the only principle that by excluding any further purpose or interest maintains the *Unparteilichkeit* (§13, 39, AA 223, 5) of a pure aesthetic judgment and opposes it to empirical and pathological judgments based upon charm and emotion. The partition of aesthetic judgments into "pure" and "empirical" follows accordingly (§14). Pure aesthetic judgments are "formal" (they are the only proper judgments of taste), while empirical aesthetic judgments are merely material (§13, 39, AA 223, 29–33).[34] To be sure, two types of nonpure judgments of

33. See KpV A 133 ff.

34. This argument grounds Kant's appreciation for "composition" and "design" as features that are purely formal and less dependent upon the materiality of sensation (§14, 42, AA 225, 16–20), as well as his considerations on the purity of colors and sounds (pure sensation).

taste are introduced by Kant's partition. On the one hand, we have *empirical* judgments of taste in which aesthetic pleasure is mingled with the sensible pleasure produced by agreeable sensations. On the other hand, Kant presents *intellectual* judgments of taste that involve a reference to the concept. This latter case opens up the possibility that aesthetic pleasure may be combined with an intellectual pleasure in the object. By opposing pure aesthetic judgments to the two types of nonpure aesthetic judgments, Kant consolidates the autonomy of the sphere of pure aesthetic judgments. He thereby excludes the possibility that charm and emotion can be the *Bestimmungsgrund* of pure aesthetic judgments (§14, 43, AA 226, 18–20); at the same time, he declares these judgments independent of any notion of purpose—be it "perfection" (as "objective internal purposiveness") or "utility" (as objective external purposiveness) (§15, 44, AA 226, 31–227, 3). We do not need to know the *concept* of the object in order to find the object beautiful—neither its function nor its purpose play a role in the assessment of the object's beauty.

The distinction between pure aesthetic judgments and intellectual judgments of taste based upon concepts grounds Kant's famous distinction between *pulchritudo vaga,* or "free beauty," and *pulchritudo adherens,* or "adherent beauty" (§16, 48, AA 229, 10–11), which is beauty that is "fixed" in and by a concept of objective purposiveness. "Free beauty" is the object of a purely aesthetic liking, while "fixed beauty" implies intellectual appreciation of the object. The former presupposes no concept of what the object is meant to be, for such a concept would limit the "freedom of the imagination" that plays with the representation of beauty (§16, 50, AA 230, 1–2). The latter, on the contrary, is based precisely on such a concept, and implies the notion of the object's perfection.

Kant's presentation of the notion of pure aesthetic judgment as independent of any concept implies the sheer impossibility of providing any objective universal rule for taste or for a model of beauty. Such a rule would have to determine through concepts what must be judged as beautiful by everyone. By opposing the notion of pure aesthetic judgment—as the only proper judgment of taste—to the two types of nonpure aesthetic judgments, Kant relegates the traditional problems raised by the aesthetic discussion of the Enlightenment to the sphere of nonpure intellectual judgments. In other words, issues concerning the criterion of taste and the ideal of beauty are no longer crucial problems for a *transcendental critique* of the aesthetic faculty of judgment. Moreover, the question of the "ideal" of beauty and its "exemplarity" presents itself only in the case of non-pure intellectual judgments of taste, in which beauty is fixed in a determinate concept of objective purposiveness (§17, 53–54, AA 232, 7–16).

The archetype, or highest model, of taste can be "only an idea" or, better, an "ideal." While idea is for Kant a concept of reason, ideal is "the representation of an individual being as adequate to an idea" (§17, 54, AA 232, 13–17). The ideal of beauty is properly an "ideal of the imagination" as the faculty of "exhibition" (§17, 54–55, AA 232, 21, 23–24). Since the ideal refers to the notion of purpose, Kant presents the figure of the human being as the highest ideal of intellectual beauty, which, however, can only be the object of an intellectual (nonpure and hence improper aesthetic judgment). The human being is the only being that carries in itself the moral purpose of its existence and is the being that through reason determines its own purposes.

The Fourth Moment (Modality): The Judgment of Taste Has Necessary Validity, §§18–22

Along with the moment of universality, the modality of the judgment of taste is crucial to Kant's demonstration of the a priori character of pure aesthetic judgments. Indeed, the modality of aesthetic judgment is considered "a principal moment for the critique of judgment"; for by revealing an a priori principle of the faculty of judgment, the critical investigation rescues the analysis of both the beautiful and the sublime from empirical psychology and turns it into the topic of transcendental philosophy (§29, 112–113, AA 266, 9–17). In the last moment of the Analytic of the Beautiful, the issue of the *Bestimmungsgrund* is transformed into the question of the "principle" (*Prinzip*) of aesthetic judgment (§20). The issue of the principle of the judgment of taste is discussed by Kant in the Deduction.[35]

What I judge as beautiful is the object of a necessary liking without a concept being involved in my evaluation. Kant's argument for the special necessity to be attributed to aesthetic judgments refers back to the development of its "remarkable" universality. This moment eventually solves the problem of the possibility of pure a priori aesthetic judgments. With regard to the *necessity* that connects beauty with a liking, Kant observes that it is a necessity "of a special kind" (§18, 62, AA 236, 21–22). Once again, its first determination is merely negative. It is neither the "theoretical objective necessity" that allows me to infer a priori that everyone will necessarily like the object that I call beautiful; nor is it the practical objective necessity that presents the object's liking as a necessary consequence of the moral law (§18, 62, AA 236, 22–237, 6). However, if the necessity of aesthetic judgment cannot derive from a concept, it is also not a necessity of empirical origin—a claim that would simply be contradictory, as no necessity can be obtained from experience. By formulating a judgment of taste, we imply that "everyone *ought to* [*soll*] give his approval to the object at hand" (§19, 63, AA 237, 22–25). Consequently, not being based upon a concept, the necessity of the *Sollen* that we express in aesthetic judgments must be merely "subjective." It must determine through a feeling (not through a concept) the object of liking or disliking (§19 title; §20, 64, AA 238, 4–6). In addition, since it cannot imply a concept, it is not an apodeictic necessity (§18, 63, AA 237, 10–18). Kant maintains that it is rather a "conditioned" necessity (§19, title). Thus, we must ask, where does the *Sollen* come from, and what is the condition that affects this necessity?[36]

---

35. See §§34–36.
36. See the "*Pflicht*" that Kant presents at the end of §40 (161, AA 296, 12).

Kant calls the peculiar necessity of the judgment of taste an "exemplary" necessity. In the case of universality, my calling something beautiful implies my taking up a "universal voice" that demands everyone's assent—whereby my judgment becomes somehow an example or an utterance of this voice. Instead, the necessity of aesthetic judgment is the "necessity of the assent of everyone to a judgment that is regarded as an example of a universal rule that we are unable to state" (§18, 62–63, AA 237, 8–10). My judgment entails necessity *because* it is considered as an example of a rule or principle that cannot be provided and therefore remains unstated. As example, my judgment derives the necessity of a universal consensus from this rule. Accordingly, Kant's suggestion is that the special subjective necessity proper to the judgment of taste lies precisely in the special relation between principle and example.

We do solicit everyone's assent in the form of a *Sollen* because we have a "ground for it that is common to all" (§19, 63, AA 237, 27–28). The assumption of this common ground is the basis for the necessity of the judgment of taste. What kind of ground is Kant referring to? It is apparent that only that which can justify everyone's duty to assent to my judgment can provide the peculiar necessity that Kant is looking for. The ground that requires universal assent constitutes the rule of approval and the basis, or principle, upon which I formulate my judgment.

At this point, Kant introduces the condition that limits the very necessity of aesthetic judgments. Indeed, we could count on everyone else's assent "if only we could always be sure that the instance had been subsumed correctly under that ground as rule for the approval" (§19, 63–64, AA 237, 28–30).[37] Why does Kant need to specify the apparently obvious condition that the subsumption must be carried through correctly? In what does the error in subsuming under the notion of beautiful consist, and in what sense does this error affect the character of judgment's necessity? From Kant's efforts at isolating pure judgments of taste from all other nonpure types of judgments, we can conclude that the error consists in subsuming either under the notion of the agreeable or the good (i.e., either under the faculty of desire or under the faculty of knowledge), thus implying the use of a concept. At stake in the correctness of the subsumption is precisely the specificity (and purity) of aesthetic judgment.[38] Hence, to formulate a *pure* aesthetic judgment is to operate a *correct* subsumption under the rule for the approval, thereby producing an example of the rule. This example carries with itself the subjective necessity of everyone's assent.

The limiting condition concerns the relation between the principle of aesthetic judgment as such and each single, individual judgment that is pronounced according to that rule. A "*conditioned*" necessity characterizes aesthetic judgments as

---

37. See L. Scaravelli, *Scritti kantiani*, Firenze, La Nuova Italia, 1968, 427–449.

38. The problem of how "subsumption" works in the case of the judgment of taste (with no concept of object involved) is addressed in the Deduction (see §35).

opposed to cognitive or logical judgments, which, being based upon an "objective determinate principle," enjoy "*unconditioned* necessity" (§20, 64, 237, 34–238, 1). In the discussion of the universal validity of aesthetic judgments, we encountered the claim that in logic a judgment that is "universally valid *objectively*" is also, at the same time, universally valid *subjectively* (§8, 23, AA 215, 3–6). An objectively universal judgment must also be valid *subjectively* for everyone who represents to herself an object by means of that concept. In the case of logical judgments, to ask whether the subsumption entailed in a given individual judgment has or has not been effected correctly is a completely irrelevant question. On the contrary, since in the case of aesthetic judgments no objective validity can be inferred from their merely subjective universal validity, the limiting condition of the correct subsumption must be related to the subjective character of judgment's necessity, thereby becoming an essential condition.

By introducing such a limiting condition in the case of aesthetic judgments, Kant raises a crucial issue. We need to ask, (i) does the assent that we demand from everyone else regard the *principle* that guides the subsumption upon which my individual judgment is constructed and of which it is an example (if the subsumption is correct); (ii) does it regard *this individual judgment* itself; or (iii) does it concern *both the principle and my individual judgment*? Evidently, if the agreement that we demand regarded our individual judgments of beautiful objects, then to add the limiting condition "provided that the subsumption had been operated correctly" would simply be tautological and trivial. But if on the contrary the condition concerns the very principle of our judgments of taste, then Kant is thereby presenting a *very special connection between the general principle and the particular judgment* formulated according to that principle. In this case, we have a *transcendental* condition that specifies the proper character of pure aesthetic judgments a priori.

We need to recall that §18 defined the necessity of aesthetic judgments as "exemplarity" (i.e., as the "necessity of the assent of everyone to a judgment that is regarded as an example *of a universal rule that we are unable to state*" (§18, 62–63, AA 237, 8–10). Unlike the synthetic a priori principles of the understanding, the principle of the aesthetic faculty of judgment can neither be exhibited nor schematized. This is the reason why the Analytic of the Beautiful is not divided into analytic of concepts and analytic of principles (instead of the latter, Kant presents the notion of genius). In the case of aesthetic judgments, the rule cannot be provided. Hence we can formulate individual judgments according to the rule, but we can never present (exhibit or schematize) the rule itself. All we can count on are our individual judgments of taste. Consequently, individual aesthetic judgments must have a different relation to the principle on which they are formulated than single cognitive judgments have to the synthetic principles of the understanding. "Exemplarity" describes precisely that different relation and provides the peculiar type of necessity of the judgment of taste. Exemplarity replaces schematization.

The "principle" of the judgment of taste is the "presupposition" of a *Gemeinsinn* as *sensus communis* (§20, 64, AA 238, 6–9).[39] This principle is an "idea" (§20 title, §22, 67, AA 239, 30; 68, 240, 15). It is apparent that Kant construes the moment of necessity parallel to the moment of universality. The idea of the "universal voice" in whose place I speak when I pronounce a pure aesthetic judgment is complemented now by the idea of the *Gemeinsinn* as a principle that I cannot exhibit but of which I can present an example in my own judgment (if and only if this judgment is correctly formed) (§22, 67, AA 239, 24). Both in the second and in the fourth moment, the assumption of the ground of aesthetic judgment in a universal voice, or *sensus communis*, is connected to the issue of "universal communicability," and hence with the subjective condition for "cognition in general" (§§9, 21). The *Gemeinsinn* is, Kant argues, the condition for the universal communicability of our feeling (§21, 66, AA 238, 4–5). We know that only cognition can be universally communicated. The state of mind in which our cognitive faculties are set in that proportional balance that is the most conducive to the mutual attunement—or free play—of imagination and understanding with no cognitive aim and no further interest in view—this *Gemützustand*—is "determined by feeling (as opposed to being determined by a concept)" (§21, 66, AA 238, 35–239, 2). Such a feeling can be universally communicated on the basis of the assumption of a *Gemeinsinn*. Logic and all forms of cognition as such must presuppose this same condition if solipsism and skepticism are to be defeated.

Against the merely individual validity of a "private feeling" (§22, 67, AA 239, 19), the feeling voiced by the *sensus communis* has a public and common validity that entails the necessity of a *Sollen*, (i.e., the necessity and even the duty) of universal approval. Since such an injunction could never be deduced from experience, *Gemeinsinn* does not express the empirical generality of a (cultural or historical) *fact*, but is rather a "necessary *idea*" (§22, 67, AA 239, 30). The "*Gemeinsinn, of whose judgment I am . . . offering my judgment of taste as an example*, attributing to it exemplary validity on that account, is an *ideal norm*" (§22, 67, AA 239, 24–26). Even though this principle is only subjectively universal, it "could, like an objective principle, demand universal assent insofar as agreement among different judging persons is concerned, *provided only we were certain that we had correctly subsumed under it*" (§22, 68, AA 239, 29–33). The limiting clause expressed at the end of §19 is now repeated since the very possibility for my judgment to be an example of the principle is affected by the condition that the subsumption by which my individual judgment is formulated must be correct. And since the principle of aesthetic judgment cannot itself be exhibited, the only possible relation to the principle lies in the exemplary character of my judgment. Under this condition, the fact that my individual aesthetic judgment en-

39. In the same passage, Kant warns not to mistake this *sensus communis* with what is generally called "sound human understanding," or common sense.

tails a *correct* subsumption decides for the very possibility of expressing, as example, the principle of the *Gemeinsinn*.

The impossibility of exhibiting the principle of aesthetic judgments has important consequences when Kant makes the transition from the problem of the *contemplation* of the beautiful to the *production* of beautiful art works. At this juncture, the necessary lack of an analytic of the principles in the Analytic of the Beautiful implies that artistic production is left without principles as it cannot follow from any. Hence, artistic production will have to be brought back to an original faculty, namely the genius that indeed operates without principles and norms and outside of all principles and norms. Thus, the faculty of the genius is eventually identical with the *Gemeinsinn* that grounds the necessity of our aesthetic judgments.

In the idea of the *Gemeinsinn*, all the elements of the judgment of taste are eventually united, and with it the task of the Analytic of the Beautiful is concluded (§22, 68, AA 240, 14–15).

4. The Analytic of the Sublime (§§23–29)

The second book of the Analytic of the Aesthetic Faculty of Judgment is dedicated to the Analytic of the Sublime. The conceptual separation between beautiful and sublime is relatively recent in the history of modern aesthetics. Kant's interest in the topic goes back to the 1764 *Observations Concerning the Beautiful and the Sublime*, where the subject is examined mainly in a psychological and anthropological perspective or, as Kant puts it, in the perspective of an observer rather than a philosopher. By isolating pure aesthetic judgments from nonpure aesthetic judgments and consequently by drawing the distinction between "free beauty" and "adherent beauty" (§16), Kant already hinted at the possible connection between the sphere of aesthetic judgment and morality as well as at the possible link between imagination and reason. Thus, he addresses for the first time the issue raised in the introduction (§§II, III, and IX) of the mediating role exercised by the reflective faculty of judgment in bridging the gap that separates the sensible from the supersensible.

In the Analytic of the Sublime the "method" of the presentation follows the main titles of the table of the categories already employed in the Analytic of the Beautiful (§24, 79, AA 247, 12). We are still dealing with a judgment of reflection that is aesthetic (and hence is not determinant), and implies a liking that depends neither on sensation nor on concepts (§23, 74, AA 244, 10–12). However, Kant announces from the outset a change in the precedence of quantity over quality. Such a change is due to the crucial difference between the judgment of the beautiful, which regards the form of the object (and hence requires to start from quality), and the judgment of the sublime, which instead deals with that which may lack any form at all (*Formlosigkeit*, §24, 79, AA 247, 15). Thereby Kant assigns to the imagination the task of a comprehension of the unity of an absolute magnitude (quantity).

Kant starts his exposition by confronting the notion of the sublime as well as the way in which we predicate it of natural objects with the different explanations of the beautiful reached in the four moments of the preceding Analytic. Both in the case of the beautiful and of the sublime, we pronounce singular judgments that claim universal and necessary validity to the "liking" thereby expressed. Hence, the Analytic of the Sublime is developed on the ground of the basic notions that resulted from the analysis of the pure judgment of taste. Yet while the cognitive faculties engaged in the judgment of the beautiful are imagination and understanding (due to the reference to an "indeterminate" concept [§23, 74, AA 244, 13] in which the form of the beautiful object finds its "limitation" or its boundaries [§23, 75, AA 244, 24]), the faculties that participate in the judgment of the sublime are imagination and reason (§23, 75, AA 244, 24–29). Since the sublime refers to objects that lack any form and boundaries, it expresses a striving toward the infinite and a claim to totality. These are, as we know, distinctive characteristics of reason as faculty of the unconditioned.

It follows that the notion of purposiveness—which describes the relation between our feeling and the cognitive faculties involved in the apprehension of the object's representation—must be different in the judgment of the beautiful and of the sublime. In the case of the beautiful, purposiveness refers to the way in which the object's form appears so as to fit our perception. Consequently, nature as a whole appears as a harmonious system shaped by a "technic of nature." Nature is judged as if it were art (§23, 77, AA 246, 5). On the contrary, in the case of the sublime the object's lack of form is experienced as *zweckwidrig* (i.e., as contra-purposive, inconvenient, and not at all suited to our capacity of presentation). The lack of form even seems to do violence to our imagination. Accordingly, we do not call nature sublime when it is present to us as an ordered systematic whole. We call sublime a wild chaos of elements (§23, 78, AA 246, 17–19).[40] The playful disposition of our cognitive faculties that we experience in the case of beautiful objects yields to the seriousness of awe and "reverence" that we feel when

40. It follows that as examples of a pure aesthetic judgment of the sublime (i.e., a judgment not mingled with teleological considerations) neither works of art nor natural objects whose concept implies a determinate purpose are allowed. Only "crude nature" can provide an example for a pure judgment of the sublime (§26, 88–89, AA 252, 32–253, 2; also General Remark on the First Division of the Analytic, 118, AA 269, 35–270, 4). In the case of the mathematically sublime, examples are provided by nature when intuition implies the "idea of the infinite" (§26, 93, AA 255, 15; 95–96, 256). In the case of the dynamically sublime, the "might" of nature is instead the focus (§28, 104, AA 261, 13–19). A perspective on the *Critique of Judgment* through Kant's examples is provided by G. Böhme, *Kants Kritik der Urteilskraft in neuer Sicht*, Frankfurt a.M., Suhrkamp, 1999. This work is explicitly placed in the aftermath of Lyotard's revival of the topic of the sublime; see F. Lyotard, *Leçons sur l'Analytique du Sublime*, Paris, Galilée, 1991. See also his "La réflexion dans l'esthétique Kantienne," in *Revue Internationale de Philosophie*, 175, (1990), 507–551.

confronting the sublime. In this case, the imagination is not free in its play but is submitted to reason and is at work as reason's "instrument" (General Remark on the First Division of the Analytic, 117, AA 269, 4, 26). Thus, the notion of the sublime indicates nothing purposive in nature itself; what is purposive is only the "use we can make of our intuitions of nature so that we can feel a *purposiveness within ourselves* entirely independent of nature" (§23, 78, AA 246, 22–25). It is precisely the feeling of our independency from nature's forces that characterizes the experience of the dynamical sublime. This is an experience of freedom in the negative sense of being the will's independency from the mechanism of nature.[41] In our judgment of the sublime, purposiveness points to a moral determination within ourselves: the sublime cannot concern sensible forms and objects, but only reason's ideas. While ideas can never be adequately exhibited in a sensible form, certain natural objects may call ideas to mind. These are the objects that we perceive as sublime, thereby pointing to the supersensible disposition (or *Zweckmäßigkeit*) that is to be found only within ourselves and does not regard, as in the case of the beautiful, the relation between the object's form and our cognitive faculties. Because of this different reference to the notion of purposiveness, which is somehow borrowed from the sphere of reason and simply used by the reflective faculty of judgment, the Analytic of the Sublime is considered by Kant a "mere appendix to our aesthetic judging of nature's purposiveness" (§23, 78, AA 246, 30–31).

While beauty is quietly contemplated in a still disposition of mind, the sublime sets the *Gemüt* in motion. We judge this motion as subjectively purposive (we like it). The imagination relates it either to the cognitive faculty (in the evaluation of magnitude) or to the faculty of desire (in the will's attempt to contrast nature's power as well as in practical reason's providing the sense for our moral destination). From these considerations Kant derives the division of the Analytic of the Sublime into "mathematically sublime" (under which the moments of quality and quantity are considered) and "dynamically sublime" (under which the moments of relation and modality are considered) (§24, 80, AA 247, 23–35).[42]

The Mathematically Sublime, §§23–27

Quantity and quality of our judgments of the sublime are presented with regard to a specifically *aesthetic* way of evaluating magnitude in intuition, which differs from all mathematical measurement of appearances by means of numbers (herein lies the reference to and the comparison with the cognitive faculty) (§26). Sublime is what is judged as "absolutely large," or large beyond all comparison, so

---

41. This connection has been explored by P. Guyer, "The Symbols of Freedom in Kant's Aesthetics," in *Kants Ästhetik/Kant's Aesthetics/L'esthétique de Kant*, op. cit., 338–355, in particular 342–345.

42. Following Kant's division, Fr. Schiller will distinguish *Theoretisch-Erhabenes* and *Praktisch-Erhabenes*. See Fr. Schiller, "Vom Erhabenen," in *Sämtliche Werke*, ed. by G. Fricke, H. G. Göpfert, München, C. Hanser, 1960, vol. 5, 490.

that no (objective) standard of measurement is externally applied to it. The sublime constitutes an absolute (subjective) standard of magnitude of its own (§25). Moreover, the standard is not set in order to logically and mathematically determine the object's magnitude (to ascertain *how* large an object is, given that every object of the senses *has* a *determinate* magnitude). At stake, rather, is a standard upon which an *aesthetic judgment of reflection* is pronounced (the different claim is made *that* something *is* an *absolute* magnitude). The concept of magnitude employed in the judgment of the sublime is neither a pure concept of understanding nor a sensible intuition nor a rational concept. It is rather a specific "concept of the faculty of judgment" (§25, 81, 248, 14–15).[43] While mathematical evaluation allows for no largest magnitude, aesthetic evaluation does indeed admit of an absolute maximum (§26, 87, AA 251, 25). The idea of the maximum brings with itself the idea of the sublime. Accordingly, the explication of the mathematically sublime is the following: "Sublime is that in comparison with which everything else is small" (§25, 84, 250, 12–13). Evidently, nothing in nature, i.e., no object of the senses can ever be adequate to the representation of an absolute magnitude (in nature everything is only relatively small or large, as proved by the use of telescopes and microscopes). Yet, the judgment of the sublime bears witness both to our imagination's stretching and expanding toward the infinite and to our reason's demand for an absolute totality as "real idea" (§25, 84, 250, 22–25).

The judgment of the sublime sees the imagination engaging in a twofold activity, namely, "apprehension (*apprehensio*) and comprehension (*comprehensio aesthetica*)" (§26, 87, AA 251, 34–35). The sublime stresses the relation of *unbalance* between the two acts. This unbalance is perceived only by a feeling, which constitutes the sublime. The case of an absolute magnitude (or the infinite) brings to light that while the apprehension has no limit and may go on *ad infinitum*, reason requires that the imagination complete the comprehension in the single graspable unity of a totality of intuition—a task that the imagination is unable to perform (§26, 92, AA 254, 21–23). The imagination's striving to comprehend the infinite in a totality dissociates it from the understanding, thereby revealing the presence of a supersensible faculty proper to the human *Gemüt* (§26, 92, AA 254, 36–37). Herein lies the reference to reason and its ideas as well as to the practical sphere. This reference allows one to understand the nature of subjective purposiveness at work in the judgment of the sublime (§26, 90, AA 253, 22–23). In the sublime, the aesthetic faculty of judgment relates the imagination to reason and its ideas so as to produce a subjective accordance among them. This accordance is an "attunement of the *Gemüt*" that conforms to (and is analogous with) the one that "an influence by practical ideas would produce on feeling" (§26, 95, AA 256, 6–11). It is precisely our imagination's inability to evaluate the absolute magnitude of natural things that arouses the "feeling of a supersensible faculty in

---

43. It is precisely this peculiarity that requires the inquiry of the Analytic of the Sublime.

us" (§25, 85, 250, 27). Thereby it also proves that what is sublime is not the object itself but the "*Geistesstimmung*" (§25, 85, 250, 31) effected by a certain representation occupying our reflective judgment. "True sublimity" is never in the object but only in the *Gemüt* of the judging subject (§26, 95, AA 256, 12).

Kant's explanation of the quality of the liking proper to our judgments of the sublime (§27) follows from the insufficiency of the imagination's striving toward reason's absolute totality in the comprehension of appearances. The feeling involved in the judgment of the sublime is a feeling of respect, or reverence. For Kant, this feeling is always related to reason's (moral) law: "Respect is the feeling of our inability to attain an idea that has for us the force of law" (§27, 96, AA 257, 9–10). As was the case in the *Critique of Practical Reason*, the feeling of respect or reverence is a feeling of humiliation and hence displeasure and even pain. Yet this feeling is accompanied, at the same time, by the pleasure of discovering our higher supersensible determination of moral beings. The feeling of the sublime in nature is a feeling of displeasure for our imagination's insufficiency in the aesthetic estimation of magnitude and, at the same time, a feeling of respect for our own supersensible (moral) determination. *Achtung* is a feeling of both pleasure and displeasure in the consciousness of striving toward ideas—a striving that is a law for us. Thus, in the motion of our *Gemüt*, the feeling of displeasure is represented as purposive (§27, 100, AA 259, 13–17) since our imagination's inability uncovers the consciousness of an unlimited ability provided by reason.

Kant contends that it is a deceiving logical "subreption" that leads us "to put a reverence for the object in place of the reverence for the idea of the humanity in the subject" (§27, 96, AA 257, 22–23). The judgment of the sublime contains a subreption that attributes to the objects dignity and value (purposiveness) that belong, instead, only to the subject. Even though in the case of the beautiful Kant was stressing the seemingly analogous operation according to which, with regard to the universality of aesthetic judgment, we predicate beauty "as if it were a property of the object" (§6, 18, AA 211, 23–24; also §23, 73, AA 245, 25–26), in this case, properly, no subreption takes place. Purposiveness belongs here to the form of the object as it is apprehended by the imagination (although it is not objective purposiveness); hence, no value is actually transferred from the subject to the object. It is only in the case of the sublime, where the object itself is perceived as lacking all form and as being indeed *zweckwidrig*, that purposiveness can be discovered only within the subject. To attribute purposiveness to the object would immediately imply contradiction.

The Dynamically Sublime, §§28–29

In characterizing the sublime according to the moments of relation and modality as "dynamically sublime," Kant further develops the relation between aesthetic judgment and reason. He addresses the issue of a possible experience of freedom (in its negative sense) and establishes a link to religion and religious feeling. The dynamically sublime concerns our aesthetic judgment of nature considered as "a might" that yet "has no dominance over us" (§28, 102, AA 260, 15–16). We consider nature sublime when it is for us an object of fear. However, Kant suggests that in order to find it sublime, we must be able to judge nature as fearful without being afraid of it.[44] As in the case of the beautiful, no pathological emotion, fear or inclination can be the ground of an aesthetic judgment of the sublime. Rather, the experience of the sublime is precisely the experience of our independence of all pathological determination. It is an experience of freedom as independence of external determination.

The process is the same as for the mathematically sublime. In both cases, nature seems to set a sensible standard (be it mathematically a standard of magnitude or dynamically of might) in front of which we feel physical impotence and humiliation. Yet in this same confrontation, we discover a supersensible standard within ourselves that allows us to consider ourselves "independent of nature," thereby revealing our superiority over nature (§28, 105, AA 261, 34–35). This standard is the moral worth of "humanity in our person" (§28, 105, AA 262, 1). All the examples that Kant provides for the dynamically sublime show a sort of personified nature raging in thunder and lightning, in volcanoes' eruptions, and in devastating hurricanes. Once again, what is called sublime in these appearances of nature is that which "elevates the imagination" and makes the mind feel its own sublimity and independence (§28, 105, AA 260, 11–13). The feeling of pleasure regards the supersensible, moral "determination of our faculty."[45] This determination is indeed a natural disposition; yet it is up to us to cultivate, develop, and exercise it (§28, 106, AA 262, 19–21).

With the latter consideration Kant starts to address the crucial issue that he raised for the first time in the concluding section of the Analytic of the Beautiful. Herein Kant shifted the question of the determining ground of our pure a priori aesthetic judgments to a question concerning the very nature of the aesthetic faculty of judgment. The answer to the former problem proved that this is an independent faculty with an a priori principle of its own. In §22, Kant asks whether "taste is *an original and natural faculty* or *only the idea of a faculty yet to be acquired and artificial*" (§22, 68, AA 240, 4–6).[46] At the end of the Analytic of the Beautiful, however, Kant simply postpones the task of addressing this important issue. In the Analytic of the Sublime, the problem of the connection between aesthetic feeling and reason brings the aforementioned issue to the fore. The question, however, will be fully addressed only after the deduction of taste's subjective principle.

---

44. An illustration of this argument is provided by the analogy with our thought of god and by religion (§28, 103, AA 260, 27–28; §29, 108, AA 263, 26 ff.). See A. Lazaroff, "The Kantian Sublime: Aesthetic Judgment and Religious Feeling," in *Kant-Studien*, 71 (1980), 202–220.

45. The Romantic sense of *Bestimmung* as vocation (which is the way in which the term is generally translated starting with Fichte) is still absent in Kant's text, although the Analytic of the Sublime will offer more than one occasion for this interpretation.

46. This issue is developed by E. Garroni, "Une faculté à acquérir: Sens et non-sens dans la Troisième Critique," in *Kants Ästhetik/Kant's Aesthetics/L'esthétique de Kant,* op. cit., 313–324.

In presenting the moment of modality of the judgment of the sublime, Kant argues that while the necessity of everyone's agreement with our judgment of the beautiful is valid with no further presupposition, the appreciation of the sublime in nature seems to require a certain "cultivation" both of the faculty of judgment and of the cognitive faculties on the basis of which aesthetic judgment operates. The *Stimmung des Gemüts* for the feeling of the sublime requires a receptivity for ideas (§29, 110, AA 265, 1–2). In other words, even though reason naturally provides us with ideas and with a natural striving toward the unconditioned, the capacity of our mind and feeling to be attuned to them so as to be *moved* by the feeling of the sublime (i.e., to feel respect and reverence in front of what we judge as sublime as opposed to being afraid and repelled by it), requires cultivation and a "development of moral ideas" (§29, 110–111, AA 265, 10–12).[47]

Kant immediately makes clear that to claim that the judgment about the sublime requires culture does not mean that it is produced by culture (§29, 111, AA 265, 24–26). For our capacity of judging the sublime has its foundation "in human nature," i.e., in the moral determination proper to our reason. This is the ground for the *necessity* of the approval claimed by the judgment of the sublime (§29, 112, AA 265, 31). The feeling of *Achtung* shows the kinship between two kinds of pure feeling—namely the feeling of the sublime and the "moral feeling." Their relation is so close that the former cannot be thought of without the latter (§29, 112–113, AA 265, 35–266, 8; General Remark on the First Division of the Analytic, 114, AA 267, 16–18; 116, 268, 31–33).[48]

---

47. See the discussion at the end of §59 of the Dialectic of the Aesthetic Faculty of Judgment, and in §60 of the Methodology. See also P. Guyer, "The Symbols of Freedom in Kant's Aesthetics," in *Kants Ästhetik/Kant's Aesthetics/L'esthétique de Kant*, op. cit., 343; Guyer provides a reason why the sublime, as opposed to the beautiful, cannot be considered as a "complete symbol of morality."

48. The relation between moral feeling and aesthetic representation is extensively developed in the General Remark on the First Division of the Analytic (see in particular 120 ff., AA 271.

Chapter 10

The Deduction of Pure Aesthetic Judgments (§§30–54): *Sensus Communis* and Genius, Nature, and Art

In the first edition of the *Critique of Judgment*, the Deduction appears as a "third book" of the Analytic of the Aesthetic Faculty of Judgment—a title that Kant successively drops as a typographical error.[1] In the Deduction, which occupies almost one half of the Critique of the Aesthetic Faculty of Judgment, Kant repeats the moments of the judgment of taste within a new frame of discussion and following a new demonstrative aim. We can distinguish two main parts of the Deduction.[2] In §§30–38, Remark, Kant provides the properly formal "deduction" of the judgment of taste (i.e., the justification and legitimization of its universal validity and necessity). The argument of the formal deduction is concluded in §38, which is entitled "Deduction of the Judgments of Taste," and confirmed by the Remark. In §§39–54, Kant draws the implications from the principles established with regard to the different spheres in which taste is practiced and exercised. The relation between aesthetic and moral feeling comes to the fore here. In this group of sections, Kant additionally turns from the problem of the nature and structure of our pleasure in the beautiful to the issue of the production of beautiful forms. Thereby Kant draws the distinction between nature and art, and thematizes the activity of genius. The issue of "communicability" of aesthetic feelings is supple-

---

1. The correction is put in the *errata corrige*; see Kant's letter to J. G. C. Kiesewetter, April 20, 1790.

2. A discussion among the interpreters regards the question of whether the deduction can be considered complete with §38 or the link between beauty and morality that Kant pursues up to §57 (245, AA 346, 13) and §59 of the Dialectic still belongs to it (the former position, with which I agree, is held by, among others, P. Guyer, *Kant and the Claims of Taste*, op. cit., 373–389 and W. Pluhar's introduction to his translation of the third *Critique*, l vi f.; the latter position is held by W. Crawford, *Kant's Aesthetic Theory*, Madison, University of Wisconsin Press, 1974, 142–159, R. Brandt, "Analytic/Dialectic," in *Reading Kant: New Perspectives on Transcendental Arguments and Critical Philosophy*, ed. by E. Schaper, W. Vossenkuhl, Oxford, Oxford University Press, 1989, 179–195). For a discussion of the most recent literature on the Deduction see S. Kemal, *Kant's Aesthetic Theory: An Introduction*, London, Macmillan, 1992, 103–115. Neither the reference to the "supersensible" nor the link to morality can provide an argument for the deduction of the judgments of taste. The former possibility is obviously excluded by the nature of the notion of the supersensible. Kant's contention that in the case of the judgments on the sublime their exposition is at the same time their deduction suffices to exclude his intention of pursuing a deduction by way of the link to morality. The reference to the moral law provides, in this case, a sufficient justification for the claim to universal and necessary validity so that no deduction is further required.

mented by the issue of the "communication" of aesthetic ideas. Herein Kant's strictly epistemological arguments open up to considerations that pertain to the observation of culture and society.

1. The Formal Deduction: How Are Pure A Priori Judgments of Taste Possible? (§§30–38 Remark)

As the traditional topic of a "critique of taste" is transformed by Kant into a "critique of the faculty of judgment" (i.e., in a transcendental inquiry into the faculty of judgment and its a priori principle), the task of the "critique of the faculty of judgment," namely to prove "how . . . judgments of taste [are] possible" (§36, 148, AA 288, 21–22) can be addressed as a specification of the "general problem of transcendental philosophy: how are synthetic judgments a priori possible?" (§36, 149, AA 289, 3–5). As was the case in the previous *Critiques*, such a question receives its definitive answer in what Kant calls the transcendental deduction. The aim of the deduction is to provide the legitimization and justification of the right (*quid juris*) of aesthetic judgments to claim universal and necessary validity (§§30–31). The "exposition" of the Analytic of the Beautiful has argued that pure aesthetic judgments entail a claim for the universal and necessary validity of the feeling of pleasure connected to the representation of an object's form (*quid facti*) and hence must be grounded upon an a priori principle. The deduction has to prove that this pretension is legitimated by a right (*mit Recht*, §38, 151, AA 290, 14). In this way, the deduction integrates the definition-task of the exposition.[3] To be sure, since in the case of aesthetic judgments neither is objective cognition of nature produced nor is action according to the idea of freedom involved, and hence no concepts (neither of understanding nor of reason) are assumed, the aim of the deduction will not consist in justifying the possibility of an a priori reference to objects or possible actions. Thus, the same reason that made the transcendental deduction of the first *Critique* so difficult will now make the deduction of the third *Critique* (relatively) "easy" (§38 Remark, 152, AA 291, 16). The aim of the transcendental deduction is not to justify the "objective validity" but only the subjective validity of our judgments. However, the deduction of aesthetic judgments still involves a certain relation to the object in its form. It regards both the *universal validity* of the "liking or disliking in the *form of the object*" (§30, 131, AA 279, 11–12), which is predicated in those judgments, and the *necessity* of the relation between such feeling and our reflection upon the form of the object. Certainly, this is a relation mediated neither through a concept (of understanding or reason) nor through sensation. However, it is still a relation to the form *of the object* and its figure that takes place in reflection and calls in the a priori principle of formal purposiveness.

---

3. For "*exposition*" as philosophical "*definition*" see KrV B 757 ff./A 729 ff. For the distinction between *quid juris* and *quid facti* in relation to the task of a deduction see KrV B 116 f./A 84 f.

If it is this feature of aesthetic judgments (i.e., the reference to the form of the object in the apprehension of its representation) that prompts the need for a transcendental deduction, then it is clear that such a deduction will be needed only in the case of pure aesthetic judgments on the beautiful, not in the case of pure aesthetic judgments on the sublime in nature. In the latter case, the deduction coincides with the exposition (§30, 133, AA 280, 8–9). For in the pure judgment of the sublime, the object is properly not involved. Therein neither form nor figure nor purposiveness of the object plays a role (rather, the sublime lacks form and figure and is contra-purposive), so that it is only "improperly" that we speak of "*nature's* sublime." The natural object provides only the occasion for bringing a character and a *Denkungsart* to the fore, which are both proper to human nature and intrinsically purposive independently of the object—and almost in spite of it (§30, 132, AA 280, 1–4). As Kant has argued in the Analytic of the Sublime, a logical "subreption" takes place in these judgments, according to which we "substitute a reverence for the object, to the reverence for the idea of the humanity in the subject" (§27, 96, AA 257, 22–23). Herein the reference to practical reason and the will as faculty of purposes sufficiently justifies our judgment's claim to universality and necessity without a deduction being required.

To say that in the case of a pure aesthetic judgment of the beautiful the deduction has to prove the legitimacy of its claim to universal validity means that the deduction has to prove the "universal *validity for the faculty of judgment in general of a singular judgment*, which expresses the subjective purposiveness of an empirical representation of the form of an object" (§31, 134, AA 280, 36–281, 3). The issue of universal validity that the deduction has to address regards precisely the *relation* between the singularity of the judgment of taste and its grounding role for the "faculty of judgment in general." For this very faculty is at stake in the legitimacy of each individual judgment's claim to universal validity. In other words, the deduction has to assess in what sense a judgment of taste is judgment in the proper sense, i.e., in what sense it stands for and is an example of the most peculiar activity of the "faculty of judgment *in general*."

By raising the issue of the deduction in this way, Kant reveals that the aesthetic faculty of judgment is indeed a "strange faculty" (§31, 136, AA 281, 27) that is characterized by a "twofold logical peculiarity" (§31, 135, AA 281, 15–16). (i) The first peculiarity consists in the claim of a "universal validity a priori," which is not logical universality but universal validity of a thoroughly autonomous and singular judgment independent of any concept. (ii) The second peculiarity consists in a "necessity (which must always rest on a priori grounds) independent of any conceptual a priori ground of proof" (§31, 135, AA 281, 16–20). It is precisely because of this twofold logical feature that Kant needs to address the judgment-structure of the pure judgment of taste in its formal character. Accordingly, the deduction will display a formal character as well. *Initially*, it will make abstraction from all content and only "compare the aesthetic form with the form of objective judgments" (§31, 135, AA 281, 24–26). Kant discusses the twofold logical peculiarity of the judgment of taste by means of "examples" (§§32–33) that show the "autonomy" of our aesthetic judgments from all empirical rules and sources, thereby providing yet another argument for the main difference between logical and aesthetic judgments (§35). In this way, Kant also restates the transcendental perspective of his inquiry from which the need for a transcendental deduction immediately follows (a physiological inquiry into the nature of taste, such as Burke's, requires no deduction).

The strangeness of the judgment of taste consists in its being neither properly objective nor properly subjective. For it is formulated both "as if it were objective" (§32, 136, AA 281, 34; also §6, 18, AA 211, 23–24: we predicate beauty "as if it were a property of the object," and §23, 73, AA 245, 25–26) and "as if it were merely subjective" (§33, 140, AA 284, 4). It should be noticed, however, that those as-if formulations are relevant to the deduction (and actually require one) only because they do not entail a subreption such as the one involved in the judgment of the sublime. With regard to the universality proper of the judgment of taste, Kant observes that judgment here is pronounced "as if it were objective." For to state "this flower is beautiful" is to judge it as if beauty were a property of the flower itself (§32, 136, AA 281, 35–282, 5). "A judgment of taste consists precisely in this, that it calls a thing beautiful only by virtue of that characteristic in which it adapts itself to the way in which we apprehend it" (§32, 136, AA 282, 8–10). The notion of formal purposiveness entails the peculiar objective reference proper to the judgment of taste (it is the form of the object that is judged as purposive)—the basis for its universal validity. The as-if clause suggests that this objective reference does not rest on an objective ground. It does not suggest that the objective reference is illusory, and hence it does not express a subreption. The notion of formal purposiveness, which is an a priori notion and does not imply any reference to experience, is the ground of the judgment of taste. This is always a singular judgment, pronounced in a radically autonomous way (§32, 137, AA 282, 30–31). Our judgments of taste are independent of the public's judgment and appreciation, as there are neither a posteriori sources for taste nor models nor empirical rules. Hence, none of the traditional empiricist explanations can replace the work of a transcendental deduction: by failing to explain taste's claim to universal validity, they instead reveal the need for one.

On the other hand, Kant argues that the judgment of taste's necessity is not based upon logical proof. In this respect, it is just "as if it were merely subjective"—just as if it were a judgment based upon private sensation or feeling. If someone does not find a certain building beautiful, nothing will ever persuade her of the contrary. The fact that other people (even people of so-called taste) like it or that alleged criteria and rules are proposed by expert *Kritiker* is not regarded as a valid proof for the contrary. Neither an empirical nor an a priori *Beweisgrund* can be provided in order to compel anyone to make a judgment of taste (i.e., a judgment in which a feeling of pleasure or displeasure is *necessarily* connected to the representation of the object). Kant contends that the taste involved in our judging of beauty is, in this regard, as subjective as the taste of the tongue, which can be only the taste of "*my* tongue," and always voices the singular judgment of *my* tongue for a certain specific dish (§33, 141–142, AA 285, 3–10). In both cases, it is only the subject's "reflection" on her own state and not an external authority, rule, or model *to determine* the judgment of taste (§34, 143, AA 286, 1–2).

According to this twofold logical peculiarity of aesthetic judgment, Kant sets out to determine the character of its principle. The deduction concerns precisely the transcendental "a priori principles of the pure faculty of judgment in *aesthetic* judgments" (§§36, 148, AA 288, 22–23)—just as the transcendental deduction of the first *Critique* regarded the "a priori principles of the pure understanding and its theoretical judgments" (§36, 147, AA 288, 8–9). While the exposition of the four moments of taste provided different definitions of beauty up to the point of formulating in the *Gemeinsinn* the principle of aesthetic judgment (§20), the deduction picks up the task of justifying that same principle (*Gemeinsinn* as *sensus communis*—§40) precisely at that point. Kant's contention is that the principle of aesthetic judgment can only be subjective. For a judgment of taste does not subsume objects under concepts and hence does not need an objective logical principle for its "subsumption." In addition, since a judgment of taste expresses a pleasure that is felt as "immediately" related to the representation of the object (§34, 143, AA 285, 29–31), any conceptual mediation (either theoretical or practical) is necessarily excluded.

However, with the title of §35, Kant suggests that the subjective nature of taste's judgment is a subjectivity of a special kind: "The principle of taste is the subjective principle of the *faculty of judgment in general*." The subjective principle of taste is the paradigmatic principle of *all* judging as such or of judging *in general*. The deduction refers to a character for which taste is judgment in the most proper and original sense: taste reveals the way in which the faculty of judgment *in general* works. In the fourth moment of the Analytic of the Beautiful, Kant argued that the principle of taste cannot be exhibited. Accordingly, all we can count on are individual judgments of taste, which, however, maintain an exemplary link to that principle. This explains why the critique of aesthetic judgment is the key moment of the critique of the faculty of judgment in general; it also explains why aesthetic judgment in its non-pure forms necessarily leads to other ways of judging in which theoretical and practical interests are intermingled.

While the exposition of the second and fourth moments of the Analytic of the Beautiful already referred to the subjective conditions sufficient for *Erkenntnis überhaupt*, the deduction more radically shifts even the conditions for cognition in general back to the employment of *Urteilskraft überhaupt*. No cognition in general is possible without a faculty of judgment in general. In order to present the subjective principle with which the deduction is concerned, Kant analyzes the formal judgment-structure proper to taste. Both cognitive and aesthetic judgments claim "universality and necessity" (§35, 145, AA 286, 34). As opposed to cognitive or practical judgment, however, aesthetic judgment does not subsume under concepts. Since concepts constitute the very "*content*" and the *objective* condition of a judgment (for the concept is that which properly belongs to cognition), we must infer that what makes the judgment-structure of a judgment of taste is exclusively the "*subjective formal* condition of a judgment in general." But the "subjective condition of *all* judgments" (not just of judgments of taste) is the "faculty to judge itself [*das Vermögen zu urteilen selbst*] or the faculty of judgment [*Urteilskraft*]" (§35, 145, AA 287, 5–7). Interestingly, in this passage *subjective* means the same as *transcendental* in the sense of operative. Formally, *all judgments*, whatever their content (concepts of nature, concepts of freedom, mere sensation, or feeling), rest on our ability to judge. In the case of aesthetic judgments, however, since no determinate concept is involved, this subjective and formal reference is the only constitutive reference to which we can appeal in trying to justify a claim to universality and necessity. Lacking the determining ground of the concept as rule for the subsumption that constitutes all judgments, taste requires only a subjective condition to be satisfied, namely the "harmony" of imagination and understanding (§35, 145, AA 287, 10). For it is this harmony that allows our cognitive faculties to work—or better to play—in the subsumption that constitutes judgment even without involving a determinate concept. The harmony of the cognitive faculties is, for Kant, the transcendental condition of *all* judging as such. This consideration sheds light on the way in which Kant essentially transforms the notion of the harmonious play of the faculties that he found in the tradition.

What is it then that is subsumed in the judgment of taste? Kant's important suggestion is that taste is a sort of meta-faculty. A judgment of taste does not subsume intuitions under concepts (cognitive judgment) but subsumes the *faculty* of intuitions (imagination) under the *faculty* of concepts (understanding). Judgment of taste consists in the "subsumption of the imagination itself under the condition for the understanding to proceed in general from intuitions to concepts." This is the only situation in which the "freedom of the imagination" is attuned to and harmonizes with the "lawfulness" of the understanding (§35, 146, AA 287, 13–28). Thus, the judgment of taste properly subsumes under the "feeling" of free play, or harmony, between imagination's freedom and understanding's lawfulness. Better yet, since the subjective principle of the faculty of judgment is at stake here, it subsumes under the "universal validity" of this feeling. Such a feeling now takes the place of the predicate in the judgment (§37, 150, AA 289, 22–23). This feeling makes us judge the object's form as "purposive," or conducive in furthering the free play of our cognitive faculties. Thus, in a judgment of taste, we subsume a "singular empirically given representation" (§37, 150, AA 289, 21) apprehended by the imagination (the subject, S) under the universal validity of a feeling (the predicate, P), so as to consider the form of the object as necessarily and universally purposive, or fit, with regard to our faculties. This is the *Rechtsgrund* that the deduction of the judgment of taste attempts to discover by focusing merely on the logical form of the judgment itself (§35, 146, AA 287, 29–32).

The Deduction of the Judgments of Taste carried out in §38 argues as follows. Its basic assumption is the formal and reflective nature of the pleasure involved in a pure judgment of taste. In such a judgment, the liking for the object is connected to the object's form so that what we perceive as pleasure is nothing but the subjective purposiveness of the object's form for the faculty of judgment, or the universal communicability of the act of self-reflection contained therein. Since this judgment is merely formal and does not depend for its construction (subsumption) on any "matter" (be it sensation or concept), it must rest exclusively on the subjective minimal conditions for the employment of the faculty of "judgment in general" (a certain proportion, balance, or harmony of the cognitive faculties). These conditions can transcendentally be found in "every human being" as conditions required for all "possible cognition in general" (§38, 150–151, AA 290, 1–9; Remark fn. 152, AA 290, 25–35; §39, 155, AA 292, 36–37) as argued already in §9 and §22. Since the pleasure involved in a judgment of taste is not a pleasure of the senses but the reflected consciousness of a subjective purposiveness, we must conclude that we are entitled to assume a priori that "*the harmony of a representation with these conditions of the faculty of judgment*" is valid for everyone else (i.e., the pleasure's universal validity has a legitimate ground).

Lending this proof an indirect formulation, we can say that to deny the universal validity of the aesthetic pleasure expressed by a pure judgment of taste would be to deny the possibility of a justified minimal employment of the faculty of judgment in general (of "all judgments"), and to deny this much would mean to deny that cognition in general is possible for us—which is, according to Kant's premises, a clear contradiction. The result of this *ad absurdum* version of the proof is precisely the "skepticism" that Kant addresses in §21. To skepticism he opposes the "necessary condition of universal communicability" that must ground all logic as well as all cognitive principle (§21, 65, 66, AA 238, 22; 239, 8–10). The basic proportion of the "equilibrium" of our cognitive faculties must be established first in order for their "different proportion" (§21, 66, AA 238, 34) to be possible, from which different forms and modes of cognition arise in relation to different given objects; those different proportions are nothing but variations of that basic equilibrium.[4] To deny the possibility of that original and simplest proportion is to fall into skepticism.

2. Sensus Communis *and Genius, Nature, and Art (§§39–54)*

Since the universal validity of the pleasure in the object that we call beautiful has an a priori ground in the subjective conditions both for judgment in general and cognition in general, the *universal validity* of the aesthetic pleasure immediately translates into its *universal communicability*. *Universal validity* and *universal*

---

4. See G. Deleuze, *La philosophie critique de Kant*, Paris, PUF, 1963 (*Kant's Critical Philosophy: The Doctrine of the Faculties*, trans. H. Tomlinson, B. Habberjan, Minneapolis, University of Minnesota Press, 1996, 23).

communicability are both constitutive conditions of the intersubjective validity of judgments of taste. Thus, the deduction of taste opens up to the intersubjective, public dimension of Kant's analysis of this faculty. *The universal subjective validity of the judgment of taste is its intersubjective communicability and hence its social validity.*[5] The issue of "communicability" leads Kant to the issue of actual human "communication."

Once the formal deduction of the principle of pure aesthetic judgments has been accomplished, Kant's argument turns to the question of how we exercise taste in the context of its social communication and in the different spheres of its application. At this point, both the question regarding the *object* that we judge as beautiful and the issue of *art production* are addressed. By introducing the distinction between "free beauty" and "adherent beauty," the Analytic of the Beautiful has already raised the issue of the application of taste to different interests of life and consequently the issue of its mingling with other types of judgments. The distinction between free beauty and adherent beauty implies the distinction between "pure judgment of taste" and "applied judgment of taste" (§16, 52, AA 231, 23–24). To these topics, Kant dedicates the last part of the Deduction.

Drawing from the result of the formal deduction, Kant analyzes the question regarding the kind of pleasure that can be universally communicated. Thereby he presents a typology of forms of pleasure that accompany the different faculties of the mind in their respective activity. This typology supports Kant's further discussion of the difference between the beautiful in nature and art (§§41–42) and accordingly justifies Kant's differentiations within the notion of art (§§43–45).

(i) The pleasure that arises from mere sensation is a passive and merely empirical "pleasure of enjoyment" (§39, 153, AA 292, 2) that certainly cannot be communicated universally since its validity is only private. (ii) In the practical sphere, the pleasure that arises from spontaneous action in accordance with the idea of freedom is indeed universally valid and universally communicable. However, this pleasure implies determinate concepts of reason and is related to a kind of purposiveness that is not "free" (in the aesthetic sense) but "lawful" (§39, 154, AA 292, 7). (iii) The pleasure that we experience in judging the sublime in nature has affinity with the moral pleasure as it refers to our moral destination, is mediated by reason, and has a moral foundation. Accordingly, its claim to universal validity is justified only by the moral law and has no independence of its own. (iv) Only the pleasure in the beautiful is a pleasure based upon mere reflection and hence independent of all other cognitive faculties. This is the pleasure in the apprehension of an object whose form is judged as purposive for our cognitive powers. In developing the implications of the act of reflection involved in our judgments of taste for human communication, Kant identifies the subjective a pri-

5. For this aspect, Kant's theory is central to H. Arendt's interpretation; see her *Lectures in Kant's Political Philosophy*, ed. by R. Beiner, Chicago, University of Chicago Press, 1982.

ori principle of taste in a *sensus communis* (§40). Thereby the *Critique of Judgment* extends the realm of pure sensibility that allows for transcendental foundation in a fundamental way, establishing a new meaning for Kant's transcendental aesthetics.

If we understand by "sense" (*Sinn*) the effect ("feeling of pleasure") that "mere *reflection* has over our *Gemüt*," then we can easily see how taste deserves the title of *sensus communis* (§40, 160, AA 295, 24–25). More precisely, Kant's contention is that taste is "a kind of" *sensus communis* (§40, title). This is for Kant the "idea of a sense that is shared [*gemeinschaftlicher Sinn*], i.e., a faculty to judge that in reflecting takes account (a priori) . . . of everyone else's way of representing, in order, as it were, to compare our own judgment with the whole of human reason" (§40, 157, AA 293, 30–34). The *sensus communis* is a sense (and a transcendental condition for sense) that we all have in common.

The act of reflection implied in all aesthetic judgments contains a comparison between our single judgment and the whole of human reason or, as Kant has argued in the formal deduction, with the faculty of judgment in general. Universal communicability is rooted in this act of comparison and reflection. In reflection, we take into account the "possible" judgment of everyone else; we make abstraction from all material conditions that pertain only to our private self; and we consider exclusively the formal character of our representation. Thus, in reflecting (i.e., in pronouncing a judgment of taste), we assume a "universal standpoint" (§40, 159, AA 295, 12).[6] As Kant claimed in the fourth moment of the Analytic of the Beautiful (§18), our singular judgment of taste is an "example" of a rule that, as such, cannot be exhibited. This rule was already stated in the principle of the *Gemeinsinn* (§20). Now what it means for each individual judgment of taste to express the *principle* of the *sensus communis*—or to provide an example thereof—becomes clear. It is in reference to this "sense" and by means of its "universal voice" that all singular judgments gain the universal communicability proper to a universal and public standpoint. "Taste is the capacity to judge a priori the communicability of the feelings that are connected with a given representation (without mediation by a concept)" (§40, 161, AA 296, 5–7). Accordingly, taste is the fundamental intersubjective faculty that grounds transcendentally human communication.

Kant contends that under *sensus communis* we should not understand what the European culture of the eighteenth century generally means by "sound (not yet cultivated) human understanding," or common sense—which, in the German language, carries with it the connotation of "vulgar" (§40, 156–157, AA 293, 20–29).[7] As "elucidation" of the new meaning proposed for the *sensus communis*,

---

6. Compare with the "universal voice" of §8.

7. For a brief history of the term *sensus communis,* see H. G. Gadamer, *Wahrheit und Methode*, Tübingen, Mohr, 1972[3] (*Truth and Method*, New York, Continuum, 1975), 39 ff.; a detailed historical account can be found in E. De Angelis, "Il buon senso. Per una storia del problema da Las Casas a Locke," in *Giornale Critico della Filosofia Italiana*, 51 (1972), 375–456. See also F. Lyotard, "Sensus communis," in *Cahiers du College International de Philosophie*, 3 (1987), 67–87.

Kant presents three subjective maxims that are not an integral part of the "critique of taste" (§40, 158, AA 294, 15) but serve to clarify the sense in which the aesthetic faculty of judgment works as a meta-faculty with regard to the exercise of all our cognitive powers. They are the maxims "1. To think for oneself; 2. to think from the standpoint of everyone else; and 3. to always think consistently" (§40, 158, AA 294, 16–18). These maxims point to the way in which we should shape a new *Denkungsart* that is free from prejudice, reaches out broadly to our fellow human beings, and is always consistent with itself. These maxims do not concern any particular faculty in its specific pursuit of cognition. They concern, instead, the very thought-way with which we must learn how to "put those cognitive faculties to a purposive use" (§40, 159, AA 295, 7). Thereby Kant presents the aesthetic faculty of judgment as the meta-faculty that teaches us, through its maxims, how to exercise all our cognitive powers in a most conducive and appropriate way.

In this connection, Kant reproposes an issue raised for the very first time at the end of the Analytic of the Beautiful and hinted at successively in the Analytic of the Sublime. In §22, Kant asked whether "taste is an original and natural faculty or only the idea of a faculty yet to be acquired and artificial" (§22, 68, AA 240, 4–6). A first answer to the question is provided by Kant's view of taste as meta-faculty of reflection. Taste is a faculty that, instead of being legislative over a domain of objects, aims at developing a new *Denkungsart* that, in turn, influences the employment of all other faculties. In this endeavor, the faculty of judgment coordinates and organizes all other powers of the mind.

The intersubjective perspective opened by the idea of taste as a kind of *sensus communis* cannot but reveal the "interest" that all our cognitive faculties take in the exercise of this peculiar "sense." The first moment of the Analytic of the Beautiful has shown the disinterested nature of pure aesthetic judgments. At this point, Kant stresses again that no interest can serve as the *Bestimmungsgrund* of a judgment of taste (§41, 161, AA 296, 17) even though taste may indeed be producing an interest or be linked to an interest either "directly" or "indirectly." This is not surprising, considering that the *sensus communis* is the ground of the social communicability of our feelings and that such a communicability is likely to imply an interest (§40, 161, AA 296, 8–13). Interest always involves the pleasure in the existence of the object. Even though no interest can be the ground of a pure judgment of taste, an interest can indeed be grounded in taste. More precisely, when taste is connected with an empirical inclination or desire (hence, with the lower faculty of desire), we have an *empirical interest* in beauty (§41); when on the contrary taste is connected with a pure practical determination of the will (hence, with the higher faculty of desire), we have an *intellectual interest* in beauty (§42). To take an interest in beauty, as opposed to pronouncing a pure judgment of taste, means to like the object's *existence*, not just its *form*. Kant claims that the beautiful is of empirical interest only in society. In this respect, taste can be regarded as a means to further human sociability (§41, 162, AA 296, 33–35).

The consideration of intellectual interest in beauty leads Kant to link aesthetic judgment to the moral sphere, taste to moral feeling. Thereby, he addresses both the issue of the asymmetry in the relation between nature and freedom and the problem of the mediating function of the faculty of judgment. These issues were raised for the first time in §IX of the introduction, and played an important role in the Analytic of the Sublime. The notions of "genius" and "spirit" by means of which Kant describes the creative function of the imagination in art will display the highest form of mediation between nature and freedom, the sensible world and the supersensible.

While up until now the analysis of our pleasure in the beautiful could make abstraction of any reference either to nature or art, at this point the aforementioned issues lead Kant to the distinction between nature and art, which occupies the rest of the Deduction. Kant's claim is that an "immediate interest"[8] for nature's beauty is always a mark or sign of a good moral disposition (§42, 16, AA 298, 33–35), or of a *schöne Seele* (§42, 168, AA 300, 6). As Kant has argued in the introduction, reason has an interest in the objective practical reality of its ideas. Therefore, it is our moral feeling that takes an "immediate interest" in beauty. Yet if the moral law is to be realized in the world of nature, nature must be so constituted as to allow for the realization of freedom. An idea of purposiveness underlies this assumption. Nature must manifest in itself at least a "trace or give a hint" that it presents a ground for our assumption of a harmony between nature's products and our disinterested aesthetic feeling of pleasure in its forms (§42, 169, AA 300, 23–29). The notion of purposiveness, or harmony between nature's forms and our faculties, displays an "analogy" (§42, 170, AA 301, 10), or "kinship" (§42, 169, 170, AA 300, 33; 301, 3–4), between reason's moral interest in the realization of freedom in the world of nature and the immediate interest that we take in the beauty and existence of nature's forms.

By acknowledging that an analogy between moral and aesthetic feeling plays an important role in aesthetic judgment, we recognize in these feelings our attempt to interpret nature's way of speaking to us through the beauty of its forms. Or in the language of the introduction, we view them as ways of making sense of the manifold of nature's empirical forms as constituting a coherent and harmonious system. Kant warns, however, that this connection holds true only of nature's beauty, not of art. For nature alone displays purposiveness *without any purpose*. Art, on the contrary, is always informed by a purpose in its production. It either imitates nature or intentionally aims at pleasing us or at being liked by us, whereby the possibility of an immediate interest in it yields to an indirect interest mediated precisely by that aim. Kant maintains that art never interests us for itself but only for its purpose (§42, 171, AA 301, 26–302, 4).[9] His account of art, art

---

8. *Immediate* here means that the interest is not mediated by a purpose of communication.

9. See P. Guyer, "Interest, Nature, and Art: A Problem in Kant's Aesthetics," in *Review of Metaphysics*, 31 (1977/78), 580–603.

production, and the discussion of the genius's activity is pervaded by a tension between the claim that art always implies a rule or an aim and responds to a kind of lawfulness, and the claim that imagination, both in the appreciation of art (in the judgment of taste) and in the creation of art, is free of any determinate concept, rule, model, and aim.[10]

Kant uses the distinction between the two forms of activity of "operating," or "acting" (*Tun*, *facere*), on the one hand, and "doing" (*Handeln, Wirken*, *agere*), on the other, to draw the distinction between art and nature.[11] In general, art indicates the purposive activity that has its source in the human will and is distinguished both from "science" since it does not imply theoretical cognition, and from craft since it enjoys the freedom of play as opposed to the constraint of work (§§43, 51). Kant argues that since art is always related to the realization of a determinate purpose (§45, 180, AA 306, 27; §48, 188, AA 311, 22–23), it sets a limitation to beauty, which in nature (and in nature alone) can be related instead to the notion of purposiveness without purpose. As we have seen in the third moment of the Analytic of the Beautiful, this notion qualifies pure judgments of taste. Kant's idea of the arts and their classification is based upon the transcendental framework developed in the Analytic and on the typology of pleasure that follows from it (§§44, 39).

Thus, "mechanical art" is distinguished from "aesthetic art," and this, in turn, is further divided into "agreeable art," whose purpose is merely "enjoyment," and "fine art" (*schöne Kunst*) (§44, 177–178, AA 305, 19–26). "Fine art is a way of representing that is purposive on its own and that furthers, even without a purpose, the culture of our *Gemütskräfte* to social communication" (§44, 179, AA 306, 3–5). Fine art is, for Kant, a vehicle of human social communication; it is that through which the universal communicability of our aesthetic pleasure is put in a social, cultural, and historical context. The "standard" of fine art is the reflective faculty of judgment since the pleasure that is thereby communicated is not pleasure of enjoyment but pleasure of reflection (§44, 179, AA 306, 8–10). In a formulation that draws important implications from the definitions of beauty provided in the Analytic, Kant claims that "*beautiful is what we like in merely judging it,*" be it in nature or in art (§45, 180, AA 306, 25–26). From this general statement it follows that the product of art must look "as if it were a product of nature" even though we must be conscious that it is art and not nature (§45, 179, AA 306, 14–17). At stake is the "feeling of freedom in the play of our cognitive faculties" that grounds the feeling that we communicate in our judgments of taste (§45, 179, AA 306, 17–18). This is freedom from concepts, interests, rules, and models, but is also freedom from any particular aim and purpose. Since art, as

10. P. Guyer in "Genius and the Canon of Art: A Second Dialectic of Aesthetic Judgment" (in *Kant and the Experience of Freedom: Essays in Aesthetics and Morality*, Cambridge, Cambridge University Press, 1993, 275–303) sees in this tension a sort of pre-Hegelian "dialectic" within Kant's theory.

11. See also introduction §§I–II.

opposed to nature, always implies a determinate aim in its production, it is this aim that art needs to conceal in trying to look like nature, so that the pleasure in the contemplation of art's products can be the free pleasure of simply judging (i.e., reflecting upon its forms), undisturbed by the intervention of sensation, concepts, aims, and interests. Correspondingly, since art must always be produced according to rules (although our judging of it cannot be deduced or inferred from any rule as its *Bestimmungsgrund*) (§46, 181, AA 307, 22–27), the artist must also conceal the rules that guided the process of artistic production. Once again, the process of art-making must be carried out with the same freedom (i.e., lack of purposes and lack of rules) with which nature produces her forms.

On the other hand, however, the beauty of nature can be judged from two different perspectives. This is true, in particular, in the case of living beings. Herein we can either judge nature as if it were art, in which case we should make abstraction from the living being's objective purpose and pronounce a *pure* aesthetic judgment, or we can judge nature in its "being really art (although a superhuman art)" and formulate a nonpure aesthetic judgment based upon a teleological judgment (§48, 189, AA 311, 35–36). Thereby, Kant expresses in yet another way the independence of aesthetic judgment from the constitution of its object. Art must look like nature, but nature must also look like art if its beauty is to be judged by a pure judgment of taste. What shall be counted as nature or art is ultimately not prescribed by the object itself but by our way of relating to it. Nature or art, we could suggest, are different ways of thinking or judging (or classifying) objects according to whether beauty is referred directly to the form of a "thing," or to the "representation of a thing" (§48, 188, AA 311, 14–15).

The analogical relation between nature and art follows from Kant's view of the transcendental structure of taste and leads to the fortunate notion of "genius."[12] In this way, Kant turns from the problem of the character of our pleasure in the beautiful to the problem of the production of beautiful works; from the problem of "communicability" of aesthetic feelings to the problem of "communication" of aesthetic ideas. In Kant's theory, genius represents the creative side of the *Gemeinsinn,* or *sensus communis,* as the principle, or "ideal norm," that grounds our judgments of taste. The characters of the genius follow from the transcendental structure of the pure judgment of taste (§§1–22). The genius expresses the active side of the same transcendental structure that underlies taste while taking up the crucial reference to reason and the supersensible that is proper to the judgment of the sublime. In the fourth moment of the Analytic of the Beautiful, Kant introduced the idea of the *Gemeinsinn* as the final "unification" of all

12. For the development of this notion in Kant's thought see G. Tonelli, "Kant's Early Theory of Genius (1770–1779)," in *Journal of the History of Philosophy*, 4 (1966), 109–131, 209–224; O. Schlapp, *Kants Lehre vom Genie und die Entstehung der Kritik der Urteilskraft*, Göttingen, Vandenhoeck & Rupprecht, 1901. For the term *genius,* see the article by J. Ritter, in *Historisches Wörterbuch der Philosophie*, vol. 3, ed. by J. Ritter, K. F. Gründer, Basel, Schönig, 1974, 279–310.

the elements in which taste had been analytically resolved throughout the four moments (§22, 68, AA 240, 14, 15). The *Gemeinsinn* is the rule of which every singular and correct (i.e., pure) judgment of taste is an example. Kant contended that, in this case, the rule itself cannot be exhibited. Consequently, as we have argued above, the principle of judgment cannot be presented as the topic of an Analytic of Principles (as was the case instead with the employment of the categories in the cognitive judgments of the first *Critique*). I can provide examples of the *Gemeinsinn*'s judgment in my own individual aesthetic judgment (if correctly formulated). However, I cannot exhibit the *Gemeinsinn*'s judgment itself since I will never be able to make abstraction from the individual instances in which the rule is embodied. Kant's notion of genius is a direct implication of this idea of *sensus communis*. The lack of a normative principle for taste that could be exhibited in a concept implies that the production of beautiful works cannot follow from any prescriptive rule but must be entrusted instead to the "talent" of the "genius" considered as a *natural* "productive faculty." We have seen that since the first *Critique* Kant has been thinking of the reflective faculty of judgment as a natural talent that can neither rest upon rules nor be taught but can only be strengthened through "examples."[13] The natural talent expressed by the genius as "productive faculty" mirrors exactly the same thought (§46, 181, AA 307, 11–15). As in the case of the *Gemeinsinn*, genius is the "unification" of the faculties of the *Gemüt*, namely imagination, understanding, and reason, which in it are brought to a determinate (ideal) balance (§49, 198, AA 316, 26–27; §50, 203, fn. AA 320, 28–29). The same idea of a free play of imagination and understanding as subjective condition for cognition in general underlies both taste's judging and the genius's creative activity (§49). In addition, however, the activity of the genius implies a fundamental reference to reason and to its ideas, whereby the mediation toward the supersensible is accomplished.

Kant's theory of the genius occupies §§46–50 of the Deduction. A first definition of the genius is provided in relation to the issue of what beauty is in art or what counts as fine art: the genius is the faculty through which nature gives the rule to art so that only the genius's creation counts as fine art (§46). A second definition follows once the relation between genius and taste has been explored (§48). Genius is the "exemplary originality of a subject's natural endowment in the free use of his cognitive faculties" (§49, 200, AA 318, 6–8). Finally, §50 presents the "connection" of taste with genius in the products of fine art (§50, title). Let us now turn to the development of Kant's argument in the two definitions of the genius.

Through the faculty of the genius, nature gives rules to art. In its "originality," the genius does not follow any determinate rule that could in turn be exhibited,[14] but gives to itself the rule. In addition, the "exemplarity" of its products provides

---

13. KrV B 172 ff./A 133 ff.

14. All imitation is excluded from the activity of the genius as well as the possibility of teaching and learning the work of the genius (§47, 183, AA 308, 20–23).

a model for inspiration that can be assumed as rule for further art making (§46, 182, AA 308, 1–5). The notion of "exemplarity" is here crucial (§46, 182, AA 308, 3). As individual judgments of taste are *examples* of the ideal norm of the *Gemeinsinn*, so the creations of the genius are *examples* of this natural talent or faculty, and the genius is an example for her followers and for the school that is formed in the genius's aftermath (§49, 200, AA 318, 17–18). In all these cases, not following any rule, this exemplarity provides itself the rule for judging. The "heautonomy" proper to the judgment of taste, taken in its productive aspect, is the free creativity of the genius. In addition, the genius's activity is independent of any cognitive or practical skill, as no knowledge (neither concept nor purpose) is involved (consequently the genius cannot teach her art, §47, 183, AA 308, 20–23). Through the genius, nature prescribes rules to art as fine art. This elicits Kant's conclusion that fine art, or beauty in art, is possible only as art produced by the genius (§46, title, 181, AA 307, 20–21). This connection sheds light on the character of the "rule" provided by the genius (as was the case for the rule contained in the principle of the *Gemeinsinn*). Such a rule is not expressed by a determinate concept but is abstracted from the genius's activity and products. It serves as a model not to be copied (*Nachmachung*) but to be imitated (*Nachahmung*) by taste (§47, 185, AA 309, 28–34). As opposed to genius, "taste" is not a "productive faculty" but only a "faculty of judgment" that when engaged in the production of works can go only as far as "useful and mechanical art," or as works whose determinate rules must be learned and precisely complied with (§48, 191, AA 313, 3–7). The work of the genius, on the contrary, serves as inspiration to other geniuses to be followed in the relation of "succession." *Nachfolge* describes the influence that a work of art exercises on other original producers of art. Genius's succession differs both from the *Nachmachung* and *Nachahmung* proper of taste as it preserves the genius's freedom and originality and yet guarantees the lineage of an historical continuity (§49, 200, AA 318, 12).

As I suggested, Kant's presentation of the different faculties of the *Gemüt* involved in the genius's productive activity displays the other, active, side of the transcendental structure of the judgment of taste. In addition, it draws on the relation to reason that we found in the structure of the sublime. I already have mentioned the aspect of unification of the cognitive faculties that characterizes both the *Gemeinsinn* and the *genius*. In the genius, however, the faculties involved are not only imagination and understanding but also reason. Kant characterizes the creative activity of the genius by means of three crucial terms that will be incredibly successful in the post-Kantian discussion, namely the notions of *Geist* (spirit), "aesthetic ideas," and aesthetic "productive imagination" (§49). These notions describe the interplay of imagination, understanding, and reason in the faculty of the genius. In cognitive judgments, the imagination is constrained by the understanding's concepts under which the subsumption takes place in view of a determinate cognition. In reflective judgments of taste, the imagination is set free in the relation of free play with the understanding since no determinate concept is provided for subsumption and the empirical laws of association exercise no constraint on it. In judging the sublime, imagination becomes reason's "instrument" (General Remark on the First Division of the Analytic, 117, AA 269, 4, 26), whereby it gains for the first time the active role of giving a supersensible meaning to the sensible content provided by nature. Finally, in the activity of the genius, the imagination is not only free (in relation to the understanding) but also productive (in relation to reason): the genius creates another nature endowed with a supersensible meaning.

In an "aesthetic sense," *Geist* is defined as the "animating principle in the *Gemüt*" (§49, 192, AA 313, 30–31). Such a *Belebung* with which the cognitive faculties are animated, enlivened, and quickened is effected through spirit's "presentation of aesthetic ideas." Spirit, as the faculty of presentation of aesthetic ideas, is the imagination taken, this time, as a free and "*productive* cognitive faculty" (§49, 192, AA 314, 9–10).[15] An "aesthetic idea" is a representation of the imagination to which no determinate concept is adequate. Aesthetic ideas constitute the counterpart of reason's own ideas as concepts to which no intuition can ever be adequate. While reason provides ideas that cannot be schematized with intuitions in order to yield knowledge, productive imagination offers intuitions that do not schematize determinate concepts and yield no knowledge. The creation of productive imagination shares with reason's ideas a *Streben* beyond the limits of experience (§49, 191, AA 314, 21–22). The imagination gives sensible body and the appearance of "objective reality" to reason's ideas. The genius's creations are sensible examples of supersensible ideas, whereby the sensible is mediated with the supersensible. Out of the material provided by "real nature," productive imagination creates another nature as it confers a new spirit to the material body of sensible nature (§49, 192–193, AA 314, 1–19). The imagination does not simply express a supersensible meaning for a sensible content as it does in the case of the sublime; in the activity of the genius, imagination creates a new supersensible or ideal nature.

An analogy regulates the relation between these two natures. The world of spirit's creation allows for an experience of freedom that is not practical but aesthetic freedom. The only access to this freedom is *feeling*. It is the freedom from the empirical laws of association as well as from the constraints of the understanding's concepts that compels us to bring an intuition to a determinate conceptual expression. In the case of the genius's activity, on the contrary, aesthetic ideas (or aesthetic "attributes") call to mind a manifold of meanings that cannot be contained in any determinate expression and hence cannot be comprehended by the understanding in a conceptual grasp. In art, imagination produces representations that concentrate in themselves an infinite number of meanings so that no determinate expression can be found for them in the conceptual language. Conceptual language lacks words or determinate expressions that could translate the richness of thinking stimulated by the imagination's aesthetic attributes. These representations dynamically bring our *Gemüt* to life (*beleben*) by opening up for

---

15. See the genius as "*productive* faculty" in §46, 181, AA 307, 12.

it "an immense realm of kindred representations." They communicate an individual feeling by giving to it the most adequate and universal expression (§49, 195, AA 315, 23–24). The imagination provides the understanding with a "wealth of undeveloped material." As the understanding does not refer to this material with an objective cognitive aim, it is enlivened by it. Thereby it relates "indirectly" to the subjective conditions of cognition in general (i.e., to the necessary formal condition for all meaning and communication) (§49, 198, AA 317, 4–6).

In this entire process of the genius's creation, the cognitive faculties display the "proportion and accordance" that we know as free play of imagination and understanding (§49, 200, AA 318, 2). As productive faculty, the imagination is free from the control of the understanding—as the imagination was free from the understanding's concepts in a pure judgment of taste. In both cases, however, understanding is still present and active. Even in the act of transcending the limits of experience by which the productive imagination borders the activity of reason, the balance, or proportion, with the understanding must be maintained. For this balance is the condition of all *sense and meaning* from which not even the genius is allowed to depart.[16] Kant warns that the genius's originality is not the originality of nonsense but the originality of "exemplarity"—the same structure of exemplarity that underlies taste and communicability (§46, 182, AA 308, 2; §50, 202–203, AA 319, 24–26). Genius is the faculty of "communication" of aesthetic ideas. In order for communication (and communicability) to be possible, the subjective condition of sense must be fulfilled. The genius is relation of imagination and reason only because it is, in the first place, free play of imagination and understanding (i.e., the balance of imagination in its freedom with understanding in its lawfulness). This balance defines taste as well as the meaningfulness of our experience. While the genius's imagination communicates spirit to the work of art, the condition of its beauty is the respect for the lawfulness of the understanding (i.e., the respect for sense and communicability) (§50, 202–203, AA 319, 18–26). Thus, both taste and judgment represent for Kant the necessary "discipline," or education, to which even the freedom of the genius must be subjected if meaningfulness is to be preserved as a necessary ingredient of art. Taste "severely clips the wings" of the genius "and makes it civilized and polished" (§50, 203, AA 319, 28–30). Thus, the unification of the faculties that are responsible for the creation of fine art, namely "imagination, understanding, spirit, and taste" can take place only "*by means*" of "taste" (§50, 203, fn., AA 320, 6–7, 28–29).

Eventually, the theory of the genius allows Kant to return to the definition of beauty, which is now presented in a general form, valid both for nature and for art as "expression of aesthetic ideas" (§51, 204, AA 320, 10–11). In beauty, aesthetic ideas are expressed and communicated. The difference between nature and art consists only in the reference, in the case of art, to an *intentional* production of repre-

16. And, Kant would say, the genius *in particular* should not depart from this condition. For the genius more than anyone else runs the risk of *Unsinn*. On this point, the later Romantics will sensibly depart from Kant.

sentations that requires consciousness of what the object ought to be. In both cases, however, the dynamic relation between aesthetic ideas and the manifold, always inadequate concepts that they call to mind holds true in the same way. At the end of the Deduction, the distinction between natural beauty and art is brought back to a common transcendental structure.

The "analogy" with the different human ways of expressing and communication through language provides Kant with the key to a partition or classification of fine arts.[17] Expression consists in "words, gestures, and tone." Accordingly, communication takes place when these three modes of expression are combined to convey the unity of thought, intuition, and sensation. Kant divides the arts into (i) "art of speech" (oratory and poetry), (ii) "visual art" (i.e., the "arts of expressing ideas in sensible intuition": plastic art and painting), and (iii) "the art of play of sensations" (which is a play that must be universally communicable in music and in the art of color). These different forms of expression can also be found combined in one and the same art work (§52). Kant's assessment of the different arts is guided by the notion of the free play of imagination and understanding, whereby the freedom from any determinate rule or model both in judging and in creating fine art, as well as the notion of "play," are drawn to the center as constitutive of all fine arts (§51, 205–306, AA 320, 27–321, 35). Further criteria of Kant's assessment are the capacity of the different arts to animate, expand, and move our mental powers, the role that sensation and sensible stimulation play in them, and the "culture" that they provide for the mind (§53, 220, AA 329, 25–26).[18] Essential to the work of all fine arts (both in production and contemplation) is the purposive character of the form. It is only the relation to the form (as opposed to the matter of sensation) that confers to aesthetic pleasure a cultural value and attunes the spirit to ideas (§52, 214, AA 326, 1–3). The connection of fine arts to moral ideas becomes the touchstone for the liking that accompanies these ideas.

---

17. The idea of a division of the arts according to an analogy between art and the modes of human linguistic expression had already been formulated by Ch. Batteaux, *Les beaux arts réduits à un même principe*, Paris, Durand, 1746, 1747^2 chapter 1, section 3. For a general consideration of the tradition that frames Kant's considerations see P. O. Kristeller, "The Modern System of the Arts," in *Renaissance Thought and the Arts*, Princeton, Princeton University Press, 1990, 163–227, who analyses the history of the five arts (painting, sculpture, architecture, music, and poetry) from antiquity up to Kant and provides an excellent bibliography.

18. Kant's consideration of music follows from the combination of these criteria. Music is high in Kant's evaluation according to its capacity of moving the mind, and yet since it concerns itself with the materiality of sensations, is regarded as a matter more of enjoyment than of culture. Hence, it receives a lower placement in Kant's assessment of the arts.

Chapter 11

The Dialectic of the Aesthetic Faculty of Judgment (§§55–60): The Analogic Logic of the Faculty of Judgment

The second division of the Critique of the Aesthetic Faculty of Judgment is dedicated to the Dialectic of the Aesthetic Faculty of Judgment. With the solution of the antinomy of taste, Kant gains reference to the idea of the supersensible and discloses the mediating function of the faculty of judgment as the faculty placed between understanding and reason, nature and freedom. While the introduction (§IV) already made clear that the faculty of judgment is the heuristic faculty through which we engage in scientific research, §59 reveals that "analogy" is the method of judgment's search for meaning. The analogic function of reflection allows Kant to establish a symbolic relation between beauty and the morally good. Thereby, Kant gives an aesthetic solution to the issue of the realization of freedom's effects in the sensible world. Aesthetic experience provides us with an analogical experience of moral freedom. The Critique of the Aesthetic Faculty of Judgment ends with a *Methodenlehre* in which Kant draws the conclusion that while there is no method of a critique of taste, a "propaedeutic" to taste can be offered by the development of moral ideas.

1. The Dialectic and Its Solution (§§55–58)

In this division of the first part of the *Critique of Judgment*, Kant develops a parallel with the dialectics of both pure theoretical reason and practical reason. The parallel is not merely extrinsic. There are three types of antinomies that involve the three higher cognitive faculties that display a priori principles, namely understanding, faculty of judgment, and reason (§57, Remark II, 243, AA 345, 3–6). In Kant's *Critiques*, the dialectic always describes the situation in which reason naturally gets caught when it passes judgment on those principles. The very nature of reason's activity, which claims the unconditioned for every given conditioned, and reason's ideas, to which no sensible content can ever be adequate and hence no objective reality can be ascribed, are responsible for this dialectic. A dialectic arises when each of our cognitive faculties, following reason's demand for the unconditioned, attempts to determine its object *unconditionally* as thing in itself rather than as appearance under its respective principles (§57, Remark II, 244, AA 345, 12–21). Thus, Kant argues, in order for a dialectic to take place in the case of the faculty of judgment we must assume that this faculty engages in "reasoning" or is itself *vernünftelnd* (§55, 231, AA 337, 5–6).[1] An antinomy in the use of the faculty of judgment will then arise as this faculty confronts reason's demand for the unconditioned (§57, Remark II, 244, AA 345, 27–28). In the third *Critique*, the dialectic ensues from the already explored connection between faculty of judgment and reason and, more precisely, once again, from the fact that the faculty of judgment confuses appearances with things in themselves. As in the other antinomies, it becomes possible to think of the supersensible substrate of the sensible world only when the sensible is recognized as mere appearance. This argument entails Kant's solution of the antinomy of taste.

Kant's presentation of the antinomy and its solution follow the methodological model developed for the first time in the dialectic of speculative reason. The result is a new assessment of the subjective principle of the faculty of judgment as well as of the role of this faculty within the system of the *Gemüt*'s powers. At the end of the Critique of the Aesthetic Faculty of Judgment, *Urteilskraft* gains an explicit relation to the supersensible. Its function, announced in the introduction (§IX), of being the faculty that effects the mediation between the sensible and the supersensible, nature and freedom, now comes to the fore. The solution of the antinomy shows that judgment mediates between the world of appearances, which presents us with individual sensible instances of our judgments, and reason's supersensible, which allows us to discover beauty and purposiveness (i.e., the supersensible meaning of those sensible instances). To be sure, the mediation does not concern the *object* of the judgment of taste but the very *transcendental structure* of the faculty of judgment itself. Kant suggests that antinomies always "compel us against our will to look beyond the sensible to the supersensible as the point of unification of all our a priori powers" (§57, 239, AA 341, 30–31). As we know from the introduction, the reflective faculty of judgment is the only faculty that can *search* for such a "point of unification" or *Vereinigungspunkt* (which can never be given).

The Dialectic revisits both the issue of the *Bestimmungsgrund* of the judgment of taste that was the key question of the Analytic, and the issue of the legitimacy proper to the subjective principle of taste addressed by the Deduction. These issues are redefined now with regard to judgment's relation to reason, to the idea of the supersensible, and to the relation between beauty and morality. The notion of *Zweckmäßigkeit* is discussed in a connection close to the more general formulations of the introduction (§§IV–V). Kant qualifies the idea of nature's subjective purposiveness for our faculty of judgment as the idea of the supersensible ground of nature and "humanity" (§57, 237, AA 340, 20–22), while he gives to the subjective principle of taste the strong connotation of being "the indeterminate idea of the supersensible in us." He announces this principle to be the "unique key for solving the mystery" of the faculty of taste, which is "concealed from us even as to its sources" (§57, 238, AA 341, 7–10).

1. See KrV B 368/A 311.

Kant maintains that in order to be subject to a dialectic, the judgments of a given faculty must raise claim to a priori universality and necessity. This implies that there is no dialectic for the aesthetic judgments based upon the agreeable, which have merely private and empirical validity. In addition, Kant contends that in a transcendental critique of taste, the dialectic properly concerns the "*critique* of taste" in relation to its principles (§55, 232, AA 337, 14–15). For, the possibility of formulating an antinomy of the principles of taste casts doubts on the very possibility of this faculty and its own lawfulness, and hence on the very possibility of a transcendental critique that assumes taste as an independent faculty resting on a priori principles of its own.

The way to conceive the twofold "peculiarity" of taste, namely the logically peculiar universal validity and necessity that Kant discusses first in the Analytic (second and fourth moments) and then in the Deduction (§§31–33), provides the ground for the formulation of the thesis and antithesis of the dialectic. The antinomy allows for a solution (in the transcendental sense) if and only if one can show that the two propositions that constitute the thesis and the antithesis respectively do not contradict each other but are both true. The solution consists in exposing the illusory character of an opposition that follows from attributing contrary predicates to one and the same concept that ought to be taken, instead, as having two quite different senses. Kant claims, however, that in our case, a solution is possible only if the antinomy is construed on the notion of taste as being a "merely reflective aesthetic faculty of judgment" (§57, 238, AA 341, 13–14). Were taste, on the contrary, to be considered with reference either to the empirical notion of the agreeable or to the concept of perfection—whereby the idea of taste as an independent reflective faculty of judgment would be lost—then both propositions of the antinomy would be utterly false. The falsity of both thesis and antithesis would then reveal that the concept on which their formulation is based (i.e., the very notion of taste) is indeed a contradictory concept. In this sense, the possibility of instituting and solving a dialectic of aesthetic judgment confirms Kant's idea of a critique of taste and its a priori principle. The solution of the antinomy proposes the transcendental perspective as the radical alternative to both the empiricist and the rationalist definitions of taste, which appear respectively as the thesis and the antithesis of the antinomy (§58).

The two propositions of the antinomy of taste arise from two commonplaces that concern both the *Bestimmungsgrund* of the judgment and its *right* to appeal to universal validity. (i) "Everyone has his own taste" (§56, 232, AA 338, 4–5) alludes to the fact that, since the determining principle of taste is merely subjective, the necessity of everyone's assent cannot be justified. (ii) "There is no disputing about taste" (§56, 233, AA 338, 10–11) grants taste the right to universal validity (i.e., the possibility for its determining principle of being objective), and yet denies that the principle can ever be expressed through concepts or supported by argumentative proof (for a dispute, as opposed to a mere quarrel, presupposes the possibility of reaching an agreement based upon objective proof). Kant suggests that between these two commonplaces, a tacitly assumed third proposition concedes that one can always quarrel, but not dispute, about taste. This proposition, which contains a claim concerning the social validity of taste, is obviously opposed to the first.

On this basis, Kant formulates the antinomy of taste. (i) The thesis, which represents the empiricist standpoint, states that "a judgment of taste is not based on concepts," for otherwise one could dispute about it. (ii) The antithesis, which represents the rationalist voice, states that "a judgment of taste is based on concepts," for otherwise we would not be able to quarrel about it as in fact we do (§56, 234, AA 338, 33–339, 2). The solution of the antinomy shows that the concept employed respectively in the thesis and the antithesis must be understood in a different sense in the two maxims. If we take taste's reference to the concept according to different specifications, both propositions turn out not to contradict each other and to be true. Kant considers the twofold perspective thereby disclosed as "necessary to our transcendental faculty of judgment."

Thus, Kant's discussion of the antinomy must turn to the nature of the "concept" involved in the activity of the judgment of taste taken as a reflective aesthetic judgment (i.e., neither as empirical nor as cognitive judgment). Thereby, Kant draws on the results of both the Analytic and the Deduction, establishing a crucial link between taste and the concepts of reason (i.e., ideas). Taste refers to the counterpart of reason's ideas, namely aesthetic ideas.[2] A judgment of taste necessarily refers to a concept since understanding must be involved therein—albeit not in a cognitive function but merely as the "faculty of concepts in general" (§57, Remark I, 242, AA 244, 10). The presence of the understanding is necessary in order to fulfill the subjective conditions of cognition in general. These conditions make of the judgment of taste a judgment in the proper sense (and hence give universal communicability to the feeling thereby expressed). Yet although the judgment of taste refers to a concept, it cannot be proved "*from* a concept" (§57, 235, AA 339, 15–16). For the concept to which it refers is not a *determinate* concept of the understanding (and proofs are always built on such concepts). What sort of concept then is involved in a judgment of taste? At the beginning of the Analytic of the Sublime, Kant intimates that taste does refer to "concepts, although it is *indeterminate* which concepts these are" (§23, 74, AA 244, 13). The very distinction between our judgments of the beautiful and the sublime rests, respectively, on the definition of beauty as "*Darstellung* of an *indeterminate* concept of the understanding" and the sublime as "*Darstellung* of an *indeterminate* concept of reason" (§23, 75, AA 244, 27–29). The reference to "*indeterminate* concepts" rectifies the meaning of the thesis and confines its validity to appearances.

In specifying the meaning of the antithesis, however, the argument of the Dialectic brings the aforementioned distinction between aesthetic judgment of the

---

2. The relation between aesthetic ideas and reason's ideas is discussed in §57, Remark I, which takes up the argument developed for the first time in §49.

beautiful and the sublime a step further. It pushes the specification of that *indeterminate* concept of the understanding to the point of disclosing the *indeterminable* dimension, or substrate, on which it rests. As opposed to the *determinate* concepts of the understanding (or, more in general, to concepts that although indeterminate are still always "*determinable*" through intuition, i.e., can always be exhibited in a corresponding intuition be it pure or empirical, §57 Remark I, 240, AA 342, 27–30), Kant presents another type of concepts, namely the "*indeterminate and at the same time indeterminable*" concepts of reason. Such is the "transcendental *Vernunftbegriff* of the supersensible" (§57, 235, AA 339, 18–21) which no intuition will ever be able to determine. Kant makes clear that there are two types of ideas, namely ideas of reason and aesthetic ideas, which are counterparts of each other. Rational ideas are "*indemonstrable* concepts of reason"; they are concepts to which no intuition will ever be adequate. Aesthetic ideas are "*unexpoundable* representations of the imagination"; they are intuitions to which no adequate concept will ever be found (§57, Remark I, 240, AA 342, 20–23). The important point, however, is that both have their principles in reason (in the same reason): the former in the objective principles of reason's employment, the latter in its subjective principles (§57 Remark I, 342, AA 244, 1–3). Kant's conclusion is that even though a judgment of taste regards objects of the senses (and hence is placed in the sensible world), the indeterminacy of the concept involved in it betrays "reason's pure concept of the supersensible." It is this concept that underlies the object as well as the judging subject both considered in their sensible nature (§57, 236, AA 340, 4–6). In other words, the free play of imagination and understanding due precisely to the freedom allowed to the imagination by the indeterminacy of the understanding's concept rests, in turn, on an indeterminacy that belongs to reason and excludes all possible sensible determination. Thus, aesthetic judgment makes possible a transcendental transition from what is theoretically indeterminate to what is practically determined as freedom.

In line with Kant's argument in the previous two *Critiques*, the grounding function of the idea of the supersensible is predicated upon the recognition that both the object and the judging subject are mere appearances. Only the reference to the indeterminate concept of reason (or to its counterpart, the aesthetic idea) allows one to save, at the same time, taste's claim to universal and necessary validity and its nature of reflective aesthetic judgment. (It is Kant's contention against the rationalist tradition that the concept involved cannot be a confused concept of perfection for, in this case, objective proof would be possible and the judgment would be cognitive, resting on a concept of the understanding.) Thereby the solution of the antinomy of taste is at hand. The thesis must be reformulated in the claim, "the judgment of taste is not based on *determinate* concepts," while the antithesis must contend more precisely that "the judgment of taste is based upon an *indeterminate* concept" (§57, 237, AA 340, 34–341, 13–14). It is clear that no opposition takes place between these two propositions and that both of them are true. Kant suggests that this solution simply follows from the consideration of taste as a "merely reflective aesthetic faculty of judgment" (§57, 238, AA 341, 13–14); that is to say from taste considered in the transcendental perspective provided by both the Analytic and the Deduction.

While the reference to the subjective conditions of judging in general describes the way in which the issue of taste's universality and necessity finds its formal proof in the Deduction, Kant's further step in the Dialectic consists in showing how the indeterminate nature of that conceptual condition opens up to the dimension of reason and to the supersensible. As Kant suggested in the introduction (§IX, LVI, 196, 12–22), it is the specific task of the faculty of judgment to fill the "gap" of indeterminacy that stands open between understanding's determinate concepts and reason's indeterminable ideas. It is at the level of the Dialectic that Kant is able to fully address this issue.

What does the supersensible, which is explicitly called into the picture under the concept of reason involved in a judgment of taste, designate at this point? Echoing the introduction's formulations, the supersensible indicates "a ground in general of nature's subjective purposiveness for our faculty of judgment" (§57, 236, AA 340, 14–15).[3] At this point, Kant presents a strong, though hypothetically attenuated, suggestion. He states that the *Bestimmungsgrund* of the judgment of taste which the Analytic has been exposing and the Deduction justifying in its legitimacy, "lies, perhaps, in the concept of what may be considered the supersensible substrate of humanity" (§57, 236–237, AA 340, 20–22). Thus, it is at the level of the Dialectic that the *Bestimmungsgrund* of the judgment of taste reveals its unknowable and indeterminable metaphysical character.

The solution of the antinomy of taste discloses the reference to a "point of unification of all our a priori powers" (§57, 239, AA 341, 30–31), which is the idea of the supersensible. Kant underscores two important points. He makes clear that this *Vereinigungspunkt* is something that *must be looked for*, not a possession given to us once and for all. And he hints at the fact that the unification regards *all* the cognitive faculties that have been respectively called into the picture at different stages in the development of the Critique of the Aesthetic Faculty of Judgment. For this faculty is actually at work with the complex of *all* the powers of our *Gemüt*. At the end of the Analytic of the Beautiful, the *Gemeinsinn* appeared as a first unification of all the moments of the judgment of taste (*vereinigt,* §22, 68, AA 240, 15). A further "unification" of the faculties of imagination, understanding, spirit, and taste under the lead of taste itself was the result of the Deduction (§50 and fn., AA 320, 6–7, 28–29). In the activity of the genius, reason was called into the picture as the faculty of aesthetic ideas. The Dialectic discloses the supersensible dimension in which this unification eventually takes place. There is a "supersensible substrate" that underlies all our cognitive faculties and serves as the condition that allows for

3. This formulation now takes the place of the more frequent formulation of the Analytic: "subjective purposiveness of the object's form for our cognitive faculties," which is, more strictly, a definition of beauty.

the harmony that we experience through feeling in taste. This supersensible substrate makes all our cognitive faculties eventually harmonize (§57, Remark I, 242, AA 344, 12–15). Such a harmony should be regarded as the ultimate purpose assigned to us by our intelligible nature. In this function, it can also be regarded as a "subjective standard" for all fine arts and taste.

With regard respectively to the three higher cognitive faculties that engage in a dialectic, the idea of the supersensible receives three different characterizations. The table of the faculties of the *Gemüt* that concludes the introduction is thereby supplemented by a sort of table of the supersensible. This is, "*first*, the idea of the supersensible in general with no further determination, as the substrate of nature; *second*, the idea of the same supersensible, as principle of the subjective purposiveness of nature for our cognitive faculties; *third*, the idea of the same supersensible as the principle of the purposes of freedom and of the harmony of these purposes with nature in the moral sphere" (§57, Remark II, 246, AA 346, 15–20). The threefold connotation of the supersensible makes clear in what sense this idea, in the significance of formal purposiveness attributed to it by the faculty of judgment, provides the key to the mediation between nature and freedom, the theoretical and the practical use of reason.

This conclusion allows Kant a final consideration with regard to the "deduction" of the judgment of taste (§57, Remark II, 246, AA 346, 13). The universal validity of taste is ultimately grounded on the idea of the supersensible in which nature's purposiveness is reconciled with freedom's purposes by means of the subjective constitution of our cognitive faculties. We can certainly neither know nor explain by means of objective proof such a "unification." Yet, we can bring it to expression through a subjective, universally communicable feeling. The means to this expression is the reflective aesthetic faculty of judgment and its a priori principle. In the same way, Kant underlined that we can neither know nor exhibit the *Gemeinsinn*'s rule for taste as an objective principle. We can only provide an example of its judging in our own individual and subjective judgment of taste, whose principle is thereby made universally valid and universally communicable.

However, Kant contends that the problem presented by the antinomy of taste can be solved only under the condition of considering the notion of purposiveness in the formal and subjective sense conferred to it by the faculty of judgment's own a priori principle. This is the position that Kant designates as "idealism of purposiveness" (§58, title; 252, AA 350, 3–15), which constitutes the critical alternative to both empiricism and rationalism (in its realistic option). By bringing his argument to a closer analysis of the notion of purposiveness, Kant moves toward the second part of the *Critique of Judgment*. The subjective purposiveness claimed by the idealistic position is merely the purposive harmony that the faculty of judgment establishes between our cognitive powers and nature's manifold forms. Such a purposiveness responds to our subjective need for meaning and orientation in the infinite variety of natural forms and empirical laws and is to be found a priori in the faculty of judgment itself (§58, 252, AA 350, 3–15). Purposiveness describes, in this case, a thoroughly contingent harmony not regulated by any determinate purpose (§58, 247, AA 347, 19–22). This view opposes the anthropocentric "realism of aesthetic purposiveness," which assumes that nature, in the production of beautiful forms, works as (mechanical) art with the purpose of pleasing our human imagination.[4] This is where the aesthetic faculty of judgment under this realistic assumption would yield to the different principle of teleology. Against the realism of teleology, which claims the existence of *objective* natural purposes, Kant proposes the idea of nature's "freedom" in the *Bildung* of beautiful forms and figures. This freedom is not determined by purposes but is merely and purely aesthetic in its purposiveness without purpose for our cognitive faculties (§58, 249, 251, 252 AA 348, 12; 349, 27–28; 350, 1–2). In this way, nature's production of beauty is rather closer to the genius's creation through aesthetic ideas. This argument confirms, on the side of nature's activity, Kant's notion of the genius. Indeed, we know from the Deduction that the genius is a power that comes from nature and expresses the way in which nature itself gives the rule to art.

2. The Analogic Logic of the Faculty of Judgment: Beauty as Symbol of Morality (§59)

In §59, Kant directly addresses the question of the "supersensible substrate" that underlies both the object and the subject in the world of appearances and constitutes the "point of unification" of all our cognitive faculties. Kant's aim is to articulate the sole possibility that we have of thinking of and reflecting upon this supersensible substrate. The first *Critique* has shown that no theoretical discursive knowledge of the supersensible is possible for us; the second *Critique* has recognized in it the practical reality of the moral law and the realm of freedom. Neither *Critique*, however, goes as far as thematizing the problem of the *relation* between the judging subject in her sensible nature and the supersensible itself. Indeed, the way freedom can be realized, in its effects or consequences, in the sensible world of mechanical nature remained an open question for practical reason. Moreover, in neither *Critique* did the supersensible appear in the qualification of a "substrate."[5]

At the end of the Dialectic of the judgment of taste, Kant addresses the issue of the realization of freedom in the sensible world by way of analogy to the issue of aesthetic judgment's realization of aesthetic ideas. He presents the way in which the faculty of judgment operates in its *search for* the indeterminate and indeterminable universal that constitutes the predicate of our judgments of reflection. In §59, Kant discusses the internal logic—or the way of thinking—proper to the reflective faculty of judgment. At stake therein is not the metaphysical prob-

4. Against this realism Kant simply recalls the need to stick to mechanistic interpretations of nature and to the maxim that forbids multiplying principles of explanations when a purely mechanistic one suffices.

5. For other occurrences of the term *Substrat* in Kant, see W. Vossenkuhl, "Schönheit als Symbol der Sittlichkeit. Über die gemeinsame Würzel von Ethik und Ästhetik bei Kant," in *Philosophisches Jahrbuch*, 99, 1 (1992), 91–104.

lem of ontological determination of the supersensible substrate of nature and humanity (a question for the determinant faculty of judgment that this faculty, however, will never be able to answer). On account of the notion of a supersensible substrate disclosed by the solution of the antinomy, the question is rather, how do we set out to *search for* something like a supersensible substrate in order to *reflect* upon our experience of the manifold forms of nature? What does our experience of beauty indirectly say about that supersensible substrate?

Kant suggests that the logic of the reflective faculty of judgment is a *logic of analogy*. Analogy designates the *heuristic* procedure followed by reflection. It provides a method for searching for what can be neither constructed a priori nor known a posteriori. Analogy is the as-if procedure whereby judgment explains the way in which judgment itself works. Here Kant uncovers a theme that has been at work throughout the whole first part of the *Critique of Judgment* and will be further investigated in its second part. The theme of analogy unifies the activity of the faculty of judgment in realms as different as the sphere of the beautiful and the sublime, empirical cognition, the cognition of life and organisms, our thinking of god, and even thinking in general (and philosophical thinking in particular) in its most diverse linguistic expression. The use of analogy always implies a certain reference to the supersensible. The analogic procedure of the faculty of judgment leads Kant to explore the issue of the "connection" and "unification" of all our faculties with regard to their common substrate. The supersensible will appear as the common territory (or, to use the language of the introduction, the "field," §II) in which all our cognitive faculties are eventually unified (§59, 258–259 AA 353, 28–34). Finally, it is by means of the analogic procedure of the faculty of judgment that Kant comes to the famous qualification of "beauty as a symbol of morality" (§59, title). The exploration of the connection between beauty and morality or aesthetic and moral judgment is, at this point, the crucial exemplification of the analogic function of reflection with regard to the problem of the realization of our concepts.[6] Thereby the conclusion of the Critique of the Aesthetic Faculty of Judgment develops the crucial suggestion with which Kant ended §IX of the introduction: "The spontaneity in the play of the cognitive faculties, whose attunement contains the ground of this [aesthetic] pleasure, makes that concept [of formal purposiveness] suitable as mediation of the connection of the domain of nature with the domain of freedom in its consequences, and also promotes at the same time the receptivity of the *Gemüt* to moral feeling" (§IX, LVII, 197, 10–15).

One of the tasks of Kant's transcendental philosophy is to distinguish the ways in which "reality," or "objective validity" is provided for our concepts in relation to the different faculties from which these concepts stem. The proof of the "objective

---

6. In other words, it is not a conclusive argument still belonging to the deduction of the judgment of taste, as suggested by interpreters such as Crawford, Brandt, and others (see chapter 10, n. 2). On this point I agree with P. Guyer, "The Symbols of Freedom in Kant's Aesthetics," in *Kants Ästhetik/Kant's Aesthetics/L'esthétique de Kant,* ed. by H. Parret, Berlin, New York, de Gruyter, 1998, 338–355, see 341.

reality" of our concepts is the crucial proof that these concepts are not empty and hence have "sense and meaning" for us. This traditional problem receives, in Kant's transcendental philosophy, a twofold formulation. In the *Critique of Pure Reason,* Kant raises first the issue of the legitimacy (*quid juris*) of the concept's reference to objects. This is the problem of the transcendental deduction of the categories. Only after the claim to objective reality has been justified in its right, can Kant move on to address the further issue of the procedure through which categories acquire objective meaning in their actual employment and application to appearances, namely in the actual formulation of judgments. This is the question that in the first *Critique* occupies the doctrine of the schematism of the understanding (Transcendental Doctrine of the Faculty of Judgment). A similar sequence is followed by Kant in the *Critique of Judgment.* The deduction of the judgments of taste (§§30–38) assesses the right for the faculty of judgment to claim universal and necessary validity for its propositions. Once this problem has been solved, Kant faces the issue of how this universal validity is actually expressed by aesthetic judgments. It is clear from the very outset that the question will receive a different solution than that of an "objective schematism of the faculty of judgment" (§9, 30, AA 218, 35–36). For judgment's aim is not determination but reflection, while the concept involved is not a category of the understanding. Moreover, in the case of aesthetic judgments, the question of the *Darstellung* of the concept cannot be addressed until the dialectic has received its solution. In facing the general problem of how concepts are applied to the objects that we call beautiful, an antinomy arises prompted by the ambiguity of the term *concept* in taste's judgments. Accordingly, the task of the dialectic is to make clear what kind of concept is involved in a judgment of taste. For up until this point the issue has been addressed only negatively. Both the Analytic and the Deduction only needed to argue what the concept appearing in a judgment of taste *is not.* (It is not a determinate concept of the understanding, and it is not reason's concept; aesthetic judgment is neither theoretical nor practical). Only after the antinomy of taste has been solved can Kant move on to the issue of the peculiar schematism proper to the faculty of judgment, i.e., to the issue of how we give sensible form to concepts in our judgments of taste. The free schematism of the imagination proper to the reflective faculty of judgment now takes the place of the schematism of the understanding required by the determinant faculty of judgment.[7]

At the beginning of §59, Kant explains that "reality" is always provided to concepts by intuitions in which the concept is exhibited (§59, 254, AA 351, 15). The faculty of intuitive representations is the imagination. In the case of *empirical* concepts, intuitions have the function of "examples." In the case of the *pure* concepts of the understanding, intuitions have the function of "schemas." For the

7. An account of these two schematisms (more in the perspective of the first *Critique* than of the third *Critique*) is provided by Fr. Kaulbach, "Der Übergang vom bestimmt-bestimmenden zum freien Schema in Kants Kritik der Urteilskraft," in *Revue Internationale de Philosophie*, 176 (1991), 76–91.

concepts of reason or ideas, no objective reality can be provided by intuition in view of theoretical cognition since no intuition can correspond to reason's concepts. Moral judgments as well exclude all intuition since practical concepts lack direct intuition. This account still leaves the possibility open to find a noncognitive and nonpractical way to associate sensible intuitions to reason's ideas. Kant works on this possibility in §59.

The issue at stake regards the *Versinnlichung* (§59, 255, AA 351, 23–24) of our concepts or, in the language of the first *Critique*, their realization by means of sensibility.[8] Exhibition, whose rhetorical figure is "hypotyposis,"[9] is the way in which concepts are rendered sensible (*Versinnlichung*). The faculty of exhibition is the imagination (§17, 55, AA 232, 24–25). There are two types of hypotyposis, "schematic" and "symbolic." Schematic hypotyposis consists in the a priori presentation of the intuition that corresponds to the understanding's concept. Schematism is the procedure followed by the imagination under the rule of the understanding in order to produce knowledge. The schema solves a problem of determination. It is the means through which the category is applied to appearances. The schema bridges the heterogeneity of sensible intuition and concept.[10] At stake in a symbolic hypotyposis is the possibility of making a concept of reason sensible in a different way than its impossible schematization. The symbol addresses a problem of reflection. In the symbol, an intuition is provided in which the faculty of judgment engages but *only in analogy* to its function in schematization. In this case, the very rule followed by the faculty of judgment in this procedure—not the intuition itself—is set in accordance to the concept. Herein the imagination is free in its relation to the understanding (no determination is required as no cognitive aim is pursued). What corresponds to reason's concept in a symbol is not directly the reality of the object provided by intuition but the way of—or the rule for—reflecting and judging with which we make sense respectively of reason's idea and of the sensible object of intuition. Symbolic hypotyposis shifts the correspondence from the determinate relation concept-reality to the reflection on a different relation in which the concept is left indeterminate and the imagination has a free range of play. As Kant puts it, in the symbol the accordance does not regard the "content" but the "form of reflection" itself (§59, 254–255, AA 351, 15–31). Schematic and symbolic hypotyposis are the two forms of our "intuitive way of representation" (i.e., the two ways in which the imagination is at work). In the case of a priori concepts, schemata proceed through demonstration, symbols through analogy. In a symbolic hypotyposis the concept is rendered sensible only "indirectly" (i.e., by means of analogy). Analogy allows us to bring to-

---

8. KrV B 186/A 147.

9. In its Greek etymology, *hypotyposis* means "outline" or "sketch"; Quintilian uses it in the sense of "illustration."

10. For both the issues of "application" and "heterogeneity," see KrV B 177/A 137.

gether elements that are different in kind (incommensurable and heterogeneous) by referring them to a common third term (§60, 263, AA 356, 15–16).[11]

In instituting an analogy, the faculty of judgment performs two distinct functions. First, it applies the concept to the object of a sensible intuition. Second, it applies the rule for reflecting upon that intuition to an entirely different object of which the first is only the symbol (§59, 256, AA 352, 13–16). Note that because of this indirect relation the analogy (and the symbolic relation) cannot be reversed. As an example, Kant discusses the relation by which we think of a constitutional monarchy in analogy to an animate body, while we think of an absolute monarchy in analogy to a mere machine (a hand mill). Thereby the animate body becomes the symbol of a constitutional monarchy while the machine symbolizes a despotic regime. Analogy and symbolic relation establish no direct similarity between the two objects (i.e., the constitutional monarchy and the animate body) as their concepts radically differ in *extension*. They establish instead an *indirect* similarity as they disclose the possibility of a *transition* from the one to the other on the ground of a reflection on the form of the two concepts (what is addressed is the *intension* of the two concepts; in Kant's example, the peculiar relation between the whole and the parts that characterizes the *totum,* as opposed to the *compositum,* both in the case of the natural and the political body).

In the *Prolegomena*, Kant observes that analogy does not designate "an imperfect similarity between two things but rather the perfect similarity of the two relations between totally unsimilar things."[12] In the example of §59, judgment's first act is to exhibit the concept of a certain relation between whole and parts in the sensible intuition of an animate body. The second act consists in transferring the rule that allows us to reflect upon the relation between whole-parts (concept) and animate body (object) to the different concept of monarchy for which no sensible object is at hand. What is similar in this case is not directly the animate body and the constitutional monarchy, but *indirectly* the relation between whole-parts in the object "animate body" and in the concept "constitutional monarchy." Thus, in the symbol, the intuition that would immediately correspond to the concept of animate body takes the place of the intuition that we lack in the case of the concept of constitutional monarchy. In the symbol, the figure of a chiasm between four terms is drawn. Three terms are given while the fourth is the lacking intuition that would correspond to a concept which cannot be exhibited. The intuition corresponding to

---

11. On the importance of analogy in the third *Critique*, see E. Garroni, introduction to his Italian translation of the *Critique of Judgment* (Torino, Einaudi, 1999). See also the more general studies by M. Guérin, "Kant et l'ontologie analogique. Recherches sur le concept kantien de l'analogie," in *Revue de Métaphysique et de Morale*, 79, 4 (1974), 516–548; by V. Melchiorre, *Analogia e analisi trascendentale*, Milano, Mursia, 1991; and P. Faggiotto, *La metafisica kantiana dell' analogia,* Trento, Verifiche, 1996.

12. *Prolegomena*, §58, AA IV, 357; see also §84 of the *Jäsche Logik,* in which Kant deals with induction and analogy as procedures proper to the faculty of judgment in its empirical use.

a demonstrable concept now takes the place of this fourth lacking term. Kant argues that analogy is an indirect procedure of inference that concerns the equality of two "*qualitative* relations" so that "from three given members we can obtain a priori knowledge only of the relation to a fourth, not of the fourth member itself."[13] Analogy presupposes a common ground that must be anticipated or constructed according to the principle of the reflecting faculty of judgment. It presupposes an aesthetic representation that does not aim at determining anything in the object but is the way of searching for the meaning of an indeterminate and indeterminable concept. This reflection must still satisfy the subjective conditions of cognition in general. To return to the problem raised by the introduction (i.e., to the issue of orientation and meaning in a world of heterogeneous things, natural forms, and empirical laws, §V), analogy is the thought-way that does not take into account only what things have in common but proceeds in thinking that in which things differ. Analogy sets out from the point of *Ungleichartigkeit*, or heterogeneity, of things (§90, 449–449, AA 464, 4–5).

Kant recognizes that analogy is the way in which the faculty of judgment is at work in the most different spheres. More generally, he points to the fact that even our language is "replete with such indirect exhibitions according to an analogy." Interestingly, Kant discusses philosophical expressions in which a pure concept of the understanding, such as substance, is seen as based upon a symbolic, not a schematic, hypotyposis. We could conclude that in a certain way the objective schematism that allows us to employ the understanding's categories for cognitive purposes ultimately rests on a reflective analogic (and hence aesthetic) use of language.

How does analogy work in the case of reason's ideas? On the premise of the analogic procedure proper to the aesthetic faculty of judgment, Kant construes his peremptory claim, "beauty is the symbol of the morally-good" (§59, 258, AA 353, 13), from which so much discussion among scholars has arisen.[14] He contends that our liking for beauty entails a claim to universal validity only because we refer beauty to the idea of the morally good as its symbol. To be sure, this statement does not regard the same question addressed in the deduction (i.e., the

---

13. KrV B 222 f./A 179–180, for the merely regulative use of the rule of the analogies of experience.

14. A good argument for the relation between beauty and the sublime as different symbols of freedom is provided by P. Guyer, "The Symbols of Freedom in Kant's Aesthetics," in *Kants Ästhetik/Kant's Aesthetics/L'esthétique de Kant*, op. cit. For the notion of beauty as symbol of morality, see in the same volume the contributions by S. Kemal, "The Practical Postulate of Freedom and Beauty as Symbol of Morality," 356–373; A. M. Roviello, "Du Beau comme symbol du Bien," 374–385; B. Recki, "Das schöne als Symbol der Freiheit," 386–402; J. Kneller, "Beauty, Autonomy, and Respect for Nature," 403–414; and T. Cohen, "Why Beauty Is a Symbol of Morality," in *Essays in Kant's Aesthetics*, ed. by T. Cohen, P. Guyer, Chicago, University of Chicago Press, 1982, 221–236. Interestingly, however, in all these contributions no specific discussion of the analogic procedure of judgment is offered.

question of the *right* of taste's claim to universal validity [*quaestio juris*]). Instead, it regards the ground of the very *fact that* we do lay claim to universal validity in judgments of taste (*quaestio facti*)—a fact that, as Kant observes, we can recognize as coming quite naturally to all of us. We even perceive the claim to universal assent as a "duty" (§59, 258, AA 353, 15; see the *Sollen* of §19, 63, AA 237, 24–25). The intersubjective agreement in judgments of taste must be viewed as the symbol of the moral community in the kingdom of freedom. This argument reveals that the "intelligible" that taste contemplates is the morally good. This is where all our cognitive faculties eventually harmonize. In his letter to Johann Friedrich Reichardt dated October 15, 1790, Kant makes a similar point. He claims that "without moral feeling, nothing would be for us beautiful or sublime," that our "legitimate claim to everyone's assent with regard to everything that can be called beautiful or sublime is based precisely upon it," and that taste itself is the capacity of judging in relation to "the subjective side of morality in our being, which is called moral feeling and is for us inscrutable." For Kant this is, once again, the sign that taste is not grounded upon the contingency of sensation but rather on an a priori principle.

The idea of the morally good is an idea to which no intuition can be adequate. No schematization (and hence no determination) is possible in this case. What is possible, instead, is a symbolization. Herein, the reflective faculty of judgment is at work analogically. The faculty of judgment constructs an analogy between our way of reflecting upon the beautiful object and our way of reflecting upon the morally good by means of the imagination, which is not constrained by the understanding's rules but is thoroughly free in its use of intuitions (whereby it draws free figures and symbols). On what is this analogy based? Certainly not on a similarity between a beautiful object and the idea of the morally good itself. For these are, as it were, two utterly incommensurable terms. The analogy regards our way of reflecting upon these objects. In assessing beauty as the object of a *pure* feeling of pleasure, the faculty of judgment enjoys a kind of freedom and autonomy that is analogous to the freedom and autonomy of practical reason in the moral sphere. It is both the negative freedom of being independent of empirical sensation and charm and the positive freedom of the autonomy of self-legislation. In experiencing beauty, the faculty of judgment discovers a possibility of harmony that brings together the object and the judging subject so as to create an alternative to both the theoretical aim of cognition and the practical perspective of freedom. The possibility of such a harmony resides, in this case, in the object as well as in the subject. The faculty of judgment finds itself referred to a *tertium comparationis* that is to be met both in the object and in the subject. Although itself neither nature nor freedom, this third term is connected with the ground of freedom in the supersensible. The third dimension thereby disclosed provides the faculty of judgment with a common unitary ground for bringing together our theoretical and practical faculties. Thus, the analogic logic of the faculty of judgment hints at the possible "transition" between nature and freedom that Kant raised in the introduction as the crucial problem of the third *Critique* (§§II, III, IX).

The claim that sets beauty as symbol of the morally good is developed in the second half of §59 and touches upon four different points (259–260, AA 353, 37–354, 17). Kant stresses the similarities and differences contained in the analogy between our ways of thinking in the two spheres of nature and freedom respectively. Thereby, he revisits the analogical argument implicitly developed by the Analytic of the Beautiful, this time bringing to the fore the way in which judgment has been at work in those previous sections. The analogic structure that connects §9 of the *Critique of Judgment* to Theorem I (§2) of the *Critique of Practical Reason* is now presented in its ultimate motivation.[15] (i) The liking for beauty is *immediate* (all concepts, interests, aims are excluded) and takes place in intuition. We find an *analogous immediacy* in our feeling toward the morally good, which pleases us immediately. The morally good is good immediately rather than mediately. Duty in its very concept should please us immediately without the mediation of subsidiary inclinations and motives. In both cases, we have a kind of *pure feeling* whose connection to the lower faculty of desire is excluded. (ii) The liking for the beautiful is bound to no interest. The morally good is necessarily connected to an interest that following from the moral judgment and not grounding it, confers to the moral judgment itself a disinterested character with regard to its motives. The disinterested character of moral maxims consists in the fact that they are undertaken for themselves rather than being mediated by a further purpose. (iii) The *freedom* of the imagination in its harmonious play with the lawfulness of the understanding is analogous to the freedom that sets the will in harmony with itself according to the universal law of reason. The former is the freedom of imagination's spontaneity and creativity; the latter is the freedom of practical autonomy. (iv) Finally, the *subjective universality* that belongs to our judging beauty and is independent of all universal concept is analogous to the *objective universality* of the moral principle, which is valid for all acting subjects as well as for all acts of the same subject but rests on a categorical concept of reason.

It is important to stress the direction that this analogy takes in invoking beauty as the symbol of the morally good (and not vice versa). The possibility of making sensible the idea of morality in an aesthetic idea by way of analogy with beauty and our experience of it in judgment opens the possibility of an *analogical experience* of moral freedom that otherwise would be utterly impossible for us.[16] Beauty brings moral freedom into the sensible world of nature. The notion of formal purposiveness—as principle of our judgments of taste—is the ground for the accordance between moral freedom and the world of nature in which freedom ought to be realized. Thereby taste overcomes the "gap"—or the "abyss"—that in the per-

---

15. See the discussion in chapter 9.

16. Kant intimated that experience of beauty is also an experience of freedom already in the General Remark that concludes the Analytic of the Beautiful.

spective of both theoretical and practical philosophy seems to lie open between nature and freedom. By means of the symbolic value of the beautiful object, our aesthetic judgment confers a sensible meaning on the supersensible realm of freedom.

In this way, we can explain Kant's suggestions at the end of §59 concerning the educational value that aesthetic experience has as sensibilization to moral ideas and means for the cultivation of humanity. The introduction already intimated that "the spontaneity in the play of the cognitive faculties," which is the core of aesthetic experience, in addition to mediating between our cognitive faculties "also promotes . . . the receptivity of the *Gemüt* to moral feeling" (§IX, LVII, 197, 10–15).[17] Kant's conclusion in §59 is that "taste enables us, as it were, to make the transition from sensible charm to the habit of moral interest" (§59, 260, AA 354, 25–26). In the very last section of the Critique of the Aesthetic Faculty of Judgment, he further elaborates on this conclusion. The transcendental argument for the transition between nature and freedom by means of aesthetic judgment of §59 yields to the empirical-anthropological argument on the moral value of aesthetic education and culture of §60.[18]

3. The Impossible Methodology of Taste as Propaedeutic to Taste (§60)

In §60, Kant presents, as appendix, a brief reflection on the "*Methodenlehre* of taste" (§60, title). Interesting in this section are the consequences drawn from the thesis of §59 concerning the connection between taste and morality, aesthetic and moral feeling. Once the opposition between nature's mechanism and freedom has been mediated by "beauty as the symbol of the morally good," reflection and its analogy face the new opposition between the freedom of nature and the constraints of culture. The mediation of this opposition is provided, in Kant's view, by history.

In Kant's philosophy, a "critique" that precedes a "science" (or doctrine) is usually divided into a "doctrine of elements" and a "doctrine of method," or methodology. However, since no "science of the beautiful" can follow the "critique of taste," that division does not apply in the case of the third *Critique*, which yields no doctrine at all (§60, 262, AA 354, 34–355, 3). Thus, Kant argues that we can speak only improperly of a method of both evaluating and producing beauty. As no objective rule of taste can be provided, so no prescriptive method

17. Compare this claim with the argument presented in the Analytic of the Sublime according to which the appreciation of the sublime in nature presupposes the mind's receptivity to moral ideas (§29, 110, AA 265, 1–2). See P. Guyer, "Symbols of Freedom in Kant's Aesthetics," op. cit., 343.

18. For this distinction, see K. Düsing, "Beauty as the Transition from Nature to Freedom in Kant's Critique of Judgment," in *Nous* 24 (1990), 79–92. Cf. Kant's claim in the preface: the present "inquiry into the faculty of taste as aesthetic faculty of judgment is not meant to form and cultivate taste but has a *transcendental* aim" (preface, IX, 170, 5–8).

can sanction how to make art. The artist, however, must still bear in mind an "ideal," and "art must keep this ideal in view even though, in practice, it will never achieve it" (§60, 262, AA 355, 11). Artistic education may still proceed with examples while avoiding examples to become models to be imitated. The freedom of the genius's imagination is here the only guiding criterion to be respected.

If no method is possible for taste, Kant proposes a "propaedeutic" to all fine arts. Such a propaedeutic does not consist in rules or precepts but in a "culture of the mental powers" (§60, 262, AA 355, 26). It is Kant's contention that the "propaedeutic that will truly establish taste is the development of moral ideas and the culture of moral feeling" (§60, 264, AA 356, 20–22). This thesis is based upon the notion of taste as the "ability to judge the way of making moral ideas sensible" by way of analogy (§60, 263, AA 356, 14–15), which is the result of §59. Kant's discussion of the true propaedeutic to all fine arts underscores the social significance of taste. At this juncture, Kant's reflection on the educational value of taste regards both the individual in her private singularity and the community in whose voice taste is always expressed. The universal validity of our aesthetic judgments plays itself out in the intersubjective social context of exchange, participation, and communication of ideas. Kant alludes to this context with the term "*humanity*," to which the traditional designation of the *humaniora* refers (§60, 262, AA 355, 27). Humanity alludes both to the possibility of sharing and participating in our feelings and to universal communication among socialized human beings. Taste as "universal human sense" (§60, 263, AA 356, 6–7) is the foremost vehicle of human socialization. This is a process that develops between the two opposites of nature's freedom and culture's constraint. Taste fulfills its function as a means of making moral ideas sensible, whereby it provides a sensible and more accessible entry into the moral kingdom of freedom.[19]

19. The historical references of Kant's argument are briefly hinted at by K. Düsing, "Beauty as the Transition from Nature to Freedom," op. cit., 83.

Chapter 12

The Analytic of the Teleological Faculty of Judgment (§61, §§62–68): The Internal Purposiveness of Natural Organisms

The second part of the *Critique of Judgment* is a critical investigation into the teleological faculty of judgment. The division of the second part follows the scheme of an Analytic, a Dialectic, and a Methodology of the teleological faculty of judgment. If compared to the critique of the aesthetic faculty of judgment, this second part attributes a different relevance to its three divisions respectively. The reason is provided by Kant's claim in the introduction according to which the key to the *Critique of Judgment* is the aesthetic faculty of judgment—the teleological faculty being just a function of judgment in general. In the case of the aesthetic faculty of judgment, the Analytic played a fundamental role while only one section was dedicated to the Methodology. In the critique of the teleological faculty of judgment, on the contrary, the Analytic plays a comparatively less central role if compared with the Dialectic and with the long Methodology (and the note that follows it). The Analytic is not clearly structured according to the moments provided by the table of the categories, although a certain parallelism with the Analytic of the Beautiful can be observed. The division into an "exposition" and a "deduction" is also not respected.[1] In the Analytic, Kant provides a typology of the different forms of "objective purposiveness" that the faculty of judgment employs in its reflection upon the manifold empirical forms of nature.

§61 works as an introductory section to the entire second part of the *Critique of Judgment*, referring back to the general considerations on the distinction between aesthetic and teleological faculty of judgment developed in §VIII of the introduction. In §§62–64 Kant presents the different forms of *Zweckmäßigkeit* and the different types of objects that can be judged according to a notion of purposiveness that is not aesthetic and subjective but logical and objective. In §§64–68, he discusses our judgments concerning the purposive structure of organisms and addresses the crucial problem of the function of teleological judgments in natural science.

1. Aesthetic and Teleological Faculty of Judgment (§61)

Kant's distinction between the subjective purposiveness of nature as principle of the aesthetic faculty of judgment and the notion of an "objective" purposiveness employed by the teleological faculty of judgment is framed in terms of the gen-

1. The reason for this has been discussed in chapter 9.

eral problem of comprehending the manifold empirical forms of nature as a lawful system of experience. Thereby, Kant goes back to the central epistemological reflections of the introduction. The principle of "subjective purposiveness of nature" is the a priori principle of the faculty of judgment that is necessary if a connection of our particular experiences of nature's forms into a coherent system is to be possible. On the ground of this subjective principle, we judge the particular forms of nature as if they were suited to our cognitive faculties. The subjectivity of the principle consists, in this case, in the harmony between the form of the object and the interplay of our cognitive powers. Accordingly, we judge those natural forms as beautiful. The reflective faculty of judgment is therein aesthetic. The critique of the aesthetic faculty of judgment becomes the fundamental part of a critique of this faculty because the original a priori principle of subjective purposiveness is necessary to the possibility of a systematic connection of our experience of nature (E §VIII, L, 193, 24–25).

Kant attributes to the teleological faculty of judgment a different function. Such a faculty refers to an objective purposiveness of nature based upon concepts of objects. The idea of nature as "complex of the objects of the senses" (§61, 267–268, AA 359, 16–17) does not legitimately allow one to infer the constitution of natural things according to purposes (i.e., the notion of an objective purposiveness in nature). While the principle of the aesthetic faculty of judgment is grounded in our own cognitive faculties and displays their "internal purposive attunement" (§61, 268, AA 359, 19), the claim of an objective purposiveness of things regards purposes that are not ours, cannot be attributed to nature as mechanism, and hence lie beyond our possible knowledge. In this case, no a priori ground can be provided for the fact that certain natural beings *must* exist as natural purposes (§61, 268, AA 359, 24–25; E §VIII, L–LI, 193, 24–34). There is no *necessary* connection between the notion of an objective purposiveness as principle for the possibility of things in nature and the notion of nature itself. On the contrary, one resorts to the notion of objective purposiveness in order to give an account of the radical *contingency* of nature's empirical forms. Nature as a mechanism is possible—and real—for us as object of the senses without needing to postulate any purpose. Nature's mechanism could have produced its forms in a thousand different ways than it actually has. The understanding would still not meet the unity of those forms in terms of a principle of purposes (§61, 269, AA 360, 16–18). Accordingly, the understanding cannot ever hope to find a ground for the notion of an objective purposiveness of nature either a priori or empirically. Yet, it is precisely the contingency of certain objects' form that leads reason to assume a principle for the explanation of the actual determinate structure of those objects. Why are these objects constituted precisely in this way and not otherwise?[2]

2. Contingent is that whose not-being or being different than it is can be thought without contradiction, see KrV B 290.

The notion of an objective purposiveness of nature is neither an original a priori principle nor an empirical concept.[3] It is rather a concept that reason uses "*in analogy*" with the aesthetic subjective ground that makes possible the connection of the representations in us (§61, 268, AA 360, 3). Our teleological reflection on nature functions in analogy with our aesthetic reflection on its beauty. In this sense, it is a merely *subjective* and "regulative" (§61, 270, AA 361, 1) principle of our judging nature. It belongs only "problematically" (§61, 269, AA 360, 21–22) to our reflection on its appearances, not constitutively to our determination of them. The principle of an objective purposiveness intervenes when mechanistic causality falls short of providing an explanation for the constitution of particular natural objects. Moreover, Kant resorts to a second analogy in order to account for the employment of the teleological faculty of judgment in these cases. He argues that we introduce a notion of purposive causality in nature that is thought "in analogy" with our own practical causality according to purposes (§61, 269, AA 360, 32). This is a causality that represents the possibility of objects through concepts. According to this analogy, we judge nature "technically" (§61, 270, AA 360, 34).

These preliminary considerations reveal the essential differences between aesthetic and teleological faculty of judgment. (i) While aesthetic judgment works without concept, teleological judgment implies a *concept* of the object as that which grounds the possibility of the object itself. (ii) Unlike aesthetic judgment teleological judgment is not referred to the conditions of "cognition in general" but to a *determinate* cognition of a particular object under a given concept. (iii) It does not rest on an immediate feeling of pleasure. "Natural beauty" is the presentation of the concept of formal subjective purposiveness through taste and is judged aesthetically by way of a feeling of pleasure. A "natural purpose," instead, is the presentation of a real objective purposiveness through understanding and reason and accordingly is judged logically by way of a concept (E §VIII).

2. A Typology of Objective Purposiveness (§§62–64)

If the teleological faculty of judgment does not present an original a priori principle of its own (as does the aesthetic faculty of judgment), nonetheless it exercises its reflection on a determinate and peculiar realm of objects of its own.[4] In order to identify the particular realm of objects proper to our teleological consideration of nature as the realm of organisms and living beings (natural products as natural purposes), Kant proceeds to a careful distinction of different kinds of objective purposiveness drawn with regard to the different objects to which these notions

---

3. Hence Kant's contention that the teleological faculty of judgment is not a peculiar faculty next to the aesthetic one but is rather the "reflective faculty of judgment in general" (E §VIII, LII, 194, 24–25).

4. See Kant's reflections on the "domain" and "territory" proper to our cognitive faculties in introduction §§I–III.

respectively apply. He considers here two categories of objects: products of art, for which geometrical figures stand, and natural products. It is only in the latter case that the teleological faculty of judgment displays a characteristic use of the principle of purposiveness distinct from merely practical purposiveness. Within the notion of objective purposiveness, Kant successively distinguishes "formal" from "material," or real, purposiveness with regard to geometrical figures (§62); "relative," "external" purposiveness from "internal" purposiveness with regard to nature (§63); and finally he reaches the idea of the peculiar internal purposiveness displayed by "natural purposes" (§64) as "organized beings" (§65).[5]

Geometrical figures, insofar as they are traced according to a principle, display a purposiveness that is not merely "subjective and aesthetic" but is "objective and intellectual" (§62, 271, AA 362, 10–11); it is not referred to the harmony of our cognitive faculties but to the object itself through the mediation of a concept. This kind of purposiveness does not regard the play of our cognitive faculties[6] but hints at the fact that a geometrical figure is suited for the solution of many different problems. This purpose, however, does not make the concept of that figure possible, as is the case for practical purposes. The ancient mathematicians investigated the properties of the parabola or the ellipse without being concerned with the possible application and use of these figures in the solution of problems. The study of these figures and their purposiveness was somehow disinterested and without any purpose (as is their aesthetic consideration). Although *objective*, the purposiveness displayed by geometrical figures is not real or material but "merely formal" in its possibility (as is the merely subjective purposiveness of aesthetic judgments). For it is not grounded on a purpose or an interest and hence, Kant argues, does not properly require "teleology" (§62, 274, AA 364, 5–6). Here, teleology, as opposed to formal purposiveness, specifically indicates a

5. The different forms and different meanings of *objective purposiveness* that occur in these sections have been broadly analyzed in the secondary literature. Explicative tables are often provided to help in classifying these forms. See G. Tonelli, "Von den verschiedenen Bedeutungen des Wortes Zweckmässigkeit in der Kritik der Urteilskraft," in *Kant-Studien*, 49, 2 (1958/59), 154–166; M. Frank/V. Zanetti, in the commentary to their edition of the *Critique of Judgment*, I. Kant, *Schriften zur Ästhetik und Naturphilosophie*, Frankfurt a.M., DKV, 1996, see 1194–1195; P. Bommersheim, "Der vierfache Sinn der Zweckmäßigkeit in Kants Philosophie des Organischen," in *Kant-Studien*, 32 (1927), 290–309; K. M. Wogau, *Vier Studien zu Kants Kritik der Urteilskraft*, Uppsala/Leipzig, Lundequistska Bokhandeln/Harrassowitz, 1938, 44–213.

6. We can certainly judge geometrical figures or numbers merely aesthetically and hence consider them beautiful and regard them according to a *subjective* purposiveness. In this case, however, no account is given of their objective purposiveness as "suitability for all sorts of purposes" (§62, 278, AA 366, 9–10) in the sciences; i.e., we do not judge these figures as beautiful *on the ground of* their *objective* purposiveness. Furthermore, Kant argues that what we judge as beautiful is properly not the figure in which we admire the objective purpose but the "demonstration" of that property. It is the demonstration that produces in us the accordance of imagination and understanding (§62, 278, AA 366, 16–20).

consideration of things that is based upon a real purposive connection of empirically given objects and events. Since geometrical figures depend upon construction, their *formal* purposiveness can be inferred a priori from the rule of their very construction in space. It is precisely the procedure of construction that distinguishes them from the existing empirical objects that we may judge, instead, according to real or material purposiveness. In the case of given existing things in which regularities and order are ascertained, neither regularity nor order can be inferred a priori. These objects cannot be constructed but must be empirically given in order to be apprehended. It follows that order and regularity can be explained only by assuming a real purpose external to them.[7]

Moving on from the consideration of geometrical figures and their objective *formal* purposiveness to the consideration of nature, Kant turns to objective *material* purposiveness, which remains the central topic both in the Analytic and the Dialectic. Within this notion, he opposes relative or external purposiveness to internal or intrinsic purposiveness (§63). In order for our judgment to be legitimately led by experience to the concept of an objective and material purposiveness (i.e., to the concept of a purpose of nature), two conditions are required. First, a relation of cause and effect must take place—and this means that we must be dealing with real existing things as opposed to merely possible ones (as is the case in mathematics). Second, the mechanistic explanation of this relation must be considered insufficient, so that the only way of seeing the relation of cause and effect as lawful must be to assume the efficacy of the cause as based upon the idea of the effect. In this case, the idea of the effect is presented as the condition for the possibility of causality itself (which is what happens in the sphere of the practical). We can think of this relation in two different ways. Either the effect is directly a product of art (i.e., is itself intrinsically a "purpose," so that the purpose that the object *is*, is at the same time the purpose that the object *has*). Or it is only the material or means for other causes to use; that is, it responds to a purposiveness that is merely external or only relative to its position within a chain of means and ends. This latter kind of purposiveness expresses the "usefulness" of something for the human being or its being of "benefit" for other beings (§63, 279–280, AA 367, 6–10). In this case, to be a purpose indicates a modality relative to the use of it by an external cause.

In the case of relative purposiveness, we judge of a determinate natural phenomenon according to a chain of purposes—each intermediate link being a relative and merely contingent purpose. Kant rejects this kind of teleological anthropocentric explanation of nature. For in all the cases in which external teleology is invoked (the claim that certain natural things exist *because* they are useful for the human being), a mechanistic explanation would be, in fact, sufficient. External purposiveness depends upon the assumption that the condition for the existence

---

7. The subjective material purposiveness of the agreeable in the Analytic of the Aesthetic Faculty of Judgment corresponds to this objective material purposiveness.

of what is useful or beneficial is a purpose of nature. More specifically, to consider that things exist *because* they are useful to the human species depends upon the hypothesis that the human species was meant to be living on earth (§63, 282–283, AA 368, 26–36). This hypothesis, however, cannot be proved.

Kant states the crucial difference between external and internal purposiveness as follows: "Judging a thing to be a natural purpose on account of its internal form is quite different from considering the existence of that thing to be a purpose of nature" (§67, 299, AA 378, 12–14). If material external purposiveness should be banned from natural science, internal purposiveness merits all our attention in Kant's view. In addressing the issue of internal purposiveness, Kant shifts from the notion of *Zweckmäßigkeit* to the notion of *Zweck* and considers respectively the products of art and natural products. At this point, he identifies organisms or organized beings as the peculiar kind of objects that the reflective faculty of judgment considers according to the notion of an objective internal purposiveness as "natural purposes" (§64). Kant asks, is there a case in which the mechanistic explanation of nature must yield to the claim that something is possible *only* as purpose? (§64, 284, AA 369, 33). To contend that something is possible *only if considered as a purpose* means to claim that its cause does not lie in the mechanism of nature but is a faculty whose causality is determined by concepts. In order to meet such a case, the following condition is required: it must be the case that the "form" of the object could not have arisen according to mere natural laws. Since its form is rather thoroughly "contingent" with regard to those laws, the only way to provide an explanation for its peculiar constitution is to resort to concepts of reason and to reason's own causality (§64, 284–285, AA 370, 1–13). An object whose form is possible only through reason is an object that is possible only as purpose. Kant sees this explanation at work first in the case of art products and then with regard to natural products. While in the first case we have to deal with reason's practical-technical causality, it is only the second case that requires the intervention of a specific teleological reflection upon nature. Such a reflection establishes the possibility of a coherent system of our experience of nature's empirical forms. The issue of a system of experience—Kant recalls right at the outset of §61—is the grounding general problem common to both parts of the *Critique of Judgment*. Thereby, the peculiar focus of the critique of the teleological faculty of judgment is attained: natural products as natural purposes provide the peculiar objective territory proper to the teleological faculty of judgment in its employment of a principle of objective internal purposiveness.

Geometrical figures are presented as the first type of objects that seem to fulfill the aforementioned condition. Kant discusses the example of a regular hexagon that someone sees drawn in the sand upon coming to a seemingly uninhabited country.[8] The observer judges that the figure could not have been produced by an

8. The historical tradition from which this example is drawn is discussed by G. Böhme, *Kants Kritik der Urteilskraft in neuerer Sicht*, Frankfurt, Suhrkamp, 1999, 108–115.

"irrational cause" (§64, 285, AA 370, 22). For it would be infinitely contingent for the mechanical processes of nature to bring about such an effect. Hence, she judges that only a concept of the hexagon provided by reason (not a mechanical interplay of natural elements and causes) can be the cause of the figure that she sees drawn in the sand. She concludes that the figure must be the purpose of a rational cause—not a natural product or a natural purpose but a "product of art" (§64, 286, AA 370, 30–31). The real theoretical challenge, however, is presented precisely by those natural products that can be neither sufficiently explained by the mechanical laws of nature nor traced back to human reason's technical causality. Since such an object cannot be explained mechanically, it is called *Zweck*; since it is not a product of art, it is "*Naturzweck*" (§64, 286, AA 370, 33–34). It is in this case that we meet the specific *objective internal* purposiveness of natural purposes.

3. In Place of a Deduction of the Concept of Natural Purpose: Organisms and Life (§§64–65)

Kant offers the following provisional definition of a *Naturzweck*: "a thing exists as a natural purpose if it is both cause and effect of itself" (§64, 286, AA 370, 36–37). Kant is aware that the notion of a natural product that follows from a type of causality that is neither nature's mechanical causality nor the practical causality of reason has the status of an "idea" (§64, 286, AA 371, 4). This idea discloses the result of a reflection in which nature is seen 'as if' it were acting in view of a purpose. Kant draws three implications from his provisional definition of a natural purpose by discussing the example of a tree. These implications express three "marvelous properties of organized beings" (§64, 288, AA 372, 11). (i) As example of the idea of a natural purpose, the tree produces itself with regard to the *species*. Within its species, the tree is both cause and effect of itself. (ii) But the tree produces itself also as *individual*. This self-production is called "growth" and is qualitatively different from a mere increase in size according to mechanical laws. The sophistication of the process of growth, Kant observes, infinitely surpasses any imaginable art. (iii) Finally, a natural product produces itself in its *parts*. This is the act of self-preservation that establishes the peculiar reciprocal relation between the parts and the whole proper to any living organism.

Kant's argument in §65 takes the place of a transcendental deduction of the concept of natural purpose.[9] The task is to show what kind of things in nature provides "objective reality" for the concept of a purpose when the purpose is not

9. Although Kant denies that a deduction is required for the concept of natural purpose, the reference to the "objective reality" provided for it on the one hand (§65) and the mention of necessity and universality of the principle of reflective judgment on the other hand (§66) allow me to designate the present step of the argument as the proof that takes the place of a deduction. See EE §XII, AA XX, 251, which still contemplates a deduction also for the teleological faculty of judgment. After the "First Introduction," one of the differences between aesthetic and teleological faculty of judgment is precisely the need for a deduction of the principle that is met by the former but not by the latter.

a practical one but a "purpose *of nature*" (§65, 295, AA 376, 1–2). The solution lies in the regulative idea that allows us to reflect upon the "peculiar character" (§64, title) and the "inscrutable property" (§65, 293, AA 374, 34–35) of organized beings. This idea serves us as a regulative "principle" for judging the internal purposiveness of organized beings. As this principle claims "universality and necessity" for nature's internal purposiveness, it must rest on an a priori ground, a proof of which is provided in §66. The principle of the teleological faculty of judgment rephrases the provisional definition of "natural purpose" (§64) in the light of the proof that has led to the concept of organized being (§65): "An organized product of nature is one in which everything is a purpose and reciprocally also a means" (§66, 295–296, AA 376, 11–13).

Following the provisional definition of a natural purpose, Kant attempts to determine the type of causality implied in this relation with regard to the only two possible kinds of causality (§65, 290, AA 373, 2–3). These are, on the one hand, the *nexus effectivus*, or the descending connection of efficient, or "real," causes proper to the understanding, in which no reciprocity is allowed[10] and, on the other hand, the *nexus finalis* of "ideal" causes or the connection according to reason's concept of a final cause, in which reciprocity is indeed allowed as in the practical-technical domain of intentional causality (§65, 289–290, AA 372, 23–373, 2). This connection displays a structure that is both ascending and descending. The question is now, can the *nexus finalis* ever be applied to nature, i.e., to a realm different from that of our intentional causality through reason, a realm in which no direct exhibition of the concept of a purpose can take place but, at the most, only an indirect (not a schematic but only a symbolic) exhibition can be carried through? How can organisms as organisms become the object of experience? While no constitutive concept of causality alternative to these two is possible for us, Kant will propose a regulative concept proper to our reflective faculty of judgment. Only this concept allows us to make sense of the internal purposiveness proper to organized beings.

Kant raises the general question regarding the set of conditions required in order to define something as a natural purpose. He contrasts, once again, products of art (this time, however, not geometrical figures but mechanical artifacts, such as a watch) and products of nature. Both in a mechanical artifact and in a natural product that should be viewed as a purpose, it must be the case that the parts are possible only through their relation to the whole. For anything that is thought of as *Zweck* is thought of under "a concept or idea" that determines it a priori (§65, 290, AA 373, 7–8). This condition, taken by itself, defines the artifact or work of art as that which is the purpose of a rational cause producing its work according to an idea. Thus, in order to define the specificity of that which is possible "*only* as a *natural* purpose" without appealing to the external causality of concepts exercised by rational beings, a second condition must supplement the first (§65, 290–291, AA 373, 16–17). The second requirement points to the problem of our *reflection upon* and *judgment of* things that are possible only as natural purposes; it

10. Obviously, in the case of a watch, its maker can only be cause, never effect.

does not concern the conditions of their objective existence or effectual production. Thereby, it reveals the regulative principle for our judging the systematic unity of nature. This requirement is that "the parts of the thing combine into the unity of the whole because they are reciprocally cause and effect of their form." In this case, the purposiveness of the whole is constitutive of the disposition of its parts (i.e., it is intrinsic or immanent to it). The type of causality involved therein is not external; rather, the causality of the cause is in this case the same causality that is proper to the effect. The idea of the whole determines reciprocally the connection and form of the parts yet not as a real cause—as in the case of the artifact—but rather as *Erkenntnisgrund*, namely as the basis for our cognition of the whole as a systematic unity of manifold parts. Kant argues that in this case a sort of combination of the two aforementioned types of causal connection (*nexus effectivus* and *nexus finalis*) takes place. "The connection of efficient causes is judged at the same time as causation through final causes" (§65, 291, AA 373, 17–34). Nature is judged as if it were producing its forms not mechanically but technically.

This formal definition of *internal* purposiveness accounts for the specificity of the structure of organized beings. In an organized being, each part or organ produces the other parts and is reciprocally produced by them; each part is there "*for*" the others and "*through*" them. The productive cause is internal to or immanent in the self-organizing whole and does not lie externally in a rational cause that acts according to concepts. An organized being differs from a mechanical artifact such as a watch since in the living being, (i) the parts produce other parts; (ii) the whole reproduces itself; and (iii) the whole produces the systematic unity of the parts.[11] As opposed to a mere machine, the organized and self-organizing being has "formative force," not just "motive force" (§65, 291–293, AA 373, 35–374, 26).

How should we think of or reflect upon such an organized being? In order to determine the transcendental status of this idea, Kant explores, once again, the possibilities offered by *analogy*. While natural beauty can be defined in analogy to art (as it implies a reflection upon an "*external* intuition"), Kant claims that an organized being is not just an "analogue of art" (§65, 293, AA 374, 28–29). Since art implies the activity of the artist as a rational cause *external* to its product, the analogy does not account for the *immanent* self-productive causality of the natural organism. A better—although still insufficient—expression is to regard the organized being as the "analogue of life" (§65, 293, AA 374, 34). In this case, however, either the peculiarity of the organized being remains unexplained or its scientific explanation is seriously threatened by metaphysical hylozoism and by the dualism of matter and soul.[12] How can dead matter ever become capable of

11. A watch, Kant argues, does not produce other watches, does not replace missing parts, does not heal itself. In other words, only organized beings are self-producing and self-regulating beings. For the historical significance of the watch analogy in teleology and for Hume's important criticism thereof, see J. D. McFarland, *Kant's Concept of Teleology*, Edinburgh, University of Edinburgh Press, 1970, chapter 3.

12. See §72 of the Dialectic.

organizing itself in living forms? Thus, Kant concludes that "strictly speaking . . . the organization of nature has nothing analogous to any causality known to us" (§65, 293–294, AA 375, 5–7).

It follows that the concept of natural purpose is not a "*constitutive* concept of understanding or reason," but only a "*regulative* concept for the faculty of judgment" that is thought of only according to a "remote analogy" with our own purposive causality (§65, 294–295, AA 375, 18–20). In this way, the concept of purposiveness employed by the teleological faculty of judgment functions indeed as an intermediary concept between the theoretical and the practical use of our faculties. We must employ this concept in judging those particular forms of nature or natural objects that display otherwise inexplicable features. We must resort to this concept if a coherent experience of the systematic unity of nature is to be possible for us. This regulative concept guides our investigation of the manifold empirical manifestations of organized nature and leads us to reflect on the "highest ground" that makes their comprehension possible. Thereby, Kant points to the supersensible basis, or "supersensible determining ground," of nature beyond nature's "blind mechanism" (§67, 297, AA 377, 11). Although no knowledge of this ground or of the system of nature will ever be possible, the reflection upon it satisfies a necessary need of our practical reason in analogy to which the notion of natural purpose is formulated. In this way, the supersensible becomes the "determining ground" of our teleological judgments on nature's contingent forms.

4. The Teleological Principle of the Faculty of Judgment (§§66–68): Organisms, the System of Nature, and the System of Science

The argument that in §65 takes the place of a deduction establishes the principle for "judging internal purposiveness in organized beings" (§66, title). This principle derives from or, better, "is occasioned by" (§66, 296, AA 376, 15) experience since it depends on our observation of nature. Insofar as it claims the universality and necessity of the notion of internal purposiveness, the principle must have an a priori ground, albeit only a regulative one. The principle of the teleological faculty of judgment is presented as a maxim (§66, 296, AA 376, 22) for our reflection upon organized beings. What is the necessity proper to the teleological principle in the investigation of nature? Kant claims that this *Grundsatz* is as necessary as the "universal physical principle" of the mechanical order of nature. While the latter grounds the possibility of "experience *in general*" so that without it nature in general would have no meaning for us as object of experience, the teleological principle provides the only possible regulative basis for a *particular* experience of nature. It furnishes the only "guiding thread in the observation of a kind of natural things" that can only be thought of as natural purposes (§66, 296–297, AA 376, 31–36). The teleological principle operates on an order that is radically different from the mechanism of nature proper to the understanding. The concept of natural purpose, implying an idea that must ground the natural product, cannot be directly exhibited in experience. Such a concept, being the internal and intrinsic purpose of nature's organization, "infinitely surpasses our ability to exhibit anything similar through art" (§68, 309–310, AA 384, 6–8). The teleological principle is a necessary maxim that provides a regulative idea to reflect upon nature as a system, not to determine it in knowledge.

In an important sense, teleology does not constitute for Kant a peculiar part of the theoretical science of nature (§68, 309, AA 383, 28–29). Teleology is not itself a science. Yet the faculty of judgment stands as the only representative of reason within the realm of human experience. By way of analogy, teleological reflection brings reason's ideas and the notion of the supersensible substrate of nature within the context of our particular experience of natural objects. Although through teleological explanations we do not come to know anything scientifically, this is the only kind of explanation that can make particular cognition possible for us. Thus, teleology remains crucial in natural sciences such as biology (and evolutionary biology), anatomy, and botany but also in history and anthropology. More generally, the notion of internal purposiveness plays a fundamental role in all the disciplines that are concerned with what is individual and contingent and that imply the systematic perspective of an organization of some kind.[13] In all these realms, the faculty of judgment brings reason's ideas to bear on our experience of the natural world.

However, the regulative principle of the reflective faculty of judgment is allowed only with regard to the *internal* purposiveness of natural products. Neither a consideration concerning the "intentionality" of nature's final cause (§67, 301, AA 379, 18; §68, 307, AA 382, 36)[14] nor the insertion of the notion of god's final purposes in creation is allowed. Teleology must be kept separate from theol-

---

13. See also Kant's remark in §65, fn. regarding the view of the political commonwealth as an organized being or a political body. For the importance of Kant's doctrine for biology, see P. Bommersheim, "Der vierfache Sinn der Zweckmäßigkeit in Kants Philosophie des Organischen," op. cit.; P. McLaughlin, *Kants Kritik der teleologischen Urteilskraft*, Bonn, Bouvier, 1989, 9–31; C. Zumbach, *The Transcendent Science: Kant's Conception of Biological Methodology*, The Hague/Boston, Nijhoff, 1984. For the more recent discussion of teleology in the natural sciences see *Nature's Purpose: Analyses of Function and Design in Biology*, ed. by C. Allen, M. Bekoff, G. Lauder, Cambridge, MIT Press, 1998; the essays in the section Teleologie und Kosmologie in *Metaphysik nach Kant?* ed. by D. Henrich, R. P. Horstmann, Stuttgart, Klett-Cotta, 1988; and the essays in part 4 of *Kant and the Sciences,* ed. by E. Watkins, Oxford, Oxford University Press, 2001 (H. Ginsborg, P. Guyer).

14. See also the division of the concept of purposiveness of nature into natural (*forma finalis naturae spontanea*) and intentional (*intentionalis*) in EE §IX, AA XX, 235, 7–9; and §72 of the Dialectic. An unintentional purposiveness would be an Aristotelian kind of purposiveness. It would be, however, quite difficult to distinguish unintentional causality from mechanism. Both Goethe's and Schopenhauer's readings of these sections of the *Critique of Judgment* are based upon an interpretation of Kant's notion of internal purposiveness as unintentional. As we will see in the following sections, Kant will move on to suggest a further hypothesis for the explanation of nature's objective purposiveness in terms of nature's intentionality.

ogy and the metaphysics of external purposiveness (§68, 305–306, AA 381, 31–382, 5).

The teleological principle that makes possible a reflection on natural organized beings leads us to reflect upon "nature in general as a system of purposes" (§67, title). Once we have discovered that nature has the capacity to produce beings that can be thought of *only* in terms of natural purposes (i.e., according to final causes), then we are entitled to go a step further. We may consider nature as a whole as if it were a system of purposes (§67, 304, AA 380, 27–301, 3). Thus, the "unity of the supersensible principle" (§67, 305, AA 381, 5–6) extends from natural products of a determinate kind (organized beings) to nature as a whole (nature as an organization in terms of final causes).

Finally, the same kind of regulative internal teleology allows us to construct science in general and physical science in particular as a systematic discipline (§68). In this regard as well, Kant underlines the need to keep teleology separate from theology and metaphysics. Kant's crucial claim regards the *analogical* nature of teleological explanations and their language: "When we apply teleology to physics, we do quite rightly speak of nature's wisdom, parsimony, foresight, or beneficence. But in speaking this way, we do not turn nature into an intelligent being . . . nor are we so bold as to posit a different, intelligent being above nature as its architect" (§68, 308, AA 383, 18–21). Kant's teleology expresses only a type of reflection according to the analogy with our own technical activity and does not commit itself to any ontological claim concerning the purposive structure of reality.

Chapter 13

The Dialectic of the Teleological Faculty of Judgment (§§69–78): Mechanism and Teleology

The Dialectic of the Critique of the Teleological Faculty of Judgment is the dialectic proper to *reflective* judgment in general (§69). Here, Kant argues for the compatibility of mechanistic and teleological explanations of nature within the perspective of our reflection on nature's manifold empirical forms (§§70–71). As in the former two *Critiques*, a dialectic arises because of the immanent constitution of our mind ("natural dialectic"). More precisely, it arises from the "discursive" character of our understanding, which strives toward the unconditioned following reason's aims even though its immanent use confines it to the realm of the conditioned. A crucial issue on the path toward a solution of the antinomy[1] regards the status of the notion of a "technic of nature" in our explanation of natural organized beings. With regard to this problem, Kant explores the two hypotheses of an objective purposiveness in which nature is seen at work unintentionally and intentionally, respectively (§§72–73). Kant establishes the "critical" validity of the notion of natural purpose for the reflective faculty of judgment (§§74–75). The solution of the antinomy links the critical validity of the principle of reflective judgment to a sort of analogy with an "intuitive understanding" for which the harmony between the manifold forms of nature and our cognitive faculty could be conceived without requiring purposes (§§76–78). If we acknowledge that the apparently opposite maxims of mechanism and teleology are due only to the limited, *discursive* constitution of our human understanding, we implicitly recognize that for a nonhuman "*intuitive* understanding" no contradiction would subsist between them. Kant solves the antinomy (§77) by referring both to an understanding different from ours and to the dimension of a "supersensible substrate" of nature thereby disclosed.

---

1. For the problem of where to locate Kant's solution of the antinomy of the teleological faculty of judgment and for the relation to the solution of the third antinomy of the first *Critique*, see McFarland's discussion: *Kant's Concept of Teleology*, Edinburgh, University of Edinburgh Press, 1970, 120 ff., 130; for the relation to the third antinomy of the first *Critique*, see V. Zanetti, "Die Antinomie der teleologischen Urteilskraft," in *Kant-Studien* 83 (1993), 341–355; a general discussion of the different interpretations of the antinomy is offered by M. Frank and V. Zanetti in their edition, I. Kant, *Schriften zur Ästhetik und Naturphilosophie*, Frankfurt a.M., DKV, 1996, 1287–1292. Various interpretations differ both with regard to the question of whether Kant's antinomy is an antinomy at all and with regard to the issues of Kant's solution for it and where to place this solution.

1. The Formulation of the Antinomy (§§69–71): Kant's View of Causality—Mechanism and Final Causes

No dialectic arises in the case of the determinant faculty of judgment since this faculty has no a priori principles of its own and merely subsumes under concepts already given by the understanding. Judgment can be mistaken in the application of concepts but cannot properly fall into an antinomy regarding the principles to be chosen since no choice is required from it. The reflective faculty of judgment, on the contrary, must subsume under laws that are "not yet given" (§69, 312, AA 385, 17), so that it must take the principles for this subsumption from itself. Thereby, the specific "heautonomy" of the reflective faculty of judgment is defined. Furthermore, while determinate judgment deals with homogeneous objects in terms of "universal laws of material nature in general," the reflective faculty of judgment attempts to unify in a thoroughgoing experience a manifold of particular empirical laws that are radically heterogeneous (§70, 313, AA 386, 18–26).[2] As Kant has shown in the Analytic, the principles of the teleological faculty of judgment are *subjective* maxims for our reflection upon certain particular forms of nature such as organized beings that seem to escape all explanation in terms of mechanical causes. These maxims are meant to account for the radical *contingency* of those natural forms in relation to nature's mechanical laws. With regard to our reflection, they are *necessary* principles. For these heuristic maxims are the only guidelines that we have for hoping to establish a coherent (although contingent) unity of nature in terms of its empirical laws. In judgment's employment of these principles, a "conflict and hence an antinomy may arise" which constitute the "natural dialectic" of the critique of the teleological faculty of judgment (§69, 312–313, AA 386, 5–8).

The conflict takes place when judgment reflects upon the contingent unity established among particular laws of nature. In so doing, it follows two different maxims that seem to contradict and exclude each other. Within the system of the cognitive faculties, the faculty of judgment may follow either understanding or reason. One of the two maxims is intimated a priori by the understanding's law of mechanism, while the other is suggested by particular experiences in which reason is involved (for example, in our encounter with natural organisms). Both Kant's presentation of the antinomy and its solution hinge upon two interrelated claims. On the one hand, the antinomy depends upon the crucial distinction between *subjective* maxims of the *reflective* faculty of judgment and *objective* principles of the *determinant* faculty of judgment. On the other hand, the solution intimates that this distinction rests precisely on the specificity of our *human* understanding. To maintain that certain maxims of our judgment are merely regulative means to acknowledge the limitation of their validity for the powers of a human mind. It follows that for an understanding different from the human, no contradiction would arise and

2. We must recall Kant's statement in the introduction that the teleological faculty of judgment is nothing but the reflective faculty of judgment in general (§VIII).

hence that also for the human understanding no contradiction would arise were it able to think 'as if' its perspective were that of a nonhuman understanding.

Because of the structure of the Dialectic, Kant formulates both the thesis and the antithesis twice: once with regard to our reflection on specific natural forms, once with regard to our objective cognition of nature in general. The aim is to show that the antinomy allows for a solution only within the perspective of the reflective faculty of judgment. Kant's suggestion is that the two propositions of the antinomy become indeed contradictory (and hence one of them necessarily must be false) only when the *regulative* maxims of the reflective faculty of judgment are illicitly "converted" into *constitutive* principles concerning the very possibility of natural objects (§70, 314, AA 387, 11). Thereby, the "autonomy" of the reflective faculty of judgment is confused with the "heteronomy" proper to determinant judgment (§71, 318–319, AA 389, 23–25). In this case, however, we no longer have an antinomy of judgment since such an antinomy, as argued in §69, can take place only for the reflective faculty of judgment. Hence, the first step in the solution of the antinomy is to show that only within the employment of the reflective faculty of judgment is a "critical" use of the principle of teleology allowed. The second step demonstrates under which condition the regulative principle of teleology can be reconciled with the principle of mechanism.

There are two extreme possible cases into which our limited human reason has no insight. On the one hand, it could be very well possible that the mechanism of nature were sufficient to produce organized beings. Yet since our knowledge of nature's manifold contingent laws is only empirical, no insight into the "first inner ground" proper to natural products (§71, 317, AA 388, 25–26) and hence into either that mechanistic possibility or its falsification is allowed to us. On the other hand, we cannot know whether natural organisms as natural purposes may not be the special product of an "entirely different kind of original causality, namely an architectonic understanding, which cannot at all lie in material nature, nor in its intelligible substrate" (§71, 317, AA 388, 22–389, 3; §75, 338, AA 400, 21–28). As in the previous case, both to affirm and to deny this possibility is prohibited to us. It is certain, however, that because of the structural limitation of our human cognitive faculty, mechanical explanation falls short of accounting for the specificity of organized beings. Repeating a claim that goes back to his 1755 *Universal Natural History and Theory of the Heavens*, Kant states: "So certain is this that we may boldly state that it is absurd for human beings even to . . . hope that perhaps some day another Newton might arise who would explain to us, in terms of natural laws unordered by an intention, how even a mere blade of grass is produced" (§75, 337–338, AA 400, 16–20; §77, 353, AA 409, 35–37). Thus, the same limitation of the human cognitive faculty that makes it impossible both to assert the existence of a universal mechanism and to assume a first intelligent cause grounds the need for a regulative principle that could serve as a "guiding thread" (§71, 318, AA 389, 14) for the explanation of the "peculiarity" of those particular forms of nature according to final causes.

Kant's formulation of the first maxim of judgment as the thesis of the antinomy reads as follows: "*All* production of material things and their forms *must be judged* to be possible in terms of merely mechanical laws." Similarly, the second maxim or antithesis claims, "*Some* products of material nature *cannot be judged* to be possible in terms of merely mechanical laws" (§70, 314, AA 387, 3–8). If maintained within the heuristic and merely regulative use of the principle of reflective judgment, these maxims do not contradict each other. The first maxim claims that mechanical explanations must be attempted in the case of *all* natural phenomena and must have priority over all other kinds of principles.[3] The second maxim expresses the limitation of our mechanistic view of nature and the need to complement it with the regulative principle of final causes in the case of *certain* natural products such as organized living beings. It is important to stress that the second maxim does not claim that the *existence* of certain things is possible only as natural purposes. It only maintains that they cannot be *thought of* or *judged* otherwise than *as* natural purposes.

The latter difference can be clearly perceived if the subjective maxims of reflective judgment are converted into objective principles of determinant judgment. In this case, the thesis is transformed as "All production of material things *is possible* in terms of merely mechanical laws," while the antithesis now would claim that "some production of material things *is not possible* in terms of merely mechanical laws" (§70, 314–315, AA 387, 13–16). These two propositions are nothing but synthetic a priori judgments, transcendental laws of nature, or constitutive principles of natural phenomena precisely in the sense of the first *Critique*.[4] Kant's reasons for rejecting this shifted formulation make up the core of the doctrine of teleological judgment's antinomy.

The crucial point can be captured by the following question: why is nature's universal mechanism, expressed by the second formulation of the thesis, insufficient in Kant's view to guide our judgment about specific natural products—this insufficiency being precisely the basis for the antinomy of the reflective faculty of judgment? The question concerns even more generally the reason why a critique of the faculty of judgment should follow the *Critique of Pure Reason*. Why is the concept of mechanical causality of the first *Critique* unable to account for our reflection on "all" natural phenomena (both in their universality and homogeneity, and in their empirical specificity and contingent heterogeneity)? The answer lies in Kant's peculiar concept of causality. It is important to underline from the outset that for Kant (as opposed, for example, to Descartes) causality is not coexten-

---

3. See also §80.

4. In the first *Critique,* Kant does not say, I have to judge all intuitions as extensive quantities, but rather, all intuitions are extensive quantities; he does not say, I have to judge all changes according to the relation of cause and effect, but rather, all changes are the effect of a cause. This crucial difference is not perceived by McFarland, who considers "puzzling" "the fact that [Kant] calls the principle" expressed by the maxim of the thesis "a *regulative* principle" (*Kant's Concept of Teleology,* op. cit., 119).

sive with mechanism. If it were so, not only the *Critique of Judgment* but also the *Critique of Practical Reason* would not have been written. Two kinds of causality different from mechanical causality (and analogically related to each other) are the basis of the last two *Critiques*. On the one hand, freedom is still defined by Kant in terms of a special kind of causality, "causality through/from freedom." On the other hand, in §63 of the third *Critique*, taking up implicitly the problem raised in introduction §V, Kant has argued that an objective material purposiveness is introduced when we have to judge the lawfulness of a relation of cause and effect that involves the essential contingency of the effect's form. The possibility of these two forms of nonmechanical causality rests on Kant's view of the mechanism of nature.

In order to measure the distance between Kant's notion of mechanical causality and the pre-Kantian idea of universal mechanism, let us consider the example of Laplace.[5] In Laplace's world, two conditions are always fulfilled. (i) In a causal chain it is always (at least *de iure*) possible to find the term that constitutes the first principle or cause, and (ii) it is always (at least *de iure*) necessary to start from that first principle or cause in order to explain all the intermediary terms of the causal chain. The world of appearances of the *Critique of Pure Reason* turns Laplace's world upside down. In the realm of Kant's "nature in general," neither of Laplace's conditions can be fulfilled. Nonetheless, Kant's world is still dominated by universal mechanical laws. In the realm of appearances, we must always start from an actual, empirically given perception, and from it go back to the conditions that make it possible until we get to the structure of the a priori. In this regressive procedure, however, we are never allowed to leave the realm of experience so that no (metaphysical) *first* cause can be attained. The doctrine of the Dialectic of the first *Critique* is meant to dissipate any illusion concerning the possibility of ever reaching a first cause. Moreover, the limitation of mechanical causality to the sphere of "possible experience" is crucial if another type of causality is to be possible at all, namely a "causality through freedom" that extends beyond the realm of appearances.

Going back to the explanation of causality in the world of appearances, the *Critique of Pure Reason* merely establishes that every effect has a cause. Yet in all scientific explanation, the further question needs to be addressed: how can we determine among a number of different candidates *which* one exactly is the cause of a particular observed phenomenon? How can we decide whether the cause of the heat of a stone is the sun or a fire lit next to it? The first *Critique* leaves this question completely unanswered. It suggests that only empirical observation or a particular experience can provide a solution to this problem. However, if we consider the way in which the problem is picked up by the third *Critique*, we must acknowl-

5. I follow here L. Scaravelli, *Scritti kantiani,* Firenze, La Nuova Italia, 369–376; see also an analogous suggestion in M. Frank, V. Zanetti, I. Kant, *Schriften zur Ästhetik und Naturphilosophie*, op. cit., 1290, who refer to P. McLaughlin, *Kants Kritik der teleologischen Urteilskraft*, Bonn, Bouvier, 1989.

edge that empirical observation does not lead us to a solution. Empirical observation is rather the very source of the new complex question addressed by Kant's 1790 work. "Empirical experience" never provides us with the *unique* cause of a given phenomenon but always produces an infinite number of possible causes. Indeed, the fact that things "are cause in an infinite number of ways" constitutes the specific problem confronted by the third *Critique* (E §V, XXXII, 183, 18).

The third *Critique* offers a twofold general claim with regard to the notion of causality. It maintains (i) that every appearance has in another appearance its cause (whereby the position of the first *Critique* is restated), and (ii) that every appearance can be connected to another appearance *in an infinite number of ways* (whereby the notion of contingency arises). Ultimately, both the relation between purposiveness and mechanism and their common reference to the concept of causality are predicated upon these two claims. This is the source of the Dialectic of teleological judgment.

The difference between the first formulation of the antinomy, which regards the subjective maxims of our reflection upon particular natural forms, and the second formulation, which leads instead to transcendental laws of nature in general in the sense of the first *Critique*, measures the profound distance between Kant's notion of causality and the pre-Kantian identity between causality and mechanism. It is precisely in the space of this distance that final causes find their place in Kant's theory. If all causality were the causality of mechanism (i.e., if all events could be always brought back to a first cause), the concept of purposiveness (and the idea of freedom) would find no place in the theory. Hence, Kant rejects the formulation that transforms the maxims of teleological judgment into universal laws of nature not only because, in this case, the two propositions would contradict each other—one of them being false. He rejects it mainly because we would have then an antinomy that would not be an antinomy of judgment but a contradiction in the legislation of reason itself. Reason can demonstrate neither that "all production of material things is possible in terms of merely mechanical laws" nor that "some production of material things is not possible" according to those mechanical laws. We cannot have determinative a priori principles for the possibility of things in terms of empirical laws. This is the condition for the possibility of an independent faculty of judgment. It follows that the only possible formulation of the antinomy between natural mechanism and objective purposiveness can be in terms of the reflective faculty of judgment.

2. "Technic of Nature" (§§72–75): Dogmatic and Critical Use of the Concept of Natural Purpose

The presentation of the antinomy of teleological judgment leads Kant to the crucial distinction between "dogmatic" and "critical" use of the principle of nature's objective purposiveness. While the former concerns the determinant faculty of judgment and implies a transcendent use of speculative reason, the latter only regards the lawfulness of our reflection on nature and leads to the employment of reason within the limits of our human cognitive faculties (§72, 323–324, AA 392, 26, 33; §74, 329, AA 395, 26–35; §75).

At this point, however, the question still remains of whether causality in terms of final causes really "proves" a special kind of causality at work in nature or whether this causality should rather be regarded as objectively one with mechanical causality itself (§72, 320, AA 390, 22–25). In the second case, final causes would be introduced in natural science not as a special kind of causality but as nothing more than a way of thinking of nature in analogy to our own practical–technical causality. At stake therein is ultimately, once again, the epistemological status of teleology. The issue can also be formulated by distinguishing a twofold notion of nature's "technic." We can think of nature either as working according to a *technica intentionalis* (i.e., as producing its forms according to an intentional causality in terms of purposes distinct from its merely mechanical causality), or we can still view nature's technique as *technica naturalis* (i.e., as a procedure that does not imply purposes and is ultimately one with mechanism) (§72, 321, AA 390, 36–37). In this case, the analogy with our own practical intentional causality would not allow us to infer the *existence* of a peculiar type of causality next to mechanism. Unintentional causality would eventually coincide with the mechanism.

How shall we explain the principle of nature's technic? Kant suggests that the history of philosophy seems to have exhausted the complete range of "dogmatic" answers to the problem (and therefore has remained trapped in the second formulation of the antinomy). The various systems have attempted to understand dogmatically the *objective* principles of the possibility of things, which they explained either in terms of unintentional final causes or in terms of intentional causes. In the former case, we have the "idealism" of unintentional natural purposes (either the systems of "casualty," such as Epicurus's and Democritus's, or of "fatalism," such as Spinoza's); in the latter case, we have the "realism" of intentional natural purposes (either "hylozoism" or "theism") (§72, 322, AA 391, 16–392, 12).[6]

Kant suggests that since the notion of natural purpose has no objective reality—neither as a concept of understanding nor as a concept of reason—it cannot be employed dogmatically in the subsumptions of determinant judgment (§74, 330, 331, AA 396, 12–13; 397, 2–3). Instead, the notion of natural purpose has only a regulative value as a "critical principle of reason for the reflective faculty of judgment" (§75, title). What is at stake is the status of the concept of a "causality of nature in terms of the rule of purposes" with regard to the distinction between (i) "the causality through purposes (of art)" (i.e., the *nexus finalis*) on the one hand, and (ii) "the causality in terms of nature's mechanism" (i.e., the *nexus effectivus*) on the other hand (§74, 332, AA 397, 13–16). While both concepts display objective real-

6. See §58 for an analogous discussion in the case of aesthetic purposiveness. The principle of "theism" has for Kant an "advantage" (despite its dogmatism) over the other systems insofar as it allows one at least to think of the ultimate ground for nature's purposiveness and to recuperate the "remote analogy" to our intentional practical causality.

ity, no objective reality can be proved for nature's objective purposiveness. It follows that this notion of purposiveness must be a merely regulative principle for the reflective faculty of judgment and that its employment can only be a critical one.

Clearly, the presentation of the antinomy has led Kant a step further in the discussion of the intentionality vs. the non–intentionality of nature's objective purposiveness—an issue that §§67–68, along with §IX of the "First Introduction," seemed to have already settled in favor of the first possibility by banning all search for an alleged intention of nature as illegitimate. To be sure, the delicate issue therein could be settled only by the Dialectic (not by the Analytic) by rejecting dogmatism of any kind. What is at stake is the only condition under which we are allowed to think of nature's purposiveness as intentional. Only after the critical use of the notion of nature's purposiveness has been established can the discussion move on to the possibility of thinking of an intention in nature's causality. Then alone will the dangers of a slip into speculative theology be avoided.

The notion of a critical use of the principle of natural purpose allows Kant the connection between teleology and theology. Within the limits of a *critical* use of the principle, the explanation of nature's productivity with regard to particular forms may indeed turn to the notion of "intention" (§75, 333, 334, AA 397, 33; 398, 13). The analogy with the "causality of an understanding that is productive" is thereby instituted (§75, 333, AA 398, 3). The faculty of judgment follows a principle of reason for the employment of our cognitive faculties and critically maintains its reflection within reason's limits. As we have learned from the first *Critique*, reason is the faculty that aims at the systematic unity of all our cognition. However, when reason refers to the understanding in this endeavor, it necessarily falls into a speculative dialectic in which its use becomes immediately "transcendent" (§76, 339, AA 401, 14–15). It is only when reason appeals to the faculty of judgment that a systematic unity of nature can be established in reflection as a regulative idea. In this case, reason is still kept within the limits of an immanent use. Within these limits, the maxim of nature's purposiveness can claim an "absolute" necessity with regard to the possibility of thinking of organized beings (§75, 334, AA 398, 16). The maxim, however, is "indeed useful but not indispensable" (§75, 334, AA 398, 23) with regard to the whole of nature conceived as a system. The whole of nature, as opposed to particular organized beings, is never given to us in experience. The "idea" of a natural purpose is, in this regard, an idea of a very special kind, since it functions as a rational principle not for the understanding but for the faculty of judgment (§77, 345, AA 405, 17, 18).[7]

The contingency that our appeal to the intention of a productive cause is meant to explain is also the ground for the connection between teleology and theology. Thereby, teleology leads to the assumption of an intelligent being outside of nature as that from whose intention the whole of nature depends in its first ori-

7. This crucial link between reason and the reflective faculty of judgment is still the missing link in the doctrine of the appendix to the transcendental Dialectic of the first *Critique*.

gin. Kant is extremely cautious in formulating his argument since all temptation to fall into dogmatism must be avoided. Hence arises a question that requires us to stop and reflect before venturing into theological speculations of any kind: "What does even the most complete teleology of all prove in the end?" (§75, 335, AA 399, 6–7). Certainly it does not prove anything about the existence of an extra-mundane intelligent being. It only proves that due to the constitution of our cognitive faculties, we cannot form any concept of the possibility of the world that we experience in its manifold empirical and contingent forms without assuming a "highest cause" working intentionally. The crucial point of Kant's argument is the reference to the specific constitution of the cognitive faculties proper to a "finite rational being in general" (§76, 339, AA 401, 23–24). Since purposiveness (in the case of the aesthetic as well as the teleological faculty of judgment) is a condition that has nothing to do with objects and their constitution but only with the subject and its cognitive faculties, then the principle thereby expressed cannot be valid for "any thinking and knowing being" in general (i.e., objectively and dogmatically) (§75, 336, AA 399, 25). Instead, it is valid exclusively for the *human* limited cognitive faculties (i.e., its validity can only be subjective and critical).

3. The Solution of the Antinomy (§§76–78): The Faculty of Judgment Between Discursive and Intuitive Understanding

In order to highlight this latter point and to show exactly what constitutes the specific limitation of the human mind, Kant discusses a contra-factual hypothesis. In this hypothesis lies the key to the final solution of the antinomy. What would a nonhuman understanding be like; how would it think; and how would the world (objects and nature) appear to it? And even more importantly for the project of transcendental philosophy as a whole, what would the elimination of the limiting condition imposed by the transcendental structures of the human mind imply for the crucial theses of transcendental philosophy in relation to both its theoretical and practical parts? Finally, given that the dialectic of teleological judgment draws to the center the peculiar function of reflective judgment in general, how does the transcendental condition intervene in the solution of the antinomy? Such are the questions that occupy Kant's discussion in the remark of §76.[8]

Kant's argument in §§76–77 identifies in the "discursive" (as opposed to "intuitive") nature of our understanding the specific character of the *human* mind (§77, 347, AA 406, 17, 25). Then it proceeds to hypothetically imagine what a mind would be like whose nature is not discursive. Consequences are drawn from

8. §§76–77 will be a crucial text for all post-Kantian philosophers precisely because they entail a consideration of Kantian philosophy from the perspective of a mind that cannot be positively thought of within the framework of Kant's thought. His successors will attempt to change the condition of the limitation to the human cognitive faculty. The results of this move are already foreseen by Kant in the present sections. With regard to the problem of freedom, see A. Nuzzo, "Transformations of Freedom in the Jena Kant-Reception (1785–1794)," in *The Owl of Minerva* 32, 2 (Spring 2001), 135–167.

this hypothesis with regard to the different thematic fields covered respectively by the three *Critiques*. Thus, the argument of §76 indirectly verifies the table of the faculties of the *human* mind that concludes the introduction to the *Critique of Judgment*. Kant's task in these sections is to construct a third term that may involve the ground for a conciliation of both the thesis and the antithesis of the antinomy of reflective judgment (the *Vereinigung* in the title of §78). For the principle of the *Vereinbarkeit* of the two types of explanation of nature "must be posited in that which rests outside of the two [maxims], i.e., in the supersensible" (§78, 357, AA 412, 9–12).

The *Critique of Pure Reason* has shown that in order for cognition to take place two radically "heterogeneous components" are required: sensibility, which provides sensible intuition of existing given objects, and understanding, which provides concepts for the possibility of objects. Only the synthesis of these two heterogeneous components can produce our cognition of objects. In their isolation from each other, neither sensibility nor understanding can lead us to any cognition of objects. In §76 of the third *Critique*, Kant summarized this fundamental thesis with the claim that it is indispensable and necessary for our human understanding to distinguish between "the possibility and the actuality of things" (§76, 340, AA 401, 31–32). The understanding, whose concepts reach only the possibility of things, needs sensible intuition in order to ascertain the actuality of its objects. Our understanding cannot take the reality of its concepts out of itself; that is, human understanding is not itself productive of the reality of the objects that it thinks. The function of understanding is thinking, not intuiting. Thus, Kant links all modal categories to the peculiar discursive character of our understanding.

(i) At this point, Kant introduces his first contra-factual statement: If cognition did not require two heterogeneous elements such as sensible intuitions and concepts, then there would be *no distinction between possibility and actuality*. In this case, we would have an "intuitive understanding." Everything that this understanding would think, it would also at the same time intuit. Such an understanding would produce in actuality whatever it could think. It would not need sensibility to fulfill any of its cognitive functions. Nothing would be sensibly given to it as actual. (ii) The second consequence drawn from the hypothetical structure of an intuitive understanding is the *elimination of the distinction between contingency and necessity*. Since whatever this understanding thinks also necessarily exists (§76, 341, AA 403, 2), then nothing can be thought by it that also could not exist (i.e., nothing contingent can be thought or can exist).

From the fact that we can think of another type of understanding that does not work *discursively* as does the human mind but is rather *intuitive*, it follows that the distinction between possibility and actuality, contingency and necessity has only a limited validity or is valid only subjectively with regard to the human mind.[9] In addition, our human understanding's limitation is further proven by reason's own

9. To make the same point in terms of the first *Critique,* human knowledge is knowledge of appearances; categories apply to objects as appearances, not as things in themselves.

striving toward an *Urgrund*, which is thought of as "something existing with unconditional necessity" (§76, 341, AA 402, 23) and in which no distinction between possibility and actuality can be found. Only if the maxim of recognizing the validity of our judgments as limited to the subjective constitution of the human understanding is respected can we be granted a "safe and immanent" (§76, 342, AA 403, 18–19)—although only regulative—use of the principles of reason.

(iii) An analogous consideration of the import of human limits plays itself out in the practical sphere, where reason presupposes its unconditioned causality (i.e., freedom). If we let the limitative condition fall, then the *distinction between obligation and action is erased.* The necessity of the practical law is the necessity of a command expressed in the form of duty—not as *Sein* but as *Sein-Sollen* (§76, 342–342, AA 403, 23–34). The reason for this lies exclusively in the possibility that human practical reason may be affected by sensibility (desires, inclinations, and passions) and not immediately determined by the law. For a "holy will" the moral law would not have the force of a command. In the case of a reason that could by no means be determined by sensibility, the moral law would not be a law (which is open to the possibility of not being respected); the distinction between what is morally necessary and what is physically contingent would not hold; and reason's causality would only take place in an intelligible world that would by necessity harmonize with the moral law. Ultimately, Kant suggests, "in such a world there would be no difference between obligation and action." (iv) But there would also be no difference "between a law that says what is possible through our doing and the theoretical law that says what is actual through our doing" (§76, 343, AA 404, 1–3). In this case, *all distinction between theoretical and practical reason would be completely eliminated.* If sensibility as an independent source of cognition were eliminated (i.e., if the distinction between possibility and actuality of things were erased) the specificity of the practical sphere and of Kant's practical reason would be lost. An intuitive understanding produces (creates) all that it thinks of and consequently all that there is. In addition, this production amounts to the only type of activity possible. In this world, everything would be actual simply because, being good, it is possible.

(v) The last consequence that Kant draws from the elimination of the restrictive condition that defines the human cognitive faculty touches upon the core doctrine of the *Critique of Judgment.* The discursive nature of our understanding requires us to move from the particular given in intuition to the universal of the concept. The universal does not itself determine the manifold particulars that are given in intuition and in sensation. The particular remains contingent in relation to the universal under which it must be subsumed (§77, 347, AA 406, 14–16), so that the particular cannot be deduced or analytically derived from the universal (§77, 348, AA 406, 36–37), hence the need for being referred to a connection in terms of purposes in order to be apprehended as a part of a unitary and systematic whole. If our understanding were intuitive, then it could go from the universal to the particular. The conceptual universal would directly determine, i.e., *produce*, the particular, which would consequently lose its contingency. In this case, no distinction between "natural mechanism" and "technic of nature" as connection in terms of purposes would take place (§76, 343, AA 404, 17–20). The determinant faculty of judgment would effect the only possible kind of subsumption, so that there would be no reflective judgment and hence no independent faculty of judgment at all. However, in this case, determination would amount to production (and even to a sort of creation). The particular would not be subsumed *under* the universal (the "analytic-universal," §77, 348, AA 407, 14–15) but contained *in* it (the "synthetic-universal," §77, 349, AA 407, 21–22). The universal would not be a concept (discursive) but an intuition (as are the forms of space and time).

The concept or, better, the idea of natural purpose is necessarily connected with the specificity and "peculiarity" of the human understanding (§77, title). A "distinguishing feature" (§77, 345, AA 405, 16–17) proper to the idea of natural purpose in relation to all other ideas corresponds to this peculiarity. The idea of natural purpose is a principle that reason gives not to the understanding but to the faculty of judgment. At issue in Kant's argument is the relation between understanding and faculty of judgment—a relation that takes place only in the case of a discursive understanding. An intuitive understanding needs neither sensibility in order for actual objects to be given to it nor reflection in order to establish a harmonious relation between the contingent forms of nature and our concepts.

We can conclude from Kant's argument in §§76–77 that if we reject the fundamental thesis of the Analytic of the first *Critique* concerning the discursive character of the human understanding then the very *raison d'être* of the third *Critique* is lost along with the crucial need for an independent faculty of judgment and its reflection. Correspondingly, if we convert the subjective maxims of judgment that constitute the antinomy of teleological judgment into transcendental laws of nature or objective principle of the understanding, then we fall into dogmatism, thereby canceling the results of critical philosophy as such. The antinomy of judgment arises precisely from the same discursive nature of the human mind that makes a faculty of judgment necessary. Yet, this same discursivity leads us to think of another understanding for which the antinomy would not hold. This is precisely Kant's way to the solution.

While in §76 the assumption of an intuitive understanding has the function of a counter-factual hypothesis meant to underline the specific limitation proper to the human discursive understanding, in §77 Kant's reference to the intuitive understanding or to "the idea of another possible understanding different from the human one" (§77, 345–346, AA 405, 26–27) becomes a sort of necessary regulative idea that grounds the employment of the principle of nature's purpose by the reflective faculty of judgment.[10] Thereby, the solution of the antinomy is complete. Kant argues that in order to at least conceive of the possibility of harmony

---

10. While Kant's argument in §76 proceeds in the form of conditionals, §77 does not hesitate to present the necessity of thinking of an intuitive understanding in terms of a *muß*.

"between the things of nature and our judgment" (§77, 348, AA 407, 5–6) "we *must* think of another understanding in relation to which we can represent the harmonious connection between the natural laws and our faculty of judgment as necessary even without the mediation of a purpose as intention" (§77, 348, AA 407, 8–12). The intuitive understanding would conceive of the whole of nature as an organism, or a system in which the whole is the condition of the possibility of the parts. For an intuitive understanding, no contradiction (and no antinomy) would subsist between mechanism and teleology. Because of the discursive character of our understanding, on the contrary, we can conceive of the whole only as the mechanical "effect of the motive forces of the parts" (§77, 349, AA 407, 29–30). Cognition and science are possible for us exclusively in this way. Yet, another possibility is available. Our faculty of judgment can assume the intuitive understanding as a sort of "model" and can follow the "standard" set by it (*nach Maßgabe*, §77, 349, AA 407, 32). In this case, we still need to adapt such a model to our limitation: "The only way that we can represent the possibility of the parts as dependent on the whole is by having the *representation* of the whole contain the ground for the possibility of the parts." The whole is the product or effect whose representation is the cause that makes the effect possible (§77, 349–350, AA 408, 1–6). This is precisely the way in which intentional causality or causality through purposes works. Hence, under the condition of a discursive understanding, the faculty of judgment's use of the principle of final causes is nothing but the surrogate for, or the translation of, the way of conceiving proper to an intuitive understanding for which no tension between mechanism and teleology would subsist. In the concept of natural purpose, judgment works as if its logic were the logic of an intuitive understanding. Hence, the reference to an intuitive understanding (i.e., to an understanding different from ours),[11] allows us first to recognize that the antinomy between mechanism and teleology is valid only subjectively for a limited human mind; second, it suggests a situation in which no contradiction would subsist between the view of nature as a mechanism and the view of nature as an organic and systematic whole (i.e., a situation in which no antinomy would arise). Finally, it leads us to assume a sort of hypothetical way of reflecting in analogy with an intuitive understanding and to refer both our maxims to a "supersensible substrate of nature" in which they may find their unification (§77, 353, AA 410, 6). This latter possibility is opened up by the limitation of our cognition to the world of appearances, which discloses the possibility of at least thinking of a "thing-in-itself" underlying it as its "supersensible real ground" (§77, 352, AA 409, 13–14, 6; §78, 359, AA 413, 14–15).[12]

11. Kant claims that we do not need to prove that such an understanding is possible but only that we can think of it in contrast to our human understanding (§77, 350, AA 408, 18–20).

12. The second formulation of the antinomy in terms of constitutive principles would render this conclusion utterly impossible.

Thus, the principle of the *Vereinigung* of mechanism and teleology "must be posited in that which rests outside" of the two maxims (§78, 357, AA 412, 9–12; 362, AA 414, 28–29); that is, in something that lies beyond all possible empirical representation of nature as well as beyond all possible determination. In the "indeterminate" (and indeterminable) concept of the "supersensible" (and in the connected notion of a "higher understanding," §78, 362, AA 414, 34), Kant locates the "*common* principle" (§78, 358, AA 412, 33–35) that explains how mechanism and teleology can be reconciled for the reflective—not for the determinant—faculty of judgment. The supersensible does not provide the ground for an "explanation" of how a product is possible in terms of given laws. It offers instead a ground for the "examination" of this possibility by means of reflection (§78, 357–358, AA 412, 17–19) and its heuristic principle of a technic of nature.

Chapter 14

The Methodology of the Teleological Faculty of Judgment (§§79–91): Faculty of Judgment and Practical Reason

Kant concluded the Critique of the Aesthetic Faculty of Judgment with a short appendix concerning the *Methodenlehre* of taste (§60). Herein a few pages were enough to argue that no methodology but, at the most, only a propaedeutic for all fine arts was feasible. For taste does not allow for universal rules, and a "science of taste" is properly an impossible discipline. In §60, however, the important issue of the relation between taste and moral ideas was developed in the aftermath of the symbolic relation between beauty and the morally good. Structurally similar is the conclusion of the Critique of the Teleological Faculty of Judgment, which also ends with a *Methodenlehre*. In this case, however, the Methodology occupies Kant at length. He dedicates to it thirteen sections and a long General Remark, which make it much longer than the Analytic and the Dialectic taken together. As was the case with the methodology of taste, the methodology of teleological judgment stays under the title of an appendix, although this title is first inserted in the second edition of the *Critique of Judgment*. In this final part of the third *Critique*, Kant deals with crucial issues such as the function played by teleology in the natural sciences, the role of living organisms within teleological systems, man's place in creation, a teleological conception of history, the relation between theology and physical teleology, and the proposal of an ethical theology. However, in a certain sense and despite the importance of the issues raised, this final discussion indeed constitutes an appendix. Nothing is added to the strictly transcendental inquiry into the a priori principle of the faculty of judgment as such. What is at stake in this part is a further and conclusive determination of the relation between the faculty of judgment and practical reason.

1. Teleology, Mechanism, and the "Adventures of Reason" in Science (§§79–81)

In the methodology, Kant takes up the fundamental results of both the Analytic and the Dialectic of the teleological faculty of judgment. He explores the various possibilities that teleology offers to natural sciences and to scientific discourses and practices as different as the analogies and hypotheses employed in evolutionary biology, comparative anatomy, geology, and taxonomy in general.[1] On the

1. For Kant's relation to the natural sciences of his time, see M. Frank and V. Zanetti in their edition, I. Kant, *Schriften zur Ästhetik und Naturphilosophie*, Frankfurt a.M., DKV, 1996, 1310–1322; see also P. McLaughlin, *Kants Kritik der teleologischen Urteilskraft*, Bonn, Bouvier, 1989, 1–36.

other hand, once the natural dialectic of the faculty of judgment has been solved and the conditions for the employment of the principle of teleology clearly stated, Kant can dwell in the presentation of the unavoidable "adventures" in which human reason ventures under the guidance of the regulative principle of nature's objective purposiveness. In all cases examined, reason and judgment proceed together along a subtle line that marks out a field in which—if reason meets no contradiction in its speculations—experience can offer no example and no support whatsoever (§80, 370, AA 419, 26–27, 35–36). These sections will prove incredibly relevant for the development of the philosophy of nature in early German Idealism.

§79 establishes the theoretical starting point of the Methodology. Returning to the issue raised right at the beginning of the introduction concerning the internal partition of philosophy as a system, Kant asks about the place occupied by teleology within the encyclopedic system of philosophy. The question already received an answer in §68 of the Analytic. As a science, philosophy is divided into a theoretical part and a practical part. The theoretical part, in turn, is either a "doctrine of nature" or a "doctrine of god," or theology. Does teleology find its place in one of these two "doctrines"? §68 has suggested that neither case applies and that a third option is rather in order. Teleology's belonging to theology is ruled out by the fact that teleology deals with natural products and their causes. From this, it follows that even though a reference to a highest cause is made, it is made not for the determinant faculty of judgment, which alone can ground a doctrine, but only for the reflective faculty of judgment. Teleology's belonging to natural science is ruled out as well and for analogous reasons. Natural science, as doctrine of nature, is the work of the determinant faculty of judgment and of the understanding in its universal laws. Teleology, instead, is a consideration proper exclusively to the reflective faculty of judgment by which no object is constituted or determined. Hence, Kant concludes that "teleology as a science does not belong to any doctrine but belongs only to critique: the critique of a special cognitive faculty, namely judgment" (§79, 366, AA 417, 15–17). As opposed to the critique of taste that can by no means be a science and hence does not allow for any methodology at all, teleology is indeed a science—albeit a quite peculiar one—and hence does contain a methodology. To the extent that teleology does follow a priori principles, method plays an important role in our judging of nature according to the principle of final causes. As Kant suggested in §68, the place of teleology in philosophy is a kind of non-place: its location is not in one of its doctrinal parts but rather in the overall structure that organizes and articulates the whole of philosophy itself. Teleology has a role in the transition from natural science to theology (§79, 366, AA 417, 22; §68, 309, AA 383, 28–30). Thus, this claim verifies the special character of the third *Critique* already stated both in the preface and in the introduction: no doctrine or metaphysics can follow the *Critique of Judgment*.

The solution of the Dialectic established a "unification" of the principles of mechanism and teleology in the concept of "technic of nature" (§78, title). Now

Kant spells out the modality of that unification, suggesting the necessity of two complementary relations between mechanism and teleology (§81, 374, AA 422, 8–9). He claims, first, the "necessary subordination" of the principle of mechanism to teleology in our explanation of natural products (§80, title). But then he complements this subordination by "associating" mechanism with the teleological principle in explaining natural purposes as *natural* products (§81, title). For, while mechanism alone cannot give a sufficient account of organized beings and their place in nature, teleology without mechanism is not able to account for organized beings as *natural* products (i.e., as products met in the world of natural phenomena and objects of a particular experience).

Referring to a central issue raised in the introduction (§V), Kant contends that the possibility of an insight into the infinite variety of particular natural forms requires that we subordinate the mechanistic principle, without which no science would be possible at all, to the idea of nature as a unitary and purposive system. Drawing from the results of both the Analytic and the Dialectic, Kant claims that the idea of nature's systematicity and organization rests on a twofold condition due to the discursive constitution of the human cognitive faculty. The first condition expresses the need for *unity* as ultimate ground of nature, while the second condition adds the *intentionality* of this first ground (i.e., the idea that the consequences or effects that proceed from this ground are related to it as its purposes) (§80, 373, AA 421, 19–22).[2] The notion of nature's technic leads to the regulative idea of an "architectonic understanding" (§80, 372, AA 420, 23–24). The two conditions, unified in Kant's idea of teleology, allow for the collaboration of reason with the reflective faculty of judgment in all those scientific enterprises that ask for the meaning of particular contingent beings within the organization of nature as a whole. These scientific explanations require heuristic hypotheses and analogies that only the reflective faculty of judgment can provide. The procedures of classification, comparison, and organization of particular natural forms and cases; the tasks of detecting kinship and similarities among different individuals or species, of recognizing patterns, and of explaining change and mutation across species—all are examples of crucial scientific practices unthinkable in terms of merely mechanistic reasoning and universal laws. They require the intervention of the reflective faculty of judgment and its capacity of explaining the particular in terms of an "analogy of forms" and of the unity of final causes (§80, 368, AA 418, 33–34). The "archaeologist of nature," in her explanation of organized matter and living beings (§80, 369, AA 419, 9), must resort to judgment and its principles by subordinating to them the understanding and the universal laws of mechanism.

On the other hand, if we want to explain organized beings as products *of nature* (i.e., as individual beings belonging to the world of phenomena and given to

2. If only the first condition is met, the "whole" problem remains unsolvable. What we have then is "pantheism" and "Spinozism" (§80, 373, AA 421, 12–22).

us in experience), teleological explanation alone is not sufficient. Only the laws of mechanism can provide an explanation in this case. Thus, we must associate mechanism to teleology while subordinating the former to the latter. We must view mechanism as the means employed by a cause that acts intentionally. In its mechanical laws, nature must be subordinated to the purpose pursued by an intentional cause (§81, 374, AA 422, 6–8). Yet we must also think of the intelligent cause as acting through nature and by means of nature. Ultimately, this is the complex meaning of the unification between teleology and mechanism that concluded the Dialectic (§78, title; §81, 374, AA 422, 6–8).[3]

2. Nature's "Ultimate Purpose" and Man's Place in Nature (§§82–83)

In light of the different notions of objective purposiveness presented in the Analytic, Kant extends the sphere of teleological investigation to two interconnected issues. On the one hand, he discusses the question of nature's "ultimate purpose" (*letzter Zweck*) (§§82–83), while on the other he raises the question of the "final purpose" (*Endzweck*) of creation (§84). The turning point of Kant's argument is the reflection on man's place in nature. Such a reflection shifts the attention from natural science to Kant's philosophy of history and more generally to practical philosophy. Thereby, Kant addresses the crucial issue regarding the intersection between nature and freedom in that particular organized natural being which is the human being. The human being must be regarded not only as a purpose of nature but also as a being capable of purposive activity.

Kant suggests that our judgment constructs a system of nature within which all particular purposes are organized and harmoniously unified. Referring back to the distinction between external and internal purposiveness of nature (§63), Kant discusses the different implications of the common sense question, "What is a thing there for?" (§82, 381, AA 425, 31). Obviously, the question is meaningful only in the framework of a teleological reflection on nature. In this case, however, it may indicate either the external relation of means to an "*ultimate* purpose" or

---

3. As examples of philosophical speculations that only assume a teleological explanation without supporting and complementing it with nature's mechanism, Kant presents "occasionalism" and the "theory of pre-established harmony, " which is represented by the "theory of evolution" and the "theory of epigenesis." In both cases (albeit in different ways), "all nature" as such "is lost entirely" in its production. For god's hand directly, not nature's formative forces, is assumed to create nature's forms (§81, 375, AA 422, 33). The risk of eliminating nature and natural explanation is what Kant calls "hyperphysics" (§81, 377, AA 423, 30). Against the theories of evolution of his time, Kant favors Friedrich Blumenbach's epigenetic theory, which leaves "an indeterminable and yet unmistakable share to natural mechanism" next to teleological explanation (§81, 379, AA 424, 28–30). See P. R. Sloan, "Preforming the Categories: Eighteenth-Century Generation Theory and the Biological Roots of Kant's Apriori," in *Journal of the History of Philosophy,* 40, 2 (2002), 229–253.

the internal purposiveness of a "*final* purpose." Kant defines *Endzweck* as "a purpose that requires no other purpose as condition of its possibility." A "final purpose" is necessarily "unconditioned" (§84, 397, AA 435, 2–6). It follows that with regard to the whole of nature, no natural thing can be considered as *Endzweck*. Yet we may still ask for nature's *letzter Zweck*, the last member of the purposive chain of means and ends that constitutes a systematic organization (§82, 382, AA 425, 15–21). In this case, the argument leads inevitably to the issue of man's place in nature and to the possibility of considering the human being as the ultimate purpose of nature.

At this point, Kant combines the distinctions of the Analytic with the results of the Dialectic and builds a sort of applied antinomy. Accordingly, he presents two opposite claims. (i) One claim sets the human being as the ultimate purpose of creation following two possible arguments, both based on external teleology. Either one maintains in an explicitly anthropocentric vein that all natural products and events exist for man's benefit, in this case dangerously trespassing in theology, or one takes the apparently different route endorsed by Linnaeus of seeing the human being both as purpose and means for a vaster balance of the whole. (ii) The opposite claim denies both that nature is a system of purposes and that man is the ultimate purpose of creation. Everything in nature is viewed as the result of mechanical revolutions that have merely mechanical causes, as the result of causes that "act wholly unintentionally," and as the product "of savage, all-powerful forces of a nature working in a state of chaos" (§82, 384, AA 427, 36–37). Nature, this time, resembles the object of our judgments on the sublime. It excludes both intention and order, or systematicity, and consequently allows for no objective purpose at all. With regard to these two claims, Kant refers to the solution of the antinomy of teleological judgment and to the unification of the principles of mechanism and final causes in that "supersensible substrate" of nature that contains the ground for the "unificability" of both mechanistic and teleological representations of the possibility of nature (§82, 387, AA 429, 16). This antinomy shows the question of nature's ultimate purpose must be posed in a different way. Such a purpose should not be searched merely in man's biological and natural existence but rather in those human dispositions that reveal what man is able to purposively do with himself in society and history.

Thus, Kant's argument leads to a view of man as the point of intersection between nature and freedom, the place in which freedom meets the natural conditions of its own sensible realization. If what is generally at stake in the Methodology is the systematic position of teleology within the encyclopedia of all the sciences, now Kant extends the realm of teleology to anthropology, philosophy of history, and practical philosophy in general. For the faculty of judgment, the human being as natural being is not only organism, or natural purpose, but also the "ultimate purpose of nature." But what is it, in the human being, that must be considered as nature's ultimate purpose? Kant presents two possibilities: either this purpose is materially a purpose that nature itself must fulfill, namely man's "happiness," or it is formally only "man's aptitude and skill" for various purposes in general (i.e., dispositions that man himself must develop and cultivate), and this is "culture" (§83, 388, AA 429, 35–430, 5). Kant's considerations on the idea of happiness confirm its exclusion from the practical sphere of freedom. Happiness belongs neither to nature strictly considered by theoretical knowledge nor to freedom or practical knowledge. In its lowest determination, happiness is restricted to the natural needs of the human species, while in its highest determination, it extends to the capacity of pursuing all imagined ends. In neither case, however, is happiness something that man can ever completely achieve in life. Yet it does constitute the "material" of all human purposes on earth (§83, 391, AA 431, 19–20). If happiness is indeed *our own* human "ultimate purpose" (§83, 389, AA 430, 21), we have no basis on which to maintain that human happiness is *nature's own* ultimate purpose, as if nature were a benevolent agent acting and producing its forms just for man's own welfare.[4]

Once the material condition of happiness has been excluded as possible ultimate purpose of nature with regard to the human being, what remains is a merely "formal and subjective condition." According to this condition, nature's purpose would be simply to make man capable of setting purposes in general and of using nature itself as a means in conformity with the "maxims of his free purposes" (§83, 391, AA 431, 25–26). Kant calls culture the "production of an aptitude for purposes in general in a rational being" (§83, 392, AA 431, 28–30). The production of this aptitude leaves the subject thoroughly free in its moral determination. Thus, culture is the only "ultimate purpose" that we can attribute to nature with regard to the human being. Nature only provides man with the formal disposition or capacity of making something out of himself, of creating value for his own life not in terms of what is naturally given but in terms of what he is capable of achieving (§83, 395 fn., AA 434, 29–36). Herein, Kant pushes the self-productive character of natural organisms to further consequences. Man is a being that is capable of self-organization not only in a natural but also in a social and political way.

Moreover, Kant distinguishes different types of "culture." The "culture of skill" is the foremost pragmatic condition for promoting purposes. This kind of culture does not assist the will in choosing which purposes should be achieved in the first place. To this aim, a "culture of discipline" is required. Such a culture is a merely negative one. It consists in the "liberation of the will from the despotism of desires" so that our choices are not completely determined by them. Arts, the sciences, and the culture of taste promote this liberation. However, Kant suggests that we must recognize, at the same time, that desires constitute the natural—even "animal"—part of ourselves, a part that we must not injure but rather reconcile with our freedom of choice (§83, 392, AA 432, 5–6). Thereby Kant takes us directly to his philosophy of history. The formal condition to promote nature's ultimate purpose (i.e., culture), is the development of man's natural dispositions in

---

4. Further, it would make no sense to assume that nature has an ultimate purpose that can never be achieved.

civil society.[5] This requires, in turn, a cosmopolitan order, a system of all states without which war becomes inevitable (§83, 393–394, AA 432, 31–433, 5). In his teleological philosophy of history, Kant sees war as an incentive for man "to develop to the utmost all the talents that serve culture" (§83, 394, AA 433, 14–15).[6] Thus, he concludes that although "war is an unintentional human endeavor . . . yet it is also a deeply hidden and perhaps intentional endeavor of the supreme wisdom" at least to prepare for the condition of lawfulness and freedom among the states on a moral ground (§83, 394, AA 435, 2–3). Thus, through culture, nature's teleology becomes historical. As such, it works as a bridge toward morality. The methodology of teleological judgment proceeds similarly to the methodology of aesthetic judgment. In the case of taste, it was the development of taste to prepare and foster a moral habit and a receptivity to moral ideas.

3. The Transition to Morality: Man as the "Final Purpose" of Creation (§84)

The inquiry into nature's "ultimate purpose" leads to the issue of the "final purpose" of creation. At stake is the possibility of identifying beyond the relativity of an ultimate purpose a purpose that has the absolute value of an *Endzweck*. The human being as subject of morality is nature's final purpose, which hints at a noumenal dimension beyond nature itself. Thereby, Kant throws a bridge between the realm of nature and that of freedom.

Once Kant has shown that a productive understanding can be at least thought as the intentional cause of nature's organized beings, then the further question necessarily arises that regards the "objective ground" that determines this cause to production. This is the question of the "final purpose" for which such things exist (§84, 397, AA 434, 17–435, 3). The final purpose—being "a purpose that requires no other purpose as condition of its possibility"—is necessarily unconditioned and set beyond the chain of empirical conditions to be met within nature (§84, 397, AA 435, 6; §86, 412–413; AA 443, 31–37). Hence, the final purpose cannot itself be a purpose of nature (both of the nature outside and within us), which is always an empirically conditioned purpose. Thus, the final purpose must be something that has in itself the condition of its own possibility. Accordingly, it must be an a priori concept of reason (§86, 415, AA 445, 10–11). If something is to exist as the final purpose of an intelligent cause, then in the order of purposes that constitutes creation, this being must depend simply on its idea (§84, 396–397, AA 435, 10–14). It is not difficult for Kant to discover the only possible candidate—"in this world"—for this description. It is the "human being—but the human being considered as noumenon," or as the "subject of morality" (§84, 398, 399 AA 435, 19–20, 34). Man is the only natural being entrusted with a "supersensible faculty," which is freedom. The law according to which causality oper-

---

5. See the thesis V of Kant's 1784 *Idea for a Universal History with Cosmopolitan Intent.*

6. See the thesis VII of the *Idea for a Universal History.*

ates is freedom. Its object and highest purpose is the highest good in the world. Thus, the "ultimate end" of creation is the human being considered not as natural being but as "moral being." In this case, it makes no sense to ask for a further, higher purpose for which man should be on earth. Rather, man's existence has the highest purpose in itself. Thereby Kant suggests a convergence between the concept of moral autonomy and the concept of *Endzweck*. As subject of morality, man is the final purpose of creation to which all other purposes and even nature as a whole "are teleologically subordinated" (§84, 399, AA 436, 1–2).

4. Moral Teleology and Ethicotheology (§§85–91)

The final sections of the Methodology, along with the General Remark to Teleology, deal with the relation between teleology and theology and with the collaboration between practical reason and the faculty of judgment. Kant's argument proceeds in two steps, accomplishing two transitions: on the one hand, Kant shows how physical teleology yields to moral teleology, while on the other, he suggests that only moral teleology can provide the basis for a theology. The key concept that allows Kant to achieve a transition from the sensible world of nature to the supersensible and from the supersensible back to the sensible is the concept of freedom. Freedom is considered this time in conjunction with a teleological reflection that addresses the issue of its realization or actualization in the world of nature by the moral agent. Freedom is no longer just *Faktum der Vernunft*. Freedom is now, quite remarkably, *Tatsache*, or "matter of fact."

At the end of the *Critique of Judgment*, the relation to practical reason comes to the fore as a central issue. The problem of our access to the "supersensible substrate" of nature and humanity, which Kant addressed first with regard to the aesthetic faculty of judgment and then in relation to our judgments on nature's objective purposiveness, now gains a fundamentally practical dimension. In the final sections of the third *Critique*, Kant discusses a problem that the second *Critique* left open, namely the issue of the actual realization of freedom in the sensible world—in the world of nature and history. In the new perspective, natural purposes become an important—albeit incidental—confirmation of the ideas of pure practical reason (§86, 415, AA 445, 3–4). Thus, retrospectively, the moral law is seen as the necessary principle for a teleological consideration of natural things—and even for the aesthetic contemplation of the beauty of nature's forms. Regressively, Kant rereads and requalifies the whole development of the third *Critique* in light of the moral foundation of teleology. It is a "moral interest" that ultimately grounds both our teleological consideration of nature in science and our aesthetic and disinterested appreciation of nature's beauty (§88 Remark, 439, AA 459, 2–9), while our aesthetic "admiration for the beauty of nature, as well as the emotion aroused by the so diverse purposes of nature," displays something in common with a "religious feeling" (General Remark to Teleology, fn. 478, AA 482, 29–32).

The argument of §84, taken up conclusively in the General Remark to Teleology, constitutes the basis for Kant's proposal of an "ethicotheology" to take the place of the traditional, metaphysical "physicotheology."[7] Physicotheology, Kant explains, is reason's attempt to infer the supreme cause of nature and its properties from the purposes of nature. "Moral theology, " instead, is reason's attempt to infer the supreme cause of nature and its properties from the *moral* purpose of rational beings in nature (§85, 400, AA 436, 5–10). Kant intimates that physicotheology is nothing but a misunderstanding of "physical teleology." It illicitly employs judgment's principle for *reflecting* upon the system of nature in the impossible task of *determining* a first intelligent cause and its attributes. Kant's critique of the metaphysical inference from physical teleology to theology is based upon the results of both the Dialectic of teleological judgment and the Dialectic of the first *Critique*. Since physicotheology always proceeds according to the principles of theoretical reason, it cannot go beyond a physical teleology. It can only reach the indeterminate and merely regulative idea of an intelligent cause of the world, but by no means can it objectively *determine* the concept of this cause. It can provide no clue regarding the intention of this cause or the final purpose of creation. Both concepts imply an inference to the supersensible to which theoretical reason has no access at all. Since physical teleology remains within the empirical realm of nature, on its ground no theology is possible. At the most, it provides a basis for deism or even "demonology" (§86, 414, AA 444, 31–32), whereby the concept of a supreme cause of the world is either left completely undetermined or is determined anthropomorphically (§89, 440, AA 459, 16–17).[8] Kant concedes that "physical teleology does induce us to look for a theology," but he recognizes that "it cannot produce one" (§85, 407, AA 440, 26–27). Physical teleology goes only as far as the idea of an "artistic understanding" in order to account for sporadic purposes as well as for the systematic constitution of nature. It does not reach the idea of a "*wisdom*" to provide a final purpose of creation (§85, 408, AA 441, 3–4). Thus, on the basis of a physical teleology—lacking any notion of the final purpose of the supreme intelligent cause—we can establish neither the properties of this supreme cause nor the degree to which the supreme cause must be entrusted with them. Without the determinate notion of a final purpose, we can claim neither that the supreme cause is omnipotent, nor all-wise, nor infinite, nor even that it is only one. All we can do—because of the limited constitution of our cognitive faculty—is to reflect upon the systematic organization of nature as a whole in terms of the principle of the reflective faculty of judgment; that is, to view nature as the product of an intelligent cause. With regard to such an intelligent cause, however, we can establish nothing more.[9]

---

7. Physicotheology indicates a common current in the culture of the seventeenth and eighteenth centuries. In the General Remark to Teleology, Kant mentions H. S. Reimarus as its representative.

8. For Kant's critique of the proofs of natural theology see also §90, 444–445, AA 461 f.

9. See the dialectic between deism and theism in the first *Critique* B 659 ff./A 631 ff.

Once the human world is brought into the field of teleology, Kant's discussion turns to the vocabulary of "value." What is the source of the value that the final purpose communicates to everything else that is judged as relating to it and as meaningful only in this relation? Kant's transcendental formulation of the question is the following: *which faculty* is responsible for attributing "value" to our "consideration of the world"—a value that furthermore is unconditioned and "absolute"? (§86, 411, AA 442, 33). (i) Kant answers by denying that the faculty in point can be the cognitive faculty or theoretical reason. For our cognitive approach to the world has a value only if value is somehow already presupposed. The fact that the world is known by us does not make it more valuable. The world is not there in order for someone to contemplate it.[10] (ii) But the source of value cannot be our feeling of pleasure, either. To defend this claim would amount to stating that the world has value only insofar as it satisfies the condition of human happiness. Yet Kant argues that in this case also the value of human existence on earth must be already presupposed in order to maintain that man's happiness can be indeed a purpose of nature. (iii) It follows that only the faculty of desire can be the faculty through which a finite rational being (not necessarily a human being, §87, 419, AA 447, 19–10) gives value to its own existence. Value is generated by a subject acting according to the law of freedom. Echoing the *Critique of Practical Reason*, Kant maintains that only a "good will" is that through which human existence gains an "absolute value" and in relation to which everything else in the world can have a final purpose (i.e., a meaning) (§86, 412, AA 443, 10–13). Thus, only the moral determination of the human being as the final purpose of creation allows Kant to move beyond physical teleology and the *impasse* of deism and demonology. Now we have a *moral* principle for conceiving of the nature and properties of the first cause so that its concept, left (theoretically) undetermined by all considerations of physical teleology, can ultimately be (practically) determined (§86, 413, AA 444, 6–8). Thus, the "original being" is determined not only as an intelligence that gives the law to nature but also as the "legislating sovereign of a moral kingdom of purposes" (§86, 413–414, AA 444, 13–15). In this *moral* perspective, we shall think of the original being as omniscient, omnipotent, omnibenevolent, just, and endorsed with all transcendental predicates that achieving the final purpose presupposes.[11] Accordingly, it is only on a moral basis that a theology becomes possible in Kant's critical project.

Thus, the moral law as the a priori principle of practical reason is also the ultimate condition of teleology. It is not only the condition that allows us to determine the idea of a supreme cause of creation but also the principle according to which *man must judge of himself* as being a "*Weltwesen* under moral laws," and *of his own life in this world* (§86, 415, AA 445, 4–5) as the life of a being neces-

10. The argument is further developed in the General Remark to Teleology, 471, AA 477, 9–19.

11. The argument is further developed in the General Remark to Teleology, 476–477, AA 481, 1–11.

sarily connected with other beings and with nature as a whole. Man must judge of himself as a being somehow responsible for the same whole of nature for which he serves as final purpose. Finally, the moral law is the principle that directs our attention to the teleological investigation of nature. Kant suggests that in this perspective, organized beings appear as an "incidental confirmation of the ideas of pure practical reason" displayed in the world of nature and given to us in a sensible experience (§86, 415, AA 445, 3–4). To a teleological consideration, nature offers "something analogous to the (moral) idea of reason" (General Remark, 474, AA 479, 11–12). Thus, "physical teleology" eventually yields to a "moral teleology" (§87, 418–419, AA 447, 16–21). A moral teleology allows us to think of the unity of nature and freedom; that is, it allows us to solve the problem that Kant was raising in the introduction regarding the relation of nature (without and within us), in its internal purposive constitution, to what is moral in us.

I want to underscore the crucial importance of the latter point as a valuable contribution to the issue of the function of science and technology in the contemporary world. A moral motivation, a sense of moral responsibility, and a moral self-consciousness must ultimately ground all scientific inquiry into the constitution of organized nature or, more generally, into all those aspects of nature that can only be explained in terms of purposes. A moral motivation, interest, and value is what ultimately justifies the employment of teleological principles in our reflection on nature. What is at stake again after the conclusion of the Critique of the Aesthetic Faculty of Judgment is the issue of a *Versinnlichung* of moral ideas. The principle of purposiveness—both in aesthetic judgment and in teleological judgment—is the means through which moral ideas become sensible in the world of nature.

At this point, moral teleology raises the crucial issue of a transition to "ethicotheology." Kant asks, does moral teleology, which is grounded on a principle that we find "in ourselves," in our practical reason, compel us to go beyond the world to seek an intelligent principle that justifies a "representation of nature as purposive also in relation to our inner moral legislation and to how we can carry it out?" (§87, 420, AA 448, 2–7). What guarantees the teleological orientation of nature toward the possible realization of freedom and the highest good? This is the question that leads to Kant's merely subjective "moral proof of god's existence" (§87, title): the issue of the "*progress* of reason" (not just the "transition") from physical teleology to theology by means of moral teleology (§87, 420, AA 448, 13–15).

Kant's moral proof of god's existence raises the issue of the realization of freedom in the world or, to put it differently, the issue of the connection between reason and the realization of a moral order possible only according to ideas. To this problem, Kant has provided an initial answer in the doctrine of the postulates of the second *Critique*. This doctrine is now reconfirmed and more precisely articulated from a different standpoint. Kant no longer attempts to disclose a possible access to the supersensible through the postulates, which was the aim in the second *Critique*. Rather, he investigates the possibility of *somehow* having an experience of the supersensible *within the sensible world*. Now this possibility is revealed by a concept of freedom thought of on the basis of teleology (§§88–89, 91). If freedom discloses a supersensible dimension of the human being as noumenon, teleology addresses the aspect of the realization of this dimension in the world of experience. Thus, Kant revisits the issue of freedom's actualization in the world in light of the idea of a purposive harmony between nature and freedom. God as "moral author of the world" is the necessary assumption that makes the actualization of the final purpose of morality *subjectively* possible (i.e., possible *for us* in our limited capacity) (§87, 429, AA 453, 4–5).

However, the moral law being unconditioned and thoroughly independent of any purpose, does not itself rest on this condition. Morality retains for Kant its radical autonomy with regard to faith, theology, and religion.[12] Morality is independent of the proof of god's existence just as moral teleology remains independent of physical teleology (General Remark to Teleology, 473–474, 482, AA 478, 28–479, 8; 485, 4–8). It is only *subjectively* that the human agent needs to assume the existence of a god as the guarantee of the realizability of freedom and of the highest good in the world and in history. The concept of god (and hence the possibility of theology and religion), on the contrary, must rest on a moral basis. For such concept can express a moral obligation only because it results from moral teleology. If the concept of god were the result of a theoretical inference of speculative reason, it would by no means allow us to see in him a moral god toward which we could feel *morally* obligated (General Remark to Teleology, 477, AA 41, 24–29).[13]

In the subjective perspective of a finite rational being, the harmony between nature and freedom translates into the possibility of becoming worthy of happiness as a consequence of following the moral law. Practical reason determines us a priori to "strive to the utmost to further the highest good in the world." The highest good consists in the "combination of universal happiness" with the supreme condition of our being good, namely, that we be moral in conformity with the moral law (§88, 429, AA 453, 16–20). Ultimately, Kant's moral proof depends upon the impossibility of a transition from nature to freedom by means of

---

12. Religion is defined in this connection as "morality in relation to god as legislator" (§89, 441, AA 460, 12–13); see also the General Remark to Teleology, 477, AA 481, 12–29.

13. This final thesis of the *Critique of Judgment* radically overturns the position that Kant still held in the *Critique of Pure Reason*. In the first *Critique,* the idea of god is still needed as guarantee for the "obligatory" character of the moral law. In the second *Critique*, the idea of god is a "postulate" that is no longer required for moral obligation but is still required as guarantee for the possibility of the highest good to be realized in this world. In the third *Critique*, the idea of god is no longer postulated. God as the cause of a world conceived as a moral world is now the result of a moral teleology. God is an inference of reflective judgment from the assumption of the moral essence of man as final purpose of the world.

mere concepts of nature. The proof rests on the notion of the purposive harmony between the world of nature and the moral order established by moral teleology. Since the legislation of nature's mechanism and that of freedom retain their radical independence, only the reference to a moral cause of the world allows us to conceive of the purposive accordance between them.

The idea of final purpose—namely, universal happiness combined with the condition of being moral (i.e., worthy of happiness)—is the purpose that practical reason sets for human life. With regard to the practical sphere, this idea has a "subjectively constitutive" value and reality (§87, 429, AA 453, 12, 16). Its first component (the possibility of happiness) is empirically conditioned, while the second component (morality) is a priori certain. Thereby Kant presents the intersection and interdependence between nature and morality in the idea of final purpose. Man's practical final purpose is linked to the final purpose of the world. For if creation has indeed a final purpose, then we have to conceive of it as being in harmony with our moral final purpose. The idea of a final purpose of creation is an idea to which only practical reason can provide "objective reality." What role does this idea play for theoretical reason? In the first and the second *Critiques*, Kant denies to theoretical reason any access to the idea of a final purpose. In §88 of the *Critique of Judgment*, he raises a more articulated question. Certainly, the notion of final purpose is inaccessible to the determinant faculty of judgment. But could it be adequate, instead, to the maxims that the reflective faculty of judgment uses in reflecting theoretically? (§88, 431, AA 454, 12–16). Kant's argument aims at securing, once again, the "primacy," or absolute priority, of practical reason. It is only from the dimension of the autonomy of practical reason that a step into theology is allowed to the faculty of judgment. Reflective judgment extends only as far as physical teleology, in which no concept of final purpose can be reached. The concept of *Endzweck* is exclusively a concept of practical reason. Kant is extremely clear in this regard: "There is no other possible use of this concept except for practical reason according to moral laws" (§88, 433, AA 454, 36–455, 1).

However, once the primacy of practical reason is recognized as laying the ground for teleology in the practical sphere, then the merely *regulative* principle of judgment becomes a principle that is indeed "*constitutive*, i.e., determinative practically" (§88, 437–438, AA 457, 35–458, 3). Once Kant has secured that the idea of final purpose belongs to the moral sphere, and to this sphere only, he can put forth the two inferences that practical reason offers to judgment's own reflection. The first inference concludes the possibility of achieving—or seeing realized—the moral final purpose in the sensible world from the fact that this goal is given to us by practical reason through the pure moral command (practical reason could not command something impossible). Nature must therefore be conceived as harmonizing with the necessity of freedom. Only the second inference, however, leads properly from moral teleology to theology. This inference provides the "idea of god" with "practical reality" (in the way the postulate of god did in the second *Critique*) (§88, 435, AA 456, 16, 21), but also with "practical reality *only*"

(§88, 436, AA 456, 35). In this case, we infer the existence of an author of the world entrusted with intelligence and morality from the conformity of things with a morally grounded final purpose. Kant underlines that these two inferences are only conclusions "for the reflective faculty of judgment" working in accordance with practical reason (§88, 433, AA 455, 22–23).

On the other hand, the indispensable contribution of the faculty of judgment in its collaboration with practical reason emerges in Kant's remark that any practical determination of the highest being can take place *only by way of analogy*, namely according to the specific method proper to reflective judgment. In its attempts to determine the attributes of the moral author of the world, practical reason resorts to reflective judgment and to its analogical thinking. Ultimately, for Kant, theology is just the manifestation of a specifically human need for moral self-comprehension and self-determination. The real task of a moral theology is not, Kant suggests, to determine the nature of the highest being "but to determine ourselves and our will" (§88, 436, AA 457, 4–5).

5. The Geography of the Human Mind Reconsidered

The conclusion of the *Critique of Judgment* establishes the new thesis—which Kant himself insistently qualifies as "very remarkable" (§91, 457, 467, AA 468, 21; 474, 20)—that the idea of freedom is *Tatsache*, a matter of fact (§91, 457, 467, AA 468, 22–30; 474, 16). Freedom is the only idea of reason whose object is a matter of fact. Even though the idea of freedom cannot be exhibited in a sensible intuition, it displays through action an objective reality in the sensible world of experience. Once the possibility of a theoretical determination of the ideas of god, the immortality of the soul, and the highest good as final purpose has been ruled out yet again in all respects (§90),[14] Kant shows the necessary dependence of all these ideas on the idea of freedom. While freedom is *Tatsache*, all other ideas are *Glaubenssachen*, or matters of faith (§91, 457, AA 469, 1–4).[15] Matters of faith are those objects that we have to think a priori in reference to our practical use of reason in conformity to duty (§91, 457, AA 469, 1–4). Faith for Kant is properly "moral faith." He defines it as "reason's moral way of thinking in assenting to [*Fürwahrhalten*] what is not accessible to theoretical cognition" (§91, 462, AA 471, 3–5).

No other idea of reason but freedom displays an objective reality in the sensible world. Yet Kant claims that through freedom even all other ideas (god, immortality of the soul) become real for us in the sensible world as they become an

---

14. Kant denies that a theoretical-speculative proof of god's existence can establish "conviction" on all levels. Neither "rigorous syllogistic inferences," nor "inference by analogy, " nor "probable opinion," nor "hypotheses" can be reached on the ground of mere theoretical proof (§90, 447, AA 463, 15–20; but see the whole §90).

15. Kant divides all possible "cognizable things" into *Sachen der Meinung* (*opinabile*), or matters of opinion; *Tatsachen* (*scibile*), or matters of fact; and *Glaubenssachen* (*mere credibile*), or matters of faith (§91, 454, AA 467, 12–14).

integral part of our morality in the form of a moral faith. The only way to determine the concepts of god and the immortality of the soul "is through predicates that, though they themselves are possible only on a supersensible ground, *must yet prove in experience that they have reality*. . . . Now the only such concept to be found in human reason is the idea of human freedom under moral laws along with the final purpose that these moral laws prescribe." This is the correction that the third *Critique* offers to the doctrine of the postulates of the second *Critique*. Through the idea of freedom and the mediation of moral teleology, even the idea of god and of the soul's immortality prove themselves somehow *in experience*. Hence, Kant concludes that "it is from this same idea of freedom that we can infer the existence and the constitution" of god and soul, namely of those beings "that are otherwise wholly hidden to us" (§91, 466, AA 473, 30–474, 7). Freedom is the only idea that, resting on the supersensible, is theoretically inaccessible and yet by presenting its realization in the world of experience allows us to gain an access—that thereby is necessarily a *practical* access—to the supersensible that grounds the ideas of god and the soul's immortality.

The "remarkable" fact that freedom is not only *Faktum der Vernunft*, as in the second *Critique*, but *Tatsache*, is a discovery of the reflective faculty of judgment.[16] We can say that freedom as *Tatsache* is the idea of freedom considered not in the perspective of pure practical reason alone but in "connection" (*Verknüpfung*) with reflective judgment; it is the idea of freedom to which our reflective judgments on nature (both aesthetic and teleological judgments) ultimately lead. Because of the causality that we think of in the concept of freedom, its idea proves "in nature that it has objective reality by the effects it can produce in it." This is precisely the point that allows us "to *connect* [*Verknüpfung*] the other two ideas with nature and to *connect* all three with one another to form a religion" (§91, 468, AA 474, 21–26). This multiple connection necessarily transforms the systematic of philosophy: theology is transformed into moral faith, while rational psychology (and pneumatology) becomes an "anthropology of the inner sense," or the self–knowledge that man reaches of himself in this life (§89, 442, AA 461, 1–5; General Remark on Teleology, 475, AA 479, 33–37). Thus, the idea of freedom and the teleological developments that it produces for our faculty of judgment become the conditions for the "*Verknüpfung* of the legislations of understanding and reason through the faculty of judgment" that programmatically concluded the introduction to the third *Critique* (§IX, title).

---

16. Note that in both of the expressions *Faktum* and *Tatsache* the origin of factuality in action is preserved—*Faktum* goes back to *facere* and *Tatsache* to *Tat*.

Bibliography

The focus of the following bibliography is the *Critique of Judgment.* Thus, it aims neither at being complete nor at comprehending all different aspects of Kant's philosophy.

1. German Editions of Kant's Works and of the Kritik der Urteilskraft

Erste Einleitung in die Kritik der Urteilskraft. Faksimile und Transkription, ed. by N. Hinske, W. Müller-Lauter, M. Theunissen, Stuttgart, Frommann, 1965.

Kant, I., *Schriften zur Ästhetik und Naturphilosophie*, ed. by M. Frank, V. Zanetti, Frankfurt a.M., DKV, 1996.

Kants Gesammelte Schriften Herausgegeben von der Preußischen Akademie der Wissenschaften zu Berlin, Berlin, de Gruyter, 1902–83, vol. 5.

Lehmann, G., "Eine Faksimile-Ausgabe von Kants Erster Einleitung in die Kritik der Urteilskraft," in *Zeitschrift für philosophische Forschung*, 21, 4, 1967, 589–599.

2. English Translations of Kant's Works

A new, complete translation of Kant's works is being pulished by Cambridge University Press (14 volumes are planned).

Anthropology from a Pragmatic Point of View, trans. Mary J. Gregor, The Hague, Nijhoff, 1974.

The Conflict of the Faculties, trans. Mary J. Gregor, New York, Arbaris Books, 1979.

Critique of Judgment, trans. J. H. Bernard, New York, Haffner, 1968.

Critique of Judgement, trans. J. Meredith, Oxford, Clarendon, 1964.

Critique of Judgment, trans. W. S. Pluhar, Indianapolis/Cambridge, Hackett, 1987.

Critique of the Power of Judgment, trans. P. Guyer, E. Matthews, Cambridge, Cambridge University Press, 2000.

Critique of Practical Reason, trans. Lewis W. Beck, Indianapolis, Bobbs-Merrill, 1956.

Critique of Practical Reason, trans. Mary J. Gregor, Cambridge, Cambridge University Press, 1997.

Critique of Pure Reason, trans. Norman Kemp-Smith, New York, St. Martin's Press, 1965.

Critique of Pure Reason, trans. P. Guyer, A. Wood, Cambridge, Cambridge University Press, 1999.

Dreams of a Spirit-Seer Elucidated by Dreams of Metaphysics, trans. E. F. Goerwitz, London, Swan Sonnenschein, 1900.

First Introduction to the Critique of Judgment, trans. J. Haden, Indianapolis, Bobbs-Merrill, 1965.

Groundwork of the Metaphysics of Morals, trans. H. J. Paton, London, Hutchinson, 1949.

Idea for a Universal History with Cosmopolitan Intent, trans. Carl Friedrich, in *The Philosophy of Immanuel Kant,* ed. by C. Friedrich, New York, Modern Library, 1949.

Kant's Philosophical Correspondence, 1759–1799, trans. A. Zweig, Chicago, University of Chicago Press, 1967.

Lectures on Ethics, trans. P. Heath, ed. by J. B. Schneewind, Cambridge, Cambridge University Press, 2001.

Lectures on Metaphysics, trans. K. Ameriks, S. Naragon, Cambridge, Cambridge University Press, 2001.

Logic: A Manual for Lectures, trans. Robert S. Hartman, W. Schwarz, Indianapolis, Bobbs-Merrill, 1974.

Metaphysical Foundations of Natural Science, trans. J. Ellington, Indianapolis, Bobbs-Merrill, 1970.

Metaphysics of Morals, trans. Mary J. Gregor, Cambridge, Cambridge University Press, 1996.

Observations on the Feeling of the Beautiful and the Sublime, trans. John T. Goldthwait, Berkeley, University of California Press, 1960.

The One Possible Basis for a Demonstration of the Existence of God, trans. G. Treash, New York, Arbaris Books, 1979.

"On the Old Saw: That May Be Right in Theory but It Won't Work in Practice," trans. E. B. Ashton, Philadelphia, University of Pennsylvania Press, 1974.

Opus Postumum, ed. by E. Förster, M. Rosen, Cambridge, Cambridge University Press, 1995.

Perpetual Peace, trans. L.W. Beck, Indianapolis, Bobbs-Merrill, 1957.

Political Writings, ed. by H. S. Reiss, trans. H. B. Nisbet, Cambridge, Cambridge University Press, 1991.

Practical Philosophy, ed. by Mary J. Gregor, Cambridge, Cambridge University Press, 1999.

Prolegomena to Any Future Metaphysics, trans. L. W. Beck, Indianapolis, Bobbs-Merrill, 1950.

Prolegomena to Any Future Metaphysics, trans. G. Hatfield, Cambridge, Cambridge University Press, 2004.

Review of Herder's *Ideas for a Philosophy of History of Mankind,* in *Kant on History*, ed. by Lewis W. Beck, Indianapolis, Bobbs-Merrill, 1963 (Recension von J. G. Herders *Ideen zur Philosophie der Geschichte der Menschheit,* Theil I, [1784] and Recension von J. G. Herders *Ideen zur Philosophie der Geschichte der Menschheit,* Theil II, [1785], AA VIII).

Religion and Rational Theology, trans. A. Wood, G. Di Giovanni, Cambridge, Cambridge University Press, 2001.

Religion Within the Boundaries of Mere Reason, ed. by A. Wood, G. Di Giovanni, Cambridge, Cambridge University Press, 1998.

Religion Within the Limits of Reason Alone, trans. Theodore M. Greene, H. H. Hudson, La Salle, Ill., Open Court, 1960.

Theoretical Philosophy, 1755-1770, ed. by D. Walford, Cambridge, Cambridge University Press, 2003.

Theoretical Philosophy after1781, trans. H. Allison, P. Heath, G. Hatfield, M. Friedman, Cambridge, Cambridge University Press, 2002.

Universal Natural History and Theory of the Heavens, trans. W. Hastie, Ann Arbor, University of Michigan Press, 1969.

"What Is Enlightenment?" trans. Lewis W. Beck, in *Kant on History*, Indianapolis, Bobbs-Merrill, 1963.

What Real Progress Has Metaphysics Made in Germany Since the Time of Leibniz and Wolff? trans. T. Humphrey, New York, Abaris Books, 1983.

Other Translations of the *Critique of Judgment*

Critique de la faculté de juger, traduction par A. Philonenko, Paris, Vrin, 1965.

Critica della facoltà di giudizio, a cura di A. Gargiulo, rev. V. Verra, Bari, Laterza, 1960.

Critica della facoltà di giudizio, a cura di E. Garroni, H. Hohenegger, Torino, Einaudi, 1999.

3. *Primary Sources*

Addison, J., "Genius," in *Spectator*, 160 (Sept. 1711), reprinted in: *Eighteenth-Century Critical Essays*, vol. 1, ed. by S. Elledge, Ithaca, Cornell University Press, 1961, 27–30.

Adelung, J. C., *Grammatisch-kritisches Wörterbuch der hochdeutschen Mundart*, Leipzig, 1796.

Akenside, M., *Pleasures of Imagination*, London, Dodsley, 1744.

Batteau, Abbé Charles, *Les beaux arts réduits à un meme principe*, Paris, Durand, 1746, 1747².

Baumgarten, A.G., *Meditationes philosophicae de nonnullis ad poema pertinentibus*, Halle, 1735.

———, *Metaphysica*, Halle, 1739.

———, *Aesthetica*, Frankfurt an der Oder, 1750–1758.

Beck, J. S., *Erläuternder Auszug aus den critischen Schriften des Herrn Prof. Kant auf Anrathen desselben, Zweyter Band, welcher die Critik der Urtheilskraft und die metaphysischen Anfangsgründe der Naturwissenschaft enthält*, Riga, bey Johann Friedrich Hartknoch, 1794.

Bendavid, L., *Vorlesungen über die Kritik der Urtheilskraft*, Wien, 1796.

Between Kant and Hegel: Texts in the Development of post-Kantian Idealism, trans. G. Di Giovanni, H. S. Harris, Indianapolis, Hackett, 2000.

Blumenbach, J. Fr., *Ueber den Bildungstrieb*, Göttingen, Dieterich, 1791.

Bodmer, J. J., *Critische Betrachtungen ueber die Poetischen Gemälde der Dichter*, Zürich, verlegts Conrad Orell und Comp., 1741.

Breitinger, J. J., *Critische Dichtkunst*, Zürich, verlegts Conrad Orell und Comp., 1740.

Burke, E., *A Philosophical Inquiry into the Origin of Our Ideas of the Sublime and the Beautiful*, London, T. Tegg, 1757, 1759[2].

Christian Wolffens Meinungen . . . und A. Rüdigers Gegen-Meinungen, Leipzig, 1727.

Crousaz, J. P., *Traité du Beau*, 2 vols., Amsterdam, F. L'Honoré, 1715.

Fichte, J. G., "Versuch eines erklärenden Auszugs aus Kants Kritik der Urtheilskraft" (1790–91), in *J. G. Fichte, Nachgelassene Schriften, 1780–1791*, ed. by R. Lauth, H. Jacob, Stuttgart, Frommann, 1992, *Gesamtausgabe* der Bayerischen Akademie der Wissenschaften, ed. by R. Lauth, H. Jacob, Stuttgart, Frommann, 1966, 2, 1.

Ficino, Marsilio, *Theologia platonica*, in *Opera*, Basileae, ex officina Henricipetrina, 1576, vol. 1.

Gellert, Ch. Fürchtegott, "Von dem Einflusse der schönen Wissenschaften auf das Herz und die Sitten," in *Sammlung vermischter Schriften*, Leipzig, in der Weidmannischen Handlung, 1756.

Gottsched, J. C., *Versuch einer Critischen Dichtkunst*, Leipzig, verlegts Bernhard Christoph Breitkopff, 1742[3].

Herder, J. G., *Sämtliche Werke*, ed. by B. Suphan, 33 vols., Berlin, Weidmann, 1877–1813.

Home, H. (Lord Kames), *Elements of Criticism*, printed for A. Miller, London, and A. Kincaid & J. Bell, Edinburgh, 1762 (German translation appears in 1763).

Hume, D., "Of the Standard of Taste," in *Essays Moral, Political, and Literary*, London, 1772, 1777.

Hutcheson, F., *An Inquiry into Our Ideas of Beauty and Virtue*, London, 1725.

Jacobi, Fr. H., *Über die Lehre des Spinoza in Briefen an den Herrn Moses Mendelssohn*, Breslau, Lowe, 1785.

Koller, J., *Entwurf zur Geschichte und Literatur der Aesthetik von Baumgarten bis auf die neueste Zeit*, Regensburg, 1799.

Materialien zu Kants Kritik der Urteilskraft, ed. by J. Kulenkampf, Frankfurt, Suhrkamp, 1974.

Meier, G. F., *Anfangsgründe aller schönen Wissenschaften*, 3. vols., Halle, verlegsts Carl Hermann Hemmerde, 1748, 1749, 1750.

———, *Auszug aus der Vernunftlehre*, Halle, J. J. Gebauer, 1752.

Mellin, G. S. A., *Enzyklopädisches Wörterbuch der kritischen Philosophie*, Züllichau/Leipzig, Frommann, 1797–1804.

Mendelssohn, M., "Betrachtungen über die Quellen und die Verbindung der schönen Künste und Wissenschaften" (1757), in *Gesammelte Schriften (Jubiläums-Ausgabe)*, Stuttgart, Frommann, 1929, vol. 1, 165–190.

———, Review of: G. F. Meier, *Auszug aus der Anfangsgründen aller schönen Künste und Wissenschaften,* (1758), in *Gesammelte Schriften*, Leipzig, 1844, vol. 4, 313–318.

Niphus, Augustinus, *De pulchro liber,* Roma, 1531.

Schiller, Fr., *Ueber die ästhetische Erziehung des Menschen in einer Reihe von Briefen*, "Die Horen," 1795.

———, "Vom Erhabenen," in *Sämtliche Werke*, vol. 5, ed. by G. Fricke, H. G. Göpfert, München, C. Hanser, 1960.

Schmid, C. Chr. E., *Wörterbuch zum leichtern Gebrauch der Kantischen Schriften*, Jena, Cröker, 1788.

Shaftesbury, Anthony Earl of, *Characteristics of Men, Manners, Opinions, Times*, 2 vols., ed. by John M. Robertson, Indianapolis, Bobbs-Merrill, 1964.

Sulzer, J. G., *Vermischte philosophische Schriften*, 2 vols., Leipzig, bey Weidmann Erben und Reich, 1773–1781.

———, *Allgemeine Theorie der Schönen Künste*, 4 vols., Leipzig, Weidmann Reich, 1771–1774; 1777–78²; 1792–99³.

Thomasius, Ch., *Von Nachahmung der Franzosen: nach den Ausgaben von 1687 und 1701*, ed. by A. Sauer, Nendeln/Liechtenstein, Kraus, 1968.

———. "Welcher Gestalt man den Frantzosen in gemeinem Leben und Wandel nachahmen solle? ein Collegium über Gratians Grund-Reguln, vernünftig, klug und artig zu leben" (1687), reprinted in *Deutsche Literaturdenkmale*, 51, 1894.

Young, E., "Conjectures on Original Composition," reprinted in M. Steinke, *Edward Young's Conjectures on Original Composition in England and Germany*, New York, Stechert, 1917.

Wolff, Ch., *Psychologia empirica*, Fracofurti & Lipsiae, in officina libraria Rengeriana, 1738.

4. Bibliographies, Lexica, General Surveys

Adickes, E., *German Kantian Bibliography: Bibliography of Writings by and on Kant Which Have Appeared in Germany Up to the End of 1887*, Würzburg, A. Liebig, 1896.

Bartuschat, W., "Neuere Arbeiten zu Kants Kritik der Urteilskraft," in *Philosophisches Rundschau*, 18, 1972, 161–189.

Beck, L. W., "A Bibliography on Kant's Ethics," in *Delaware Notes*, 1945, 23–43.

Brandt, R., Stark, W., "Kant-Archiv Marburg," in *Information Philosophie*, 1983, 49–52.

De Vleeschauwer, J.-H., "A Survey of Kantian Philosophy," in *Review of Metaphysics*, 11, 1957/1958, 122–142.

The Cambridge Companion to Kant, ed. by P. Guyer, Cambridge, Cambridge University Press, 1992.

Eisler, R., *Kant-Lexicon*, Hildesheim, Olms, 1964.

Grimm, J., Grimm, W., *Deutsches Wörterbuch*, Leipzig, Verlag von S. Hirzel, 1860.

Guerra, A., *Introduzione a Kant*, Bari, Laterza, 1980.

Hinske, N., "Die Kantausgabe der Preußischen Akademie der Wissenschaften und ihre Probleme," in *Il cannocchiale*, 3, 1990, 229–254.

Lehmann, G., *Beiträge zur Geschichte und Interpretation der Philosophie Kants*, Berlin, de Gruyter, 1969.

Malter, J., "Kant-Bibliographie 1965–1969," in *Proceedings of the Third International Kant-Congress*, 1970, ed. by L.W. Beck, Dordrecht, Riedel, 1972, 16–46.

Mellin, G. S. A., *Enzyklopädisches Wörterbuch der kritischen Philosophie*, Züllichau/Leipzig, Frommann, 1797–1804.

Ratke, H. *Systematisches Handlexikon zu Kants Kritik der reinen Vernunft*, Hamburg, Meiner, 1965.

Rezensionen zur Kantischen Philosophie, 1781–1787, vol. 1, Bebra, A. Landau, 1991.

Ritter, J., *Historisches Wörterbuch der Philosophie*, ed. by J. Ritter, K. F. Gründer, Basel, Schönig, 1974 ff.

Schmid, C. Chr. E., *Wörterbuch zum leichtern Gebrauch der Kantischen Schriften*, Jena, Cröker, 1788.

Walsh, W. H., "A Survey of Work on Kant," in *The Philosophical Quarterly*, 3, 1953, 257–270.

Wood, A., *Kant*, Oxford, Blackwell, 2004.

5. Kant's Biography

Cassirer, E., *Kants Leben und Lehre*, Berlin, Verlag Bruno Cassirer, 1918 (*Kant's Life and Thought*, trans. J. Haden, New Haven, Yale University Press, 1981).

Immanuel Kant im Rede und Gespräch, ed. by R. Malter, Hamburg, Meiner, 1990.

Immanuel Kant. Sein Leben in Darstellungen von Zeitgenossen. Die Biographien von L. E. Borowski, R. B. Jachmann und A. Chr. Wasianski, ed. by F. Gross, Berlin, 1912.

Kuehn, M., *Kant: A Biography*, Cambridge, Cambridge University Press, 2001.

Stuckenberg, J. H. W., *The Life of Immanuel Kant*, London, Macmillan, 1882.

Vorländer, K., *Immanuel Kant. Der Mann und das Werk*, 2 vols., Leipzig, Meiner, 1924.

6. Kant's Age, the Genesis of Kant's Philosophy, and the Pre-Critical Period

Allison, H., *The Kant-Eberhard Controversy*, Baltimore, Johns Hopkins University Press, 1973.

Beck, Lewis W., *Studies in the Philosophy of Kant*, Indianapolis, Bobbs-Merrill, 1965.

———, ed., *Kant's Studies Today*, La Salle, Ill., Open Court, 1967.

———, *Early German Philosophy,* Cambridge, Mass., Harvard University Press, 1969.

Beiser, Frederick C., *The Fate of Reason: German Philosophy from Kant to Fichte*, Cambridge, Harvard University Press, 1987.

———, "Kant's Intellectual Development, 1746–1781," in *The Cambridge Companion to Kant*, ed. by P. Guyer, Cambridge, Cambridge University Press, 1992, 26–61.

———, *German Idealism: The Struggle Against Subjectivism (1781–1801)*, Cambridge, Mass., Harvard University Press, 2002.

Berlin, I., "David Hume and the Sources of German Anti-Rationalism," in *David Hume: Bicentenary Papers*, ed. by G. P. Morice, Edinburgh, Edinburgh University Press, 1977, 95–116.

Buroker, Jill V., *Space and Incongruence: The Origin of Kant's Idealism*, Dordrecht/London, Riedel, 1981.

Campo, M., *La genesi del criticismo kantiano*, Varese, Magenta, 1953.

Cassirer, E., *The Philosophy of the Enlightenment*, trans. C. A. Koelln, J. P. Pettegrove, Princeton, Princeton University Press, 1951.

Dessoir, M., *Geschichte der neueren deutschen Psychologie*, Berlin, Duncker, 1902.

De Vleeschauwer, H.-J., *L'évolution de la pensée kantienne*, Paris, Alcan, 1939.

Ebbinghaus, J., "Kant und Swedenborg," in *Jahrbuch des Auslandsamtes der deutschen Dozentenschaft*, 1943.

Erdmann, B., *Martin Knutzen und seine Zeit. Ein Beitrag zur Geschichte der wolffischen Schule und insbesondere zur Entwicklungsgeschichte Kants*, Leipzig, L. Voss, 1876.

Gregor, Mary J., "Baumgarten's Aesthetica," in *Review of Metaphysics*, 37, 1983–84, 357–385.

Hearing, Th., *Der Duisburg'sche Nachlass und Kants Kritizismus um 1775*, Leipzig, J. B. Hirschfeld, 1910.

Heimsoeth, H., "Metaphysik und Kritik bei Ch. A. Crusius," in *Studien zur Philosophie Immanuel Kants. Metaphysische Ursprünge und ontologische Grundlagen*, Köln, Kölner Universitätsverlag, 1956, 125–188.

Henrich, D., *Der ontologische Gottesbeweis. Sein Problem und seine Geschichte in der Neuzeit*, Tübingen, Mohr, 1960.

Hinske, N., *Kants Weg zur Transzendentalphilosophie. Der dreißigjährige Kant*, Stuttgart, Kohlhammer, 1970.

Laywine, A., *Kant's Early Metaphysics and the Origins of the Critical Philosophy*, North American Kant Society Studies, vol. 3, Atascadero, Ridgeview, 1993.

———, "Kant in Reply to Lambert on the Ancestry of Metaphysical Concepts," in *Kantian Review*, 5, 2001, 1–48.

Merlan, P., "From Hume to Hamann," in *Kleine philosophische Schriften*, ed. by F. Merlan, Hildesheim, New York, de Gruyter, 1976, 506–518.

Nuzzo, A., "Transformations of Freedom in the Jena Kant-Reception, 1785–1794," in *The Owl of Minerva*, 32, 2, Spring, 2001, 135–167.

The Reception of Kant's Critical Philosophy, ed. by S. Sedgwick, Cambridge, Cambridge University Press, 2001.

Reich, K., *Kants Einzig mögliche Beweisgrund zu einer Demonstration des Daseins Gottes*, Hamburg, Meiner, 1937.

———, "Kants Behandlung des Raumbegriffs in den 'Träume eines Geistersehers' und im 'Unterschied der Gegenden im Raum,'" in I. Kant, *Träume eines Geistersehers*, Hamburg, Meiner, 1975, v–xviii.

Schmucker, J., *Die Ursprünge der Ethik Kants in seinen vorkritischen Schriften und Reflektionen,* Meisenheim a.G., A. Hain, 1961.

Schneewind, J. B., *Moral Philosophy from Montaigne to Kant*, Cambridge, Cambridge University Press, 1990.

Vorlesungsverzeichnisse der Universität Königsberg, 1720–1804, ed. by M. Oberhausen, R. Pozzo, Stuttgart, Frommann, 1999.

Wellek, R., *A History of Modern Criticism: I., The Later Eighteenth Century*, New Haven, Yale University Press, 1955.

Wundt, M., *Die deutsche Schulphilosophie im Zeitalter der Aufklärung*, Tübingen, Mohr, 1945.

7. **Critique of Pure Reason—*Kant's Theoretical Philosophy***

Allison, H., *Transcendental Idealism*, New Haven, Yale University Press, 1983.

———, "The Originality of Kant's Distinction between Analytic and Synthetic Judgments," in *The Philosophy of Immanuel Kant*, ed. by R. Kennington, Washington, D.C., Catholic University of America Press, 1985, 15–38.

———, "Transcendental Idealism: The Two Aspect View," in *New Essays on Kant,* ed. by B. den Ouden, M. Moen, New York, Peter Lang, 1987, 155–78.

Ameriks, K., "Kant's Transcendental Deduction as a Regressive Argument," in *Kant-Studien*, 69, 1978, 273–287.

———, *Kant's Theory of Mind: An Analysis of the Paralogisms of Pure Reason*, Oxford, Clarendon Press, 1982.

Aquila, R., *Matter in Mind: A Study of Kant's Transcendental Deduction,* Bloomington, Indiana University Press, 1989.

Baum, M., "Erkennen und Machen in der 'Kritik der reinen Vernunft,'" in *Probleme der"Kritik der reinen Vernunft,"* ed. by B. Tuschling, Berlin, De Gruyter, 1984, 161–177.

———, *Deduktion und Beweis in Kants Transzendentalphilosophie. Untersuchungen zur "Kritik der reinen Vernunft,"* Königstein/Ts., Hain, 1986.

———, "Dinge an sich und Raum bei Kant," in *Akten der siebenten Internationalen Kant-Kongresses*, Bonn, Bouvier, 1991, 63–72.

———, "Kant on Pure Intuition," in *Minds, Ideas, and Objects*, ed. by Ph. D. Cummins, G. Zöller, Atascadero, Ridgeview, 1992, 303–316.

Bennett, J. *Kant's Analytic*, Cambridge, Cambridge University Press, 1966.

Brandt, R., *Die Urteilstafel. Kritik der reinen Vernunft A 67–76; B 92–101*, Hamburg, Meiner, 1991.

Buroker, Jill V., *Space and Incongruence: The Origin of Kant's Idealism*, Dordrecht/London, Riedel, 1981.

Centi, B., *Coscienza, etica e architettonica in Kant. Uno studio attraverso le Critiche,* Pisa/Roma, Istituti Editoriale e Poligrafici, 2002.

De Vleeschauwer, H.-J., *La déduction transcendentale dans l'oeuvre de Kant*, 1., Antwerpen-Paris, De Sikkel, 1934.

Findlay, J. N., *Kant and the Transcendental Object: A Hermeneutic Study*, Oxford, Clarendon Press, 1981.

Friedman, M., "Kant on Laws of Nature and the Foundations of Newtonian Science," in *Proceedings: Sixth International Kant Congress*, ed. by G. Funke, Th. Seebohm, Washington, D.C., University Press of America, 1990, 97–107.

———, *Kant and the Exact Sciences*, Cambridge, Mass., Harvard University Press, 1992.

Gigliotti, G., "'Vermögen' e 'Kraft'. Una rilettura del concetto di 'sintesi' nella Critica della ragion pura di Kant," in *Rivista di storia della filosofia*, 2, 1995, 255–275.

Guyer, P., *Kant and the Claims of Knowledge*, Cambridge, Cambridge University Press, 1979.

———, "The Unity of Reason: Pure Reason as Practical Reason in Kant's Early Conception of the Transcendental Dialectic," in *The Monist*, 72, 1989, 139–167.

Henrich, D., "The Proof-Structure of Kant's Transcendental Deduction," in *Review of Metaphysics*, 22, 1969, 640–659.

———, "Kant's Notion of a Deduction and the Methodological Background of the First Critique," in *Kant's Transcendental Deductions*, ed. by E. Förster, Stanford, Stanford University Press, 1989, 29–47.

———, *The Unity of Reason: Essays on Kant's Philosophy*, Cambridge, Mass., Harvard University Press, 1994.

Holzhey, H., *Kants Erfahrungsbegriff*, Basel/Stuttgart, Schwabe, 1970.

Kant's Transcendental Deductions, ed. by E. Förster, Stanford, Stanford University Press, 1989.

Kemp-Smith, N., *A Commentary to Kant's Critique of Pure Reason*, London, Macmillan, 1918.

Longuenesse, B., *Kant and the Capacity to Judge: Sensibility and Discursivity in the Transcendental Analytic of the Critique of Pure Reason*, Princeton, Princeton University Press, 1998.

Mathieu, V., *Kants Opus Postumum*, Frankfurt a.M., Klostermann, 1989.

Nuzzo, A., "'Idee' bei Kant und Hegel," in *Das Recht der Vernunft. Kant und Hegel über Denken, Erkennen, und Handeln*, ed. by C. Fricke, P. König, Th. Petersen, Stuttgart, Frommann, 1995, 81–120.

———, "Idea and Ideal in Kant's De mundi sensibilis atque intelligibilis forma et principiis (1770)," in *New Essays on the Precritical Kant*, ed. by T. Rockmore, Amherst, N.Y., Humanity Books, 2001, 224–239.

———, "Soul and Body—Plato in Kant's Theory of Ideas," in *Platonismus im Idealismus. Die platonische Tradition in der klassischen deutschen Philosophie,* ed. by O. Summerell, B. Mojsisch, München, Saur Verlag, 2003, 33–58.

Paton, N. H. J., *Kant's Metaphysics of Experience: A Commentary on the First Half of the Kritik der reinen Vernunft*, London, Allen & Unwin, 1936.

Probleme der "Kritik der reinen Vernunft," ed. by B. Tuschling, Berlin, de Gruyter, 1984.

Reich, K., *Die Vollständigkeit der Kantischen Urteilstafel*, Berlin, Schoetz, 1948 (*The Completeness of Kant's Table of Judgments*, trans. by J. Kneller and M. Losonsky, foreword by L. W. Beck, Stanford, Stanford University Press, 1992).

Scaravelli, L., *Scritti kantiani*, Firenze, La Nuova Italia, 1968.

Strawson, P., *The Bounds of Sense: An Essay on Kant's Critique of Pure Reason*, London, Methuen, 1966.

Vahinger, H., *Commentar zu Kants Kritik der reinen Vernunft*, Stuttgart, Spemann, 1881–1892.

Westphal, K., *Kant's Transcendental Proof of Realism,* Cambridge, Cambridge University Press, 2004.

Wolff, M., *Die Vollständigkeit der Kantischen Urteilstafel*, Frankfurt a.M., Klostermann, 1995.

8. Critique of Practical Reason—*Kant's Practical Philosophy*

Allison, H., *Kant's Theory of Freedom*, Cambridge, Cambridge University Press, 1990.

Ameriks, K., "Kant's Deduction of Freedom and Morality," in *Journal of the History of Philosophy*, 19, 1981, 53–79.

Beck, L. W., *A Commentary on Kant's Critique of Practical Reason*, Chicago, University of Chicago Press, 1960.

Bohatec, J., *Die Religionsphilosophie Kants in der "Religion innerhalb der Grenzen der bloßen Vernunft." Mit besonderer Berücksichtigung ihrer theologisch-dogmatischen Quellen*, Hamburg, Hoffmann u. Campe, 1938.

Fackenheim, E., "*Kant and Radical Evil*," in *University of Toronto Quarterly*, 23, 1954, 439–453.

———, "Kant's Concept of History," in *Kant-Studien* 48, 1956–1957, 381–398.

Greene, T. M., *The Historical Context and Religious Significance of Kant's Religion: Introductory Essay to Religion Within the Limits of Reason Alone*, New York, Harper, 1960.

Gregor, Mary J., *Laws of Freedom: A Study of Kant's Method of Applying the Categorical Imperative in the "Metaphysik der Sitten,"* Oxford, Oxford University Press, 1963.

Henrich, D., "Der Begriff der sittlichen Einsicht und Kants Lehre vom Faktum der Vernunft," in *Die Gegenwart der Griechen im neueren Denken*, Festschrift f. H. G. Gadamer, Tübingen, Mohr, 1960, 75–115.

Herman, B., "On the Value of Acting from the Motive of Duty," in *The Philosophical Review*, 90, 1981, 354–382.

———, "The Practice of Moral Judgment," in *The Journal of Philosophy*, 82, 1985, 414–436.

———, *The Practice of Moral Judgment*, Cambridge, Mass., Harvard University Press, 1993.

Kant's Practical Philosophy Reconsidered, ed. by Y. Yovel, Dordrecht, Kluwer, 1989.

Kersting, W., *Wohlgeordnete Freiheit. Kants Rechts- und Staatphilosophie*, Frankfurt a.M., Suhrkamp, 1983.

Kofman, S., "The Economy of Respect: Kant and Respect for Women," in *Social Research*, 49, 1982, 383–404.

König, P., *Autonomie und Autokratie. Über Kants Metaphysik der Sitten*, Berlin, de Gruyter,1994.

———, "Kants Postulate der Vernunft und Hegels 'Verstellung der Sache,'" in *Das Recht der Vernunft. Kant und Hegel über Denken, Erkennen, und Handeln*, ed. by Ch. Fricke, P. König, Th. Petersen, Stuttgart, Frommann, 1995, 121–155.

Korsgaard, C., *Creating the Kingdom of Ends*, Cambridge, Cambridge University Press, 1996.

Landucci, S., *La "Critica della ragion pratica" di Kant. Introduzione alla lettura*, Roma, La Nuova Italia Scientifica, 1993.

Materialien zur Kritik der praktischen Vernunft, ed. by R. Bittner, K. Cramer, Frankfurt a.M., Suhrkamp, 1975.

Neiman, S., *The Unity of Reason: Rereading Kant*, Oxford, Oxford University Press, 1994.

O'Neill, O., "Agency and Anthropology in Kant's Groundwork," in *Kant's Practical Philosophy Reconsidered,* ed. by Y. Yovel, Dordrecht, Kluwer, 1989, 63–82.

———, *Constructions of Reason: Explorations of Kant's Practical Philosophy*, Cambridge, Cambridge University Press, 1989.

Paton, H. J., *The Categorical Imperative: A Study in Kant's Moral Philosophy*, London, Hutchinson, 1947.

Prauss, G., *Kant über Freiheit und Autonomie*, Frankfurt a.M., Klostermann, 1983.

Rawls, J., "Kantian Constructivism in Moral Theory," in *The Journal of Philosophy*, 11, 1980, 515–572.

Ross, D., *Kant's Ethical Theory: A Commentary on the Groundwork of the Metaphysics of Morals*, Oxford, Clarendon Press, 1954.

Shell, Susan M., *The Rights of Reason: A Study of Kant's Philosophy and Politics*, Toronto, University of Toronto Press, 1980.

———, *The Embodiment of Reason: Kant on Spirit, Generation, and Community*, Chicago, University of Chicago Press, 1996.

Van de Pitte, F., *Kant as Philosophical Anthropologist*, The Hague, Nijhoff, 1971.

Wood, A.W., *Kant's Moral Religion*, Ithaca, Cornell University Press, 1970.

9. Critique of Judgment

A. General Studies

Allison, H., *Kant's Transcendental Idealism*, New Haven, Yale University Press, 1983.

———, "Is the Critique of Judgment 'Post-Critical'?" in *The Reception of Kant's Critical Philosophy*, ed. by S. Sedgwick, Cambridge, Cambridge University Press, 2001, 78–92.

Bartuschat, W., *Zum systematischen Ort von Kants Kritik der Urteilskraft*, Frankfurt a.M., Klostermann, 1972.

Cassirer, H. W., *A Commentary on Kant's Critique of Judgment*, London, Methuen, 1836.

Deleuze, G., *La philosophie critique de Kant*, Paris, PUF, 1963 (*Kant's Critical Philosophy: The Doctrine of the Faculties*, trans. by H. Tomlinson, B. Habberjan, Minneapolis, University of Minnesota Press, 1996).

De Vleeschauwer, H.-J., *L'évolution de la pensée kantienne*, Paris, Alcan, 1939 (*The Development of Kantian Thought*, trans. by A. R. C. Duncan, London/New York, T. Nelson, 1962).

Lebrun, G., *Kant et la fin de la métaphysique. Essai sur la critique de la faculté de juger*, Paris, Colin, 1970.

Lehmann, G., *Beiträge zur Geschichte und Interpretation der Philosophie Kants*, Berlin, de Gruyter, 1969.

Materialien zu Kants Kritik der Urteilskraft, ed. by J. Kulenkampf, Frankfurt a.M., Suhrkamp, 1974.

Mathieu, V., "Opus postumum e Critica del Giudizio," in *La filosofia trascendentale e l'"Opus postumum" di Kant*, Torino, Edizioni di Filosofia, 1958, 149–160.

Menegoni, F., *Introduzione alla Critica del giudizio*, Roma, La Nuova Italia Scientifica, 1995.

Model, A., *Metaphysik und reflektierende Urteilskraft bei Kant*, Frankfurt a.M., Athenaeum, 1987.

Pluhar, W., "How to Render Zweckmäßigkeit in Kant's Third Critique," in *Interpreting Kant*, ed. by Moltke S. Gram, Iowa City, University of Iowa Press, 1982, 85–98.

Scaravelli, L., *Scritti kantiani*, Firenze, La Nuova Italia, 1968.

Souriau, M., *Le jugement réflechissant dans la philosophie critique de Kant*, Paris, F. Alcan, 1926.

Tonelli, G., "La formazione del testo della Kritik der Urteilskraft," in *Revue Internationale de Philosophie*, 30, 4, 1954, 423–448.

———, *Dall'estetica metafisica all'estetica psicoempirica. Studi sulla genesi del criticismo (1754–1771) e le sue fonti*, Torino, Memorie della Accademia delle Scienze di Torino, 1955.

Windelband, W., "Einleitung," in AA, V, 512–527.

Zammito, J. H., *The Genesis of Kant's Critique of Judgment*, Chicago, University of Chicago Press, 1992.

B. Critique of the Aesthetic Faculty of Judgment

Allison, H., *Kant's Theory of Taste. A Reading of the Critique of Aesthetic Judgment,* Cambridge, Cambridge University Press, 2001.

Ameriks, K., "How to Save Kant's Deduction of Taste," in *Journal of Value Inquiry*, 16, 295–302, 1982.

———, "Kant and the Objectivity of Taste," in *British Journal of Aesthetics*, 23, 1983, 3–17.

Amoroso, L., "Kant et le nom de l'esthétique," in *Kants Ästhetik/Kant's Aesthetics/ L'esthétique de Kant*, ed. by H. Parret, Berlin/New York, de Gruyter, 1998, 701–705.

Anceschi, L., *Autonomia ed eteronomia dell'arte*, Firenze, Vallecchi, 1936.

Arendt, H., *Lectures in Kant's Political Philosophy*, ed. by R. Beiner, Chicago, University of Chicago Press, 1982.

Baeumler, A., *Das Irrationalitätsproblem in der Ästhetik und Logik des 18. Jahrhunderts bis zur Kritik der Urteilskraft*, Tübingen, Niemeyer, 1967.

Basch, V., *Essai critique sur l'Esthétique de Kant*, Paris, 1897.

Baum, M., "Subjektivität, Allgemeingültigkeit, und Apriorität des Geschmacksurteils bei Kant," in *Deutsche Zeitschrift für Philosophie*, 39, 3, 1991, 272–284.

Biemel, W., *Die Bedeutung von Kants Begründung der Ästhetik für die Philosophie der Kunst, Kant-Studien*, Ergänzungsheft 77, 1959.

Böhme, G., *Kants Kritik der Urteilskraft in neuerer Sicht*, Frankfurt, Suhrkamp, 1999.

Brandt, R., "Analytic/Dialectic," in *Reading Kant: New Perspectives on Transcendental Arguments and Critical Philosophy*, ed. by E. Schaper, W. Vossenkuhl, Oxford, Oxford University Press, 1989, 179–195.

———, "The Deductions in the Critique of Judgment: Comments on Hampshire and Horstmann," in *Kant's Transcendental Deductions*, ed. by E. Förster, Stanford, Stanford University Press, 1989, 177–190.

———, "Die Schönheit der Kristalle und das Spiel der Erkenntniskräfte. Zum Gegenstand und zur Logik des ästhetischen Urteils bei Kant," in *Autographen, Dokumente und Berichte. Kant Forschungen*, 5, 1994, 19–54.

Cagyll, H., *Art of Judgment*, Oxford, Blackwell, 1989.

Cohen, H., *Kants Begründung der Ästhetik*, Berlin, Dummler, 1889.

Cohen, T., "Why Beauty Is a Symbol of Morality," in *Essays in Kant's Aesthetics*, ed. by T. Cohen, P. Guyer, Chicago, University of Chicago Press, 1982, 221–236.

Crawford, D., *Kant's Aesthetic Theory,* Madison, University of Wisconsin Press, 1974.

———, "The Place of the Sublime in Kant's Aesthetic Theory," in *The Philosophy of Immanuel Kant*, ed. by R. Kennington, Washington, D.C., Catholic University of America Press, 1985, 161–183.

———, "Kant's Principles of Judgment and Taste," in *Proceedings of the Sixth International Kant Congress*, ed. by G. Funke, Thomas M. Seebohm, Washington, D.C., University Press of America, 1990, 87–109.

Crawter, P., *The Kantian Sublime*, Oxford, Clarendon Press, 1989.

Dumouchel, D., "La découverte de la faculté de juger réfléchissante. Le role heuristique de la 'Critique du gout' dans la formation de la Critique de la faculté de juger," in *Kant-Studien*, 85, 1994, 419–442.

———, "L'esthétique pré-critique de Kant. Genèse de la théorie du 'gout' et du beau," in *Archives de Philosophie*, 60, 1997, 59–86.

———, "Genèse de la troisième Critique. Le role de l'esthétique dans l'achèvement du système critique," in *Kants Ästhetik/Kant's Aesthetics/L'esthétique de Kant*, ed. by H. Parret, Berlin/New York, de Gruyter, 1998, 18–41.

Düsing, K., "Beauty as the Transition from Nature to Freedom in Kant's Critique of Judgment," in *Nous*, 24, 1990, 79–92.

Elliot, R. K., "The Unity of Kant's 'Critique of Aesthetic Judgment,'" in *British Journal of Aesthetics*, 8, 1968, 244–250.

Essays in Kant's Aesthetics, ed. by T. Cohen, P. Guyer, Chicago, University of Chicago Press, 1982.

Faggiotto, P., *La metafisica kantiana dell' analogia,* Trento, Verifiche, 1996.

Frank, M., "Kants 'Reflexionen zur Ästhetik.' Zur Werkgeschichte der 'Kritik der ästhetischen Urteilskraft,'" in *Revue Internationale de Philosophie*, 4, 1990, 552–580.

Fricke, C., *Kants Theorie der reinen Geschmacksurteils*, Berlin, de Gruyter, 1990.

Frost, W., *Der Begriff der Urteilskraft bei Kant*, Halle, Niemeyer, 1906.

Gadamer, H. G., *Wahrheit und Methode*, Tübingen, Mohr, 1972[3] (*Truth and Method*, trans. G. Barden, J. Cumming, New York, Continuum, 1975).

Garroni, E., *Estetica ed epistemologia. Riflessioni sulla "Critica del Giudizio"*, Roma, Bulzoni, 1976.

———, *Senso e paradosso. L'estetica filosofia non speciale*, Bari, Laterza, 1986.

———, "Une faculté à acquérir. Sens et non-sens dans la Troisième Critique," in *Kants Ästhetik/Kant's Aesthetics/L'esthétique de Kant*, ed. by H. Parret, Berlin, New York, de Gruyter, 1998, 313–324.

Gasché, "Of Mere Form: On Kant's Analytic of the Beautiful," in *Interrogating the Tradition: Hermeneutics and the History of Philosophy*, ed. by Ch. Schott, Albany, SUNY Press, 2000, 211–234.

Gigliotti, G., "Il rispetto di un tulipano. Riflessioni sul sistema kantiano delle facoltà," in *Rivista di storia della filosofia*, 1, 2001, 26–63.

Gregor, Mary J., "Baumgarten's Aesthetica," in *Review of Metaphysics*, 37, 1983–84, 357–385.

———, "Aesthetic Form and Sensory Content in the Critique of Judgment," in *The Philosophy of Immanuel Kant,* ed. R. Kennington, Washington, D.C., Catholic University of America Press, 1985, 185–199.

Guérin, M., "Kant et l'ontologie analogique. Recherches sur le concept kantien de l'analogie," in *Revue de Métaphysique et de Morale*, 79, 4, 1974, 516–548.

Guillermit, L., *Critique de la faculté de juger esthétique de Kant. Commentaire*, Paris, Editions Pedagogie moderne, 1981.

———, *L'élucidation critique du jugement de gout selon Kant*, Paris, Editions du Centre nationale de la recherche scientifique, 1986.

Guyer, P., "Interest, Nature and Art: A Problem in Kant's Aesthetics," in *Review of Metaphysics*, 31, 1978, 580–603.

———, "Kant's Distinction Between the Beautiful and the Sublime," in *Review of Metaphysics*, 35, 1982, 753–783.

———, "The Unity of Reason: Pure Reason as Practical Reason in Kant's Early Conception of the Transcendental Dialectic," in *The Monist*, 72, 1989, 139–167.

———, "Reason and Reflective Judgment: Kant on the Significance of Systematicity," in *Nous*, 24, 1990, 17–43.

———, *Kant and the Experience of Freedom: Essays in Aesthetics and Morality*, Cambridge, Mass., Harvard University Press, 1993.

———, *Kant and the Claims of Taste*, Cambridge, Mass., Harvard University Press, 1997[2].

———, "The Symbols of Freedom in Kant's Aesthetics," in *Kants Ästhetik/Kant's Aesthetics/L'esthétique de Kant*, ed. by H. Parret, Berlin, New York, de Gruyter, 1998, 338–355.

———, ed., *Kant's Critique of the Power of Judgment. Critical Essays*, Lanham, Rowman & Littlefield, 2003.

Hampshire, S., "The Social Spirit of Mankind," in *Kant's Transcendental Deductions: The Three Critiques and the Opus Postumum*, ed. by E. Förster, Stanford, Stanford University Press, 1989, 145–156.

Henrich, D., "Kant's Explanation of Aesthetic Judgment," in *Aesthetic Judgment and the Moral Image of the World: Studies in Kant*, Stanford, Stanford University Press, 1992, 29–56.

Horstmann, R. P., "Why Must There Be a Deduction in Kant's Critique of Judgment?" in *Kant's Transcendental Deductions*, ed. by E. Förster, Stanford, Stanford University Press, 1989, 157–176.

Juchem, H. G., *Die Entwicklung des Begriffs des Schönen bei Kant. Unter besonderer Berücksichtigung des Begriffs der verworrenen Erkenntnis*, Bonn, Bouvier, 1970.

Kants Ästhetik/Kant's Aesthetics/L'esthétique de Kant, ed. by H. Parret, Berlin, New York, de Gruyter, 1998.

Kaulbach, F., "Weltorientierung, Welterkenntnis und pragmatische Vernunft bei Kant," in *Kritik und Metaphysik. H. Heimsoeth zum 80. Geburtstag*, Berlin, de Gruyter, 1966.

———, "Der Übergang vom bestimmt-bestimmenden zum freien Schema in Kants Kritik der Urteilskraft," in *Revue Internationale de Philosophie*, 176, 1, 1991, 76–91.

Kemal, S., *Kant's Aesthetic Theory: An Introduction*, London, Macmillan, 1992.

———, "The Practical Postulate of Freedom and Beauty as Symbol of Morality," in *Kants Ästhetik/Kant's Aesthetics/L'esthétique de Kant*, ed. by H. Parret, Berlin, New York, de Gruyter, 1998, 356–373.

Kneller, J., "Beauty, Autonomy, and Respect for Nature," in *Kants Ästhetik/Kant's Aesthetics/L'esthétique de Kant*, ed. by H. Parret, Berlin, New York, de Gruyter, 1998, 403–414.

Kulenkampff, J., *Kants Logik des ästhetischen Urteils*, Frankfurt a.M., Klostermann, 1978.

Künemann, E., *Kants und Schillers Begründung der Ästhetik*, München, C. H. Beck, 1895.

Kuypers, K., *Kants Kunsttheorie und die Einheit der Kritik der Urteilskraft*, Amsterdam and London, North Holland Pub. Co., 1972.

Lazaroff, A., "The Kantian Sublime: Aesthetic Judgment and Religious Feeling," in *Kant-Studien*, 71, 1980, 202–220.

Lyotard, F., "Sensus communis," in *Cahiers du College International de Philosophie*, 3, 1987, 67–87.

———, "La réflexion dans l'esthétique Kantienne," in *Revue Internationale de Philosophie*, 175, 4, 1990, 507–551.

———, *Leçons sur l'Analytique du Sublime,* Paris, Galilée, 1991.

Makkreel, R., "Imagination and Temporality in Kant's Theory of the Sublime," in *Journal of Aesthetics and Art Criticism*, 42, 1984, 303–315.

———, *Imagination and Interpretation in Kant,* Chicago, University of Chicago Press, 1990.

McCloskey, Mary A., *Kant's Aesthetics*, London, Macmillan, 1987.

Meerbote, R., "Reflection on Beauty," in *Essays in Kant's Aesthetics*, ed. by T. Cohen, P. Guyer, Chicago, University of Chicago Press, 1982, 55–86.

Melchiorre, V., *Analogia e analisi trascendentale*, Milano, Mursia, 1991.

Menzer, P., *Kants Aesthetik in ihrer Entwicklung*, Berlin, Akademie Verlag, 1952.

Meredith, J. C., "Last Stages of the Development of Kant's Critique of Taste," in *Kant's Critique of Aesthetic Judgment: Translated with Seven Introductory Essays, Notes, and Analytical Index*, Oxford, Oxford University Press, 1911.

Model, A., "Zur Bedeutung und Ursprung der 'reflektierenden Urteilskraft' bei Kant," in *Akten des Siebenten Internationalen Kant-Kongresses, 1990*, ed. by G. Funke, Bonn, Bouvier, 1991, 135–141.

Pareyson, L., *L'estetica di Kant. Lettura della "Critica del giudizio,"* Milano, Mursia, 1984.

Pillow, K., *Sublime Understanding: Aesthetic Reflection in Kant and Hegel*, Cambridge, Mass., MIT Press, 2003.

Recki, B., "Das schöne als Symbol der Freiheit," in *Kants Ästhetik/Kant's Aesthetics/L'esthétique de Kant*, ed. by H. Parret, Berlin, New York, de Gruyter, 1998, 386–402.

Ritter, J., "'Genius,'" in *Historisches Wörterbuch der Philosophie*, ed. by J. Ritter, K. F. Gründer, vol. 3, Basel, Schönig, 1974, 279–310.

Roviello, A. M., "Du Beau comme symbol du Bien," in *Kants Ästhetik/Kant's Aesthetics/L'esthétique de Kant*, ed. by H. Parret, Berlin, New York, de Gruyter, 1998, 374–385.

Savile, A., *Aesthetic Reconstructions*, Oxford, Basil Blackwell, 1987.

Scaravelli, L., "Osservazioni sulla Critica del giudizio," in *Scritti kantiani*, Firenze, La Nuova Italia, 1968, 336–528.

Schlapp, O., *Kants Lehre vom Genie und die Entstehung der Kritik der Urteilskraft*, Göttingen, Vandenhoeck & Rupprecht, 1901.

Shaper, E., ed., *Pleasure, Preference, and Value*, Cambridge, Cambridge University Press, 1983.

———, *Studies in Kant's Aesthetics*, Edinburgh, Edinburgh University Press, 1979.

———, "Taste, Sublimity, and Genius: The Aesthetics of Nature and Art," in *The Cambridge Companion to Kant*, ed. by P. Guyer, Cambridge, Cambridge University Press, 1992, 367–394.

Strube, W., "Der Begriff des Erhabenen in der deutschsprachingen Ästhetik des 18. Jahrhunderts," in *Aufklärung und Skepsis. Studien zur Philosophie und Geistesgeschichte des 17. und 18. Jahrhunderts*, ed. by L. Kreimendahl, Stuttgart, Frommann-Holzboog, 1995, 272–302.

Tonelli, G., "Zabarella inspirateur de Baumgarten ou l'origine de la connexion entre esthétique et logique," in *Revue d'Esthétique*, 9, 1956, 182–192.

———, "Die Umwälzung von 1769 bei Kant," in *Kant-Studien*, 54, 1963, 369–373.

———, "Kant's Early Theory of Genius, 1770–1779," in *Journal of the History of Philosophy*, 4, 1966, 109–131, 209–224.

———, Review of N. Hinske, et al.'s edition of Kant's *Erste Einleitung in der Kritik der Urteilskraft*, Stuttgart, Frommann, 1965, in *Philosophy and History*, 1968, 167–172.

Uehling, Th., *The Notion of Form in Kant's Critique of Aesthetic Judgment*, The Hague, Mouton, 1971.

Vossenkuhl, W., "Schönheit als Symbol der Sittlichkeit. Über die gemeinsame Würzel von Ethik und Ästhetik bei Kant," in *Philosophisches Jahrbuch*, 99, 1, 1992, 91–104.

Wogau, K. M., *Vier Studien zu Kants Kritik der Urteilskraft*, Uppsala/Leipzig, A. B. Lundequistska Bokhandeln, Harrassowitz, 1938.

C. Critique of the Teleological Faculty of Judgment

Adickes, E., *Kant als Naturforscher*, Berlin, de Gruyter, 1924/1925.

Allison, H., "Kant's Antinomy of Teleological Judgment," in *Southern Journal of Philosophy*, 30, 1991, 25–42.

Auxter, T., "The Teleology of Kant's Ectypal World," in *Proceedings of the Ottawa Congress on Kant*, 1974, Ottawa, University of Ottawa Press, 1976, 488–493.

———, *Kant's Moral Teleology,* Macon, Mercer University Press, 1982.

Bateson, G., *Steps to an Ecology of Mind*, San Francisco, Chandler, 1972.

Baumanns, P., *Das Problem der organischen Zweckmäßigkeit,* Bonn, Bouvier, 1965.

Bauer-Drevermann, I., "Zufälligkeit in Kants Kritik der Urteilskraft," in *Kant-Studien*, 56, 1965–66, 497–504.

Bommersheim, P., "Der Begriff der organischen Selbstregulation in Kants Kritik der Urteilskraft," in *Kant-Studien*, 23, 1919, 209–220.

———, "Der vierfache Sinn der Zweckmäßigkeit in Kants Philosophie des Organischen," in *Kant-Studien*, 32, 1927, 290–309.

Buchdal, G., "Der Begriff der Gesetztmäßigkeit in Kants Philosophie der Naturwissenschaft," in *Zur Kantforschung der Gegenwart*, ed. by P. Heintel, L. Nagl, Darmstadt, Wissenschaftliche Buchgesellschaft, 1981.

Butts, R., "Teleology and Scientific Method in Kant's Critique of Judgment," in *Nous*, 24, 1990, 1–16.

Düsing, K., *Die Teleologie in Kants Weltbegriff*, Bonn, Bouvier, 1968.

Eisler, R., *Der Zweck: Seine Bedeutung für Natur und Geist*, Berlin, Mittler und Sohn, 1914.

Final Causality in Nature and Human Affairs, ed. by R. F. Hassing, Washington, D.C., The Catholic University of America Press, 1997.

Friedman, M., *Kant and the Exact Sciences*, Cambridge, Mass., Harvard University Press, 1992.

Frost, W., "Kants Teleologie," in *Kant-Studien*, 11, 1906, 297–347.

Hermann, I., *Kants Teleologie*, Budapest, Akadémiai Kiadò, 1972.

Kant and the Sciences, ed. by E. Watkins, Oxford, Oxford University Press, 2001.

Lovejoy, Arthur O., *The Great Chain of Being,* New York, Harper, 1936.

———, "Kant and Evolution," in *Forerunners of Darwin, 1745–1859,* ed. by Bentley Glass, et al., Baltimore, Johns Hopkins University Press, 1959, 173–206.

Löw, R., *Philosophie des Lebendigen: Der Begriff des Organischen bei Kant, sein Grund und seine Aktualität*, Frankfurt a.M., Suhrkamp, 1980.

McFarland, J. D., *Kant's Concept of Teleology*, Edinburgh, University of Edinburgh Press, 1970.

McLaughlin, P., *Kants Kritik der teleologischen Urteilskraft*, Bonn, Bouvier, 1989.

Menegoni, F., *Finalità e destinatione morale nella "Critica del Giudizio,"* Trento, Verifiche, 1988.

Menzer, P., *Kants Lehre von der Entwicklung in der Natur und Geschichte*, Berlin, Reimer, 1911.

Metaphysik nach Kant? ed. by D. Henrich, R. P. Horstmann, Stuttgart, Klett-Cotta, 1988.

Nature Purposes: Analyses of Function and Design in Biology, ed. by C. Allen, M. Bekoff, G. Lauder, Cambridge, Mass., MIT Press, 1998.

Pfannkuche, A., "Der Zweckbegriff bei Kant," in *Kant-Studien*, 5, 1901, 51–72.

Philonenko, A., "L'antinomie du jugement téléologique chez Kant," in *Revue de Métaphysique et de Morale*, 82, 1977, 13–37.

Pleines, J.-E., *Teleologie als metaphysisches Problem*, Würzburg, Königshausen & Neumann, 1995.

Roqué, A. J., "Self-Organization: Kant's Concept of Teleology and Modern Chemistry," in *Review of Metaphysics*, 39, 1985, 107–135.

Schrader, G., "The Status of Teleological Judgment in the Critical Philosophy," in *Kant-Studien*, 45, 1953–54, 204–235.

Stadler, A., *Kants Teleologie und ihre erkenntnistheoretische Bedeutung*, Berlin, Dümmler, 1874.

Teleologie, Neue Hefte für Philosophie, 20, 1981.

Tonelli, G., "Von den verschiedenen Bedeutungen des Wortes Zweckmässigkeit in der Kritik der Urteilskraft," in *Kant-Studien*, 49, 2, 1958/1959, 154–166.

Tufts, J. H., *The Sources and Development of Kant's Teleology*, Chicago, University of Chicago Press, 1892.

Ungerer, E., *Die Teleologie Kants und ihre Bedeutung für die Logik der Biologie*, Berlin, Borntraeger, 1922.

White, D., "Unity and Form in Kant's Notion of Purpose," in *Final Causality in Nature and Human Affairs*, ed. by R. F. Hassing, Washington, D.C., Catholic University of America Press, 1997, 125–150.

Wogau, K. M., *Vier Studien zu Kants Kritik der Urteilskraft*, Uppsala/Leipzig, Lundequistska Bokhandeln/Harrassowitz, 1938.

Zanetti, V., "Die Antinomie der teleologischen Urteilskraft," in *Kant-Studien*, 83, 1993, 341–355.

———, *La nature a-t-elle une fin? Le problème de la téléologie chez Kant*, Bruxelles, Ousia, 1994.

Zumbach, C., *The Transcendent Science: Kant's Conception of Biological Methodology*, The Hague/Boston, Nijhoff, 1984.

10. History of Aesthetics

Bergmann, E., *Ernst Platner und die Kunstphilosophie des 18. Jahrhunderts,* Leipzig, Meiner, 1913.

Bosanquet, B., *A History of Aesthetic*, London, S. Sonnenschein, 1892, 1917[4].

Cassirer, E., *Die Philosophie der Aufklärung*, Tübingen, Mohr, 1932.

Cavell, S., "Aesthetic Problems of Modern Philosophy," in *Must We Mean What We Say?* Cambridge, Cambridge University Press, 1976, 73–96.

De Angelis, E., "Il buon senso. Per una storia del problema da Las Casas a Locke," in *Giornale Critico della Filosofia Italiana*, 51, 1972, 375–456.

Dewey, J., *Art as Experience*, New York, Milton, Balch, 1934.

Draper, John W., "Aristotelian 'Mimesis' in Eighteenth Century England," in *PMLA*, 36, 1921, 372–400.

de Duve, Thierry, *Kant after Duchamp*, Cambridge, Mass., MIT Press, 1998.

Eighteenth-Century English Aesthetics: A Bibliography, Heidelberg, C. Winter, 1931.

Ferraris, M., *L'immaginazione*, Bologna, Il Mulino, 1996.

Franke, U., *Kunst als Erkenntnis. Die Rolle der Sinnlichkeit in der Ästhetik des Alexander Gottlieb Baumgarten*, Wiesbaden, Steiner, 1972.

Goldstein, L., *Moses Mendelssohn und die deutsche Aesthetik*, Königsberg, Grafe u. Unzer, 1904.

Goodman, N., *Languages of Art: An Approach to a Theory of Symbols*, Brighton, The Harvester Press, 1981.

Gregor, Mary J., "Baumgarten's Aesthetica," in *Review of Metaphysics*, 37, 1983–1984, 357–385.

Gross, K. J., *Sulzers Allgemeine Theorie der Schönen Künste*, diss., Berlin, 1905.

Hartmann, E. v., *Die deutsche Aesthetik seit Kant*, Leipzig, Haacke, 1886.

Heym, L. M., *Darstellung und Kritik der aesthetischen Ansichten Johann Georg Sulzers*, diss., Leipzig, 1894.

Hildebrand, R., "Geschmack in Anwendung auf das Schöne," in *Beiträge zum deutschen Unterricht*, 1897.

Kannegiesser, G., *Die Stellung Moses Mendelssohn's in der Geschichte der Aesthetik*, diss., Marburg, 1868.

Kristeller, P. O., "The Modern System of the Arts," in *Renaissance Thought and the Arts*, Princeton, Princeton University Press, 1990, 163–227.

Leo, J., *Zur Entstehungsgeschichte der "Allgemeinen Theorie der Schönen Künste" J.G. Sulzers*, diss., Heidelberg/Berlin, 1906.

Nahm, M. C., "The Theological Background of the Theory of the Artist as Creator," in *Journal of the History of Ideas*, 8, 1947, 363–372.

Pevsner, N., "The Term *Architect* in the Middle Ages," in *Speculum*, 17, 1942, 549–562.

Pozzo, R., *Georg Friedrich Meiers "Vernunftlehre." Eine historisch-systematische Untersuchung*, Stuttgart, Frommann-Holzboog, 2000.

Riemann, A., *Die Ästhetik Alexander Gottlieb Baumgartens*, Halle, Niemeyer, 1928.

Schmidt, J., *Die Geschichte des Genie-Gedankens in der deutschen Literatur, Philosophie, und Politik 1750–1945*, 2 vols., Darmstadt, Wissenschaftliche Buchgesellschaft, 1988.

Schott, Robin M., *The Gender of Enlightenment*, in: *What Is Enlightenment? Eighteenth-Century Answers and Twentieth-Century Questions*, ed. by J. Schmidt, Berkeley, University of California Press, 1996.

Yaeger, P., "Toward a Female Sublime," in *Gender and Theory*, ed. by L. Kaufman, Oxford, Blackwell, 1989.

Zielsel, E., *Die Entstehung des Geniebegriffs*, Tübingen, Mohr, 1926.

Index

References to Kant's text and translation of the Introduction to the *Critique of Judgment* are italicized.